Fodor's

BUDAPEST

2nd Edition

**Where to Stay and Eat
for All Budgets**

**Must-See Sights
and Local Secrets**

Ratings You Can Trust

Fodor's Travel Publications   New York, Toronto, London, Sydney, Auckland
www.fodors.com

FODOR'S BUDAPEST
Editor: Jacinta O'Halloran

Editorial Production: Linda K. Schmidt
Editorial Contributors: Susan MacCallum-Whitcomb, Betsy Maury, Paul Olchváry
Maps: David Lindroth, *cartographer*; Rebecca Baer and Bob Blake, *map editors*
Design: Fabrizio La Rocca, *creative director*; Guido Caroti, *art director*; Moon Sun Kim, *cover designer*; Melanie Marin, *senior picture editor*
Production/Manufacturing: Colleen Ziemba
Cover Photo (Opera House, Budapest): Jim Doberman/The Image Bank/Getty Images

COPYRIGHT
Copyright © 2007 by Fodor's Travel, a division of Random House, Inc.

Fodor's is a registered trademark of Random House, Inc.

All rights reserved under International and Pan-American Copyright Conventions. Published in the United States by Fodor's Travel, a division of Random House, Inc., and simultaneously in Canada by Random House of Canada, Limited, Toronto. Distributed by Random House, Inc., New York.

No maps, illustrations, or other portions of this book may be reproduced in any form without written permission from the publisher.

Second Edition

ISBN 978–1–4000–1740–9

ISSN 1554–3455

SPECIAL SALES
This book is available at special discounts for bulk purchases for sales promotions or premiums. Special editions, including personalized covers, excerpts of existing books, and corporate imprints, can be created in large quantities for special needs. For more information, write to Special Markets/Premium Sales, 1745 Broadway, MD 6-2, New York, New York 10019, or e-mail specialmarkets@randomhouse.com.

AN IMPORTANT TIP & AN INVITATION
Although all prices, opening times, and other details in this book are based on information supplied to us at press time, changes occur all the time in the travel world, and Fodor's cannot accept responsibility for facts that become outdated or for inadvertent errors or omissions. So **always confirm information when it matters,** especially if you're making a detour to visit a specific place. Your experiences—positive and negative—matter to us. If we have missed or misstated something, **please write to us.** We follow up on all suggestions. Contact the Budapest editor at editors@fodors.com or c/o Fodor's at 1745 Broadway, New York, NY 10019.

PRINTED IN THE UNITED STATES OF AMERICA

10 9 8 7 6 5 4 3 2 1

Be a Fodor's Correspondent

Your opinion matters. It matters to us. It matters to your fellow Fodor's travelers, too. And we'd like to hear it. In fact, we *need* to hear it.

When you share your experiences and opinions, you become an active member of the Fodor's community. That means we'll not only use your feedback to make our books better, but we'll publish your names and comments whenever possible. Throughout our guides, look for "Word of Mouth," excerpts of your unvarnished feedback.

Here's how you can help improve Fodor's for all of us.

Tell us when we're right. We rely on local writers to give you an insider's perspective. But our writers and staff editors—who are the best in the business—depend on you. Your positive feedback is a vote to renew our recommendations for the next edition.

Tell us when we're wrong. We're proud that we update most of our guides every year. But we're not perfect. Things change. Hotels cut services. Museums change hours. Charming cafés lose charm. If our writer didn't quite capture the essence of a place, tell us how you'd do it differently. If any of our descriptions are inaccurate or inadequate, we'll incorporate your changes in the next edition and will correct factual errors at fodors.com *immediately.*

Tell us what to include. You probably have had fantastic travel experiences that aren't yet in Fodor's. Why not share them with a community of like-minded travelers? Maybe you chanced upon a beach or bistro or B&B that you don't want to keep to yourself. Tell us why we should include it. And share your discoveries and experiences with everyone directly at fodors.com. Your input may lead us to add a new listing or highlight a place we cover with a "Highly Recommended" star or with our highest rating, "Fodor's Choice."

Give us your opinion instantly at our feedback center at www.fodors.com/feedback. You may also e-mail editors@fodors.com with the subject line "Budapest Editor." Or send your nominations, comments, and complaints by mail to Budapest Editor, Fodor's, 1745 Broadway, New York, NY 10019.

You and travelers like you are the heart of the Fodor's community. Make our community richer by sharing your experiences. Be a Fodor's correspondent.

Happy traveling!

Tim Jarrell, Publisher

CONTENTS

UNDERSTANDING BUDAPEST

CLOSEUPS

MAPS

ABOUT THIS BOOK

Our Ratings

Sometimes you find terrific travel experiences and sometimes they just find you. But usually the burden is on you to select the right combination of experiences. That's where our ratings come in.

As travelers we've all discovered a place so wonderful that its worthiness is obvious. And sometimes that place is so unique that superlatives don't do it justice: you just have to be there to know. These sights, properties, and experiences get our highest rating, **Fodor's Choice**, indicated by orange stars throughout this book.

Black stars highlight sights and properties we deem **Highly Recommended,** places that our writers, editors, and readers praise again and again for consistency and excellence.

By default, there's another category: any place we include in this book is by definition worth your time, unless we say otherwise. And we will.

Disagree with any of our choices? Care to nominate a place or suggest that we rate one more highly? Visit our feedback center at www. fodors.com/feedback.

Budget Well

Hotel and restaurant price categories from ¢ to **$$$$** are defined in the opening pages of each chapter. For attractions, we always give standard adult admission fees; reductions are usually available for children, students, and senior citizens. Want to pay with plastic? **AE, D, DC, MC, V** following restaurant and hotel listings indicate whether American Express, Discover, Diners Club, MasterCard, and Visa are accepted.

Restaurants

Unless we state otherwise, restaurants are open for lunch and dinner daily. We mention dress only when there's a specific requirement and reservations only when they're essential or not accepted—it's always best to book ahead.

Hotels

Hotels have private bath, phone, TV, and air-conditioning and operate on the European Plan (aka EP, meaning without meals), unless we specify that they use the Continental Plan (CP, with a Continental breakfast), Breakfast Plan (BP, with a full breakfast), or Modified American Plan (MAP, with breakfast and dinner) or are all-inclusive (AI, including all meals and most activities). We always

list facilities but not whether you'll be charged an extra fee to use them, so when pricing accommodations, find out what's included.

Many Listings	
★	Fodor's Choice
★	Highly recommended
✉	Physical address
✛	Directions
⬩	Mailing address
☎	Telephone
🖷	Fax
⊕	On the Web
✍	E-mail
🖼	Admission fee
⊘	Open/closed times
▶	Start of walk/itinerary
Ⓜ	Metro stations
▭	Credit cards

Hotels & Restaurants	
🏨	Hotel
⬑	Number of rooms
⬢	Facilities
⦿◎	Meal plans
✕	Restaurant
⬧	Reservations
🏛	Dress code
⬎	Smoking
🕮	BYOB
✕🏨	Hotel with restaurant that warrants a visit

Outdoors	
🏌	Golf
⛺	Camping

Other	
☙	Family-friendly
🛈	Contact information
⇨	See also
✉	Branch address
☞	Take note

WHAT'S WHERE

BUDAPEST

Várhegy (Castle Hill): Literally and figuratively, you can't miss Castle Hill: a UNESCO-designated neighborhood that boasts narrow cobbled streets and some of the city's most stunning sites. Its crowning glories are the Royal Palace and ornate Matthias Church. Both were originally built in the 13th century—"originally" being the operative word. Though Castle Hill seems serene now, it has been the site of 30 devastating sieges: most recently, in the winter of 1944–45, when the Nazi's took their last stand here. As a result, buildings are more a product of architectural reconstruction than preservation *per se*. But they are stunning nonetheless.

Elsewhere in Buda: The area south of Várhegy has a handful of historic attractions—like the Citadella and Liberation Monument. To the north lies the 16th-century tomb of Gül Baba; and to the west is Szobor, the Soviet statue park. However, some of the most memorable sites in this neck of the woods are the natural ones: specifically, Buda's verdant rolling hills. Visitors can hike around them; sigh over the views granted by them; and tour the labyrinthine caves that wind beneath them.

Downtown Pest & the Small Ring Road: Hungary's Parliament, a neo-Gothic structure top heavy with ornamental stonework, visually dominates this part of town. The neighborhood around it serves as the nation's administrative nerve center. But the tone changes farther south, where the sacred and the secular collide. St. Stephen's opulent basilica is here; as are Budapest's oldest sanctuary (the 12th-century Inner City Parish Church) and Europe's largest synagogue (the 3,000-seat Nagy Zsinagóga). Yet even devout souls might be distracted by Budapest's most famous and unabashedly touristy shopping street, Váci utca, which runs from Vörösmarty tér right down to the Vásárcsarnok (Central Market).

Along Andrássy út: Starting near the basilica, Andrássy út extends over a mile, getting grander, greener, and less commercial the farther northeast it goes. Like much of Pest, the boulevard was constructed in the late 19th century, and its pedigree shows. Underneath it lies the continent's first metro line, opened in 1896, while above ground are scores of gorgeous *fin de siécle* buildings. Andrássy út ends with a bang at Hősök tere (Heroes' Square). Just behind it is City Park, which contains the Széchenyi Baths, the glorious Museum of Fine Arts, and the city's top children's sites.

WHAT'S
WHERE

Eastern Pest & the Large Ring Road: This area is understandably less touristed than other parts of Pest: after all, swathes of it have long been better known for seediness than sites. But this is changing due to a major urban revitalization effort. The Holocaust Memorial Center, for instance, opened here in 2004; while the new National Theater and adjacent Palace of Arts (home of the National Concert Hall, Festival Theatre, and Ludwig Contemporary Arts Museum) opened in 2002 and 2005, respectively. The renewal process makes older cultural gems—like the Erkel (Budapest's "other" opera house) and the Vígszínház Theater—ripe for rediscovery.

Óbuda & Margitsziget (Margaret Island): In 1873 Óbuda—the area first settled by the ancient Romans—was united with Buda and Pest to form the present-day city. Located on the Danube's west bank, upriver from the main sights, Óbuda today is a barrage of highways and concrete housing blocks. Yet the 2,000-year-old ruins of Aquincum stand as reminders of its more illustrious past. In the Danube, across from Óbuda, is Margaret Island. Anchored by bridges at both ends, this tranquil 250-acre parkland has gardens, paths, pools, an outdoor theatre, and two classic hotels.

BEYOND BUDAPEST

The Danube Bend: OK. So the Danube River isn't exactly blue anymore. But it is still beautiful, especially above Budapest, where it curves gracefully past a string of postcard-perfect towns. Proximity to the city combined with a high "cute quotient" (think cobblestone squares, candy-colored houses, and a surfeit of crafts shops) makes Szentendre the most popular of the lot. However, Visegrád (with its 13th-century citadel) and Esztergom (Hungary's first capital) are also rewarding destinations. Of course, none of these villages can be classified as well-kept secrets, so you should expect to encounter crowds—particularly in high season.

Lake Balaton: Central Europe's largest lake is seen as prized real estate in landlocked Hungary, and in summer it seems as if the entire populace congregates here. If you plan to join them, bear in mind that more than water separates the southern and northern shores: each has its own distinct character. The former is flatter and focuses largely on waterfront "amusements" (which means it attracts beach babies of both the diapered and bikinied variety). On the more attractive north shore, lakeside strands are backed by scenic hills. So discerning guests have

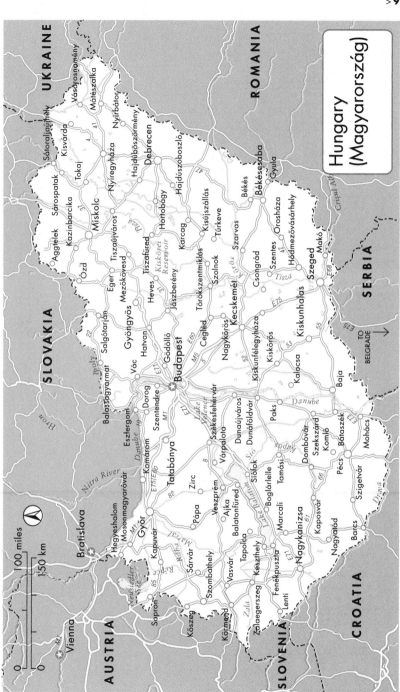

Hungary (Magyarország)

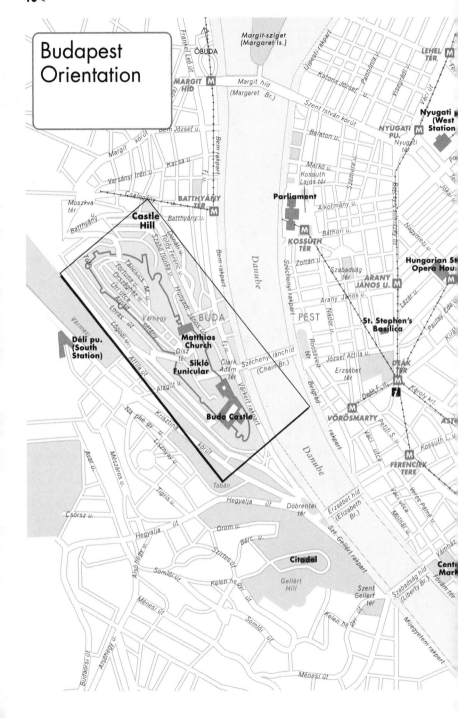

Budapest Orientation

Margit-sziget (Margaret Is.)

ÓBUDA

Frankel Leó út

MARGIT HÍD Ⓜ

Margit híd
(Margaret Br.)

LEHEL TÉR

Katona József u.

Pannónia u.

Visegrádi u.

Váci út

Nyugati (West Station)

Szent István körút

NYUGATI PU. Ⓜ

Nyugati tér

Bem József u.

Balaton u.

Margit körút

Bem rakpart

Markó u.

Szemere u.

Bajcsy-Zsilinszky út

Jókai u.

Moszkva tér

Csalogány

BATTHYÁNY TÉR Ⓜ

Kossuth Lajos tér

Parliament

Alkotmány u.

Markó u.

Varsányi Irén u.

Kacsa u.

Fő u.

Batthyány u.

Batthyány u.

Báthori u.

Nagymező u.

Castle Hill

Donáti u.

Toldy Ferenc u.

KOSSÚTH TÉR Ⓜ

Zoltán u.

Szabadság tér

Markó u.

Hungarian St Opera Hou

Táncsics M. u.

Szabó Ilonka u.

Hunyadi János u.

Bem rakpart

Széchenyi rakpart

ARANY JÁNOS U. Ⓜ

Lázár u.

Fortuna u.

Országház u.

Úri utca

Arany János u.

Tárnok

Lovas út

BUDA

Nádor u.

PEST

Pauláy Ede u.

Király

Várhegy sétány

Matthias Church

Fő u.

Danube

Roosevelt

St. Stephen's Basilica

Vérmező

Logodi u.

Attila u.

Dísz tér

Siklő Funicular

Clark Ádám tér

Széchenyi lánchíd (Chain Br.)

József Attila u.

DEÁK TÉR Ⓜ

Károly krt.

Déli pu. (South Station)

Várkert rakpart

Erzsébet tér

Belgrád rakpart

Deák F. u.

A

Alagút u.

Krisztina körút

Buda Castle

VÖRÖSMARTY Ⓜ

Petőfi S. u.

Kossuth L. u.

Na phe gy u.

Lisznyai u.

Avar u.

Mészáros u.

Tabán

Danube

Váci utca

FERENCIEK TERE Ⓜ

Veres Pálné u.

Tigris u.

Hegyalja út

Döbrentei tér

Erzsébet híd (Elizabeth Br.)

Molnár u.

Csörsz u.

Hegyalja út

Orom u.

Szirtes út

Bérc u.

Citadel

Szt. Gellért rakpart

Vámház

Alsóhegy u.

Somlói út

Kelen he gy ú.

Gellért Hill

Szent Gellért tér

Szabadság híd (Liberty Br.)

Fővám tér

Centr Mark

Ménesi út

Somlói út

Kelen he gy ú.

Budaörsi út

Alsóhegy u.

Ménesi út

Muegyetem rakpart

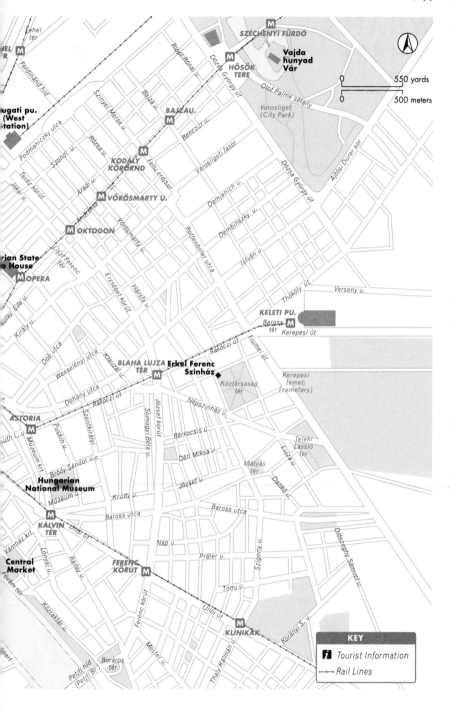

WHAT'S WHERE

an opportunity to explore traditional hillside villages, hiking trails, and vineyards as well the waterfront. Upscale spa resorts are an added bonus.

Sopron: This northwestern city makes an easy day-trip—assuming you're based in Vienna! Austria's capital is just 37 mi away, while Hungary's is 137. Nevertheless, if you want some fresh mountain air (and after smoke-wreathed Budapest you might), this is a great place to get it. Crystalline lakes, pine-covered slopes, and a range of sporting facilities invite outdoorsy types. But Sopron welcomes history buffs, too. Tucked within the city walls is a remarkably high concentration of antique buildings and monuments (355 to be exact).

Pécs: Considering it has just 160,000 inhabitants, this Transdanubian city packs quite a punch. Attractions include a fabled porcelain factory (Zsolnay's); Christian sites that run the gamut from a 4th-century mausoleum to a stellar 19th-century basilica; and some of Hungary's best Ottoman architecture. The fact that Pécs has been a university town since 1367 further adds to its cachet by enabling it to support more museums, symphonies, theaters, and ballet companies than you'd otherwise expect in a centre of this size. The good news, then, is that Pécs delivers many of Budapest's delights on a more intimate scale. The bad news is that it's about three hours away by train.

The Great Plain: With its grazing animals and amber fields of grain, the vast expanse of land south and east of Budapest calls to mind the American West. It's also been mythologized in much the same way, with *csikós* (Hungary's heroes on horseback) subbing for cowboys. Hungary's second-largest urban center (Debrecen); its largest national park (Hortobágy); its largest water park (Mediterrán Elményfürdő); and its sunniest city (Szeged, which records over 2,000 hours of sunshine annually).

Northern Hungary: The midsize mountains of Northern Hungary are definitely picturesque. However, for many travelers the grapes growing on the slopes and valleys below them are a bigger draw. You see, the country's two best-known wine centers—the city of Eger and village of Tokaj—are located here. Happily, tasting opportunities abound in both. Eger also appeals to teetotalers thanks to the wealth of baroque and rococo buildings in its well-preserved Old Town.

WHEN TO GO

°F BUDAPEST °C

Dreaming of visiting Budapest on your summer vacation? Well, be careful what you wish for. Summer certainly does have its charms: the days are sunny and long, the gardens are in full bloom, and the chairs are set out invitingly at all the sidewalk cafés. Moreover, the activities calendar is packed. But so is everything else. In July and August—the peak vacation season for Hungarians as well as foreign tourists—Budapest gets crowded. The same goes for popular excursion areas like Danube Bend towns and the entire Lake Balaton region. Special events only compound matters. For instance, the Hungarian Formula One Grand Prix (held annually in August) maxes out Budapest's hotel capacity, raising room prices in the process.

Traveling in winter also involves trade-offs. Admittedly, crowds and costs drop; however, the mercury in local thermometers does, too. Lake Balaton resorts are boarded up for an extended period (being as shallow as it is, parts of the lake routinely freeze) and even in the city certain tourist services are offered on a limited basis. So the ideal time to come to Budapest is in the spring (May through June) or late summer into autumn (the end of August through October). During these months you'll find the weather pleasant, the crowds manageable, and the landscape glorious. An extra incentive is that some of Hungary's major fairs, festivals, and cultural events take place in this period: including the Spring Festival, which runs from mid-March to early April, and the myriad wine-harvest festivals that are held in late summer and early fall.

Climate

Hungary has the standard Continental climate. November into March is typically the lowest season for tourism—and justifiably so. Shortened hours of daylight coupled with cold, overcast weather can make Budapest seem quite dreary. Overall, May, June, September, and October have the optimal weather for sightseeing, June being both the warmest and the wettest of the four.

🔲 Forecasts **Weather Channel Connection** (☎ 900/932–8437 95¢ per minute from a Touch-Tone phone ⊕ www.weather.com).

QUINTESSENTIAL BUDAPEST

The Life Aquatic

Although the Danube is Budapest's most famous body of water, it's the therapeutic H_2O spewed up daily by 100-odd hot springs that sets local hearts aflutter. Ancient Romans—the guys who coined the word "spa" (an acronym for "*solus per aqua*" or "health by water")—were the first to exploit the springs by building baths around them 2,000 years ago. Simply put: they came, they saw, they conquered . . . and then they soaked. Later occupiers followed suit: including the Ottoman Turks, who built their own dramatically domed facilities, and the Habsburgs, who erected oh-so-atmospheric Beaux Arts beauties. Add in the later contributions of communists and capitalists, and Budapest has over a dozen thermal baths. More than mere monuments, these are part of the fabric of life. And, on any given day a large percentage of the city's population seems to take a dip in one.

Not Your Average Joe

Budapesters have been drinking copious amounts of coffee ever since the Turks introduced it in 1579. But they seldom grab a cup to go: city coffeehouses are elegant affairs designed for lingering. Indeed, in the 19th and early 20th centuries they served as extended living rooms for impoverished intellectuals. The communists, fearing cafés were hotbeds of sedition, closed most of them down. A few—like Gerbaud—survived, while others—like the Café Central—have been revived. All offer an extensive coffee menu. (Ask for standard "kávé" to get espresso; specify "amerikai kávé" to get a weaker brew and a disdainful stare.) All, moreover, boast an absurd array of decadent tortes, fruit-filled strudels, and fanciful marzipan creations. Sure they're fattening, but given how much goose liver and goulash you'll consume on your trip, extra calories hardly matter.

Chances are you'll never master the Hungarian language, a notoriously difficult tongue that is so obscure it's related only to Finnish and Estonian. Luckily, penetrating the mysteries of day-to-day life in the Hungarian capital is much easier. You just need to know a few **fundamentals.**

Hungary's Right-Hand Man

It's hard to ignore Szent István (St. Stephen to the tongue-tied). Stamps and forints bear his image; places and people bear his name; and statues of him pop up everywhere. Admittedly István wasn't Hungary's most devout saint: that distinction goes to Margaret, who entered a convent as a child and swore she'd rather cut off her nose than leave it. Nor was he the most spectacularly martyred (St. Gellért wins that award for rolling downhill in a spike-lined barrel). But as Hungary's first king, István remains the hands-down favorite. After being crowned in 1000, he turned loosely linked tribes into a centralized state and converted his pagan subjects to Christianity, thereby allying Hungary with the burgeoning powers of western Europe. Curiously, citizens express their undying gratitude each St. Stephen's Day (August 20) by parading his mummified right hand around Szent István Bazilika.

Seeing Red

You cannot appreciate how much has been achieved in Budapest in recent years until you acknowledge the not-so-distant Soviet domination. Though a generation has come of age since the Iron Curtain parted in 1989, reminders of the regime are relatively easy to find. Observe the dispiriting blocks of Soviet-built housing. Note the older edifices still bullet-pocked from World War II and the 1956 Hungarian Uprising. Walk through Szobor Park, where overbearing statutes of Lenin, Marx, and assorted comrades were exiled after Communism collapsed. Or visit the controversial—and undeniably disturbing—Terror Háza. Once headquarters of the State Security Police, it's now a museum that uses propaganda posters, arresting displays (including a re-created "interrogation" room), and video-taped interviews with victims to make the past palpable.

IF YOU LIKE

Thermal Spas

Nothing quite compares to a long, hot soak in the Gellért Baths. After all, it's impossible to remain blasé amid such Art Nouveau opulence (especially when you only pay $14 a day for the pleasure). The main pool is a marble extravaganza rimmed with sensuous statuary and capped by a vaulted glass roof. But the star attraction is the sublime stuff that fills it: naturally-heated mineral-rich water. Devotees claim it can cure almost any ill. Whether that's true or not, the Gellért Baths certainly do relax and revitalize. Yet there are numerous others that also deserve a dip.

Take the Rudas Gyógyfürdő: built by a 16th-century Turkish pasha, it has recently been restored—and opened to women! Then there's the neo-baroque Széchenyi Gyógyfürdő: a super-sized indoor-outdoor bathing complex much loved by locals. Beyond Budapest, another hot pick is the century-old spa resort at Hévíz, the world's second-largest thermal lake. The downside with such historic spots is that cultural differences can cause confusion. Ditto for entrance policies (many are single-sex or have alternate days for men and women).

Furthermore, since all focus on health—not hedonism—you'll typically need a doctor's prescription if you hope to follow your bath with anything more stimulating than a sauna-and-massage combo. So for full-on pampering, Budapest's Western-style spas are a better bet. One of the best, Aphrodite Health & Wellness Center in the five-star Corinthia Aquincum Hotel, blissfully combines trendy treatments (think lava-stone massages and lavish body wraps) with traditional thermal bathing.

Classical Music

Maybe the symphonic sweep of its history inspires them. Maybe having so convoluted a language motivates them to communicate by more melodic means. In any case, a number of imposing classical musicians have been bred in Hungary, most notably Béla Bartók, Zoltán Kodály, and Ferenc Liszt (familiar to the rest of us as Franz). Prodigious talents aside, what's most impressive about the music scene here is that it's not monopolized by the tux-and-tiara crowd. On the contrary, *everyone* seems to know the score.

Hence both programming and ticket pricing are designed for a demographically diverse audience. The internationally acclaimed Budapest Festival Orchestra, for instance, strikes an equalitarian chord by offering One-Forint Concerts for the cash-strapped (basically midday dress rehearsals) and Cocoa Concerts for kids. These are usually held in the National Concert Hall, part of the über-modern "concrete colossus" known as the Palace of Arts (Mûvészetek Palotája). But there are also plenty of other places where you can hear the sound of music.

Budapest alone has two opera houses, 12 concert halls, plus a host of intimate chamber-style venues. Add in festival stages—to say nothing of street corners—and the possibilities seem limitless. When architecture matters as much as acoustics, opt for the Magyar Állami Operaház (a glittering confection that ranks as one of the world's most beautiful opera houses) or the Liszt Ferenc Zeneakadémia: home to the country's most prestigious music conservatory and the city's premier concert hall, the academy has been a local landmark since 1907.

Wine

Hungarians, to put it bluntly, like to drink. And so do many of the tourists who visit their country. Some, in fact, seem to come solely for that purpose. Prospective imbibers, though, should pick their poison wisely. As far as Eastern Bloc beer goes, Hungary's can't match those brewed in the Czech Republic. Meanwhile its bitter national liqueur, Unicum, is—hmmm, how shall we say it?—an *acquired* taste. Domestic wines, on the other hand, can meet even an oenophile's grape expectations.

The two most celebrated are sweet white Tokaji Aszü and a full-bodied red that's fittingly dubbed Eger Bull's Blood (Egri Bikavér). Connoisseurs wishing to sample these at their source can contact regional "wine route" associations (⊕ www. wineroads.hu has links) for help plotting a vintage countryside vacation complete with winery tours and vineyard visits. Plan on sticking close to the capital? Try timing your trip to coincide with the Budapest International Wine and Champagne Festival, a suitably bacchanalian event held each year in early September.

Of course, the easiest option is to take part in a two-hour tasting session at the House of Hungarian Wines (Magyar Borok Háza) on Castle Hill. Within its labyrinthine cellars guests are invited to help themselves to representative wines from each of Hungary's 22 regions: all for the princely sum of $19. Considering that there are more than 50 different varieties to choose from, you might want to practice saying "Egészségedre" (slowly now, *eg - eeS - SHE - ged - re*)—"to your health!"

Shopping

These days Budapesters are reveling in consumerism, so it seems almost unsporting not to join the fun by doing a little shopping. A logical first stop is Váci utca: the pedestrian-only thoroughfare in Pest where 19th-century facades and attractive storefront displays compete for your attention. Along the street, boutiques selling local luxury items like lead crystal and hand-painted Herend porcelain are interspersed with the same "high street" stores found in other European centers (Britain's Marks and Spencer, Sweden's H&M, Spain's Zara: you get the picture).

Treasure hunters may try their luck elsewhere in town. Although most Hungarian attics were emptied out a decade ago, goodies are still being discovered. (In 2003, for example, 40 of composer Joseph Haydn's libretti surfaced in a second-hand bookshop.) If your pocketbook is well padded, sift through the eclectic selection on Falk Miksa utca (aka "Antique Row"). Otherwise, haggle to your heart's content at Ecseri Piac on Budapest's southeast edge. Billed as Central Europe's largest flea market, it has everything from the family jewels to military paraphernalia.

Whatever your tastes, don't miss the *fin-de-siècle* Vásárcsarnok Market. Under its Zsolnay-tiled roof, you'll find butchers, bakers—even a few candlestick makers. Browse the mezzanine level for intricately-patterned lace, embroidered linens, and ceramics decorated with folk-art designs; then head to the ground floor to check out the chockablock food stalls. Piled behind hanging garlands of paprika are smoked sausages, pungent cheeses, and all the other fixings for a picnic on the riverfront promenade.

GREAT ITINERARIES

HITTING THE HIGHLIGHTS

Let's be honest: you can blow through Budapest's big-ticket attractions in three days and still have time to quaff down the requisite bowl of goulash. But this city has as many "must-dos" as "must-sees." So if you want to really experience Hungary's capital, plan on spending six days, setting a seventh aside for outbound travel.

Day 1: Take It from the Top

There's a good reason why Castle Hill is the undisputed first stop on everyone's itinerary. This UNESCO World Heritage Site has a genuine "wow factor," yet it is compact enough for jet-lagged—or late-arriving—visitors to cover on their first day. Begin by poking around the Royal Palace (time permitting, tour the Hungarian National Gallery in its center block). Next, stroll along the cobblestone streets between colorful baroque, Gothic, and Renaissance facades, stopping in for a look at Matthias Church; then head for Fishermen's Bastion. The view from its Disneyesque turrets isn't just achingly beautiful: it will help you get your bearings! If you need a caffeine fix to keep you going—or just want to get a fix on Budapest's coffee culture—drop into Ruszwurm, the city's oldest café.

Day 2: On the Boulevard

Today, turn your back on hilly Buda and get acquainted with blessedly flat Pest. Start with a look inside massive Szent István Bazilika. Views from the cupola are worth the climb; though you may want to save your energy for the walk along Andrássy út, another UNESCO World Heritage Site. En route, pick and choose between the attractions (the Operaház and Terror Háza are favorites), leaving time to ogle other architectural treasures. The boulevard comes to a climatic finish at Hősök tere, where the Millennial Monument is flanked by two more museums. After perusing Old Masters in the Fodor's-recommended Szépművészeti, take the Millennial Underground back to the opera house for an evening performance. Then wrap things up by toasting the good life with an alfresco nightcap (and some world-class people-watching) on nearby Liszt Ferenc tér.

Day 3: Playing in Pest

Time for a little self-indulgence! Kick off your day the Budapest way by breakfasting at Café Gerbeaud on Vörösmarty tér; then spend the morning browsing around Váci utca. Even if shopping's not your bag, you'll find the street to be a fascinating study in contrasts as it runs south past Euro-style boutiques, through the university area, to the venerable Vásárcsarnok Market. In the afternoon, treat yourself to a tour. Commercial ones cater to almost every taste—and cover almost every mode of transportation, from boats and bikes to balloons. Major sites, like Parliament, also offer tours. Prefer to be independent? Www.budapestinfo.hu outlines self-guided walks relating to subjects like Bauhaus architecture and Jewish history.

Day 4: Parking Permitted

Budapesters *love* their parks—and you will, too, because the best of the bunch offer both gorgeous greenery and plentiful bathing opportunities. If you happen to be staying at either the Grand Hotel Margitsziget or Thermal Hotel Margitsziget, Margaret Island is a serendipitous place to take the plunge. Otherwise, head for City Park, at the northeast end of Andrássy út. Developed as the centerpiece of Hungary's 1896 millennial celebrations, this urban oasis is the setting for the Széchenyi Baths. You could while away hours in its indoor and outdoor thermal pools. But before your toes get too wrinkled, consider City Park's other attractions. Beyond the baths, kids can kick back at the zoo, fun fair, and circus. Adults, meanwhile, can enjoy a smattering of museums and concert venues, plus one of Budapest's best-loved restaurants (Gundel).

Day 5: Around the Bend

By now you've probably crisscrossed the Danube on countless occasions. So it's high time you actually got out on the water. The ideal way to do it is by taking a leisurely two-hour boat trip upriver to Szentendre. Although it's known primarily as an artists' colony, there's more to this picturesque little town than galleries and cutesy crafts shops. For instance, Hungary's Open-Air Ethnographic Museum (a site that re-creates village life from centuries past) is located on the outskirts. Those who wish to take everything in can gain precious sightseeing time by opting for the shorter land route when returning to Budapest. Once back, you can compensate for your abbreviated boat trip by booking a moonlight dinner cruise through the city itself.

Day 6: Head for the Hills

Want to escape the urban scene without leaving the city limits? No problem. Gellért Hill is the laced with trails leading up—waaay up—to the towering Liberation Monument and the Citadella behind it. (Don't worry about aching muscles. You can lounge later in one of three vintage baths located on the hill). More outdoorsy adventures are available in the Buda Hills: and you don't have to be die-hard hiker to

take advantage of them. János Hill, for example, can be accessed via a panoramic chairlift or a narrow-gauge train that's operated primarily by children. You'll find equally intriguing sites *beneath* these hills: namely some 200 caves, several of which are open to sightseers and spelunkers. Whatever you choose, reward yourself afterward with a down-home Hungarian dinner, complete with noodle pudding and live Gypsy music.

TIPS

❶ If you're not staying on Castle Hill, getting up it may seem daunting. So spare your tired legs by taking the funicular between the Chain Bridge and the Castle Hill district.

❷ Many shops close Saturday afternoon and all day Sunday. Museums tend to close on Monday. So depending on your timing, it may be prudent to re-shuffle these daily itineraries.

❸ You can only be admitted to Parliament on a guided tour; English-language tours run daily at 10, 12, and 2. To avoid long lines, it is advisable to reserve a place in advance. See ⊕ www. parlament.hu for booking information.

❹ Another advantage of City Park is that it is an all-season destination. Its rowing pond doubles as a skating rink in winter and its outdoor thermal pools remain open year-round.

❺ Do-it-yourselfers can skip the cruise and paddle around Budapest by canoe or kayak. In summer you'll find rental facilities on Margaret Island.

GREAT ITINERARIES

ADD-ON EXCURSIONS

If you're lucky enough to have days to spare, use them to check out more of Hungary's highlights. Many areas that are popular with tourists can be seen on day trips from Budapest. But if you don't want to end up feeling like a contestant in "The Amazing Race," it's wiser to do them as separate one- or two-night excursions. Think of each as a vacation within your vacation.

Add 2 Nights: Lake Balaton
Siofók, the closest lakeside resort, is just 65 mi from Budapest. So it is possible to zip in for a few hours. But if you're hoping for more than a fast "fun in the sun" experience, it's preferable to follow the scenic secondary roads through southern Transdanubia to Keszthely (on the lake's northwestern tip); then spend two nights working your way back east. Considering that the region features ample parklands, traditional villages with thatched-roof cottages, and picturesque hiking and biking paths, there's no shortage of activity options. Badacsony (with its vineyard-carpeted volcanic slopes) and Balatonfüred (Hungary's oldest spa resort) are good bets for Night One and Night Two, respectively. Both destinations have Fodor's Choice hotels.

Add 1 Night: Sopron
Sopron is one of those places that really does have something for everyone. Perched in Hungary's hilly northwest corner, it provides access to outdoor adventures— hiking, fishing, canoeing, even summer bobsledding. Meanwhile, the city itself ranks second only to Budapest when it comes to heritage buildings. If you can't decide between the great outdoors and Sopron's great Old Town, simply follow the lead of the day-tripping Austrians who come here to shop. (They also come to have dental work done, but we don't suggest you try that).

Add 1 Night: Pécs
It's no surprise that Pécs has several important historic sites: after all, the place has been around for 2,000 years. What *is* surprising is that so small a city would have such a vibrant arts community. Its orchestra and ballet companies have international reputations, and the scene will heat up even more as Pécs prepares to assume the title "European Capital of Culture" in 2010. As a result, this city is a solid choice for visitors who want to see the countryside without scrimping on artsy amenities. There's much else to recommend it (including an enviable selection of restaurants and hotels), so you'll have no trouble filling in time before or after a performance.

Add 2 Nights: The Great Plain
Venture out to the Puszta to see the legendary *csikós* demonstrate their equestrian skills. In season, Hortobágy National Park (near Debrecen), Kiskunság National Park (near Kecskemét), and Opusztaszer National Historical Memorial Park (equidistant from Kecskemét and Szeged) all host regularly scheduled stunt shows. Are they kitschy? Yes. Are they cool nonetheless? Absolutely! Spend the rest of the day exploring your chosen park. Then overnight nearby—ideally in a riding pension where you can practice horsemanship yourself. For proof that the Great Plain has urban attractions, too, spend your second night in Debrecen, Kecskemét, or Szeged.

Exploring
Budapest

WORD OF MOUTH

"Some people compare Budapest to Prague. I like Prague. I like it a lot. But it is really doing Budapest a disservice to say it is like Prague. Budapest is perhaps one of the best cities I've been to, and only Rome, in my opinion, is a better capital city. . . . [It] is like a tiny Paris with only the good parts."
—alyssamma

"Váci utca is a pedestrian street with Americanized shops. It has no real European flavor. Spend your time around the Jewish triangle, Heroes' Square . . . along the Pest bank of the Danube between the chain bridge and the Parliament building, take in all the wonderful Buda sites, walk through Margaret Island, and enjoy the steep ascent and descent of the subway system."
—Syl

By Paul
Olchváry

SITUATED ON BOTH BANKS OF THE DANUBE, amid an embarrassing wealth of geographic and architectural splendor that accounts for its reputation as one of the world's most panoramic and charismatic cities, Budapest (pronounced "*boo*-duh-pesht") unites the colorful hills of Buda and the wide, relatively bustling boulevards of Pest. Though it was the site of a Roman outpost during the 1st century AD, the city per se was not officially created until 1873, when the towns of Óbuda, Pest, and Buda united. By the turn of the 20th century Budapest was among the world's fastest-growing cities. Its newly developing face was modeled after Paris—which meant wide boulevards; eclectic, Art Nouveau architecture; elegant cafés aplenty; and a dynamic literary and arts scene. Since then Budapest has remained the cultural, political, intellectual, and commercial heart of Hungary. To this day it is—in terms of architecture and layout, at least—an amazingly similar urban landscape for its inhabitants as it was back in its pre-World War I "golden age." For the 20% of the nation's population who live in the capital, anywhere else is simply *vidék* ("the country").

Budapest has suffered many ravages in the course of its long history—and yet it has always arisen from the ashes. It was totally destroyed by the Mongols in 1241; captured by the Turks in 1541; ravaged more than a century later when retaken from the Turks; nearly destroyed by a combination of Allied bombing, retreating Germans, and advancing Soviet troops in 1944–45; and, as is still apparent on some downtown buildings, in the 1956 revolution Soviet tanks shot up the city once again. But this bustling industrial and cultural center survived as the capital of the People's Republic of Hungary after the war—and then, gradually from the 1960s on and especially into the 1980s, it became renowned for "goulash socialism," a phrase used to describe the state's tolerance of an irrepressible entrepreneurial spirit. Hungary, thanks in no small part to a whole boatload of foreign loans it subsequently struggled to repay, was the economic star of the Soviet bloc.

Budapest has undergone a radical makeover since the free elections of 1990. As more and more restaurants, bars, shops, and boutiques open their doors—and with fashion-conscious youth parading the streets—almost all conspicuous traces of communism have disappeared. While European Union membership in 2005 was accompanied by high hopes, it is fair to say that most Hungarians continue to view their prospects through glasses

PAUL'S TOP 5

Várhegy. Its cobblestone streets are clustered with beautifully preserved baroque, Gothic, and Renaissance houses and museums.
Andrássy út. Budapest's Champs-Élysées, this wide, straight boulevard is lined with plane trees, cafés, and grand old architecture.
Széchenyi Baths. This complex of indoor and outdoor thermal baths is open year-round.
The Bridges. There's nothing quite like strolling over the Danube.
Margit-sziget. This island oasis is where Budapesters stroll, swim, sunbathe, and snuggle in its plethora of parks and gardens, cafés, and clubs.

that are anything but rose-colored. Budget cuts and higher taxes announced by the government in 2006—a necessity, if Hungary's debt-ridden economy is to get in shape to adopt the euro as its currency around 2010 (later, say some pundits)—serve to ensure that cynicism won't vanish anytime soon from the Hungarian psyche.

Much of the charm of a visit to Budapest lies in unexpected glimpses into shadowy courtyards and in long vistas down sunlit cobbled streets. Although some 30,000 buildings were destroyed during World War II and in the 1956 revolution, the past lingers on in the often crumbling architectural details of the antique structures that remain.

The city's principal sights fall roughly into three areas, each of which can be comfortably covered on foot. The Buda hills are best explored by public transportation. Note that, by tradition, the district number—a Roman numeral designating one of Budapest's 22 districts—precedes each address. For the sake of clarity, in this book the word "District" precedes the number. Districts V, VI, and VII are in downtown Pest; District I includes Castle Hill, Buda's main tourist district.

VÁRHEGY (CASTLE HILL)

Most of Buda's major sights are on Várhegy (Castle Hill), a long, narrow plateau laced with cobblestone streets, clustered with beautifully preserved baroque, Gothic, and Renaissance houses, and crowned by the magnificent Royal Palace. The area is banned to private cars (except for those of neighborhood residents and Hilton hotel guests), but the streets manage to be lined bumper to bumper with shiny new Opels, Suzukis, Mercedes, and (the once ubiquitous and now uncommon) Trabants all the same—the only visual element to verify you're not in a fairy tale. As in all of Budapest, thriving urban new has taken up residence in historic old; international corporate offices, diplomatic residences, restaurants, and boutiques occupy many of its landmark buildings. The most striking example, perhaps, is the Hilton Hotel on Hess András tér, which has incorporated remains of Castle Hill's oldest church (a tower and one wall), built by Dominican friars in the 13th century.

Numbers in the text correspond to numbers in the margin and on the Castle Hill (Várhegy) map.

A GOOD WALK

Castle Hill's cobblestone streets and numerous museums are best explored on foot. Most of the transportation options for getting to Castle Hill deposit you on Szent György tér or Dísz tér, toward the southern end of Castle Hill and a short walk from most of its museums and grandest sights. If you're already on the Buda side of the river, you can take the Castle bus—*Várbusz*—from the Moszkva tér metro station, northwest of Castle Hill. If you're starting out from Pest, you can take a taxi or Bus 16 from Erzsébet tér or, the most scenic alternative, cross the Széchenyi Lánchíd (Chain Bridge) on foot to Clark Ádám tér and ride the *Sikló* (funicular) up Castle Hill. ■ TIP→ You could also hoof it up the hill in 10 minutes and save yourself the 700-forint ticket.

Begin your exploration at the **Királyi Palota** ❶ at the southern end of the hill. Of the palace's wealth of museums, the Ludwig Múzeum, the Magyar Nemzeti Galéria, the Budapesti Történeti Múzeum, and Országos Széchenyi Könyvtár are all interesting. Take in the stunning view of Pest from up here and stop for a look at the **Statue of Prince Eugene of Savoy** ❷ outside the entrance to Wing C before moving on. From here, you can cover the rest of the area by walking north along its handful of cobbled streets.

From Dísz tér, you can walk over to the **Nemzeti Táncszínház** ❸ on Szinház utca, then go up Tárnok utca, whose houses and open courtyards offer glimpses of how Hungarians have integrated contemporary life into Gothic, Renaissance, and baroque settings. Of particular interest are the houses at No. 16, now the Aranyhordó restaurant, and at No. 18, the 15th-century Arany Sas Patika (Golden Eagle Pharmacy Museum), with a naïf Madonna and child in an overhead niche. Modern commerce is also integrated into Tárnok utca's historic homes; you'll encounter numerous folk souvenir shops and tiny boutiques lining the street. Tárnok utca funnels into **Szentháromság tér** ❹ and the Trinity Column; this is also where you'll find the **Mátyás templom** ❺ and, just behind it, the **Halászbástya** ❻.

After exploring them, double back to Dísz tér and set out northward again on **Úri utca** ❼, which runs parallel to Tárnok utca; this long street is lined with beautiful, genteel homes. The **Budavári Labirintus** ❽, at No. 9, is worth a stop, as is the amusing little Telefónia Múzeum, at No. 49. At the end of Úri utca you'll reach **Kapisztrán tér** ❾, where you'll find the **Hadtörténeti Múzeum** ❿.

■ **TIP**→ To take in a little-explored yet lovely corner of Castle Hill, go beyond the museum to the northwest corner of the hill and walk along the castle wall (behind the museum) back toward Vienna Gate. Move on from the Hadtörténeti Múzeum toward Castle Hill's more notable sights by walking south again on Országház utca (Parliament Street), the main thoroughfare of 18th-century Buda; it takes its name from the building at No. 28, which was the seat of Parliament from 1790 to 1807. You'll end up back at Szentháromság tér, with just two streets remaining to explore.

You can stroll up to the end of Fortuna utca where you'll find **Bécsi kapu tér** ⓫, opening to Moszkva tér just below. Head back on Táncsics Mihály, where you will find the **Középkori Zsidó Imaház** ⓬. Continue down this street, and you'll find yourself in front of the Hilton Hotel, back at Hess András tér, bordering Szentháromság tér.

THE BEST VIEWS

You can either pay a modest fee to enter the Halászbástya (Fishermen's Bastion)—right by Mátyás templom (Matthias Church)—or else walk 10 minutes (or hop on any Várbusz) to the Királyi Palota (Royal Palace), where the lovely vistas are free. To soak in the sublimity of the Buda hills, meanwhile, go to the other side of the castle district (a two-minute walk) and walk along Tóth Árpád sétány (Árpád Tóth Promenade).

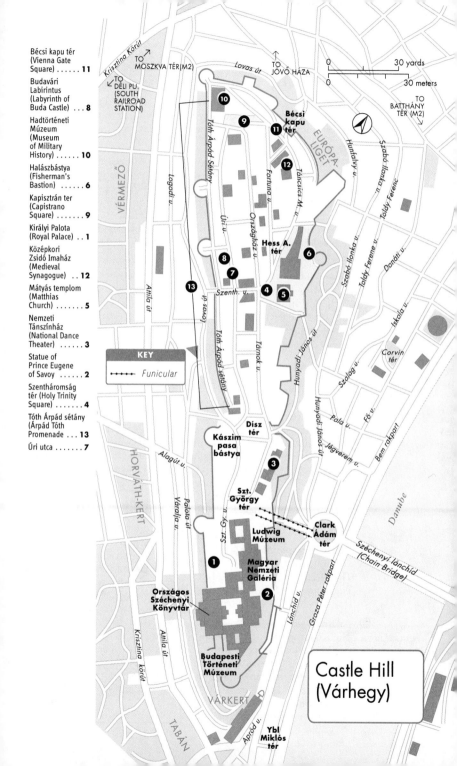

KEY

•••••• Funicular

Castle Hill (Várhegy)

Those whose feet haven't protested yet can finish off their tour of Castle Hill by strolling south back to Dísz tér on **Tóth Árpád sétány** ⑬, the romantic, tree-lined promenade along the Buda side of the hill.

TIMING   Castle Hill is small enough to cover in a two- to three-hour power walk, but perusing it at a leisurely pace and visiting its major museums and several tiny exhibits will require a full day.

What to See

⑪ **Bécsi kapu tér** (Vienna Gate Square). Marking the northern entrance to Castle Hill, the stone gateway (rebuilt in 1936) called Vienna Gate opens toward Vienna—or, closer at hand, Moszkva tér a few short blocks below. The square named after it has some fine baroque and rococo houses, but is dominated by the enormous neo-Romanesque (1913–17) headquarters of the **Országos Levéltár** (Hungarian National Archives), a cathedral-like shrine to paperwork. ⊠ *District I* Ⓜ *Várbusz (2nd stop after M2: Moszkva tér).*

⑧ **Budavári Labirintus** (Labyrinth of Buda Castle). Used as a wine cellar during the 16th and 17th centuries and then as an air-raid shelter during World War II, this 16-meter (52-foot) deep, 1,200-meter (3,900-foot) long labyrinth—entered at Úri utca 9 below an early-18th-century house—can be explored with a tour or, if you dare, on your own. English-language brochures are available. ⊠ *District I, Úri utca 9* ☎ *1/212–0207 Ext. 34* 🖾 *1,400 HUF* ☉ *Daily 9:30–7:30* Ⓜ *Várbusz (4th stop from M2: Moszkva tér).*

⑩ **Hadtörténeti Múzeum** (Museum of Military History). Fittingly, this museum is lodged in a former barracks, on the northwestern corner of Kapisztrán tér. The exhibits, which include collections of uniforms and military regalia, trace Hungary's military history from the original Magyar conquest in the 9th century through the period of Ottoman rule to the mid-20th century. Families or couples can arrange an English-language group tour in advance for 2,500 HUF, and for larger groups it's 3,000 HUF. There is a charge to use a camera or video camera. ⊠ *District I, Tóth Árpád sétány 40* ☎ *1/325–1647, 1/325–1600, or 1/344–1000* ⊕ *www.militaria.hu* 🖾 *Museum free, photos 600 HUF, videos 1,200 HUF* ☉ *Apr.–Sept., Tues.–Sun. 10–6; Oct.–Mar., Tues.–Sun. 10–4* Ⓜ *Várbusz (3rd stop from M2: Moszkva tér).*

⑥ **Halászbástya** (Fishermen's Bastion).
Fodor'sChoice   The wondrous porch overlooking
★   the Danube and Pest is the neo-Romanesque Fishermen's Bastion, a merry cluster of white stone towers, arches, and columns above a modern bronze statue of St. Stephen, Hungary's first king. Al-

> ## WORD OF MOUTH
>
> "The Castle Labyrinth is one of the weirdest places I've ever visited. It's a labyrinth of connected caves under the castle area. No history or anything, this seems to be all about the atmosphere and the experience. It was creepy and scary with sound effects and no signs to guide you through. I got there right when they opened and was the only one there, which added to the creep factor. If you're claustrophobic or easily weirded out, skip it.   —Jackee

though you must pay to wander over most of it during the day over much of the year (as has been the practice since 2000), the price is reasonable. Medieval fishwives once peddled their wares here, but now you see merchants selling souvenirs and crafts, musicians, and—less visible but always present—pickpockets. Buy your tickets at the tiny office beside the Tourinform by the adjacent park. ■ TIP→ Our sources tell us that should you happen to arrive outside of open hours (i.e., when the ticket office is closed), chances are no one will mind if you step over the modest barrier and wander around for free. Don't say we told you so! ⊠ *District I, East of Szentháromság tér* ☎ *330 HUF Mar.–Oct. 15, 9 AM–9 PM daily; free Nov.–Feb.* ⊙ *Daily 24 hrs* Ⓜ *Várbusz (4th stop from M2: Moszkva tér).*

> **DON'T MISS**
>
> Just behind wing C on the palace's western side is one of Castle Hill's most striking sculptures—Alajos Strobl's multi-level, patina-covered work Mátyás's Kútja (Matthias's Well), complete with a little waterfall, hunting dogs, king's helpers, and a triumphant King Matthias topping off the scene—above a felled stag, that is.

❾ Kapisztrán tér (Capistrano Square). Castle Hill's northernmost square was named after St. John of Capistrano, an Italian friar who in 1456 recruited a crusading army to fight the Turks who were threatening Hungary. There's a statue of this honored Franciscan on the northwest corner; also here are the Museum of Military History and the remains of the 12th-century Gothic Mária Magdolna templom (Church of St. Mary Magdalene). Its *torony* (tower), completed in 1496, is the only part left standing; the rest of the church was destroyed by air raids during World War II. Ⓜ *Várbusz (3rd stop from M2: Moszkva tér).*

★ ❶ Királyi Palota (Royal Palace). A palace originally built on this spot in the 13th century for the kings of Hungary was reconstructed in Renaissance style under the supervision of King Matthias during the 15th century. That, in turn, was demolished as Buda was recaptured from the Turks in 1686. The Habsburg empress Maria Theresa directed the building of a new palace in the 1700s. It was damaged during an unsuccessful attack by revolutionaries in 1849, but the Habsburgs set about building again, completing work in 1905. Then, near the end of the Soviets' seven-week siege in February 1945, the entire Castle Hill district of palaces, mansions, and churches was reduced to rubble. Decades passed before reconstruction and whatever restoration was possible were completed. Archaeologists were able to recover both the original defensive walls and royal chambers, due in part to still surviving plans and texts from the reigns of Holy Roman Emperor Sigismund and King Matthias.

Freed from mounds of rubble, the foundation walls and medieval castle walls were completed, and the ramparts surrounding the medieval royal residence were re-created as close to their original shape and size as possible. If you want an idea of the Hungarian home-life of Franz Josef and Sissi, however, you'll have to visit the baroque Gödöllő Palace. The Royal Palace today is used as a cultural center and museum complex.

The Royal Palace's baroque southern wing (Wing E) contains the **Budapesti Történeti Múzeum** (Budapest History Museum), displaying a fascinating permanent exhibit of modern Budapest history from Buda's liberation from the Turks in 1686 through the 1970s. Viewing the vintage 19th- and 20th-century photos and videos of the castle, the Széchenyi Lánchíd, and other Budapest monuments—and seeing them as the backdrop to the horrors of World War II and the 1956 revolution—helps to put your later sightseeing in context.

Through historical documents, objects, and art, other permanent exhibits depict the medieval history of the Buda fortress and the capital as a whole. This is the best place to view remains of the medieval Royal Palace and other archaeological excavations. Some of the artifacts unearthed during excavations are in the vestibule in the basement; others are still among the remains of medieval structures. Down in the cellars are the palace's original medieval vaults; portraits of King Matthias and his second wife, Beatrice of Aragon; and many late-14th-century statues that probably adorned the Renaissance palace. ⊠ *District I, Királyi Palota (Wing E), Szent György tér 2* ☎ *1/225–7815* ⊕ *www.btm.hu* 🖅 *800 HUF* ☉ *mid-May–mid-Sept., daily 10–6; Mar.–mid-May and mid-Sept.–Oct., Wed.–Mon. 10–6; Nov.–Feb., Wed.–Mon. 10–4* Ⓜ *Várbusz (5th stop from M2: Moszkva tér).*

FodorśChoice
★

The **Magyar Nemzeti Galéria** (Hungarian National Gallery), which comprises the immense center block of the Royal Palace (Wings B, C, and D), exhibits Hungarian fine art, from medieval ecclesiastical paintings and statues through Gothic, Renaissance, and baroque art, to a rich collection of 19th- and 20th-century works. Especially notable are the works of the romantic painter Mihály Munkácsy, the impressionist Pál Szinyei Merse, and the surrealist Mihály Tivadar Kosztka Csontváry, whom Picasso much admired. There is also a large collection of modern Hungarian sculpture. Labels and commentary for both permanent and temporary exhibits are in English. If you contact the museum in advance, you can book a tour for up to five people with an English-speaking guide for 3,200 HUF (more for a larger group). There is a charge to use a camera or video camera. ⊠ *District I, Királyi Palota (entrance in Wing C), Dísz tér 17* ☎ *1/201–9082 or 20/439–7325* ⊕ *www.mng.hu* 🖅 *Museum free; special exhibits 1,200 HUF; photos 1,500 HUF, videos 2,000 HUF* ☉ *Tues.–Sun. 10–6* Ⓜ *Várbusz (5th stop from M2: Moszkva tér).*

> **TIGHT ON TIME IN THE NATIONAL GALLERY?**
>
> Go right to the rooms with the great19th-century Hungarian masters, László Munkácsy and László Pá. Don't miss Pál Szinyei Merse, who quite on his own pursued a style akin to French impressionism but was not appreciated in his own era. If you're a fan of early ecclesiastical art, the medieval triptychs are something to behold. Have 15 minutes to spare yet? Go to the rooms displaying the work of the Nagybánya School painters of the early 20th century, whose village and mountain scenes from a single Transylvanian town had a great influence on the nation's art.

The western wing (F) of the Royal Palace is the **Országos Széchenyi Könyvtár** (Széchenyi National Library), which houses more than 2 million volumes. Its archives include well-preserved medieval codices, manuscripts, and historic correspondence. This is not a lending library, but the reading rooms are open to the public (though you must show a passport); the most valuable materials can be viewed only on microfilm, however. Temporary exhibits on rare books and documents, for example, are usually on display; the hours for these special exhibits vary, and admission for smaller exhibits is sometimes free, though major exhibits usually have a charge of around 600 HUF. Note that the entire library closes for one month every summer, usually in August. ⊠ *District I, Királyi Palota (Wing F), Dísz tér 17* ☎ *1/224–3745, 1/224–3700 to arrange English-language tours* ⊕ *www.oszk.hu* 🖭 *Museum 600 HUF; sometimes a separate fee for special exhibits; one-day pass to the reading rooms 600 HUF* ☉ *Reading rooms Tues.–Fri. 9–9, Sat. 10–8; exhibits Mon. 1–6, Tues.–Sat. 10–6* Ⓜ *Várbusz (5th stop from M2: Moszkva tér).*

⑫ **Középkori Zsidó Imaház** (Medieval Synagogue). The excavated one-room medieval synagogue is now used as a museum. On display are objects relating to the Jewish community, including religious inscriptions, frescoes, and tombstones dating to the 15th century. ⊠ *District I, Táncsics Mihály utca 26* ☎ *1/225–7816* 🖭 *400 HUF* ☉ *May–Oct., Tues.–Sun. 10–6* Ⓜ *Várbusz (2nd stop from M2: Moszkva tér).*

FINE-WINE TIME

Whether **Magyar Borok Háza** (House of Hungarian Wines; ⊠ District 1, Szentháromság tér 6, across the street from the Budapest Hilton ☎ 1/212–1030 or 1/212–1031) is more properly called a museum or simply a self-promoting venture by the Hungarian wine industry is open to question, but it's the best place in Budapest to *liberally* sample a comprehensive selection of the country's finest wines while still appearing to be a respectable traveler. A ticket (which costs 4,000 HUF) is good for a two-hour, self-guided tour through a cellar, with more than 700 wines on display arranged by 22 wine regions and with classical music in the background; you may pour as you wish from some 50 open bottles, but you may not get visibly smashed. It's open daily from noon to 8 PM.

---

⑤ **Mátyás templom** (Matthias Church). The ornate white (er, sooty white)

Fodor'sChoice
★

steeple of the Matthias Church is the highest point on Castle Hill. It was added in the 15th century, above a 13th-century Gothic chapel. Officially the Buda Church of Our Lady, it has been known as the Matthias Church since the 15th century, in remembrance of the so-called "just king" who greatly added to and embellished it during his reign. Many of these changes were lost when the Turks converted it into a mosque. The intricate white stonework, mosaic roof decorations, and some of its geometric patterned columns seem to suggest Byzantium, yet it was substantially rebuilt again in the neo-baroque style 87 years after the Turkish defeat in 1686. One fortunate survivor of all the changes was perhaps the finest example of Gothic stone carving in Hungary, the Assumption of the Blessed Virgin Mary, visible above the door on the side of the church that faces the Danube.

The **Szentháromság Kápolna** (Trinity Chapel) holds an *encolpion,* an enameled casket containing a miniature copy of the Gospel to be worn on the chest; it belonged to the 12th-century king Béla III and his wife, Anne of Chatillon. Their burial crowns and a cross, scepter, and rings found in their excavated graves are also displayed here. The church's **treasury** contains Renaissance and baroque chalices, monstrances, and vestments. High Mass is celebrated every Sunday at 10 AM, sometimes with full orchestra and choir—and often with major soloists; get here early if you want a seat. During the summer there are usually organ recitals on Sundays at 7:30 PM. ⊠ *District I, Szentháromság tér 2* ☎ *1/355-5657* ☾ *Church weekdays 9–5, Sat. 9–3:30 (often closed to the public on Sat. afternoon), Sun. 3–5; treasury daily 9–5* 🚋 *Church and treasury 550 HUF; treasury only 330 HUF* Ⓜ *Várbusz (4th stop from M2: Moszkva tér).*

❸ **Nemzeti Táncszínház** (National Dance Theater). This former Franciscan church was transformed into a more secular royal venue in 1787 under the supervision of courtier Farkas Kempelen. The first theatrical performance in Hungarian was held here in 1790. Heavily damaged during World War II, the theater was rebuilt and reopened in 1978. While the building retains its original late-baroque facade, the interior was renovated with marble and concrete. It is now used for performances of Hungarian contemporary dance, including ballet, as well as concerts. There is usually an art exhibit or a historical exhibition in its foyer—usually theater-related, such as a display of costumes. ⊠ *District I, Színház utca 1–3* ☎ *1/201–4407* ⊕ *www.nemzetitancszinhaz.hu* 🚋 *Free (foyer exhibit)* ☾ *Daily 1–6* Ⓜ *Várbusz (5th stop from M2: Moszkva tér).*

❷ **Statue of Prince Eugene of Savoy.** In front of the Royal Palace, facing the Danube by the entrance to Wing C, stands an equestrian statue of Prince Eugene of Savoy, a commander of the army that liberated Hungary from the Turks at the end of the 17th century. From here there is a superb view across the river to Pest. ⊠ *District I, Királyi Palota (by Wing C entrance), Dísz tér 17* Ⓜ *Várbusz (5th stop from M2: Moszkva tér).*

❹ **Szentháromság tér** (Holy Trinity Square). This square is named for its baroque Trinity Column, erected in 1712–13 as a gesture of thanksgiving by survivors of a plague. The column stands in front of the famous Gothic Matthias Church, its large pedestal a perfect seat from which to watch the wedding spectacles that take over the church on spring and summer weekends: from morning until night, frilly engaged pairs flow in one after the other and, after a brief transformation inside, back out onto the square. As of this writing, the column was removed for renovation. But it should be back in place by spring 2007. ⊠ *District I* Ⓜ *Várbusz (4th stop from M2: Moszkva tér).*

★ ⓭ **Tóth Árpád sétány** (Árpád Tóth Promenade). This romantic, tree-lined promenade along the Buda side of the hill is often mistakenly overlooked by sightseers. Beginning at the Museum of Military History, the promenade takes you "behind the scenes" along the back sides of the matte-pastel baroque houses that face Úri utca, with their regal arched windows and wrought-iron gates. On a late spring afternoon the fragrance of the cherry

GOOD TO KNOW

What not to say to a Hungarian: That Hungary is great because everything is so inexpensive. Hearing visitors say this sends a chill up Hungarians' spines: it is a double reminder not only of their shaky economy but also of how folks elsewhere are relatively well off. Instead, tell Hungarians you love Hungary because it is lovely, because the people and places are bright and beautiful, because their language sounds so sumptuous, and because the food is scrumptious—likewise good reasons to love Hungary, after all.

Which bath? For a veritable Turkish experience, try the Rudas (popular with everyone) or the Király (previously a favorite of gay men, reportedly less so these days)—or the Rácz, if, that is, it ever reopens after years of reconstruction. For a host of services plus an outdoor wave pool at one of Budapest's grand old hotels, go to the Gellért, though it's the most crowded of all. For an unforgettable outdoor-indoor experience in a wide array of pools, set in halcyon City Park, the Széchenyi—the capital's only major bath that's fully coed every day of the week—is the one.

Where do I park? Parking downtown is, generally speaking, not nearly as hard as it may seem. Although you'll find parking garages here and there (e.g., near the basilica on Sas utca and on Aranykéz utca, right by the Váci utca shopping district), parking curbside is relatively easy even downtown if you have the patience to drive around a promising block several times. On business days you must pay for the appropriate time (up to 2-3 hours at a time, 120-400 HUF per hour) at a nearby ticket machine and display the ticket in your windshield.

Which line should I stand in at the post office? No sense wasting a half-hour in line with your postcards when everyone in front of you wants to pay their utility bills. So be sure you stand in line for a window with an envelope pictured above it; i.e., a window that accepts mail! Then again, since post offices here put your stamps on for you, if there are folks ahead of you with stacks of envelopes in their hands, you may be in for a long wait.

Is it okay to jaywalk? Yes—that is, Hungarians have nothing against breaking such rules. But look both ways.

What to do when people stare at you? Stare back, smile, or look the other way. Whether out of plain old curiosity or envy (you're the tourist, you have it easy) or both, some Hungarians are apt to stare, especially on public transport. Of course it's possible you're being stared at because you've caught someone's eye (in the romantic sense). Then it's for you to decide what to do. . . .

Tipping vs. "keep the change"? At a restaurant, give your server at least a 10% tip (customarily done by telling them the total, but it's fine to do subsequently). On your way out of a thermal bath, give a 100 forint coin to the person who locks (and then unlocks) your cabin. But when buying a newspaper or magazine for 390 forints, for example, give a wave of your hand to indicate that the clerk should keep that 10 forints.

Travels by Tram

Trams (*villamos*) are abundant and convenient, covering the entire city from around 5 AM to 11 PM, or a bit later. Though comfortable, you might well have to stand and grab a handhold for lack of a seat; trams can get crowded, particularly after around 7 AM and then throughout the day until early evening. Schedules, though not available in printed form, are posted at stops, and trams generally stick to them, although rush-hour traffic may sometimes throw a wrench into the otherwise smoothly functioning mechanism of public transport in the capital.

Tickets are widely available in metro stations and at many newsstands and (sometimes malfunctioning) sidewalk automats. The accepted method of payment is cash. Your best bet is simply to buy a pass, which you can do at a metro station. If you do opt to buy individual tickets instead (do so if you'll take only a handful of rides during the day and saving a couple of dollars is an issue), each ticket must be validated on board by inserting it, downward-facing, into the little device provided for that purpose, then pulling the knob; with newer devices, just insert the ticket. ■ TIP→ Hold on to whatever ticket you have throughout the length of the ride; spot checks by undercover checkers—who slip on red armbands just before getting down to their highly unpopular task—are numerous, and often target tourists.

MUST I VALIDATE MY TICKET IF THE TRAM OR BUS IS TOO CROWDED TO EVEN MOVE?
Jostle your way to that red or orange validation box no matter how thick the crowd, rules are rules. That said, as many thrifty Budapesters know as they warily clutch an unvalidated ticket in their hand, the chances of an inspector bothering to board at such crowded times are low—so you can accept the substantially reduced risk of being caught, especially if you're going just a stop or two or three. PS: don't tell the inspector that we told you so!

TRAM NO. 56 TO THE BUDA HILLS
If you have at least an hour to spare, hop aboard Tram No. 56, which sets out from Moszkva tér for a lovely 20-minute ride into the heart of the Buda Hills—perhaps the most economical scenic excursion in all of Budapest at a cost of two public transport tickets (or nothing if you have a pass). The *Fogaskerekű vasút* (cogwheel railway) station, from where you can ride up into the hills all the way to the beginning point of the scenic *Gyermek vasút* (Children's Railway), is on your left at the third stop. Before long the greenery becomes lush on your left, and the stately, if worn, apartment houses give you a sense of what Buda might have been like a century ago. At the fifth stop (Nagyajtai utca), look to your right for a statue of Raoul Wallenberg in a small, shaded park. From the seventh stop on, the lovely, forested Buda Hills are increasingly visible to your right; by the 12th stop it's as if the tram were passing through a forest; and, finally the tram reaches its 13th and final stop, at Hüvösvölgy, near the terminus of the Children's Railway and close to several trailheads.

OTHER SCENIC TRAM RIDES
For beautiful riverside views of Pest (including the Parliament building), hop aboard Tram 19 at Batthány tér and take it for 10 minutes or so to Gellért tér.

For stunning views of Buda (from Pest), get on Tram 2 at the Parliament building and take it 15 minutes or so to Fővám tér at the foot of Szabadság híd.

trees and the sweeping view of the quiet Buda neighborhoods below may be enough to revive even the most weary. ✉ *District I, from Kapisztrán tér to Szent György utca* Ⓜ *Várbusz (3rd stop from M2: Moszkva tér).*

❼ **Úri utca** (Úri Street). Running parallel to Tárnok utca, Úri utca has been less commercialized by boutiques and other shops. The longest and oldest street in the castle district, it is lined with many stately houses, all worth special attention for their delicately carved details. Both gateways of the baroque palace at Nos. 48–50—like those at Nos. 54–56—are articulated by Gothic niches from the 14th and 15th centuries.

▌ NEED A BREAK?
A few yards west of Szentháromság tér, the **Ruszwurm** (✉ Szentháromság utca 7 ☎ 1/375–5284) is Budapest's oldest surviving café, dating from the early 19th century. It's known for its excellent pastries and reasonable prices.

TABÁN & GELLÉRT-HEGY (GELLÉRT HILL)

Spreading below Castle Hill is the old quarter called Tabán (from the Turkish word for "armory"). A onetime suburb of Buda, it was known at the end of the 17th century as Little Serbia (*Rác*) because so many Serbian refugees settled here after fleeing from the Turks. It later became a district of vineyards and small taverns. Though most of the small houses characteristic of this district have been demolished—mainly in the interest of easing traffic—a few traditional buildings remain.

Gellért-hegy (Gellért Hill), 761 feet high, is the most beautiful natural formation on the Buda bank. It takes its name from St. Gellért (Gerard) of Csanád, a Venetian bishop who came to Hungary in the 11th century and, legend has it, was rolled off the top of the hill in a cart by pagans. The walk up can be tough, but take solace from the cluster of hot springs at its foot; these soothe and cure bathers at the Rác, Rudas, and Gellért baths.

Numbers in the text correspond to numbers in the margin and on the Central Budapest map.

▌ A GOOD WALK
From the **Semmelweis Orvostörténeti Múzeum** ⓮, walk around the corner to Szarvas tér, where you will find the **Szarvas-ház** ⓯ at No. 1, and a few yards toward the river the **Tabán plébánia-templom** ⓰. Walking south on Attila út and crossing to the other side of Hegyalja út, you can continue on to the foot of Gellért Hill. On the other side of the **Erzsébet híd** ⓱ is the Turkish Bath **Rudas Fürdő** ⓲. You might be in need of a good soak after climbing the stairs to the top of the hill (a strenuous 30-minute walk), but keep in mind that most days at the Rudas are men-only. Here, overlooking Budapest, is the **Citadella** ⓳, with its panoramic views of Budapest and the nearby Liberty Statue. You can return the way you came, or go down the southeastern side of the hill to the **Gellért Szálloda és Thermál Fürdő** ⓴ at its southeastern foot. If you don't feel like walking to the Gellért baths, you can also take Bus 27 down the back of the hill to Móricz Zsigmond körtér and walk back toward the Gellért on busy Bartók Béla út, or take Tram 47, 49, 18, or 19 a couple of stops to Szent Gellért tér. This is your best bet if you want to soak your

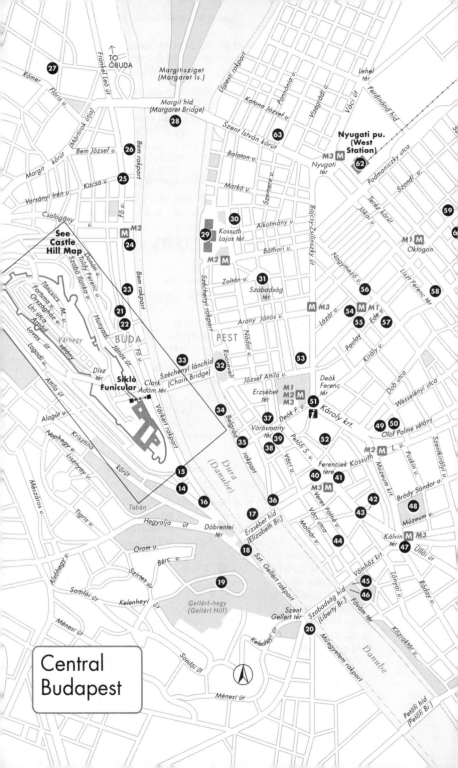

KEY

M Metro stops

ℹ Tourist information

⊢−−−⊣ Rail lines

0 _____ 500 yards

0 _____ 500 meters

aching bones after the long walk, as the baths are open to both men and women on any day.

TIMING The Citadella and Szabadság szobor are lit in golden lights every night, but the entire Gellért-hegy is at its scenic best every year on August 20, when it forms the backdrop to the spectacular St. Stephen's Day fireworks display. On a more practical note, should you wish to take advantage of the area's inviting baths, remember that not all baths are open on Sunday or Saturday afternoon, and they all close by 6 or 7.

What to See

★ ⓳ **Citadella.** The sweeping views of Budapest from this fortress atop the hill were once valued by the Austrian army, which used it as a lookout after the 1848–49 War of Independence. Some 60 cannons were housed in the citadel, though never used on the city's resentful populace. In the 1960s the Citadel was converted into a tourist site. Its outer perimeter includes a café and a beer garden. Within the walls you'll find a small graphic exhibition (with some relics) of Budapest's 2,000-year history, and a "World War II bunker exhibition" you can enter for 1,200 HUF (under 14 free), as well as a surprisingly hard-to-locate hotel.

Visible from many parts of the city, the 130-foot-high **Szabadság szobor** (Liberty Statue), just below the southern edge of the Citadella, was originally planned as a memorial to a son of Hungary's then-ruler, Miklós Horthy, whose warplane had crashed in 1942. However, by the time of its completion in 1947 (three years after Horthy was ousted), it had become a memorial (known until recently as the Liberation Monument) to the Russian soldiers who fell in the 1944–45 siege of Budapest; and hence for decades it was associated chiefly with this. From afar it looks light, airy, and even liberating. A sturdy young girl, her hair and robe swirling in the wind, holds a palm branch high above her head. During much of the communist era, and for a couple of years after its close, she was further embellished with sculptures of giants slaying dragons, Red Army soldiers, and peasants rejoicing at the freedom that Soviet liberation promised (but failed) to bring to Hungary. Since 1992 her mood has lightened: in the Budapest city government's systematic purging of communist symbols, the Red Combat infantrymen who had flanked the Liberty Statue for decades were hacked off and carted away. A few are now on display among the other evicted statues in Szobor Park in the city's 22nd district. ■ TIP→ **Just behind the statue is a small, open-air exhibit of Soviet artillery used in the 1944–45 seige of Budapest.** ✉ *District XI, Citadella sétány, Gellért-hegy and Tabán* ☎ *No phone* 🎫 *Free* ⊙ *Fortress daily* Ⓜ *47 or 49 tram.*

COFFEE STOP **Erzsébet híd eszpresszó** (✉ District I, Döbrentei tér 2–1, Gellért-hegy and Tabán ☎ 1/212–2127) may not be Budapest's most elegant café-cum-beer garden, but it sure is popular. Near the foot of the bridge after which it is named and close to Tabán's major sights (and baths), this is a convenient and inviting place to sit down in the shade at one of the many tables out front on a warm day for a beer, wine, espresso, mineral water, or soft drink. Despite the traffic roaring by, it is a longtime favorite with young Budapesters.

1

⑰ Erzsébet híd (Elizabeth Bridge). This bridge was named for Empress Elizabeth (1837–98), called Sissi, of whom the Hungarians were particularly fond. The beautiful but unhappy wife of Franz Joseph, she was stabbed to death in 1898 by an anarchist while boarding a boat on Lake Geneva. The bridge was built between 1897 and 1903; at the time, it was the longest single-span suspension bridge in Europe. Ⓜ *M3: Ferenciek tere.*

★ **⑳ Gellért Szálloda és Thermál Fürdő** (Gellért Hotel & Thermal Baths). At the foot of Gellért Hill the beautiful Art Nouveau Danubius Hotel Gellért is the oldest spa hotel in Hungary, with hot springs that have supplied curative baths for nearly 2,000 years. Its baths are the most popular among tourists, both because you don't need reservations, as you do at most other hotel-based thermal spas, and also because there's a wealth of treatments—including chamomile steam baths, salt-vapor inhalations, and hot mud packs. Many of these treatments require a doctor's prescription; prescriptions from foreign doctors are accepted. Most staff speak English. Men and women have separate steam and sauna rooms; both the indoor pool and the outdoor wave pool are coed. ⊠ *District XI, Gellért tér 1, at the foot of the hill, Gellért-hegy and Tabán* ☎ *1/466–6166 baths* 🖃 *2,900 HUF, 3,200 HUF with a private cabin; treatments extra* ⊙ *Baths Apr.–Oct., weekdays 6 AM–7 PM, weekends 6 AM–5 PM; Nov.–Mar., weekdays 6 AM–6 PM, weekends 6 AM–4 PM* Ⓜ *M3: Kálvin tér, then 47 or 49 tram 2 stops across the Danube.*

⑱ Rudas Fürdő (Rudas Baths). This bath is on the riverbank, the original Turkish pool making its interior possibly the most dramatically beautiful of Budapest's baths, though after its 2005 renovation some former fans say it has lost some of its magic. A high, domed roof admits pinpricks of bluish-green light into the dark, circular stone hall with its austere columns and arches. Fed by eight springs with a year-round temperature of 44°C (111°F), the Rudas's highly fluoridated waters have been known for 1,000 years. The thermal part is open by day Monday and Wednesday–Friday to men only and Tuesday to women only, and Saturdays to both sexes. Notably, it is coed also from 10 PM to 4 AM on Friday and Saturday. A less interesting outer swimming pool is open to both sexes. ⊠ *District I, Döbrentei tér 9, at the northern foot of the hill, Gellért-hegy and Tabán* ☎ *1/356–1322* 🖃 *2,000 HUF (200 HUF refund on your way out within 2 hrs, 300 HUF back within 3 hrs); 15-min. massage 2,400 HUF* ⊙ *weekdays 6 AM–8 PM, weekends 8 AM–5 PM* Ⓜ *M3: Ferenciek tere, then a 10-minute walk to Buda, across Erzsébet híd.*

OFF THE BEATEN PATH

SZOBOR PARK (STATUE PARK) – After the collapse of the Iron Curtain, Hungarians were understandably keen to rid Budapest of the symbols of Soviet domination. The communist statues and memorials that once dotted Budapest's streets and squares have been moved to this open-air "Disneyland of Communism." As well as the huge figures of Lenin and Marx, there are statues of the Hungarian worker shaking hands with his Soviet army comrade, and Hungarian puppet prime minister János Kádár. Somewhat tacky but amusing souvenirs are for sale, and songs from the Hungarian and Russian workers' movements play on a tinny speaker system. To get there, first go to Etele tér in Buda via either a red Bus 7 or Bus 173 from Ferenciek tere, Tram 49 from Deák tér, or Tram 19 from Batthyány tér; then catch the yellow Volán bus from Platform 2 (but ask here to be sure). ⊠ *District XXII, Balatoni út, corner of Szabadkai út, South Buda* ☎ *1/424–7500* ⊕ *www.szoborpark.hu* ✉ *600 HUF* ☉ *Daily 10–dusk.*

⓮ Semmelweis Orvostörténeti Múzeum (Semmelweis Museum of Medical History). This splendid baroque house was the birthplace of Ignác Semmelweis (1818–65), the Hungarian physician who proved the contagiousness of puerperal (childbed) fever. It's now a museum that traces the history of healing. Semmelweis's grave is in the garden. Just to the left is a bust of József Antall, a former director of the museum who went on to serve as Hungary's first prime minister in the post-communist era, from 1990 until he succumbed to cancer three years later. ⊠ *District I, Apród utca 1–3, Gellért-hegy and Tabán* ☎ *1/201–1577* ✉ *Free* ☉ *Mar.–Oct., Tues.–Sun. 10:30–6; Nov.–Feb., Tues.–Sun. 10:30–4* Ⓜ *M3: Ferenciek tere, then a 15-minute walk to Buda, across Erzsébet híd.*

⓯ Szarvas-ház (Stag House). This pale yellow, Louis XVI–style building is named for the former Szarvas Café or, more accurately, for its extant trade sign, with an emblem of a stag not quite at bay, which can be seen above the arched entryway. The structure houses the Aranyszarvas restaurant, which preserves some of the mood of the old Tabán. ⊠ *District I, Szarvas tér 1, Gellért-hegy and Tabán* Ⓜ *M3: Ferenciek tere, then a 15-minute walk to Buda, across Erzsébet híd.*

⓰ Tabán plébánia-templom (Tabán Parish Church). This church, whose steeple is a symbol of the old Tabán neighborhood, arose between 1728 and 1736 on the site of a Turkish mosque and was subsequently expanded several times, its present facade dating to 1880–81. Its form—mustard-colored stone with a rotund, green clock tower—could be described as restrained baroque. ⊠ *District I, Attila utca 1, Gellért-hegy and Tabán* Ⓜ *M3: Ferenciek tere, then a 15-minute walk to Buda, across the Erzsébet híd.*

HERE'S WHERE   Named after architect Miklós Ybl (1814–1891), the eerily quiet square, **Ybl Miklós tér,** is right along the Danube, midway between the Erzsébet híd and the Lánchíd. With the exception of Ybl's spiffy-looking Várkert Casino at No. 9, much of it looks almost forgotten by time. Ybl's building at No. 2, built between 1875 and 1880, features a plaque in memory of writer, member of Parliament, and director of Hungarian Radio Gyula Somogyváry, who lived there from 1937 to 1950 and was "taken from here by the Gestapo in 1944, and then in 1950 by the communist secret police." ⊠ *District I, Gellért-hegy and Tabán* Ⓜ *M3: Ferenciek tere, then a 15-minute walk to Buda, across the Erzsébet híd.*

NORTH OF VÁRHEGY

Most of these sights are along Fő utca (Main Street), a long, straight thoroughfare that starts at the Chain Bridge and runs parallel to the Danube. It is lined on both sides with multistory late-18th-century houses—many darkened by soot and showing their age more than those you see in sparklingly restored Castle Hill. This northbound exploration can be done with the help of Bus 86, which covers the waterfront, or on foot, although this is a fairly large area.

Numbers in the text correspond to numbers in the margin and on the Exploring Budapest map.

A GOOD WALK

Begin your walk along Fő utca. Stop first to take in the arresting beauty of the **Corvin tér** ㉑; just a block down Fő utca is the **Kapucinus Templom** ㉒, which was originally a Turkish mosque. Continue your walk up Fő utca, stopping at two other scenic squares, **Szilágyi Dezső tér** ㉓ and **Batthyány tér** ㉔, with its head-on view of Parliament across the Danube. From there, continue north on Fő utca, passing (or stopping to bathe at) the famous Turkish **Király-fürdő** ㉕. From **Bem József tér** ㉖, go one block north, turn left (away from the river) and walk up Fekete Sas utca, crossing busy Margit körút and turning right, one block past, up Mecset utca. This will take you up the hill to **Gül Baba türbéje** ㉗. From here, walk back to the river and cross the **Margit híd** ㉘. You might also wish to explore Margit-sziget in the middle of the Danube.

TIMING

Expect the walk from Bem József tér up the hill to Gül Baba türbéje to take about 25 minutes. Fő utca and Bem József tér can get congested during rush hours (from around 7:30 AM to 8:30 AM and 4:30 PM to 6 PM). But add 1½ hours for a good soak at the baths. Remember that museums are closed Monday and that the Király Baths are open to men and women on different days of the week.

What to See

㉔ **Batthyány tér.** There are tremendous views of Parliament from this square named after Count Lajos Batthyány, the prime minister shot dead in the 1848 revolution. The M2 subway, the HÉV electric railway from Szentendre, and various suburban and local buses converge on the square, and there's even a supermarket here. At No. 7 Batthyány tér is the beautiful, baroque twin-tower **Szent Anna-templom** (Church of St. Anne), dating from 1740–62, its oval cupola adorned with frescoes and statuary. ✉ *District I, Fő utca at Batthyány utca, Around Batthyány tér* Ⓜ *M2: Batthyány tér.*

NEED A BREAK?

The **Angelika kávéház** (✉ District I, Batthyány tér 7, Around Batthyány tér ☎ 1/212–3784), in the rectory of the Church of St. Anne, quickly became a popular hangout for writers, poets, and other artists after its establishment in 1973. Elegant yet homey, rather touristy, and a bit smoky, it serves everything from traditional pastries to gourmet appetizers and grilled meats. You can sit inside in one of several large rooms, or at one of the umbrella-shaded tables outdoors.

㉖ **Bem József tér.** This square near the river is not particularly picturesque and can get heavy with traffic, but it houses the statue of its important namesake, Polish general József Bem, who offered his services to the 1848 revolutionaries in Vienna and then Hungary. Reorganizing the rebel forces in Transylvania, he was the war's most successful general. It was at this statue on October 23, 1956, that a big demonstration exploded into the

Hungarian uprising suppressed by the Red Army. ⊠ *District II, Fő utca at Bem József utca, Around Batthyány tér* Ⓜ *M2: Batthyány tér.*

㉑ Corvin tér. This small, shady square on Fő utca is the site of a turn-of-the-20th-century building that houses the Hungarian Cultural Institute and, at No. 8, the Budai Vigadó concert hall. There's also a pleasant little café. From Corvin tér you can see the spires of the Halászbástya (Fishermen's Bastion) up above, on Castle Hill. ⊠ *District I, Fő utca at Ponty utca, Around Batthyány tér* Ⓜ *M2: Batthyány tér.*

㉗ Gül Baba türbéje (Tomb of Gül Baba). Gül Baba, a 16th-century dervish and poet whose name means "father of roses" in Turkish, was buried in a tomb built of carved stone blocks with four oval windows. He fought in several wars waged by the Turks and fell during the siege of Buda in 1541. The tomb remains a place of pilgrimage; it is considered Europe's northernmost Muslim shrine and marks the spot where he was slain. Set at an elevation on Rózsadomb (Rose Hill), the tomb is near a good lookout for city views. ⊠ *District II, Mecset utca 14, North Buda* 🎫 *500 HUF* ☉ *May–Sept., Tues.–Sun. 10–6; Oct., Tues.–Sun. 10–4* Ⓜ *M2: Batthyány tér or Moszkva tér.*

OFF THE BEATEN PATH

GYERMEK VASÚT – The 12-km (7-mi) Children's Railway—so called because it's operated primarily by children—runs from Széchenyi-hegy to Hűvösvölgy. The sweeping views make the trip well worthwhile for children and adults alike. Departures are from Széchenyi-hegy. To get to Széchenyi-hegy, take Tram 56 from Moszkva tér, and change to the cog railway (public transport tickets valid) at the Fogaskerekű Vasút stop. Take the cog railway uphill to the last stop and then walk a few hundred yards down a short, partly forested road to the left, in the direction most others will be going. The railway terminates at Hűvösvölgy, where you can catch Tram 56 back to Moszkva tér. ⊠ *District XII, Szilágyi Erzsébet fasor and Pasaréti út, Buda Hills* ☎ *1/397–5392* ⊕ *www.gyermekvasut. com* 🎫 *400 HUF one-way* ☉ *Late Apr.–Oct., weekdays 9–6, weekends 9–8; Nov.–late Apr., daily 9–5 (sometimes closed Tues.). Trains run hourly on weekdays, every 45 min on weekends* Ⓜ *M2: Moszkva tér.*

JÁNOSHEGY – A *libegő* (chairlift) will take you to János Hill—at 1,729 feet the highest point in Budapest—where you can climb a lookout tower for the best view of the city. To get there, take Bus 158 from Moszkva tér to the last stop, Zugligeti út. *Chairlift* ⊠ *District XII, Zugligeti út 97, Buda Hills* ☎ *1/394–3764* 🎫 *500 HUF one-way* ☉ *Mid-May–mid-Sept., daily 9–5; mid-Sept.–mid-May (depending on weather), daily 10–4; closed every other Mon.* Ⓜ *M2: Moszkva tér.*

㉒ Kapucinus templom (Capuchin Church). This church was converted from a Turkish mosque at the end of the 17th century. Damaged during the revolution in 1849, it acquired its current romantic exterior when it was rebuilt a few years later. ⊠ *District II, Fő utca 32, Around Batthyány tér* Ⓜ *M2: Batthyány tér.*

㉕ Király-fürdő (Király Baths). In 1565 Sokoli Mustapha, the Turkish pasha of Buda, ordered the construction of Turkish baths within the old city walls, to ensure that the Turks could still bathe in the event of siege. A stone cupola, crowned by a golden moon and crescent, arches over the steamy, dark pools indoors. It is open to men on Tuesday, Thursday, and Saturday; to women on Monday, Wednesday, and Friday. These baths are popular with the gay male community. ⊠ *District II, Fő utca 84, Around Batthyány tér* ☎ *1/202–3688* 💰 *1,000 HUF for 1½ hrs* ☉ *Weekdays 9–8 for men (admission until 7), 7–6 for women (admission until 5); Sat. 6:30–noon* Ⓜ *M2: Batthyány tér.*

㉘ Margit híd (Margaret Bridge). At the southern end of Margaret Island, the Margaret Bridge is the closer of the two island entrances for those coming from downtown Buda or Pest. Just north of the Chain Bridge, the bridge walkway provides gorgeous mid-river views of Castle Hill and Parliament. The original bridge was built during the 1840s by French engineer Ernest Gouin in collaboration with Gustave Eiffel. Toward the end of 1944, the bridge was blown up by the retreating Nazis while crowded with rush-hour traffic. It was rebuilt in the same unusual shape—forming an obtuse angle in midstream, with a short leg leading down to the island. ⊠ *Margit-sziget* Ⓜ *M2: Batthyány tér or M1: Nyugati Train Station (then Tram 4 or 6).*

㉙ Szilágyi Dezső tér. This is another of the charming little squares punctuating Fő utca. At its center is the striking, neo-Gothic **Budai Református Templom** (Buda Reformed Church), designed by Samu Pecz and built in 1893–96; rising above the deep-red brickwork of its facade, both its steeple and a massive dome above the main part of the church are covered with colorful tilework from the famous Zsolnay factory in Pécs. ■ TIP→ Also on the square is the building where composer Béla Bartók lived, **No. 4.** ⊠ *District I, Fő utca at Székely utca, Around Batthyány tér* Ⓜ *M2: Batthyány tér.*

DOWNTOWN PEST & THE SMALL RING ROAD

Budapest's urban heart is full of bona fide sights plus innumerable tiny streets and grand avenues where you can wander for hours admiring the city's stately old buildings—some freshly sparkling after their first painting in decades, others silently but still gracefully crumbling.

Dominated by the Parliament building, the district surrounding Kossuth tér is the legislative, diplomatic, and administrative nexus of Budapest; most of the ministries are here, as are the National Bank and Courts of Justice. Downriver, the romantic Danube promenade, the Duna korzó, extends along the stretch of riverfront across from Castle Hill. With Vörösmarty tér and pedestrian shopping street Váci utca just inland, this area forms Pest's tourist core. Going south, the korzó ends at Március 15 tér. One block in from the river, Ferenciek tere marks the beginning of the university area, spreading south of Kossuth Lajos utca. Here the streets are narrower, and the sounds of your footsteps echo off the elegantly aging stone buildings.

However, another stretch of Váci utca, pedestrianized in the 1990s and rivalling the older, more famous section with a rich array of antiques stores, bookshops, cafés, and restaurants, continues on the other side of busy Szabad sajtó út all the way to the next bridge, Szabadság híd, and the indoor food market, the Vásárcsarnok. From here it's just a few blocks to yet another vibrant, Pest-side street revitalized in the 1990s, Ráday utca.

Pest is laid out in broad circular *körúts* ("ring roads" or boulevards). Vámház körút is the first sector of the 2½-km (1½-mi) Kis körút (Small Ring Road), which traces the route of the Old Town wall from Szabadság híd (Liberty Bridge) to Deák tér. Construction of the inner körút

> ### THE BEST VIEWS
>
> Stand anywhere downtown along the Danube. More specifically, you might take a walk along the corso from Roosevelt tér to Ferenciek tere; walk to the middle of the Lánchíd (Chain Bridge); or else work your way to the foot of Szabadság-híd (Liberty Bridge), from where the relatively close-up view of Freedom Hill only adds to the effect.

began in 1872 and was completed in 1880. Changing names as it curves, after Kálvin tér it becomes Múzeum körút (passing by the National Museum) and then Károly körút for its final stretch ending at Deák tér. Deák tér, the only place where all three subway lines converge, could be called the dead center of downtown. East of Károly körút are the weathered streets of Budapest's former ghetto.

A GOOD WALK

After starting at Kossuth tér to see the **Országház** ㉙ and the **Néprajzi Múzeum** ㉚, it's worth walking a few blocks southeast to take in stately **Szabadság tér** ㉛ before heading back to the Danube and south to **Roosevelt tér** ㉜, which is at the foot of the **Széchenyi Lánchíd** ㉝. As this tour involves quite a bit of walking, you may want to take Tram 2 from Kossuth tér a few stops downriver to Roosevelt tér to save your energy. While time and/or energy may not allow it just now, at some point during your visit, a walk across the Chain Bridge is a must.

From Roosevelt tér go south, across the street, and join the **Korzó** ㉞ along the river, strolling past the **Vigadó** ㉟ at Vigadó tér, all the way to the **Belvárosi plébánia templom** ㊱ at Március 15 tér, just under the Elizabeth Bridge. Double back up the korzó to Vigadó tér and walk in from the river on Vigadó utca to **Vörösmarty tér** ㊲. Follow the crowds down pedestrian-only **Váci utca** ㊳, and when you reach Régiposta utca, take a detour to the right to see the **Görög Ortodox templom** ㊴. Return to Váci utca and continue south; at Ferenciek tere, look for the grand **Párizsi udvar** ㊵ arcade. Across busy Kossuth Lajos utca, you will find the **Ferenciek templom** ㊶. From here, stroll Petőfi Sándor utca, passing the Greek Orthodox temple, and continue along Károlyi Mihály utca past the **Petőfi Irodalmi Múzeum** ㊷ and **Egyetem tér** ㊸. Take a right on Szerb utca until you get to Veres Pálné utca, where you will find a 17th-century **Szerb Ortodox templom** ㊹. Continuing down Szerb utca, you'll find yourself at the southern end of Váci utca, facing **Vásárcsarnok** ㊺, the huge market.

Across Vámház körút is the campus of the **Közgazdasági Egyetem** ㊻, the University of Economics. From here you can either walk or take Tram 47 or 49 to **Kálvin tér** ㊼. One block before Kálvin tér is Ráday utca, which in recent years has been transformed into a lively, largely pedestrian thoroughfare of cafés and restaurants.

Just north of Kálvin tér on Múzeum körút is the **Magyar Nemzeti Múzeum** ㊽. The **Nagy Zsinagóga** ㊾ is about ¾ km (⅓ mi) farther north along the Kis körút (Small Ring Road)—a longish walk or one short stop by tram; around the corner from the synagogue is the **Zsidó Múzeum** ㊿. ■ TIP→ **There's a beautiful little park, so easily missed, right across the street from Múzeum körút No. 4. There are plenty of benches, birdsong, plane trees, and a playground.** From here, more walking along the körút, or a tram ride brings you to Pest's main hub, Deák tér, where you'll find the **Evangelikus templom** (51), Budapest's main Lutheran church.

From Deák tér it's a short walk to the **Városház** (52), Budapest's old city hall building. The **Szent István Bazilika** (53) is an extra but rewarding 500-yard walk north on Bajcsy-Zsilinszky út.

TIMING This is a particularly rich part of the city; the suggested walk will take the better part of a day, including time to visit the museums, stroll on the Korzó, and browse on Váci utca—not to mention time for lunch. Keep in mind that the museums are closed on Monday.

What to See

★ ㊱ **Belvárosi plébánia templom** (Inner City Parish Church). Dating to the 12th century, this is the oldest—and, in terms of architectural history, the most extraordinary—ecclesiastical building in Pest. It's actually built on even older structures–an 11th-century Romanesque church commissioned by Hungary's first king, Saint Stephen, plus the remains of the Contra Aquincum (a third-century Roman fortress and tower), parts of which are visible. There is hardly any architectural style that cannot be found in some part or another, starting with a single Romanesque arch in its south tower. The single nave, with an equally high transept and unusually slender columns, still has its original Gothic chancel and some frescoes from the 14th–15th centuries. Two side chapels contain beautifully carved Renaissance altarpieces and tabernacles of red marble from the early 16th century. During Budapest's Turkish occupation the church served as a mosque—a *mihrab,* a Muslim prayer niche, is a reminder. During the 18th century the church was given two baroque towers and its present facade. In 1808 it was enriched with a rococo pulpit. From 1867 to 1875 Franz Liszt lived in a town house a few steps away, where he held regular "musical Sundays" at which Richard and Cosima Wagner were frequent guests. Liszt's own musical Sunday mornings often began in this church. He conducted many masses here, including the first Budapest performance of his *Missa Choralis* in 1872. The church contains the relics of Saint Gellért, the bishop who was initially buried here in 1046 after pagans pushed him off a hill across the river. And in 2006 the relics of the legendary 11th-century Hungarian king, Saint László, found their way here as well. Talkative, sweet little old ladies receive you at the door and hand out brochures (which include English-language text). ✉ *District V, Március 15 tér 2, Around Váci utca* ☎ *1/318–3108* 🎫 *Free* ⏲ *Weekdays 9–7, weekends during services* Ⓜ *M3: Ferenciek tere.*

43 **Egyetem tér** (University Square). Budapest's University of Law sits here in the heart of the city's university neighborhood. On one corner is the cool gray-and-green marble **Egyetemi Templom** (University Church), one of Hungary's most beautiful baroque buildings. Built between 1725 and 1742, it has an especially splendid pulpit and an elaborately carved door. ⊠ *District V, Around Ferenciek tere* Ⓜ *M3: Ferenciek tere.*

NEED A BREAK?

Though billed as a café, **Centrál** (⊠ District V, Károlyi Mihály utca 9, Around Ferenciek tere ☎ 1/266–2110) is actually more a living museum. It enjoyed fame as an illustrious literary café during Budapest's late-19th- and early-20th-century golden age and, after years of neglect, was finally restored to its original luster a few years ago. Centrál's menu includes, with each main dish, a recommended wine by the glass—as well as a good selection of vegetarian dishes and desserts. (And it has some of the most spotless toilets in all of Budapest.)

---

51 **Evangélikus Templom & Evangélikus Múzeum** (Lutheran Church & Lutheran Museum). The neoclassical Lutheran Church sits in the center of it all on busy Deák tér. Classical concerts are regularly held here. The church's interior designer, János Krausz, flouted then-traditional church architecture by placing a single large interior beneath the huge vaulted roof structure. The adjoining school is now the Lutheran Museum, which traces the role of Protestantism in Hungarian history and contains Martin Luther's original will. ⊠ *District V, Deák Ferenc tér 4, Around Deák Ferenc tér* ☎ *1/317–4173* 🎟 *Museum 300 HUF, including a tour of church* ☉ *Museum Mar.–Oct., Tues.–Sun. 10–6; Nov.–Feb., Tues.–Sun. 10–5. Church daily 2–6* Ⓜ *M1, M2, M3: Deák Ferenc tér.*

41 **Ferenciek templom** (Franciscan Church). This pale yellow church was built in 1743. On the wall facing Kossuth Lajos utca is a bronze relief showing a scene from the devastating flood of 1838; the detail is so vivid that it almost makes you seasick. A faded arrow below the relief indicates the high-water mark of almost 4 feet. ⊠ *District V, Felszabadulás tér, Around Ferenciek tere* Ⓜ *M3: Ferenciek tere.*

39 **Görög Ortodox templom** (Greek Orthodox Church). Built at the end of the 18th century in late-baroque style, the Greek Orthodox Church was remodeled a century later by Miklós Ybl, who designed the Opera House and many other important Budapest landmarks. The church retains some fine woodcarvings and a dazzling collection of icons by late-18th-century Serbian master Miklós Jankovich. ⊠ *District V, Petőfi tér 2/b, Around Váci utca* Ⓜ *M3: Ferenciek tere.*

47 **Kálvin tér.** Calvin Square takes its name from the neoclassical Hungarian Reformed (Calvinist) church that tries to dominate this busy traffic hub; this is a hard task, what with the dull-as-can-be glass facade of the Kálvin Center office building across the square. The Kecskeméti Kapu, a main gate of Pest, once stood here, as well as a cattle market that was a notorious den of thieves. At the beginning of the 19th century this was where Pest ended and the prairie began. ⊠ *District V, Around Kálvin tér* Ⓜ *M3: Kálvin tér.*

46 **Közgazdasági Egyetem** (University of Economics). Just below Szabadság híd (Liberty Bridge) on the waterfront, the monumental neo-Renaissance building was once the Customs House. Built in 1871–74 by Miklós Ybl, it is now also known as *közgáz* ("econ."), following a stint during the Communist era as Karl Marx University. ⊠ *District V, Fővám tér, Around Kálvin tér* Ⓜ *M3: Kálvin tér.*

★ **34** **Korzó** (Promenade). The neighborhood to the south of Roosevelt tér has regained much of its past elegance—if not its architectural grandeur— with the erection of the Sofitel (formerly the Hyatt Regency), Inter-Continental, and Marriott luxury hotels. Traversing all three and continuing well beyond them is the riverside *korzó,* a pedestrian promenade lined with park benches and appealing outdoor cafés from which one can enjoy postcard-perfect views of Gellért Hill and Castle Hill directly across the Danube. Try to take a stroll in the evening, when the views are lit up in shimmering gold lights. ⊠ *District V, from Eötvös tér to Március 15 tér, Around Váci utca* Ⓜ *M3: Ferenciek tere (or M1, M2, M3: Deák Ferenc tér).*

★ **48** **Magyar Nemzeti Múzeum** (Hungarian National Museum). Following an overhaul early in the new millennium, this museum's permanent exhibit is no longer its relatively dry old self but a real treat: a stimulating journey into the heart of the everyday Hungarian experience from the recent to the more distant past. Among the highlights are the 20th-century exhibit, including an early cinema replete with films of the era, an old schoolroom, a 1960s apartment interior, and a host of historical posters— all of which takes you right up to the end of communism and the much-celebrated exodus of Russian troops. Many of the museum's previous main attractions also remain as part of this mix, including masterworks of cabinetmaking and woodcarving (e.g., church pews from Nyírbátor and Transylvania); a piano that belonged to both Beethoven and Liszt; and, in the treasury, masterpieces of goldsmithing. ⊠ *District IX, Múzeum körút 14–16, Around Kálvin tér* ☎ *1/338–2122* 💲 *Free* ☉ *Tues.–Sun. 10–6* Ⓜ *M3: Kálvin tér.*

49 **Nagy Zsinagóga** (Great Synagogue). Seating 3,000, Europe's largest synagogue was designed by Ludwig Förs and built between 1844 and 1859 in a Byzantine-Moorish style described as "consciously archaic Romantic-Eastern." Desecrated by German and Hungarian Nazis, it was painstakingly reconstructed with donations from all over the world; its doors reopened in the fall of 1996. While used for regular services during much of the year, it is generally not used in midwinter, as the space is too large to heat; between December and February, visiting hours are erratic. In the courtyard behind the synagogue a weeping willow made of metal honors the victims of the Holocaust. Liszt and Saint-Saëns are among the great musicians who played the synagogue's grand organ. ⊠ *District VII, Dohány utca 2–8, Around Astoria* ☎ *1/342–8949* 💲 *Free* ☉ *Mon.–Thurs. 10–5, Fri. and Sun. 10–2* Ⓜ *M2: Astoria.*

FodorsChoice ★

30 **Néprajzi Múzeum** (Museum of Ethnography). The 1890s neoclassical temple formerly housed the Supreme Court. Now an impressive permanent exhibition, "The Folk Culture of the Hungarian People," explains all

FodorsChoice ★

aspects of peasant life from the end of the 18th century until World War I; explanatory texts are provided in both English and Hungarian. Besides embroideries, pottery, and carvings—the authentic pieces you can't see at touristy folk shops—there are farming tools, furniture, and traditional costumes. The central room of the building alone is worth the entrance fee: a majestic hall with ornate marble staircases and pillars, and towering stained-glass windows. ⊠ *District V, Kossuth tér 12, Parliament* ☎ *1/473–2400* ⊕ *www.neprajz.hu* ⊠ *700 HUF* ☉ *Tues.–Sun. 10–6* Ⓜ *M2: Kossuth tér.*

★ ㉙ **Országház** (Parliament). The most visible symbol of Budapest's left bank is the huge neo-Gothic Parliament. Mirrored in the Danube much the way Britain's Parliament is reflected in the Thames, it lies midway between the Margaret and Chain bridges and can be reached by the M2 subway and waterfront Tram 2. A fine example of historicizing, eclectic fin-de-siècle architecture, it was designed by the Hungarian architect Imre Steindl and built by a thousand workers between 1885 and 1902. The grace and dignity of its long facade and 24 slender towers, with spacious arcades and high windows balancing its vast central dome, lend this living landmark a refreshingly baroque spatial effect. The exterior is lined with 90 statues of great figures from Hungarian history; the corbels are ornamented by 242 allegorical statues. Inside are 691 rooms, 10 courtyards, and 29 staircases; some 88 pounds of gold were used for the staircases and halls. These halls are also a gallery of late-19th-century Hungarian art, with frescoes and canvases depicting Hungarian history, starting with Mihály Munkácsy's large painting of the Magyar Conquest of 896.

Since early 2000 Parliament's most sacred treasure has not been the Hungarian legislature but the **Szent Korona** (Holy Crown), which reposes with other royal relics under the cupola. The crown sits like a golden soufflé above a Byzantine band of holy scenes in enamel and pearls and other gems. It seems to date from the 12th century, so it could not be the crown that Pope Sylvester II presented to St. Stephen in the year 1000, when he was crowned the first king of Hungary. Nevertheless, it is known as the Crown of St. Stephen and has been regarded—even by communist governments—as the legal symbol of Hungarian sovereignty and unbroken statehood. In 1945 the fleeing Hungarian army handed over the crown and its accompanying regalia to the Americans rather than have them fall into Soviet hands. They were restored to Hungary in 1978. The crown can be seen in the course of daily tours of the Parliament building, which is the only way you can visit the Parliament, except during ceremonial events and when the legislature is in session (usually Monday and Tuesday from late summer to spring). Lines may be long, so it's best to call in advance for reservations. The building can also be visited as part of a four-hour city tour led by IBUSZ Travel at 10 and 11 AM daily for 9,900 HUF. ⊠ *District V, Kossuth tér, Parliament* ☎ *1/441–4412, 1/441–4415, 1/441–4904 for info and tour reservations, 1/485–2722 for IBUSZ Travel* ⊟ *1/441–4801* ⊕ *www.mkogy. hu* ⊠ *2,070 HUF* ☉ *Mon. 8–11 AM, Tues.–Fri. 8–6, Sat. 8–4, Sun. 8–2; daily tours in English at 10 and 2, starting from Gate No. 10, just right of main stairs* Ⓜ *M2: Kossuth tér.*

40 **Párizsi Udvar** (Paris Court). This glass-roof arcade was built in 1914 in richly ornamental neo-Gothic, Renaissance, and arabesque styles. Sorely in need of an overhaul to restore its former brilliance, nowadays it's filled with touristy boutiques. ⊠ *District VI, corner of Petőfi Sándor utca and Kossuth Lajos utca, Around Ferenciek tere* Ⓜ *M3: Ferenciek tere.*

42 **Petőfi Irodalmi Múzeum** (Petőfi Literary Museum). Founded in 1954 as the national museum of 19th- and 20th-century Hungarian literature, this lovely venue—named after Hungary's famous poet of the 1848 revolution, Sándor Petőfi—is well worth a visit regardless of what you know (or don't know) about Hungarian literature. For one thing, it's in the ravishing Károlyi Palota. Bestowed with a new facade and interior beginning in the late 18th century by its owners, the Károlyi family, the palace has some grand staircases and stunning rooms that were renovated in recent years. A ticket allows you to visit not only the literary exhibits, which include a fascinating collection of objects relating to the lives of some of Hungary's dearest writers and poets, but also other parts of the building. ■ **TIP→** Behind the palace is its lovely onetime park, Károlyi kert, which has long been open to the public at no charge. ⊠ *District IX, Károly Mihályi utca 16, Around Ferenciek tere* ☎ *1/317–3611* ⊕ *www. pim.hu* ⊠ *Permanent collection free, special exhibits 350 HUF* ⊙ *Tues.–Sun. 10–6* Ⓜ *M3: Ferenciek tere.*

32 **Roosevelt tér.** This square opening onto the Danube is less closely connected with the U.S. president than with the progressive Hungarian statesman Count István Széchenyi, dubbed "the greatest Hungarian" even by his adversary Kossuth. The neo-Renaissance palace of the **Magyar Tudományos Akadémia** (Academy of Sciences) on the north side was built between 1862 and 1864, after Széchenyi's suicide. It is a fitting memorial, for in 1825 the statesman donated a year's income from all his estates to establish the academy. Another Széchenyi project, the Széchenyi Lánchíd, leads into the square; there stands a statue of Széchenyi near one of another statesman, Ferenc Deák, whose negotiations led to the establishment of the dual monarchy after Kossuth's 1848–49 revolution failed. Both men lived on this square. The spectacular, Art Nouveau **Gresham Palota** is situated ideally on the square's east side facing the bridge. Designed by Zsigmond Quittner and completed in 1906, it reopened in 2004 as a luxury hotel. ⊠ *District V, Around Váci utca* Ⓜ *M1, M2, M3: Deák Ferenc tér.*

★ **31** **Szabadság tér.** The sprawling Liberty Square is dominated by the longtime headquarters of **Magyar Televízió** (Hungarian Television), a former stock exchange with what look like four temples and two castles on its roof. Across from it is a solemn-looking neoclassical shrine, the **Nemzeti Bank** (National Bank). The bank's Postal Savings Bank branch, adjacent to the main building but visible from behind Szabadság tér on Hold utca, is another exuberant Art Nouveau masterpiece of architect Ödön Lechner, built in 1901 with colorful majolica mosaics, characteristically curvaceous windows, and pointed towers ending in swirling gold flourishes. In the square's center remains a gold hammer and sickle atop a white stone obelisk, one of the few monuments to the Russian "liberation" of Budapest in 1945. There were mutterings that it, too, would be pulled down, which prompted a Russian diplomatic protest; the monument, after all, marks a gravesite of fallen Soviet troops. With the Stars and Stripes flying out in front, and a high-security presence, the **United States Embassy** is at Szabadság tér 12. ✉ *District V, Parliament* Ⓜ *M2: Kossuth tér or M3: Arany János utca.*

❸❸ **Széchenyi Lánchíd** (Chain Bridge). This is the oldest and most beautiful of the seven road bridges that span the Danube in Budapest. When lit up at night, it captures Budapest's radiance as do few other scenes. Before it was built, the river could be crossed only by ferry or by a pontoon bridge that had to be removed when ice blocks began floating downstream in winter. It was constructed at the initiative of the great Hungarian reformer and philanthropist Count István Széchenyi, using an 1839 design by the English civil engineer William Tierney Clark. This classical, almost poetically graceful and symmetrical suspension bridge was finished by the Scotsman Adam Clark (no relation to William Tierney Clark), who also built the 383-yard tunnel under Castle Hill, thus connecting the Danube quay with the rest of Buda. After it was destroyed by the Nazis, the bridge was rebuilt in its original form (though widened for traffic) and was reopened in 1949, on the centenary of its inauguration. ■ TIP➔ **At the Buda end of the bridge is Clark Ádám tér (Adam Clark Square), where you can zip up to Castle Hill on the Sikló funicular.** ✉ *District I, linking Clark Ádám tér with Roosevelt tér, Around Váci utca* 📞 *Funicular 700 HUF one-way* ☉ *Funicular daily 7:30 AM–10 PM (closed every other Mon.)* Ⓜ *M2: Batthyány tér or M1, M2, M3: Deák Ferenc tér.*

❺❸ **Szent István Bazilika** (St. Stephen's Basilica). Handsome and massive, this is one of the chief landmarks of Pest and the city's largest church—it can hold 8,500 people. Its very Holy Roman front porch greets you with a tympanum bustling with statuary. The basilica's dome and the dome of Parliament are by far the most visible in the Pest skyline, and this is no accident: with the Magyar Millennium of 1896 in mind (the lavishly celebrated thousandth anniversary of the settling of the Carpathian Basin in 896), both domes were planned to be 315 feet high.

FodorśChoice ★

The millennium was not yet in sight when architect József Hild began building the basilica in neoclassical style in 1851, two years after the revolution was suppressed. After Hild's death, the project was taken over in 1867 by Miklós Ybl, the architect who did the most to transform modern Pest into a monumental metropolis. Wherever he could, Ybl shifted Hild's motifs toward the neo-Renaissance mode that Ybl favored. When the dome collapsed, partly damaging the walls, he made even more drastic changes. Ybl died in 1891, five years before the 1,000-year celebration, and the basilica was completed in neo-Renaissance style by József Kauser—but not until 1905.

Below the cupola is a rich collection of late-19th-century Hungarian art: mosaics, altarpieces, and statuary (what heady days the Magyar Millennium must have meant for local talents). There are 150 kinds of marble, all from Hungary except for the Carrara in the sanctuary's centerpiece: a white statue of King (St.) Stephen I, Hungary's first king and patron saint. Stephen's mummified right hand is preserved as a relic in the **Szent**

Jobb Kápolna (Holy Right Chapel); press a button and it will be illuminated for two minutes. You can also climb the 364 stairs (or take the elevator) to the top of the cupola for a spectacular view of the city. Extensive renovation work here has, among other things, returned the cathedral from a sooty gray to an almost bright tan. Guided tours (available in English) cost 2,000 HUF and leave five times a day on weekdays (the first at 9:30) and twice on Saturdays (at 9:30 and 11). ⊠ *District V, Szt. István tér, Szent István Bazilika* ☎ *1/311–0839* 🕙 *Church and Szt. Jobb Chapel free, cupola 500 HUF* ☉ *Church Mon.–Sat. 9–5:30, Sun. 1–5:30. Szt. Jobb Chapel Apr.–Oct., Mon.–Sat. 9–5, Sun. 1–5; Nov.–Mar., Mon.–Sat. 10–4, Sun. 1–4. Cupola Apr. and Sept.–Oct., daily 10–5; May–Aug., daily 9–6* Ⓜ *M1, M2, M3: Deák Ferenc tér or M3: Arany János utca.*

㊹ Szerb Ortodox templom. Built in 1688, this lovely burnt-orange church, one of Budapest's oldest buildings, sits in a shaded garden surrounded by thick stone walls decorated with a large tile mosaic of St. George defeating the dragon. Its opening hours are somewhat erratic, but if the wrought-iron gates are open, wander in for a look at the beautiful hand-carved wooden pews. ⊠ *District V, Szerb utca, Around Váci utca* Ⓜ *M3: Kálvin tér.*

㊳ Váci utca. Immediately north of Elizabeth Bridge is Budapest's best-known shopping street and most unabashed tourist zone, Váci utca, a pedestrian precinct with electric 19th-century lampposts and smart shops with credit-card emblems on ornate doorways. No bargain basement, Váci utca gets its special flavor from the mix of native furriers, tailors, designers, folk-craft shops, china shops, bookstores, and internationally known boutiques. On Régi Posta utca, just off Vái utca, you'll find Hungary's first McDonald's, which opened in 1988. Váci utca's second half, south of Kossuth Lajos utca, was transformed into another pedestrian-only zone in the 1990s. On both halves of Váci utca, beware of inflated prices *and* pickpockets. ⊠ *District V, from Vörösmarty tér to Fővám tér, Around Váci utca* Ⓜ *M3: Ferenciek tere or M1: Vörösmarty tér.*

㊾ Városház (City Hall). The monumental former city council building, which used to be a hospital for wounded soldiers and then a home for the elderly, is now Budapest's city hall. You can freely enter its courtyard, but just how far you'll get beyond that may depend on whether the concierge woke up on the right side of his bed. Once Budapest's largest building, it is enormous enough to loom over the row of shops and businesses lining Károly körút in front of it but can only be entered through courtyards or side streets (it is most accessible from Gerlóczy utca). The Tuscan columns at the main entrance and the allegorical statuary of *Atlas, War,* and *Peace* are especially splendid. There was once a chapel in the center of the main facade, but now only its spire remains. ⊠ *District V, Városház utca 9–11, Around Deák Ferenc tér* ☎ *1/327–1000* 🕙 *Free* ☉ *Weekdays 6 AM–6:30 PM* Ⓜ *M1, M2, M3: Deák Ferenc tér.*

㊺ Vásárcsarnok (Central Market Hall). The magnificent hall, a 19th-century iron-frame construction, was reopened in late 1994 after years of renovation (and disputes over who would foot the bill). Even during the leanest years of communist shortages, the abundance of food came as a revelation to shoppers from East and West. Today the cavernous, three-story market, which is near the southern end of Váci utca, once again teems with people browsing among stalls packed with salamis and red-paprika chains. Upstairs you can buy folk embroideries and souvenirs and have your fill of Hungarian-style fast food. ⊠ *District IX, Vámház körút 1–3, Around Kálvin tér* ☎ *1/217–6067* ⊙ *Mon. 6 AM–5 PM, Tues.–Fri. 6 AM–6 PM, Sat. 6 AM–2 PM* Ⓜ *M3: Kálvin tér.*

❸❺ **Vigadó** (Concert Hall). Designed in a striking romantic style by Frigyes Feszl and inaugurated in 1865 with Franz Liszt conducting his own *St. Elizabeth Oratorio,* Budapest's premier city-center concert hall—whose facade was being renovated as of this writing—is a curious mixture of Byzantine, Moorish, Romanesque, and Hungarian motifs, punctuated by dancing statues and sturdy pillars. Brahms, Debussy, and Casals are among the other phenomenal musicians who have graced its stage. Mahler's *Symphony No. 1* and many works by Bartók were first performed here. You can go into the lobby on your own, but the rest is open only for concerts. ■ TIP→ There's a little park out front, fountain and all—a great place for a breather from the nearby Váci utca rush. ⊠ *District V, Vigadó tér 2, Around Váci utca* ☎ *1/318–7932 box office* Ⓜ *M1: Vörösmarty tér.*

▌ **NEED A BREAK?**   If you only visit one café in Budapest, stop on Vörösmarty Square at **Gerbeaud** (⊠ District V, Vörösmarty tér 7, Around Váci utca ☎ 1/429–9000), a café and pastry shop founded in 1858 by Hungarian Henrik Kugler and a Swiss, Emil Gerbeaud. The decor (green-marble tables, Regency-style marble fireplaces) is as sumptuous as the tempting selection of cake and sweets. The Gerbeaud's piano was originally intended for the *Titanic,* but was saved because it wasn't ready in time for the voyage.

★ ❸❼ **Vörösmarty tér.** Downtown revitalization since the early 1990s has de-centralized things somewhat, but this large, handsome square at the northern end of Váci utca is still the heart of Pest's tourist life in many respects. Street musicians, sidewalk cafés, and ice-cream-toting tourists make this one of the liveliest places in Budapest and a good spot to take it all in. At its center is a white-marble statue of the 19th-century poet and dramatist Mihály Vörösmarty, and nearby is an elegant former pis-soir—today a lovely kiosk displaying gold-painted historic scenes of the square's golden days. Stores and businesses occupy the perimeter, and as of this writing a grand new "multifunctional" building was rising on the square' west side. In June the square plays host to Budapest's annual "Book Week" and in the run-up to Christmas it is awash with gift stands. ⊠ *District V, at northern end of Váci utca, Around Váci utca* Ⓜ *M1: Vörösmarty tér.*

❺⓿ **Zsidó Múzeum** (Jewish Museum). The four-room museum, around the corner from the Great Synagogue, has displays explaining the effect of the Holocaust on Hungarian and Transylvanian Jews. (There are labels in English.) In late 1993 burglars ransacked the museum and got away with approximately 80% of its priceless collection; several months later, the stolen objects were found in Romania and returned to their rightful

home. ✉ *District VII, Dohány utca 2, Around Astoria* ☎ *1/343–6756*
💷 *1,000 HUF* ☉ *Mid-Mar.–mid-Oct., Mon.–Thurs. 10–5, Fri. and Sun.
10–2; mid-Oct.–mid-Mar., weekdays 10–3, Sun. 10–1* Ⓜ *M2: Astoria.*

ALONG ANDRÁSSY ÚT

Behind St. Stephen's Basilica, at the crossroad along Bajcsy-Zsilinszky
út, begins Budapest's grandest avenue, Andrássy út. For too many years
this broad boulevard bore the tongue-twisting name Népköztársaság útja
(Avenue of the People's Republic) and, for a while before that, Stalin
Avenue. In 1990, however, it reverted to its old name honoring Count
Gyula Andrássy, a statesman who in 1867 became Hungary's first con-
stitutional premier. The boulevard that would eventually bear his name
was begun in 1872, as Buda and Pest (and Óbuda) were about to be
unified. Most of the mansions that line it were completed by 1884. It
took another dozen years before the first underground railway on the
Continent was completed for—you guessed it—the Magyar Millennium in 1896. Though preceded by London's Underground (1863),
Budapest's was the world's first electrified subway. Only slightly mod-
ernized but refurbished for the 1996 millecentenary, this "Little Metro"
is still running a 4-km (2½-mi) stretch from Vörösmarty tér to the far
end of City Park. Using tiny yellow trains with tanklike treads, and stopping at antique stations marked FÖLDALATTI (Underground) on their
wrought-iron entranceways, Line 1 is a tourist attraction in itself. Six
of its 10 stations are along Andrássy út.

**A GOOD
WALK**

A walking tour of Andrássy út's sights is straightforward: begin at its
downtown end, near Deák tér, and stroll its length (about 2 km [1 mi])
all the way to Hősök tere, at the entrance to Budapest's popular City
Park. Of course, if your feet are weary, you can always hop on the Little Metro at one of its stations every few blocks and go one or more
stops that way. The first third of the avenue, from Bajcsy-Zsilinszky út
to the eight-sided intersection called Oktogon, is framed by rows of eclectic city palaces with balconies held up by stone giants. First stop is the
imposing **Magyar Állami Operaház** ❺❹ and across the street the **Drechsler
Kastély** ❺❺. A block or two farther, on "Budapest's Broadway," Nagymező
utca, where you'll find theaters, nightclubs, and cabarets, is the **Magyar
Fotógráfusok Háza (Mai Manó Ház)** ❺❻ photographic museum, to the left
of Andrássy út; and a block-and-a-half to the right is the **Ernst Múzeum** ❺❼,
with its exhibits of modern art. Walk to the next block here and you'll
find yourself on Király utca, a bustling narrow street rich in local flavor; walk even farther, and you'll be on Klauzál tér, the square at the
heart of Budapest's wartime Jewish ghetto. Continuing down Andrássy,
turn right onto Liszt Ferenc tér, a pedestrian street dominated by the
Liszt Ferenc Zeneakadémia ❺❽.

The Parisian-style boulevard of Andrássy alters when it crosses the
Nagy körút (Outer Ring Road), at the Oktogon crossing. Four rows of
trees and scores of flower beds make the thoroughfare look more like
a garden promenade, but its cultural character lingers. Two blocks beyond the Oktogon, on your left, is the **Terror Háza** ❺❾, a relatively new,

state-of-the-art museum dedicated to victims of terror. Continue until you come to Vörösmarty utca, where a short detour right will take you to the **Liszt Ferenc Emlékmúzeum** ⑥. Farther up, past **Kodály körönd** ⑥, the rest of Andrássy út is dominated by widely spaced mansions surrounded by private gardens and ends at **Hősök tere** ⑥. Finish your tour by browsing through the **Műcsarnok** ⑥ and/or the **Szépművészeti Múzeum** ⑥, and then perhaps take a stroll into **Városliget** ⑥. Before exploring the park and its many attractions, however, you might want to turn back in the direction of the Oktogon for a moment and go left a couple blocks along Dózsa György út to a great big parking lot bordering the park; here you'll find the area's newest wonder, the **Időkerék** ⑥. You can return to Deák tér on the Millenniumi Földalatti (Millennial Underground).

TIMING Most museums are closed Monday so it's best to explore Andrássy út on a weekday or early Saturday, when stores are also open for browsing. During opera season you can time your exploration to land you at the Operaház stairs just before 7 PM to watch the spectacle of operagoers flowing in for the evening's performance. City Park is best explored on a clear day.

What to See

⑤ **Drechsler Kastély** (Drechsler Palace). Across the street from the Operaház is the French Renaissance–style Drechsler Palace. An early work by Ödön Lechner, Hungary's master of Art Nouveau, it was formerly the home of the National Ballet School. As of this writing, it was being remodeled to begin a new life as a hotel. ⊠ *District VI, Andrássy út 25, Around Andrássy út* Ⓜ *M1: Opera.*

⑤ **Ernst Múzeum.** A block-and-a-half to the right of Andrássy út, on Nagymező utca, this is Budapest's finest gallery of 20th-century and contemporary art and cultural objects of all sorts. The exhibits change frequently. This stretch of Nagymező utca has also some good cafés. Be careful crossing the street, though—the trolleys barrel down the road like wildfire. ⊠ *District VI, Nagymező utca 8, Around Andrássy út* ☎ *1/341–4355* 💴 *500 HUF* ⊗ *Tues.–Sat. 11–7.*

★ ⑥ **Hősök tere.** Andrássy út ends in grandeur at Heroes' Square, with Budapest's answer to Berlin's Brandenburg Gate. Cleaned and refurbished in 1996 for the millecentenary (1100th anniversary), the **Millenniumi Emlékmű** (Millennial Monument) is a semicircular twin colonnade with statues of Hungary's kings and leaders between its pillars. Set back in its open center, a 118-foot stone column is crowned by a dynamic statue of the archangel Gabriel, his outstretched arms bearing the ancient emblems of Hungary. At its base ride seven bronze horsemen: the Magyar chieftains, led by Árpád, whose tribes conquered the land in 896. Before the column lies a simple marble slab, the **Nemzeti Háborús Emlék Tábla** (National War Memorial), the nation's altar, at which every visiting foreign dignitary lays a ceremonial wreath. England's Queen Elizabeth upheld the tradition during her royal visit in May 1992. In 1991 Pope John Paul II conducted a mass here. Just a few months earlier, half a million Hungarians had convened to recall the memory of Imre Nagy, the reform-minded communist prime minister who partially inspired the 1956 revolution. Little would anyone have guessed then that in 1995, palm trees—and Madonna—would spring up on this very square in a scene from the film *Evita* (set in Argentina, not Hungary), or that Michael Jackson would do his part to consecrate the square with a music video. ⊠ *District VI, Városliget* Ⓜ *M1: Hősök tere.*

⑥⑧ Időkerék (Time Wheel). Against a lovely backdrop of tall plane trees and spruces at the edge of City Park just off Felvonulás tér—a huge parking lot along Dózsa György út that in decades past was used for communist rallies—is the world's largest hourglass. Aimed more at portraying time rather than measuring it, the Time Wheel is made of granite, stainless steel, and glass that allows you to watch (or imagine) a fine trickle of sand flow from top to bottom, it is 8 meters (26 feet) in diameter and weighs a whopping 60 tons. Once a year, on December 31, the top chamber empties out, and then the wheel is turned a half-circle along the track it is set in, always the same way, so the upper and lower chambers switch places, and the sand begins flowing once again. ⊠ *District XIV, Városliget, Around Andrássy út* Ⓜ *M1: Hősök tere.*

⑥① Kodály körönd. A handsome traffic circle with imposing statues of three Hungarian warriors—leavened by a fourth one of a poet—Kodály körönd is surrounded by plane and chestnut trees. Look carefully at the towered mansions on the north side of the circle—behind the soot you'll see the fading colors of ornate frescoes peeking through. The circle was named for the composer Zoltán Kodály, who lived just beyond it, at Andrássy út 89. ⊠ *District VI, Andrássy út at Szinyei Merse utca, Around Andrássy út* Ⓜ *M1: Kodály körönd.*

⑥⓪ Liszt Ferenc Emlékmúzeum (Franz Liszt Memorial Museum). Andrássy út No. 67 was the original location of the old Academy of Music and Franz Liszt's last home; entered around the corner, it now houses a museum. Several rooms display the original furniture and instruments from Liszt's time there; another room shows temporary exhibits. The museum hosts excellent, free classical concerts year-round, except August 1–20, when it is closed. ⊠ *District VI, Vörösmarty utca 35, Around Andrássy út* ☎ *1/322–9804* ⊕ *www.lisztmuseum.hu* ⊠ *400 HUF* ☉ *Weekdays 10–6, Sat. 9–5. Classical concerts (free with admission) Sept.–July, Sat. at 11 AM* Ⓜ *M1: Vörösmarty utca.*

⑤⑧ Liszt Ferenc Zeneakadémia (Franz Liszt Academy of Music). This magnificent Art Nouveau building presides over the cafés and gardens of Liszt Ferenc tér. Along with the Vigadó, this is one of the city's main concert halls. On summer days the sound of daytime rehearsals adds to the sweetness in the air along this pedestrian oasis of café society, just off buzzing Andrássy út. The academy itself has two auditoriums: a green-and-gold 1,200-seat main hall and a smaller hall for chamber music and solo recitals. Farther along the square is a dramatic statue of Liszt Ferenc (Franz Liszt) himself, hair blown back from his brow, seemingly in a flight of inspiration. Pianist Ernő (Ernst) Dohnányi and composers Béla Bartók and Zoltán Kodály were teachers here. ⊠ *District VI, Liszt Ferenc tér 8, Around Andrássy út* ☎ *1/462–4600* Ⓜ *M1: Oktogon.*

★ ❺❹ **Magyar Állami Operaház** (Hungarian State Opera House). Miklós Ybl's crowning achievement is the neo-Renaissance Opera House, built between 1875 and 1884. Badly damaged during the siege of 1944–45, it was restored for its 1984 centenary. Two buxom marble sphinxes guard the driveway; the main entrance is flanked by Alajos Strobl's "romantic-realist" limestone statues of Liszt and of another 19th-century Hungarian composer, Ferenc Erkel, the father of Hungarian opera (his patriotic opera *Bánk bán* is still performed for national celebrations). (⇨ See also Strobl's magnificent sculpture "Mathias's Well" behind the Királyi Palota, *in* Várhegy [Castle Hill] *above.*)

Inside, the spectacle begins even before the performance does. You glide up grand staircases and through wood-paneled corridors and gilt lime-green salons into a glittering jewel box of an auditorium. Its four tiers of boxes are held up by helmeted sphinxes beneath a frescoed ceiling by Károly Lotz. Lower down there are frescoes everywhere, with intertwined motifs of Apollo and Dionysus. In its early years the Budapest Opera was conducted by Gustav Mahler (1888–91), and after World War II by Otto Klemperer (1947–50).

The best way to experience the Opera House's interior is to see a ballet or opera; and while performance quality varies, tickets are relatively affordable and easy to come by, at least for tourists. And descending from *La Bohème* into the Földalatti station beneath the Opera House was described by travel writer Stephen Brook in *The Double Eagle* as stepping "out of one period piece and into another." There are no performances in summer, except for the weeklong BudaFest international opera and ballet festival in mid-August. You cannot view the interior on your own, but 45-minute tours in English are usually conducted daily; buy tickets in the Opera Shop, by the sphinx at the Hajós utca entrance. (Large groups should call in advance.) ✉ *District VI, Andrássy út 22, Around Andrássy út* ☏ *1/331–2550 Ext. 156 for tours, 1/331–8197 for other info* ⊕ *www.opera.hu* 🎫 *Tours 2,500 HUF* ☉ *Tours daily at 3 and 4* Ⓜ *M1: Opera.*

❺❻ **Magyar Fotográfusok Háza (Mai Manó Ház)** (Hungarian Photographers' House [Manó Mai House]). This ornate turn-of-the-20th-century building was built as a photography studio, where the wealthy bourgeoisie would come to be photographed by imperial and royal court photographer Manó Mai. Inside, ironwork and frescoes ornament the curving staircase leading up to the exhibition space, the largest of Budapest's three photo galleries. Right next door, by the way, is the impeccably fashionable little Mai Manó Café. ✉ *District VI, Nagymező utca 20, Around Andrássy út* ☏ *1/473–2666* 🎫 *500 HUF* ☉ *Weekdays 2–7, weekends 11–7* Ⓜ *M1: Opera.*

❻❻ **Műcsarnok** (Palace of Exhibitions). The city's largest hall for special exhibitions is a striking 1895 temple of culture with a colorful tympanum. Its program of events includes exhibitions of contemporary Hungarian and international art and a rich series of films, plays, and concerts. Admission is free on Tuesday. ✉ *District XIV, Hősök tere, Városliget* ☏ *1/460–7000* ⊕ *www.mucsarnok.hu* 🎫 *700 HUF* ☉ *Tues., Wed., Fri., and Sun. 10–6, Thurs. 10–8* Ⓜ *M1: Hősök tere.*

NEED A BREAK?

The **Müvész Café** (⊠ District VI, Andrássy út 29, Around Andrássy út ☎ 1/352–1337) is perhaps the only surviving "writer's café" where you will occasionally see an actual writer at work. The combination of low lighting and striped, dark gold-green wallpaper gives it an elegant yet chic appeal. Sit at a table outside in summer to watch the world passing by on Andrássy út.

64 **Szépművészeti Múzeum** (Museum of Fine Arts). Across Heroes' Square

FodorśChoice from the Palace of Exhibitions and built by the same team of Albert ★ Schickedanz and Fülöp Herzog, the Museum of Fine Arts houses Hungary's best art collection, rich in Flemish and Dutch old masters. With seven fine El Grecos and five beautiful Goyas as well as paintings by Velázquez and Murillo, the collection of Spanish Old Masters is probably the best outside Spain. The Italian school is represented by Giorgione, Bellini, Correggio, Tintoretto, and Titian masterpieces and, above all, two superb Raphael paintings: *The Eszterházy Madonna* and his immortal *Portrait of a Youth,* rescued after a world-famous art heist. Nineteenth-century French art includes works by Delacroix, Pissarro, Cézanne, Toulouse-Lautrec, Gauguin, Renoir, and Monet. There are also more than 100,000 drawings (including five by Rembrandt and three studies by Leonardo), and Egyptian and Greco-Roman exhibitions. A 20th-century collection was added to the museum's permanent exhibits in 1994, comprising an interesting series of statues, paintings, and drawings by Chagall, Le Corbusier, and others. The special exhibits are outstanding and frequent. Labels are in both Hungarian and English; there's also an English-language booklet for sale about the permanent collection. ⊠ *District XIV, Hősök tere, Around Andrássy út* ☎ *1/469–7100 or 1/363–4654* ⊕ *www.szepmuveszeti.hu* ⊠ *Free, special exhibits each 600–1,600 HUF, entry to all 2,000 HUF* ☉ *Tues.–Sun. 10–5:30* Ⓜ *M1: Hősök tere.*

★ **59** **Terror Háza** (House of Terror). The most controversial museum in post-communist Hungary was established at great cost, with the support of the center-right government in power from 1998 to 2002. Some critics alleged that its exhibits are less than objective, sensational attacks on those even loosely associated with the communist-era dictatorship and place less emphasis on the terrors of the fascist era and the Holocaust in particular. The museum director replied that the collection is dedicated to the victims of both regimes (fascist and communist)—noting that there is an exhibit on the atrocities against Jews before and during World War II—and that it was painstakingly researched and designed by experts. The building itself has a terrible history. Starting in 1939 it was headquarters of the Arrow Cross; from 1945 to 1956 the notorious communist state security police, the ÁVO (later succeeded by the ÁVH), used it as its headquarters and as its interrogation-cum-torture center. A powerful visual and sensual experience, this state-of-the-art, multimedia museum features everything from videos of sobbing victims telling their stories to a full-size Soviet tank. An English-language audio guide is available for 1,000 HUF per person above the ticket price; larger groups needing them for each member should call several days or more in advance to reserve, as the number of units is limited. ⊠ *District VI, Andrássy út 60, Around Andrássy út* ☎ *1/374–2600* ⊕ *www.terrorhaza.hu* ⊠ *1,500 HUF* ☉ *Tues.–Fri. 10–6, weekends 10–7:30* Ⓜ *M1: Vörösmarty utca.*

🌀 **⑥** **Városliget** (City Park). Heroes' Square is the gateway to a square kilometer (almost ½ square mi) of recreation, entertainment, beauty, and culture. A bridge behind the Millennial Monument leads across a boating basin that becomes an artificial ice-skating rink in winter; to the south of this lake stands a statue of George Washington, erected in 1906 with donations by Hungarian emigrants to the United States. You can soak or swim at the lovely, turn-of-the-20th-century Széchenyi Fürdő, jog along the park paths, or careen on Vidám Park's roller coaster. There's also the Petőfi Csarnok, a leisure-time youth center and major concert hall on the site of an old industrial exhibition. The Gundel restaurant charms diners with its turn-of-the-20th-century ambience. Fair-weather weekends, when the children's attractions are teeming with youngsters and parents and the Széchenyi Fürdő is brimming with bathers, are the best times for people-watchers to visit the park; if you go on a weekday, the main sights are rarely crowded. ⊠ *District XIV, Andrássy út, Városliget* 🎟 *Park free, admission charged for attractions* ⊙ *Daily* Ⓜ *M1: Városliget.*

🌀 The renovation of the once-depressing **Budapesti Állat-és Növénykert** (Budapest Zoo & Botanical Garden), which began in the late 1990s, was still underway as of this writing, but the place is already cheerier, especially for humans. The petting opportunities are aplenty, and a new monkey house allows endearing, seemingly clawless little simians to climb all over you (beware of pickpockets). Don't miss the elephant pavilion, decorated with Zsolnay majolica and glazed ceramic animals. Note that the last tickets are sold one hour before closing, and animal houses don't open until an hour after the zoo gates. ⊠ *District XIV, Városliget, Állatkerti körút 6–12* 🕾 *1/273—4901* ⊕ *www.zoobudapest.com* 🎟 *1,400 HUF; tropical greenhouse and aquarium 300 HUF each* ⊙ *May–Aug., Mon.–Thurs. 9–6, Fri.–Sun. 9–7; Mar.–Apr. and Sept.–Oct., daily 9–5; Nov.–Feb., daily 9–4.*

🌀 At the **Fővárosi Nagycirkusz** (Municipal Grand Circus), colorful performances by local acrobats, clowns, and animal trainers, as well as by international artists, are staged in a small ring. ⚠ **Beware of pickpockets out front by the timeworn snack-bar.** ⊠ *District XIV, Városliget, Állatkerti körút 7* 🕾 *1/343–8300 or 1/344–6008* ⊕ *www.maciva.hu* 🎟 *1,300–2,000 HUF* ⊙ *July–Aug., Wed. and Fri. at 3 and 7, Thurs. at 3, Sat. at 10:30, 3, and 7, Sun. at 10:30 and 3; Sept.–June, schedule varies.*

Széchenyi Fürdő (Széchenyi Baths), the largest medicinal bathing complex in Europe, is housed in a beautiful neo-baroque building in the middle of City Park. There are several thermal pools indoors as well as two outdoor pools, which remain open even in winter, when dense steam hangs thick over the hot water's surface—you can just barely make out the figures of elderly men, submerged shoulder deep, crowded around waterproof chessboards. To use the baths, you pay a deposit: a portion of which may be returned depending on how long you stay. Facilities include medical and underwater massage treatments, carbonated bath treatments, and mud wraps. ⊠ *District XIV, Városliget, Állatkerti körút 11* 🕾 *1/363–3210* 🎟 *2,000 HUF (600 HUF back within 2 hours, 300 HUF within 3 hours); changing room 300 HUF, cabin 700 HUF*

⊙ *May–Sept., daily 6 AM–7 PM; Oct.–Apr., weekdays 6 AM–7 PM, weekends 6 AM–5 PM.*

Beside the City Park's lake stands **Vajdahunyad Vár** (Vajdahunyad Castle), a fantastic medley of Hungary's historic and architectural past, starting with the Romanesque gateway of the cloister of Jak, in western Hungary. A Gothic castle whose Transylvanian turrets, Renaissance loggia, baroque portico, and Byzantine decorations are all guarded by a spooky modern (1903) bronze statue of the anonymous medieval "chronicler," who was the first recorder of Hungarian history. Designed for the millennial celebration in 1896, it was not completed until 1908. This hodgepodge houses the surprisingly interesting Mezőgazdasági Múzeum (Agricultural Museum), which touts itself as Europe's largest such museum. Twelve permanent exhibitions (and frequent temporary ones) cover animal husbandry, forestry, horticulture, viticulture, hunting, fishing, and more. There are regular arts and crafts activities for kids. ⊠ *District XIV, Városliget, Széchenyi Island* ☎ *1/363–1117* ⊕ *www.mmgm. hu* ☎ *300 HUF* ⊙ *Mar.–Nov. 15, Tues.–Fri. 10–5, Sat. 10–6, Sun. 10–5; Nov. 15–Feb. 15, Tues.–Fri. 10–4, weekends 10–5.*

Budapest's somewhat weary amusement park, **Vidám Park,** is next to the zoo and is crawling with happy children with their parents or grandparents in tow. In addition to the rides, there are game rooms and a scenic railway. In all, there are 35 different attractions, including Europe's longest wooden roller coaster and a merry-go-round dating from 1906 and beautifully restored in 1998. That said, the advertising is more glittery than the park itself. Next to the main park is a separate, smaller section for toddlers. There is a nominal admission charge, and then you buy individual tickets for rides; rides take one to three tickets. Kids under 120 cm (3.9 feet) tall get in for free. ⊠ *District XIV, Városliget, Állatkerti körút 14–16* ☎ *1/363–8310* ⊕ *www.vidampark.hu* ☎ *300 HUF general admission, 250 HUF for a ride ticket, though most rides require two such tickets* ⊙ *July–Aug., Mon.–Thurs. and Sun. 10–8, Fri.–Sat. 10–10; May–June, weekdays 11–7, Sat. 10–10, Sun. 10–8; Apr. and Sept., weekdays noon–7, weekends 10–7:30; Mar. and Oct., weekdays 10–6, weekends 10–7.*

EASTERN PEST & THE LARGE RING ROAD

Pest's Large Ring Road (Nagy körút) was laid out at the end of the 19th century in a wide semicircle, anchored to the Danube at both ends; an arm of the river was covered over to create this 114-foot-wide thoroughfare. The large apartment buildings on both sides also date from this era. Along with theaters, stores, and cafés, they form a boulevard unique in Europe for its "unified eclecticism," which blends several different historic styles into a harmonious whole. Its entire length of almost 4½ km (2¾ mi) from the Margaret Bridge to the Petőfi bridge is traversed by Trams 4 and 6, but strolling it in stretches is also a good way to experience the hustle and bustle of Budapest's busy, less-touristy urban thoroughfares full of people, cars, shops, and the city's unique urban flavor.

Beginning a few blocks from the Elizabeth Bridge, Kossuth Lajos utca was once Budapest's busiest shopping street, and though its star stores have tended to fade away as shopping malls have seized the new day, it still retains much of its past élan. Try to look above and beyond the store windows to the turn-of-the-20th-century architecture and activity along Kossuth Lajos utca and its continuation, Rákóczi út, which begins when it crosses the Kis körút (Small Ring Road) at the busy intersection called Astoria. Most of Rákóczi út is lined with hotels, shops, cinemas, and cafés, and it ends at the grandiose Keleti (East) Railway Station, on Baross tér.

Like its smaller counterpart, the Kis körút (Small Ring Road), the Large Ring Road comprises sections of various names. Beginning with Ferenc körút at the Petőfi Bridge, it changes to József körút at the intersection marked by the Museum of Applied Arts, then to Erzsébet körút at Blaha Lujza tér. Teréz körút begins at the busy Oktogon crossing with Andrássy út and ends at the Nyugati (West) Railway Station, where Szent István takes over for the final stretch to the Margaret Bridge.

A GOOD WALK

Beginning with a visit to the **Iparművészeti Múzeum** 🕖, near the southern end of the Large Ring Road, walk or take Tram 4 or 6 north (away from the Petőfi Bridge) to **Köztársaság tér** 🕖. The neo-Renaissance **Keleti pályaudvar** 🕖 is a one-metro-stop detour away from Blaha Lujza tér. At the corner of the Nagy körút and Dohány utca you can stop to admire the newly restored **New York Palota** 🕖 and perhaps wander in for a coffee. Continuing in the same direction on the körút, go several stops on the tram to **Nyugati pályaudvar** 🕖 and walk the remaining sector, Szent István körút, past the **Vígszínház** 🕖 to Margaret Bridge. From the bridge, views of Margaret Island, to the north, and Parliament, Castle Hill, the Chain Bridge, and Gellért Hill, to the south, are gorgeous.

As an alternative, you might explore the newly revitalized neighborhood of Mester utca and environs along the Large Ring Road just one tram stop south of the Iparművészeti Múzeum. Walk or take Tram 4 or 6 south (toward Petőfi Bridge) three short blocks to Mester utca, on your left. This wide, lovely street, shaded by plane trees, has lots of small shops, grocery stores, and local flavor, including one of Budapest's best *rétes* (strudel) stands. Take the third street to your left, Páva utca, and go two blocks to the **Holocaust Emlékközpont** 🕖. From here you're within a block of Üllői út, where you can take a left for a short walk back toward the museum. If you'd prefer to have a look at Hungary's stunning new national theater, the **Nemzeti Színház** 🕖, go one tram stop farther, to Petőfi Bridge, and walk from Boráros tér, which is beside the bridge, 20 minutes south along the Danube. You'll walk by several long, massive apartment buildings that utterly block the view of Pest beyond, evoking communist-era architectural monstrosities—until 2004 this area was a long, narrow stretch of green space. You can also take the HÉV electric railway (runs at 10–20 min. intervals) one stop to the national theater.

TIMING As this area is packed with stores, it's best to explore during business hours—weekdays until around 5 PM and Saturday until 1 PM. Saturday will be most crowded. Keep in mind that the Iparművészeti Múzeum is closed Monday.

What to See

73 **Holocaust Emlékközpont** (Holocaust Memorial Center). On the 60th anniversary of the closing off of Budapest's Jewish ghetto, April 15, 2004,
Fodor's Choice   Hungary's first major center for Holocaust research and exhibits opened
★   in the presence of Hungarian statesmen and the Israeli president. The stone
facade of this onetime synagogue is an eerily high, windowless wall; the
entrance comprises two tall, massive iron doors. Just inside the courtyard is a black wall bearing the names of all known Hungarian victims
of the Holocaust, including both Jews and many Romas (Gypsies). From
there you go downstairs into a cellar, where you proceed through a com-
pelling and haunting blend of family and individual stories told through
photos, films, original documents, personal objects, and touch-screen computers (with all text also in English). You are taken from 1938, when the
Hungarian state first began depriving Jews and others of their rights; to
1944, by which time these people were being systematically deprived of
their freedom and their lives; to liberation in 1945. On reaching the final
space, a small synagogue, you can still hear the wedding music from the
first rooms: a poignant reminder of the pre-Holocaust era. Unlike the
Terror háza (House of Terror), which honors victims of both nazism and
communism, nothing at all about this feels forced. It is just right. This
is a moving and dignified testament to genocide. ✉ *District IX, Páva utca
39, North of Blaha Lujza tér* ☎ *1/455–3333* ⊕ *www.hdke.hu* ✉ *Free*
☉ *Tues.–Sun. 10–6* Ⓜ *M3: Üllői út.*

★ **72** **Iparművészeti Múzeum** (Museum of Applied & Decorative Arts). The tem-
plelike structure is indeed a shrine to Hungarian Art Nouveau, and in
front of it, drawing pen in hand, sits a statue of its creator, Hungarian
architect Ödön Lechner. Opened in the Magyar Millennial year of 1896,
it was only the third museum of its kind in Europe. Its dome of deep
green and golden tiles is crowned by a majolica lantern from the same
source: the Zsolnay ceramic works in Pécs. Inside its central hall are play-
fully swirling whitewashed, double-decker, Moorish-style galleries and
arcades. The museum, which collects and studies objects of interior decoration and use, has five departments: furniture, textiles, goldsmithing,
ceramics, and everyday objects. ✉ *District VIII, Üllői út 33–37, North
of Blaha Lujza tér* ☎ *1/456–5100* ⊕ *www.imm.hu* ✉ *600 HUF*
☉ *Tues.–Sun. 10–6* Ⓜ *M3: Üllői út.*

**OFF THE
BEATEN
PATH**
GÖDÖLLŐI KIRÁLYI KASTÉLY (ROYAL PALACE OF GÖDÖLLŐ) – Gödöllői
Királyi Kastély has been referred to as the Hungarian Versailles, and while
this baroque mansion and former royal residence may not be quite that,
extensive restoration early in the new millennium has restored some of
the glitter it lost while being used as a barracks by Soviet troops after
1945. In particular, the royal quarters have come out looking positively
royal anew. Built in 1735 by local nobleman Antal Grassalkovich I, the
palace was bought by the Hungarian state in 1867 and given as a wedding present to Emperor Franz Josef I and his beautiful and charismatic
wife Elizabeth (known as Sissi). Sissi's violet-colored rooms contain secret doors, which allowed her to avoid tiresome guests. For a rewarding half-day excursion here, go to the Örs Vezér tere—last stop on the
red metro line, and take the HÉV suburban train to the Szabadság tere

stop. The palace is across the street. ⊠ *Grassalkovich Kastély, Gödöllő*
☎ *28/410–124 or 28/420–331* ⊕ *www.royalpalace-godollo.com* 🖼 *1,400
HUF* ⊙ *Apr.–Oct., Tues.–Sun. 10–6 (tickets until 5 PM), Nov.–Mar. 10–5*
Ⓜ *M2: Örs Vezér tere, then HÉV to Szabadság tere.*

㊉ Keleti pályaudvar (East Railway Station). The grandiose, imperial-look-
ing station was built in 1884 and was considered Europe's most modern until well into the 20th century. Its neo-Renaissance facade, which
resembles a gateway, is flanked by statues of two British inventors and
railway pioneers, James Watt and George Stephenson. ⊠ *District VIII,
Baross tér* Ⓜ *M2: Keleti Train Station.*

㉛ Köztársaság tér. Surrounded by an extraordinary mix of faceless concrete
monstrosities and lovely old buildings, the vast Square of the Republic
has a serene, somewhat shaded park at its center. Its 20th-century historical significance stems from the fact that it was where the Communist Party
of Budapest had its headquarters (today the Socialist Party offices), and
saw heavy fighting in 1956. Here also is the city's second opera house,
and Budapest's largest, the Erkel Ferenc színház (Ferenc Erkel Theater).
⊠ *District VIII, between Luther utca and Berzeriyi utca, Around Keleti
Train Station* Ⓜ *M2: Blaha Lujza tér or Keleti Train Station.*

㊞ **㊲ Nemzeti Színház** (National Theater). No area of downtown Budapest has
undergone as much revitalization since the early 1990s as the corner of
Eastern Pest that stretches from Petőfi Bridge to Budapest's newest
bridge, Lágymányosi híd, between the Danube and Mester utca. A key
attraction here, the new National Theater, was completed in 2000.
Round and colonnaded in front and square in back, the massive building is a spectacular blend of modern and classical. The spacious square
out front and to the side is something to behold—though, admittedly,
different folks behold it differently. The large reflecting pool contains a
toppled-over, life-size ancient theater facade and three eternal flames.
The bow of a ship, which you can walk on, overlooks the pool. Elsewhere on the square, scattered about, some on benches, others standing, are eight metal statues of late, great Hungarian thespians of the 20th
century, each performing a legendary role. If you take the HÉV commuter railway, you get off a short distance beyond the theater, and you
must walk back over a small bridge spanning the tracks. On the way
you'll pass by a compellingly round structure that's aptly nicknamed
the Tower of Babel and that houses a small exhibit gallery. In no time
you can walk up the path that winds around its outer perimeter to the
top for a modest view of the Buda hills and of the surrounding new architecture on the Pest side—and, notably, of a fascinating little labyrinth
of hedges at the foot of the tower that kids just love to get lost inside
⊠ *District IX, Bajor Gizi Park 1, Around Boráros tér* ☎ *1/476–6800*
⊕ *www.nemzetiszinhaz.hu* Ⓜ *M3: Üllői út.*

㊉ New York Palota (New York Palace). *The* architectural wonder everyone in Budapest was waiting to see again—after years of scaffolding-
encased limbo—is beautiful and bustling anew (as a hotel and café) as
of 2006. Commissioned by the New York Insurance Company and designed in eclectic styles with an Italian Renaissance edge by Alajos Haus-
man, Flóris Korb, and Alajos Giegl, the palace first opened in 1894

and soon became famous for its New York Café. With a steeple-like central tower that rises resplendently above the Large Ring Boulevard, a small clock set in the facade just below, two colonnaded floors below that, and two mini-towers on each side of the central one, it positively radiates when lit up at night. Nowadays the café is back in business—even if the pastry selection is not what it used to be, and even if many Budapesters, including the literary sorts who used to frequent the place, are pooh-poohing the new glitter and the mirror-topped tables that reflect the painfully restored ceiling frescoes above you. The owner, Italy's Boscolo group, operates much of the palace as a luxury hotel and, yes, a stylish restaurant. So then, if you're passing by the intersection of the Large Ring Boulevard and Dohány utca, it's worth stopping in for a coffee (reasonably priced for such a place) and a croissant—if only so you can say you've been there. It's the thing to do these days in Budapest, after all. ⊠ *District VII, Erzsébet körút 9–11, near Blaha Lujza tér* ☎ *1/886–6111* ⊕ *www.newyorkpalace.hu* Ⓜ *M2: Blaha Lujza tér.*

㊽ Nyugati pályaudvar (West Railway Station). The iron-laced glass hall of the West Railway Station is in complete contrast to—and much more modern than—the newer East Railway Station. Built in the 1870s, it was designed by a team of architects from Gustav Eiffel's office in Paris. ⊠ *District XIII, Teréz körút, Around Nyugati Train Station* Ⓜ *M3: Nyugati Train Station.*

No longer do you have to wait to take off from Ferihegy Airport nor do you have to climb Gellért-hegy for a bird's-eye view of Budapest. Simply hop aboard the city's very own **Helium Balloon** (⊠ District XIII, West End Shopping Center, Váci út 1–3, Around Nyugati Train Station ☎ 1/238–7623), which floats 150 meters (487 feet) above Nyugati pályaudvar at the end of a metal cable for 30 minutes at a stretch. You can take the ride for 3,000 HUF; it's open from 10 to 10 daily in fair weather (i.e., when there is little or no wind), with rides leaving every 20 minutes.

㊆ Művészetek Palotája (Palace of the Arts). Situated in southern Pest, at the foot of the Lágymányosi Bridge, right beside the similarly grand National Theater (which opened five years earlier), this monumental (750,000-square-foot) venue is not just a place where the capital's nouveau riche can spend their forints on a wide array of musical, theatrical, and dance performances in addition to dining in style. As per the title of a brochure advertising its splendors, it is also an "experience in every sense"—much of which is accessible free of charge to anyone who wants to wander around inside. Of course, you first have to make your way to Boráros tér and take the HÉV commuter train one stop—a bit of a bother, but worth it, if you have several days in Budapest. On the outside the place does indeed look palatial, in a very modern sense. The inside, as spacious and as sparkling as it is, contains plenty of intimate, well-cushioned little nooks on all floors on both sides of its National Concert Hall—which occupies its center—where you can take a seat and ponder life and/or art. ⊠ *District IX, Komor Marcell utca 1, Around Boráros tér* ☎ *1/555–3000* ⊠ *Free to enter, admission for events* ⊕ *www.mupa.hu* Ⓜ *M3: Üllői út.*

Fodor's Choice
★

In addition to housing the National Concert Hall, the Festival Theatre, a restaurant, and a couple of stores, the Palace is home to the Ludwig Múzeum, a venue of contemporary art that moved here in 2005 from its former home in Castle Hill's Royal Palace. The permanent collection covers American Pop Art (e.g., Warhol); the German, French, and Italian trans-avant-garde; and Eastern and Central European art (including, of course, Hungarian art from the 1960s to the present day.) ⊠ *District IX, Komor Marcell utca 1, Around Boráros tér* ☎ *1/555–3444* ▧ *Free, special exhibits 1,000 HUF* ☉ *Tues., Fri., and Sun. 10–6, Wed. 12–6, Thurs. 12–8, and Sat. 10–8, until 10 the last Sat. of each month)* ⊕ *www.ludwigmuseum.hu* Ⓜ *M3: Üllői út.*

★ ⑥ **Vígszínház** (Comedy Theater). This neo-baroque, late-19th-century, gemlike theater twinkles with just a tiny, playful anticipation of Art Nouveau and sparkles inside and out since its 1994 refurbishment. The theater hosts primarily musicals, such as Hungarian adaptations of *Cats,* as well as dance performances and classical concerts. ⊠ *District XIII, Pannónia utca 1, Parliament* ☎ *1/329–2340 box office* ⊕ *www. vigszinhaz.hu* Ⓜ *M3: Nyugati pu.*

Just 1½ blocks from Blaha Lujza tér and the Large Ring Road, going away from the river, **Hauer Cukrászda** (⊠ District VIII, Rákóczi út 47–49, Around Blaha Lujza tér ☎ 1/323–1476) has been around since 1890. Last renovated in 2002, it is one of Budapest's most elegant such establishments. The best-looking sweets here include the tiramisu and the *borkrém-rolády* (wine-cream roll).

ÓBUDA & MARGIT-SZIGET (MARGARET ISLAND)

Until its unification with Buda and Pest in 1872 to form the city of Budapest, Óbuda (meaning Old Buda) was a separate town that used to be the main settlement; now it is usually thought of as a suburb. Although the vast new apartment blocks of Budapest's biggest housing project and busy roadways are what first strike the eye, the historic core of Óbuda has been preserved in its entirety. Margit-sziget itself is an island in the middle of the Danube.

Numbers in the text correspond to numbers in the margin and on the Óbuda & Margaret Island map.

▌ A GOOD
WALK

Begin your tour on the Margit híd, entering **Margit-sziget** ㉖ on its southern end. Stroll up the island, toward the Árpád híd, where you can catch the streetcar or just walk over to Óbuda. Once you're there, covering all the sights on foot involves large but manageable distances along major exhaust-permeated roadways. One way to tackle it is to take Tram 17 from its southern terminus at the Buda side of the Margaret Bridge. Óbuda really begins after the third stop; and the fourth stop marks a charming commercial subcenter of this part of town; after this, keep your eyes open to the right, as the tram soon passes by the ruins of the **Római amfiteátrum** ㉗. At the seventh stop, Szent Margit Korház, get off and walk back a short distance to Kiscelli utca; from there, walk uphill to the **Kiscelli**

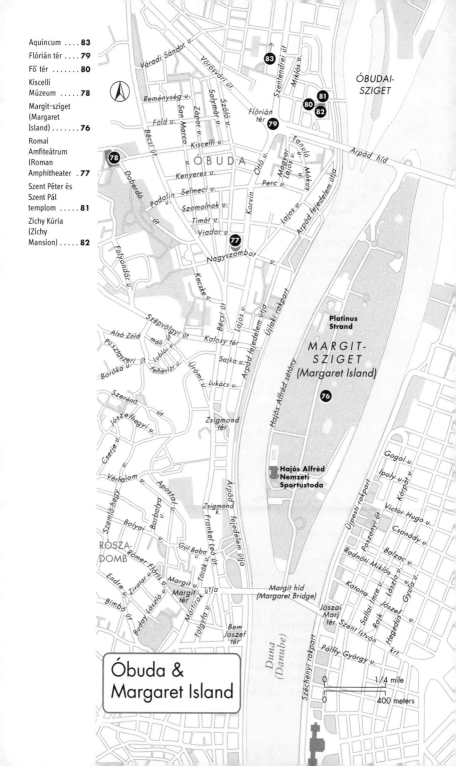

ÓBUDAI-
SZIGET

ÓBUDA

Platinus
Strand

MARGIT-
SZIGET
(Margaret Island)

Hajós Alfréd
Nemzeti
Sportuszoda

RÓSZA-
DOMB

Margit híd
(Margaret Bridge)

Bem
Joszef
tér

Duna
(Danube)

Óbuda &
Margaret Island

1/4 mile

400 meters

Múzeum 🔟. Then walk back down the same street all the way past **Flórián tér** 🔟, continuing toward the Danube and making a left onto Hídfő utca or Szentlélek tér to enter **Fő tér** 🔟. A short detour south will get you to **Szent Péter és Szent Pál templom** 🔟. On the south side of the square is the **Zichy Kúria** 🔟, a cultural center and museum. After exploring the square, walk a block or two southeast to the HÉV suburban railway stop and take the train just north to the museum complex at **Aquincum** 🔟 and the Hercules Villa, nearby.

TIMING   A leisurely stroll from one end of Margit-sziget to the other takes 45–60 minutes, but it's nice to spend some extra time wandering. Margit-sziget is most lively on a weekend, when the city's residents take full advantage of the island's green expanses; on a weekday it's a much quieter place, and that can have its own rewards. Avoid Monday, when museums are closed.

What to See

🔟 **Aquincum.** This complex comprises the reconstructed remains of a Roman settlement dating from the first century AD and the capital of the Roman province of Pannonia. Careful excavations have unearthed a varied selection of artifacts and mosaics, providing a tantalizing inkling of what life was like in the provinces of the Roman Empire. A gymnasium and a central heating system have been unearthed, along with the ruins of two baths and a shrine to Mithras, the Persian god of light, truth, and the sun. The **Aquincum múzeum** (Aquincum Museum) displays the dig's most notable finds: ceramics; a red-marble sarcophagus showing a triton and flying Eros on one side and on the other, Telesphorus, the angel of death, depicted as a hooded dwarf; and jewelry from a Roman lady's tomb. Near the main Aquincum ruins—but functioning as a separate museum—a fine third-century Roman dwelling, **Hercules Villa** (⊠ District III, Meggyfa utca 19–21), takes its name from the myth depicted on its beautiful mosaic floor. The ruin was unearthed between 1958 and 1967 and is now only open by request (inquire at the Aquincum Museum). ⊠ *District III, Szentendrei út 139, Óbuda* ☎ *1/250–1650* ⧈ *Aquincum Museum 800 HUF, Hercules Villa 100 HUF* ☉ *Aquincum Museum mid- to late Apr. and Oct., Tues.–Sun. 10–5; May–Sept., Tues.–Sun. 10–6 (grounds open an hour earlier than museum). Hercules Villa mid-Apr.–Oct., Tues.–Sun. 10–5.*

🔟 **Flórián tér** (Flórián Square). The center of today's Óbuda is Flórián tér, where Roman ruins were first discovered when the foundations of a house were dug in 1778. Two centuries later, careful excavations were carried out during the reconstruction of the square, and today the restored ancient ruins lie in the center in mind-boggling contrast to the racing traffic and cement-block housing projects. In the middle of the large, grassy park stretching from the square toward Kiscelli utca is an eerie, black metal angel-like sculpture pointing one hand skyward and holding a wreath in the other. This is the **Memorial to the Victims of Road Accidents.** In case the title isn't enough, a wrecked car at the foot of the main statue and a list of annual highway death tolls from 1984 to the present further ensures that the point gets across, compliments of the National Police Headquarters' Accident Prevention Committee. ⊠ *District III, Vörösvári út at Pacsirtamező utca, Óbuda.*

80 **Fő tér** (Main Square). Óbuda's old main square is its most picturesque part. There are several good restaurants and interesting museums in and around the baroque Zichy Mansion, which has become a neighborhood cultural center. Among the most popular offerings are the summer concerts in the courtyard and the evening jazz concerts. Toward the southern end of the square (on the way out to Árpád út and the HÉV is the elaborate **Óbudai Szentháromság Szobor** (Óbuda Trinity Statue), built originally in 1740, razed in 1950, and rebuilt in 2000. ⊠ *District III, Kórház utca at Hídfő utca, Óbuda.*

78 **Kiscelli Múzeum** (Kiscelli Museum). A short climb up the steep sidewalk of Remetehegy (Hermit Hill) will deposit you at this elegant, mustard-yellow baroque mansion. It was built between 1744 and 1760 as a Trinitarian monastery. Today, it holds an eclectic mix of paintings, sculptures, engravings, old clocks, antique furniture, and other items related to the history of Budapest. Included here is the printing press on which poet and revolutionary Sándor Petőfi printed his famous "Nemzeti Dal" ("National Song"), in 1848, inciting the Hungarian people to rise up against the Habsburgs. There are concerts here every Sunday in July. ⊠ *District III, Kiscelli utca 108, Óbuda* ☎ *1/368–7917 or 1/388–7817* 💰 *600 HUF* ⊗ *Nov.–Mar., Tues.–Sun. 10–4; Apr.–Oct., Tues.–Sun. 10–6.*

76 **Margit-sziget** (Margaret Island).
FodorsChoice More than 2½ km (1½ mi) long
★ and covering nearly 200 acres, this island park is ideal for strolling, jogging, sunbathing, or just loafing. In good weather it draws a multitudinous cross section of the city's population out to its gardens and sporting facilities. The outdoor pool complex of the Palatinus Baths, built in 1921, can attract tens of thousands of people on a summer day. Nearby are a tennis stadium, a youth athletic center, boathouses, sports grounds, and, most impressive of all, the Nemzeti Sportuszoda (National Sports Swimming Pool), designed by the architect Alfred Hajós (while still in his teens, Hajós won two gold medals in swimming at the first modern Olympic Games, held in Athens in 1896). The island's natural curative hot springs have given rise to the Danubius Grand and Thermal hotels on the northern end of the island and are piped into two spa hotels on the mainland, the Aquincum on the Buda bank and the Hélia on the Pest side.

> **WORD OF MOUTH**
>
> This island in the Danube is a park, and a beautiful one at that. Very lush and green—really an oasis in the city.   –Patti

To experience Margaret Island's role in Budapest life fully, go on a Saturday or Sunday afternoon to join and/or watch people whiling away the day. Sunday is a particularly good choice for strategic sightseers, who can utilize the rest of the week to cover those city sights and areas that are closed on Sunday. On weekdays you'll share the island only with joggers and children playing hooky from school.

The island was first mentioned almost 2,000 years ago as the summer residence of the commander of the Roman garrison at nearby Aquincum. Later known as Rabbit Island (Insula Leporum), it was a royal hunting ground during the Árpád dynasty. King Imre, who reigned from 1196 to 1204, held court here, and several convents and monasteries were built here during the Middle Ages. (During a walk round the island, you'll see the ruins of a few of these buildings.) It takes its current name from St. Margaret (1242–71), the pious daughter of King Béla IV, who at the ripe old age of 10 retired to a Dominican nunnery situated here from the 13th to the 16th centuries.

Through the center of the island runs the **Művész sétány** (Artists' Promenade), lined with busts of Hungarian visual artists, writers, and musicians. Shaded by giant plane trees, it's a perfect place to stroll. The promenade passes close to the **rose garden** (in the center of the island), a large grassy lawn surrounded by blooming flower beds planted with hundreds of kinds of flowers. It's a great spot to picnic or to watch a game of soccer. Just east of the rose garden is a small, free game farm, the **Margit-sziget Vadaspark.** A fenced-in compound houses a menagerie of goats, storks, rabbits, deer, ducks, a bunch of sad-looking falcons in a tiny cage, and other assorted birds, including gargantuan peacocks that seem to have the run of the place, getting in your way on the paths.

At the northern end of the island is a copy of the water-powered **Marosvásárhelyi zenélő kút** (Marosvásárhely Musical Fountain), which plays songs and chimes. The original was designed more than 150 years ago by a Transylvanian named Péter Bodor. It stands near a serene, artificial rock garden with Japanese dwarf trees and lily ponds. The stream coursing through it never freezes, for it comes from a natural hot spring, causing it instead to give off thick steam in winter that enshrouds the garden in a mystical cloud. ✉ *Margit-sziget* Ⓜ *M3: Árpád híd.*

(77) **Római amfiteátrum** (Roman Amphitheater). Probably dating back to the second century AD, Óbuda's Roman military amphitheater once held some 16,000 people and, at 144 yards in diameter, was one of Europe's largest. A block of dwellings called the Round House was later built by the Romans above the amphitheater; massive stone walls found in the Round House's cellar were actually parts of the amphitheater. Below the amphitheater are the cells where prisoners and lions were held while awaiting confrontation. ✉ *District III, Pacsirtamező utca at Nagyszombat utca, Óbuda.*

(81) **Szent Péter és Szent Pál templom.** (Saint Peter and Saint Paul Church). Its pale yellow steeple being one of Óbuda's core landmarks, this church—a tad more impressive on the outside than the inside—was built by the Zichy family from 1744 to 1749 as the successor to a previous church established here by Hungary's first king, Saint Stephen, in 1010. Situated in a peaceful neighborhood a couple minutes' walk from Fő tér and behind the Corinthia Aquincum Hotel, it features a red-marble altar (1774) and striking wooden statues of Christ and the church's patron saints (1884). ✉ *District III, northern end of Lajos utca, Óbuda* Ⓜ *M3: Kálvin tér.*

(82) **Zichy Kúria** (Zichy Mansion). Weatherbeaten but beautifully baroque with a pleasingly pink second-floor facade, the 18th century Zichy Mansion

CLOSE UP

What's Free

THE PERMANENT COLLECTIONS of many of Budapest's museums can be visited for free, though admission is charged for special exhibits. These include the **Hadtörténeti Múzeum, Ludwig Múzeum,** and **Magyar Nemzeti Galéria,** all of which are on Várhegy (Castle Hill); the **Semmelweis Orvostudoáyi Múzeum** in Tabán; the **Magyar Nemzeti Múzeum,** near the Small Ring Road; the **Ráth György Múzeum** and the **Szépművészeti Múzeum,** both of which are just off Andrássy út; the Vajdahuyad Vár in Varosliget (City Park); and the **Hercules Villa** and **Kassák Múzeum** in Óbuda.

There's never a charge for the exceptional view from the Citadella on Gellért Hill, and even the popular Halászbástaya is free during the off-season, from November through March.

is deep in a courtyard at the exalted if neglected-looking address of Fő tér 1. As you walk in the courtyard, you'll see another building to your right: this houses the **Óbudai Helytörténeti Gyüjtemény** (Óbuda Local History Collection). Permanent exhibitions here include traditional rooms from typical homes in the district of Békásmegyer and a popular exhibit covering the history of toys from 1860 to 1960. The Zichy Mansion itself is home to the **Kassák Múzeum,** which honors the literary and artistic works of a pioneer of the Hungarian avant-garde, Lajos Kassák. The museum also has a new permanent collection of 10th-century Hungarian art from the estates of the nation's authors. The courtyard hosts a popular series of summer concerts and evening jazz performances. ✉ *District III, Fő tér 1, Óbuda* ☎ *1/437–8682 or 1/388–2534 for Local History Collection, 1/368–7021 for Kassák Museum* ✆ *Local History Collection 120 HUF, Kassák Museum free* ☾ *Local History Collection mid-Mar.–mid-Oct., Tues.–Fri. 10–6, weekends 10–6; mid-Oct.–mid-Mar., Tues.–Fri. 2–5, weekends 10–5. Kassák Museum Tues.–Sun. 10–6.*

Where to Eat

2

WORD OF MOUTH

"We ordered 3 dishes and shared them, we laughed because we kept moaning about how good the food was à la *When Harry Met Sally*. We ordered stuffed peppers in a paprika sauce—AMAZING—meat-filled crepes in a paprikash sauce with I think sour cream on top—AMAZING—and chicken breast in an apricot sauce with apricot slices and candied walnuts—REALLY AMAZING. These people know how to eat!"

–laartista

By Betsy
Maury

DINING OUT IN BUDAPEST feels more sophisticated and diverse than it used to. Gone are the days when one had to choose between expensive grand dining rooms and tired communist-era taverns. These days dynamic dining options abound, and Budapest enjoys a lively restaurant scene. The best news has to do with variety. A typical night out can begin in a cozy Spanish tapas bar and end up at a rustic Tuscan trattoria on a terrace overlooking the Danube. Young chefs trained abroad are having the biggest impact on the restaurant scene just now, and in truth some of the best places to eat in Budapest aren't Hungarian. In addition to very good Italian restaurants, many of the most popular new places in Budapest serve well-prepared international dishes.

As if in defense, throughout the city Hungarian chefs seem determined to bring their cuisine into a new era and are at once creating innovative dishes and seeking to prevent a few classics from disappearing from modern menus. In many of District V's newer establishments, for instance, menus include well-prepared Hungarian dishes that use new ingredients to complement traditional flavors. Pork, long a Hungarian staple, gets dressed up both with traditional *lecsó* (pepper, onion, and tomato ragout flavored with paprika) and trimmed with Asian spices (rolled and stuffed with bok choy and hoisin sauce). Some standbys, such as *gulyás leves* (goulash soup) and *paprikás csirke* (chicken paprikash) are on the menu at even the most stylish restaurants. Other Hungarian favorites like goose remain popular everywhere, and you'll find that a crispy goose leg (*sült libacomb*) served with sautéed red cabbage has a devoted following. Long-celebrated goose liver (*libamaj*) also survives on virtually every menu in the city. You'll find it prepared in one of many traditional Hungarian styles as well as in myriad new ways, for example soaked in aged cognac and served with onion relish. Fish eaters will also find more options than the local lake *fogas* (pike perch). Tuna, salmon, and even sea bass are now widely available on most menus, although consistent cooking remains a challenge for the land-locked chef.

Dining aesthetics overall are better now in Budapest restaurants, too. Upscale bistros look and feel Parisian; trendy restaurants have low lighting and serve dishes using funky tableware. Service is markedly improved all over town, and while you're unlikely to find a waiter or waitress too chummy, professional service is now the norm in most good restaurants. Thankfully, the pace in Budapest restaurants remains decidedly European and therefore considerably slower than at an average American establishment. Glasses of wine are finished before dessert is discussed, and you're allowed to linger in most restaurants for quite some time before paying the bill. In most cases you will need to ask for the bill; it will not be brought spontaneously.

BETSY'S TOP 5

Weekend morning on the quiet leafy terrace at Gerlóczy Kávéház.
Sunday afternoon lunch is a family affair at Trattoria Toscana.
Splurge at Pava. The service and views make any occasion special.
Good old Menza is communist-cool and good anytime.
Heart attack waiting to happen—Lángos at the Vásárcsarnok.

WHAT IT COSTS in Forints				
$$$$	$$$	$$	$	¢
AT DINNER over 3,500	2,500–3,500	1,500–2,500	800–1,500	under 800

Prices are per person for a main course at dinner and include 15% tax, but not service.

Downtown Pest & the Small Ring Road

★ **$$$$** ╳ **Fausto's.** Of all the excellent Italian restaurants now to be found in Budapest, this elegant one across from the Dohány utca synagogue has been in business the longest. Its fans are unwavering on its consistently excellent cuisine, so this place is a good bet if you feel like a splurge. Authentic Italian delicacies like salmon carpaccio and homemade tagliatelli with rabbit ragout are lovingly prepared. The white-glove service is impeccable and surprisingly friendly. ⊠ *District VII, Dohány utca 5, Around Deák Ferenc tér* ☎ *1/269–6806* ⌖ *Reservations essential* ⊟ *AE, DC, MC, V* ۞ *Closed Sun.* Ⓜ *M2: Astoria.*

$$$–$$$$ ╳ **Cyrano.** This slick bistro just off Vörösmarty tér has an arty, contemporary bent, with wrought-iron chairs, black and gold wallpaper, and a chandelier of feather boas festooning the dining room. The creative kitchen sends out elegantly presented Hungarian and Continental dishes, from standards such as goose liver and duck breast to more adventurous monkfish and tuna. Though the prices are high for what you get, the restaurant is in the heart of the Váci utca shopping district. There's a flash VIP room upstairs for private parties. ⊠ *District V, Kristóf tér 7–8, Around Váci utca* ☎ *1/226-3096* ⊟ *AE, DC, MC, V* Ⓜ *M1, M2, M3: Deák tér.*

$$$–$$$$ ╳ **Óceán Bar & Grill.** If you're looking for an elegant seafood dinner, you'll find it here. You'll also find rope accents in the dining room, colorful fish tanks in the atrium, crisp white-linen table settings and shell napkin rings. The first-rate service does justice to the food, innovatively prepared fish dishes like Caribbean tuna with spicy bean salad and mango salsa or scallop ceviche with tabouleh. All fish can be cooked to order. If plain and simple is what you like, go for the grilled *branzino* (Adriatic sea bass). ⊠ *District V, Petőfi tér 3, Around Váci utca* ☎ *1/266–1826* ⊟ *AE, MC, V* Ⓜ *M1: Vórósmarty tér.*

★ **$$–$$$** ╳ **Café Bouchon.** You won't find friendlier or more attentive service in Budapest than in this French-inspired bistro in the edgy Sixth District. Café tables, parquet floors, and a daily menu written on butcher paper all set the mood for a casual but sophisticated meal. The well-chosen wine list highlights some of Hungary's best and most interesting wines by the glass. Smoked duck-breast salad and steak au poivre are classics on the menu, but the daily specials—usually seasonally inspired—are the real draw. The flourless French chocolate cake on the regular menu is a treat any time of the year. ⊠ *District VI, Zichy Jenő utca 33, Around Andrássy út* ☎ *1/353–4094* ⊟ *No credit cards* ۞ *Closed Sun.* Ⓜ *M3: Arany János utca.*

۞ **$$** ╳ **Wasabi.** If you're looking for dinner and a distraction, try this Asian restaurant where the tables are set in front of a conveyer belt that

KNOW-HOW

MEALTIMES

Dinner hours in Budapest are typically from around 7 to 9 PM, although bustling downtown restaurants will serve until about 10. Lunch, the main meal for many, is served from noon to 2. Many restaurants are closed on Sunday.

RESERVATIONS

Reservations for dinner are necessary in most of the nicer restaurants in Budapest. A day or two in advance is usually time enough to secure a good table. Reservations are mentioned in listings only when we feel you absolutely will not be able to get a table otherwise. You will nearly always find an English speaker at the restaurant who can competently book a table. Reservations are generally not necessary for lunch.

SMOKING

Budapest's smoking policy is typically European. Smokers are welcome everywhere, and many restaurants do not have designated no-smoking sections. Some do, however, and you can request a no-smoking table at those places. Small restaurants and cafés can be quite smoky in the winter time.

WHAT TO WEAR

At most moderately priced and inexpensive restaurants, casual but neat dress is acceptable. In restaurant listings we mention dress only when men are expected to wear a jacket or a jacket and tie.

WINE

Hungarian wines make up the bulk of the offerings on most Budapest wine lists. While not cheap, most wines are affordable and nearly all are quite drinkable. Some visitors to Hungary find the local wines very good indeed. *Tokaj aszú*, Hungary's unique dessert wine, excites enthusiasts, and you shouldn't miss the chance to taste at least one glass while you're in Hungary. Most restaurants offer at least one white, one red, and one rosé by the glass (called a *pohár*). Wines to choose include whites and Rieslings from Lake Balaton, reds from Villány or Eger, rosés from Szekszárd, and Tokaj aszú from Tokaj. A popular aperitif in Hungary is *pezsgő* (sparking wine), which can be ordered dry (*száraz*) or sweet (*édes*).

PRICES

Although prices are steadily increasing, there are plenty of good, affordable restaurants offering Hungarian and international dishes. Even though prices in Budapest have increased tremendously in recent years, eating out can provide you with some of the best value for the money of any European capital. In almost all restaurants an inexpensive prix-fixe lunch called a *napi menü* (daily menu) is available, usually for as little as 1,500 HUF. It includes soup or salad, a main course, and a dessert. Taxes (ÁFA) are included in menu prices but usually broken out on the final bill. There's a 25% tax on drinks and 15% tax on food. Service is generally not included, so an additional tip of 10% to 15% is customary in all restaurants. While rip-offs are less common in Budapest than they once were, it's best to scrutinize your bill in all establishments; restaurants in high-traffic tourist areas have been known to help themselves to a 10% tip before presenting you with the bill.

On the Menu

Csirke paprikás (chicken paprikash). This famous dish is made from cubed chicken breast or chicken legs covered in creamy paprika sauce.

Desszertek (desserts). Hungarian desserts can be cakes, pancakes, or fresh fruit in season.

Galuska (semolina dumplings). These thimble-sized dumplings are served with popular stews such as *borjúpaprikás* (veal paprikash).

Gesztenyepüré (chestnut puree). Chestnuts are ground with sugar, cream, and nutmeg to create this mound of light brown puree. It's usually served as a dessert in winter.

Gulyás leves (goulash soup). While goulash is known outside of Hungary as a stew, it's mostly served in Hungary as a soup made of paprika-flavored beef broth, cubed beef, parsnips, and carrots.

Gundel palacsinta (Gundel pancakes). Made famous by Gundel restaurant, these light dessert crepes are stuffed with walnuts and served with chocolate sauce.

Halászlé (spicy fish soup). This soup is made from carp fillets and seasoned with spicy paprika.

Hortobágyi palacsinta (Hortobagy pancakes). These meat-stuffed pancakes get their name from a village in the Great Plain. The light pancakes are stuffed, rolled, and covered with a creamy paprika sauce. They are heavy and are usually served as an appetizer.

Lángos (fried dough). This popular but greasy street food is available at most Hungarian markets. It comes plain or with cheese, cabbage, or dill, and you can smear it with sour cream and garlic.

Lecsó (a vegetable compote made of peppers, onions, tomato, and paprika). Lecsó is a multi-purpose Hungarian vegetable dish, which can be served as a sauce on top of steaks, as an accompaniment to seared goose liver, or even mixed in with eggs for breakfast.

Libamaj (goose liver). One of the celebrated culinary treats in Hungary, goose liver is made into rich pâtés or seared whole and served with a light fruit sauce.

Pálinka (fruit spirits). This homegrown brandy is a popular drink to start off a Hungarian meal. *Barack* (apricot) and *szliva* (plum) are the two most widely available flavors.

Pogácsa (scones). These irresistible baked biscuits can be plain or savory and are available in most bake shops. Different flavors include *sajtos* (cheese) or *tepertős* (spicy crackling).

Rétes (strudel). Light pastry is filled with cheese, apples, raisins, or sour cherries and is a popular cake with coffee.

Sült libacomb (crispy-fried goose leg). A popular main course in many Hungarian restaurants, succulent goose legs are usually served with steamed red cabbage.

Téliszalámi (Hungarian salami). This delicious long-life salami from Szeged is made of 100% pork and has a very strong, smoky flavor. There are two big manufacturers, Pick and Herz.

Töltött káposzta (stuffed cabbage). Boiled cabbage is stuffed with meat and rice; this is a popular winter main course.

whizzes by with such dim sum treats as sushi rolls, chicken satay, egg rolls, and canned peaches, of all things. The theme is vaguely Asian, but the conveyer-belt gimmick is the real show. One price gets you as many courses as you'd like, and evenings find this place lively withcurious diners. Kids are wild for the place. ⊠ *District VI, Podmanicsky utca 21, Near Nyugati pu.* ☎ *1/374–0008* ⊟ *MC, V* Ⓜ *M3: Nyugati pu.*

$–$$ ✕ **Gerlóczy Kávéház.** The green-and-yellow cane chairs and cafe tables of this elegant bistro remind you of a scene out of your favorite French movie. The terrace in the summertime is about the prettiest location for lunch in Budapest, on a quiet, leafy square tucked behind Váci utca. The menu has seasonal Hungarian favorites like *sült libacomb* (crispy goose leg) with red cabbage in winter, asparagus soup in the spring, but there are customers here all day long, drinking coffee and using the free wireless Internet service. Breakfast draws a big crowd on weekends. Get there early for some of the city's fluffiest croissants. ⊠ *District V, Gerlóczy utca 1, Around Váci utca* ☎ *1/235–0953* ⊟ *MC, V* Ⓜ *M1, M2, M3: Deák tér.*

$ ✕ **Castro.** The biggest surprise here may be that—despite the name—the specialty at this communist-theme bar and restaurant is Serbian, not Cuban, food. It's crowded, it's smoky, but there's a fun vibe of Magyar teen spirit. Tasty *pleskavica* (spicy hamburgers) and *čevapčiči* (spicy meatballs) are served all day to a largely student crowd, who come mainly for the cheap draft beer. Ask for the *ajvar* (sweet red-pepper and garlic pesto) with everything. ⊠ *District VII, Madách Imre tér, Around Deák tér* ⊟ *No credit cards* Ⓜ *M1, M2, M3: Deák tér.*

$ ✕ **Kádár Étkezde.** This home-style family restaurant has been around for
Fodor'sChoice a while, as have its generations of fans. The walls are decorated with
★ photos of celebrities from years gone by and the tables are topped with old-fashioned spritzer bottles from which you serve yourself water. Good old-fashioned Hungarian Jewish cooking is the thing here (not kosher, though); think stuffed kohlrabi, *káposztás kocka* (cabbage pasta), and lots of boiled beef. Everyone orders the tasty raspberry *(málna)* drink. Tell the cashier what you ate including how many slices of bread, and pay at the door. It's only open from 11:30 to 3:30. ⊠ *District VII, Klauzá tér 9, Around Király utca* ☎ *1/321–3622* ⊟ *No credit cards* ☉ *Closed Sat.–Mon. No dinner* Ⓜ *M2: Blaha Lujza tér.*

¢–$ ✕ **Noa Grill.** This clean, spacious Israeli-owned fast-food restaurant is the best choice for falafel or döner kebab in the bustling Nyugati area. Midnight finds a crowd of partygoers fueling up for the night with tasty Middle Eastern dishes like grilled eggplant salad and hummus. There's usually a line at the take-away area on the street, but you can enjoy your meal in a pleasant seating area inside. ⊠ *District VI, Terez Körút, Around Nyugati pu.* ☎ *1/354–1671* ⊟ *No credit cards* Ⓜ *M3: Nyugati pu.*

Near St. Stephen's Basilica

$$$$ ✕ **Pava.** The opening of the Gresham Palace, the city's first true five-
Fodor'sChoice star hotel, brought world-class dining to Budapest. The hotel's premier
★ restaurant is everything you'd expect from the Four Seasons chain: discreet luxury in a unique and historic building. The international menu hardly let's you know you're in Hungary, but the food is so expertly

Where to Eat in Central Budapest

50

49 **Vajda-
hunyad
Vár**

M Hösök
M1 tere Olof Palme sétány

48

Ripai-Rónai u.

Szinyei Merse u.

Balza u.

Benczúr u.

Dózsa György út

Aradi u.

Andrássy út

Felsö erdösor

Városligeti fasor

Damjanich u.

Rózsa u.

Rottenbiller utca

Vörösmarty u.

Dembinszky u.

Erzsébet

körút

Hársfa u.

István u.

M2 M Baross
tér

Rákóczi út

Fiumei út

Klauzál u.

M2 M **Erkel Ferenc
szinház** ♦

Köztársaság
tér

Rákóczi út

József körút

Somogyi Béla u.

Népszínház u.

Bérkocsis u.

Luiza u.

Sándor u.

Szentkirályi u.

Déri Miksa u.

Mátyás
tér

Krúdy u.

József u.

Dankó u.

Baross utca

KEY

Nap u.

M Metro stops

i Tourist information

Üllöi út

Rail lines

M3 M

Tömö u.

Üllöi út

Ferenc körút

Thaly Kálmán u.

Mester u.

Boráros
tér

0 ────── 500 yards

0 ────── 500 meters

prepared you're willing to settle for the breathtaking views of the Chain Bridge and Budapest Castle as a reminder. Service is friendly but white-glove all the way. The menu changes frequently and there's usually a five or six course prix-fixe option. For a truly memorable evening, splurge here and begin your evening with an aperitif in the bar or adjacent Art Nouveau arcade. ⊠ *District V, Roosevelt tér 5–6, St. Stephen's Basilica* ☎ *1/268–5100* ⌨ *Reservations essential* ⊟*AE, MC, V* Ⓜ *M1: Vörösmarty tér.*

> **FUEL UP!**
>
> Just about every market, grocery store, and *pékség* (bakery) in Budapest is open bright and early selling a wide selection of baked goods (*sütemények*) to kick-start your morning of sightseeing. *Pogácsa* (Hungarian scones) are a local favorite, and come plain, with cheese, or with cracklings. You can also choose from *kifli* (simple rolls), croissants, and *beigli* (rolls stuffed with filling like nuts or poppy seeds).

$$$–$$$$
FodorśChoice
★
✕ **Tom-George Restaurant & Bar.** Well situated in the heart of downtown, Tom-George is Budapest's answer to urban chic. The spacious bar blends blonde wood and wicker, giving the interior a relaxed yet sophisticated feel. Evenings find a young and stylish crowd choosing from the expansive cocktail menu. Minimalism at the table, though, belies exotic creativity in the kitchen. House specialties include Indian green curry chicken with naan, and sirloin goulash soup. Sushi—perhaps Budapest's best—is glamorously prepared in a corner of the dining room. Service is stylish and professional. ⊠ *District V, Október 6 utca 8, St. Stephen's Basilica* ☎ *1/266–3525* ⌨ *Reservations essential* ⊟ *AE, V* Ⓜ *M3: Arany János utca.*

$$–$$$$ ✕ **Café Kör.** The wrought-iron tables, vaulted ceilings, and crisp white tablecloths give this chic bistro a decidedly downtown feel. In the heart of the busy Fifth District, Café Kör is ideal for lunch or dinner when touring nearby St. Stephen's Basilica, although it's best to go early, since the place enjoys a loyal local following. True to bistro aspirations, the daily specials are scribbled on the wall, in both Hungarian and English. Let the friendly waitstaff guide you—even if steamed leg of veal sounds a bit less than tempting, it's heavenly. Grilled ewe-cheese salad is a favorite with regulars. ⊠ *District V, Sas utca 17, St. Stephen's Basilica* ☎ *1/311–0053* ⌨ *Reservations essential* ⊟ *No credit cards* ☉ *Closed Sun.* Ⓜ *M3: Arany János utca.*

$$–$$$ ✕ **Negro.** Location, location, location is the thing to remember at this slick bar-cum-restaurant right smack in the middle of St. Stephen's Square; you won't get a better view of Budapest's famous basilica anywhere. Tables are crowded all day long with flashy locals and tourists alike enjoying salads, tapas plates, milky coffees, and sexy cocktails in the evening. The food's a bit better than what you'd expect at this location, but the service can be hit-or-miss. There's a really good-looking waitstaff, though. ⊠ *District V, Szent István tér 11, St. Stephen's Basilica* ☎ *1/302–0136* ⊟ *AE, MC, V* Ⓜ *M1: Bajcsy-Zsilinsky utca.*

$$–$$$ ✕ **PomoD'oro.** Real Italian pizzas made to order in a brick oven attract a hungry business crowd during the week. Weekends find just as many people enjoying pastas like ravioli with Gorgonzola and walnut sauce or the "priest strangler"—homemade pasta in tomato ragout flambéed with Parmesan cheese. It makes quite a spectacular presentation. The seating here has rustic tables on many levels fenced in by wrought iron. Exposed bricks and hanging plants give the place a Tuscan patio feel. ⊠ *District V, Arany János utca 9, St. Stephen's Basilica* ☎ *1/302–6473* ⊟ *AE, MC, V* Ⓜ *M3: Arany János utca.*

$$–$$$ ✕ **Spoon Café.** For a world-class view of Castle Hill, the Chain Bridge, and the Danube, step aboard this hip restaurant and café boat moored in the heart of downtown Pest across from the Inter-Continental Hotel. Cocktail hour is crowded with tourists and residents enjoying the spectacular view. Stylishly prepared international food like lemon chicken Caesar salad keep the crowds happy. There are tempting choices here for vegetarians, like grilled goat-cheese sandwiches and homemade pastas. Take notice of the bill, though, before you pay; unlike most other places in the city, service here is included. ⊠ *District V, Vigado tér, Around Vörösmarty tér* ☎ *1/411–0933* ⊟ *AE, MC, V* Ⓜ *M1: Vörösmarty tér.*

$$ ✕ **Salaam Bombay.** Of the Indian restaurants now crowding District V, this upscale eatery has become a local favorite. The airy interior is decked out with modern Indian furnishings like funky mosaic floors and woven orange placemats. The menu concentrates on curries and "sizzlers" (kebabs), most of which can be made of beef, lamb, or chicken, but all the vegetable dishes like *saag paneer* (spinach with fresh cheese) and *daal* (lentils) are expertly done. Unlike the traditional Indian family-style servings, portions here are served per person, so if you want to share, let your server know when you order. ⊠ *District V, Mérleg utca 6, St. Stephen's Basilica* ☎ *1/411–1252* ⊟ *MC, V* Ⓜ *M1: Vörösmarty tér.*

¢ ✕ **Duran Szendvics.** You feel almost like a kid in a candy store standing outside the window of this take-away sandwich shop at lunchtime. Beautiful rows of canapés are delicately piled with fluffy egg salad, ham with black caviar, pickled herring salad, and spicy pepperoni, each with a pretty sprig of curly parsley. Take a box of four, six, or eight and walk one block around the corner to the benches in front of St. Stephen's and enjoy a lovely picnic. It gets crowded at lunch, and the inventory is usually cleaned out by 4. ⊠ *District V, Október 6 utca 15, St. Stephen's Basilica* ☎ *1/332–9348* ⊟ *No credit cards* ☉ *Closed Sun. No dinner* Ⓜ *M3: Arany János utca.*

¢ ✕ **Kisharang Étkezde.** There are only three tables and a counter at this tiny home-style restaurant not far from the basilica. It gets a lunch crowd early and bustles well into the late afternoon with downtown professional types, closing right after early dinner (by 8 PM). Dishes Hungarian grandmothers make, including goose-dumpling soup and stuffed cabbage with pork, elicit smiles from most patrons. Daily specials generally come in two sizes, but even the biggest is cheaper than anything else in this area. ⊠ *District V, Október 6 utca 17, St. Stephen's Basilica* ☎ *1/269–3861* ⊟ *No credit cards* ☉ *No dinner weekends* Ⓜ *M3: Arany János utca.*

Parliament

$–$$$ ✕ **Iguana.** People have been going to Iguana for its friendly service, big draft beers, and satisfying Mexican food for so long now that it's become almost a Budapest institution. Tex-Mex classics include whoop-ass chili and jalapeño poppers; locals rave about the taquitos. It's a good place to go for a light bite and a beer, as well as a full lunch or dinner. Jenő's favorite quesadilla is chock-full of chorizo, cheese, tomatoes, and guacamole and is perfect with a margarita. In summer there's an easy-going mixed bar scene that spills out onto the street. ☒ *District V, Zoltán utca 16, Parliament* ☎ *1/331–4352* ☐ *AE, MC, V* Ⓜ *M2: Kossuth Lajos tér.*

$–$$$
Fodor'sChoice
★

✕ **Kiskakkuk.** The Art Deco facade of the Little Cuckoo restaurant evokes the history of this once-fashionable residential neighborhood. The setting today is comfortable; wood-paneled walls and leather-upholstered chairs give the place a sophisticated, albeit homey, feel. Sunday finds multigenerational Hungarian families enjoying the familiar and attentive service. All the classic Hungarian poultry dishes are well done, including goose and duck leg with cabbage, and there are a few refined dishes, too, such as veal medallions in cream sauce and lamb with rosemary. This is a good place to take visiting relatives. ☒ *District XIII, Pozsonyi utca 12, Parliament* ☎ *1/450–0829* ☐ *MC, V* Ⓜ *M3: Nyugati pu.*

¢–$
✕ **Momotaro.** You'll find very few empty lunchtime tables at this bustling Asian greasy spoon not far from Parliament. Big bowls of steaming *ramen* satisfy most diners, but scallion pizza and pork dumplings steamed in a bamboo pot also have their fans. There's a big range of sautéed fresh vegetables available as well. The seating area isn't much, just a few low wooden tables and a counter, but turnover is quick most days. ☒ *District V, Széchenyi utca 16, Parliament* ☎ *1/269–2037* ☐ *No credit cards* Ⓜ *M2: Kossuth Lajos tér.*

¢–$
✕ **Poszonyi Kisvendéglő.** Rock-bottom prices ensure a crowd most days for lunch and dinner at this well-loved neighborhood *vendeglő* (restaurant serving home-cooking). Big bowls of *jókai bableves* (bean soup) are sopped up with fresh white bread, and classics like *borjúpaprikás* (veal paprikash) are made the way Hungarian grandmothers used to make them—with plenty of lard. ☒ *District XIII, Radnóti Miklos utca 38, Parliament* ☎ *1/329–2911* ⌲ *Reservations essential* ☐ *No credit cards* Ⓜ *M3: Nyugati pu.*

Around Andrássy út

$$$$
Fodor'sChoice
★

✕ **Baraka.** The new digs for this celebrated Budapest restaurant couldn't be more inviting. The leafy outside terrace looks onto majestic Andrássy út and Heroes Square; the spacious interior dining room is all grown-up big-city glamour. Dimmed crystal chandeliers, sleek black tables, and massive vases filled with calla lillies suggest a sophisticated evening in store. Expect innovative seasonal dishes like caramelized Belgian endive with fresh peaches, and blue-cheese and sweet-corn bisque, as well as creative fish courses. Prices match the ambition of the place, but there's a reasonable two-course lunch special daily. ✉ *District VI, Andrássy út 11, Andrássy út* ☎ *1/483–1355* ✍ *Reservations essential* ⊟ *AE, MC, V* ⊗ *Closed Sun.* Ⓜ *M1: Hősök tere.*

$$$–$$$$ ✕ **Krizia.** Locals rate this Italian restaurant as one of the best in town for its homemade pastas like pumpkin ravioli and tagliatelli with asparagus and lemon. Other Italian classics like veal saltimbocca and carpaccio with *rucola* (arugula) and Parmesan are perennial favorites. The wine list here includes a reasonably priced selection of Italian vintages. Though the owners have done their best to make the cellar space feel rustic and authentically Italian, it's hard not to notice you're in a basement. ✉ *District VI, Moszár utca 12, Around Andrássy út* ☎ *1/331–8711* ⊟ *MC, V* ⊗ *Closed Sun.* Ⓜ *M1: Oktogon.*

$$–$$$ ✕ **Goa Café.** The airy, monochromatic design of this two-floor modern restaurant on Andrássy út has a decidedly Asian feel. Light-colored stone floors, rattan vases and placemats, and minimalist lighting all evoke Asia, though no specific region. The bar, which faces the streetside window, is a popular place for drinks. The kitchen turns out some high-quality fusion food, including blackened ahi tuna with wasabi soy dressing and Goan pork vindaloo, as well as some offbeat Mediterranean dishes such as shiitake ravioli. You can order smaller salads and sandwiches at the bar all day. ✉ *District VI, Andrássy út 8, Around Andrássy út* ☎ *1/302–2570* ⊟ *AE, MC, V* Ⓜ *M1: Opera.*

$$–$$$ ✕ **Két Szerecsen.** Long a local favorite, Két Szerecsen keeps diners happy all day long with fresh and affordable soups, salads, and daily specials. The kitchen has a light touch with cold soups, especially the cucumber, dill, and gazpacho varieties. There's a Middle Eastern–influenced menu with meze plates like *tzatziki* (garlic cheese spread) topped with marinated olives, and *köfte* (lamb meatballs), as well as daily quiches. The cozy orange and burgundy interior has café tables and copper lamps with vintage posters on the walls. It can get a bit smoky inside in winter, but there's outdoor seating in summer. It's open daily for breakfast. ✉ *District VI, Nagymező utca 14, Around Andrássy út* ☎ *1/343–1984* ⊟ *MC, V* Ⓜ *M1: Oktogon.*

$$–$$$ ✕ **Vörös és Fehér.** Hungarian wines are showcased in this modern yet cozy bistro on bustling Andrássy út, close to the Opera and the Music Academy. The cement floors and minimalist lights give the place a soft industrial feel. Owned by the Budapest Wine Society, this place takes wines seriously. Order one of the *borozó* (wine snacks) like a plate of sauteed almonds or a hearty country pâté to pair with Hungary's best vintages, many available very reasonably by the glass. Main courses are seasonally inspired, and there's an emphasis on Hungarian favorites such as duck and game. ✉ *District VI, Andrássy út 41, Around Andrássy út* ☎ *1/413–1545* ⊟ *MC, V* Ⓜ *M1: Opera.*

$–$$ ✕ **Balletcipő.** Tucked away on Hajós utca a few blocks behind the Opera, this local hangout is a popular place for a light bite during the day. An innovative menu of sandwiches, including the tasty turkey mango quesadilla as well as a cheap daily lunch menu are perfect for refueling when sightseeing on Andrássy út has tuckered you out. It's located on the corner of pedestrianized Hajós utca where a lively bar scene develops on summer evenings. ⊠ *District VI, Hajós utca 14, Around Andrássy út* ☎ *1/269–3114* ⊟ *MC, V* Ⓜ *M1: Opera.*

$–$$ ✕ **Kispipa.** If you find yourself wandering the streets of Andrássy, near Király utca, this old-time favorite is a good stop for lunch and a glimpse of old Pest. Don't be surprised if other patrons don't look at menus; most of them have been lunching here for decades. It's a somewhat shabby interior, but the wizened staff is authentic and really perfect for the place. Venison tarragon ragout soup is a crowd-pleaser, as is the *birka pörkölt* (mutton stew). There are cheap and hearty daily lunch specials. ⊠ *District VII, Akácfa út 38, Around Király utca* ☎ *1/342–3969* ⊟ *AE, MC, V* Ⓜ *M1: Oktogon.*

$–$$
Fodor'sChoice
★
✕ **Menza.** Somebody's clever vision of a 1970s-style communist-era cafeteria right in the heart of trendy Liszt Ferenc tér is a big hit. Details like retro table settings, orange and olive green Formica, and the very worst in communist lighting design miraculously come together to give this place a cool hipster vibe. Quirky dishes like homemade Hungarian soups served with cereal croutons get a giggle from most diners, and greasy childhood treats like *langós* (fried dough) get reinvented and stuffed with chicken and mushrooms. In spite of the grooviness, there's good old-fashioned Hungarian comfort food here and pretty attentive, non–communist-era service. Check out the Kádár-era soft-drink list at the bar, and try *meggy marka*, a surprisingly refreshing sour cherry soda. ⊠ *District VI, Liszt Ferenc tér 2, Around Andrássy út* ☎ *1/413–1482* ⊟ *MC, V* Ⓜ *M1: Oktogon.*

$ ✕ **Al Amir.** When poking in shops along Király utca, treat yourself to the tastes of the Middle East in this long-standing Syrian restaurant popular with Budapesters. The interior feels decidedly Arab with *sheeshas* (water pipes) and elaborate tea services decorating the dining room and a mural of the Aleppo citadel in the back. There are the usual *meze*—including hummus and eggplant dip—as well as a light lentil soup to start. Main courses are heavy on lamb, but the chicken is popular, too, and the *sistauk* (kebabs) come with homemade lemony mayonnaise. Save room for fresh honey-and-pistachio pastries and mint tea for dessert. If you're on the move, you can get a *shawarma* to go from the take-away shop in front. ⊠ *District VII, Király utca 17, Around Andrássy út* ☎ *1/ 352–1422* ⊟ *MC, V* Ⓜ *M1: Oktogon.*

$ ✕ **M.** This no-frills restaurant in the edgy Seventh District not far from the popular *kerts* (summer bars) has a certain charm. The walls are draped in brown paper bags, with things like windows and pictures frames drawn on; bare tables have single candles and mismatched chairs. The daily Hungarian menu is limited to only three or four specials a night, and if you don't get there early you won't have much choice; they run out of most dishes by 9. It's popular with students and budget-minded writers and journalists, who can be found there most evenings, drinking glasses of cheap red wine. ⊠ *District VII, Kertész utca 48, Around Andrássy út* ☎ *1/342–8991* ⊟ *No credit cards* ⊘ *No lunch* Ⓜ *M1: Oktogon.*

¢–$ ✕ **Falafel.** This tiny take-away joint is one of Budapest's original salad bars and still one of the best. It is possible to get a seat upstairs but you have to be *very* lucky during the lunch hour, when the place is packed to the gills with health-conscious young professionals. Lots of Middle Eastern

PAPRIKA IS THE SPICE OF LIFE

Hungarian food is closely identified with bright-red paprika. Hungary's two most famous dishes, *gulyás leves* (goulash soup) and *csirke paprikás* (chicken paprikash), are brought to life with the rich, red spice. It comes in many forms, from light and sweet to bold and fiery. Many Hungarian dishes, such as chicken paprikash, begin with paprika mixed with oil, onions, and flour, making a roux. Meat is cooked with the paprika roux and then mixed with cream to give the dish its light color and rich depth. While its rich flavor is only released in hot oil, many a Hungarian *néni* (great aunt) will warn novice chefs to use paprika judiciously. Removing the pan from heat when adding the delicate spice prevents paprika from burning and turning bitter.

Paprika is available in all Hungarian supermarkets. The varieties include *különleges* (special), the highest-quality version, which has a pleasantly spicy aroma and is very finely ground; *édes* (sweet), which has a rich color, mild aroma, and is somewhat coarsely ground; *csipős* (hot), which is light brown with yellowish tones, has a fiery flavor, and is coarsely ground; *rózsa* (rose), bright red in color, medium spicy, and medium-ground; and *csemege* (mild), which is light red in color, has a rich aroma, and is medium-ground.

options like falafel and hummus are here, as well as fresh vegetables and legumes. A few holdovers from the good old days can be had, too, like frozen carrot and pea "salad" in a bath of mayonnaise. ⊠ *District VI, Paulay Ede utca 53, corner of Nagymező, Around Király utca* ☎ *1/351–1243* ⊟ *No credit cards* ☽ *Closed weekends* Ⓜ *M1: Oktogon.*

Around Kálvin tér

★ **$$$** ✕ **Trattoria Toscana.** Visiting Italians tell us this popular trattoria feels pretty authentic, with its bustling waiters, rustic interior, and wooden tables filled with families on Sunday. An antipasti bar in front overflows with marinated artichokes, white-bean salad, and other classic Tuscan treats, and there's a well-worn brick pizza oven in back. The extensive menu boasts some of the best fish in town, including several sea bass options. The little understood mozzarella *ventigli* pasta with San Marzano tomatoes and fresh oregano (homemade cheese-filled ravioli with garlicky tomatoes and lots of oregano) is a dish to die for. ⊠ *District V, Belgrád Rakpart 13, Around Fővam tér* ☎ *1/327–0045* ⚑ *Reservations essential* ⊟ *AE, DC, MC, V* Ⓜ *M3: Kálvin tér.*

$$–$$$ ✕ **Biboros.** This upscale Hungarian wine bar makes the best of its location on the Pest side of the Danube: large floor-to-ceiling windows give you a spectacular view of Gellért Hill, and if you're there for an early dinner, the setting sun. The menu here is modern Hungarian, which means all the beef, duck, and goose liver you'd expect with slightly lighter and more refined sauces. The duck-liver pâté with tokay marinated grapes is an elegant way to start. Five Hungarian whites and reds are on the menu by the glass. ☒ *District V, Belgrád Rakpart 18, Around Fővam tér* ☎ *1/411–1909* ▭ *MC, V* Ⓜ *M3: Kálvin tér.*

$$–$$$ ✕ **Múzeum.** This old-timer is a surprisingly affordable option for traditional cuisine served in turn-of-the-20th-century style. A beautifully frescoed ceiling and tables set with sterling silver and Zsolnay porcelain provide an elegant, if somewhat faded, grandeur. Hungarian classics here, such as *Hortobágyi palacsinta* (pancakes), and crispy goose leg with steamed cabbage, are accomplished, but the menu also includes a few ill-conceived fish dishes like sushi. Stick with pork or veal paired with a good red wine from Villány (Bock or Gere are always safe choices); the wine list is extensive and well chosen. ☒ *District VIII, Múzeum körút 11, Around Kálvin tér* ☎ *1/338–4221* 🏛 *Jacket and tie* ▭ *MC, V* ☾ *Closed Sun.* Ⓜ *M2: Kálvin tér.*

$$–$$$ ✕ **Pampas Argentine Restaurant.** Feel like a side of beef? You'll be spoiled for choice at this dedicated steak house specializing in imported Argentine beef. Cuts difficult to find in Hungary like rib-eye and New York strip are aged and lovingly grilled in this sophisticated restaurant in central Pest. Steaks can be ordered by weight and come with classic side dishes like jacket potatoes and creamed spinach. The mostly Hungarian wine list is affordable and suited to juicy beef dinners. The cheesecake, while not quite Junior's, isn't bad for Central Europe. ☒ *District V, Vámház körút, Around Kálvin tér* ☎ *1/411–1750* ▭ *AE, MC, V* Ⓜ *M3: Kálvin tér.*

$$–$$$ ✕ **Soul Cafe.** Big club chairs and mustard-colored walls covered with framed textiles warm up this Mediterranean restaurant on lively Ráday utca. Grilled sandwiches and ample salads please vegetarians, and there's a good range of chicken and turkey dishes if you want to go non-veg. The zucchini cake with Camembert and sun-dried tomatoes wins just about everyone over. ☒ *District IX, Ráday utca 11–13, Around Kálvin tér* ☎ *1/217–6986* ▭ *MC, V* Ⓜ *M3: Kálvin tér.*

$–$$ ✕ **Pata Negra.** The colorful Spanish tiles on the wall, the big legs of *ibérico jámon*, and a full wall stacked with rioja tip you off to the authenticity of this tapas bar just off Ráday utca. The Black Trotter is the real thing, serving imported Spanish goodies like marinated anchovies and chorizo in small portions in an easygoing setting. There are all the things you'd expect to nibble on, like *bacalao* (salted codfish) and squid in black ink, and if your order enough of them, you can make a full meal. There's eggy flan and *crème catalan* for dessert. ☒ *District IX, Kálvin tér 8, near Kálvin tér* ☎ *1/215–5616* ▭ *MC, V* Ⓜ *M3: Kálvin tér.*

North Buda & the Buda Hills

$$$$ ✕ **Uhu Villa.** Once you find this elegant restaurant in a villa in the hills around Hűvösvölgy, you'll feel like you're in a distant relative's country estate, and you may even want to spend the night in the attached hotel. Whether in the intimate dining room or on the breezy terrace, you'll find well executed Italian food the mainstay here. The sophisticated menu of antipasti, homemade pasta, and fish is selective; the chef relies on fresh ingredients found at local markets to make a new menu each day. The gracious owners make your trip to the hills worthwhile by welcoming you with genuine Italian hospitality. ☒ *District II, Ke-*

selý utca 1/a, Buda Hills ☎ *1/398–0570* ⊕ *www.uhuvilla.hu* ⊟ *AE, MC, V* ⊘ *Closed Sun.*

$$–$$$$ ✕ **Fuji Japan.** An aura of Zenlike calm permeates this long-standing Japanese restaurant in the affluent Rószadomb district of Upper Buda. Comfortable club chairs and big windows make you feel miles away from the hustle and bustle of downtown Pest. Tables are set a comfortable distance apart, so that you can watch the Japanese and Hungarian chefs work their craft in this full-service restaurant. Sushi and sashimi are expertly prepared, as are other Japanese specialties such as teriyaki tenderloin with sesame and mushroom tempura. There's even

a separate dining room where you can eat at low tables, in traditional Japanese style. ⊠ *District II, Csatárka utca 54/b, Buda Hills* ☎ *1/325–7111* ⊟ *AE, DC, MC, V.*

$$ ✕ **Náncsi Nénivendéglője.** "Auntie Nancsi" has built a loyal following by serving up straightforward, home-style Hungarian dishes in rustic surroundings. Chains of paprika and garlic dangle from the low wooden ceiling above tables set with red-and-white gingham tablecloths. Big tables of Hungarian families can be found here on summer weekends enjoying well-prepared Hungarian food. Sunday chicken soup and catfish paprika are well-loved by regulars. Try the popular *túrógombóc* (sweet cheese dumpling) dessert; it's the biggest and best in town. There is a garden dining area open during warmer months, when reservations are essential. ⊠ *District III, Ördögárok út 80, North Buda* ☎ *1/397–2742* ⊟ *AE, DC, MC, V* ⚲ *Reservations essential.*

Around Moskva tér & Castle Hill

☉ **$$$–$$$$** ✕ **Remiz.** The facade of this upscale restaurant in leafy Buda is fashioned out of an old tram depot. The spacious restaurant includes a dining room to suit any season, including a *söröző* (beer cellar), a glass-enclosed room, a richly paneled dining room, and an outdoor terrace. There's a jungle gym and sandbox outside for kids, and that makes the terrace *very* popular in summer. Buda families like the grilled meat cooked on a lava stone, including mouth-watering spare ribs. It's no surprise that the chocolate profiteroles are popular with children, not to mention their parents. ⊠ *District II, Budakeszi út 5, Around Moszkva tér* ☎ *1/275–1396 or 1/200–3843* ⚲ *Reservations essential* ⊟ *AE, DC, MC, V.*

$$–$$$$ ✕ **Rivalda.** On summer nights you can choose to dine outside in an 18th-century courtyard or in the restaurant's rather rococo interior—with poplin stage curtains, theatrical masks, and peach-colored walls. The location couldn't be more romantic, on a quiet street in the Castle District. The food is a lighter take on Hungarian cuisine, with some excellent seafood dishes including cream of pumpkin bisque with smoked salmon, and fillet of pike perch. A terrific place for a celebration, whether intimate or with a group, Rivalda has a substantial vegetarian menu, still something of a rarity in Budapest. ⊠ *District I, Színház utca 5–9, Castle Hill* ☎ *1/489–0236* ▭ *AE, DC, MC, V.*

$$–$$$ ✕ **Café Pierrot.** When touring the sights of Castle Hill, tuck into this inviting café for a relaxing lunch. You may not want to leave once you hear the soothing live jazz piano and see the charming interior—walls covered with paintings of harlequins and fresh flowers on the tables. This is definitely an elegant refueling stop. The menu includes updated Hungarian favorites, as well as inventive pastas and sandwiches. This all comes at a price you'd expect in one of the main tourist areas of the city, but the restaurant does offer free wireless Internet access to its customers. ⊠ *District I, Fortuna utca 14, Castle Hill* ☎ *1/375–6971* ▭ *AE, DC, MC, V.*

$–$$ ✕ **Café Gusto.** Hidden away on a leafy street not far from the Margit Bridge, this tiny café turns out some of the best salads in town. The Italian-influenced menu is limited, but you won't find better carpaccio or tiramisu in Budapest. The always-crowded spot only offers cold salads and light seafood dishes. ⊠ *District II, Frankel Leó utca 12, Around Moszkva tér* ☎ *1/316–3970* ⌘ *Reservations essential* ▭ *No credit cards* ⊘ *Closed Sun.*

Óbuda

$$–$$$ ✕ **Kéhli.** This pricey but laid-back, sepia-toned neighborhood tavern is on a hard-to-find street near the Óbuda end of the Árpád Bridge. Practically all the food here arrives in huge servings, which was just the way that Hungarian writer Gyula Krúdy (to whom the restaurant is dedicated) liked it when he was a regular customer. Dishes like the hot pot with marrow bone and toast, or *lecsó* (a stew with a base of onions, peppers, tomatoes, and paprika) are great comfort food on a cool day. ⊠ *District III, Mókus utca 22, Óbuda* ☎ *1/250–4241 or 1/368–0613* ▭ *AE, DC, MC, V* ⊘ *No lunch weekdays.*

★ $$–$$$ ✕ **Kisbuda Gyöngye.** Considered by many the finest restaurant in Óbuda, this intimate place is filled with antique furniture and decorated with an eclectic but elegant patchwork of carved wooden cupboard doors and panels. The mood is set by the veteran pianist, who can serenade guests in a dozen languages, but who is at his best with Hungarian ballads. Meat and game dishes stand out here. Try the tarragon ragout of game, or sample the goose wedding feast, a richly flavorful dish that includes a crispy goose leg with braised red cabbage, grilled goose liver, and lightly fried goose cracklings. ⊠ *District III, Kenyeres utca 34, Óbuda* ☎ *1/368–6402 or 1/368–9246* ⌘ *Reservations essential* ▭ *AE, DC, MC, V* ⊘ *Closed Sun.*

Gellért-hegy & the Tabán

$$$–$$$$ ✕ **Arcade Bistro.** Upscale residents of the 12th District pay regular patronage to this modern, sophisticated bistro on a leafy intersection not far from Déli Pályaudvar (Train Station). The floor-to-ceiling waterfall smack in the middle of the dining room soothes as it keeps conversations discreet and complements the unfussy interior. Classy starters, such

Market Eats

MOST HUNGARIAN FOOD markets have stalls in the back (or upstairs in the Vásárcsarnok) where busy shoppers can get a bite to eat. These are usually simple kiosks where you stand and eat off a paper plate. You'll find little elbow room at lunchtime when locals crowd around eating *főzelék* (pureed vegetables), *töltött káposzta* (stuffed cabbage), and other home-style dishes. Piles of fluffy white bread accompany everything, to sop up the heavy and sometimes greasy sauce. One market favorite is *rántott hal* (fried fish), deep-fried catfish, carp, or pike. If fish doesn't appeal, there's usually an exhaustive *rántott* (breaded and fried) selection: cauliflower, cheese, mushrooms, you name it.

Of course no market would be complete without a *lángos* (fried dough) stand, the uncelebrated mainstay of Hungarian market dining. Try this at least once while here. Dough is fried in very hot oil until crisp on the outside and light and airy on the inside. When it's hot it's delicious, but the enjoyment doesn't come without a price; all that grease can fill even the heartiest Magyar with woe and heartburn to boot. Lángos can be topped with a variety of condiments, cheese, sour cream, cabbage, or garlic. Best to wash it all back with a good Hungarian beer!

Rétes (strudel) stands can usually be found in most markets or street fairs in Budapest. They resemble the Austrian variety of strudel—sheets of filo dough wrapped around fruit topped with powdered sugar. There's a local preference for *meggyes rétes* (sour cherry strudel) and *túros rétes* (farmer's cheese strudel) in Hungary, and they make quite unusual ones like *kaposztás rétes* (cabbage strudel) and *mak rétes* (poppyseed strudel). In addition to being available at most markets, just about every *cukrászda* (cake shop) has a good selection available.

If your trip to Budapest falls before Christmas or Easter or during the August 20th holiday, you'll find Vörösmarty tér decked out with stands selling both handicrafts and market food. One perennially popular treat here is *kürtőskalács* (sweet funnel cake). It's made by pouring batter onto a funnel, basting it with honey and baking it until golden brown. They're sweet and gooey but perfect for an afternoon of market browsing.

---

as tuna carpaccio and duck breast and ruccola (arugula) salad, prepare you for innovative game dishes and seasonal specialties. The smart and courteous staff will help you choose a wine from the refined list, all available by the glass. ☒ *District XII, Kíss János Alt. utca 38, Around Déli Train Station* ☎ *1/225–1969* ▤ *MC, V* ☉ *No dinner Sun.* Ⓜ *M2: Déli Train Station.*

$$–$$$$ ✕ **Hemingway.** It takes some brio to pull off a restaurant with the style of Ernest Hemingway, but when that restaurant is housed in what looks like a 19th-century hunting lodge—complete with wooden balcony and lake views—the odds for success start to look better. The menu includes several kinds of seafood cooked on Mediterranean lava stone. Fans of heroic consumption will also appreciate a cocktail menu with 100-some drinks, and a selection of after-dinner cigars. ✉ *District XI, Kosztolányi Dezso tér 2, on Feneketlen Lake, South Buda* ☎ *1/489–0236* ♿ *Reservations essential* 🍽 *AE, DC, MC, V.*

$$–$$$ ✕ **Paulaner Brauhaus.** There's a lively mood at this German brewery and beer hall most nights, even though it's hidden away in a shopping mall. Big wooden tables fill three separate rooms, and there's space enough for impromptu dancing if the band gets you going. Solid Bavarian classics like *Weisswurst* with honey mustard and frankfurters with sauerkraut keep the crowd happy, and there's a wide selection of

Paulaner beers on draft, including amber ales, pilsners, and light lagers. The classic *Weissbier* is served in a huge mug with a lemon. ✉ *District XII, Mom Park Shopping Center, Alkotás utca, Around Déli Train Station* ☎ *1/224–2020* ♿ *Reservations essential* 🍽 *AE, MC, V.*

$–$$ ✕ **Tabáni Gösser Étterem.** For a refined Hungarian meal without all the kitsch of hanging peppers or pomp of crystal chandeliers, check out this favorite eatery in the quiet Tabán area just below the Castle District. There's not much to the interior, but the excellent *marha pörkölt* (beef stew) with red wine and *borjú paprikas* (veal paprikash) draw regulars for Sunday lunch. There's a pleasant terrace facing a park for dining in nice weather. ✉ *District I, Attila út 19, Tabán* ☎ *1/375–9482* 🍽 *MC, V.*

Városliget (City Park)

$$$$ ✕ **Gundel.** This is probably Hungary's most celebrated restaurant, both for its history (opened in 1894) as well as its renovation in the 1990s by Hungarian-American restaurateur George Lang. The gorgeous setting in the City Park includes an Art Nouveau bar designed by Adam Tihany. Fin-de-siècle grandeur shines through in the glorious dining room, tastefully adorned with 19th- and 20th-century Hungarian paintings, and a 10-piece gypsy band adds an earnest nostalgia to the place. The food, sadly, is just a bit above average, though some classics such as goose liver pâté and Gundel pancakes are well executed. Nevertheless, a visit is a uniquely memorable experience. ✉ *District XIV, Állatkerti út 2, Városliget* ☎ *1/321–3550* ♿ *Reservations essential* 👔 *Jacket and tie* 🍽 *AE, DC, MC, V* Ⓜ *M1: Hősök tere.*

$$$–$$$$ ✕ **Robinson Restaurant.** Robinson can certainly lay claim to one of the more exotic locations in Budapest dining—on wooden platforms atop an artificial lake, looking across to the delightful architectural folly of Vajdahunyad Castle. You can sit outside on the terrace during summer or enjoy the warm pastel interior in colder months. The menu includes some Hungarian highlights such as goose liver and *becsi szelet* (Wiener schnitzel), but also has some innovative dishes like sirloin stew with sherry sauce and wok-fried shrimp. Unlike most restaurants in Budapest, you can pay in euros here at the daily rate. ✉ *District XIV, Városliget-tó*

Városliget ☎ *1/422–0222* ⚓ *Reservations essential* 🚭 *AE, DC, MC, V* Ⓜ *M1: Hősök tere.*

Coffeehouses

The coffeehouse has a long tradition in Budapest. At the turn of the 20th century there were more than 400 coffeehouses in the city, many of them patronized by struggling writers. Important journals and books were produced here, and the coffeehouse itself was a cornerstone of Budapest literary life. Though by no means vital to intellectual life today, the coffeehouse is still a popular institution. It is home to occasional writers but it's equally patronized by tourists, students, and grandmothers chatting over coffee and cake. In general, most *kávéházak* (coffeehouses) serve a wide range of coffees and a small list of spirits, wine, and beer. The more traditional ones serve a dizzying array of cakes, all made fresh daily. The modern ones serve cakes as well, but may also serve sandwiches, soups, and light dishes. You will find both styles of grand turn-of-the-20th-century coffeehouses in Budapest, as well as quite a few modern cafés.

> ### IN A PICKLE
>
> Traditional Hungarian salads are made up of pickled vegetables *savanyúság*: cucumbers, cabbage, peppers, and even beets, melons, and cauliflower. These salads are served together with the main course, the idea being that the heaviness of the main course is cut by the acidity of the salad. This taste combination works very well with rich Hungarian food. So when you're in a traditional restaurant, order a *uborka saláta* (cucumber salad) or *vegyes saláta* (mixed pickle salad) with your *csirke paprikás* (chicken paprikash) or *sült libacomb* (crispy goose leg). *Jó etvagyot!* (bon appetit!)

Angelika. This four-room café gets even bigger in the summer, when six small graduated terraces with awnings open up outside. You can get a full range of cakes here and an over-the-top iced coffee with ice cream and whipped cream. The terraces themselves have one of the best views of Parliament in the city. ✉ *District I, Batthyány tér 7, Around Batthyány tér* ☎ *1/212–3784* 🚭 *No credit cards* Ⓜ *M2: Batthyány tér.*

Auguszt Cukrászda. This old-fashioned pastry shop has a loyal following for some of the lightest, most buttery pastries in Budapest. All the classic Hungarian cakes like *rétes* (strudel filled with sour cherries, apples, or cheese) and *dobos torta* (chocolate cream cake with caramel) can be enjoyed here. ✉ *District V, Kossuth Lajos utca 14–16, Around Váci utca* ☎ *1/337–6379* 🚭 *No credit cards* ☉ *Closed Sun.* Ⓜ *M2: Astoria.*

Café Picard. Antiques dealers and local artists can be found here most mornings chatting over short black coffees and croissants in this friendly café in the antiques district. Lunchtime finds the same crowd, plus a few shoppers enjoying homemade soups, tasty panini, and mixed cheese and salami plates. Some days there are a few romantic lunchers, discreetly sipping champagne in the back booths. ✉ *District V, Falk Miksa utca*

10, Parliament ☎ *1/473–0939* ▭ *No credit cards* Ⓜ *M2: Kossuth Lajos tér.*

Café Vian. This trendy café in the heart of Liszt Ferenc tér is popular for coffee in the afternoon and cocktails in the evening. There's a good range of warm sandwiches and salads, as well as a plentiful array of cakes and boutique teas. The mascarpone cheesecake is a killer. ⊠ *District VI, Liszt Ferenc tér 9, Around Andrássy út* ☎ *1/268–1154* ▭ *AE, MC, V* Ⓜ *M1: Oktogon.*

Fodor's Choice   **Centrál Kávéház.** For 19th-century grandeur in 21st-century comfort, this
★   popular café can't be beat. Coffees are served on silver trays with glasses of mineral water just like the old days, but these days it's enjoyed in an air-conditioned, no-smoking room. The menu includes substantial dishes like *hortobágyi palacsinta* (meat pancakes with paprika sauce) and beef Stroganoff all day. ⊠ *District V, Károlyi Mihály utca 9, Around Váci utca* ☎ *1/235–0599* ▭ *AE, MC, V* Ⓜ *M3: Ferenciek tere.*

Eckermann. The coffees are served in mugs with lots of milk at this popular spot directly across the street from Művész. You won't find much to eat on the menu, but you will find a few European intellectual types looking very serious. The café is attached to the Goethe Institute. ⊠ *District VI, Andrássy út 24, Around Andrássy út* ☎ *1/269–2542* ▭ *No credit cards* ☉ *Closed Sun.* Ⓜ *M1: Opera.*

Farger Kávézo. The staff at this modern coffee shop near Szabadság tér look like they could have stepped off the set of *Friends*; good-looking, friendly, mostly English-speaking kids whipping up frothy cappuccinos and decaf lattes. It's a good place to grab a sandwich or salad and use the free wireless Internet connection. ⊠ *District V, Zoltán utca 18, Around Parliament* ☎ *1/373–0078* ▭ *No credit cards* Ⓜ *M2: Kossuth tér.*

Gerbeaud. It's hard to miss this grand coffeehouse, which has been selling its magnificent cakes at the north end of Vörösmarty tér since 1858. Accept that there are lots of tourists here at all times of the year. However, while the afternoon coffee and cake are pricey, the experience is pure Budapest. ⊠ *District V, Vörösmarty tér 7, Around Deák Ferenc tér* ☎ *1/429–9000* ▭ *AE, MC, V* Ⓜ *M1: Vörösmarty tér.*

Művész. While service at this grand coffeehouse can be less than cheery, its interior can't be beat for a faded-grandeur feel. In summer the terrace spills out onto Andrássy út, and it's a premier place for people-watching. All the classic Hungarian cakes are here, as well as a moist, not-too-sweet *alma torta* (apple cake). ⊠ *District VI, Andrássy út 29, Around Andrássy út* ☎ *1/352–1337* ▭ *No credit cards* Ⓜ *M1: Opera.*

Where to Stay

By Paul
Olchváry

BUDAPEST HAS SEEN A STEADY increase in both the quantity and quality of its accommodations since 1989, when the country broke away from communism, but the first years of the 21st century have seen an extraordinary number of new hotels opening their doors. Long gone are the old days when you had to settle for what was available. Theoretically, the advantage is shifting to the traveler, who is increasingly benefiting from not only more sheer options but also from stiff competition keeping rates lower. That said you have to know where to look. Indeed, the evidence of this visitor-friendly trend is much more apparent on side streets, on the edge of downtown Budapest, and farther out than it is on the main thoroughfares of the city center. Minus private rooms, which are still available as a budget alternative, and lower-priced alternatives tucked away in not necessarily conspicuous places, the salient heart of Hungary's capital has become ever more dominated by high-class hotels to which low prices are a foreign language.

Luxury hotels are making a bit of a splash in Budapest. Where once the Hotel Kempinski single-handedly dominated, now there are many five-star properties from which to choose. Most are painstaking, multimillion dollar resurrections of faded glories, like the Méridien, the Corinthia Grand Hotel Royal, and the Four Seasons Budapest. As of this writing, the most recent arrival on this scene is the legendary New York Palace, which re-opened as a five-star hotel in May 2006. The word on the street is that the next big luxury overhaul will be the Drechsler Palace, across the boulevard from the Opera House. Formerly the home of the Hungarian National Ballet, this property was more recently purchased by an Israeli investment firm that (as of this writing) seemed to be in no big hurry to follow through on its plans to turn it into a hotel.

Numerous small and medium-sized private hotels have opened on the side streets of inner Pest, some in lovely old 18th- and 19th-century buildings refurbished to modern standards. Earlier it wasn't possible to stay so centrally without paying through the nose for a modern chain hotel or risking your safety in less expensive, but seedy, places. Indeed, the very definition of "central Pest" may need to be further calibrated, as the number of downtown properties grows.

In upper price ranges you can expect top international-standard service, facilities, and amenities. Many of these high-priced hotels cater to business travelers, offering relatively new extras (to Hungary, at least)

> ## PAUL'S TOP 5
>
> **Four Seasons Gresham Palace Budapest.** Centrally located, this stunning 1906 Art Nouveau palace has some of the loveliest views in town.
> **Andrássy Hotel.** Budapest's best boutique hotel, with an Art Deco lobby and a hip young staff.
> **Hotel Victoria.** This small, family-run, reasonably priced hotel has a choice Buda-side location on the Danube riverbank.
> **Danubius Grand Hotel Margitsziget.** Built in 1873 by Opera House architect Miklós Ybl, this hotel has free access to spa facilities.
> **Kalmár Bed & Breakfast.** This treasure trove of elegant, old Budapest is a must for those who appreciate original ambience over amenities.

KNOW-HOW

RESERVATIONS

Advance reservations are strongly advised in summer, especially at the smaller, lower-priced hotels and during the week in August that Formula I racing descends upon Budapest. In winter it's not anywhere near as difficult to find a hotel room, even at the last minute, and prices are usually reduced by 20% to 30%. The best budget option is to book a private room or an entire apartment. Expect to pay between €30 and €40 for a double room. Visitors who prefer a room unsullied by cigarette smoke will be happy to know that most of Budapest's large hotels offer some smoke-free rooms, and in some cases entire wings or floors. The situation changes dramatically, however, once you travel far from the capital.

PRICES

All room rates indicated here are based on double-occupancy rack rates in high season. It's important to note, however, that these rates often double during the week Formula I racing comes to Budapest every year, usually in mid-August. On the other hand, most large hotels offer significant discounts, frequently including breakfast, for weekend bookings and during special sale periods throughout the year. If a property seems too expensive at first glance, it's worth looking into special rates by calling them as well as checking their Web site. Most hotels include all taxes as well as breakfast in their regular quoted rates. Luxury hotels usually do not include VAT of 15% and a tourist tax of 3% in the room rate, nor do they usually include breakfast. We note in the review when taxes are not included; each review indicates whether breakfast is included in the rates or not.

Assume that all hotels operate on the **European Plan** (EP, with no meals), unless we specify that they use the **Breakfast Plan** (BP, with a full breakfast) or **Continental Plan** (CP, with a Continental breakfast).

Most hotels allow children under 16 to stay in their parents' room for free, though age limits vary from property to property. For single rooms with bath, count on paying about 80% of the double-room rate. Most hotels in Budapest set their rates and expect payment in euros. With very few exceptions (mostly family-run pensions), credit cards are widely accepted.

WHAT IT COSTS In Euros and Forints				
$$$$	**$$$**	**$$**	**$**	**¢**
FOR 2 PEOPLE IN EUROS				
over 225	175–225	125–175	75–125	under 75
FOR 2 PEOPLE IN FORINTS				
over 56,000	44,000–56,000	31,000–44,000	18,500–31,000	under 18,500

Prices are for two people in a standard double room with a private bath and breakfast during peak season (May through October).

LODGING ALTERNATIVES

APARTMENTS & PRIVATE ROOMS

Apartments, available for short- and long-term rental, are often an economical alternative to staying in a hotel, with an increasing number of options available, as Hungarian entrepreneurs find uses for old family homes and inherited apartments. The Internet is teeming with apartment offers. A short-term rental in Budapest will probably cost from €40 to €60 a day in high season.

Accommodations can also be arranged in private rooms, sometimes with the option of breakfast. Since this usually involves sharing someone's home—your host is most often a kindly elderly Hungarian lady—it is an appealing possibility for those who want to meet the locals. The typical two-person, high-season rate for a private room is approximately €30 a night.

Both apartments and private rooms usually come with bed linens and towels. Payments generally need to be made in cash, but some bookings made through accommodation agencies allow use of credit cards.

IBUSZ Private Accommodation Service (✉ District V, Ferenciek tere 10, Around Ferenciek tere ☎ 1/485–2700 or 06-40/428–794 (toll-free within Hungary) 🖷 1/338–4987 🌐 www.ibusz.hu ✉ District V Vörösmarty tér 6 ☎ 1/317–0532 🖷 1/317–1474), with offices throughout the city, rents out apartments in downtown Budapest, most consisting of two rooms plus a fully equipped kitchen and bathroom. Private rooms are also available. You can explore some of your options on the IBUSZ Web site. The main office, on Ferenciek tere, is closed on weekends and only open until 4 PM Monday through Thursday, until 3 PM Friday. **Non-Stop Hotel Service** (✉ District V, Apáczai Csere János utca 1, Around Váci utca ☎ 1/318–3925 or 1/266–8042 🖷 1/317–9099 🌐 www.non-stophotelservice.hu) has the advantage of being the only accommodation service open 24 hours a day. The agency books apartments as well as rooms in private homes, and can also make hotel reservations. **Panaco Tours** (☎ 1/430–0831 or [last-minute reservations] 06-30/210–9951 🖷 1/430–0833 🌐 www.budapesthotels.com) is best known for its Web site, a thorough and professional Internet accommodation service with lots of helpful extra information about traveling in Budapest thrown in for good measure. **To-Ma Tours** (✉ District V, Október 6 utca 22, Around St. Stephen's Basilica ☎ 1/353–0819 🖷 1/269–5715 🌐 www.tomatour.hu) arranges private apartments and rooms and is open on weekends.

HOME EXCHANGES

If you would like to exchange your home for someone else's, join a home-exchange organization, which will send you its updated listings of available exchanges for a year and will include your own listing in at least one of them. It's up to you to make specific arrangements.

There are two major U.S.-based home exchange organizations. **HomeLink International** (✉ 2937 NW 9th Terrace, Fort Lauderdale, FL

33311 ☎ 954/566−2687 or 800/638−3841 ⊕ www.homelink.org); $125 yearly for a listing, online access, and catalog; $80 without catalog. **Intervac U.S.** (✉ 30 Corte San Fernando, Tiburon, CA 94920 ☎ 800/756−4663 ⊕ www.intervacus.com); $126 yearly for a listing, online access, and a catalog; $79 without catalog.

HOSTELS

No matter what your age, you can save on lodging costs by staying at hostels. In some 4,500 locations in more than 70 countries around the world, Hostelling International (HI), the umbrella group for a number of national youth-hostel associations, offers single-sex, dorm-style beds and, at many hostels, rooms for couples and family accommodations. Membership in any HI national hostel association, open to travelers of all ages, allows you to stay in HI-affiliated hostels at member rates; one-year membership is about $28 for adults (C$35 for a two-year minimum membership in Canada, £14 in the U.K., A$52 in Australia, and NZ$40 in New Zealand); hostels charge about $10−$30 per night. Members have priority if the hostel is full; they're also eligible for discounts around the world, even on rail and bus travel in some countries.

In Hungary most hostels are geared toward the college crowd. For further information, consult the free annual accommodations directory published by Tourinform or the listings in *Budapest in Your Pocket*, available at newsstands, or visit the Web site ⊕ Backpackers.hu or, indeed, the site of the Hungarian Youth Hostels Association

⊕ miszsz.hu. At the Internet-equipped **Back Pack Guesthouse** (✉ District XI, Takács Menyhért utca 33, South Buda ☎ 1/385−8946 ⊕ www.backpackbudapest.hu) rates range from 3,000 HUF for a bed in a 7- to 11-bed room to 3,500 HUF for a bed in a 4- to 5-bed room. You can get your own double for 8,000 HUF. The **Sirály Youth Hostel** (✉ District XIII, Margitsziget, Margaret Island ☎ 1/329−3952), situated in the relative peace, quiet, and clean air of an island park in the Danube, charges 2,000 HUF per person for a bed in a 12-bed room.

For more information about hosteling, contact your local youth hostel office. **Hostelling International–USA** (✉ 8401 Colesville Rd., Suite 600, Silver Spring, MD 20910 ☎ 301/495−1240 🖷 301/495−6697 ⊕ www.hiusa.org). **Hostelling International–Canada** (✉ 205 Catherine St., Suite 400, Ottawa, Ontario K2P 1C3 ☎ 613/237−7884 or 800/663−5777 🖷 613/237−7868 ⊕ www.hihostels.ca). **YHA England and Wales** (✉ Trevelyan House, Dimple Rd., Matlock, Derbyshire DE4 3YH, U.K. ☎ 0870/870−8808, 0870/770−8868, or 0162/959−2600 🖷 0870/770−6127 ⊕ www.yha.org.uk). **YHA Australia** (✉ 422 Kent St., Sydney, NSW 2001 ☎ 02/9261−1111 🖷 02/9261−1969 ⊕ www.yha.com.au). **YHA New Zealand** (✉ Level 1, Moorhouse City, 166 Moorhouse Ave., Box 436, Christchurch ☎ 03/379−9970 or 0800/278−299 🖷 03/365−4476 ⊕ www.yha.org.nz).

3

like wireless Internet hot spots and automated check-in and check-out. Perks like thicker mattresses and swankier bathrooms are more common. Generally, the older, less expensive properties can be a bit worn, with quintessential brown-and-orange communist-era decor, flimsy shower stalls instead of bathtubs, and low-riding single beds that are pushed together to make a double. There are plenty of exceptions, however, in newer and refurbished budget hotels—more of which are opening year by year—and family-run pensions and bed-and-breakfasts. Almost all of Budapest's least expensive hotels have cable TV and telephones in the rooms, and most have at least a few air-conditioned rooms.

> **DOUBLY SWEET DREAMS**
>
> Regardless of the price range, Hungarian hotels tend to count two single beds pushed together as a double bed. If it's important to you, be sure to specify you want a double mattress, often referred to as a *francia ágy* (French bed).

The probability of higher taxes and other government-imposed economic austerity measures (to bring the economy up to speed to adopt the euro by 2010) means that travelers can expect higher than usual rate increases in the immediate future. Although in recent years many hotels here have increased rates only minimally, if at all, increases of 10% or more are in the cards for 2007.

Something important to keep in mind when planning your trip to Budapest is that every year for a week in mid-August the Formula 1 auto races descend upon the city, literally doubling the hotel rates and maxing out occupancy. If you're not a racing fan and can afford to be flexible, it's best to avoid this period in Budapest.

Addresses below are preceded by the district number (in Roman numerals) and include the Hungarian postal code. Districts V, VI, and VII are in downtown Pest; District I includes Castle Hill, the main tourist district of Buda.

BUDA HOTELS

Castle Hill and Around Batthyány tér

The fairytale surroundings of Castle Hill make it a delightful place to stay, and it doesn't even have to cost an arm and a leg anymore. The only downside is that because it's Budapest's number one tourist area the district's restaurants and shops tend to be touristy and more expensive. Walking home is a strenuous uphill affair, but buses, taxis, and the *sikló* funicular can help out. Hotels on the Danube near Batthyány tér have great river views of Parliament and Pest, or of Castle Hill itself, and easy metro access to the rest of the city.

★ ☺ 🖬 **Budapest Hilton.** You'll have to decide for yourself if this hotel, built
$$–$$$$ in 1977 around the remains of a 17th-century Gothic chapel and adjacent to the Matthias Church, is a successful integration or not. The exterior certainly betrays the hotel's 1970s origins, but the modern and

tasteful rooms and great views from Castle Hill will soothe the most delicate of aesthetic sensibilities. While the minimal fitness facilities leave much to be desired, the 24-hour business center and free airport shuttle service make the Hilton stand out among its peers. Rooms with the best Danube vistas cost more. Children, regardless of age, stay free when sharing a room with their parents. VAT and tourist tax are not included in the rates. ⊠ *District I, Hess András tér 1–3, Castle Hill H-1014* ☎ *1/889–6600, 800/445–8667 in the U.S. and Canada* ⊟ *1/889–6644* ⊕ *www.budapest.hilton.com* ☞ *298 rooms, 24 suites* ⌂ *Restaurant, café, bar, room service, in-room safes, Wi-Fi, cable TV with video games, in-room data ports, gym, hair salon, sauna, bar, wineshop, shops, babysitting, dry cleaning, laundry service, concierge, Internet, business services, convention center, airport shuttle, travel services, parking (fee), some free parking, some pets allowed (fee), no-smoking floor* ⊟ *AE, DC, MC, V* ⦶ *EP* Ⓜ *M2: Moszkva tér, then Várbusz.*

3

★ **$$$** ⌂ **art'otel.** Travelers bored with bland, business-hotel decor may get more excited by this mod lodging's snazzy design. Everything—from the multimillion-dollar art collection on the walls to the whimsical red-and-white carpeting and even the cups and saucers—is the work of one man, American artist Donald Sultan. Encompassing one new building and four 18th-century baroque houses on the Buda riverfront, the art'otel adroitly blends old and new. Rooms are on the small side, but some have splendid views of Fisherman's Bastion and the Matthias Church. ⊠ *District I, Bem rakpart 16–19, Around Batthyány tér H-1011* ☎ *1/487–9487* ⊟ *1/487–9488* ⊕ *www.artotel.de* ☞ *155 rooms, 9 suites* ⌂ *Restaurant, café, bar, room service, in-room safes, minibars, cable TV, Wi-Fi, gym, hair salon, sauna, shop, dry cleaning, laundry service, concierge, Internet, meeting rooms, travel services, parking (fee), no-smoking rooms* ⊟ *AE, DC, MC, V* ⦶ *BP* Ⓜ *M2: Batthyány tér.*

$–$$ ⌂ **Burg Hotel.** You don't have to splurge on the Hilton to stay on Szentháromság tér. This prime piece of real estate opened in 2000, making it the third hotel on Castle Hill's most famous square. The only downside is having the peak-season crowds thronging under your window, but then the quiet nights are that much more magical. Rooms have green wall-to-wall carpeting, beige wallpaper, and blue-tiled bathrooms with either tubs or shower stalls. ⊠ *District I, Szentháromság tér 7, Castle Hill H-1014* ☎ *1/212–0269* ⊟ *1/212–3970* ⊕ *www.burghotelbudapest. com* ☞ *24 rooms, 2 suites* ⌂ *Minibars, cable TV, bar, Internet, travel services, parking (fee), no-smoking rooms* ⊟ *AE, DC, MC, V* ⦶ *BP* Ⓜ *M2: Moszkva tér, then Várbusz.*

★ **$** ⌂ **Carlton Hotel.** The Carlton is proof that you can stay in the Castle Hill district—even nestled at the foot of the hill itself—without paying a fortune. Rooms on the upper floors offer lovely views over rooftops to Castle Hill, leaving one only to wish the smallish windows were larger. Request a newly refurbished room to avoid the adequate but stark gray furnishings of the earlier design. With downtown just a walk across the Chain Bridge away and the Castle Hill district rising in your backyard, it's hard to do better for location and price. A large buffet breakfast is served every morning. ⊠ *District I, Apor Péter utca 3, Castle Hill H-1011* ☎ *1/224–0999* 🖷 *1/ 224–0990* ⊕ *www.carltonhotel.hu* 🔊 *95 rooms* ⚒ *In-room safes, minibars, cable TV, Wi-Fi, bar, dry cleaning, laundry service, Internet, business services, meeting room, parking (fee), some pets allowed (fee), no-smoking rooms* ▤ *AE, DC, MC, V* ⦿ *BP* Ⓜ *M2: Batthyány tér.*

> ### HYPO-NICE ROOMS
>
> Many properties keep a few so-called "bio" rooms aside for people with severe allergies. These rooms don't have the otherwise ubiquitous wall-to-wall carpeting and are specially fitted with hypo-allergenic linens and pillows. In theory, they are also no-smoking rooms.

$ 🖬 **Hotel Kulturinov.** This relatively inexpensive hotel can be found in rather noble quarters—one wing of a magnificent 1902 neo-baroque castle in the heart of the luxurious Castle District. The building's main tenants are a cultural foundation and a large wine center, so part of the charm is navigating your way through the cavernous entry hall, up the sweeping staircase, and down the hallway to finally reach the hotel's small reception desk. Rooms come with two or three beds and are very basic but peaceful; they have showers but no tubs. Children under 14 can share their parents' room for free. The neighborhood is simply magical, even if it is often overrun with tourists. Reserve well in advance. ⊠ *District I, Szentháromság tér 6, Castle Hill H-1014* ☎ *224–8102* 🖷 *1/375–1886* ⊕ *www.mka.hu* 🔊 *16 rooms* ⚒ *Snack bar, some fans, minibars, cable TV, meeting rooms, parking (fee); no a/c* ▤ *DC, MC, V* ⦿ *BP* Ⓜ *M2: Moszkva tér, then Várbusz or Bus 16.*

★ $ 🖬 **Hotel Victoria.** This small, family-run hotel has had a loyal following since it opened shortly after the Iron Curtain came down. Taking advantage of a choice Buda-side location on the Danube riverbank, each room has a small seating area in front of floor-to-ceiling windows looking across the river to Parliament. The reception staff is kind and able, and can direct you to the nearby restaurants where you can charge your meals to your room. Request a no-smoking room when reserving to avoid overlapping with a heavy smoker. ⊠ *District I, Bem rakpart 11, Around Batthyány tér H-1011* ☎ *1/457–8080* 🖷 *1/457–8088* ⊕ *www.victoria.hu* 🔊 *27 rooms* ⚒ *In-room safes, minibars, cable TV, Wi-Fi, sauna, bar, dry cleaning, laundry service, Internet, business services, meeting room, travel services, parking (fee)* ▤ *AE, DC, MC, V* ⦿ *BP* Ⓜ *M2: Batthyány tér.*

Gellért Hill and South Buda

In addition to offering easy access to the famed Gellert Hotel's thermal bath complex, the area around and south of Gellért Hill offers less hectic, greener surroundings than those of Pest, particularly as you move away from busy Bartók Béla út and the bridge traffic around Szent Gellért tér. The verdant slopes of Gellért Hill and its hilltop citadel and monument make for lovely views from hotel windows looking onto it. There is no metro in this part of Buda, but extensive tram and bus service make it still easily accessible.

★ **$$–$$$** ⊞ **Danubius Hotel Gellért.** Budapest's most renowned Art Nouveau hotel is undergoing a painfully slow, incremental overhaul, aimed at restoring the original Jugendstil style popular when it was built during World War I. Rooms are elegant and spacious. Be sure to request a refurbished room when you reserve for optimal comfort; unrenovated rooms are a good value, if you don't mind a little Iron Curtain sternness. Regardless, ask about options—and perhaps bargains—as rooms in this quirky building come in all shapes, sizes, and prices. Everyone staying here also has free access to the monumental and ornate thermal baths, with a dedicated elevator to whisk you directly to the premises. ⊠ *District XI, Szent Gellért tér 1, Gellért-hegy and Tabán H-1111* ☎ *1/889–5500* 🖷 *1/889–5505* ⊕ *www.danubiusgroup.com* ⇴ *220 rooms, 14 suites* ⚑ *2 restaurants, café, bar, room service, in-room safes, minibars, cable TV, Wi-Fi, 3 outdoor pools, 10 indoor pools, hair salon, spa, Turkish bath, shops, babysitting, dry cleaning, laundry service, concierge, Internet, business services, meeting rooms, travel services, parking (fee), no-smoking rooms; no a/c in some rooms* ⊟ *AE, DC, MC, V* �🍽 *BP* Ⓜ *Tram 18, 19, 47, 49 to Szent Gellért tér.*

$–$$ ⊞ **Park Hotel Flamenco.** This glass-and-concrete socialist-era leviathan is right across the street from the supposedly (but not) bottomless Feneketlen Lake. Happily, once inside, you can almost forget the Stalinist architecture, due to the pleasant, contemporary furnishings. It's a bit out of the way (a good 20-minute tram ride will get you across the river into Pest), but the location is at least relatively bucolic, what with the lake and park surrounding it. ⊠ *District XI, Tas Vezér utca 7, South Buda H-1113* ☎ *1/889–5600* 🖷 *1/889–5651* ⊕ *www.danubiusgroup.com* ⇴ *347 rooms, 8 suites* ⚑ *2 restaurants, 2 cafés, in-room safes, minibars, cable TV, Wi-Fi, 2 indoor tennis courts, indoor pool, health club, hair salon, gym, sauna, bar, shop, dry cleaning, laundry service, concierge, Internet, business services, meeting rooms, travel services, parking (fee), some pets allowed (fee), some no-smoking rooms* ⊟ *AE, DC, MC, V* �🍽 *BP* Ⓜ *Tram 19, 49 to Kosztolányi Dezső tér.*

$ ⊞ **Kalmár Bed & Breakfast.** This treasure trove of elegant, old Budapest is a 1900 stone mansion on the lower slopes of Gellért Hill, right behind the Hotel Gellért. Those who appreciate original ambience over amenities will be pleased. While cheaper doubles on the ground floor are relatively small and dark, there are also antique-filled suites and opulent, full-scale apartments that can accommodate two couples. Some rooms come with a kitchen, others with a terrace. Ask Eszter (who speaks English) to help you choose a room to fit your budget and standards. The Kalmár family has been running the house as a B&B since 1964, slowly buying back rooms and apartments that were partitioned off during the communist era. Breakfast is served on delicate matching porcelain. ⊠ *District XI, Kelenhegyi út 7–9, Gellért-hegy and Tabán H-1118* ☎ *1/372–7530, 1/271–9312 English-speaking* 🖷 *1/385–2804* ⇴ *5 rooms, 2 suites, 2 apartments* ⚑ *Minibars, cable TV* ⊟ *No credit cards* �🍽 *BP* Ⓜ *Tram 18, 19, 47, 49 to Szent Gellért tér.*

Fodor's Choice ★

¢ ▦ **Hotel Citadella.** Housed within the historical Citadella fort that crowns Gellért Hill, this hotel and hostel combination is geared towards low-maintenance, budget-minded travelers who don't mind an uphill hike at the end of their sightseeing day. Its origins as an army barracks still come through loud and clear: windows are small, and half the rooms share a WC. But the vaulted stone ceilings and marvelous views from many of the rooms make it unique in Budapest. Of the twelve rooms with private bath, two have a bathtub, the rest simple showers. While the location is as on top of the city as possible, finding your way to it is quite another matter, for there are no signs. Your best bet is to walk under an archway that leads to the "Panoráma Múzeumok" (Panorama Museums). ⊠ *District XI, Citadella sétány, Gellért Hill H–1118* ☎ *1/466–5794* 🖷 *1/386–0505* ⊕ *www.citadella.hu* ➷ *12 private rooms (two–four beds each), 1 14-bed hostel room* ♢ *Restaurant, shop, some free parking, some pets allowed (fee); no a/c, no room phones, no room TVs* ▭ *No credit cards* |◯| *CP* Ⓜ *Bus 27 to Szirtes út.*

PEST HOTELS

Around Deák Ferenc tér

Budapest's poshest and priciest hotels line the Danube riverbank just south of the Chain Bridge. The area is hard to beat: central to major sights, restaurants, and business—Deák tér metro hub is nearby—and offering postcard-perfect views from your bedroom window.

$$$$ ▦ **Four Seasons Hotel Gresham Palace Budapest.** It doesn't get much bet-
Fodor'sChoice ter than this: a centrally located, super-deluxe hotel in a museum-qual-
★ ity landmark with the prettiest views in town. No detail has been spared in restoring this stunning 1906 Art Nouveau palace to its original majesty: delicate wrought-iron vents in the hallways, exquisite gold mosaic tiles on the facade, stained-glass windows, and cupolas. Three magnificent stairwells are so grand that you may not want to use the elevators. Rooms, some with balconies and vaulted ceilings, are similarly large and plush. Spanish-marble bathrooms—unlike any in Budapest—have both showers and deep soaking tubs. The lobby café is modeled after the building's original. Taxes are not included. ⊠ *District V, Roosevelt tér 5–6, Around Váci utca H-1051* ☎ *1/268–6000* 🖷 *1/268–5000* ⊕ *www.fourseasons.com* ➷ *165 rooms, 14 suites* ♢ *Restaurant, café, room service, in-room safes, minibars, cable TV, Wi-Fi, ethernet, indoor pool, gym, health club, sauna, spa, steam room, bar, lobby lounge, shops, babysitting, dry cleaning, laundry service, concierge, Internet, business services, convention center, travel services, parking (fee), no-smoking floors* ▭ *AE, DC, MC, V* |◯| *EP* Ⓜ *M1: Vörösmarty tér.*

$$$$ ▦ **Kempinski Hotel Corvinus Budapest.** Budapest's best business hotel
Fodor'sChoice doesn't cater only to the international CEO set. Though rather cold and
★ futuristic-looking on the outside, the Kempinski has exceptionally spacious rooms and suites, with custom-made art deco fittings and furniture, as well as an emphasis on functional touches like three phones in every room. Large, sparkling bathrooms have tubs and separate shower stalls and come stocked with every toiletry. The state-of-the-art "Kempin-

ski spa" that opened in April 2005 features Thai and Balinese massage and handcrafted furniture from Indonesia and China. The buffet breakfast is said to be the best and most bountiful in Budapest. ⊠ *District V, Erzsébet tér 7–8, Around Deák Ferenc tér H-1051* ☎ *1/429–3777, 800/426–3135 in the U.S. and Canada* ☒ *1/429–4777* ⊕ *www.kempinski-budapest.com* ⬚ *335 rooms, 30 suites* ⚇ *3 restaurants, room service, in-room safes, minibars, cable TV, Wi-Fi, ethernet, indoor pool, gym, 2 hair salons, hot tub, sauna, spa, bar, lobby lounge, shops, dry cleaning, laundry service, concierge, Internet, business services, convention center, travel services, parking (fee), some pets allowed (fee), no-smoking floors* ⊟ *AE, DC, MC, V* ⍟ *EP* Ⓜ *M1, M2, M3: Deák tér.*

★ **$$$$** ▥ **Le Méridien Budapest.** There could scarcely be more contrast between the stately Méridien (where George W. Bush and company occupied 15 rooms on a 2006 presidential visit to Hungary) and its pointedly modern neighbor, the Kempinski. The rooms of this entirely renovated, early-20th-century building are decorated in the French Empire style and are both comfortable and plush, with king-sized beds in every double room and large bathrooms with separate shower stalls and bathtubs. Rooms on the higher floors are slightly smaller but come with an individual balcony. Taxes are not included. ■ **TIP→** **Substantial discounts are available online.** ⊠ *District V, Erzsébet tér 9–10, Around Deák Ferenc tér H-1051* ☎ *1/429–5500, 800/543–4300 in U.S. and Canada* ☒ *1/429–5555* ⊕ *www.lemeridien.com* ⬚ *218 rooms, 26 suites* ⚇ *Restaurant, 2 cafés, room service, in-room safes, minibars, cable TV, ethernet, indoor pool, gym, hot tub, massage, sauna, steam room, bar, lobby lounge, shops, babysitting, dry cleaning, laundry service, concierge, Internet, business services, convention center, travel services, parking (fee), no-smoking floors* ⊟ *AE, DC, MC, V* ⍟ *EP* Ⓜ *M1, M2, M3: Deák tér.*

$$$$ ▥ **Sofitel Atrium Budapest.** The former Hyatt-Regency's spectacular 10-story atrium—a mix of glass-capsule elevators, blinding mini-chandeliers that run the length of the reception desk, cascading greenery, and an actual prop plane suspended over a fake library and a tiny bar—is impressive albeit not at all representative of the city it's in. Quintessentially Budapest, however, are the postcard views across the Danube to Castle Hill. A thorough makeover in 2005 added plush maroon carpeting and silky down-filled duvets. Taxes are not included, but substantial Internet discounts are available. ⊠ *District V, Roosevelt tér 2, Around Váci utca H-1051* ☎ *1/266–1234* ☒ *1/266–9101* ⊕ *www.sofitel.com* ⬚ *350 rooms, 54 suites* ⚇ *Restaurant, 2 cafés, room service, in-room safes, minibars, cable TV, Wi-Fi, ethernet, indoor pool, gym, hair salon, hot tub, sauna, spa, 2 bars, casino, shops, babysitting, dry cleaning, laundry service, concierge, Internet, business services, convention center, meeting rooms, travel services, parking (fee), no-smoking rooms, some pets allowed (fee)* ⊟ *AE, DC, MC, V* ⍟ *EP* Ⓜ *M1: Vörösmarty tér.*

$$$–$$$$ ▥ **Hotel InterContinental Budapest.** Its days as the socialist-era Fórum Hotel now firmly consigned to the past, the InterContinental appeals to the modern business traveler. Every room has a work desk, and some even have a printer. Additional executive-friendly perks include a 24-hour business center and wireless Internet in the lobby. The hotel is right next to the Chain Bridge in Pest, and 60% of the rooms have views across the Danube to Castle Hill (these are about €50 more expensive but worth it, considering the view). Rooms on higher floors ensure the least noise. All are decorated in pleasant pastels and furnished in the Biedermeier style typical of Central Europe. Taxes are not included. ⊠ *District V, Apáczai Csere János utca 12–14, Around Váci utca H-1052* ☎ *1/327–6333* 🖶 *1/327–6357* ⊕ *www.ichotelsgroup.com* 🛏 *398 rooms, 16 suites* ♿ *2 restaurants, café, room service, in-room safes, minibars, cable TV, Wi-Fi, ethernet, indoor pool, health club, bar, Internet, business services, meeting rooms, car rental, parking (fee), no-smoking floors* ⊟ *AE, DC, MC, V* ⦿ *EP* Ⓜ *M1: Vörösmarty tér.*

$$$ ⊡ **Starlight Suites.** The Chain Bridge, Danube promenade, St. Stephen's Basilica, and the heart of the banking and business districts are all within walking distance of this all-suites hotel, making it ideal for independent travelers and executives who prefer to come and go on foot. Rooms are spacious, with two TVs, microwaves, and separate sleeping and working areas. Some have bathtubs and some only showers. The staff is efficient and friendly, and, upon request, they will deliver breakfast to your room for free. A no-groups policy keeps the hotel staff free to focus on meeting each individual's needs. ■ TIP→ This hotel is an excellent choice if you want to be practically next door to the Gresham Palace but without that hotel's much higher rates. ⊠ *District V, Mérleg utca 6, St. Stephen's Basilica H-1051* ☎ *1/484–3700* 🖶 *1/484–3711* ⊕ *www.starlighthotels.com* 🛏 *54 suites* ♿ *Café, in-room safes, minibars, microwaves, cable TV, Wi-Fi, gym, sauna, steam room, Internet, travel services, parking (fee)* ⊟ *AE, DC, MC, V* ⦿ *CP* Ⓜ *M1, M2, M3: Deák tér.*

$$-$$$ ⊡ **Budapest Marriott.** North American–style hospitality on the Pest side of the Danube begins with a buffet of pastries served daily in the lobby. The hotel building is rather drab but its prime Danube location makes for some breathtaking views. Gellért Hill, the Chain and Elizabeth bridges, and Castle Hill are visible from every guest room, as well as the lobby, ballroom, and even the impressive hotel fitness center. Taxes are not included. ⊠ *District V, Apáczai Csere János utca 4, Around Váci utca H-1052* ☎ *1/266–7000, 800/228–9290 in the U.S. and Canada* 🖶 *1/266–5000* ⊕ *www.marriott.com* 🛏 *342 rooms, 20 suites* ♿ *2 restaurants, room service, in-room safes, minibars, cable TV with movies, Wi-Fi, ethernet, health club, massage, squash, hair salon, bar, shops, babysitting, dry cleaning, laundry service, concierge, concierge floors, Internet, business services, convention center, car rental, travel services, parking (fee), no-smoking rooms* ⊟ *AE, DC, MC, V* ⦿ *EP* Ⓜ *M1: Vörösmarty tér.*

Around Andrássy út and Király utca

The city's grandest boulevard is thriving with new restaurants, hotels, and shops, yet still maintains its Old World grandeur. The Opera House, Heroes' Square, hip Liszt Ferenc tér, and the theater district are just some of Andrássy út's local treasures, all navigable on foot or by the charming "little metro." The leafy side streets of the diplomatic

> **WORD OF MOUTH**
>
> "I enthusiastically endorse the Marriott hotel, with its beautiful balconies overlooking the Danube, its daily pastry cart in the lobby, and its incredibly good and bounteous breakfast."   –GirlTravel

district near Heroes' Square provide a gentler pace, while the boulevard's other end is full of city-center buzz. Nearby and running parallel to Andrássy út is grittier, up-and-coming Király utca, full of dark, atmospheric side streets and blending into the city's old Jewish quarter. Restaurants and nightspots abound.

$$$$
Fodor'sChoice
★

Andrássy Hotel. Budapest's best boutique hotel has come a long way from its origins as a 1930s-era orphanage. Opened as a hotel in 2001, it exudes grand style. In the bright Art Deco lobby the sound of rushing water from a glass-window waterfall blends artfully into soft jazz music playing on the sound system, and hip young staff receive guests at the funky orange-lit front desk. Done up in terra-cotta, blue, and cream, rooms are large and well appointed; most have lovely balconies overlooking the trees and mansions of the Andrássy út. With colorful, coordinated tilework, bathrooms follow the room design. The hotel lacks health and fitness facilities, but free access to a nearby center is available. A surcharge applies to children staying with their parents. Taxes are not included. ⊠ *District VI, Andrássy út 111, Around Andrássy út H-1063* ☎ *1/462–2118* 🖶 *1/322–9445* ⊕ *www.andrassyhotel.com* 🛏 *62 rooms, 8 suites* ⚘ *Restaurant, room service, in-room safes, minibars, cable TV, Wi-Fi, bar, dry cleaning, laundry service, concierge, Internet, business services, meeting rooms, travel services, parking (fee), no-smoking rooms* 🚭 *AE, DC, MC, V* ⏍ *EP* Ⓜ *M1: Bajza utca.*

★ **$$$**
K+K Hotel Opera. Location, location, location: the K+K Hotel Opera has it all, around the corner from Budapest's beautiful opera house and just far enough away from busy Andrássy út to block out the noise of traffic. Sunflower-yellow walls and bamboo and wicker furniture coupled with all-round warm hues, fresh flowers, and striking rectangular lamps all over the place, give the rooms—and, indeed, the entire hotel—a cheerful-cum-squarishly-modern look. Better, smiling staff are willing to go the extra mile, and a hearty breakfast buffet will set you up well for a day's sightseeing. ⊠ *District VI, Révay utca 24, Around Andrássy út H-1065* ☎ *1/269–0222* 🖶 *1/269–0230* ⊕ *www.kkhotels.com* 🛏 *203 rooms, 2 suites* ⚘ *Restaurant, room service, in-room safes, minibars, cable TV, Wi-Fi, ethernet, gym, massage, sauna, steam room, bar, babysitting, dry cleaning, laundry service, concierge, Internet, business services, meeting rooms, parking (fee), some pets allowed (fee), no-smoking rooms* 🚭 *AE, DC, MC, V* ⏍ *BP* Ⓜ *M1: Opera.*

$$
Domina Hotel Fiesta. On a typical cobblestone street near Pest's old Jewish quarter, this young hotel provides modern comforts in a nicely restored turn-of-the-20th-century building. Rooms are larger than at other city-center hotels, with high ceilings and simple yellow and navy-blue decor, but the bathrooms have flimsy shower stalls rather than tubs. Inner-facing rooms can be dark; for more natural light, request one of the street-facing rooms, which are quiet despite the car and bus traffic. Breakfast is served in the vaulted cellar restaurant. A pianist entertains in the lobby bar every evening. ⊠ *District VI, Király utca 20, Around Király utca H-1061* ☎ *1/328–3000* 🖶 *1/266–6024* ⊕ *www.ahotelfiesta.hu* 🛏 *108 rooms, 4 suites* ⚘ *Restaurant, room service, in-room safes, minibars, cable TV, Wi-Fi, gym, sauna, bar, shop, dry cleaning, laundry service,*

Internet, business services, meeting rooms, parking (fee), some pets allowed (fee), no-smoking rooms ⊟ *AE, DC, MC, V* †◯| *BP* Ⓜ *M1, M2, M3: Deák tér.*

$$ 🖭 **Hotel Liget.** With majestic Heroes' Square and the Museum of Fine Arts just across the street, and City Park—with the zoo, the Széchenyi Baths, and Gundel restaurant—a short walk away, the location couldn't be more ideal. The distance seems even shorter should you choose to borrow one of the free bicycles. Rooms are blandly modern, with green wall-to-wall carpeting and blond-wood furniture. Request an upper-floor room facing Dózsa György út for views of the museums. ⊠ *District VI, Dózsa György út 106, Around Andrássy út H-1068* ☎ *1/269–5300* 🖷 *1/ 269–5329* ⊕ *www.liget.hu* ↪ *139 rooms* ⚖ *Restaurant, room service, some in-room safes, minibars, cable TV, Wi-Fi, sauna, bicycles, bar, dry cleaning, laundry service, Internet, meeting room, parking (fee), some free parking, some pets allowed (fee), no-smoking floors* ⊟ *AE, DC, MC, V* †◯| *BP* Ⓜ *M1: Hősök tere.*

$$
Fodor'sChoice
★
🖭 **Hotel Pest.** Echoes of true, old Pest are preserved in this once-crumbling—now imaginatively refurbished—18th-century apartment building. In typical Budapest style, rooms open off an inner courtyard shared with the private building next door, where thick, green ivy spills over wrought-iron railings. In the guest rooms daylight filters discretely through sheer curtains and homey brown wood window frames. Decor is a soothing mix of dark wood and sage-colored textiles. Only some bathrooms have tubs, but all have heated towel racks. The breakfast room's stone walls are covered by a central glass skylight. Stepping out to the street through the heavy wood door, you find yourself in the heart of inner Pest, just two blocks from the Opera House. ⊠ *District VI, Paulay Ede utca 31, Around Andrássy út H-1061* ☎ *1/343–1198* 🖷 *1/351– 9164* ⊕ *www.hotelpest.hu* ↪ *25 rooms* ⚖ *Minibars, cable TV, ethernet, bar, laundry service, Internet, meeting rooms, travel services, parking (fee), no-smoking floor; no a/c in some rooms* ⊟ *AE, DC, MC, V* †◯| *BP* Ⓜ *M1: Opera.*

Around Nyugati Train Station

The area immediately around Nyugati Train Station is bustling nearly 24 hours a day with travelers' comings and goings. On foot or by way of the frequently running 4/6 Tram zipping along Szent István körút, you are just minutes away from Buda and Margaret Island in one direction and Andrássy út in the other. Areas north of Szent István körút are less touristed, so they're a good place to stay for those who like to be slightly off the beaten track.

$$$$ 🖭 **Hilton Budapest WestEnd.** Once you get over the fact that you are staying in a shopping mall—the swanky West End City Centre—you should be very happy indeed at this modern glass tower. Despite its bustling location next to Nyugati Train Station, the public spaces and guest rooms are hushed and peaceful owing to exceptional sound-proofing and structural planning. Facilities and amenities are top-notch, worthy of any international-standard business hotel. The aubergine and teal room decor is at once funky and understated. Rooms overlook the train station, the mall roof garden, or busy Váci út. ✉ *District VI, Váci út 1–3, Around Nyugati Train Station H-1062* ☎ *1/288–5500, 800/445–8667 in the U.S.* 🖷 *1/288–5588* 🌐 *www.budapest-westend.hilton.com* 🛏 *223 rooms, 7 suites* ♨ *Restaurant, café, room service, in-room safes, mini-bars, cable TV, Wi-Fi, ethernet, gym, bar, babysitting, dry cleaning, laundry service, concierge, Internet, business services, convention center, travel services, parking (fee), some pets allowed (fee), no-smoking floors* ▤ *AE, DC, MC, V* ⦿ *EP* Ⓜ *M3: Nyugati Train Station.*

☪ **$$$–$$$$** ▦ **Adina Apartment Hotel.** Although half the clientele here are business executives on longer-term stays, that shouldn't deter you from choosing these impeccably stylish, spacious apartments with such amenities as self-catering kitchens and one of the nicest indoor pools in town. The very helpful 24-hour front-office service can even arrange for groceries or local restaurant meals to be delivered to your kitchen. The extra space makes these apartments a good deal for families as well. ✉ *District XIII, Hegedűs Gyula utca 52–54, Around Nyugati Train Station H-1133* ☎ *1/236–8888* 🖷 *1/236–8899* 🌐 *www.adina.hu* 🛏 *21 rooms, 76 suites* ♨ *In-room safes, kitchens, minibars, cable TV, Wi-Fi, ethernet, indoor pool, gym, hot tub, massage, sauna, steam room, dry cleaning, laundry facilities, laundry service, Internet, meeting rooms, travel services, parking (fee), some pets allowed (fee), no-smoking floor* ▤ *AE, DC, MC, V* ⦿ *EP* Ⓜ *M3: Lehel tér.*

★ **$$–$$$** ▦ **NH Budapest.** Extra-thick mattresses, a pick-your-own pillow bar, and free ironing service are some of the welcome extras that set this new Spanish-owned business hotel apart. In the eight-story atrium lobby an up-to-the-minute flight schedule monitoring any changes is streamed in from Ferihegy onto the television screen behind the front desk. Dark-wood and gray-tone rooms, though on the small side, are slick and professional, each with a whimsical cherry-red easy chair for relaxing, either post-work or post-sightseeing. The NH is central to sights and business, just behind the Vígszínház theater. ✉ *District XIII, Vígszínház utca 3, Around Nyugati Train Station H-1137* ☎ *1/814–0000* 🖷 *1/814–0100* 🌐 *www.nh-hotels.com* 🛏 *160 rooms* ♨ *Restaurant, room service, in-room safes, minibars, cable TV, Wi-Fi, ethernet, gym, massage, sauna, bar, dry cleaning, laundry service, Internet, meeting rooms, travel services, parking (fee), some pets allowed (fee)* ▤ *AE, DC, MC, V* ⦿ *EP* Ⓜ *M3: Nyugati Train Station.*

$$–$$$ ▦ **Radisson SAS Béke Hotel Budapest.** If you are arriving in Budapest's Nyugati Train Station from Prague or Berlin, the Radisson could scarcely be better located, situated as it is within walking distance, on a bustling stretch of the körút. Once you've passed through the impressive reception area and ascended the sweeping marble staircase, you'll discover bland though comfortable and modern rooms. Snappy service and a great location compensate. ✉ *District VI, Teréz körút 43, Around Nyugati Train Station H-1067* ☎ *1/889–3900* 🖷 *1/889–3915* 🌐 *www.radissonsas.com* 🛏 *239 rooms, 8 suites* ♨ *Restaurant, room service, in-room safes, minibars, cable TV, in-room data ports, indoor pool, gym, massage, sauna, 2 bars, babysitting, dry cleaning, laundry service, concierge, Internet, business services, meeting rooms, travel services, parking (fee), no-smoking floors* ▤ *AE, DC, MC, V* ⦿ *EP* Ⓜ *M3: Nyugati Train Station.*

$$ 🏨 **Danubius Thermal & Conference Hotel Helia.** While this well-known spa hotel's upriver location offers a less hectic pace, it also positions you in an uninteresting neighborhood among depressing, Soviet-era housing blocks. So choose the Helia for what's inside. The spa facilities are the most spotlessly clean in Budapest, and an on-site medical clinic caters to English-speaking clients. Rooms are reasonably spacious and kitted out in IKEA-influenced, Scandinavian style. To make the most of the location, request a newly renovated room on the Danube side with a downriver view. All rates include unlimited use of the thermal bath and free parking. Town is a few stops south on Bus 79. ⊠ *District XIII, Kárpát utca 62–64, Around Nyugati Train Station H-1133* ☎ *1/889–5800* 📠 *1/889–5801* ⊕ *www.danubiusgroup.com/helia* 🛏 *254 rooms, 8 suites* ⚐ *Restaurant, café, some in-room safes, minibars, cable TV, Wi-Fi, 3 indoor pools, gym, health club, hair salon, hot tub, spa, Turkish bath, bar, shops, dry cleaning, laundry service, concierge, Internet, business services, convention center, travel services, free parking, some pets allowed (fee), no-smoking floors* 🖃 *AE, DC, MC, V* �"⊙⏐ *BP* Ⓜ *M3: Dózsa György út.*

WORD OF MOUTH

"Kempinski has a better location, but Hotel Aquincum is not a bad starting point for sightseeing tours either. (It is easy to get around by public transport.) By the way, Corinthia (the chain Aquincum belongs to) has just opened a 5-star hotel in downtown Budapest. It is the Corinthia Grand Hotel Royal. It looks great, though its services are not as 'broad' as those of Aquincum (it has no thermal pool at the moment). —Angelita

$ 🏨 **Fortuna Boat Hotel.** For a change of pace, you can bed down on this retired 1967 vessel, which once plied the waters of the Danube and is now anchored near the Pest side of the Margaret Bridge. Snug cabins, each named after a different nautical persona (Jacques Cousteau, Captain Cook), open off narrow, wood-paneled corridors with tiny chandeliers. Furnishings are basic, and miniature bathrooms are almost too small to shower in. Request a Danube-facing room; the other side looks onto the cement and traffic of the Pest quay. Headroom is low and stairways are narrow, making this a poor choice for people with mobility issues (or for the merely tall). A 14-room hostel section is downstairs in the hold; these cheaper but tiny rooms have shared baths. ⊠ *District XIII, Szent István Park, Lower Quay, Around Nyugati Train Station H-1137* ☎ *1/288–8100* 📠 *1/270–0351* ⊕ *www.fortunahajo.hu* 🛏 *58 rooms, 44 with private bath* ⚐ *Restaurant, room service, minibars, cable TV, bar, dry cleaning, laundry service, Internet, meeting rooms, travel services, free parking; no smoking* 🖃 *AE, MC, V* ⏐⊙⏐ *BP* Ⓜ *M3: Lehel tér.*

Around Blaha Lujza tér and Ferenc körút

Less touristy than its other end, the area around this section of the "big" ring road thrums with real-life Budapest, full of traffic and grit and interesting less-trodden side streets. With a growing number of new boutiques, restaurants, and nightspots, it's undergoing a real renaissance, but parts can still be dodgy at night, especially east of the körút.

$$$$ 🏨 **Corinthia Grand Hotel Royal.** One of the newer five-star properties in
Fodor'sChoice Budapest—and, with 414 rooms, the biggest—the Royal is back to its
★ 1896 origins when it opened as a luxury hotel for the Magyar Millennium. Josephine Baker stayed here in 1928; her guestbook entry is displayed in a case the near the entrance. The expansive atrium lobby is
full of Italian marble and wrought-iron ornamentation, and the hotel's
luxurious Royal Spa—in part a dazzling reconstruction of a spa designed
and built in the late 1880s that operated here until 1944—opened in
July 2006 replete with a swimming pool, saunas, steam room, Jacuzzis,
massage salons, treatment facilities, and tropical showers. (The spa is
free to guests, 10,000 HUF a day for others.) Guest rooms are stylish
with dark woods and jewel-tone upholstery; bathrooms are all-Italian,
from marble floors to gleaming fixtures. Some rooms look inward onto
the lobby. Brasserie Royal's Sunday "V.I.K." (Very Important Kids)
brunch is very popular. ⊠ *District VII, Erzsébet körút 43–49, Around
Blaha Lujza tér H-1073* ☎ *1/479–4000* 🖷 *1/479–4333* ⊕ *www.
corinthiahotels.com* ⇗ *363 rooms, 51 suites* ⚃ *3 restaurants, café,
room service, in-room safes, minibars, cable TV, ethernet, indoor pool,
hair salon, spa, bar, dry cleaning, laundry service, concierge, Internet,
business services, convention center, travel services, parking (fee), no-
smoking floors* ▭ *AE, DC, MC, V* ⍥*EP* Ⓜ *M2: Blaha Lujza tér.*

★ **$$$$** 🏨 **New York Palace.** After years behind scaffolding, the New York is not
only back in business as the grand old café it once was, but now also
as Budapest's newest luxury hotel. Opened in May 2006 by Italy's Boscolo Hotels, this mostly pleasing (sometimes weird) mix of tradition and
high fashion confronts you first in the yellow-and-gold cavernous atrium
punctuated with several headless mannequins. Clerks stand around a
glass reception desk staring at laptops as pop music carries from the adjacent New York Café (part of the hotel but with a separate entrance
from the street). Phones are answered first in Italian, then Hungarian,
and not surprisingly, the restaurant specializes in Italian cuisine. Golden
hues predominate, and all rooms have full baths, bidets, and two sinks.
Commissioned by the New York Insurance Company and designed in
eclectic styles with an Italian Renaissance edge, the palace—whose
steeple-like tower and colonnaded facade rises loftily above the Large
Ring Boulevard—opened originally in 1894, and was long most famous
for its café. A spa and fitness center is planned for the near future. ⊠ *District VII, Erzsébet körút 9–11, Around Blaha Lujza tér H-1073* ☎ *1/
886–6111* 🖷 *1/886–6199* ⊕ *www.newyorkpalace.hu or www.
boscolohotels.com* ⇗ *73 rooms, 34 suites* ⚃ *Restaurant, café, breakfast lounge, room service, in-room safes, minibars, cable TV, Wi-Fi, ethernet, bar, laundry service, concierge, Internet, business services,
convention center, travel services, business center, babysitting service,
parking (fee), no-smoking rooms* ▭*AE, DC, MC, V* ⍥*EP* Ⓜ *M2: Blaha
Lujza tér.*

$$ 🏨 **Hotel Sissi.** This little hotel is next door to the Hotel Corvin in Pest's
once edgy Ninth District, a few blocks from the Museum of Applied
Arts. Tiny rooms are decorated in cheery blue and yellow with IKEA-
style blond-wood furniture. Blue-and-white checked tiles in the bath-
rooms—some with shower stalls, some with tubs—are a sweet touch.

Those sensitive to street noise may prefer a room facing the backyard. ⌧ *District IX, Angyal utca 33, Around Ferenc körút H-1094* ☎ *1/215–0082* 📠 *1/216–6063* ⊕ *www.hotelsissi.hu* 🛏 *44 rooms* ♨ *Room service, in-room safes, minibars, cable TV, Wi-Fi, bar, laundry service, Internet, meeting room, travel services, parking (fee), no-smoking floors* 🖃 *AE, DC, MC, V* |⊖| *BP* Ⓜ *M3: Ferenc körút.*

$$ 🏨 **Ramada.** Budapest's first Ramada—on a quiet street a few blocks farther from downtown and the Large Ring Boulevard than the Hotel Sissi and Hotel Corvin—was reopened under the Ramada banner in 2004 after thorough renovation. Standard rooms, some of which have showers only, are small, with brown carpeting, brown-and-black-striped bedspreads, and red armchairs. About half the rooms have two single beds pushed together; the rest have double mattresses or, as in Hungarian, a *francia ágy* (French bed). Rooms rated superior and above have minibars. ■ TIP➔ There's a large, playground-equipped park right next door, so this hotel may be a good choice if you're traveling with little ones. ⌧ *District IX, Tompa utca 30–34, Around Ferenc körút H-1094* ☎ *1/477–7200* 📠 *1/477–7272* ⊕ *www.ramadabudapest.com* 🛏 *167 rooms, 15 suites* ♨ *2 restaurants, room service, in-room safes, cable TV, Wi-Fi, sauna, gym, bar, laundry service, concierge, Internet, meeting rooms, travel services, parking (fee), no-smoking wings* 🖃 *AE, DC, MC, V* |⊖| *BP* Ⓜ *M3: Ferenc körút.*

$ 🏨 **Hotel Corvin.** This small, Hungarian-owned property is tucked into a calm side street off busy Ferenc körút, next door to the slightly more expensive Hotel Sissi (the two refer guests to each other when one is full), a once seedy, now up-and-coming area. Rooms come with two or three single beds and have simple, floral pastel decor. Those overlooking the hotel's courtyard are quieter than those opening onto the street. ⌧ *District IX, Angyal utca 31, Around Ferenc körút H-1094* ☎ *1/218—6566 or 1/218–6564* 📠 *1/218–6562* ⊕ *www.corvinhotelbudapest.hu* 🛏 *44 rooms, 3 suites* ♨ *Dining room, minibars, cable TV, Wi-Fi, bar, meeting rooms, travel services, parking (fee), no-smoking floors* 🖃 *AE, DC, MC, V* |⊖| *BP* Ⓜ *M3: Ferenc körút.*

Around Kálvin tér, Ferenciek tere, and Astoria

This bustling downtown area can get clogged with traffic, but myriad side streets offer quick escape. Home to loads of shops, restaurants, nightspots, and cafés, not to mention the Nemzeti Múzeum, and with excellent transport links, this area is a good place to stay for those who like to be in the thick of things.

$$$ 🏨 **Hotel Astoria.** Constructed between 1912 and 1914, the Astoria has a fascinating and turbulent history. The first independent Hungarian government was formed here in 1918, but later the Nazi high command used the Astoria more or less as its headquarters, as did the Soviet forces during the ill-fated revolution of 1956. Nowadays, rooms—refurbished in 2005—are genteel, spacious, and comfortable, with renovations faithful to the original Empire-style decor. The Café Mirror, with its dripping chandeliers and pink marble columns, is a wonderful place to relive the Central European coffeehouse tradition, even if it is, sadly, often empty. ⊠ *District V, Kossuth Lajos utca 19–21, Around Astoria H-1053* ☎ *1/889–6000* 🖷 *1/889–6091* ⊕ *www.danubiusgroup.com* 🛏 *126 rooms, 5 suites* ♿ *Restaurant, café, room service, in-room safes, minibars, cable TV, Wi-Fi, shop, babysitting, dry cleaning, laundry service, Internet, business services, meeting rooms, travel services, parking (fee), no-smoking rooms; no a/c in some rooms* ▭ *AE, DC, MC, V* ⍾⍾ *EP* Ⓜ *M2: Astoria.*

$$–$$$ 🏨 **Hotel Mercure Korona.** The downside of a big chain hotel on one of Budapest's busiest squares is that rooms are tiny and traffic outside is fierce. The upside, however, is you are central to all the sights and experiences of bustling downtown Pest, including the National Museum and some of the city's hottest nightlife. Rooms refurbished in 2004 are the nicest, decorated in a Scandinavian style with patterns in geometric beiges and browns. ⊠ *District V, Kecskeméti utca 14, Around Kálvin tér H-1053* ☎ *1/486–8800* 🖷 *1/318–3867* ⊕ *www.mercure-korona.hu* 🛏 *400 rooms, 24 suites* ♿ *Restaurant, tapas bar, room service, in-room safes, minibars, cable TV, Wi-Fi, ethernet, indoor pool, massage, sauna, bar, shops, babysitting, dry cleaning, laundry service, Internet, business services, meeting rooms, travel services, parking (fee), no-smoking floors* ▭ *AE, DC, MC, V* ⍾⍾ *EP* Ⓜ *M3: Kálvin tér.*

$ 🏨 **City Hotel Mátyás.** This low-frills hotel serves breakfast in one of the most famous (and touristy) restaurants in town, sharing neoclassical quarters with the Mátyás Pince eatery. Newer rooms are standard pastel-contemporary and have small bathrooms with shower stalls. The hotel's older section is still inhabited by some private tenants and is accessed by a tiny elevator. Converted from apartments, these rooms are spacious and have soaring ceilings, but are best taken by those who find exposed heating units and other such quirks atmospheric rather than off-putting. Some rooms have stunning views over the Elizabeth Bridge, Belvárosi Church, and beyond to Castle Hill. ⊠ *District V, Március 15 tér 7–8, Around Ferenciek tere H-1056* ☎ *1/338–4711* 🖷 *1/317–9086* ⊕ *www.taverna. hu/matyas* 🛏 *79 rooms, 6 suites* ♿ *Restaurant, minibars, cable TV, laundry service, Internet, travel services, parking (fee), no-smoking floor; no a/c in some rooms* ▭ *AE, MC, V* ⍾⍾ *BP* Ⓜ *M3: Ferenciek tere.*

Near Parliament

$ 🏨 **Hotel Hold.** A fantastic location on a lovely street behind the American Embassy and across from the ornately mosaicked Hungarian National Bank gives this low-key little hotel its appeal. Parliament and the basilica are a few minutes' walk away. Converted from private apartments in the turn-of-the-20th-century building, most guest rooms are quite small, but have soaring ceilings and tall windows with translucent white curtains. Furnishings are flimsy but adequate; there's royal-blue wall-to-wall carpeting throughout. Avoid the rooms on the ground floor, as they open directly onto the courtyard restaurant. Most bathrooms have showers only, no tubs. ⊠ *District V, Hold utca 5, Parliament H-1054* ☎ *1/472–0480* 🖷 *1/472–0484* ⊕ *www.hotelhold.hu* 🛏 *25 rooms, 3 suites* ♿ *Restaurant, minibars, cable TV, Internet, travel services* ▭ *AE, DC, MC, V* ⍾⍾ *BP* Ⓜ *M3: Arany János utca.*

MARGARET ISLAND HOTELS

A veritable oasis of grass and trees, Margaret Island in the Danube is a lovely change of pace from the typical city visit. Downtown is 20–25 minutes away by bus, less by taxi, making it good for those who like to see the sights but not sleep in them. The island's thermal bath complexes are an added benefit.

$$$ 🏨 **Danubius Thermal Hotel Margit-sziget.** Bubbling up from ancient thermal springs, curative waters fill the pools of this established spa hotel on the island's northern end. Rates include the use of spa facilities and also complex health and beauty treatments. Every guest room has a balcony, where you can sit and watch the sun set or rise. Buda-facing (sunset) rooms have the nicest views. Having been renovated in 2001, the shining, spacious lobby and contemporary guest rooms come as a pleasant surprise given the hotel's homely, Iron Curtain cement-block exterior. ✉ *District XIII, Margit-sziget, Margaret Island H-1138* 🕾 *1/889–4700* 🖷 *1/889–4988* ⊕ *www.danubiusgroup.com* ⬛ *259 rooms, 8 suites* ⚴ *Restaurant, café, room service, in-room safes, minibars, cable TV, Wi-Fi, outdoor pool, indoor pools, health club, hair salon, spa, 2 bars, shops, dry cleaning, laundry service, Internet, business services, meeting rooms, travel services, parking (fee), some pets allowed (fee), no-smoking floors* ▤ *AE, DC, MC, V* ⦿️ *BP* Ⓜ *Bus 26 to northern end of Margaret Island.*

★ **$$–$$$** 🏨 **Danubius Grand Hotel Margit-sziget.** The older, much more attractive (and a tad less pricey) next-door neighbor of the Thermal Hotel Margit-sziget was built in 1873 by Opera House architect Miklós Ybl in neo-Renaissance style. Ceilings are high here, and rooms are decorated in Empire style, with red- or blue-upholstered antique-looking wood furnishings. Guests have free admission to the thermal's spa facilities, directly accessed by a heated, underground walkway. It was here that the Hungarian writer János Arany, a regular guest in the late-19th century, composed some of his greatest novels. ✉ *District XIII, Margit-sziget, Margaret Island H-1138* 🕾 *1/889–4700* 🖷 *1/889–4988* ⊕ *www. danubiusgroup.com* ⬛ *154 rooms, 10 suites* ⚴ *Restaurant, café, room service, in-room safes, minibars, cable TV, Wi-Fi, bar, pub, shops, babysitting, dry cleaning, laundry service, Internet, business services, meeting rooms, travel services, parking (fee), some pets allowed (fee), no-smoking rooms* ▤ *AE, DC, MC, V* ⦿️ *BP* Ⓜ *Bus 26 to northern end of Margaret Island.*

ÓBUDA HOTELS

$$$$ 🏨 **Corinthia Aquincum Hotel.** Capital of the Roman province of Pannonia in the first century AD, this part of Buda is more on the outskirts these days. With the HÉV railway just outside the door, the Corinthia Aquincum is well situated for easy trips to Szentendre, as well as into town; the ancient sights of Óbuda are just around the corner. Rooms in this huge, rectangular, red-brick property are fairly small for a hotel of this category, but they are sufficiently comfortable. The main draws are the

A Short History of the Gresham Palace

THE MASSIVE ART NOUVEAU palace that is now the Four Seasons Hotel began its life near the turn of the 20th century as, of all things, the headquarters of an insurance company. The London-based Gresham Life Assurance Company hired eminent architect Zsigmond Quittner and almost every prominent craftsman working in Hungary to create the building. Miksa Róth made the beautiful glass mosaics and the stained-glass windows, while the wrought-iron railings of the main staircases and the three large peacock gates opening onto the courtyard were the work of Gyula Jungfer. The Zsolnay Ceramics Factory in Pécs produced the tiles for the walls of the ground-floor passage and the courtyard, and the interior wall and floor tiles. The palace was a luxurious meeting point for British aristocrats, away from the politically charged atmosphere of Vienna and Berlin. In 1944 the building was severely damaged by the retreating German army. In 1948 Hungary's communist government subdivided the palatial suites into tiny units to house both state offices and residential tenants; the building quickly fell into disrepair. By the 1970s it had been named a national protected landmark, but continued its slow decline; passersby would collect the precious Zsolnay tiles that had crumbled off the facade. After the overthrow of the communists in 1990, the City of Budapest took ownership of the palace. Long-term tenants, including the flamboyant actress Ida Turay, refused to vacate and filed lawsuits against the city, which finally won its case. The building was purchased by a private investment group that, along with Four Seasons, finally received permission to create the hotel. Construction commenced in 2000, and the hotel opened in June 2004.

sparkling spa and thermal baths, fed by ancient springs on Margaret Island, which is a short walk or bike ride across the nearby bridge. Although it's right on the Danube, the immediate surroundings are rather drab: a busy highway, the suburban railway, and the concrete Árpád Bridge. ⊠ *District III, Árpád fejedelem útja 94, Óbuda H–1036* ☎ *1/ 436–4100* 🖷 *1/436–4156* ⊕ *www.corinthia.hu or www.corinthiahotels. com* ⇌ *302 rooms, 8 suites* ⚐ *Restaurant, room service, minibars, cable TV, Wi-Fi, ethernet, 3 indoor pools, gym, hair salon, hot tub, sauna, spa, steam room, 2 bars, shops, dry cleaning, laundry service, concierge, Internet, business services, meeting rooms, travel services, some free parking, some pets allowed (fee), no-smoking rooms* ⊟ *AE, DC, MC, V* ⍝️*BP* Ⓜ *HÉV: Árpád híd.*

Nightlife &
the Arts

WORD OF MOUTH

"The opera was a fantastic experience. The opera house is gorgeous and the performance was very impressive. Cheaper than going to a movie. Amazing. Reserve your tickets in advance online—www.jegymester.hu/index_eng.html"

—sgny

By Paul
Olchváry

NOT EVERYTHING IN BUDAPEST GOES TO SLEEP WITH THE SUN. In addition to particularly rich cultural offerings—the city has several classical orchestras and not only the Liszt Ferenc Music Academy, one of central Europe's greatest performance spaces, but, as of 2005, the world-class Béla Bartók National Concert Hall in its Palace of the Arts—there are also a host of bars and clubs, where the cultural offerings are less than classical. Now that communism has passed out of the realm of *Realpolitik* and into the realm of kitsch, there's even a small subdivision of bars with a retro-communist theme.

Although heavily subsidized during the communist years, most cultural groups have been able to find their own footing with private funding. As of this writing, the prospect of severe state budget cuts into 2007 and 2008—and for private foundations that support the arts—has more than a few such organizations wondering anew what the future holds. Though tickets are not as cheap as they were in years gone by, you can still go to a concert or opera for a song—by Western standards, that is. The price of the most expensive opera box seat is still less than half what you'd pay in New York or London or Paris, even if, for most Hungarians, this represents a formidable expense.

In summer everyone seems to practically live outdoors. Cafés on virtually every major square are open until the wee hours, and open-air pubs and beer gardens seem to pop up everywhere, particularly in Pest.

NIGHTLIFE

The streets of Budapest might seem mysteriously quiet late at night, but that doesn't mean Hungarians—those without kids and those well away from retirement, at any rate—are home in bed. Quite the contrary. This is a nation of heavy drinkers and smokers—and of an ever increasing number of nonsmokers and light drinkers who like to have fun, too, but are compelled to tolerate their more indulgent peers—who stay up late doing both nearly every night of the week. This is the case especially from late spring to early fall (May to September), when it seems that everyone in the capital is sometimes spilled across the terraces and outdoor seating areas of Pest. While the city's nightlife is typically concentrated in Pest, where the majority of watering holes are located, Buda also boasts some excellent spots, although nighttime there is typically much quieter and concentrated in neighborhood pubs.

PAUL'S TOP 5

Liszt Ferenc tér. With its chic cafés and ample outdoor seating, this is *the* place to socialize in Budapest.

Gödör Klub. This spacious club in the heart of downtown has live jazz and lively youth.

Magyar Állami Operaház. The glittering Hungarian State Opera House is Budapest's main venue for opera and classical ballet.

Liszt Ferenc Music Academy and the **Béla Bartók National Concert Hall.** One steeped with historical elegance and the other magnificently modern.

Fészek Artists Club. Bohemian Budapest is alive and well at this huge 100-year-old club.

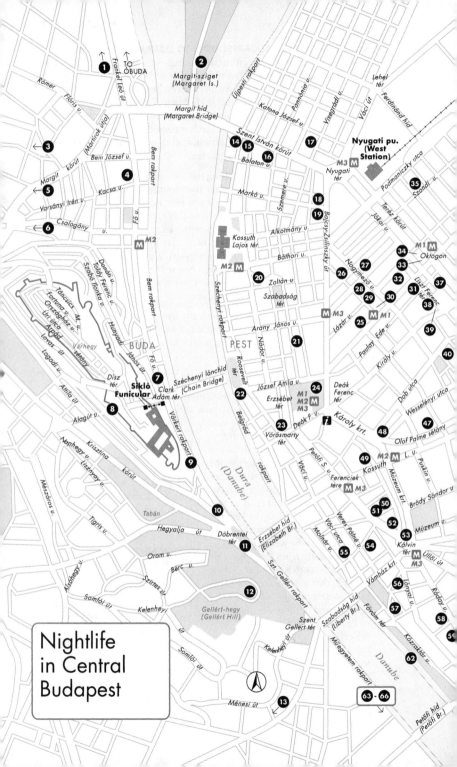

Nightlife
in Central
Budapest

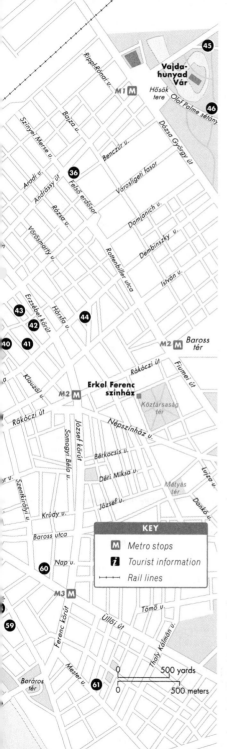

KEY

🅜 Metro stops

🅘 Tourist information

⊢⊢⊢⊢ Rail lines

Budapest as a whole, however, seems to have every kind of drinking establishment you might imagine, from discos and bars to quiet indoor courtyards, live-music joints, and artsy bohemian spaces. Karaoke has also become all but ubiquitous in recent years. Local pubs, where you can get mostly beer and wine, called *söröző* (beer joints) or a *borozó* (wine bars), are scattered across the city. ■ TIP→ **Knowing a few words of basic Hungarian will help you, as these places cater more to locals than to tourists.**

Thursday night is a big party night in Budapest, especially in Pest, and is often busier than a weekend evening—a tradition begun by students who preferred to party on Thursday night after most of the week's classes were finished and before they headed to their parents' home in the provinces on Friday afternoon. Most nighttime spots in Budapest are open past midnight, some until 4 or 5 AM, with the exception of several outdoor terrace squares, where bars close around midnight or 1 AM. There are also numerous bars that stay open 24 hours.

Most nightspots and clubs have both bars and dance floors, and some also have pool tables. Although some places do accept credit cards, it is still much more common to pay in cash for your night on the town. As is the case in most cities, the life of a club or disco in Budapest can be somewhat ephemeral. We recommend places that are popular and seem to have some staying power. But for the very latest on the more transient "in" spots, consult the "Nightlife" section of the weekly *Budapest Sun,* or *Budapest in Your Pocket,* which is published six times a year.

Bars & Pubs

Budapest has a wide selection of nightlife spots. Popular among creative types is a vast array of bohemian pubs and cafés where you can find writers and artists debating politics, poetry, and art well into the night. But there are also a good many flashy—and not very expensive—cocktail and lounge bars, particularly on pedestrianized Liszt Ferenc tér, a big outdoor square on the Pest side of the city, just off Andrássy út, with a handful of cafés that spill out onto the square; this is the best spot in the city to people-watch. Also rising in popularity is the nearby theater district, comprising the stretch of Nagymező utca that lies immediately west of Andrássy út; and, a 25-minute walk south but likewise downtown, Ráday utca, a less touristy cobblestone street in Pest that is loaded with outdoor restaurants and cafés. Watch your bags and belongings in these areas—in fact in all bars in Budapest—as petty theft is common. Many Hungarian pubs stay open until 2 AM or much later, although most pubs on Liszt Ferenc tér, Nagymező utca, and Ráday utca close around 1 AM.

While Hungarian beer is nothing to write home about from a European perspective (suffice it to say that young Brits and Germans don't come to Budapest for the brew), star-quality European beers (some made under license in Hungary) are widely available. But of course Hungary is more of a wine culture, and indeed wine—most of it Hungarian, and much of it decent quality and affordable—flows every bit as much, if not more, in Budapest's bars than does beer. You might also try the country's national liquor, *Unicum,* a bitter concoction of more than 50 herbs drunk for pleasure but with the dubious notion that it wards off ailments.

Becketts. Conveniently located near the center of Budapest, Becketts Irish pub attracts a mostly male expat crowd and is a great place for lunch, an afternoon pint while watching a soccer match, or a rollicking good time in the evening, when bands come on and the place fills up. ⊠ *District V, Bajcsy-Zsilinszky út 72, Around Nyugati Train Station* ☎ *1/311–1035 or 1/311–1033* Ⓜ *M3: Nyugati.*

Cactus Juice. The interior is rustic American "Wild West." The pub serves lunch and dinner during the day but turns into a popular dance spot for Hungarians at night. It is usually open until dawn. ⊠ *District VI, Jókai tér 5, Around Andrássy út* ☎ *1/302–2116* Ⓜ *M1: Oktogon.*

> ### DRINK-A PÁLINKA
>
> No trip to Budapest would be complete without a taste of the fruit spirit *pálinka,* the local headache-inducing firewater. These days high-quality pálinka aged in oak barrels can be found in some of Budapest's upmarket restaurants. Look for the Agárdi boutique pálinkas from near Lake Velence. These spirits come in unusual flavors like raspberry and *cigany meggy* (gypsy cherry). All restaurants in Budapest stock the traditional *barackpálinka* (apricot brandy) and *szilvapálinka* (plum brandy). Hungarians enjoy palinka before a meal and as a drink to celebrate good fortune. Be forewarned: this strong brandy is not for the weak of stomach.

Cafe Vian. Of all the see-and-be-seen cafés in Budapest, Vian was among the first to gain wide renown after the fall of the Iron Curtain (a status it continues to hold much of today), partly because of its unbeatable spot in the heart of Liszt Ferenc tér. It's a great place to while away the hours chatting and people-watching, either inside and surrounded by an ever-changing exhibit of modern art, or outside under a canopy in summer. ⊠ *District VI, Liszt Ferenc tér 9, Around Andrássy út* ☎ *1/ 268–1154* Ⓜ *M1: Oktogon.*

Castro. A good mix of locals and expats can be found at Castro any given night of the week. The popular Cuban-themed bar, with movie posters and artwork dotting the walls, tends to get extremely smoky, but is well-positioned along Ráday utca. Castro also serves heavy, grease-laden Serbian food. Internet access is available on several computer terminals in the back, and you'll find outdoor seating along the street in warmer months. ⊠ *District IX, Ráday utca 35, Around Kálvin tér* ☎ *1/215– 0184* Ⓜ *M3: Kálvin tér.*

Chagall Café. Just one block over from another hot spot with a painterly name, Picasso Point, this hip little drinking place that opened in May 2006 is hard to miss: look for the giant Chagallish mural on the building's facade. Inside are two spacious rooms (one with a Chagall-adorned wall) with not terribly comfy, straight-backed white chairs; and, yes, there's outdoor seating. ⊠ *District VI, Hajós utca 27, Around Andrássy út* ☎ *1/ 302–4614* Ⓜ *M1: Opera.*

Ellátó. On the main square in the heart of the onetime Jewish ghetto, "the Supplier" is the place to get your night's supply of Staropramen, a good Czech beer (or your choice of a small handful of other fine brews, wines, and stronger drinks)—while admiring the artsy black-and-white photos on the walls, the well-worn wood floors, and the old wood chairs with their little round seats. As of this writing, plans called for the second-floor space to become an "Arabian café" with live music before too long. ⊠ *District VII, Klauzal tér 1–2, Around Király utca* 🕾 *No phone* Ⓜ *M2: Blaha Lujza tér.*

FodorśChoice **Fészek Artists' Klub.** Bohemian Budapest is alive and well at Fészek, a
★ huge club that dates back 100 years and attracts writers, artists, and other creative souls. A large enclosed drinking garden that transports you back a century or more is covered with a canopy during the winter and heated with large outdoor lamps. A pizzeria is also outside, above the garden; a restaurant inside serves up delicious meals. The cellar, which has live musical acts from jazz to blues to hard rock most nights, is open 24 hours a day. ⊠ *District VII, Kertész utca 36, Around Király utca* 🕾 *1/342–6549* Ⓜ *M1: Oktogon.*

Iguana. Aside from the only decent Mexican food in town, Iguana is a popular nightlife spot for expats, where strong margaritas are quickly gulped down. The pub also hosts several outdoor street parties during the year, including the annual "Cinco de Mayo" block party. ⊠ *District V, Zoltán utca 16, Parliament* 🕾 *1/331–4352* Ⓜ *M2: Kossuth Lajos tér.*

Komédiás Kávéház. Also called Café le Comédien, this ravishingly elegant little café in the heart of the main theater district, next door to the Thália Theater and near the Opera House, has live piano music daily from 7 PM and has an impressive cherry-wood-like staircase leading up to its small second-floor room. Open until midnight, it's just the place to have a drink in high style—and perhaps a slice of one of several delicious cakes—after or before taking in a nearby performance. ⊠ *District V, Nagymező út, Around Andrássy út* 🕾 *1/302–0910* Ⓜ *M1: Opera.*

★ **Lánchíd Söröző.** Next to Clark Ádám tér, a large square in Buda at the end of the Lánchíd (Chain Bridge), this tiny pub attracts tourists and locals alike. The walls are covered with black-and-white photos from Budapest and Paris. Ask for owner Róbert Nagy, who speaks excellent English and loves to meet visitors from abroad. ⊠ *District 1, Fő utca 4, Around Batthyány tér* 🕾 *1/214–3144.*

Manna Euthenic Lounge. Nestled serenely on the west side of Castle Hill, right above the tunnel that leads to the Chain Bridge, is one of Budapest's comfiest, nay, most euthenics-minded cafés. After trekking all over the Castle just above you, this capacious, covered terrace—with its large white armchairs, intimate lighting, and Mediterranean plants—is just right for kicking back and relaxing in. There's "lounge" music every evening (sometimes live, sometimes compliments of DJs), from swing to jazz to Latin. If you're hungry, there's a restaurant with an open kitchen, too. Go up the short flight of steps to the right of the tunnel entrance on Alagút utca (Tunnel Street). ⊠ *District I, Palota út 17, Castle Hill* 🕾 *06–20/ 999–9188 (mobile)* Ⓜ *M2: Déli Train Station.*

★ **Menza.** The name, which means "canteen" in Hungarian, refers to student cafeterias that were free of charge when the country was still under communism. The Menza at this location boasts a funky, retro style in green, orange, and black, and it's a bit cheaper than most of the other outdoor spots on Liszt Ferenc tér. ⊠ *District VI, Liszt Ferenc tér 2, Around Andrássy út* ☎ *1/413–1482* Ⓜ *M1: Oktogon.*

Negro. Conveniently situated on the square next to the Szent István Basilica, Negro is a sleek black and metal upscale cocktail bar with funky orange ceiling lamps. Plenty of outdoor seating is available during the warmer months, where you can gaze at the basilica while drinking away. The bar's name, by the way, appears to derive from a popular Hungarian cough drop that happens to be black and is pronounced "neh-grow" (i.e., not racist at all in the Hungarian context). ⊠ *District V, Szent István tér 11, St. Stephen's Basilica* ☎ *1/302–0136* Ⓜ *M3: Arany János.*

Oscar American Bar. Attracts a mixed Hungarian and international crowd, who venture over the Danube to what is, perhaps, Buda's most jumping neighborhood bar. Old-time Hollywood movie stills adorn its walls. ⊠ *District I, Ostrom utca 14, Around Moszkva tér* ☎ *1/212–8017* Ⓜ *M2: Moszkva tér.*

Picasso Point. Close to Budapest's opera and theater district, Picasso Point is a spacious, unpretentious pub with some brightly colored walls where you can kick back for a few drinks. There's dancing in the basement at night with a DJ usually spinning the tunes, and there are regular karaoke nights. ⊠ *District VI, Hajós utca 31, Around Andrássy út* ☎ *1/312–1727* Ⓜ *M3: Arany János.*

Portside de Cuba. This large underground cocktail bar and restaurant, which packed in a yuppie crowd a few blocks from Deák tér, was being given a Cuban facelift as of this writing, but one that appears targeted at the same sort of crowd. Regardless of whether you dine here also, it seems likely that this is set to be a more than decent spot to nurse a daiquiri or a champagne and dance the night away to live Latin tunes. ⊠ *District VII, Dohány utca 7, Around Astoria* ☎ *1/351–8405* Ⓜ *M2: Astoria.*

★ **Pótkulcs.** The name of this pub means "spare key," and this one attracts a hip, bohemian crowd. There is no sign outside, just a metal door bearing the name and address. Walk through the door and down the small pathway to find outdoor seating in warm months and a bit of respite from the smoky bar inside. At midnight on Friday and Saturday, gypsy bands play inside. Soups and open-faced sandwiches are also available. ⊠ *District VI, Csengery utca 65/b, Around Nyugati Train Station* ☎ *1/269–1050* Ⓜ *M3: Nyugati.*

Rigoletto. This bar packs them in weeknights as well as weekends, with a tempting two-for-one regu-

TALK IS [NOT] CHEAP

The city has its share of seedy go-go clubs and "cabarets," some of which are known for scandalous billing and physical intimidation. Male tourists should get real and generally assume that attractive young women who approach them on the street and suggest that they go have a drink—sometimes shyly asking for directions first—are up to no good; chances are that they are in cahoots with venues where the drinks come at a heavy price indeed. To avoid such rip-offs, check the American Embassy in Budapest for places to avoid, which are posted at ⊕ www.budapest.usembassy.gov.

lar cocktail special. The music program is more varied—some nights live, mellow jazz, on weekends commercial disco. ⊠ *District XIII, Visegrádi utca 9, Around Nyugati Train Station* ☎ *1/237–0666* Ⓜ *M3: Nyugati.*

Szimpla. This is yet another bohemian hot spot—just around the corner from Sark—where a host of local creative types gather in the large underground cellar, sprawling over an eclectic mix of furniture. Live jazz music is offered several nights a week in an extremely smoky environment. ⊠ *District VII, Kértesz utca 48, Around Király utca* ☎ *1/342–1034 or 30/275–7616* Ⓜ *M1: Oktogon.*

Teaház a Vörös Oroszlánhoz. Okay, there's neither alcohol nor a raucous atmosphere here, but the "Teahouse at the Red Lion" is nonetheless a enchanting space in which to while away an evening while sipping one or more of its many fine teas. Head through the downstairs tea shop up the stairs to a spacious, intimately lit room or one of its cozy nooks draped with red gossamer curtains. Open until 11 PM, after which you can take a quiet stroll along the Danube before turning in or else switch to bar-hopping mode. There's also a branch across downtown, likewise in Pest, at Ráday utca 9 (☎ 215–2101). ⊠ *District VI, Jókai tér 8, Around Andrássy út* ☎ *1/269–0579* Ⓜ *M1: Oktogon.*

Dance Clubs & Discos

When Hungarians go out dancing, they typically stay out—until dawn, evidenced by the variety of late-night dance clubs and discos around the capital city. Hungarians strut out in style, donning their best outfits, with women in stiletto heels and men generous with hair gel. Some of the liveliest nightlife in Budapest hinges around the electronica scene: trance, techno, drum 'n' bass, etc. Most dance clubs charge a cover, which usually ranges between 1,000 HUF and 1,500 HUF.

A38. A large ship permanently moored on the Buda side of the Danube has a restaurant upstairs and a large dance floor downstairs. There's a different band on hand every night, from jazz to Latin, retro to electronic. ⊠ *District XI, Near the Petőfi Híd, on the Buda side of the river, South Buda* ☎ *1/464–3940.*

Barokko. The former Pesti Est café on bustling Liszt Ferenc tér still looks like just another swarming, stylish café in which to pass the night away, but Wednesday through Friday you get a broad mix of live music to boot—and if you look beyond the outside seating and the loungelike ground floor and head downstairs, you'll discover a dance

THIS CITY'S SMOKIN'

A word of warning to the smoke-sensitive: although a 1999 law requiring smoke-free areas in many public establishments has had a discernible impact in restaurants, the bar scene is a firm reminder that Budapest remains a city where smokers still feel quite at home. Compared to 10 or 15 years ago, considerably fewer members of the adult, club-hopping population smoke (maybe 25%), and though the smoke is clearing just a tad, the smokers do still constitute a sufficiently strong minority to have their way until stricter legislation comes into force (not out of the question in the next few years).

floor where DJs bring you retro disco, house, and funky disco nightly from 11 PM to 3 AM. ⊠ *District VI, Liszt Ferenc tér 5, Around Andrássy út* ☎ *1/322–0700.*

★ **Café del Rio.** Calling itself a "fancy club for fancy people," one of Budapest's largest and hottest dance clubs—home to two dance floors, a "VIP lounge," and a restaurant—is near the Buda side of the Petőfi Bridge, close to the popular outdoor drinking garden Zöld Pardon. ⊠ *District XI, Goldmann György tér 1, South Buda* ☎ *06–30/297–2158.*

★ **Cha-Cha-Cha.** This tiny, sweatspot/dance club in the Kálvin tér metro station packs in partygoers until dawn, and it's often so crowded that people pour out of the club onto the metro station walkway. DJs are featured Thursday through Saturday nights. A seasonal branch with an open-air dance space, the Cha-Cha-Cha Terasz, opened in 2006 on Margaret Island not far from the island's southern end at Margit híd (Margaret Bridge). ⊠ *District IX, Kálvin tér underpass, Around Kálvin tér* ☎ *1/215–0545* Ⓜ *M3: Kálvin tér.*

Citadella Dance Club. From the top of Budapest's beautiful Gellért Hill you can gaze at the city's landscape through large windows while cutting a rug on the dance floor. Be warned that drinks are expensive, and so are the taxis waiting outside to take you back down the hill. ⚠ **Unless you traipse back down to the tram/bus stops in front of the Gellért Hotel, public transportation is not available from here in the late-night hours.** ⊠ *District XI, Citadella sétány 2, Gellért-hegy and Tabán* ☎ *1/209–3271.*

Dokk Backstage. Budapest's version of a truly glitzy international disco is great for people-watching, especially if you wish to observe the get-rich-quick set and their trophy dates at play. Dokk is more expensive than most dance and disco bars, with cocktails averaging around 3,000 HUF apiece. ⊠ *District III, Hajógyári sziget 122, Óbuda* ☎ *1/457–1023.*

Közgáz Pince Club. This large, underground dance club at the Budapest Economics University attracts a younger crowd. ⊠ *District IX, Fővám tér 8, Around Kálvin tér* ☎ *1/215–4359* Ⓜ *M3: Kálvin tér.*

Nincs Pardon ("No excuse"). There are plenty of reasons and perhaps even good excuses to come here and dance until dawn. Watch the steep steps coming into the underground dance club, though. Once you are past the bar, you'll find a series of several dance floors in back. ⊠ *District VII, Almássy tér 11, Around Blaha Lujza tér* ☎ *1/351–4351* Ⓜ *M2: Blaha Lujza tér.*

★ **Piaf.** Only two blocks from Budapest's opera and theater district, Piaf is one of the city's most interesting late-night clubs, with red-velvety decor, a smokey piano bar, a singer upstairs, and a small dance floor underground where you can dance the night away with locals to a mix of current latino beats and '80s hits. Watch for the small, sometimes unlit red PIAF sign above the entrance. ■ **TIP→ You may have to ring the doorbell to get in.** The entrance fee includes the first drink. Piaf is open from about 10 PM to 7 AM. ⊠ *District VI, Nagymező utca, between nos. 25 and 27, Around Andrássy út* ☎ *1/312–3823* Ⓜ *M3: Arany János.*

Tracadero. It's billed as the only Latin disco in town, and weekends are the best nights to dance here. Occasional live acts include salsa and merengue shows. Be careful to enter the sign for Tracadero, as the place next door is for the "Nirvana Bar," a strip club known to be run by the Mafia, which you should plan to avoid. ✉ *District V, Szent István körút 15, Around Nyugati Train Station* ☎ *1/311–4691* Ⓜ *M3: Nyugati.*

Retro-Communist

Although communism is long gone in Hungary, the following spots either make their living off a nostalgia for the past or never got around to updating their interiors. Either way, time spent at one of the following is a trip down Budapest's memory lane.

★ **Bambi Eszpresszó.** A neighborhood presence since 1960, this is the perfect place to sip Dreher, the popular Hungarian beer, and watch older Hungarian men pass the day playing chess. Sit inside the bare-bones establishment on red plastic–covered chairs and peer out through white lace curtains that appear decades old, or outside on the terrace during warmer months. Rude service is free of charge, and adds to Bambi's character. ✉ *District I, Frankel Leó utca 2–4, Around Batthyány tér* ☎ *1/212–3171* Ⓜ *M2: Batthyány tér.*

Jaffa. Named after an orange soda popular under communism, Jaffa is laid-back cool, with a retro orange and black interior. Order a glass of Jaffa for yourself and decide. ✉ *District IX, Ráday utca 39, Around Kálvin tér* ☎ *1/219–5285* Ⓜ *M3: Kálvin tér.*

Marxim. Across the street from Budapest's Millenáris Park, this bar and pizza parlor is a tribute to socialism, including graffiti-scrawled walls, chicken wire, and black and red paint smeared everywhere. Try the "Gulag Pizza," covered in spicy red paprika, ham, and corn; it also comes with a bottle of ketchup to pour on top—a popular condiment Hungarians slather on their pizza. ✉ *District II, Kisrókus utca 23, Around Moszkva tér* ☎ *1/316–0231* Ⓜ *M2: Moszkva tér.*

FodorśChoice
★ **Mélypont.** If you ever wondered what Hungarian interior design looked like under communism, look no farther. A walk into this basement bar is a carefully stylized step back into 1970s Hungary, with decor mostly in black, orange, and lacquered wood. Old clocks, rugs, uncomfortable reclining chairs, and an espresso machine the size of a desk are all on hand to see. The drinks here are simple, as are the snacks, but the ambience is a winner. ✉ *District V, Magyar utca 23, Around Kálvin tér* ☎ *06–30/812–4064 (mobile)* Ⓜ *M3: Kálvin tér.*

Seasonal

Warm weather in Budapest means outdoor pubs and outdoor *kertek* (gardens), many of which offer live music and DJs on most nights. The kertek typically open in early May, when warm weather approaches, and close for the season around mid-September. Most places stay open daily until dawn.

Buddha Beach. The main attraction in one of Budapest's newest outdoor nightspots is in fact not so much a beach as a cluster of thatched-roof bars with plenty of space to mill about, complemented by likewise thatched-roof but wall-less seating cubicles along the adjacent Danube river. With a focus on Latin, retro, and hip-hop, the Beach has live music some nights and DJs spinning the tunes most nights. This space is also the site of other clubs, including one titled retroBeach. Though hard to tell which club you're in, the atmosphere and fine nighttime views of Buda are worth a visit. Located in the onetime home of the city's largest food market, this club complex is accessible via a drab riverside path you enter by one of two gates between the Szabadság Bridge and the Petőfi Bridge. ☒ *District V, Közraktár utca 9–11, Around Kálvin tér* ☎ *1/210–4872* Ⓜ *M3: Kálvin tér.*

Érzsébet Híd Eszpresszo. At the foot of its namesake bridge in Buda, near the Rudas baths, the Érzsébet Bridge Eszpresszo pub has a large outdoor terrace with green plastic tables at the foot of a grand old apartment building. Despite the traffic roaring by, this is a great place to chat away while sipping a beer a stone's throw from the Danube; and it's just a five-minute stroll north of the Rómkert, a much louder, music-enhanced, party-oriented club (*see below*). ☒ *District I, Döbrentei tér 1, Gellért-hegy and Tabán* ☎ *1/212–2127.*

Liget Café & Grill. In the heart of Városliget (City Park), this delightful open-air club has reasonable drink prices, salsa music, and Mediterranean-style foods. Open until 4 AM. ☒ *District XVI, Olof Palme sétány, City Park* ☎ *06–30/408–8030 (mobile)* Ⓜ *M1: Hősök tere.*

Rómkert. Five minutes south of the more intellectual, conversation-oriented Érzsébet Híd Eszpresszo (via a stroll under the foot of the Elisabeth Bridge), this comparatively raucous outdoor pub adjoining the Rudas baths specializes in cocktails. It's usually packed with yuppies and young scantily clothed Hungarian women. Rómkert is open daily and extremely crowded on weekends, when the crowd grinds to the dance music. ☒ *District I, Döbrentei tér 9, Gellért-hegy and Tabán* ☎ *No phone.*

Sark-kert. Sark-kert is the summer location of the Sark pub, which grills up Hungarian food on an outdoor barbecue nightly. Enjoy a tranquil evening under the stars on Margaret Island. From the Margit híd (Margaret Bridge), walk straight down the island following signs for the "Margaret Island Youth Hostel," Sark-kert is adjacent to the hostel. ☒ *District XIII, Margit-sziget, Margaret Island* ☎ *No phone* Ⓜ *M3: Nyugati.*

West Balkan. This great outdoor dance spot is a bit tricky to find. From the Buda side of the Lágymányos Bridge, walk south for about 10 to 15 minutes, following the Danube. You can also take a bicycle rickshaw from the bridge or from Zöld Pardon. ☒ *District XI, Kopaszi gát, South Buda* ☎ *No phone.*

Zöld Pardon. The largest outdoor drinking garden in Budapest, which is located near the Buda side of the Petőfi Bridge, opens daily in the afternoon and stays open until dawn, serving breakfast and other food. Big-name Hungarian musical acts are featured on a regular basis, as well as DJs spinning house and drum 'n' bass music nightly. ☒ *District XI, Goldmann György tér, South Buda* ☎ *1/279–1880.*

Wine Bars

Budapest has literally hundreds of wine bars around the city, called *borozó*, but the majority are smoky little joints packed with older Hungarians from open until close. A borozó is perfectly safe to stop at to sample a slice of everyday Hungarian life; you can often get a small sampling of snacks to go with your wine. The places recommended here are good spots to try Hungarian wines, which, according to many wine experts, are among the top wines produced in Europe.

Fodor'sChoice
★

BorBíróság (Wine Court). Tucked behind the *Vásárcsarnok* (Central Market Hall) in downtown Budapest, this is among the best places in Budapest to sample a range of quality Hungarian wines, unless you are planning a visit to the wine regions yourself. It's not exactly your typical, working-class *borozó* and it's a bit pricey by Hungarian standards—a small glass of wine costs the equivalent of several dollars, on average. But the owners pride themselves on selecting the best 150 wines Hungary has to offer, and it's true. You can easily spend an entire afternoon or evening sampling different great wines here. Also check out the daily "Wine Happy Hour" from 4 to 5 PM, where every glass of wine is half-price. Open until 10 PM Monday–Thursday, 11 PM Friday and Saturday, closed Sunday. ⊠ *District IX, Csarnok tér 5, Around Kálvin tér* ☎ *1/219–0902* Ⓜ *M3: Kálvin tér.*

Egri Borozó. This borozó specializes in wine from the northern Hungarian city of Eger. In the warmer months you can order a small or large pint of the famed red *Bikavér* (Bull's Blood) while sitting on the terrace outside, or when the weather is less nice you can stay in the cellar-level bar. ⊠ *District V, Bajcsy-Zsilinszsky út 72, Around Nyugati Train Station* ☎ *1/302–1724* Ⓜ *M3: Nyugati.*

Magyar Bortársaság (Hungarian Wine Society). Though technically not a wine bar, this shop has a wide selection of local vintages as well as locations in both Pest and Buda. It sells wine from every region of the country, and there are plenty of opportunities to try different wines at the free wine tastings each Saturday from 2 to 5. ⊠ *District 1, Batthyány utca 59, Around Moszkva tér* ☎ *1/212–2569* Ⓜ *M3: Moszkva tér* ⊠ *District IX, Ráday utca 7, Around Kálvin tér* ☎ *1/219–5647* Ⓜ *M3: Kálvin tér.*

Sandaken Lisboa. The name might make you think this bar specializes in port, but in fact this small wine bar along the pedestrianized Hajos utca, behind the Hungarian State Opera House, serves mostly Hungarian wines plus a couple of Portuguese varieties thrown in to justify its name. ⊠ *District VI, Hajós utca 23, Around Andrássy út* ☎ *1/302–7002* Ⓜ *M1: Oktogon.*

Tokaji Borozó. This extremely smoky, packed-to-the-gills underground wine bar offers Hungarian whites from the eastern Tokaj region plus snacks. It has more than its share of middle-aged and older Hungarians debating politics or, sometimes, playing cards or chess. ⊠ *District V, Falk Miksa utca 32, Around Nyugati Train Station* ☎ *No phone* Ⓜ *M3: Nyugati, or M2: Kossuth Lajos tér.*

Vörös és Fehér Wine Bar & Restaurant. True wine lovers can choose from more than 150 types of Hungarian and international wines. Owned and operated by the Hungarian Wine Society, which also has popular wine shops in Budapest, "Red & White" is one of the best upscale wine bars and restaurants in Budapest. *See also* the review *in* Where to Eat. ⊠ *District VI, Andrássy út 41, Around Andrássy út* ☎ *1/413–1545.*

Gay & Lesbian

Outward public affection among gays is pretty much taboo in Budapest—even hand-holding is rarely seen on the streets despite a surprising degree of open-mindedness on such matters among Hungarians young and old. The gay club scene, however, is quite lively, even though (or because?)

most of it is literally underground, in cellar venues; and many of the discos listed below are packed on weekends and a bit more mellow on weekdays. Virtually all gay bars and discos charge a cover of 1,500 HUF to 2,500 HUF, or have a drink minimum. With the exception of Café Eklektika, Budapest's gay bars are mainly male-dominated, although Capella and Club Bohemian Alibi have some lesbian and straight clientele. Check out ⊕ www.gayguide.net and ⊕ www.gay.hu for the latest on gay clubs and happenings in the city. The major gay event is the annual Gay Pride Budapest festival and parade, held in early July.

Action Bar. Action is the perfect name for this cellar bar in the city center, which features a popular dark room and video room, as well as go-go and erotic dance shows starting at midnight. The crowd is all-male, and this is mostly a pick-up scene, definitely not a place to go for a quiet drink. ⊠ *District V, Magyar utca 42, Around Kálvin tér* ☎ *1/266–9148* Ⓜ *M3: Kálvin tér.*

Café Capella. Open Wednesday through Saturday, the club attracts a mixed gay-straight crowd clustered in this basement disco for frequent, glittery drag shows. There's also great music and lots of floor space to dance until dawn. ⊠ *District V, Belgrád rakpart 23, Around Ferenciek tere* ☎ *1/318–6231.*

Café Eklektika. A mixed straight and gay clientele frequents this gay-friendly classy café-cum-restaurant at its new location (as of April 2006) in a historic café-, museum-, and theater-rich neighborhood near Andrássy út. With pastel walls and funky 1960s wooden chairs and benches, Eklektika is a soothing spot in which to while away a couple of hours as jazz music plays softly in the background. ⊠ *District VI, Nagymező utca 30, Around Andrássy út* ☎ *1/266–1226* Ⓜ *M1: Opera.*

Club Bohemian Alibi. One of the most popular gay bars in Budapest, Alibi is a basement club with three bars. Entertainment is provided by DJs and a midnight "Best Bohemian Transvestite" show that features singing, dancing, and occasional guest stars from the theater community. It also serves food until 11 PM. ⊠ *District VIII, Üllői út 45, Around Ferenc József körút* ☎ *1/219–5260* Ⓜ *M3: Ferenc József körút.*

CoXx Club. This men-only bar is in a huge cellar with an industrial-looking brick-and-metal motif. There's a small dance floor with a nightly DJ. Formerly called Chaos, CoXx also hosts a monthly leather-and-fetish sex party. ⊠ *District VII, Dohány utca 38, Around Astoria* ☎ *1/344–4884* Ⓜ *M2: Astoria.*

Live Music Venues

Jazz & Blues

Fat Mo's. Established Hungarian jazz headliners and young up-and-comers play from Thursday through Saturday in the popular, though small, stylishly brick-walled cellar pub. The music is good, but the audience is mainly expats and tourists. ⊠ *District V, Nyári Pál utca 11, Around Ferenciek tere* ☎ *1/267–3199* Ⓜ *M3: Ferenciek tere.*

FodorśChoice ★ **Gödör Klub.** Emblematic of the transformation of Budapest public space of recent years at its very best, the spacious, jazzy "Ditch Club" is right in the heart of downtown—on what used to be the drab parking lot of the city's communist-era bus station and was later a hollowed out, sorry-looking abandoned construction site (for the National Theater, which ended up elsewhere) dubbed "the ditch." On a fine summer evening it seems that all the under-30 faces for a mile around are here, sitting about with plastic cups of wine or beer on the broad flight of steps leading down into the "ditch" or dipping their feet in a big pool of water right above the club—that is, if they're not actually inside listening to live jazz on the club's small stage. ⊠ *District V, Erzsébet tér, Around Deák tér* ☎ *06–20/201–3868* Ⓜ *M1, M2, M3: Deák tér.*

Jazz Garden. The basement jazz club/restaurant presents well-known Hungarian jazz musicians on a regular basis. ⊠ *District V, Veres Pálné utca 44/a, Around Ferenciek tere* ☎ *1/266–7364* Ⓜ *M3: Ferenciek tere.*

Morrison's Music Pub. Only a few yards to the west of the Opera House, this long-popular cellar venue hosts karaoke and disco in its two rooms, with DJs regularly on hand. Closed Monday. Mugs of good beer are sold for around 150 HUF one evening a week (as of this writing, Thursday). ⊠ *District VI, Révai utca 25, Around Andrássy út* ☎ *1/269–4060* Ⓜ *M1: Opera.*

Old Man's Music Pub. One thing you can't fault this dimly lit cellar pub for is consistency; it's packed even on Monday night. Of course in Hungary that means you'll be inhaling a fair bit of second-hand smoke. If that doesn't ruin your fun, enjoy the live bluesy rock and jazz, as well as the friendly chaos behind the bar—while everyone squeezes onto the small dance floor. ⊠ *District VII, Akácfa utca 13, Around Blaha Lujza tér* ☎ *1/322–7645* Ⓜ *M2: Blaha Lujza tér.*

Trafó Bár Tangó. In the basement of the Trafó House of Contemporary Arts, this bar features regular live jazz performances from some of Budapest's best jazz musicians, including Mihály Dresch and Elemér Balázs. ⊠ *District IX, Liliom utca 41, Around Ferenc József körút* ☎ *1/456–2040* Ⓜ *M3: Ferenc körút.*

Rock & Eclectic

Benczúr Klub. With a nice outdoor terrace in summer months, the Benczúr features local rock, folk, and jazz acts on a near-weekly basis indoors year-round. ⊠ *District VI, Benczúr utca 27, Around Andrássy út* ☎ *1/321–7334* Ⓜ *M1: Kodály Körönd.*

Petőfi Csarnok. In City Park, this is a venue where local and mid-level international acts play regularly—everything from popular to folk music. However, the best time to drop in is in the summer, when the outdoor amphitheater is open, affording a pleasant switch from the drab interior. ⊠ *District XIV, Zichy Mihály út 14, City Park* ☎ *1/363–3730* Ⓜ *M1: Széchenyi Fürdő.*

Rocktogon. A large, bright yellow–walled basement club that features local rock, punk, and other acts every week. When there isn't a live act, the club regularly hosts DJs spinning dance and punk tunes into the wee hours of the night. ⊠ *District V, Mozsár utca 9, Around Andrássy út* ☎ *1/353–0443* Ⓜ *M1: Oktogon.*

Süss Fel Nap. Typically hosting a younger crowd, this is a good place to see up-and-coming rock, punk, techno, and electronic music acts. The colorful, busy interior is decorated with murals, paintings, and lots of

LATE-NIGHT BITES

After-hours food options in Budapest remain somewhat limited. Even with numerous gyro and Turkish food stands open 24 hours a day, it remains a challenge to find Western, breakfast-type foods in a country that does not eat a Western-style breakfast. But after a long night of clubbing or bar-hopping, you can expect several decent places to be open for some kind of late-night snack.

Hepicentrum. This floating salad bar on a boat near the Buda side of the Margit híd offers salads, pasta, and grilled meats 24 hours daily. ⊠ *District II, Bem Alsó Rakpart, Around Batthyány tér* ☎ *1/212–4479.*

Nagyi Palacsintázója. Choose from more than 50 kinds of *palacsinta*, the Hungarian pancake that tastes and looks like a crepe and can be filled with everything imaginable. The place is dirt cheap and open 24 hours. ⊠ *District I, Batthyány tér 5, Around Batthyány tér* ☎ *1/212–4866.*

Noa Caffé. The best falafel in the city can be found at this Israeli café. It's open Sunday to Thursday until 2 AM, Friday and Saturday until 5 AM. ⊠ *District VI, Teréz körút 54, Around Nyugati Train Station* ☎ *06-30/288–3854 (mobile).*

Szent Jupát. The popular basement restaurant is open 24 hours a day, serving massive portions of Hungarian food to clog your arteries and send you rolling home to bed. ⊠ *District II, Retek utca 16, at Dékán utca, around Moszkva tér* ☎ *1/212–2923.*

tables, benches, and chairs. ⊠ *District V, Corner of Honvéd utca and Szent István körút, Around Nyugati Train Station* ☎ *1/374–3329* Ⓜ *M3: Nyugati.*

Wigwam. Although outside the city center, this is one of the few bars featuring live rock and heavy metal acts on a large stage. When the music's not live, you can twist and thrash on the dance floor while rock DJs spin the tunes, from rock 'n roll to salsa; and Wigwam, like many a Budapest bar these days, also has regular karaoke nights. ⊠ *District XI, Fehévári út 202, South Buda* ☎ *1/208–5569.*

Casinos

There are literally hundreds of casinos in Budapest, but most are small establishments on side streets and are best avoided—as many are money laundering operations for the Mafia. The casinos we list here are the largest in Budapest and are perfectly legal and safe to visit. You must be 18 to enter; if you don't necessarily look it, bring a photo ID.

Las Vegas Casino. The centrally located casino is inside the Sofitel Atrium. It's open 24 hours a day and features 26 table games as well as slots. ⊠ *District V, Sofitel Atrium Budapest, Roosevelt tér 2, Around Váci utca* ☎ *1/317–6022* Ⓜ *M1: Vörösmarty tér.*

Tropicana. Next to Vörösmarty tér, the Tropicana is popular with locals as well as tourists. Sit outside during warmer months under palm trees.

It's open daily from 11 AM to 6 AM. ⊠ *District V, Vigádó utca 2, Around Váci utca 1/266–3062* Ⓜ M1: Vörösmarty tér.

Várkert Casino. An 1879 building designed by prolific architect Miklós Ybl—who also designed the State Opera House—the Várkert is the most visually striking of the city's casinos. It's open daily from 11 AM to 6 AM. ⊠ *District I, Miklós Ybl tér 9, Gellért-hegy and Tabán* ☎ *1/202–4244.*

PERFORMING ARTS

Budapest is a city deeply rooted in its love and appreciation for the performing arts. During the main season, which runs from September through June, you can find ballet, opera, classical music, and theater performances any night of the week. And compared to those for performances in many European cities, tickets to events in Budapest are affordable indeed to Western pocketbooks.

Hungarians have kept the arts in full swing. Nearly every theater and performing arts house that existed under socialism—and was heavily subsidized by the state—is still in operation today, even though many have since been privatized, and only a handful remain subsidized by the state or local governments. A night out at the opera or ballet is no casual affair. Hungarians dress for the occasion, and that usually means business or formal attire. Nor are the arts reserved only for older members of society. It is quite common to see teenagers and young adults in full regalia for the opera or the ballet.

Hungary is, perhaps, best known for modern classical music, having produced two of the most famous composers of the 20th century, Béla Bartók and Zoltán Kodály, both of whose works are widely played throughout the city by numerous orchestras. Budapest is also home to the world-renowned Liszt Ferenc Music Academy, named after Hungarian composer Franz Liszt, which has by far the city's finest classical concert hall.

The Hungarian State Opera House, a grandiose hall on the beautiful, tree-lined Andrássy út in the city center, is one of Budapest's most famous buildings, built in 1884 and celebrated at that time as the most modern opera house in all of Europe. It is home to the Hungarian State Opera and the National Ballet, which, in addition to their regular performance schedules, put on a special Summer Opera & Ballet Festival for two to three weeks in July or August.

As for tradition, Hungarians celebrate their folk-music history through a handful of folkloric dance ensembles, which perform regularly. You can even try your hand at learning a few steps at several community centers that teach the art.

For the latest on arts events, consult the entertainment listings of the English-language press. Detailed entertainment calendars map out all that's happening in Budapest's arts and culture world—from thrash bands in wild clubs to performances at the Opera House. Hotels and tourist offices will also provide you with a copy of the monthly publication *Bu-*

CLOSE UP

Festivals & Events

FROM MUSIC AND THEATER to folk art and film, Hungarians milk every occasion possible to host a celebration.

Budapest International Wine & Champagne Festival. In mid-September, a wine exhibition in the Buda castle features the country's best wine producers, including a wine auction. The arts component includes classical and jazz concerts each evening. ☎ 1/203-8507 ⊕ www.winefestival.hu.

Budapest Spring Festival. The most popular of Hungarian festivals is held for two weeks beginning in mid-March, and is the pride of Hungarian classical music. Spread across 50 to 60 venues around the city, the festival hosts renowned musicians, performers, and orchestras from across Europe and beyond, and also includes various theater productions, performances, and film screenings. Tickets to its more than 200 events go fast, so it's wise to check out the festival's Web site and order online if you plan to be in Budapest in March. The Budapest Spring Festival celebrated its 25th anniversary in March 2005. ☎ 1/486-3300 ⊕ www.festivalcity.hu.

Danube Carnival International Cultural Festival. Folk dancing, classical music, wind bands, world music, and contemporary dance performances are held at a variety of venues across the capital city for two weeks in mid-June. ☎ 1/201-6613 ⊕ www.dunaart.hu/carnival.

Danube Water Carnival. On the weekend in mid-June closest to the anniversary of the construction of Hungary's *Lánchíd* (Chain Bridge), the oldest and most stunning of the five bridges connecting Buda and Pest, a variety of aquatic events, competitions, and air shows take place along and above the Danube. Make sure to catch a glimpse of the Chain Bridge at night, when it's lit up in all its splendor. Check with Tourinform for details.

Parliament Dome Concerts. On about six occasions annually, the Hungarian Virtuosi Chamber Orchestra, founded by graduates of the Liszt Ferenc Music Academy, gives performances in the Dome Hall of the Hungarian Parliament. Concerts start at 6 PM, with the option of a Parliament tour beginning at 5:15 PM. Tickets and dates are available at most ticket agencies in Budapest, including Ticket Express and the Liszt Ferenc Music Academy itself.

Sziget Festival (Island Festival). For one week in early to mid-August, one of Europe's biggest music festivals, hosting hundreds of local and international artists, is staged on the northern reaches of Óbuda Island, north of the Árpád Bridge. Some 15 stages and numerous venues host nearly every musical genre as well as theater, film, art exhibitions, and sports competitions. Tickets are available at numerous ticket offices in Budapest and at Tesco megastores. ☎ 1/372-0684 ⊕ www.sziget.hu.

4

dapest Panorama (⊕ www.budapestpanorama.com), which contains details of all cultural events.

TICKETS Tickets for arts events can be bought at the venues themselves, but many ticket offices across the city sell them without an extra charge. Prices are still low by Western standards, so mark-ups of even 30% shouldn't dent your wallet substantially if you book through the concierge at your hotel. Inquire at Tourinform if you're not sure where to go. It's usually possible to get tickets a few days before most shows, but performances by major international artists sell out early. Tickets to Budapest Spring Festival events also go particularly quickly. Virtually every performance and concert is listed on the Web site ⊕ www. koncertkalendarium.hu. A booklet copy is also available at Tourinform and other ticket agencies across the city.

Központi Jegyiroda (Central Ticket Office). This agency specializes in tickets to Hungarian theater productions. ⊠ *District VI, Andrássy út 15, Around Andrássy út* ☎ *1/267–1267.*

Liszt Ferenc Zeneakadémia. You can purchase tickets to all performances and classical music concerts held at the music academy through the ticket office. Given the large number of performances here, this is a major agency in Budapest for cultural tickets. ⊠ *District VI, Liszt Ferenc tér 8, Around Andrássy út* ☎ *1/342–0179 or 1/462–4600* ⊕ *www.liszt.hu.*

Magyar Állami Operaház (Hungarian State Opera House). Tickets for the Hungarian State Opera, National Ballet, or the Erkel Theater can be purchased on-site. ⊠ *District VI, Andrássy út 20, Around Andrássy út* ☎ *1/331–2250 or 1/331–8197* ⊕ *www.opera.hu.*

Magyar Telekom Jegyiroda (Hungarian Telecom Ticket Office). The Hungarian Telecom Symphony Orchestra sells tickets to its own performances, as well as for the National Philharmonic, Budapest's Summer Opera & Ballet Festival, and other pop music and festival events around town. ⊠ *District VI, Nagymező utca 19, Around Andrássy út* ☎ *1/428–0791 or 1/302–3841* ⊕ *www.ticket.axelero.hu.*

Művészetek Palotája (Palace of the Arts). Tickets for concerts and theatrical events at Hungary's newest and largest cultural center—which, most prominently, is home to the Béla Bartók National Concert Hall—are available on-site or at ticket offices. ⊠ *District IX, Komor Marcell utca 1, Around Boráros tér* ☎ *1/555–3000* ⊕ *www.mupa.hu* Ⓜ *M3: Üllői út.*

National Philharmonic Ticket Office. The Philharmonic's service sells tickets for classical music, ballet, and opera, as well as tickets for major pop and rock shows. ⊠ *District VII, Madách utca 3, Around Deák Ferenc tér* ☎ *1/321–4199* ⊕ *www.filharmonikusok.hu.*

Ticket Express. The biggest agency in Budapest sells tickets to nearly every show or performance happening in Hungary, including theater, opera, musicals, and concerts. ⊠ *District VI, Andrássy út 18, Around Andrássy út* ☎ *1/312–0000 or 06–30/303–0999 (mobile)* ⊕ *www.tex.hu.*

Major Performance Venues

Budapest has a wide range of performance venues, offering classical music, theater, ballet, and folk-dancing performances. The best place to see a classical music concert is the Liszt Ferenc Music Academy, which reg-

How Now, Blue Cow?

WHETHER IN THE BURGEONING of outdoor pubs or monumental (and sometimes controversial) new arts centers, public space in Budapest has undergone a sea change in recent years. The question has arisen repeatedly: Is a square or a street just something to pass through or also to experience? If the latter, just *how* should it be experienced? Calmly? Clamorously? Shockingly? Can it (or should it) be art? Does conceiving of public spaces this way mean that an elite minority imposes its often secular ideas on the silent majority? Well, in summer 2006 the "silent majority"—if indeed it is a majority, which is open to question in largely liberal Budapest—struck back. They had a cow—over a cow.

On the heels of previous such events in cities from New York to London, from Prague to Tokyo, Budapest was among those European cities in 2006 that hosted a so-called CowParade. The objective: to put the public into direct contact with art—in particular, with life-size, fiberglass cow sculptures conceived by local artists. Many of the cows are then auctioned off for good causes after a few months on public spaces. In Hungary more than 50 winners were chosen from some 900 applications, and from June 30 until September 10, 2006, their works were on display—outdoors, that is—all over Budapest.

But one cow in particular didn't sit well with everyone. Inspired by the dog days of summer and by the novelty of a strikingly colored cow, artists András Hajdu, Balázs Magashegyi, and Krisztián Imre made "Melting Popsicle." Picture an upside-down, dazzlingly blue bovine whose upper body appears to be melting into the pavement while a popsicle stick protrudes from its behind (reading: "Don't Lick Me"). Their creation was a favorite with the public—which was invited to register its opinions on the cows. The problem: "Melting Popsicle" ended up—apparently by chance, and unbeknownst to the artists—on Szent István tér, the square in front of Budapest's basilica. What's worse, the popsicle stick in its behind was pointing at the holy edifice. Cathedral officials made it clear that they were none too happy, but event organizers in Hungary stood their ground, insisting that the cow would remain right where it was.

Then, on the night of July 3, one or more unknown perpetrators removed the blasphemous blue bovine and deposited the damaged beast a few blocks away in front of the Liberálisok Háza (House of the Liberals). The media had a field day over it all, but compromise prevailed, as the offending cow, after some repair, was put to pasture well away from its former, contentious site.

---

ularly features Hungary's most talented musicians. The elegant Hungarian State Opera House is the venue for not just opera, but also ballet. The Trafó House of Contemporary Arts puts on dance productions nearly every night of the week.

Bartók Béla Emlékház (Bartók Béla Memorial House). The tiny recital room hosts intimate Friday-evening chamber-music recitals by well-known ensembles from mid-March to June and September to mid-December. As of this writing it was under renovation, but was expected to reopen before long. ✉ *District II, Csalán út 29, Buda Hills* ☏ *1/394–4472 or 1/394–2100* ⊕ *www.bartokmuseum.hu.*

Budapest Kongresszusi Központ (Budapest Convention Center). One of the city's largest-capacity (but least atmospheric) classical concert venues, this hosts a wide range of events, including some that are part of the Spring Festival. ✉ *District XII, Jagelló út 1–3, Gellért-hegy and Tabán* ☏ *1/209–1990.*

Erkel Színház (Erkel Theater). The homely little sister of the Opera House, the Erkel is Budapest's other main opera and ballet venue. There are no regular performances in summer, however. The unattractive, vast Soviet-style building never appears to be filled. ✉ *District VIII, Köztársaság tér 30, Around Blaha Lujza tér* ☏ *1/333–0540* Ⓜ *M2: Blaha Lujza tér.*

Folklór Centrum. The center has been a major venue for folklore performances for more than 30 years. It hosts regular traditional folk concerts and dance performances from spring through fall. ✉ *District XI, Fehérvári út 47, South Buda* ☏ *1/203–3868.*

★ **Fonó Budai Zeneház** (Fonó Buda Music House). Although it's a bit of a trek from the city center to Fonó, on the outskirts of Buda, it is a great place to see live folk acts. The music house has its own bar, several performance stages, and even its own folk-music CD shop. Concerts are held on a near-nightly basis, and tickets are bought when you enter the music house. ✉ *District XI, Sztregova utca 3, South Buda* ☏ *1/206–5300* ⊕ *www.fono.hu.*

IBS (International Buda Stage). Performances here include English- and Hungarian-language theater in addition to movies, dance, and concerts. English-only shows are typically once a month, although there is simultaneous translation into English during Hungarian-language events. ✉ *District II, Tárogató út 2–4, Buda Hills* ☏ *1/391–2525* ⊕ *www.ibs-b.hu.*

Jövő Háza (House of the Future). Built for the year 2000 and originally called Millennium Park, this capacious park comprises not just open space—refreshing enough in this architecturally congested district of Buda—but also a series of several buildings that (in addition to housing two science and technology museums) host arts performances from film and dance to music and theater. In warmer months a large stage for concerts is constructed outside in the park near several small, man-made lakes. ✉ *District II, Lövőház utca 39, Around Moszkva tér* ☏ *1/438–5335* ⊕ *www.jovohaza.hu* Ⓜ *M2: Moszkva tér.*

Fodor'sChoice **Liszt Ferenc Zeneakadémia** (Franz Liszt Academy of Music). Usually re-
★ ferred to as the Music Academy, this is Budapest's premier classical concert venue, hosting orchestra and chamber music concerts in its splendid main hall. It's sometimes possible to grab a standing-room ticket just before a performance here. ✉ *District VI, Liszt Ferenc tér 8, Around Andrássy út* ☏ *1/342–0179 or 1/462–4600* ⊕ *www.liszt.hu* Ⓜ *M1: Oktogon.*

Fodor'sChoice **Magyar Állami Operaház** (Hungarian State Opera House). The glitter-
★ ing opera house is Budapest's main venue for opera and classical ballet, and presents an international repertoire of classical and modern works

as well as such Hungarian favorites as Kodály's *Háry János*. Except during the two-week international opera and ballet festival in mid-August, the Opera House is closed during the summer. ⊠ *District VI, Andrássy út 22, Around Andrássy út* ☏ *1/331–2250 or 1/331–8197* ⊕ *www.opera. hu* Ⓜ *M1: Opera.*

Művészetek Palotája (Palace of the Arts). One of the world's biggest and brightest cultural centers opened on the outskirts of downtown Budapest in 2005 right beside the likewise relatively new National Theater. At its center is the Béla Bartók National Concert Hall, which has world-class acoustics. ⊠ *District IX, Komor Marcell utca 1, Around Boráros tér* ☏ *1/555–3000* ⊕ *www.mupa.hu* Ⓜ *M3: Üllői út.*

Nemzeti Színház (National Theater). Completed in 2000 on the outskirts of downtown—and outdone in 2005 by an even grander neighbor, the Palace of the Arts—Hungary's preeminent national theatrical venue is a spectacular blend of modern and classical whose construction (and out-of-the-way site) sparked no little controversy at the time. The huge square out front includes a large reflecting pool with a toppled-over, life-size ancient theater facade and eternal flames; and, scattered about, in eerily lifelike poses, eight metal statues of late, great Hungarian thespians of the 20th century. There are nightly performances on at least one of two stages inside the theater. ⊠ *District IX, Bajor Gizi Park 1, Around Boráros tér* ☏ *1/476–6800* Ⓜ *M3: Üllői út* ⊕ *www. nemzetiszinhaz.hu.*

Nemzeti Táncszínház (National Dance Theater). The theater stages modern dance productions and ballet; it is also a venue for performance by popular folk bands. ⊠ *District I, Színház utca 1–3, Castle Hill* ☏ *1/ 302–3841* ⊕ *www.nemzetitancszinhaz.hu* Ⓜ *M2: Moszkva tér.*

Pesti Vigadó (Pest Concert Hall). Classical concerts are held regularly here, as well as occasional opera, operetta, and ballet series. ⊠ *District V, Vigadó tér 2, Around Váci utca* ☏ *1/318–7932* Ⓜ *M1: Vörösmarty tér.*

Thália Theater. This is the third site for performances by the Hungarian State Opera. This first is the State Opera House and the second is the Erkel Theater. ⊠ *District VI, Nagymező utca 22–24, Around Andrássy út* ☏ *1/331–0500* ⊕ *www.thalia.hu* Ⓜ *M1: Oktogon.*

★ **Trafó Kortárs Művészetek Háza** (Trafó House of Contemporary Arts). A former electrical transformer station in Pest, the Trafó building today showcases contemporary and alternative dance performances by Hungarian and international companies. It also serves as the venue for one or two monthly musical concerts. ⊠ *District IX, Liliom utca 41, Around Ferenc József körút* ☏ *1/215–1600* ⊕ *www.trafo.hu* Ⓜ *M2: Ferenc körút.*

Fodor'sChoice **Vígszínház** (Comedy Theater). Built in 1896, the sparkling Vígszínház ★ is the pride of the Hungarian theater world, seating over 1,000 people. The theater hosts modern European and American plays from playwrights such as Arthur Miller, Tennessee Williams, and Friedrich Dürrenmatt, but always in Hungarian. The theater is also a venue for musicals, such as Hungarian translations of *West Side Story* and a musical version of the *Jungle Book*. ⊠ *District XIII, Pannónia utca 1, Around Nyugati Train Station* ☏ *1/329–2340* ⊕ *www.vigszinhaz.hu* Ⓜ *M3: Nyugati.*

Dance

Ballet

Ballet has a strong following in Hungary despite the fact that the National Ballet Theater, formerly across the street from the Hungarian State Opera House, was bought by foreign investors to turn into a hotel in the early 2000s—a project that, as of this writing, is still in limbo. The best time to catch a performance is during Budapest's annual Summer Opera & Ballet Festival in early August.

Győri Balett (Győr Ballet). Founded in 1979, the Győr Ballet is the troupe to watch in Hungary, and is by far the most talented of the major ballets countrywide. Although the Győr Ballet is based in Győr in western Hungary, it does perform premieres in Budapest several times a year. The company has also given shows throughout Europe, performed at the Olympic Games in Seoul, and staged the production of *Purim* in 2002 at the Joyce Theater in New York. ☎ 96/523–217 ⊕ *www.gyoribalett.hu.*

Magyar Fesztival Balett (Hungarian Festival Ballet). The company was formed in September 1996 as Europe's biggest private dance troupe. Since 2002, choreography has been accompanied by music from famed Hungarian composers Franz Liszt, Béla Bartók, and Zoltán Kodály. The company performs mainly at the National Dance Theater. ☎ 1/319–9855 ⊕ *www.magyarfesztivalbalett.hu.*

Magyar Nemzeti Balett (Hungarian National Ballet). Performing at the Hungarian State Opera House, or on occasion at the Erkel Theater, the company began in 1884. Though this ballet company has been called "lifeless" by some critics—and does not come out on top when compared to the Győr Ballet—they perform on a regular basis in Budapest. ☎ 1/353–0170 ⊕ *www.opera.hu.*

Pécsi Balett (Pécs Ballet). The first modern ballet ensemble in Hungary began in the 1960s, on the basis of classical ballet mixed with pantomime, folk dance, and a language of gestures. The Pécs Ballet, although based outside Budapest, gives several major openings in the capital city throughout the year. ☎ 72/512–660 ⊕ *www.pnsz.hu.*

Folk Dancing

Many of Budapest's district cultural centers regularly hold traditional regional folk-dancing evenings, or *táncház* (dance houses), often with general instruction at the beginning. These sessions provide a less touristy way to taste Hungarian culture. Check out ⊕ www.tanchaz.hu for information on folk performers and the local scene.

Almássy téri Szabadidő központ (Almássy Square Recreation Center). The center holds numerous folk-dancing evenings, representing Hungarian as well as Greek and other ethnic cultures. ⊠ *District VII, Almássy tér 6, Around Blaha Lujza tér* ☎ 1/352–1572 Ⓜ *M2: Blaha Lujza tér.*

Belvárosi Ifjúsági Művelődési ház (City Youth Cultural Center). Traditionally, the city's wildest táncház is held Saturday night at the Belvárosi, where the stomping and whirling go on way into the night. The center, like many such venues, closes from mid-July to mid-August. ⊠ *District*

V, Molnár utca 9, Around Ferenciek tere ☎ *1/317–5928* Ⓜ *M3: Ferenciek tere.*

Marczibányi Téri Művelődési Központ (Marczibányi Square Cultural Center). A well-known Transylvanian folk ensemble, Tatros, hosts a weekly dance house at the center, from 8 until midnight on Wednesday night. ✉ *District II, Marczibányi tér 5/a, Around Moszkva tér* ☎ *1/212–2820 or 1/212–5789* Ⓜ *Around Moszkva tér.*

Modern Dance

The systematic changes in Hungary since the early 1990s have created a hunger for contemporary dance. Today Hungarian dance companies have begun to take development into their own hands and are forming strategies for long-term survival. Finally given the room to flourish, modern-dance companies are thriving in Budapest and seeking out broader audiences throughout Hungary and abroad. Most of these companies perform at the National Dance Theater or Trafó House of Contemporary Arts.

The Artus Company. One of the most popular dance companies in Hungary, the Artus incorporates computers and video into dance performances. The company also began an "art laboratory" in the late 1990s, where 32 dancers, performers, choreographers, actors, costume designers, painters, sculptors, and architects work together on their projects in a 2,000-square-meter space. ☎ *204–3755* ⊕ *www.artus.hu.*

Compagnie Pál Frenák. Choreographer Pál Frenák, a Hungarian who studied and lived in France for many years, bases his company in both Budapest and Paris, and has performances in Budapest every year. ☎ *30/966–2464 (mobile)* ⊕ *www.ciefrenak.org.*

★ **Közép Europai Táncszínház** (Central European Dance Theater). This small, contemporary modern dance company incorporates traditional roots, rituals, and folklore into its performances, which are held four to five times monthly at its own theater. ✉ *District VII, Bethlen Gábor tér 3, Around Király utca* ☎ *1/342–7163* ⊕ *www.cedt.hu* Ⓜ *M2: Keleti.*

La Dance Company. A classically trained ballerina who performed with the Győr Ballet, the company's founder and choreographer, Andrea Ladányi, headed to Toronto, New York, and Los Angeles to train in modern dance. A former solo dancer for the Helsinki City Theater in Finland, Ladányi is one of Hungary's most acclaimed dancers. She founded La Dance in 1995, a small group of five dancers. ☎ *1/342–7163.*

Yvette Bozsik Company. After making a name for herself as a solo performer, Yvette Bozsik went on to perform her own choreographies and founded her own company in 1983. Based in the Katona József Theater (⇨ Theater), the company tours extensively throughout Europe, performing any number of the more than one dozen pieces Bozsik has choreographed for the troupe. ☎ *1/394–4386* ⊕ *www.ybozsik.hu.*

Classical Music

Budapest is a must-visit city for the classical music lover. Not only did Hungary produce Bartók, Kodály, and Liszt, but there are more than 20 active symphony orchestras just in Budapest. Hungarians are so deeply devoted in their love and appreciation of classical music that, aside from numerous top-notch music academies across the country, they put on a two-week Spring Festival each March.

Orchestras

The most noteworthy orchestras are the Budapest Festival Orchestra and Hungarian Radio Symphony. Most play at the Liszt Ferenc Music Academy, but for up-to-date information, pick up *Fidelio*, a free monthly booklet listing every classical music event available at ticket and Tourinform offices.

Fodor'sChoice **Budapest Festival Orchestra.** World-renowned conductor Iván Fischer, who
★ is still music director, formed the group with famed Hungarian conductor Zoltán Kocsis in 1983. The orchestra has won international accolades and is hands-down your best bet for classical music in Budapest. International soloists and conductors are often invited to perform with the orchestra. Its home base was previously Liszt Ferenc Music Academy, but since 2005 the orchestra has also performed regularly at the new Béla Bartók National Concert Hall in the Palace of the Arts. Tickets can be purchased online or at several locations around Budapest, including Ticket Express and the Liszt Ferenc Academy. ☒ *Budapest Festival Foundation, District XII, Alkotás utca 39/c, South Buda* ☎ *1/355–4015 or 1/489–4332* ⊕ *www.bfz.hu.*

Budapest Philharmonic Orchestra. The oldest Hungarian orchestra, the Budapest Philharmonic was founded in 1853 by Hungarian composer Ferenc Erkel. Its long and rich musical history and traditions have been formed by outstanding musicians including János Richter, Gustav Mahler, Johannes Brahms, Ernst von Dohnányi, and János Ferencsik. The Budapest Philharmonic is also famous for its first performances of works—some of them written originally for the orchestra—by Liszt, Brahms, Goldmark, Mahler, Bartók, Kodály, and Dohnányi. Tickets can be purchased at the Hungarian State Opera House. ☒ *Hajós utca 8–10, Around Andrássy út* ☎ *1/353–0170 or 1/332–7914* ⊕ *www.bpo.hu.*

Danube Symphony Orchestra. Founded in 1961, this orchestra consists of about 60 professional musicians. Their repertoire covers almost every musical style from the baroque to the 20th century. The orchestra performs at the Duna Palace. ☒ *Duna Palota, District V, Zrinyi utca 5, Parliament* ☎ *1/317–3142* Ⓜ *M2: Parliament.*

Hungarian National Philharmonic Orchestra. Formerly the Hungarian State Symphony Orchestra, it began performing in 1923. The orchestra, with 105 musicians, is currently directed by one of Hungary's most famous conductors, Zoltán Kocsis. The orchestra performs regularly at the Liszt Ferenc Music Academy, the National Concert Hall in the Palace of the Arts, the Budapest Convention Center, and sometimes in St. Stephen's Basilica. ☎ *1/411–6600* ⊕ *www.hunphilharmonic.org.hu.*

Hungarian Radio Symphony Orchestra. Considered one of the best in Europe and right up there with the Budapest Festival Orchestra, the Hungarian Radio Symphony—which was founded in 1943 and goes by the name "Budapest Symphony Orchestra" on its foreign labels—has been bestowed much praise from critics worldwide, especially for its Beethoven concert series. Also well known for playing and recording Hungarian contemporary music, the orchestra has toured 45 countries on four continents thus far. The orchestra regularly plays at the Liszt Ferenc Music Academy and the Budapest Convention Center. ☏ *1/328–8326.*

Hungarian Telecom Symphony Orchestra. With the appointment of András Ligeti as music director in 1997, the symphony took on a new artistic conception and extended its diversity to include contemporary pieces, oratorios, and even youth concerts. The orchestra plays mainly at the Liszt Ferenc Music Academy. The orchestra's ticket office sells a wide selection of performance tickets (*see* ⇨ Tickets, *above*). ✉ *District VI, Nagymező utca 19, Around Andrássy út* ☏ *1/302–3841* ⊕ *www. telekomzenekar.hu* Ⓜ *M1: Oktogon.*

Church Concerts

Several of Budapest's most famous churches host concerts by pianists, orchestras, and sometimes singers, mostly during the summer months from May to September, for an average 600 HUF entry fee. We highly recommend taking in an orchestra concert in the Gothic Mátyás Templom in the Castle District, as it overlooks the entire city and the Danube River.

Budai Capuchin Templom (Buda Capuchin Church). The Capuchin Church holds monthly concerts on the last Thursday of every month starting at 7:30 PM. ✉ *District 1, Fő utca 30–32, Around Batthyány tér* ☏ *No phone* Ⓜ *M2: Batthyány tér.*

Deák Tér Templom (Deák Square Church). In the Pest city center, the yellow Deák Church has organ music the first and last Sunday of the month in summer. The church dates back to 1809 and was used as a warehouse for military uniforms during World War II. It reopened in 2003 with a facelift inside and out after a years-long closure. ✉ *District V, Deák tér 4, Around Deák tér* ☏ *1/317–4173* Ⓜ *M1, M2, M3: Deák tér.*

★ **Mátyás Templom** (Matthias Church). The 13th-century Gothic chapel on Castle Hill is host to orchestra concerts every Saturday night from May through the end of September, usually starting at 8 PM. ✉ *District 1, Szentháromság tér 2, Castle Hill* ☏ *1/489–0717* ⊕ *www.matyastemplom.hu* Ⓜ *Around Moszkva tér.*

Szent Anna Templom (St. Anne's Church). The historic baroque church, which was built in 1761, hosts a Friday night organ concert series throughout the year. Performances start at 8 PM. ✉ *District I, Batthyány tér 7, Around Batthyány tér* ☏ *1/201–3404* Ⓜ *M2: Batthyány tér.*

Film

Budapest is a good destination for film-lovers. You'll find everything from shiny new multiplexes to a vast array of art-house theaters that continue to thrive. Hollywood, independent, foreign, low-budget, and Hungarian films can be seen around town any night of the week. With the notable exception of those films that are also screened in independent and art cinemas, most of the English-language blockbusters and children's movies that come to Budapest are dubbed into Hungarian rather than subtitled. Independent and art films, meanwhile, which are generally shown in smaller cinemas to begin with, are more often subtitled. ■ TIP→ Generally speaking, look for smaller cinemas if you want an English-language film to reach your ears in English. But always confirm this fine point before buying your tickets. Tickets are inexpensive by Western standards (about 600 HUF to 1,100 HUF). Consult the movie matrix in the *Budapest Sun* (⊕ www.budapestsun.com) or ⊕ www.xpatloop.com for a weekly list of what's showing.

Corvin Budapest Filmpalota. Inside a beautifully restored and historic building, the Corvin multiplex houses several theaters and is typically packed, showing Hollywood and foreign films as well as works from independent directors. The Corvin is also the site for the annual Hungarian Film Festival. ⊠ *District VIII, Corvin köz 1, Around Ferenc József körút* ☎ *1/459–5050* ⊕ *www.corvin.hu* Ⓜ *M3: Ferenc körút.*

★ **Művész.** One of the most popular art cinemas in Budapest is centrally located and shows independent and foreign films on five screens. There's also a CD and art-book shop in the foyer where you buy tickets. ⊠ *District VI, Teréz körút 30, Around Andrássy út* ☎ *1/459–5050* ⊕ *www.artmozi.hu* Ⓜ *M1: Oktogon.*

Palace Mammut. In addition to loveseats in some of the theaters, the Mammut has 10 large, modern movie screens, which mainly show Hollywood and other big-budget films in their original languages with Hungarian subtitles. ⊠ *District II, Lövöház utca 2–6, Around Moszkva tér* ☎ *1/999–6161* ⊕ *www.palacecinemas.hu* Ⓜ *M2: Moszkva tér.*

Palace WestEnd. The centrally located multiplex usually has several mainstream movies playing in their original languages with Hungarian subtitles. ⊠ *District VI, Váci út 1–3, Around Nyugati Train Station* ☎ *1/999–6161* ⊕ *www.palacecinemas.hu* Ⓜ *M3: Nyugati.*

★ **Uránia.** Hungary's national cinema, a showcase for Hungarian film, reopened after a major renovation in 2002. It is definitely worth a glimpse inside the beautifully restored Moorish interior. Aside from Hungarian films, the Uránia shows independent and foreign films, many of which are in English. ⊠ *District VIII, Rákóczi út 21, Around Blaha Lujza tér* ☎ *1/486–3413* ⊕ *www.urania-nf.hu* Ⓜ *M2: Blaha Lujza tér.*

Folklore Performances

Folklore performances involve a large group of dancers who stage a grand folk-dancing show, as opposed to more local, neighborhood folk dance groups. Folk performances are a tradition in Hungary dating back hundreds of years, and are always accompanied by Hungarian or gypsy folk music. If you have time, it is worth checking out one of the ensembles listed below, as performers dress in traditional outfits, the women in peasant dresses with bright colors and men in white blouses and brown knickers.

Budapest Dance Ensemble. The group has performed since 1958 with the aim of reviving national folk traditions and bringing them to the stage. The group performs at the National Theater, at the edge of the city. ⊠ *District I, Nemzeti Színház, Színház utca 19, Castle District* ☎ *1/201–4407* Ⓜ *Around Moszkva tér.*

Danube Folk Ensemble. Formed in 1957, the 30-member Danube dance troupe and 7-member folk orchestra aim for a certain artistic vision through its performances, combining music and theater. Aside from presenting its own repertoire, the ensemble participates in various theater productions, including musicals and rock operas. Like the Danube Symphony Orchestra, the ensemble performs at the Duna Palace. ⊠ *District V, Duna Palota, Zrínyi utca 5, Parliament* ☎ *1/235–5500* Ⓜ *M2: Parliament.*

Hungarian State Folk Ensemble. The 30-member ensemble, formed in 1951, performs at the Budai Vigadó. Choreography is based on authentic dances that date back hundreds of years. It's considered to be one of the top folk groups worldwide, having performed in 44 countries. The ensemble gives between 90 and 100 shows in Budapest annually at their venue. ⊠ *District 1, Budai Vigadó, Corvin tér 8, Around Batthyány tér* ☎ *1/201–3766* Ⓜ *Around Batthyány tér.*

Rajkó Folk Ensemble. This fiery group of 60 dancers uses both ballet and modern dance forms as well as combining folklore and operetta programs. They perform at the Budapest Bábszínház. ⊠ *District VI, Andrássy út 69, Around Andrássy út* ☎ *1/303–6505* Ⓜ *M1: Oktogon.*

Opera & Operetta

Belvárosi Színház. Centrally located on the Small Ring Boulevard right across from the main synagogue, the Central Theater has, since 2005, carried on the summertime tradition (formerly at the Pesti Vigadó) of hosting performances of classical Hungarian and Austrian operettas several times a week. As of this writing such entertainment can be had Tuesday, Wednesday, Thursday, and Saturday evenings. ⊠ *District VII, Károly körút 3/a, Around Astoria* ☎ *1/517–5067 or 1/266–7130* Ⓜ *M2: Astoria.*

Magyar Állami Operaház. The National Opera Company has a solid reputation among listeners, and the group sometimes performs at various outdoor stages and festivals during the summer, and can be heard almost nightly on several local classical radio stations. At the Opera House, the company has performed works from the likes of Bártok, Bellini, and Donizetti. The main season runs from September to mid-June, and includes about 50 major productions, including about five new opera premieres a year. The Hungarian State Opera House is one of Budapest's most famous landmarks. ⊠ *District VI, Andrássy út 22, Around Andrássy út* ☎ *1/353–0170* ⊕ *www.opera.hu* Ⓜ *M1: Opera.*

Operetta Theater. Colorful Hungarian-language operettas, such as those by Lehár and Kálmán, are performed here. The libretto is displayed above the stage in English- and German-language subtitles. ⊠ *District VI, Nagymező utca 17, Around Andrássy út* ☎ *1/269–3837* ⊕ *www. operettszinhaz.hu* Ⓜ *M1: Oktogon.*

Operetthajó (Operetta Ship). From March through October, soloists from the National Opera Company perform popular songs from operas, operettas, musicals, and more on a ship that sets out on a two-hour voyage—on Mondays, Wednesdays, Fridays, and Sundays—through nighttime Budapest (from 8 to 10 PM) from Vigadó tér. The price is 12,500 HUF including dinner, 8,500 HUF without dinner. ⊠ *District V, Vigadó tér, Around Váci utca* ☎ *06–20/332–9116 (mobile)* ⊕ *www.operetthajo. hu* Ⓜ *M1: Vörösmarty tér.*

Theater

Budapest's theater scene thrives from September to mid-August, with on-stage performances every night even in the remotest corner of the city. With nearly 100 small companies and theaters in Budapest alone, theater is one more important cornerstone of Hungarian art and culture.

Bárka Színház (Ark Theater). This company of actors, most of whom are in their early thirties, stage classics by Shakespeare and Chekhov, as well as Hungarian plays, all in Hungarian. ⊠ *Üllői út 82 Around Ferenc József körút* ☎ *1/303–6505* ⊕ *www.barka.hu* Ⓜ *M3: Ferenc körút.*

Ⓒ **Budapest Bábszínház** (Budapest Puppet Theater). These are colorful shows that both children and adults can enjoy, even if they don't understand Hungarian. Watch for showings of such timeless favorites as *The Wizard of Oz* (*Óz, a nagy varázsló*) and the Hungarian classic *John the Valiant* (*János Vitéz*), part of the theater's regular repertoire. ⊠ *District VI, Andrássy út 69, Around Andrássy út* ☎ *1/321–5200* ⊕ *www. budapest-babszinhaz.hu* Ⓜ *M1: Oktogon.*

Katona József Theater. Funded by the City of Budapest, the Katona stages three premieres each year, usually adaptations of foreign classics, which have included plays by Dostoyevsky, Orwell, and Kleist. In operation since 1982, the company also regularly tours Europe. ⊠ *District V, Petőfi Sándor utca 6, Around Ferenciek tere* ☎ *1/318–6599* ⊕ *www.szinhaz/ katona.hu* Ⓜ *M3: Ferenciek tere.*

Ⓒ **Kolibri Színház** (Hummingbird Theater). This children's theater company gives some 450 performances annually, including puppet shows, at its own theater. ⊠ *District VI, Jókai tér 10, Around Andrássy út* ☎ *1/353– 4633* ⊕ *kolibri.szinhaz.hu* Ⓜ *M1: Oktogon.*

Madách Theater. The Madách features a regular bill of Hungarian-language plays and musicals, including popular adaptations of *Cats, Fiddler on the Roof,* and *A Christmas Carol.* Beginning in 2002, the Madách added an English-language version of Andrew Lloyd Webber's *Phantom of the Opera,* which is the theater's only English-language production. ⊠ *District VII, Erzsébet körút 29–33, Around Király utca* ☎ *1/478–2041* ⊕ *www.madachszinhaz.hu* Ⓜ *M2: Blaha Lujza tér.*

Merlin International Theater. Budapest's only full-time English-language theater is situated in downtown Pest. Extremely popular not only with locals but also with the expat community since opening in 1990, the two-stage theater hosts both Hungarian and foreign actors. ⊠ *District V, Gerlóczy utca 4, Around Deák Ferenc tér* ☎ *1/317–9338* ⊕ *www. szinhaz.hu* Ⓜ *M1, M2, M3: Deák Ferenc tér.*

Pesti Színház (Pest Theater). The chamber theater, a subsidiary of the Vígszínház (Comedy Theater), has its own resident company and stages several plays and musicals in English each season. ⊠ *District V, Váci utca 9, Around Váci utca* ☎ *1/266–5557* Ⓜ *M3: Ferenciek tere.*

Radnóti Színház (Radnóti Theater). This theater's company is a more literary stage, which aims to introduce works of Hungarian literature, including contemporary writers and poets. The company unveils four premieres each season. ✉ *District VI, Nagymező utca 11, Around Andrássy út* ☎ *1/321–0600* ⊕ *www.radnotiszinhaz.hu* Ⓜ *M1: Oktogon.*
Vidám Színpad (Comedy Stage). This small, yet popular, back-alley comedy theater occasionally puts on shows in English. ✉ *District VI, Révay utca 18, Around Andrássy út* ☎ *1/301–2060* ⊕ *www.vidamszinpad.hu* Ⓜ *M1: Opera.*

4

Thermal Spas & Sports

WORD OF MOUTH

"While the Gellért baths are prettier and older, I prefer the Széchenyi. They are much more modern, and the water was hotter."

—L84SKY

"The Széchenyi is historic, too, though—a splendid Beaux Arts pavilion from around 1900. Great setting in the main city park."

—tedgale

"The Lukács is [also] worth visiting. It is rather modest in comparison to the Széchenyi, but it has the best thermal (healing) water in Budapest. That is why it is the most popular among the locals. The Gellért is a bit rundown and nowadays it is mostly an overpriced tourist attraction."

—okszi

By Paul
Olchváry

WITH MORE THAN 100 THERMAL SPRINGS bubbling up alongside the Danube River, Budapest is one of Europe's oldest spa destinations. The Romans were the first to develop public baths in Budapest at the site of Aquincum, which they called Ak-Ink, meaning plentiful water. Bathing culture really took root though during the Turkish occupation (1541–1686), when the Ottomans built large spa complexes like the Király, Rudás, and Rác (the Rác is under renovation at this writing) in traditional Turkish style. These baths today are among the most important Ottoman ruins in Budapest.

In 1891 the Hungarian Balneological Society discovered the benefits of Budapest's mineral water and began to develop medicinal water treatments, further advancing bathing culture. The turn of the 20th century saw the building of grand thermal baths, including the Lukács, Széchenyi, and Gellért baths in beautiful Secessionist style. Budapest enjoyed yet another bathing heyday in the 1930s, when these baths were considered among the most fashionable in Europe.

Thermal baths remain a popular and egalitarian Hungarian institution, and taking the waters in Budapest is an activity not to be missed. In 2006 the Hungarian Government earmarked 7 billion HUF for the restoration of several baths, including the Gellért, the Széchenyi, and the Lukács by late 2008. Even in the depth of winter, spending an afternoon chin-deep in 36°C (97°F) water certainly will get the Central European chill out of one's bones. And sitting in a lounge chair amid Art Nouveau fountains at one of the outdoor thermal complexes in the summer is a pleasant way to cool off and also experience a bit of history. In any season, a soak in the thermal waters will leave you feeling relaxed and refreshed, ready for a big plate of *borjúpaprikás* (veal paprikash) and a nap.

The Turkish-era baths are the oldest and most atmospheric, with ancient domed cupolas positioned over a collection of small steaming pools of water. The grand complexes of Lukács, Gellért, and Széchenyi all have both indoor thermal baths and outdoor swimming pools and grounds for sitting and relaxing. Although Budapest's modern wellness hotels don't have the most character, they deliver the most luxurious day of spa-going, with thermal baths and swimming pools plus all the services—including massages, mud baths, and pedicures—of a well-staffed spa hotel.

PAUL'S TOP 5

Széchenyi Gyógyfürdő. This indoor and outdoor thermal bath complex has that glorious Old World feel.

Rudas Gyógyfürdő. This has been a favorite spot for Budapest men since the 16th century.

Royal Spa. Opened in July 2006 as part of the Corinthia Grand Hotel Royal, this compact spa brings to life the splendor of one that existed here in 1886.

Mandala Day Spa. There's so much here to relax you in this oasis of calm.

Csillaghegy. Budapest's loveliest outdoor swimming complex—several pools set on a tranquil forested hillside.

THERMAL BATHS

At this writing, the Rác was closed for substantial renovations, with its reopening by 2007 questionable. The Rudás baths, meanwhile, not only reopened in 2005 after thorough renovation but now offer women-only days as well as coed weekends and two coed all-nighters.

Fodor'sChoice **Király Gyógyfürdő** (Király Baths). The Király baths don't have their own
★ source of thermal water, but they are the oldest in Budapest. The Turks built them here in 1565 inside the city walls and piped the water to this location so that in case of a siege they would still be able to enjoy a good bath. Although they do show their age, you still get a feeling of the Orient in these baths, perhaps Budapest's most atmospheric. Men and women bathe on separate days in small pools underneath the Turkish cupola. Men get Tuesday, Thursday, and Saturday; women, Monday, Wednesday, and Friday. Though long popular with gay men on men's days, in 2005 an enterprising Hungarian TV reporter secretly filmed men engaging in unbecoming behavior; which led the Király to the drastic step of requiring swimming suits on all days, for men and women alike. Note also that a ticket here allows 1½ hours of thermal bathing on weekdays and 1 hour on weekends. ⊠ *District II, Fő utca 84, Lower Buda* ☎ *1/202–3688* ⊕ *www.spasbudapest.com* ⊠ *1,100 HUF* ⊙ *Mon., Wed., Fri. 7–6 for women only; Tues., Thurs., Sat. 9–8 for men only.*

Lukács Gyógyfürdő (Lukács Baths). These thermal baths are popular with aging Hungarian film stars, who can be found lolling around the leafy outdoor mixed-sex pools on weekday afternoons. There's a full range of thermal baths in various temperatures here, with two swimming pools and lounge chairs to rest and recover in. White-coated medical attendants administering treatments to pensioners give the place a somewhat clinical feel. In addition to soaking, you can drink the mineral water, which is especially recommended for gastroenterological disorders. ⊠ *District II, Frankel Leó utca 25–29, Lower Buda* ☎ *1/326–1695* ⊕ *www.spasbudapest.com* ⊠ *1,500 HUF (partial refunds if you leave within 3 hours)* ⊙ *Weekdays 6–7, weekends 6–5.*

Rudas Gyógyfürdő (Rudas Baths). The thermal baths at the Rudas have been a favorite spot for Budapest men since the 16th century, when the Turks restored themselves and made their daily ablution along the marble floors. And now, reopened in 2005 after lengthy restoration, women are welcome, too—one day a week without males present, and on coed weekends and two nights. The central octagonal pool catches the light from the glass-tiled cupola and casts it around the surrounding six pools, capturing the feeling of an ancient Turkish *hammam*. ⊠ *District I, Döbrentei tér 9, Gellért Hegy* ☎ *1/356–1322* ⊕ *www.spasbudapest. com* ⊠ *2,000 HUF (partial refunds on single-gender days if you leave within 3 hours)* ⊙ *Men only Mon., Wed., and Fri. 6–8; women only Tues. 6–8; coed weekends 8–5 and Fri. & Sat. 10 PM–4 AM.*

Fodor'sChoice **Széchenyi Gyógyfürdő** (Széchenyi Baths). Over 2 million visitors to Bu-
★ dapest have taken the waters at this glorious indoor and outdoor thermal bath complex, one of Europe's largest. The turn-of-the-20th-century baths in the heart of City Park have that Old World feel, with yellow-

KNOW HOW

ARRIVING

The entrance procedure to *gyógyfürdők* (thermal baths) in Budapest can be baffling to visitors. Some baths post prices and treatments in English, but it remains unclear what kind of ticket you need and what you're actually getting. Sadly, in most of the state-run baths there's not much help from the staff. Much of the information on the price list pertains to medical treatments offered at the spa for patients with prescriptions from their doctors. There's also a lengthy explanation of the refund policy, which entitles you to a refund of the ticket price if you stay no more than around three hours. In general, buy a *belépő jegy* (entrance ticket), then choose a locker or cabin (cabins are slightly more expensive). An entrance ticket allows you to use both the thermal baths and the swimming pools. Most places issue small bits of paper as tickets. Hold on to these because you'll need them for the refund you can receive at the cashier's desk upon leaving.

GETTING READY

Once you've paid, follow the directions to the locker room, where you will change. Once you have changed into your swimsuit—or disrobed completely if you're in a single-sex spa—a locker attendant will lock your cabin and give you a key. You might have to go looking for him or her, so keep an eye on your belongings meanwhile. Make sure to tie this key around your wrist or attach it to your swimsuit. With the exception of the Király, where swimsuits are now required all the time, in the single-sex places you'll be given a sheet, or a cotton frock of some kind to wear when you walk between the locker room and the thermal bath. Signs posted in all thermal baths instruct you to shower before entering the water.

WHAT TO BRING

As a rule, bring shower shoes to all thermal baths and a towel to all but the big wellness hotels. Swimsuits are required in mixed company (at wellness hotels; at the Lukács, the Rudas, and the Széchenyi thermal baths; and at the swimming pool at the Gellért), and a bathing cap is required in most swimming pools.

■ TIP➔ **Keep some small change (100 HUF–200 HUF) with you to tip locker attendants on your way out and in case you want a beverage in between soaks (another 200 HUF–400 HUF).** Check all your other valuables in a safe, which you can ask for when you buy your ticket. It's useful to bring your own shampoo, body lotion, and a comb for showering afterward, but most thermal baths have hair dryers.

HEALTH SPAS

Visits to hotel wellness centers are more straightforward, and you will often find a cheerful, English-speaking receptionist who can guide you on the treatments offered. Most hotels accept credit cards as well. In general, wellness hotels in Hungary feel more like medical facilities—with spotless, somewhat clinical interiors—than the soft-lighted spas in the United States. There's no water-dripping music or incense burning, and the staff works in white coats. The treatments are first-rate, though, and guaranteed to bring an overall sense of relaxation and well-being.

5

and-white Secessionist-style architecture, beautiful grounds, and lots of fountains and loggias. There are a big swimming pool and two thermal baths outside, plus thermal pools, a cold shock pool, and the hottest steam room in Budapest on the inside. On any given day, you will find wizened Hungarian men playing chess in one of the steaming thermal outdoor baths, which open all winter. ✉ *District XVI, Állatkerti körút 11, City Park* ☎ *1/363–3210* ⊕ *www.spasbudapest.com* ✆ *2,000 HUF (partial refunds if you leave within 3 hours, and discounted admission beginning 3 hours before closing)* ⊙ *Weekdays 6 AM–10 PM (smaller thermal pools close by 7 PM or earlier).*

★ **Szent Gellért Gyógyfürdő** (Saint Gellért Baths). Budapest's most famous thermal baths were built in 1918 as part of the grand Gellért Hotel. They have long been a favorite in the city for their architectural beauty as well as their innovative outdoor wave pool, which was added in 1927 and is immensely popular to this day. The elegant Art Nouveau complex includes separate men's and women's thermal baths, mixed indoor and outdoor swimming pools, steam rooms, and saunas. There's a full range of treatments available here, including a well-established Thai massage center. Due to its popularity, these are probably the most crowded baths in Budapest, especially on summer weekends. ✉ *District XI, Kelenhegyi út 4, Gellért-hegy and Tabán* ☎ *1/466–6166* ⊕ *www.spasbudapest. com* ✆ *2,500 (partial refunds if you leave within 3 hours) HUF* ⊙ *Oct.–Apr., weekdays 7 AM–7 PM, weekends 7–5; May–Sept., daily 6–7.*

Spas & Wellness Hotels

Aphrodite Spa. Families flock to this luxury hotel wellness center on winter weekends for its thermal baths and swimming pool plus a pleasant seating area serving healthy meals all day. The layout provides spacious resting areas and comfortable lounge chairs nicely set apart, so it never feels too crowded here. The big swimming pool keeps the kids happy, and there's a full range of wellness treatments for adults (at extra charges), including several types of massage, a Dead Sea salt bath, and aromatherapy treatments. In addition, there are infrared saunas, steam rooms, a Thalaxion bath, a Jacuzzi, and a solarium. ✉ *District III, Corinthia Aquincum Hotel, Árpád fejedelem útja 94, Óbuda* ☎ *1/436–4130* ⊕ *www.corinthiahotels.hu* ✆ *Weekdays, 2,500 HUF for morning session (6:30–10), 4,100 for the day; weekends and holidays, 4,900 HUF for the day* ⊙ *Daily 6:30 AM–10 PM.*

FodorśChoice **Danubius Thermal & Conference Hotel Helia.** There's an exhaustive well-
★ ness program available at this spotless hotel not far from the Danube, and you don't need to be a guest to enjoy it. Aside from the thermal baths, sauna, steam room, and 17-meter swimming pool, there are seven kinds of massage, hydrotherapy, electrotherapy, and mud treatments, plus on-site medical check-ups available as well, making this one of the most full-service places in town to take in the waters. The resident pedicurist has a loyal local clientele. There's also a fitness room with daily aerobics classes. ✉ *District XIII, Kárpát utca 62–64, Duna Plaza* ☎ *1/889–5800* ⊕ *www.danubiushotels.com* ✆ *Weekdays, 3,700 HUF for morning session (7–3), 4,700 HUF for afternoon session (3–10); weekends, 5,200 HUF for the day* ⊙ *Daily 7 AM–10 PM.*

Spa Smarts

HERE ARE SOME common terms you will see on signs in thermal spas and wellness hotels throughout Hungary.

Caldarium. A hot-water tub or tiled room of 40°C–50°C (104°F–122°F).

Értékmegőrző. Safe-deposit box. (⇨ Páncélszekrény.)

Gőzfürdő. Steam room.

Gyógyfürdő. Any thermal bath that has naturally occurring water above 30°C (86°F). Most thermal baths contain minerals, which are listed at the entrance to the bath.

Hőlégfürdő. Sauna.

Iszapfürdő. Mud bath.

Kezelés. Treatment.

Kleopátra Fürdő. Cleopatra Bath. A bath of milk and essential oils, known to be a moisturizing skin treatment.

Kneipp cure. This body of treatments is based on the theories of Sebastian Kneipp, a German priest who believed in the importance of water and herbs in treating stress and exhaustion. Treatments are designed for the individual based on a medical exam and are offered at most wellness hotels. An average treatment uses alternating hot and cold stimuli to increase blood circulation, followed by wrapping the body in herb infusions.

Laconium. A dry sauna of 55°C.

Masszázs. Massage. In general, massages are performed with light aromatic oil. Some, such as Thai massage, are performed with no oil.

Medence. Pool or basin—generally a thermal pool rather than a swimming pool (see *Uszómedence*).

Nyirokcsomó kezelés. Lymph drainage. This treatment restores balance to the lymph system and rids the body of accumulated toxins.

Öltöző. Changing room.

Páncélszekrény. Literally "safe," but in this context refers simply to a safe-deposit box. (See also *Értékmegőrző.*)

Szakorvosi vizsgálatok. Medical examination, which is required for some treatments.

Száraz kefe masszázs. Dry brush massage. This massage is performed with a soft bristle brush. It helps exfoliate the skin and increase blood circulation.

Szekrény. Locker.

Thalasso. This general term refers to any treatment using seaweed or sea algae, known to help combat cellulite.

Uszoda. Swimming (pool) facility (with one or more pools).

Uszómedence. Swimming pool.

Víz alatti masszázs. Underwater massage. This massage is performed under jets of cold and warm water treating specific body parts.

Danubius Thermal Hotel Margit-sziget. The location of this spa hotel couldn't be better for relaxation. It's at the northern end of Margaret Island, nestled among leafy walking paths and flower gardens and far away from the noise of downtown Pest. The full-service wellness hotel offers thermal baths and swimming pools plus all the things you need for a complete rehabilitation, including a fitness center, dentistry clinic, and cosmetic surgery department. The Thermal is connected by a passageway to the Danubius Grand Hotel, a slightly more elegant hotel in a historic building. ⊠ *District XIII, Margit-sziget, Margaret Island* ☎ *1/889–4700* ⊕ *www.danubiushotels.com* ☝ *Weekdays 5,500 HUF, weekends 6,700 HUF* ⊙ *6:30 AM–9:30 PM.*

FodorśChoice **Mandala Day Spa.** There are no thermal waters to take in at this day spa, but you'll find plenty here to relax you in this oasis of calm housed in an apartment complex in the 13th District. An attentive staff guides you to a service that's best for you and then hands you a fluffy robe and sends you inside for some herbal tea while you await your treatment. There's an Indonesian theme here, with soothing music, neutral-colored tiles, and plenty of comfortable rattan lounging chairs. Massages and mud baths are given in luxurious treatment rooms, and cosmetic treatments use high-end Clarins products. Count on spending at least 10,000 HUF for every hour you're there; the various treatments range from around one to three hours. ⊠ *District XIII, Ipoly utca 8 (in Kleopátra Ház), Duna Plaza* ☎ *1/801–2566* ⊕ *www.mandaladayspa.hu* ⊙ *weekdays 10–10, Sat. 10–10, Sun. 10–6.*

★ **Royal Spa.** Opened in July 2006 as part of the Corinthia Grand Hotel Royal, this compact but captivating spa is a worthy successor to one that existed here from 1886 to 1944. Not only do you get much of the original architectural splendor, but also a 15-meter swimming pool, saunas, a steam room, Jacuzzis, eight massage salons, treatment facilities, and, yes, tropical showers. The Royal Spa uses seaweed- and other marine-based products from the noted French spa firm Algotherm. As of this writing, precise fees for nonguests of the hotel had yet to be determined, but a clerk estimated that it may be as much as 10,000 HUF per day. ⊠ *District VII, Erzsébet körút 43–49, Around Blaha Lujza tér, H-1073* ☎ *1/479–4650* ⊕ *www.corinthiahotels.com* ⊙ *Daily 6:30 AM–10 PM.*

SPORTS & THE OUTDOORS

Bicycling

Biking is a popular sport in Hungary, and Budapest has several places where you can rent the newest models.

Bringóhintó. This rental outfit on Margaret Island offers popular four-wheel pedaled contraptions called *bringóhintók*, as well as traditional two-wheelers; standard bikes cost about 590 HUF per half-hour or 900 HUF an hour. Bikes can be rented overnight with a 10,000 HUF deposit. ⊠ *District VIII, Hajós Alfréd sétány 1, across from Thermal Hotel, Margaret Island* ☎ *1/329–2073* ⊕ *www.bringohinto.hu.*

Magyar Kerékpáros Túrázók Szövetsége (Bicycle Touring Association of Hungary). The organization can give you brochures and general information on bicycling conditions and suggested routes. ⊠ *District V, Bajcsy-Zsilinszky út 31, 2nd floor, Apt. 3* ☎ *1/311–2467* ⊕ *www.mktsz.hu.*

Yellow Zebra Bikes. The company with two central locations just a few blocks apart offers bike tours of Budapest as well as bike rentals. Bicycle rental prices are 1,500 HUF for 1–5 hours, 2,500 HUF for 5+ hours (return the same day), and 3,500 HUF for 24 hours. What is more, the shop behind the Opera House also provides space for Budapest's only Segway tours operation: for 12,000 HUF you get 30–45 minutes of training plus a roughly 2-hour tour of downtown; tours usually 10 AM and 6:30 PM, but call beforehand to confirm. ⊠ *District V, Sütő utca 2, Around Deák Ferenc tér* ☎ *1/266–8777* ⊠ *District VI, behind the Opera House Lázár utca 16, Around Deák Ferenc tér* ☎ *1/269–3843* ⊕ *www.yellowzebrabikes.com.*

Golf

Golf is a growing sport in Hungary, and the country now has several first-class courses, a couple of which are reasonably close to Budapest.

Golftanya. True, all you get at the Golf Farm is a driving range, but then again, it's a hop, skip, or a (short) drive from downtown, on the southern end of Óbudai-sziget (Óbuda Island), also called Hajógyári-sziget. The range is visible on your right along the island's shore between the two bridges that provide access to the island from Buda. For 1,500 HUF you get 48 balls and your choice of 70 clubs. ⊠ *Hajógyári-sziget 410, Budapest* ☎ *1/437–9038.*

Old Lake Golf & Country Club. About 40 km (25 mi) from Budapest, this course is built on the grounds of an estate once owned by Count Ezsterházy. The course is well kept, and there's a par-3 executive course as well as driving range. The golf course is attached to a hotel, which has a swimming pool and tennis courts. ⊠ *Remeteségpuszta, Tata* ☎ *34/587–620* ⊕ *www.oldlakegolf.com* ▣ *Weekdays, 7,000 HUF for 9 holes, 9,000 HUF for 18 holes, 3,500 HUF for the par-3; weekends, 10,000 HUF for 9 holes (from 4:30 PM only), 14,500 HUF for 18 holes, 4,500 HUF for the par-3.*

★ **Pannonia Golf & Country Club.** This Austrian-owned, semiprivate club is also about 40 km (25 mi) outside of Budapest in the direction of Vienna. A top-class 18-hole golf course, the greens are hard and well manicured. The club has excellent practice facilities, including a driving range and chipping range. The policy is to accept golfers with a minimum 36 handicap. ⊠ *Alcsútdoboz, Máriavölgy* ☎ *22/594–200* ⊕ *www.pannoniagolf.hu* ▣ *Weekdays, 8,000 HUF for 9 holes, 13,500 HUF for 18 holes; weekends, 11,200 HUF for 9 holes, 18,000 HUF for 18 holes.*

Horseback Riding

English saddle, not Western, is the standard in Hungary.

Budapesti Lovas Klub (Budapest Equestrian Club). Experienced riders can ride at the club for about 2,500 HUF per hour. Call about two weeks ahead to assure yourself a horse. ⊠ *District VIII, Kerepesi út 7, Városliget* ☎ *1/313–5210.*

⚲ **Petneházy Lovas Centrum** (Petneházy Equestrian Center). In the verdant outskirts of Buda, the club offers pony rides to kids at 2,000 HUF for 15 minutes. ⊠ *District II, Feketefej út 2, Adyliget* ☎ *1/397–5048.*

Swimming

Hungarians are enthusiastic about water sports, and there's no shortage of swimming pools in Budapest. Most pools require swim caps.

★ **Csillaghegyi Strand.** Set on a lovely, verdant hillside with two big pools and one children's pool, Budapest's most captivating swimming complex can be yours for a 20-minute HÉV (commuter train) ride from Batthány tér plus a short walk from there. A short walk uphill along a path—past the pools and through some pretty woods—will get you to a large, open-air naturist sunbathing area; swimsuits are required down below and in the pools. A daily ticket costs 1,000 HUF. Open 9–7 daily, May–September. To get here, take the HÉV to the Csillaghegy stop, cross the tracks to your left, go back a bit on the other side, and then walk a couple of minutes down Fürdő utca, at the end of which the complex will be visible across Pusztakúti út. ⊠ *District III, Pusztakúti út 3* ☎ *1/250–1533.*

Hajós Alfréd Nemzeti Sportuszoda. Margaret Island is home to the national swimming pool, which is named after the celebrated Hungarian swimming champ. The walls here testify to Hungarian prowess in the pool, with the names of Olympians etched in the walls. There are two outdoor pools with sunbathing terrace and one indoor pool. The national water polo team practices here. A daily ticket costs 800 HUF. ⊠ *District XIII, Margit-sziget, Margaret Island* ☎ *1/311–4046.*

Palatinus Strand. On summer days you'll find half the city frolicking at the giant swimming complex on Margaret Island, drinking beer, eating hot dogs, and dipping into one of the seven swimming pools. It's a huge complex but it can get crowded. Entrance is 1,500 HUF, and you can rent everything, including swimsuits, towels, and swimcaps. ⊠ *District XIII, Margit-sziget, Margaret Island* ☎ *1/312–3069.*

Tennis & Squash

There are some 30 tennis clubs in Budapest, and some hotels also rent courts out to nonguests.

Hungarian Tennis Association. For those who can't travel without playing, the association produces a yearbook with a complete list of the country clubs with courts in Hungary. ⊠ *District XIV, Istvánmezei út 1–3* ☎ *1/460–6807.*

Rózsadomb Squash Club. Hourly rates at this facility on the 5th floor of the Rózsadomb Center shopping mall—accessible by car or bus in about 10 minutes from Moszkva tér in Buda—run from 2,100 HUF to 2,600 HUF weekdays during the day and 4,200 HUF weekdays after 5 PM; and 2,700 HUF on weekends. The club rents equipment and stays open until 1 AM on weekdays and midnight on weekends. ⊠ *Törökvész út 87, Around Moszkva tér* ☎ *1/345–8490.*

Városmajor Tennis Academy. The club has five outdoor courts (clay and hexapet) available weekdays from 7 AM to 10 PM, Saturdays 7 AM to 7 PM, and Sundays 8 AM to 7 PM. They are lit for night play and covered by a tent in winter. Court fees run around 2,500 HUF per hour in summer, 2,700 HUF to 4,400 HUF per hour in winter. Racket rentals and lessons are also offered. ⊠ *District VII, Városmajor utca 63–69, Around Moszkva tér* ☎ *1/202–5337.*

World Class Fitness Center. The health club has one excellent squash court available for 2,500 HUF an hour; be sure to reserve it a day or two in advance. ⊠ *District V, Marriott Hotel, Apáczai Csere János utca 4, Around Váci utca* ☎ *1/266–4290.*

Shopping

WORD OF MOUTH

"As a tour guide and a big lover and collector of antiques I can reassure you, you will find zillions of antiques at the Ecseri flea market. The market is open all year round, every single day, even on Sundays. Absolutely the best day to go there is Saturday, early in the morning before the tourist crowds. As for the City Market near the Freedom Bridge, well it definitely has a gorgeous architectural look and is worth visiting in terms of a sightseeing spot and stockpiling some food. Otherwise it is a REAL Tourist Trap. Most of the quite expensive souvenirs are imported."

–Bela

By Betsy
Maury

STRICTLY SPEAKING, BUDAPEST IS NOT A SHOPPING TOWN. There are interesting things to buy, of course, but a weekend in Budapest doesn't promise the same shopping thrill that, say, a weekend in Istanbul or Paris does. Major European and American retailers have outposts here and show the latest fashions, but prices are generally about the same as anywhere else in Europe and the selections can be limited.

That said, a day of shopping can have rich rewards in Budapest, and you can leave the city with uniquely Hungarian treats if you look beyond the big high-street shops. In general, folk arts are high quality and traditional crafts are well done. The antiques shops clustered around Falk Miksa utca will provide an enjoyable half-day browse even though bargains are long gone for the most part. Interesting and reasonable bric-a-brac can be found in nearly all of Budapest's antiques shops and markets. Ever-changing Váci utca is worth a stroll as well for its vibrant downtown feel; there's a good mix of older shops and trendy new ones. Some of the big foreign fashion houses like Max Mara, Zara, Furla, and Hugo Boss are in this neighborhood.

Meandering around District V can delight with unusual treasures, too, and perhaps the best shopping can be done in Pest's side streets and *udvars* (passages). In a nutshell, there are two types of shops to look for in Budapest: older shops selling classic goods such as leather gloves, woolen hats, wooden toys, and antique silver, and newer shops run by artistic upstarts selling their own designs. Often, both kinds of shops are really unique. The areas around Király utca and Ferenciek tere are dotted with stylish design shops. The streets off Váci utca, toward Petőfi Sándor are good places to poke around in for both old-style shops and ateliers. Andrássy út—perhaps Budapest's most beautiful shopping boulevard—is a must for strolling in any case, and serious shoppers will certainly enjoy the many upscale furniture and housewares shops lining the street between Oktogon and Deák Ferenc tér.

> **BETSY'S TOP 5**
>
> **Nadortex** for the warmest, fluffiest, most lightweight goose-down duvets.
> **Feyérzsuzsa** for unique, affordable gifts like evening bags and change purses.
> **Magma** for linen and silk placemats and table runners.
> **Ékes** or **Balogh Kesztyű** for sturdy, beautiful leather gloves.
> **BomoArt** for a leather-bound travel diary.

Shops are generally open until 5 or 6 on weekdays and 1 on Saturdays (only shops in the malls are open on Sundays, for the most part).

Major Shopping Districts

You'll find plenty of expensive boutiques, folk-art and souvenir shops, foreign-language bookstores, and high-end foreign fashion shops on or around touristy **Váci utca**, Budapest's famous, pedestrian-only promenade in District V. Some of the most interesting shops though, are tucked away on the side streets between Váci and **Petőfi Sandor utca.**

CLOSE UP

Budapest Blitz Tour

BEGIN THE DAY IN BUDAPEST bright and early by going to the **Vásárcsárnok,** which is at its liveliest in the morning. Admire the building itself, but then stock up on paprika, salami, or tinned goose liver at one of the stalls downstairs. While upstairs, enjoy a coffee and lángos (fried dough with cheese and sour cream) at one of the *büfé* stands to fortify you for a full day of shopping. Then head north by walking on **Váci utca.** You'll pass **Manier, V-50 Design Art Studio,** and **Folkart Centrum.** Turn right on Irányi utca before you reach the underpass (you'll see the Erzsébet bridge to your left), and check out the whimsical designs at **Naray Tamás** before circling back towards Váci on Kigyó utca, where you'll pass a branch of **Herend.**

Once back on Váci, crisscross between there and Petőfi Sándor utca for the next few blocks and you'll come across the highly recommended design emporium **Magma,** leather-glove shop **Balogh Kesztyű,** bespoke shoe shop **Vass,** jewelry designer **Varga Design,** and the stationer **BomoArt.** Finish off your morning in the Váci utca area by having a coffee and light sandwich at **Gerbeaud.** From this point, you have two options. For antiques, head north to the largest concentration of antiques shops in the city, or if you want to look at a wider variety of stores, head off on foot to the Király utca neighborhood. Either way, you'll end up in the major square Deák Ferenc tér.

If you choose antiques, go north by Tram No. 2 or 2A from Eötvös tér (near the Danube in front of the Hotel InterContinental) toward Falk Miksa utca, get off on Szalay utca, and walk north to the antiques district. You'll pass **Pintér Antik Diskont, Studio Agram, Anna Antikvitás,** and **Nagyházi Galéria,** as well as the interesting **Wladis Galéria és Műterem** jewelry shop. Once you reach St. István Körút, turn right until you get to Nyugati Pályaudvar. To the left is **West End City Center** if you're up for more shopping. Otherwise, take the metro Line 3 back to centrally located Deák Ferenc tér.

The other option is to walk through József Nádor tér and turn right onto József Attila utca, where you'll pass another branch of **Herend, Nádortex,** and **Ajka Kristály.** Continue east on Jozsef Atilla, cross Bajcsy-Zsilinsky út, and begin walking up lovely Andrássy út. Before long you'll pass the high-end shoe shop **La Boutique.** Walk as far as Liszt Ferenc tér, turn right, and then turn right again on Paulay Ede utca. Work your way back towards Deák Ferenc tér on Paulay Ede. Along the way you'll find **Brinkus Design.** Cross over to Király utca on Nagymező and stroll down one of Budapest's most interesting shopping streets. Here you'll find housewares at **Goa Home,** groovy goods at **ÉK,** women's clothing at **Siptár,** and flowers at **Arioso.** Király utca ends at Deák Ferenc tér.

6

Inner Pest
Shopping

0   250 yards

0   250 meters

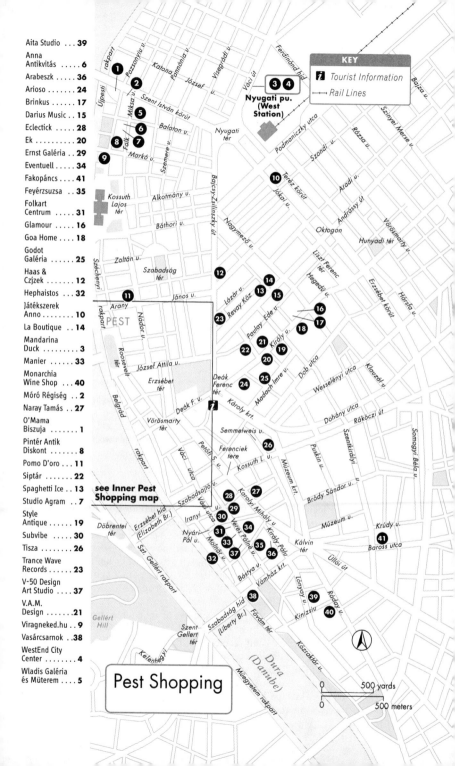

KEY

𝐢 Tourist Information

⊢—⊣ Rail Lines

Nyugati pu.
(West
Station)

see Inner Pest
Shopping map

Pest Shopping

0 ___ 500 yards
0 ___ 500 meters

Although a stroll along Váci utca is integral to a Budapest visit, browsing among some of the smaller, less touristy, more typically Hungarian shops in Pest—on the **Kis körút** (Small Ring Road) and **Nagy körút** (Large Ring Road)—may prove more interesting and less pricey.

Budapest's luxury boulevard, **Andrássy ut,** which runs from Ferenc Deák tér to Heroes Square, is lined with many high-end furniture stores. Interior design and housewares shops have sprung up in the section of District VI around **Király utca.** In District V the areas **toward the Danube** and around **Kálvin tér** are good places to wander for unique, arty boutiques. **Falk Miksa utca,** also in District V, running south from Szent István körút, is one of the city's best antiques districts, lined on both sides with charming little shops and galleries.

Department Stores & Malls

Shopping malls are popular in Budapest. Winter weekends find many Hungarian families happily strolling the corridors of most Budapest malls, shopping, browsing, eating, and going to the movies. It's cold outside, after all. Although there are other downtown shopping areas, big branch stores of upscale chains are in just about every mall. If you're looking for a specific item, heading to a mall like West End City Center, which has nearly 400 shops, is a good way to maximize your effort.

Mammut. This cornerstone of Buda shopping, near Moszkva tér, is popular with young Hungarian women for its high-fashion shops. On the first floor alone there are trendy Mexx and Promod, and preppy Jackpot & Cottonfield. Shoes are easy to find here as well, since there are over 10 shoe stores. The mall is referred to as Mammut 1 and Mammut 2, the older section having a sports club and the newer one a multiplex. Although each section of the mall is relatively small, high-quality shops are the norm. A good fruit and vegetable market (known as the Fény utca piac) sets up behind the mall every morning except Sunday, selling top-notch produce. The mall is on the 4 and 6 tram lines. It is open from 10 to 9 Monday through Saturday, until 6 on Sunday. ⊠ *District II, Lövőház 2, Around Moszkva tér* ☎ *1/345–8020* Ⓜ *M2: Moszkva tér.*

> ## CHRISTMAS IN JULY
>
> Even if you visit Budapest in the heat of summer, visit one of the folk-art shops and take a look at the handmade Christmas ornaments. There are beautiful felt appliqué Wise Men, angels made of walnut shells, and hand-painted red and green wooden eggs with traditional motifs.

★ **Mom Park.** Spacious corridors and lots of light appeal to shoppers at this modern mall in affluent District XII. You'll find the overall shopping mood here remarkably relaxed. Goa Home is here, selling Asian-inspired furniture and home accessories. There are high-end children's clothing stores, including the only outlet in Budapest of French favorite Jacadi. Locals flock to the Paulaner Brauhaus after the movies for hearty German fare in a fun-loving Bavarian setting. The nine-screen cinema at the top is home to Budapest's only digital cinema. Tram 61 stops right in front of the mall. ✉ *District XII, Alkotás út 53, Around Déli Train Station* ☏ *1/487–5501.*

West End City Center. Central Europe's largest shopping mall is home to many luxury retailers, including Italian handbag maker Mandarina Duck, Austrian lingerie purveyor Palmer, high-end watchmaker Orex, and fashion-forward but relatively low-priced Mango (in the same league as Zara). There's a good offering of sports apparel here as well, with Nike, Champion, Puma, Adidas, and Quicksilver shops. The mall's roof is thoughtfully landscaped with benches and paths, providing welcome relief from the sometimes teeming floors below. The 14-screen cinema on the top floor is abuzz with activity most nights, with popular restaurants and bars right beside the box office. In addition to the metro, the mall is served by the 4 and 6 trams. It is open until 11 PM nightly. ✉ *District VI, Váci út 1–3, Around Nyugati Train Station* ☏ *1/238–7777* Ⓜ *M3: Nyugati pu.*

Markets

Ecseri Piac. For true bargains and possibly an adventure, make an early-morning trip to the vast and meandering flea market on the outskirts of the city. A colorful, chaotic market that shoppers have flocked to for decades, it is an arsenal of secondhand goods, where you can find everything from frayed Russian army fatigues to Herend and Zsolnay porcelain vases to antique silver chalices. Goods are sold at permanent tables set up in rows, from trunks of cars parked on the perimeter, and by lone, shady characters clutching just one or two items. As a foreigner, you may be

> ### NO RETURN
>
> Returning or exchanging items at most shops in Budapest is the exception, not the rule. If you are unsure of a purchase, or if it's a gift, ask at the shop to find out whether an exchange or return is possible. For some shops in Budapest, the notion of an exchange is completely novel!

overcharged, so prepare to haggle—it's part of the flea-market experience. Also, watch out for pickpockets. Ecseri is open weekdays from 6 AM to 1 PM, Saturday from 8 to 3. Although the best selection is on Saturday morning, when the market is generally livelier, prices are said to be 10% to 20% higher than on weekdays. Haggle hard. ✉ *District XIX, Nagykőrösi út 156, Kispest* ☏ *1/282–9563* Ⓜ *Bus 54 from Boráros tér.*

Petőfi Csarnok. A colorful outdoor flea market is held weekend mornings from 7 to 2 in this somewhat rundown group of buildings in City Park. The quantity and selection are smaller than at Ecseri Piac, but it's a fun flea-market experience closer to the city center. Red-star medals, Russian military watches, and other memorabilia from communist days are popular buys here. East German postcards are worth looking at for their excellent kitsch value. Other more modern items, including car radios and mobile phones, often wind up here. ✉ *District XIV, Zichy Mihály út 14, City Park* ☏ *1/251–7266* Ⓜ *M1: Mexikói út.*

★ **Vásárcsarnok.** A trip to Budapest wouldn't be complete without a visit to this spectacularly renovated grand food hall. Pictures on the east wall show the history of this market, when it was Budapest's central location for meat and produce coming in from the countryside. Today the food stalls are still patronized by Hungarians, and like most markets in Hungary, seasonal products prevail. In summer tomatoes and peaches are abundant; in November celeriac and pumpkin. The stalls on the ground floor sell meat and produce as well as prepared food. This is the place to buy Hungarian delicacies such as piquant salamis, robust paprika, and buttery goose or duck liver pâtés. Upstairs is filled with folk-art vendors, souvenir shops, and a few fast-food kiosks. Handmade tablecloths, painted boxes, and traditional embroidery are the best buys among the handcrafts. The market is open Monday from 6 AM to 5 PM, Tuesday through Friday from 6 AM to 6 PM, and Saturday from 6 AM to 2 PM. ⊠ *District IX, Vámház körút 1–3, South end of Váci utca* ☎ *1/ 217–6067.*

Vörösmarty tér Christmas Market. If you are lucky enough to be in Budapest in December, you may be able to get all your Christmas shopping done in one fell swoop at this old-fashioned market at Vörösmarty tér, in front of the famous Gerbeaud coffeehouse. The facade of Gerbeaud itself is blanketed with a colorful Advent calendar that counts the days to Christmas. The city of Budapest wisely restricted the goods sold at this market to include only handmade, traditional crafts so you won't find any tacky, plastic holiday kitsch here. Handmade paper diaries, wrought-iron candle sticks, fur hats, wooden toys, and an exquisite array of handmade ornaments are for sale. Many Hungarian ceramic artists have stalls here as well. ■ TIP➔ **Concerts take place most evenings, when shoppers are keeping warm with hot mulled wine and Christmas sweets.** The market is open from 9 AM to 7 PM every day beginning the first weekend in December. ⊠ *District V, Vörösmarty tér, Around Deák Ferenc tér* Ⓜ *M1: Vörösmarty tér.*

> **WORD OF MOUTH**
>
> "Be sure to go to the Central Market Hall and marvel at how many things can be marinated in vinegar! Don't forget the fish market downstairs.   –offwego

Specialty Stores

Art & Antiques

Antiques stores are clustered around **Falk Miksa utca,** a leafy street north of the Parliament that's a browser's delight. A few auction houses and artisan's boutiques can be found on side streets as well as on **St. István körút.** The side streets off **Váci utca** are a good place to hunt for antique decorative items such as vases, tablecloths, and silver.

Anna Antikvitás. The shelves and tables at this tiny shop are stacked with exquisite antique textiles—from heavily embroidered wall hangings to dainty lace gloves to turn-of-the-century Christening dresses. The ceiling is dressed with a canopy of antique cotton umbrellas. ⊠ *District V, Falk Miksa utca 18–20, Parliament* ☎ *1/302–5461.*

BÁV Műtárgy. The State Commission Trading House has a network of shops around Budapest. The following are worth a visit for bric-a-brac, sets of sterling silver, old crystal vases, paintings, and furniture. ⊠ *District V, Szent István körút 3, Parliament* ☏ *1/331–4534* ⊠ *District V, Párizsi u. 2, Around Váci utca* ☏ *1/318–6217.*

Ernst Galéria. This small, elegant antiques shop a few blocks from Váci utca is worth visiting for its first-rate painting collection as well as its furniture. Paintings are more beautifully framed and displayed here than anywhere else in Budapest. ⊠ *District V, Irányi utca 27, Around Ferenciek tere* ☏ *1/266–4016.*

Godot Galéria. A well-chosen selection of contemporary Hungarian artists' work is exhibited here. ⊠ *District VII, Madách Imre út, Around Deák Ferenc tér* ☏ *1/322–5272.*

Móró Régiség. If antique weapons are your thing, then check out this esoteric shop, which specializes in 18th-century weaponry. A curious array of militaria and firearms and even torture devices will keep even the casual browser interested. ⊠ *District V, Szent István körút 1, Parliament* ☏ *1/311–0814.*

Nagyházi Galéria. A side street off Falk Miksa is home to one of Hungary's most prestigious auction houses. An impressive array of Old Master paintings, antique furniture, and carpets lines the aisles here, with a small corner of the shop dedicated to nude paintings. ⊠ *District V, Balaton utca 8, Parliament* ☏ *1/475–6000.*

Pintér Antik Diskont. Take a deep breath before you head into this cavernous antiques store. Just when you think you've seen everything, you enter yet another basement room filled with a dining room set for twenty or a Bohemian chandelier. The specialty here is furniture, everything from Biedermeier to Art Deco, with a good selection of antique pine armoires. Pieces are well restored and reasonably priced. ⊠ *District V, Falk Miksa utca 10, Parliament* ☏ *1/311–3030.*

Polgár Galéria és Aukciósház. Auctions are held once or twice a year at this well-established auction house. You can find everything from jewelry and furniture to antique porcelain. ⊠ *District V, Kossuth Lajos utca 3, Ferenciek tere* ☏ *1/318–6954.*

Fodor's Choice ★ **Studio Agram.** If urban Art Deco is your aesthetic, head straight to where you'll find the most refined collection in Budapest. Vintage club chairs as well as silver coffee sets are exquisitely restored. ⊠ *District V, Falk Miksa utca 10, Parliament* ☏ *1/428–0653.*

Style Antique. This French-Hungarian partnership has been working wonders with pine since the early 1990s, expertly restoring and selling antique pine furniture. Custom-made furniture can be made from either new or old wood and chosen from an expansive computerized catalog. ⊠ *District V, Király utca 25, Király utca* ☏ *1/322–8884.*

V.A.M. Design. Step into this vast showroom to see the latest furniture creations by Hungarian and European designers. ⊠ *District VI, Király utca 26, Around Király utca* ☏ *1/267–9540.*

Books

English-language newspapers can be found in most bookstores in Budapest. The bookstores listed here cater to English speakers.

★ **Bestsellers.** The stock at this popular bookshop consists almost entirely of English-language books and periodicals, including Hungarian classics translated into English, popular British and American best-sellers, and newspapers. There's a French-language section as well. ⊠ *District V, Október 6 utca 11, St. Stephen's Basilica* ☎ *1/312–1295.*

Central European University Bookshop. The bookshop housed in the Central European University building should be your first stop for books concerned with Central European politics and history. There's a decent collection of classics and travel books here, too. ⊠ *District V, Nádor utca 9, St. Stephen's Basilica* ☎ *1/327–3096.*

Király Books. French cookbooks as well as English-language newspapers are available at this large bookshop in lower Buda, not far from the French Institute. ⊠ *District I, Fő utca 79, Around Batthyány tér* ☎ *1/214–0972.*

THE ART OF SHOPPING

Looking for an unusual antique souvenir or in the market for a 19th-century Hungarian painting? For expert help in procuring just the right objet d'art from Hungary, contact Taylor Art Advisors ⊕ www.taylorartadvisors.com ☎ 06–20–933–5240 or 06–30/924–4748. The Hungarian-American team will find just about anything for you, from rustic pine cupboards to Art Deco tea sets to Biedermeier settees. They can arrange buying tours in the Hungarian country-side, bid in art auctions for you, and for a reasonable fee organize restoration and shipping of your newfound treasures back home.

Párisi Udvar Könyvesbolt. To find this bookstore, tuck into one of Budapest's most beautiful arcades behind Váci utca. The shop specializes in foreign-language books, especially maps and travel-related writing. ⊠ *District V, Petőfi Sándor utca 2, Around Ferenciek tere* ☎ *1/235–0380.*

Pen Dragon. A friendly staff keeps expats happy at this English-language bookstore off St. István körút, not far from Falk Miksa utca. There's a big selection of coffee-table books and cookbooks, plus self-help and New Age titles. ⊠ *District XIII, Pozsonyi utca 21–23, Parliament* ☎ *1/ 340–4426.*

Red Bus Bookstore. Although the shop seems small from the outside, you'll find thousands of English-language used books waiting to be discovered inside. Fiction, history, and classics are usually well stocked. The store buys used books as well. ⊠ *District V, Semmelweis utca 14, Around Deák Ferenc tér* ☎ *1/337–7453.*

Tree Hugger Dan's Bookstore Café. There's a green vibe at this coffee shop and English-language bookstore in the edgy 7th District. The café only sells brews that are procured through fair-trade practices, and there's a good trade-in policy on used books. The shelves are lined with a broad range of titles, everything from activism and environmentalism to last year's literary fiction bestseller. ⊠ *District VII, Csengery utca 48, Near Andrássy út* ☎ *1/322–0774.*

Clothing

Many of the big European and American retailers have branches in shopping malls like the West End City Center and Mammut and show the latest styles. High-fashion favorites like Mango, Zara, and H & M have trendy shops on Váci utca. Uniquely Hungarian shops are scattered throughout the city and often sell the styles of a group of designers. These are good places to check for the one-off purse, pullover, or accessory to remind you of Budapest. Secondhand clothing (*használt ruhák*) stores selling everything from last year's Gap T-shirts to 1940s ermine stoles are plentiful in the city as well.

Aqua-tick. You may encounter a steady stream of students from neighboring CEU (Central European University) at this downtown shop selling the whimsical designs of two Hungarian designers. Bright colors and mod prints are the look, with very retro accessories to match. ⊠ *District V, Zrínyi utca 12, St. Stephen's Basilica* ☏ *No phone.*

Fodor'sChoice
★ **Eclectick.** This shop bills itself as a Shop of Young Hungarian Designers and the place is stocked with the hip, colorful creations of five upstart designers who are hard at work on the second floor. The casual clothes range from patchwork skirts to handbags made from LPs to groovy print leisure suits for men. ⊠ *District V, Irányi utca 20, Around Váci utca* ☏ *1/266–3341.*

ÉK. Thick handknit sweaterlike striped trousers and halter tops are just a couple of things you'll find in this tiny shop owned by a French-Hungarian design team. There's an offbeat collection of imported goods as well, like skin handbags, print skirts from Thailand, and a line of shirts made by German prisoners. ⊠ *District VII, Király utca 11, Around Király utca* ▭ *no credit cards* ☏ *06–20/371–1054.*

Feyérzsuzsa. Tucked away on a quiet corner a few blocks off Váci utca is this handbag shop selling the playful designs of Zsuzsa Feyér. There are foldable shopping sacks as well as sweet evening bags made of silk and grosgrain ribbon. ■ TIP➡ **The print change purses make lovely gifts.** ⊠ *District V, Király Pál utca, Around Váci utca* ☏ *06–30/430–1253.*

Glamour. Inside this tiny shop you'll find the best collection of brightly colored feather boas this side of Greenwich Village. There's also a good selection of sequined things, including halter tops and briefs, not to mention humorous underwear. ⊠ *District VI, Nagymező utca 6, Around Andrássy út* ☏ *1/321–5161.*

Manier. This popular atelier run by talented Hungarian designer Anikó Németh sells women's clothing, with designs ranging from quirky to totally outrageous. The haute-couture salon and personal shopping department is just down the street, off Váci utca. ⊠ *District V, Váci utca 68, Around Váci utca* ☏ *1/411–0852* ⊠ *District V, Nyári Pál utca 4, Around Váci utca* ☏ *1/483–1140.*

Naray Tamás. A walk through Tamás Naray's colorful corner shop is a feast for the eyes. Rich fabrics, fanciful accessories, and seamless tailoring characterize his designs; no one would quarrel with the idea that Naray has an eye for dressing women with a "wow." Black polka-dot skirts offset by lacy lingerie blouses get a giant red flower belt to hold them together. These clothes are not for the off-the-rack crowd. ⊠ *District V, Károlyi Mihály utca 12, Around Ferenciek tere* ☏ *1/266–2473.*

Siptár. You'll find loose-fitting women's clothes all designed by Réka Siptar in this tasteful shop on Király utca. The designer hand-dyes the all-natural materials and decorates them with her cursive designs. There

6

are children's clothes and accessories as well. ⊠ *District VII, Király utca 24, Around Király utca* ☎ *1/321–9686.*

FodorśChoice ★ **Tisza.** For a uniquely Hungarian souvenir, check out this home-grown shoe company named for a beloved river that flows through southern Hungary. The company is known for its rubber-soled shoes, boots, and sneakers, which were all the rage behind the Iron Curtain in the 1970s. Tisza soles provided the basis for scores of "domestic" shoes then as well, providing workers in Hungary with sturdy and comfortable shoes in which to toil. These days, new groovy designs make the sneakers popular with the hipster crowd. ⊠ *District VII, Károly körút 1, Around Deák tér* ☎ *1/266–3055* ⊠ *West End City Center, Váci út 1–3* ☎ *1/238–7505.*

Van Laack. If you're looking for a really top-notch men's dress shirt, check out this German purveyor of pinpoint, broadcloth, and linen shirts. The impeccable details around the cuffs and collars are worlds better than what you'll find in almost any department-store shirt, with prices that reflect the workmanship. ⊠ *District V, Váci utca 19–21, In the Millennium Center on Váci utca* ☎ *1/267–3294.*

V-50 Design Art Studio. If you've got a thing for hats, don't miss this shop carrying the unusual designs of Valéria Fazekas. Her brightly colored cloth hats range from elegant to pixyish, but all of them are functionally constructed. ⊠ *District V, Váci utca 50, Around Váci utca* ☎ *1/337–5320* ⊠ *Belgrád Rakpart 16* ☎ *1/337–0327.*

Crystal & Porcelain

Hungary is famous for its age-old Herend porcelain, which is hand-painted in the village of Herend near Lake Balaton. High-quality, hand-cut crystal is considerably less expensive here than in the United States. Crystal and porcelain dealers also sell their wares at the Ecseri Piac flea market, often at discount prices, but those looking for authentic Herend and Zsolnay should beware of imitations.

★ **Ajka Kristály.** Hand-cut lead crystal isn't as cheap as it once was in Hungary, but for a uniquely Central European gift, head to this leading Hungarian manufacturer for fine crystal. The huge selection of colored glasses—martini to cognac—comes in rich reds and blues, as well as pastel pinks and yellows. All can be packed for a long trip home. There are several outlets around town. ⊠ *District V, Jószef Atilla utca 7, St. Stephen's Basilica* ☎ *1/317–8133.*

Haas & Czjzek. This professional shop has been in business for more than 100 years, selling porcelain, glass, and ceramic pieces in traditional and contemporary styles. Today you can find the best names in Hungarian porcelain as well as Villeroy & Boch from Germany, and the top companies from Limoges. If you're looking for a one-off piece (without a set), check upstairs, where among other odd pieces, there are marvelous soup tureens. ⊠ *District VI, Bajcsy-Zsilinszky út 23, St. Stephen's Basilica* ☎ *1/311–4094.*

Herend. You can get a glimpse of the world-famous Herend porcelain that has graced the tables of royal houses for centuries at one of several branches in Budapest. Carefully hold a saucer up to the light and see how nearly transparent the finely worked porcelain is. All the brightly hand-painted animal figurines as well as most patterns can be picked up directly or ordered here. Sadly, prices are competitive with prices abroad. The multilingual staff is at the ready with calculators, though, for easy currency conversion. ⊠ *District VI, Andrássy út 16, Andrássy út* ☎ *1/374–0006* ⊠ *District V, József Nádor tér 11, St. Stephen's Basilica* ☎ *1/317–2622* ⊠ *District V, Kigyó utca 5, Around Váci utca* ☎ *1/318–3439* ⊠ *District I, Szentháromság utca 5, Castle District* ☎ *1/225–1051.*

Herend Village Pottery. For the Herend name and quality without the steep price tag, visit this small shop where you can choose from Herend's practical line of informal ceramic cups, dishes, and table settings, all hand painted. The colorful pasta bowls are perfect for outdoor summer entertaining. ⊠ *District II, Bem rakpart 37, Around Batthyány tér* ☎ *1/356–7899.*

Zsolnay Porcelain Shop. If you're unfamiliar with Zsolnay, Hungary's second most famous porcelain manufacturer, have a look at the tile roof of the Applied Arts Museum in downtown Pest to see the exquisite weatherproof mosaics. The hand-painted tile and porcelain are still made today in Pécs. Unfortunately, the company is not what it was in its heyday, when its Art Deco designs were internationally celebrated. Nevertheless, you can get an unusual hand-painted plate or vase that evokes the memory. ⊠ *District V, Váci utca 19–21, Around Váci utca* ☎ *1/266-6305.*

Flowers

Hungarians are flower bearers for even the smallest of occasions, and Budapest has many small flower shops where you can buy a single flower and have it wrapped in pretty ribbon and cellophane. All of these florists are professionally run and can create pleasing arrangements.

Arioso. Stark bouquets of calla lilies, beautifully full topiary plants, or simple cactus arrangements are the kinds of things you're likely to find in this sophisticated flower shop on Király utca. The Swiss owners are known for their innovative and classy designs. They have a small shop selling elegant vases and other small housewares next door. This is the place to go for an impressive gift bouquet. ⊠ *District VII, Király utca 9, Around Király utca* ☎ *1/266–3555.*

Moha és Páfrány. This flower-cum-gift shop across the street from Buda's Déli Train Station displays potted plants and arrangements all over the sidewalk outside, so it's hard to pass by and not be tempted by something, like big cut sunflowers or a potted azalea. ■ TIP➡ **They gift-wrap quite beautifully here, even for a single rose.** ⊠ *District XII, Magyar Jakobinusok tere 1, Around Déli Train Station* ☎ *1/356–7328.*

Viragneked.hu. A young and attentive staff puts together pretty arrangements at this well-stocked flower shop not far from the Parliament. Even in the winter, the store has a better selection than many other florists in Budapest. ⊠ *District V, Kossuth Lajos tér 18, Parliament* ☎ *06–30/954–4200.*

Folk Art

There are many folk-art vendors along Váci utca, selling hand-painted wooden eggs and embroidered fabrics. For tablecloths and traditional Hungarian costumes, head to the second floor of the Vasárcsárnok.

Blue Bird. If you like the color blue, you'll notice this shop on Váci utca right away, because the doors and windows are swung wide open every day to display the single-color inventory. Traditional folk crafts, such as blue-painted wooden eggs and blue-and-white painted ceramics are plentiful here, as well as beautiful hand-dyed blue tablecloths and napkins. ⊠ *District V, Váci utca 13, Around Váci utca* ☎ *1/313–4690.*

Folkart Centrum. If you are looking for an embroidered vest fit for a Hussar, this is the place to stop and browse. Beautifully embroidered fabrics in traditional motifs make handsome souvenirs from any trip to Hungary. Decorative wooden eggs and hand-painted ceramics are equally pleasing. ⊠ *District V, Váci utca 58, Around Váci utca* ☎ *1/318–5840.*

★ **Folkart Kézműveshóz.** All the best Hungarian handicrafts are on display in this two-room shop off Váci utca. Heavily embroidered pillow cases and tablecloths, hand-painted ceramics, and traditional peasant clothing for children are just a few of the things you'll find. Nativity crèches made of corn husks have a holiday appeal. ⊠ *District V, Régiposta utca 12, Around Váci utca* ☎ *1/318–5143.*

Holló Műhely. László Holló is a master wood craftsman who has resurrected traditional motifs and styles of earlier centuries and sells beautiful handicrafts in his shop not far from Váci utca. You'll find lovely hope chests, chairs, jewelry boxes, candlesticks, and more, all hand-carved and hand-painted with cheery folk motifs—a predominance of birds and flowers in reds, blues, and greens. ⊠ *District V, Vitkovics Mihály utca 12, Around Váci utca* ☎ *1/317–8103.*

Food & Wine

Most supermarket chains in Budapest carry a good selection of Hungarian wines and Hungarian epicurian specialties like paprika, Pick-brand salami, and tinned goose liver. There's no need to purchase these items in touristy shops, any supermarket has them. ■ TIP→ Paprika comes in two varieties: *édes* is sweet and *csipős* is hot.

★ **Budapest Bortársaság** (Budapest Wine Society). A good place to start looking for Hungarian wines is in this cellar shop at the base of Castle Hill. There's an excellent selection of Hungarian vintners represented here, and the shop is open all day on Saturday. The knowledgeable staff is always available to guide you on Hungary's wines, like this year's tokaji or kékoporto, and they'll deliver orders of a case or more free of charge anywhere in Budapest. There's a good selection of wine accessories as well, from oak wine racks to high-tech bottle openers. ⊠ *District I, Batthyány utca 59, Castle Hill* ☎ *1/212–2569 or 1/212–0262* ☐ *1/212–5285.*

Culinaris. The traffic in and out of this gourmet warehouse moves briskly, as customers snatch up Hungarian-made goat cheeses just in from the countryside or pick up exotic Sri Lankan cinnamon. The shelves are lined with a selective array of gourmet foods and wines. Fresh-baked breads and garden herbs are highlights. The friendly owner, Zoltán Bogáthy, is often on hand to advise you of a porcini delivery or just what to do with ginger paste, handily serving customers in both Hungarian and English. ✉ *District III, Perc utca 6–8, Lower Buda* ☎ *1/345–0780* ✉ *District VI, Hunyadi tér 3, Around Andrássy út* ☎ *1/341–7001.*

Monarchia Wine Shop. One of the best distributors of wine in Hungary, Monarchia stocks an excellent selection of Hungarian and international wines. A very knowledgeable staff and long hours on Saturday (when it's open until 6) make this shop a favorite of local wine enthusiasts. ✉ *District IX, Kinizsi utca 30–36, Around Kálvin tér* ☎ *1/456–9898.*

Nagy Tamás Sajtüzlete. The oldest seller of imported cheeses in Budapest, "Big Tom" now has a modest selection of Hungarian cheeses to celebrate. Be sure to try one of the very fresh goat cheeses from the Molnár farm. All the things you need for a smart cocktail party or sumptuous picnic can be found here, including fresh-baked olive focaccia. ✉ *District V, Gerlóczy utca 3, Deák Ferenc tér* ☎ *1/317–4268.*

Pomo D'oro Gastronomia. This café cum deli has some of the best Italian salamis and cheeses in downtown Budapest. There are other goodies here as well, like imported anchovies and Tuscan biscotti. They make focaccia and homemade pastas daily, and you can get authentic panini to go. ✉ *District V, Arany Janos utca 11, St. Stephen's Basilica* ☎ *1/302–6473.*

Szega Sajtszaküzlet (Szega Cheese Shop). This cheese and salami importer, one of Budapest's best, has outlets in all the tony Buda shopping centers. It's worth the trip if you can't put down that craving for Parma ham or French Muenster cheese. There are lots of other goodies here, including homemade duck and goose-liver pâtés, and hot Hungarian peppers stuffed with goat cheese. ✉ *District II, Budagyöngye Shopping Center, Szilágyi Erzsébet fasor 121, North Buda* ☎ *1/200–6777* ✉ *District II, Fény utca piac, behind Mammut I shopping center, Around Moszkva tér* ✉ *District II, Rózsakert shopping center, Gábor Áron utca 74–78, Buda Hills.*

Furs & Leather Goods

Balogh Kesztyű. Although leather gloves are widely available in most American retail stores, this store specializes in handmade and hand-dyed leather gloves made in Hungary. Some of the men's gloves have shearling lining and will keep you warm in near-Arctic temperatures. The buttery ladies' models are lined with cashmere or wool. ✉ *District V, Haris Köz 2, Around Váci utca* ☎ *1/266–1942.*

Clara Liska. The furs in the window of this established Viennese shop are the picture of elegance. There's a good choice of skins and colors here, with beautiful tailoring to match. This is the place to walk away with a truly luxurious fur coat. ✉ *District V, Semmelweis utca 9, Around Váci utca* ☎ *1/317–3449.*

Ékes kesztyűkeszitő. This old-fashioned shop sells high-quality men's and women's leather gloves. The two friendly Hungarian ladies will dote on you until you find just the right pair. The gloves, which are all made in Hungary, are well-constructed and come in a wide variety of colors and leathers. ✉ *District V, Régisposta utca 14, Around Váci utca* ☎ *1/266–0986.*

Klein Furs. A well-known name for fur in Budapest. You can look through styles and have a fur coat custom made. ⊠ *District V, Millennium Center, Váci utca 19–21, Around Váci utca* ☎ *1/266–1332.*

La Boutique. A wide range of designer shoes is sold here, including Ferragamo, Dolce & Gabbana, and Prada. There are a few Hungarian knock-offs as well, for about half the price. Thankfully, they have two blowout sales a year, usually in summer and winter. ⊠ *District VI, Andrássy út 16, Around Andrássy út* ☎ *1/302–5646* ⊠ *District V, Le Méridien Hotel, Deák Ferenc utca, Deák Ferenc tér* ☎ *1/266–7585.*

Mandarina Duck. This small, first-rate Italian handbag maker has made a name for itself by designing stylish yet incredibly durable leather goods. The leather quality can't be matched for easy upkeep and resistance to all kinds of wear and tear, making the pricey bags well worth the investment. There are wallets and small leather goods for sale here, as well as a range of non-leather handbags and luggage. ⊠ *District VI, West End City Center, Váci utca 1–3, Around Nyugati Train Station* ☎ *1/ 238–7579.*

Scandic Retail. Some very high-end fur brands such as Marina Rinaldi and Gianfranco Ferre can be found in this shop, which also sells designer leather jackets. ⊠ *District V, Galamb utca 6, Around Váci utca* ☎ *1/ 318–4866.*

Vass. If you are looking for a really luxurious indulgence, why not consider a pair of handmade leather shoes, specifically measured to your feet? You can choose from a variety of traditional styles, from cordovan to nubuck. Though wildly expensive when compared to the cost of ready-made shoes, prices are still very competitive with bespoke shoes in Europe and the United States. There's a small selection of ready-to-wear shoes available as well. ⊠ *District V, Haris Köz 2, Around Váci utca* ☎ *1/318–2375.*

Home Decor & Gifts

Aita Studio. Imported Italian pewter decanters, silver picture frames, and wrought-iron andirons are just a few of the things you'll find in this warehouse-cum-shop on low-rent Lónyay utca. You're spoiled for choice in decorative table accessories; handsome caviar bowls and tasteful salt and pepper shakers can be had at almost garage-sale prices. It's hard to leave empty-handed. ⊠ *District IX, Lónyay utca 24, Around Kálvin tér* ☎ *1/ 216–1673.*

Arabeszk. Handmade silk lampshades—and mosaic tables and mirrors—are the things to seek out in this tiny shop off the beaten path a few blocks behind Váci utca. A few other handicrafts dot the place, and one or two of the designing artists can usually be found on the premises. ⊠ *District V, Királyi Pál utca 9, Around Kálvin tér* ☎ *1/317–9577.*

Fodor'sChoice
★
BomoArt. When walking in the Váci utca area, take a minute to step into this closet-size shop selling handmade paper diaries, address books, and stationery. There are old-fashioned letter-writing accessories here, too, including bottled ink, quills, and sealing wax. The diaries are so nice that even if you're not a writer you'll be tempted to become one. ⊠ *District V, Régiposta utca 14, Around Váci utca* ☎ *1/318–7280* ⊠ *District VI, West End City Center, Váci utca 1–3, 1st floor, Around Nyugati Train Station* ☎ *1/238–9701.*

Brinkus Design. Even if you're not in the market for a carpet, check out this offbeat shop near Liszt Ferenc tér, where Hungarian designers create unique rugs by cobbling together colorful carpet remnants in geometric patterns. They're one-of-a-kind pieces that will add pizzazz to any room. There are other packable things like gorgeous bed linens and pillow cases as well. ⊠ *District VI, Paulay Ede utca 56, Around Király utca* ☎ *1/321–2138.*

Demko Feder. Natural-fiber housewares, rattan serving trays, and sheared wool blankets are just a few of the things you'll find in this eco-friendly shop. ⊠ *District V, József Atilla utca 20, St. Stephen's Basilica* ☎ *1/438–3039* ⊠ *District II, Margit körút 29a* ☎ *1/212–4408.*

★ **Eventuell Galériá.** This little shop off Váci utca selling the work of several Hungarian applied-arts designers is a feast for the eyes. There are colorful appliqué pillow and bedcover sets, gauzy curtains, and velvety throws and shawls. The store has a limited inventory, but you can speak with the designer directly and custom order anything. There's a small collection of funky jewelry as well. ⊠ *District V, Nyári Pál utca 7, Around Váci utca* ☎ *1/318–6926.*

Goa Home. All the furniture and housewares in this large showroom have an Asian aesthetic. There are big wooden beds from Indonesia, tin alms bowls, rattan placemats, lovely Chinese silk pillow covers, and lots of votive candleholders. Part of the shop—Goa Botanicus—is devoted to indoor gardening and sells lush plants, clay pots, and the makings for a rock garden. ⊠ *District VII, Király utca 19–21, Around Király utca* ☎ *1/352–8442* ⊠ *District XII, Mom Park shopping center, Alkotás utca 53, Around Déli Train Station* ☎ *1/352–8442.*

Hephaistos. Esther Gál's wrought-iron designs are a far cry from the staid stuff of traditional blacksmiths. Her loopy candlesticks and tables are playful and modern, not to mention one of a kind. Gorgeously upholstered furniture and silk textiles are another attraction in this two-floor emporium behind Váci utca. If the colorful table runners and placemats don't make you want to throw a lavish dinner party, then the hand-dripped candles available in every possible color will. ⊠ *District V, Mólnar utca 27, Around Váci utca* ☎ *1/266–1550.*

Interieur Stúdió. Just down the street from the Holló Műhely, this old-fashioned shop sells wooden brushes, bookmarks, and even birdcages; candles of all shapes and sizes; and sundry other objects for the home. There's a good selection of dried flowers and pretty hat boxes as well. ⊠ *District V, Vitkovics Mihály utca 6, Deák Ferenc tér* ☎ *1/266–1666.*

Fodor'sChoice **Magma.** To understand who's who in Hungarian applied arts, step into
★ this professionally run collective of the best textile, jewelry, and furniture designers working in Hungary today. There are silk throw pillows and gorgeous satin and linen tablecloths, as well as sleek oak card tables and ceramic figurines. Stop in and chat with the owners, who are happy to talk about any of the artists. ⊠ *District V, Petőfi Sándor utca 11, Around Váci utca* ☎ *1/235–0277.*

Nádortex. Hungarian goose down is prized the world over for its featherweight warmth. Pillows and duvets made in factories in Szeged are sold at this old-fashioned but friendly textile store. Duvets come in winter, spring, and summer weights, offering varying degrees of warmth.

Sizes are made to fit Hungarian standard beds, but with a little imagination you can find one that suits your needs. The veteran staff tries to speak a bit of English, but it's best to do some homework on what you need in advance. ✉ *District V, József Nádor tér, St. Stephen's Basilica* ☎ *1/317–0030.*

Jewelry

M. Frey Wille. This Viennese jeweler has a world-class name for beautifully enamelled gold jewelry. Some of the designs are geometric, while others evoke Art Nouveau paintings. Although the style is not for everyone, bright colors and unusual materials set these pieces apart from other more traditional jewelry. ✉ *District V, Régiposta utca 19, Around Váci utca* ☎ *1/318–7665.*

O'Mama Biszuja. Garnet rings in Art Deco settings and pendants in the shape of birds are among the many delightful things you'll find in this antique jewelry shop. Budapesters know O'Mama for her excellent taste and fair prices. ✉ *District V, Szent István körút 1, Parliament* ☎ *1/312–6812.*

Varga Design. Award-winning Miklos Varga's flagship store off Váci utca is a big and welcoming one. Expensive gold and platinum necklaces with Tahitian pearls are showcased in the front of the store, but don't miss the unusual sterling silver collection in the back. There are some lovely pieces for everyday wear. ✉ *District V, Haris Köz 1, Around Váci utca* ☎ *1/318–4089.*

★ **Wladis Galéria és Műterem.** Bulky sterling silver is the medium of Péter Vladimir, a jewelry designer and artist par excellence. His oversized pieces—sometimes made of half a pound of silver or more—are one-of-a-kind or limited issues. Big, clunky rings with cut-crystal stones, solid silver chokers, or pendants with primitive motifs make an eye-popping statement. ✉ *District V, Falk Miksa utca 13, Parliament* ☎ *1/354–0834.*

Music

Recordings of Hungarian folk music or of pieces played by Hungarian artists are widely available on compact discs throughout Budapest. Most shopping malls have at least one CD store.

Darius Music. This well-established shop doesn't sell recordings. They deal in fine and rare violins. ✉ *District VI, Paulay Ede utca 58, Around Liszt Ferenc tér* ☎ *1/352–6159 or 06–20/944–1938.*

Hungaroton Records Megastore. It's a bit out of town, but this music store in the Duna Plaza shopping center has one of the largest selection of CDs in the city. The metro will get you there in 10 minutes from downtown Pest. ✉ *District XIII, Váci utca 178, Duna Plaza* ☎ *1/239–4409* Ⓜ *M3: Gyöngyösi út.*

Rózsavölgyi Zenebolt. This is an old, established music store carrying the best selection of Hungarian composers on CD, as well as a good selection of sheet music. There's a small number of recordings by the best Hungarian classical performers as well, including celebrated pianist Zoltán Koscis. ✉ *District V, Szervita tér 5, Deák Ferenc tér* ☎ *1/318–3500.*

Subvibe. There's a good collection of mainstream and alternative CDs here, and a helpful staff to help you find what you're looking for. ✉ *District V, Irányi utca 5, Around Váci utca* ☎ *1/266–6581.*

Trance Wave Records. There's an alternative vibe at this tiny store not far from St. Stephen's Basilica. The shop is separated into two sections, Wave and Trance. One sells underground dance music (Trance) and one sells indie guitar rock (Wave). The Web site—in Hungarian only—has listings of concerts in Budapest. ⊠ *District VI, Revay köz 2, St. Stephen's Basilica* ☎ *1/269–3135* ⊕ *www.trancewave.hu.*

Pastries & Sweets

While it's fun to participate in the local káveház (coffeehouse) culture in Budapest—drinking coffee and eating cake in the late afternoon—most cukrázsdas will pack up a piece of cake to go (often beautifully) if you'd like to save it for dinner.

★ **Daubner Cukrászda.** It's with good reason that this popular confectioner has lines outside the door each morning. Every pastry here is delicate and light. Even a novice can taste the real butter cream in the famous Eszterhazy torta, which is a truly magnificent cake. Locals say the Sacher torte is every bit as good as it is in the famous Sacher Hotel in Vienna. It's usually crowded on weekends with families eating ice cream. ⊠ *District II, Szépvölgyi út 50, Buda Hills* ☎ *1/335–2253.*

Gerbeaud Ház. Around the corner from the famous Gerbeaud coffeeshop is the Gerbeaud Ház, where you can buy cakes to take away. There's a full selection of sweets, including chocolates, and everything can be packed up to travel. The Gerbeaud cake, only available here, is a moist chocolate and apricot creation that lasts for 3 to 4 weeks. There's a delivery service (cleverly called "Gerboy") that can get a cake anywhere in Budapest for a fee. ⊠ *District V, Vörösmarty tér 7–8, Around Váci utca* ☎ *1/429–9026.*

Spaghetti Ice. The line outside this popular ice-cream shop can easily be 20 deep on a hot summer weekend. There's real Italian gelato here in loads of flavors. There are other Italian favorites, too, like tiramisu and profiteroles. Everything can be packed to go. ⊠ *District VI, Andrássy út 14, Around Andrássy út* ☎ *1/332–4559.*

Szamos Marzipán. Marzipan has always been a favorite in Central Europe, and this well-loved confectioner has turned out marzipan cookies, cakes, and candies since the late 1940s. The store has always been most famous for its edible marzipan roses, but today just as many people come for the ice cream. ⊠ *District V, Párizsi utca 3, Around Váci utca* ☎ *1/317–3643.*

Toys

Fakopáncs. There's a big selection of Hungarian-made wooden toys as well as puzzles here. You can find wooden chess and backgammon replacement pieces, too. ⊠ *District VIII, Baross utca 46, Around Kálvin tér* ☎ *1/337–0992.*

Játékszerek Anno ("Toys Anno"). For a look back into the world before video games and action figures, stop in at this tiny store, where fabulous reproductions of antique European toys are sold. From simple paper puzzles to lovely stone building blocks to 1940s wind-up metal monkeys on bicycles, these "nostalgia toys" are beautifully simple and exceptionally clever. Even if you're not a collector, it's worth a stop just to browse. ⊠ *District VI, Teréz körút 54, Around Nyugati Train Station* ☎ *1/302–6234.*

6

The Danube Bend

WORD OF MOUTH

"To see Budapest and the surrounding area properly, I think seven nights is not long at all, as Budapest is larger than Prague, and nearby Szentendre, Visegrád, Esztergom, and Vác are all ideal for day trips."

–Judy C

"Szentendre is fun and charming. . . . Walk a block off the touristy drag and the village is very medieval, with churches, art studios, and museums. . . . Szentendre is worth at least half a day."

–joegri

By Paul
Olchváry

ABOUT 40 KM (25 MI) NORTH OF BUDAPEST the Danube abandons its eastward course and turns abruptly south toward the capital, cutting through the Börzsöny and Visegrád hills. This area is called the Danube Bend, and includes the baroque town of Szentendre, the hilltop castle ruins and town of Visegrád, and the cathedral town of Esztergom, all on the Danube's west bank. The most scenically varied part of Hungary, the region is best known for a chain of riverside spas and beaches, bare volcanic mountains, and limestone hills. Here, in the heartland, are traces of the country's history—the remains of the Roman Empire's frontier, the battlefields of the Middle Ages, and the relics of the Hungarian Renaissance.

The district can be covered by car in one day, the total round-trip no more than 112 km (70 mi), although this affords only a cursory look around. A day-trip to Szentendre from Budapest plus two days for Visegrád and Esztergom, with a night in either (both have lovely hotels small and large), would be best.

On the Danube's eastern bank, Vác is the prime cultural-commercial center. No bridges span the river in the Danube Bend until Esztergom, where you can cross the Mária Valéria Bridge to Slovakia on the opposite bank and head back into Hungary (a few miles to the east). But throughout the Danube Bend there are also numerous ferries (between Visegrád and Nagymaros, Basaharc and Szob, Szentendre Island and Vác), making it possible to combine a visit to both sides of the Danube on the same excursion, even if you don't wish to go as far as Esztergom.

Though the Danube Bend's west bank contains the bulk of historical sights, the less-traveled east bank has the excellent hiking trails of the Börzsöny mountain range, which extends along the Danube from Vác to Zebegény before curving toward the Slovak border. The Pilis and Visegrád hills on the Danube's western side and the Börzsöny Hills on the east are popular nature escapes.

About the Hotels & Restaurants

The Danube Bend offers a broad range of accommodations, but most are relatively small (and affordable), pensionlike hotels that often exude a charm hard to find these days in Budapest. The only serious rival (in both quality and price) to Budapest's large, luxury venues is the Danubus Spa & Conference Center Hotel Visegrád, which opened in April 2004. But with market pressures being what they are, the future may see some now-

---

PAUL'S TOP 5

Bazilika, Esztergom. Hungary's largest cathedral stands on a hill overlooking town.

Fellegvár, Visegrád. Crowning the top of a 1,148-foot hill overlooking the Danube, the dramatic citadel was built in the 13th century.

Aranysárkány, Szentendre. A favorite of early-20th-century Hungarian writer Frigyes Karinthy.

Szentendre. A romantic, lively little town with colorful baroque houses, and a long history as a haven for artists.

Kisoroszi. A captivating, albeit isolated, village.

quiet hotels lose some of their charm as they strive to keep from losing guests to their larger rivals.

Rates may be up to 20 percent lower in the colder months—between October and April, which roughly corresponds to the region's low season. Only a few hotels in this region set and advertise their rates in euros. That said, even these places will do a quick conversion for you and accept your forints. As for air-conditioning, most hotels in this region, as elsewhere outside of Budapest, are apt to offer just a few rooms with a/c.

The pressures of Hungary's burgeoning tourist industry in the past decade have seen some once "authentic" little restaurants expand into tourist mills, with tour groups passing through in assembly-line fashion; this is particularly the case in Szentendre; to a lesser extent in Visegrád and Esztergom; and least of all in Vác, which has been relatively unscathed by the tackiest side of tourism (though the tenuous local economy is none the better for this). Prices are often between 10 and 20 percent lower than those in Budapest for equivalent quality.

Although the menus are much the same as in the capital, the Danube theme inevitably yields a relatively high number of restaurants that offer fish specialties (though one might hope the fish aren't really from the long not-so-blue Danube); and, since the Bend is, after all, situated in the "countryside" (i.e., beyond Budapest), you won't have to look far to find restaurants of the *csárda,* or country tavern, variety—where you can generally be assured of a bowl of *gulyás, halászlé* (fisherman's soup), or, say, *pacalpörkölt* (tripe stew), often for under 1,000 HUF or not much more.

WHAT IT COSTS In Euros & Forints				
$$$$	**$$$**	**$$**	**$**	**¢**
HOTELS IN EUROS				
over 225	175–225	125–175	75–125	under 75
HOTELS IN FORINTS				
over 56,000	44,000–56,000	31,000–44,000	18,500–31,000	under 18,500
RESTAURANTS IN FORINTS				
over 3,500	2,500–3,500	1,500–2,500	800–1,500	under 800

Hotel prices are for two people in a standard double room with a private bath and breakfast during peak season (June through August). Restaurant prices are per person for a main course at dinner and include 15% tax but not service.

Numbers in the margin correspond to numbers on the Szentendre and Danube Bend maps.

SZENTENDRE

21 km (13 mi) north of Budapest.

A romantic, lively little town with a long history as a haven for artists—a rather touristy haven—Szentendre is the highlight of the Danube Bend

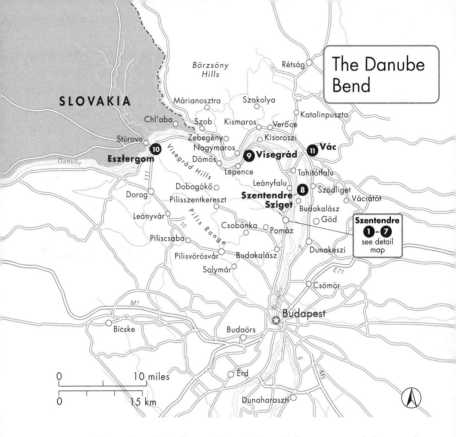

(although, technically speaking, it is well downstream of the actual bend). With its church steeples, colorful baroque houses, and winding, narrow cobblestone streets, it's no wonder Szentendre attracts swarms of visitors, tripling its population in peak season. The only drawback of a visit here is the prospect of finding yourself shoulder to shoulder with people speaking all languages but Hungarian.

Szentendre was first settled by Serbs and Greeks fleeing the advancing Turks in the 16th and 17th centuries. They built houses and churches in their own style—rich in reds and blues seldom seen elsewhere in Hungary. To truly savor Szentendre, duck into any and every cobblestone side street that appeals to you. (Indeed, you may have to do so simply to escape the crowds.) Baroque houses with shingle roofs (often with an arched eye-of-God upstairs window) and colorful stone walls will enchant your eye and pique your curiosity. And the river-

> ### WORD OF MOUTH
>
> "Szentendre is the last stop on the HEV railway, which departs from Bathyanyi Terr metro stop on the red line. You need a separate ticket as the HEV is a commuter railway and not part of the metro system. The ticket office is right where you go down the stairs.
> —s.fowler

front, right across from an amazingly untouched green paradise, Szentendre Island, is something to behold.

A GOOD
WALK

If you arrive in Szentendre from Budapest by the HÉV commuter railway—the most convenient way of traveling there short of driving—go straight ahead at the HÉV station in the direction the train was going and cross the busy road ahead of you by going through the underpass. Then, keep going straight—well, straight with respect to the stairs you go up on, but left with respect to the HÉV—along Kossuth utca. (You'll pass by a small park on your left immediately after exiting the underpass.) Within five minutes you'll cross tiny Bükkös-*patak* (stream), where the road continues as Dumtsa Jenő utca. By this point you have entered the historic district, and in a couple of minutes you'll reach the main square, Fő tér ❶, the small town's compact hub.

At the far right of **Fő tér** you'll see the **Görög templom** ❷; a right here, into Görög utca, will take you to the **Kovács Margit Múzeum** ❸. Tour the museum, then go back to Fő tér, from where a steep walk up Váralja lejtő to the top of Vár-domb (Castle Hill) will get you to the **Római Katolikus plébánia templom** ❹; from the church, it's a short walk to the **Szerb Ortodox Egyházi Gyüjtemény** ❺ and the adjacent **Szerb Ortodox Bazi-**

lika ⑥. If you are inspired to do some more walking on the relatively quiet residential hillside before heading back toward tourist-filled Fő tér, you can wind your way north along streets such as Hunyadi utca and then Bartók Béla utca, which, here and there, provide splendid views of the town and river below. Head back down anywhere, all the way to the river, and saunter north a bit, as far as (or beyond) the dock of the Szentendre Island ferry, before walking back to the town center along the lovely Duna korzó (Danube promenade). If you have a couple of hours to spare after taking in the heart of Szentendre, you may want to head out of town a tad to the **Szabadtéri Néprajzi Múzeum ⑦** by catching a bus back at the HÉV station.

TIMING   Szentendre is compact enough to allow you to cover it in half a day, unless you choose to take an additional side trip and cross by ferry to Szentendre sziget (Szentendre Island)—though you'd best have a bicycle for that unless you're fine with walking a couple of miles down lush green, uninhabited roads into the sleepy village of Szigetmonostor (*see* ⇨ Szentendre Sziget, *below*). (If you're getting about by car, you can take the bridge from Tahi, north of Szentendre.) Plan to leave Budapest via HÉV in the late morning for the 45-minute trip, so that you get there by lunch, and can then spend the afternoon looking around; or else go sometime in the afternoon and stay for dinner. Or, of course, you can make more of a day of it and have both lunch and dinner in this charming but sometimes crowded town (less so on weekdays, but in summer there's no telling). Either way, plan on an excursion of six hours or more.

What to See

❶ Fő tér is Szentendre's main square, the centerpiece of which is an ornate **Memorial Cross** erected by Serbs in gratitude because the town was spared from a plague. The cross has a crucifixion painted on it and stands atop a triangular pillar adorned with a dozen icon paintings.

Every house on Fő tér is a designated landmark, and three of them are open to the public for 400 HUF each. The **Ferenczy Múzeum** (Ferenczy Museum; ⊠ Fő tér 6 ☉ Mid-Mar.–Sept., Tues.–Sun. 10–6; Oct.–mid-Mar., Wed.–Sun. 9–5) has paintings of Szentendre landscapes. The **Kmetty Múzeum** (Kmetty Museum; ⊠ Fő út 21 ☉ Apr.–Oct., daily 1–5) displays the work of János Kmetty, a pioneer of Hungarian avant-garde painting. The **Szentendrei Képtár** (Municipal Gallery; ⊠ Fő út 2–5 ☉ Apr.–Oct., Wed.–Sun. 9–5) has an excellent collection of local contemporary art and changing exhibits of international art. Gracing the corner of Görög utca (Greek Street) and Szentendre's main square, Fő **❷** tér, the so-called **Görög templom** (Greek Church, or Blagovestenska Church) is actually a Serbian Orthodox church that takes its name from the Greek inscription on a red-marble gravestone set in its wall. This elegant edifice was built between 1752 and 1754 by a rococo master, Andreas Mayerhoffer, on the site of a wooden church dating to the Great Serbian Migration (around AD 690). Its greatest glory—a symmetrical floor-to-ceiling panoply of stunning icons—was painted between 1802 and 1804 by Mihailo Zivkovic, a Serbian painter from Buda. ⊠ *Görög utca, at Fő tér* ☎ *26/313–917* 🎟 *200 HUF* ☉ *Mar.–Oct., Tues.–Sun. 10–5.*

★ ❸ If you have time for only one of Szentendre's myriad museums, don't miss the **Kovács Margit Múzeum,** which displays the collected works of Budapest ceramics artist Margit Kovács, who died in 1977. She left behind a wealth of richly textured work that ranges from ceramics to life-size sculptures. Admission to the museum is limited to 15 persons at a time, so it is wise to line up early or at lunchtime, when the herds of tour groups are occupied elsewhere. ⊠ *Vastagh György utca 1, off Görög utca* ☎ *26/310–244 Ext. 112* ⊕ *pmmi.hu/muzeumok/ kovacsmargit/index.htm* ⊠ *700 HUF* ☉ *Apr.–Sept., daily 10–6; Oct., Tues.–Sun. 10–6; Jan.–Feb., Tues.–Sun. 9–5; Mar., daily 9–5; closed Nov.–Dec.*

❹ Perched atop Vár-domb (Castle Hill) is Szentendre's oldest surviving monument, the **Római Katolikus plébánia templom** (Roman Catholic Parish Church). According to some sources, there was a church here dating to the 13th century, but church or no church, it was apparently destroyed in some conflict in 1294. What's certain is that between 1332 and 1337 a new church was built here, though this was heavily damaged during the Turkish occupation in the 16th and 17th centuries. After many reconstructions, the church's oldest visible part is a 15th-century sundial in the doorway. The church's small cobblestone yard hosts an arts-and-crafts market and, often on weekends in summer, street entertainment. From here, views over Szentendre's angular tile rooftops and steeples and of the Danube beyond are superb. ⊠ *Templom tér (enter from Alkotmány utca), Vár-domb* ☎ *26/312–545* ⊠ *Free* ☉ *Mid-Mar.–Oct., daily 10–6, sometimes sporadic.*

❼ Szentendre's farthest-flung museum is the **Szabadtéri Néprajzi Múzeum** (Open-Air Ethnographic Museum), the largest open-air museum in the country. It is a living re-creation of 18th- and 19th-century village life from different regions of Hungary—the sort of place where blacksmith shops and a horse-powered mill compete with wooden houses and folk handicrafts for your attention. During regular crafts demonstrations you can sit back and watch or give it a try yourself. A new permanent exhibition on the village architecture of Hungary's northwestern farming towns opened in 2006. Five kilometers (3 mi) northwest of the city center, the museum is accessible by bus from the Szentendre terminus of the HÉV suburban railway; as of this writing, the bus leaves from stand No. 7 (ask for a ticket to the *Skanzen,* as this museum is also called). Throughout the year the museum has regularly scheduled activity days on Thursday through Sunday, as well as special festivals. If you arrive by car, parking will cost you at least 350 HUF. ⊠ *Sztaravodai út* ☎ *26/ 502–500, 26/317–965, or 26/317–966* ⊕ *www.skanzen.hu* ⊠ *Open-Air Exhibits: Apr.–Oct., free Tues. and Wed., 650 HUF Thurs. and Fri., 800 HUF weekends, 1,200 HUF on festival days. Gallery: Apr.–Oct., free; mid-Jan.–Mar. and Nov.–mid-Dec., 300 HUF* ☉ *Apr.–Oct., Tues.–Sun. 9–5; Nov.–mid-Dec. and early Jan.–Mar., Tues.–Sun. 9–4 (special exhibition gallery only).*

❻ The crimson steeple of the handsome **Szerb Ortodox Bazilika** (Serbian Orthodox Cathedral) presides over a restful tree-shaded yard crowning the hill just north of Vár-domb (Castle Hill). It was built in the 1740s with a much more lavish but arguably less beautiful iconostasis than is found in the Greek Church below it. ⊠ *Pátriárka utca 5* ☎ *26/314–456* 🔲 *Admission with ticket to Szerb Ortodox Egyházi Gyüjtemény* ⊙ *Same as for Szerb Ortodox Egyházi Gyüjtemény.*

★ ❺ The **Szerb Ortodox Egyházi Gyüjtemény** (Serbian Orthodox Collection of Religious Art) displays exquisite artifacts relating to the history of the Serbian Orthodox Church in Hungary. Icons, altars, robes, 16th-century prayer books, and a 17th-century cross with (legend has it) a bullet hole through it were collected from all over the country, after being sold or stolen from Serbian churches that were abandoned when most Serbs returned to their homeland at the turn of the 20th century and following World War I. The museum shares a tranquil yard with the imposing Serbian Orthodox Cathedral. ⊠ *Pátriárka utca 5* ☎ *26/312–399* 🔲*400 HUF* ⊙ *Mar.–Oct., Tues.–Sun. 10–6; Nov.–Dec. Tues.–Sun. 10–4; Jan.–Feb., Fri.–Sun. 10–4.*

NEED A BREAK?

For a quick cholesterol boost, grab a floppy, freshly fried *lángos* (flat, salty fried dough) drizzled with sour cream or brushed with garlic at **Piknik Büfé** (⊠ Dumtsa Jenő utca 22), a family-owned business that has been here since 1978 and is right next door to the Tourinform office.

A bit beyond the Piknic Büfé, farther into town toward the main square, is the **Múzeum cukrászda** (⊠ Dumtsa Jenő utca 14 ☎ 26/310–545), renovated in 2003 to recapture its elegance as a traditional café. Featuring glazed-tile artwork on the walls plus regular photo exhibits and musical performances, here you can choose from a wide selection of delectable pastries—with the *mogyorós linzer* (walnut linzer), the buttery-walnuty Eszterházy torta, and the green-topped, chocolately *Narancslikőr torta* (Orange Liquor Cake) among the most irresistible of all.

Where to Stay & Eat

$$–$$$$
Fodor'sChoice
★

✕**Aranysárkány.** A favorite of early-20th-century Hungarian writer Frigyes Karinthy, the Golden Dragon has seen more recent high-profile guests including Laura Bush (who visited Hungary years before her husband dropped by in June 2006). The food is all prepared in an open kitchen. Since there are only eight tables, be prepared to share on a busy night. Begin with *sárkány erőleves* (dragon's bouillon) with quail eggs. Main-course specialties include trout fillets steamed in campari, and venison steak in an almond crust. If you can still accommodate dessert, try the poppy-seed-spiked "opium" pudding or the cottage-cheese pudding with cranberries. A wine list with 60 varieties will tempt the inquisitive palate. Reservations are a must in the summer. ⊠ *Alkotmány utca 1/a* ☎ *26/301–479 or 26/311–670* 🗖 *AE, DC, MC, V* ⊙ *Closed mid-Dec.–mid-Jan.*

$$–$$$
✕**Régimódi.** This restaurant which has an excellent wine list and specializes in fishand game dishes is practically on Fő tér. Lace curtains, antique knickknacks, and lovely old paintings give the small upstairs dining room—which is air-conditioned and no-smoking—a homey in-

timacy; and, perhaps, the restaurant its name: Old-Fashioned (in the best sense, mind you). The downstairs dining room also has a certain antiques-induced charm to it, while the comparatively colorless seating out front carries only the advantage of allowing you to people-watch. The summer terrace, likewise upstairs, is a delightful place to dine alfresco and look out over the red-tile rooftops. ☒ *Dumtsa Jenő utca 2* 📧 *26/ 311–105* ▭ *MC, V.*

★ **$–$$** ✕ **Rab Ráby.** Hungarian home-style cooking with an emphasis on freshwater fish is the mark of this hospitable and often busy restaurant. Old lanterns, cowbells, and musical instruments decorate the walls of this converted 18th-century blacksmith's workshop. Reservations are a must during the busy summer months. There's live piano music every summer evening from 6 to 10. ☒ *Kucsera Ferenc utca 1/a* 📧 *26/310–819* ▭ *MC, V.*

★ **¢** 🔲 **Bükkös Hotel & Restaurant.** Just west of the main square and across the bridge over tiny Bükkös Brook, this is a neat, well-run establishment on a quiet side street a hop, skip, and jump from the center of town. The narrow staircase and small rooms with their peach bedspreads and overbearing red curtains—all but one of them no-smoking, by the way— give it a genuinely homey feel. As of this writing plans were in the works to add a sauna and a Jacuzzi. ☒ *Bükkös part 16, H-2000* 📧 *26/312– 021* 🖨 *26/310–782* ⊕ *www.bukkoshotel.hu* 🔄 *16 rooms* ⚘ *Restaurant, minibars, cable TV, laundry service, free parking; no a/c* ▭ *DC, MC, V* ❙◎❙ *BP.*

★ **¢** 🔲 **Centrum Panzió.** Szentendre's newest and most pristine B&B has only six rooms, but two are family-sized, and all are pleasantly furnished in shades of blue and gray. Ideally located practically but not quite in the center of things, the aptly named Centrum has pleasant Danube views, but service could be a tad friendlier. The maroon-and-pink rooms (showers only) are spotless and bright. ☒ *Bogdányi utca 15 (entrance off Rév utca), H-2000* 📧🖨 *26/302–500* 🖨 *26/500–562* ⊕ *www.hotelcentrum. hu* 🔄 *6 rooms* ⚘ *Cable TV, laundry service, free parking, some pets allowed* ▭ *AE, MC, V* ❙◎❙ *BP.*

¢ 🔲 **Horváth Fogadó.** This pension is on a quiet hillside conveniently within a 10-minute walk of Fő tér but refreshingly removed from the throngs of tourists in the center of town. The slightly frayed but clean, simply furnished rooms—two of them smaller, four extremely spacious, and one outright family-sized—are modern and reasonably priced. (Some have showers only.) Combine that with friendly service and lovely views of the town and the river below, and you've got a good place to stay. ☒ *Darupiac 2, H-2000* 📧🖨 *26/313–950* ⊕ *www.option.hu/ horvath* 🔄 *7 rooms* ⚘ *Restaurant, free parking; no a/c in some rooms* ▭ *MC, V* ❙◎❙ *EP.*

¢ 🔲 **Kentaur Hotel & Restaurant.** This handsome, modern, chalet-style hotel is less than a one-minute walk from the Danube and two minutes from Fő tér, on what may be Hungary's last surviving square still to bear Karl Marx's name. (As the manager explained, Fő tér, Szentendre's main square, used to be Marx tér, but when it was renamed Main Square, this end of Kert utca inherited the dubious honor of the Marx moniker.) Rooms are clean and simple, with unfinished-wood paneling and pastel-pink,

CLOSE UP

When the Wild West Came East

HIDDEN AWAY IN THE HEAVENLY little village of Kisoroszi on the northern tip of Szentendre Island is Hungary's most unlikely museum. The **"Baktay Ervin" Western Játékok Emlékhelye** (Ervin Baktay Western Games Memorial Site), housed in Kisoroszi's cultural center, is the creation of József Lorencz, an affable gentleman who in 1998 opened this unassuming two-room venue in memory of the most seriously intentioned but also most eccentric games of Cowboys and Indians that Hungary—and quite possibly the world—has ever seen.

As a youth, Lorencz explains, he used to hang out in summer at a nearby "Indian camp" led by one Ervin Baktay (1890–1963), whom most Hungarians know as a distinguished Hinduologist. Influenced by fashionable novels about the American West, Baktay and his friends began their adventure in the mid-1920s by holding "Wild West" meetings in their Budapest "saloon." After intensive ethnographic research into what life in the real West was like, not only for cowboys but also for Indians, Baktay took the bolder step of setting up a camp well removed from the capital, in the picturesque Danube Bend village of Zebegény, in 1931.

Led by Baktay—aka Chief Lazy Buffalo—and friends who went by such names as Little Hamster and Shaggy Wolf, these Budapest high-brows whiled away their summer vacations for years in tepees, with costumes, accoutrements, and canoes they themselves made. They sat by open fires and paddled the river in Indian headdress. Everyone played their chosen role; before long, some tired of being Indians and became

cowboys, marshals, or gold prospectors instead. Eventually, however, the locals on the mainland had had quite enough of these big-city ne'er-do-wells acting as oddly as they thought possible. It was then time to break camp and find a more isolated spot—which is how they eventually settled on Szentendre Island.

On stepping into this museum, you might at first think that the dazzling Native American regalia on a handful of mannequins; the beadwork; the headdresses; and even the bark canoe were somehow imported from North America. Think again. It was all made by Baktay and his friends. Lorencz himself proudly takes credit for the canoe, while acknowledging that for lack of birchbark, he used canvas. The black-and-white photos of Native Americans on horses or in canoes could be straight out of a history book (or a Western film), but in fact they depict Baktay and crew. One corner of the room is occupied by a saloon, replete with a very real-looking cowboy at each end of the bar.

A detailed English-language brochure explains everything you may want to know. There are, by the way, still Hungarians who continue the tradition on Szentendre Island each summer (just look for the tepees), but, says Lorencz, most people these days are too busy trying to make money to devote the time it takes to really become Indians. *Hősök tere 1, H-2024 Kisoroszi* ☎ *26/392-365 (József Lorencz) or 26/392-015 (mayor's office)* 🎫 *140 HUF* 🕐 *May–Oct., Wed. and weekends 10–2, or by prior arrangement (call at least 1 day in advance)* yellow, or blue walls hung with original paintings by local artists. The bathrooms were remodeled and new carpeting was added in 2004, and plans call for 10 more rooms to be added. Children under 10 stay for free. ⊠ *Marx tér 3–5, H-2000* ☎ *26/318–184* 📠 *26/312–125* ⊕ *www. hotels.hu/kentaur* ➡ *16 rooms* ⟳ *Restaurant, café, room service, minibars, cable TV, bar, meeting room, free parking, some pets allowed; no a/c* ⊟ *No credit cards* ⎮⊙⎮ *BP.*

Nightlife & the Arts

Most of Szentendre's concerts and entertainment events occur during the spring and summer. The annual **Spring Festival,** usually held from mid-March through early April, offers classical concerts in some of Szentendre's churches, as well as jazz, folk, and rock performances in the cultural center and other venues about town. In July the **Szentendre Summer Days** festival brings open-air theater performances and jazz and classical concerts to Fő tér and the cobblestone courtyard fronting the town hall. Although the plays are usually in Hungarian, the setting alone can make it an enjoyable experience.

Bohemia. On a short side street a two-minute walk from either Fő tér or the Danube, this pub lives up to its name as a popular, easygoing, intellectual, bohemian drinking-cum-cultural-political club. The bespectacled, bearded, blithe owner Ferenc Doór is a salty character who makes his living in other ways but just loves to hang around "this money-losing place." The large main room, with intimate lighting, a fair amount of smoke, worn wooden floors, and a couple of stuffed pheasants perched on a wall, is a splendid place to have a beer and to discuss the meaning of life—until 2 AM and, if you wish, with heated canned food you've chosen from a basket on hand at the bar (600 HUF/can). As an added plus, four computers are available near the bar for free Internet use; just sit down and log on. Hungarian luminaries from politicians to the national police chief regularly hold talks in the adjoining room. ⊠ *Bercsényi utca, near Duna korzó* ☎ *No phone.*

Shopping

Flooded with tourists in summer, Szentendre is saturated with the requisite souvenir shops. Among the attractive but overpriced goods sold in every store are dolls dressed in traditional folk costumes, wooden trinkets, pottery, and colorful hand-embroidered tablecloths, doilies, and blouses. The best bargains are the hand-embroidered blankets and bags sold by dozens of elderly women in traditional folk attire, who stand for hours on the town's crowded streets. (Because of high weekend traffic, most Szentendre stores stay open all day on weekends, unlike those in Budapest. Galleries are closed Monday and accept major credit cards, although other stores might not.)

Erdész Galéria. This sophisticated gallery on Szentendre's main square (not to be confused with the similarly named Gallery Erdész) displays paintings, statues, and other works by some 30 local artists. ⊠ *Fő tér 20* ☎ *26/310–139.*

Gallery Erdész. The gallery displays an impressive selection of contemporary Hungarian art, as well as gifts such as leather bags, colored-glass vases, and handmade paper—not to mention some unique, curvaceous silver pieces made by a famous local jeweler. ⊠ *Bercsényi utca 4* ☎ *26/ 317–925.*

Herend. For an impressive selection of Hungary's finest, most famous porcelain, check out the company shop, a one-minute stroll from Fő tér. ⊠ *Bogdányi út 1* ☎ *26/505–288.*

Kovács kékfestő. The Kovács Blue-Dyer is *the* place to stock up on shrink- and fade-resistant cotton fabric, tablecloths, skirts, aprons, shirts, and more dyed a deep, inviting blue by owner Mária Kovács, her husband Ferenc Panák, and others who carry on a proud family tradition that began way back in 1878. ⊠ *Bogdányi út 36* ☎ *26/314–388.*

László Vincze Paper Mill. Beautiful stationery, booklets, and other handmade paper products are displayed and sold at this small workshop at the top of a broken cobblestone street. Mr. Vincze lovingly creates his thick, watermarked paper using traditional, 2,000-year-old bleaching methods. ⊠ *Angyal utca 5* ☎ *26/314–328.*

Palmetta Design Galéria. Traditional crafts take a back seat in this onetime wine cellar to refreshingly contemporary designs, including textiles, ceramics, lamps, jewelry, and artwork by Hungarian and international artists and designers. ⊠ *Bogdányi út 14* ☎☎ *26/313–649.*

SZENTENDRE SZIGET

⑧ *6 km (4 mi) north of Szentendre to bridge at Tahi; 27 km (17 mi) north of Budapest to the bridge at Tahi.*

Looking for some tranquillity after a couple of hours of squeezing through the crowds in downtown Szentendre? The answer is Szentendre sziget (Szentendre Island), the lush green oasis right across the river. At the time of the Hungarian conquest of the Carpathian Basin in AD 896, the flat island—33 km (21 mi) long and 3.8 km (2.4 mi) wide at its widest point—was used as pasture land. It subsequently became a key agricultural, ship-building, and fishing center that helped link the otherwise hilly Danube Bend with Buda to the south. Only after the end of the 120-year Turkish occupation of Hungary in the late 17th century did a loose-knit web of settlements develop; and from the mid-19th century on, resort districts began to spring up here and there for city-weary Budapesters. Beginning in the 1890s, agriculture was forced in toward the island center as the Budapest waterworks acquired much of the land on the island's perimeter to preserve as a natural aquifer, and by the 1970s Szentendre Island had become the prime source of water for the capital's two-million-plus residents. As a result, in stark contrast to other flat areas near Budapest, development here has been tightly restricted.

Though most of Szentendre Island comprises nature preserves and bucolic countryside—this is a rich habitat and stopping-off point for waterfowl—it also has four villages, each separated by a few miles of sparsely traveled roads, and several distinct, sweeping districts of summer homes small and large. From quaint Kisoroszi on its northern tip to the larger but lovely Szigetmonostor on the southern end, the island is a real gem that is surprisingly untouched and ripe for exploration.

Although you can access the island farther down the Danube Bend by crossing the bridge at Tahi or at one of several car-carrying ferries, it's easy to make a little excursion from Szentendre on foot, but even more doable by bicycle. Walk past downtown Szentendre along the Danube a few hundred yards to the second set of docks. (The first docks are for boats that run regularly between Szentendre and Budapest, though at a much more leisurely pace than the HÉV railway.) Here, a small, noisy little boat takes pedestrians and bicyclists across for 130 forints per person one-way (double if you have a bicycle); pay as you board. The ferry embarks for the island at 35 minutes past every hour from 8:35 AM until 7:35 PM, and returns at half-past, the last trip leaving the island at 7:30 PM. Getting to the island's inhabited areas is far easier by bicycle; if you're on

> ### A BERRY MERRY TIME
>
> If you're around during the first or second weekend in June, when the island's many strawberries are at their peak, don't miss this two-day annual tradition, Eperfeszivál (Strawberry Festival). Kicking off with a parade led by a brass band and majorettes as well as folk-costumed locals on horseback and in carriages, the festival is held by the bridge that connects the mainland village Tahi with the island's largest village, Tahitótfalu. There is something for all: music and shows, a flea market, an amusement park, a classic tug-of-war on the bridge between the two villages, and a "super party" of concerts on Saturday night. Check with Szentendre's Tourinform office for details.

foot, you will see mostly lush young forests and open meadows unless you walk 3 mi or so into the lovely, quiet village of Szigetmonostor. There's only one way to go from the ferry landing; after several hundred yards the main road curves to the right, and before long you'll reach a little four-way intersection. If you wish to encounter more people, go left.

Where to Stay & Eat

$–$$ ✕ **Pázsit tó Étterem & Pub.** Pázsit Lake Restaurant and Pub is the perfect place to stop on a hot summer day if you find yourself driving or bicycling around the middle of this lovely island. Just off the island's main road, on the side road that leads to the charming village of Pócsmegyer, here you can not only have your fill of traditional cuisine and, indeed, fish fare—including catfish, carp, or pike-perch straight from the pretty little quarry lake the restaurant's terrace looks out upon—but, at your own risk, and at a modest cost of 500 HUF (1,200 HUF for a family), you can take a dip in the lake after you dine. ⊠ *Nagyduna sétány 83, Pócsmegyer* ☎ *26/395–298* ▭ *No credit cards.*

¢ ✕ **Sarokház Cukrászda.** A bit more than a mile down the road from the Rosinante Lodge, this café is easy to find and well worthwhile to visit. Opened in 2004, it is the only café of note at the southern edge of Szigetmonostor (which helps explain its popularity). Here you'll find a fine selection of scrumptious-looking pastries combined with a bright, airy atmosphere and wood tables and floors. (If you enter town from the north—which you will if you arrive by car from the bridge at Tahi—you'll pass by a similar café on the village outskirts there, called Laki Cuki.) ⊠ *Fő út 66, Szigetmonostor* ☎ *26/393–625.*

Inspiration in the Bend

LONG AFTER HUNGARY'S KINGS made their homes in Esztergom and Visegrád, the Danube Bend was to become a haven of rest and relaxation—and of inspiration—for Hungarian painters and writers. For example, the hopeless romantic Sindbad, immortalized in a story by Gyula Krudy (1878–1933) called "By the Danube," rested, "healing his broken-down brain and his hammering heart" on the shores of the great river.

Though Hungarian painters these days are more apt to escape to retreats farther from Budapest and the crowds, Szentendre has a century-plus history as an artists' haven. Károly Ferenczy, Hungary's foremost master of *plein-air* impressionism, lived there from 1889 to 1892. The Danube Bend's most famous 20th-century painter was István Szőnyi (1894–1960), a former student of Ferenczy's who spent much of life in Zebegény, a picturesque village set against the Börzsöny Hills across the river from Pilismarót (midway between Visegrád and Esztergom). His works include "The Danube Bend at Zebegény" (1927). Szőnyi's former home is today a museum in Zebegény.

Whether or not you choose to dine at Szentendre's Rab Ráby restaurant, you should know its name comes from one of Hungary's most famous historical novels, *Rab Ráby* (Ráby the Prisoner), by Mór Jókai (1825–1904), which is set in Szentendre. The profound impact on Hungarian letters of this romanticized account of Mátyás Ráby, a civil servant in Szentendre jailed in 1786 for opposing corrupt local officials, prompted another Hungarian writer to remark that all Hungarians should have two books by their bedside, the Bible and *Rab Ráby*. But this was hardly the only literary work focused on this region of Hungary.

Zsigmond Móricz (1879–1942), a novelist known mostly for his realistic portrayal of peasant life, moved to Leányfalu, just north of Szentendre, and his home there became a quasi-retreat for many other literary luminaries. Another Leányfalu resident was Ferenc Karinthy (1921–92), whose one-act play "Danube Bend" is set not on the river but in a bar.

Visegrád, meanwhile, was home to the famous poet Lajos Áprily (1887–1967) beginning in 1937; like Móricz's home, Áprily's functioned as a haven for other poets and writers.

The great poet Mihály Babits (1883–1941) was so inspired by Hungary's largest Roman Catholic church that he wrote "Dal az esztergomi bazilikáról" ("Song about the Esztergom Basilica"). More recently, the great contemporary Hungarian novelist Péter Nádas lived for years in charming Kisoroszi, on Szentendre Island's southern tip.

Beyond the matter of its rich history and breathtaking scenery, perhaps the ubiquitous idea among Hungarians that their nation is a cultural crossroads between East and West helps explain why the Danube's turn of course here—as it proceeds from Western Europe toward the Balkans—has resounded with such symbolic significance for painters and writers alike.

¢ 🖼 **Rácz Fogadó.** This charming and surprisingly affordable little inn opened in 2005 in lovely though isolated Kisoroszi, which has long been the secret of Hungarians looking to avoid more touristy places. The simply furnished, mostly shower-equipped rooms (you get a TV on request) are spacious, with pine floors and pretty little green or yellow bed lamps; one room is extra large and has a bathtub. Breakfast is served (for a minimal charge) in the popular restaurant downstairs, which otherwise serves its traditional fare from around mid-June through September. (Note that the phone number is shared with a nearby grocery store; if it sounds like they've answered, say the inn's name and try calling back; the store clerk will then hopefully let it keep ringing until the inn picks it up.) ⊠ *Hősök tere 3, H-2024 Kisoroszi* ☎ *26/592–010 or 20/981–8071 (mobile)* 🖷 *26/592–011* ⇌ *19 rooms, 2 suites* ⚐ *Restaurant; no a/c* ▭ *No credit cards* ⊙ *EP.*

¢ 🖼 **Rosinante Fogadó.** This cloistered gem—also called the Rosinante

Fodor'sChoice Lodge—opened in 1999 in the middle of a vast natural area over a mile

★   from the nearest town. Rooms, which have showers only, have bright, modern furnishings, wood floors, checkered-quilt bedspreads, and a decidedly homey atmosphere. The restaurant menu (printed on parchment-like paper) offers delicious, French-style fare ($$–$$$). A 10-minute walk from the landing for the Szentendre ferry, the lodge can be reached by car if you cross over by ferry at Leányfalu or by the bridge a bit farther north, at Tahi. Drive about 1 km (½ mi) south past Szigetmonostor on the main (and only) road; the hotel will be on your left. Reserve at least one month in advance. ⊠ *Szigetmonostor* ☎ *26/722–000 or 20/961–1843* 🖷 *26/722–010* ⊕ *www.rosinante.hu* ⇌ *19 rooms, 2 suites* ⚐ *Restaurant, minibars, pool, sauna, Jacuzzi, meeting room; no a/c* ▭ *AE, MC, V* ⊙ *BP.*

Sports & the Outdoors

HORSEBACK RIDING   **Zablakert lovarda.** One of many stables on the island where you can ride a horse for around 2,500 HUF an hour (this fee includes a trainer), this ☾ one is 2½ km (1½ mi) north of Tahitótfalu, on the main road to Kisoroszi. ⊠ *Kisoroszi országút, Tahitótfalu* ☎ *30/961–5797.*

Less readily accessible by bus but well worth a look is the Native American–themed Halápi Lovarda, whose thatched roof structures (beyond an entrance gate fringed by totem poles and other Indian motifs) are hard to miss on your left about 2½ km (1½ mi) south of Kisoroszi (i.e., before you reach the village). ⊠ *Szécheni út, 89/1 hrsz. Kisoroszi* ☎ *30/974–0615 or 20/918–1068.*

VISEGRÁD

➒ *23 km (14 mi) north of Szentendre, 44 km (27 mi) north of Budapest.*

Visegrád was the seat of the Hungarian kings during the 14th century, when a fortress built here by the Angevin kings became the royal residence. Today the imposing fortress at the top of the hill towers over the peaceful little town of quiet, tree-lined streets and solid old houses. The forested hills rising just behind the town offer popular hiking possibilities. For a taste of Visegrád's best, climb to the Fellegvár, and then wander and take in the views of the Danube curving through the country-side; but make time to stroll around the village center a bit—on Fő utca and other streets that pique your interest.

★ Crowning the top of a 1,148-foot hill, the dramatic **Fellegvár** (Citadel) was built in the 13th century and served as the seat of Hungarian kings in the early 14th century. In the Middle Ages the citadel was where the Holy Crown and other royal regalia were kept, until they were stolen by a dishonorable maid of honor in 1440; 23 years later King Matthias had to pay 80,000 HUF to retrieve them from Austria. (For the fore-seeable future, the crown is safe in the Parliament building in Budapest.) A *panoptikum* (akin to slide projection) show portraying the era of the kings is included with admission. The breathtaking views of the Danube Bend below are ample reward for the strenuous 40-minute hike up. Then again, you can always drive up the hill from the center of Visegra/ac/d in five minutes. ☒ *Fellegvár Nagyvillám* ☎ *26/398–101* ☒ *Fellegvár 850 HUF, Fellegvár and panoptikum 1,150 HUF* ☉ *Daily 10–6, closed in snowy conditions.*

In the 15th century, King Matthias Corvinus had a separate palace built on the bank of the Danube below the citadel. It was eventually razed by the Turks, and not until 1934 were the ruins finally excavated. Nowa-days you can see the disheveled remnants of the Királyi palota (Royal Palace) and its Salamon torony (Salamon Tower), which are part of the **Mátyás Király Múzeum** (King Matthias Museum). The Salomon Tower has two small exhibits displaying ancient statues and well structures from the age of King Matthias. Especially worth seeing is the red-marble well, built by a 15th-century Italian architect. Above a ceremonial courtyard rise the palace's various halls; on the left you can still see a few fine orig-inal carvings, which give an idea of how magnificent the palace must once have been. Inside the palace is a small exhibit on its history, as well as a collection of gravestones dating from Roman times to the 19th century. Fridays in May, the museum hosts medieval crafts demonstrations. ☒ *Fő utca 29* ☎ *26/398–026* ⊕ *www.visegrad.hu/muzeum* ☒ *Free (75 HUF to use the toilet)* ☉ *Royal Palace Tues.–Sun. 9–6 (entry until 5:30). Sa-lomon Tower May–Sept., Tues.–Sun. 9–6 (entry until 5:30).*

Like a tiny, precious gem, the miniature **Millennial Chapel** sits in a small clearing, tucked away on a corner down Fő utca, Visegrád's main street. The bite-size, powder-yellow church was built in 1896 to celebrate the Magyar Millennium, and is open only on Pentecost and a few other hol-idays. ☒ *Fő utca 113.*

Where to Stay & Eat

$$–$$$ ✕ **Sirály Restaurant.** With low lighting and funky, colorful, illuminated marsh scenes by your table mitigating its overall tourist-trap nature, this big but cramped restaurant opposite the ferry landing—which op-erates jointly with the Hotel Visegrád's adjacent Renaissance Restau-rant—specializes in wild game while also offering traditional fare and some well-intended vegetarian dishes (e.g., fried soy steak in mayon-naise sauce with vegetables). In summer, when cooking is often done on the terrace overlooking the Danube, expect barbecued meats and stews, soups, and gulyás served in old-fashioned pots. ⊠ *Rév utca 15* ☏ *26/398–376* ⊟ *AE, MC, V.*

★ **$–$$** ✕ **Gulyás Csárda.** This cozy little restaurant decorated with antique folk art and memorabilia complements its eight indoor tables with additional seating outside during the warmer months. The cuisine is typical home-style Hungarian, with a limited selection of tasty traditional dishes. Try the *halászlé* (spicy fish soup), served in a pot and kept warm on a small spirit burner; or, if you're adventurous, *pacalpörkölt* (tripe stew) with boiled parsley potatoes. ⊠ *Nagy Lajos király utca 4* ☏ *26/398–329* ⊟ *No credit cards.*

¢–$$ ✕ **Don Vito Pizzeria & Ristorante.** The pizza is okay, the ambience is A-OK. Yards from the Millennial Chapel in the village center, this is *the* place to eat if you're game for a setting inspired by *The Godfather.* In addition to almost 30 creative pizzas, there's plenty of pasta, poultry, and beef—including "Bloody Vendetta Steak," which the menu describes in English as "fatally hot tenderloin in a sauce red as blood." You can sit on the terrace out front or in one of three small rooms adorned with paintings and photos of underworld characters as well as a piano and a plethora of objects, including a sawed-off shotgun from Sicily; a few folksy Hungarian baskets are thrown in to confuse matters. The bathroom door looks likes the door of a safe. The American-Sicilian gangster theme is, meanwhile, complemented by jazzy Hungarian background music. ⊠ *Fő utca 83* ☏ *26/397–230* ⊟ *No credit cards.*

★ **$$** ▦ **Thermal Hotel Visegrád.** The Danube Bend's newest, priciest, and largest hotel, the Visegrád Superior, as it's also called, has in pomp, luxury, and breathtaking views what it lacks in charm. Opened in 2004, it's actually 3 km (2 mi) from Visegrád on Route 11 as you go toward Esztergom, facing the Danube and right beside a lovely outdoor swimming complex (*see* Sports & the Outdoors), though it also has its own such facilities. One might be tempted to call it a big, ultra-modern blight on an otherwise idyllic landscape if it weren't so nice in other ways. Most rooms—which, though a bit ordinary looking and tight on space, have pleasantly peach carpeting and light green bedspreads, plus terraces and great views—have full baths. Rates vary depending on whether the rooms face the Danube or the forested hillside behind the hotel. Suites are about twice the price of a regular room. ⊠ *Lepencevölgy hrsz. 1213, H-2025* ☏ *26/801–900* 🖷 *26/801–918* ⊕ *www.thv.hu* ⇥ *164 rooms, 10 suites* ⌂ *2 restaurants, café, minibars, in-room safes, in-room data ports, refrigerators, cable TV, 2 pools (1 indoor), hair salon, massage, sauna, Turkish bath, Ping-Pong, squash, 2 bars, shop, meeting rooms, car rental, free parking* ⊟ *AE, DC, MC, V* ⊺⃝ *BP.*

$–$$ ▦ **Beta Hotel Silvanus.** Situated ideally on Fekete Hill, with commanding forest and Danube views, this is Visegrád's highest-altitude hotel and one of its finest. The amenities include a wellness center with tepidarium (salt therapy). Although getting here by car is easiest, a bus does stop nearby three times daily. Hikers and bikers will find linking trails in the forest behind. Only suites are air-conditioned, though the somewhat pricier rooms facing the Danube (which get more sun) are equipped with special sun shades. A new wing opened in fall 2006. ⊠ *Fekete-hegy, H-2025* ☏🖷 *26/398–311* ⊕ *www.hotelsilvanus.hu* ⇥ *128 rooms, 10* *suites & Restaurant, café, room service, minibars, cable TV with movies, indoor pool, hair salon, massage, sauna, steam room, bowling, bar, playground, dry cleaning, laundry service, meeting rooms, free parking, some pets allowed; no a/c in some rooms ⊟ AE, DC, MC, V ⧀ BP.*

★ ¢ ▦ **Hotel Honti.** This 23-room hotel and an older, alpine-style pension (where the rooms are on the lower end of the price scale) share the same yard in a quiet residential area, a five-minute walk from the town center. Apple trees and a gurgling brook create a peaceful, rustic ambience, and the service is as friendly. The pension has seven tiny, clean rooms tucked under sloping ceilings with balconies, some with lovely Danube views; rooms in the hotel are more spacious and more expensive, some with balconies affording a splendid view of the citadel in the distance. Only two rooms in the hotel have a/c. ⊠ *Fő utca 66, H-2025* ☎ *26/398–120* 🖷 *26/397–274* ⊕ *www.hotelhonti.hu* ⇆ *28 rooms & Restaurant, minibars, cable TV, meeting room, free parking, some pets allowed, no-smoking rooms; no a/c in some rooms* ⊟ *No credit cards* ⧀ *BP.*

¢ ▦ **Hotel Visegrád.** This centrally located hotel, built in the late 1990s, also has an in-house travel agency that organizes local excursions in the area for both groups and individuals. Every room has a balcony with views of the Danube or the citadel, and all are pristine yet comfortable, many in warm lemony and ochre hues. The suites are suitable for a family with three children. The hotel's Renaissance Restaurant is a slightly tacky but likable renaissance-theme restaurant. An indoor pool was planned as of this writing and should be ready by 2007. ⊠ *Rév út 15, H-2025* ☎ *26/397–034* 🖷 *26/597–088* ⊕ *www.visegradtours.hu* ⇆ *33 rooms, 7 suites & Restaurant, in-room safes, minibars, cable TV, meeting room, travel services, free parking* ⊟ *AE, DC, MC, V* ⧀ *BP.*

¢ ▦ **Patak Fogadó.** At a shaded bend in the road on the right, just beyond Visegrád's center leading up the hill to the citadel, this is a friendly, reasonably priced little pension. On a forested hillside overlooking a babbling brook, it has four bright, modern rooms with wood floors and ceilings; each room has a double-mattress bed and a shower. If the owners' plans to eventually add dozens of new rooms, a pool, and a fitness room bear fruit, the place may lose a bit of its charm, but for now, at least, the combination of location, tranquillity, and affordable rates make this a good place to stay. The restaurant, which serves traditional Hungarian fare, is closed on Mondays. ⊠ *Mátyás Király utca 92, H-2025* ☎ *26/397–486* 🖷 *26/397–102* ⊕ *www.patakfogado.hu* ⇆ *4 rooms & Restaurant, cable TV, bar; no a/c* ⊟ *AE, MC, V* ⧀ *EP.*

Nightlife & the Arts

The **Visegrád International Palace Games,** held annually on the second weekend in July, take the castle complex back to its medieval heyday, with horseback jousting tournaments, archery games, a medieval music and crafts fair, and other festivities.

Sports & the Outdoors

HIKING Visegrád makes a great base for exploring the trails of the Visegrád and Pilis hills. A hiking map is posted on the corner of Fő utca and Rév utca, just above the pale-green Roman Catholic Parish Church. A well-trodden, well-marked hiking trail (posted with red signs) leads from the edge of Visegrád to the town of Pilisszentlászló, a wonderful 8½-km (5⅓-mi) journey that takes about three hours, through the oak and beech forests of the Visegrád Hills into the Pilis conservation region. Deer, wild boars, and mouflons (a type of wild sheep) roam freely here, and there are fields of yellow-blooming spring pheasant's eye and black pulsatilla.

SWIMMING   The outdoor thermal pools at **Lepence,** 3 km (2 mi) southwest of Visegrád on Route 11, combine good soaking with splendrous Danube Bend views. Those able to get there by 6 AM can get in for an early-morning swim that ends at 8 for just 550 HUF (less than half-price); the same price applies if you go after 4 PM. ☒ *Lepence-völgyi Termál és Strandfürdő, Lepence* ☎ *26/398–208* ☒ *1,200 HUF* ☉ *June–Aug., daily 9–6:30; May and Sept., daily 9–6.*

TOBOGGAN SLIDE   Winding through the trees on Nagy-Villám Hill is the **Wiegand Toboggan Run,** one of the longest slides you've ever seen. You ride on a small cart that is pulled uphill by trolley, then careen down the slope in a small, steel trough that resembles a bobsled run. ☒ *Panoráma út, ½ km (¼ mi) from Fellegvár* ☎ *26/397–397* ☒ *320 HUF; 1,600 HUF for six runs* ☉ *May–Aug., weekdays 9–6, weekends 9–7; Apr. and Sept.–Oct., daily 11–4; Nov.–Mar. (weather permitting), weekends 11–4.*

ESZTERGOM

⑩ *21 km (13 mi) west of Visegrád, 65 km (40 mi) northwest of Budapest.*

Esztergom stands on the site of a Roman fortress, at the westernmost curve of the heart-shaped Danube Bend, where the Danube (and a bridge built in 2001) marks the border between Hungary and Slovakia. St. Stephen, the first Christian king of Hungary and founder of the nation, was crowned here in AD 1000, establishing Esztergom as Hungary's first capital, which it remained for the next 250 years. The majestic Bazilika, Hungary's largest, is Esztergom's main draw, situated on the Vár (Castle) hill, which was home of a series of royal palaces and churches for centuries. Likewise not to be missed is the fine-art collection of the Primate's Palace. If you like strolling, leave yourself a little time to explore the narrow streets of Viziváros (Watertown) below the Bazilika, lined with brightly painted baroque buildings.

To the south of the cathedral, on **Szent Tamás Hill,** is a small church dedicated to St. Thomas à Becket of Canterbury. From here you can look down on the town and see how the Danube temporarily splits, forming an island, **Prímás-sziget,** that locals use as a base for waterskiing and swimming, in spite of the pollution. To reach it, cross the Kossuth Bridge.

Fodor'sChoice   Esztergom's **Bazilika** (basilica), the largest in Hungary, stands on a hill ★   overlooking the town; it is the seat of the cardinal primate of Hungary. Completed in 1856—after decades of work—on the site of a medieval cathedral that had been largely destroyed during the wars against the Turks centuries before, this was where the famous anti-communist cleric Cardinal József Mindszenty was finally reburied in 1991 (he was originally buried in Austria when he died in 1975), ending decades of religious intolerance by the communists. Its most interesting feature is perhaps the Bakócz Chapel (1506), named for a primate of Hungary who only narrowly missed becoming pope. On your left as you enter, the chapel—which was taken apart piece by piece and put back together again when the cathedral around it was built—is the most beautiful work of Renaissance ar-

chitecture in Hungary; note its red marble and magnificent carvings. Other highlights include the sacristy, which contains a valuable collection of medieval ecclesiastical art; the vast crypt, where the cathedral's builders and its key priests are buried; and, for a great view of Esztergom and environs after a steep climb up a long, winding staircase, the observation platform in the cathedral's cupola. The bell tower is also open to the public. If your timing is lucky, you could attend a concert during one of the various classical music festivals held here in summer. The adjacent **Vármúzeum** (Castle Museum) is also worth a look, with rooms full of archaeological ruins and displays on the history of the castle, but with practically no English text. Its several entrances are all off a courtyard to the left of the cathedral. As of this writing, a grand new square, including a memorial site to Cardinal Mindszenty, was under construction beside the cathedral. ⊠ *Szent István tér 1* ☏ *33/311–895 or 33/402–354* ⊕ *www.bazilika-esztergom.hu* ✉ *Church and Vármúzeum free, crypt 100 HUF, sacristy 500 HUF, cupola 200 HUF, bell tower 200 HUF* ☉ *Church Mar.–Oct., daily 6–6; Nov.–Feb., daily 6–4. Crypt Mar.–Oct., daily 9–4:30; Nov.–Feb., daily 10–3. Sacristy Mar.–Oct., daily 9–4:30; Nov.–Dec., Tues.–Fri. 11–3:30; weekends 10–5:30. Cupola Apr.–Oct., daily 9–4:30.*

Considered by many to be Hungary's finest art gallery, the **Keresztény Múzeum** (Museum of Christian Art), in the Primate's Palace, has a thorough collection of early Hungarian and Italian paintings (the 14th- and 15th-century Italian collection is unusually large for a museum outside Italy). Unique holdings include the *Coffin of Our Lord* from Garamszentbenedek (today Hronský Beňadik, Slovakia); the wooden statues of the Apostles and of the Roman soldiers guarding the coffin are masterpieces of Hungarian baroque sculpture. The building also holds the Primate's Archives, which contain 20,000 volumes, including several medieval codices. Permission to visit the archives must be obtained in advance. ⊠ *Primate's Palace, Mindszenty tér 2* ☏ *33/413–880* ⊕ *www.keresztenymuzeum.hu* ✉ *500 HUF* ☉ *Apr.–Oct., Tues.–Sun. 10–6; Nov.–Dec. and Mar., Tues.–Sun. 11–3.*

NEED A BREAK? A visit to Esztergom wouldn't be complete without a walk along **Kis Duna sétány**, the parklike promenade that passes along a peaceful little side branch of the Danube between Esztergom's mainland and the island called Prímás-sziget, and the **Dunakorzó Kávézó Söröző** (Danube Promenade Café and Pub)–

with three giant plane trees near its outdoor seating—is a splendid place to sit down for a cappuccino, a beer, or a shot of pálinka while doing so; and perhaps, to dig into a slice of delectable *almás pite* (apple pie). (⊠ Kis Duna sétány 7 ☎ 33/311–710)

Where to Stay & Eat

$$–$$$ ✕ **Csülök Csárda.** With its hearty Hungarian fare, cozy rustic atmosphere, and unbeatable location in view of the basilica (just as you enter downtown Esztergom from the direction of Visegrád), the Ham Knuckle Tavern is still popular after reopening in 2006 following a thorough makeover. While rumor has it that the money spent on renovation was at the expense of a top-notch kitchen staff, there are only so many ways to crack knuckles, which are a specialty here. Bean soup with knuckle is quite enough for a small meal. To fill up some more, try the "Baking Dish Knuckle," a scrumptious mix of smoked, sliced knuckle fried with potatoes, smothered with a garlicky sour-cream sauce, and served in a baking dish with bits of bacon sprinkled on top. ⊠ *Batthyány utca 9* ☎ *33/412–420* ▭ *AE, DC, MC, V.*

$$–$$$ ✕ **Prímás Pince.** Vaulted ceilings and brick walls make a charming setting for refined Hungarian fare at this wine cellar–like, touristy—but good—restaurant built right into the imposing, 30-foot brick wall below the basilica. Try the sirloin tips in cream, with asparagus and goose liver plus corn, rice, and potatoes; or perhaps the turkey strips cooked in a brew of marjoram-laced white wine with potato croquettes and almonds. ⊠ *Szent István tér 4* ☎ *33/313–495* ▭ *AE, DC, MC, V* ☺ *No dinner Jan.–Feb.*

★ $–$$ ✕ **Padlizsán Étterem.** The Eggplant Restaurant, which opened in 2004 on a quiet side street at the foot of Castle Hill behind the basilica, is Esztergom's best-kept secret—though its enduring quality may hinge on the presence of amiable owner-cum-chef Ferenc Jakab. You might begin with an eggplant salad with balsamic dressing, goat cheese, olives, and pepperoni; and move on to braised venison knuckle with juniper, stuffed savoy cabbage, and potato noodles; or a steak that, says Jakab, comes from British beef. The hazelnut-cherry strudel and the palacsinta soufflé are scrumptious. The wine list includes a wide range of choice Hungarian varieties. The soft hues and yellow walls of the two elegant inside rooms are complemented by a long-stem rose on every table and jazz music playing softly in the background. In the courtyard, the castle looms above you; even the chairs outside, though plastic, are somehow tasteful. ⊠ *Pázmány utca 21* ☎ *33/311–212 or 30/388–1549 (mobile)* ▭ *DC, MC, V.*

¢ ✕▭ **Szalma Csárda & Panzió.** This restaurant and pension is on a tranquil, fairly undeveloped stretch of the Danube—even if it is beyond the more striking scenery to the west of Esztergom. The 20-room pension, which resembles a ranch house, has small, double, shower-equipped rooms that are clean and bright and furnished simply with low, summer-camp-style pine beds. ■ TIP➔ **A 60-bed hostel opened next door recently under the same management; beds there are just 2,300 HUF per night, although you do share a room with three to five other guests.** The restaurant ($–$$) is splendidly rustic, complete with a large earthenware stove in the main room and strings of dried red peppers hanging all over the place. Listen to live Gypsy music while enjoying "long-forgotten peasant dishes," such as chicken paprikash with wax beans and dill-spiced dumplings on the side. ⊠ *Prímás-sziget, Nagyduna sétány 2, H-2500* 🏧 *33/315–336 or 33/ 403–838* ⊕ *www.szalmacsarda.hu* 🗗 *19 rooms* ♤ *No a/c, TV in some rooms* ▤ *No credit cards* ⟦⊙⟧ *BP.*

¢ 🎯 **Alabárdos Panzió.** Conveniently downhill from the basilica, this cozy remodeled home provides excellent views from upstairs. Rooms (doubles and quads) are small but less cramped than at other small pensions. ⚠ **A hearty breakfast including homemade cold cuts is included for 1,000 HUF more per room; if you don't need this, be sure to make this clear when reserving.** ⊠ *Bajcsy-Zsilinszky út 49, H-2500* 🏧 *33/312–640* 🗗 *24 rooms* ♤ *Cable TV, laundry facilities, meeting room; no a/c* ▤ *No credit cards* ⟦⊙⟧ *EP.*

¢ 🎯 **Hotel Esztergom.** The furnishings may be a bit old, but this hotel has an unbeatable setting on Prímás-szíget, what with the Danube on one side, the basilica on another, and a modern watersports complex on yet another side. All rooms have balconies, though the largest—and nicest— rooms face away from the river. Both suites and two rooms on each floor have mobile a/c units. ⊠ *Prímás-szíget, Nagyduna sétány, H-2500* ☎ *33/412–883 or 33/412–555* 🖷 *33/412–853* ⊕ *www.hotel-esztergom. hu* 🗗 *34 rooms, 2 suites* ♤ *Restaurant, cable TV, meeting room; no a/c in some rooms* ▤ *AE, DC, MC, V.*

Nightlife & the Arts

Every two years Esztergom hosts the **Nemzetközi Gitár Fesztivál** (International Guitar Festival), during which renowned classical guitarists from around the world hold master classes and workshops for participants. Recitals are held nearly every night in various venues in Esztergom and also in Budapest, and neighboring towns. The climax of it all is the glorious closing concert, held in the basilica, in which the hundreds of participants join together and perform as a guitar orchestra. The festival runs for two weeks, usually beginning in early August in odd-numbered years. Tickets and information are available at tourist offices. ⊕ *www. guitarfestival.hu.*

Sports & the Outdoors

SWIMMING Esztergom's new aquatic wonder world, **Aquasziget** (Aqua Island), opened in 2005 on Prímás-sziget a short walk from the bridge to Slovakia. Also called an *élményfürdő* (Sensation Spa) ("World of Adventures" as per its glossy brochure) for its host of facilities and treatments, this huge glass-walled structure includes an indoor pool complete with a waterfall and a little tropical rain forest, from which you can swim through (if you dare) to the outside pools. Inside you'll also find several saunas, a Jacuzzi, a Turkish-style bath where you can get a massage, and a fitness room. ■ TIP➔ **If you seek a simpler, lower-cost (600 HUF) swimming experience, head for the Szent István Strandfürdő on Kis Duna sétány right across from Prímás-sziget.** ⊠ *Táncsics Mihály utca 5* ☎ *33/511–100* 🏊 *pools and "infrasauna" 1,800 HUF before 4, 1,250 HUF after 4; other facilities extra* ⊙ *Daily 8–8.*

7

VÁC

⑪ *34 km (21 mi) north of Budapest; 20 km (12 mi) east of Nagymaros, which is accessed by ferry from Visegrád.*

With its lovely riverfront promenade, an imposing cathedral, an attractive main square, and a less delightful triumphal arch, the sleepy town of Vác, on the Danube's east bank, is well worth a short visit if only to watch the sun slowly set from the promenade. It is certainly a more relaxing place to saunter than Szentendre, as you probably won't find yourself shoulder-to-shoulder with other tourists. While Vác's historic town center is not as compact as Szentendre's—nor as overflowing in historic sites—and it lacks the scenic hill that makes Szentendre that much more of a tourist attraction, it is nonetheless replete with pretty baroque buildings in matte yellows and reds, offering visual rewards and photo opportunities for those who wander onto a few of its narrow cobblestone side streets heading in toward the river. If you arrive by train in late April or early May, you'll be greeted outside the station by a lovely pink promenade of cherry blossoms. Walk straight from here, and in 10 minutes you'll be on the main square, Március 15 tér—which as of this writing was undergoing extensive reconstruction that should leave it prettier than ever.

Vác's 18th-century **Székesegyház** (Cathedral) on Konstantin tér is an outstanding example of Hungarian neoclassicism. It was built between 1763 and 1777 by Archbishop Kristóf Migazzi to the designs of the Italian architect Isidor Carnevale; the most interesting features are the murals by the Austrian Franz Anton Maulbertsch, both on the dome and behind the altar. Exquisite frescoes decorate the walls inside. Due to break-ins, you can view the interior only through a locked gate, except during Mass (daily 8–9 AM and 6–7 PM). Across the street, by the way, is the building that houses the local Bishop's headquarters, with a lovely park behind it. ⊠ *Konstantin tér 11* ☎ *27/317–010* ✉ *Free* ⊙ *Daily 8–7.*

The pale yellow baroque facade of the **Fehérek temploma** (Church of the White Friars) towers over one corner of Március 15 tér. Built by the Dominican order between 1699 and 1755, the inside is a mix of baroque and rococo styles. ⊠ *Március 15 tér 20–24.*

A fascinating if somewhat macabre discovery of the **Memento Mori,** which adjoins the Fehérek temploma, was made in 1994 during renovation work on the Church of the White Friars, and the result is this unusual museum. Workers happened upon the largely forgotten, sealed entrance to a crypt that had been used by the Dominicans (who built and formerly owned the church) to bury clergy and local burghers from 1731 to 1801. Inside were numerous ornately decorated coffins with surprisingly well-preserved, still-clothed mummies and burial accessories inside. The coffins (mostly closed) were moved to a nearby cellar on the same square. A steep staircase leads downstairs to the cold exhibit room. ⊠ *Március 15 tér 19* ☎ *27/313–463 or 27/500–750* ⊕ *www.muzeum.vac.hu* ⊙ *Mar.–Oct., Tues.–Sun. 10–6.*

■ NEED A
BREAK? On the spacious main square, **Noztalgia Cukrászda** (Nostalgia Pastry Café;
⊠ Március 15 tér ☎ 27/313–539) is Vác's most elegant venue in which to sa-
tiate a sweet tooth, with historic photos on the walls.

Just around the corner from the main square, right behind the Fehérek temploma (Church of the White Friars), is Vác's outdoor food market. It's easy to
navigate your way around this delightful place and, yes, to grab a bite to eat.
(⊠ Káptalan utca 3 [main entrance] ⊙ Weekdays 6–4, Sat. 6–1, Sun. 6–10).

In 1764, when Archbishop Migazzi heard that Queen Maria Theresa
planned to visit his humble town, he hurriedly arranged the construction of a **triumphal arch.** The queen came and left, but the awkwardly
situated arch remains, at the edge of the city's historic core next to a ce-
ment-and-barbed-wire prison complex. ⊠ *Köztársaság út just past
Barabás utca.*

The **promenade** along the Danube is a wonderful place to stroll or picnic, looking out at the glistening river or back toward the pretty historic town. The main entrance to the riverfront area is from Petróczy
utca, which begins at the cathedral on Konstantin tér and feeds straight
into the promenade.

Vácrátóti Arborétum (4 km [2½ mi] from Vác) is Hungary's biggest and
best botanical garden, with more than 12,000 plant species. The ar-
boretum's top priority is botanical research, and the collection falls under
the auspices of the Hungarian Academy of Sciences. You're welcome
to stroll along the paths and sit on benches in the leafy shade. The greenhouse opens a bit later and closes earlier than the surrounding garden.
If you're driving from Vác, follow the signs toward Gödöllő, then toward Vácrátóti. ⊠ *Alkotmány utca 2–4* ☎ *28/360–122 Ext. 120*
⊠ *500 HUF* ⊙ *Apr.–Oct., daily 8–6; Nov.–Mar., daily 8–4. Greenhouse daily 9–4.*

Where to Eat

$$ ✕ **Halászkert Étterem.** The large terrace of this contemporary riverfront
restaurant some 100 yards from the ferry landing is a popular place for
a hearty lunch or dinner in warmer months. The menu includes an un-
usually large selection of Hungarian fish specialties, from catfish and
pike to trout and, indeed, pike-perch stuffed with catfish and bathed in
white-wine sauce (a dish that appears in unintelligible, half-Hungarian-
half-English language on the menu: "fogash fillet filled with sheathfish").
⊠ *Liszt Ferenc sétány 9* ☎ *27/315–985* ⊟ *AE, DC, MC, V.*

Nightlife & the Arts

In July and August a series of outdoor classical concerts are held in the
verdant **Vácrátóti Arborétum.** The last weekend in July brings the **Váci
Világi Vígalom** (Vác World Jamboree) festival, with folk dancing, music,
crafts fairs, and other festivities throughout town.

Sports & the Outdoors

Vác is the gateway to hiking in the forests of the Börzsöny Hills, rich
in natural springs, castle ruins, and splendid Danube Bend vistas. Con-

sult the Börzsöny hiking map, available at Tourinform offices, for planning a walk on the well-marked trails. The Tourinform office in Vác can also give you details on the three delightful "tourist trains" that chug in charming fashion deep into the Börzsöny; the closest one heads out from the village of Kismaros, just two train stops north of Vác on the same side of the Danube

Shopping

Duna-p'Art Galéria. On the riverfront promenade near the ferry landing and near the Halászkert Étterem, this art gallery has four exhibit rooms that display a wide variety of paintings and other works by more than 100 artists. (The capital "A" in the name, by the way, is a play on words, as *part* means "bank" in this context in Hungarian; and so "bank" melds with "art.") ⊠ *Liszt Ferenc sétány 3* ☎ *27/301–837.*

DANUBE BEND ESSENTIALS

BICYCLE TRAVEL

The Danube Bend is a great place to explore by bike, since most towns are relatively close together. Some routes have separate bike paths, while others run along the roads. (Szentendre sziget, with one arrow-straight flat road that runs the length of this parklike island, has so little traffic that it is a veritable bicyclist's paradise for those with half a day or, better yet, a full day plus a night, to spare.) Consult the "Danube Bend Cyclists' Map" (available at local Tourinform offices) for exact information. A perfect option is to rent a bicycle in Budapest and take it by the HÉV commuter railway—on the car that allows bikes, that is—to Szentendre, and ride from there; or else to rent in Szentendre.

BOAT & FERRY TRAVEL

If you have enough time, you can travel to the west-bank towns by cruise boat or jet foil from Budapest, a leisurely and pleasant journey, especially in summer and spring. Boating from Budapest to Esztergom takes five-and-a-half hours, to Visegrád three-and-a-half hours; the return trips (i.e., going downstream) are an hour or more shorter. Boats leave from the main Pest dock at Vigadó tér. The disadvantage of boat travel is that a round-trip by slow boat doesn't allow much time for sightseeing; the Esztergom route, for example, allows only under two hours before it's time to head back. And, as one traveler observed on Fodor's *Forum,* there's not much in the way of sights along the way but for lots of greenery—until you get beyond Szentendre, where the hills offer relatively dramatic vistas. Many people head upriver by boat in the morning and back down by bus or train as it's getting dark. There is daily service from Budapest to Visegrád, stopping in Szentendre. Less frequent boats go to Vác, on the east bank, as well.

Crossing the bridge between Esztergom and Stúrovo, on the Slovak side of the river, is a convenient way of accessing the opposite side of the Danube Bend in Hungary. (The Hungarian town of Szob, on the Slovak border along the east bank, is a five-minute drive from Stúrovo.) A scenic option is the regular daily passenger-and-car ferry service between several points on opposite sides of the Danube (except in winter when the river is too icy and the bridge is the only way to go). The crossing generally takes about 10 minutes and costs around 1,200 HUF per car and driver, 350 HUF per additional passenger. The crossing between Nagymaros and Visegrád is recommended, as it affords gorgeous views of Visegrád's citadel and includes a beautiful drive through rolling hills on Route 12 south and then west of Nagymaros. Mahart operates all these ferry services.

▶ **Mahart PassNave Passenger Shipping** ⊠ District V, Vigadó tér, Budapest ☎ 1/ 484–4013 (main info line) or 1/318–1223 (boat landing at Vigadó tér) ⊕ www. mahartpassnave.hu.

BUS TRAVEL

Buses, which are relatively inexpensive and fairly comfortable—if you get a seat and don't have to stand—run regularly between Budapest's Árpád híd bus station and most towns along both sides of the Danube. The ride to Szentendre takes about half an hour in easy traffic. (For an extra 10 minutes or so, the HÉV commuter train offers a more scenic ride.) If you don't have a car, this is the only way to get beyond Szentendre toward points along the Danube on the same side of the river, as there is no train service there.

CAR TRAVEL

Route 11 runs along the western shore of the Danube, connecting Budapest to Szentendre, Visegrád, and Esztergom. Route 2 runs along the eastern shore for driving between Budapest and Vác.

TOURS

Cityrama runs its popular "Danube Tour" (€56, or around 16,000 HUF) daily during the high season (May through September) from Wednesday to Sunday; from October to May, the tour is offered only once a week, so call ahead for exact dates and times. Departing from Budapest, the full-day tour begins with sightseeing in Visegrád, then Esztergom. After lunch, the tour moves on to Szentendre for a guided walk and makes a scenic return to Budapest down the Danube. (The tour returns by bus when the water level is low.) The company also offers half-day tours of Szentendre alone, for €44 (around 12,500 HUF). IBUSZ Travel organizes day-long bus trips from Budapest along the Danube (from April to October, Tuesday–Saturday; from November to March on Wednesday and Saturday only), stopping in Esztergom, Visegrád, and Szentendre. There's commentary in English; the cost per person, including lunch and admission fees, is €76 (around 21,500 HUF).

▶ **Cityrama** ☎ 1/302–4382 in Budapest ⊕ www.cityrama.hu. **IBUSZ Travel** ☎ 06–40/ 428–794 (toll-free) ⊕ www.ibusz.hu.

TRAIN TRAVEL

Vác and Esztergom have frequent daily express and local train service to and from Budapest's Nyugati (West) Station, but there is no service between Szentendre and Esztergom. Trains do not run to Visegrád either. The HÉV suburban railway runs between Batthyány tér (or Margaret Island, one stop north) in Budapest and Szentendre about every 10 to 20 minutes daily; the trip takes 40 minutes, and a *kiegészítő* (supplementary) ticket—which you need in addition to a Budapest public transport pass or ticket—costs 312 HUF one-way. Bicycles cost an extra 185 HUF; ask for a *bicikli pótjegy* (bicycle ticket). Bear in mind that not all trains go all the way to Szentendre; some go only as far as Békásmegyer, the last stop in the Budapest city limits, where you have to transfer to the next train that goes all the way (but you can do so with the same ticket). ■ TIP➔ On a hot summer day, one advantage of this HÉV journey is the opportunity to take a break in Csillaghegy to go for a swim at the beautiful outdoor swimming facility there, just a block from the HÉV station.

VISITOR INFORMATION

Esztergom Grantours ✉ Széchenyi tér 25, Esztergom 🖃🖨 33/417-052. **IBUSZ** ✉ Kossuth L. utca 5, Esztergom 🖨 33/411-643 or 520-920 ⊕ www.ibusz.hu ✉ Bogdány utca 11, Szentendre 🖨 26/500-178. **Komtourist** ✉ Lőrinc utca 6, Esztergom 🖨 33/414-152. **Tourinform** ✉ Dumtsa Jenő utca 22, Szentendre 🖨 26/317-965 or 26/317-966 ⊕ www.tourinform.hu/ ✉ Március 15 tér 17-18, Vác 🖨 27/316-160. **Visegrád Tours** ✉ Sirály Restaurant, Rév utca 15, Visegrád 🖨 26/398-160.

Lake Balaton

WORD OF MOUTH

"Tihany was very pleasant. Yes, it is touristy, but it is very nicely put together for a day of touring. . . . The village is protected as a national monument, so little change has taken place. . . . Szigliget is another village worth a stop. It has many thatched-roof houses and vineyards, and the lakeside here has a Mediterranean look. . . . We loved Keszthely, especially the Festetics mansion."

–Joe

By Paul
Olchváry

LAKE BALATON, THE LARGEST LAKE IN CENTRAL EUROPE, stretches 80 km (50 mi) across Hungary. Its vast surface area contrasts dramatically with its modest depths: averaging only 9¾ feet deep, the lake is just 52½ feet at its deepest point in the center of the lake along the northern shore at the Tihany Félsziget (Tihany Peninsula). The Balaton—the most popular playground of this landlocked nation—lies just 90 km (56 mi) to the southwest of Budapest, so it's within easy reach of the capital by car, train, bus, and even bicycle. On a hot day in July or August it seems the entire country and half of Germany are packed towel to towel on the lake's grassy public beaches, paddling about in the warm, clean, silky-soft water, and consuming fried meats and beer at the omnipresent snack bars. The Balaton is also a major wine-producing region, and scores of vineyards and wine-tasting cellars can be found in many villages.

Called the "Hungarian Sea" and accordingly revered as a national treasure by Hungarians, the Balaton was formed millions of years ago following volcanic eruptions and tectonic sagging. Today freshwater flows in from several creeks and a river to feed the lake, and scientists estimate that the water in the lake is completely refreshed every two years.

On the lake's hilly northern shore, where you'll also find most of the region's wineries, is Balatonfüred, Hungary's oldest spa town, famed for natural springs that bubble out curative waters. The national park on the Tihany Peninsula lies just to the south, and regular boat service links Tihany and Balatonfüred with Siófok and other towns on the southern shore. Flatter and more crowded with resorts, cottages, and trade-union rest houses, the southern shore (beginning with Balatonszentgyörgy) has fewer sights and is not as attractive as the northern one: north-shore locals say the only redeeming quality of the southern shore is its views back across the lake to the north. Families with small children prefer the southern shore for its shallower, warmer waters—you can walk for almost 2 km (1 mi) before it deepens. The water warms up to 25°C (77°F) in summer. ⚠ As pleasant as its water generally is, the Balaton is famous for hazardous whitecaps that can kick up with little notice, so take care when venturing far out. Warning lamps all around the lake notify bathers and boaters alike of oncoming troubled waters.

Every town along both shores has at least one *strand* (beach). The typical Balaton strand is a complex

---

PAUL'S TOP 5

Tihany. This ravishing town and the surrounding peninsula is perhaps the most historic part of the Balaton area.

Club Hotel Badacsony. A private beach is just a step away from this hotel right on the shore of Lake Balaton. The Club Hotel is the largest in the area.

Club Imola. An exquisite break from the hustle of the nearby Balatonfüred strand.

Oliva Panzió. This restaurant and garden pub in downtown Veszprém is as charming as they come.

Szigliget. A tranquil, picturesque town with fine thatch-roof wine-press houses and a small beach.

of blocky wooden changing cabanas and snack bars, fronted by a grassy, flat stretch along the water for sitting and sunbathing. Most have paddleboat and other simple boat rentals. A small entrance fee—generally between 300 and 600 HUF—is usually charged.

If you're interested in exploring beyond the beach, you can set out by car or bicycle along numerous well-groomed bike paths that follow the shores on beautiful village-to-village tours—stopping to view lovely old baroque churches, photograph a stork family perched high in its chimney-top nest, or climb a vineyard-covered hill for sweeping vistas. Since most vacationers keep close to the shore, a small amount of exploring into the roads and countryside heading away from the lake will reward you with a break from the summer crowds.

About the Hotels & Restaurants

The high season for hotels in the Lake Balaton region generally runs from June through September, and while off-season means lower rates, many hotels in the area close during winter months, from November to April, as the Balaton is quite barren during colder months. Most hotels are large, resort-style complexes with their own pools and saunas a short distance from the lakeshore. Hévíz, with its own thermal lake and spas, is one of the most-visited spa resorts in all of Europe. The majority of Balaton hotels quote rates in euros.

Menus in Balaton restaurants are certainly not wanting in freshwater fish, and a trip to Balaton is not complete without sampling fish from its waters. The most popular is the *Balatoni fogas* (pike-perch); also popular is *harcsa* (catfish). Hungarian *halaszlé* (fish soup) is usually served in large bowls with *ponty* (carp), pasta, and spicy red paprika. Aside from fresh fish, the selection of food in Balaton is traditional Hungarian: lots of meat, battered vegetables, and salads laden with mayonnaise. Dress is casual at most restaurants.

WHAT IT COSTS In Euros & Forints				
$$$$	$$$	$$	$	¢
HOTELS IN EUROS				
over 225	175–225	125–175	75–125	under 75
HOTELS IN FORINTS				
over 56,000	44,000–56,000	31,000–44,000	18,500–31,000	under 18,500
RESTAURANTS IN FORINTS				
over 3,500	2,500–3,500	1,500–2,500	800–1,500	under 800

Hotel prices are for two people in a standard double room with a private bath and breakfast during peak season (June through September). Restaurant prices are per person for a main course at dinner and include tax (15% as of this writing) but not service.

Numbers in the margin correspond to numbers on the Lake Balaton map.

VESZPRÉM

❶
Fodor'sChoice
★
116 km (72 mi) southwest of Budapest. 18 km (11 mi) north of Lake Balaton.

Hilly Veszprém is the center of cultural life in the northern half of the Balaton region and often serves as the starting point for trips around Balaton, even if it is a bit removed from the lake itself. The city was established during the 11th century AD under Hungary's King St. Stephen, but it was destroyed by the Turks during their occupation and again during Hungarian-Austrian independence battles. Veszprém was rebuilt in the early 18th century, but its castle was never reconstructed. This charming small city has several lovely pedestrian squares with cafés and outdoor seating in the summer months.

★ **Várhegy** (Castle Hill) is the most picturesque part of town, north of Szabadság tér. It's where you'll find all the sights worth seeing. The Hősök kapuja (Heroes' Gate) at the entrance to the castle commemorates those who died during World War I, and also houses a small exhibit on Hungary's history. Vár utca, just off Óváros tér, is the only street in the castle area, and it's off this little cobblestone street that all the sights can be found, including the cathedral and bishop's palace. The cathedral has been destroyed and rebuilt a handful of times since the 11th century, the current structure dating from the early 1900s. Vár utca continues past the square by the cathedral—where the *ünnepi játékok* open-air music festival (mostly classical and jazz) is held for several days in early August—up to a terrace erected on the north staircase of the castle.

During reconstruction of the cathedral in the early part of the 20th century workers unearthed a vaulted chamber believed to be part of a palace that stood on the site until the 14th century and once belonged to St. Stephen's queen, Gizella. The baroque chapel, called the **Gizella kápolna** (Gizella Chapel) was reconstructed in 1938, on the 900th anniversary of St. Stephen's death; its Byzantine-style frescoes of the apostles, which date from the 13th century, were restored. ⊠ *Vár utca* ☏ *88/426–088* 🖃 *200 HUF* ☉ *May–Oct., Tues.–Sun. 10–5.*

Just past the Heroes' Gate and down a little alley to the left is the **Tűztorony** (Fire Tower). You'll see that the lower level is medieval, although the upper stories are baroque. There is a good view of the town from the balcony. ⊠ *Vár utca 17* ☏ *88/425–204* 🖃 *300 HUF* ☉ *Early Mar.–early May, daily 10–5; mid-May–Oct., daily 10–6.*

OFF THE
BEATEN
PATH
HEREND PORCELAIN FACTORY – Hungary's reputation for creating fine pieces of porcelain began with a purchase by England's Queen Victoria in 1851, when Windsor Castle ordered a dinner set from Herend. Following the celebrated purchase, the chosen pattern of colorful and detailed butterflies and flowers was coined the "Victoria" collection. Some 600 mold-makers, potters, and painters are still trained at the company's headquarters to craft numerous patterns associated with Herend's high-quality dinnerware, decorative items, and figurines. The factory, founded

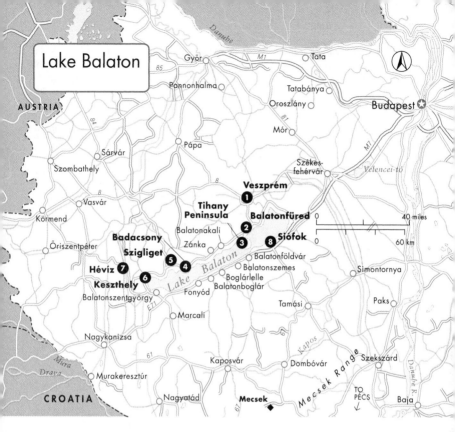

Lake Balaton

in 1839, welcomes the porcelain-prone public in its Porcelanium visitors' complex. After a short film you enter the Mini-Manufactory, where you can see how porcelain is made. Across the aptly named Porcelanium Square is the Herend Porcelain Museum with its treasure trove of precious pieces. In the adjoining Apicius Restaurant you can even dine off their collection of porcelain, worth several million forints. The town of Herend lies 16 km (10 mi) northwest of Veszprém on Road 8. ⊠ *Kossuth Lajos utca 137–139, Herend* ☎ *88/523–190* ⊕ *www.porcelanium. com* ▣ *Mini-Manufactory and museum 1,500 HUF; museum only, 500 HUF* ☉ *Apr.–Oct., Mini-Manufactory daily 9–5:30, Museum daily 9–4:30; Nov.–Mar., Mini-Manufactory Tues.–Sat. 9:30–4:15, Museum Tues.–Sat. 9–3:30. Museum closed Christmas–mid-Jan.; restaurant closed Mon. Apr.–Oct., Sun. and Mon. Nov.–Mar.*

Where to Stay & Eat

$–$$ ✕ **Elefánt Bisztró.** Next door to Cafe Piazza, the Elefánt offers a wider variety of pastas and pizzas at slightly higher prices; there is also a large selection of grilled poultry dishes, all loaded with vegetables. In nice weather you can sit outdoors; indoors is a large, built-in aquarium housing tropical fish. ⊠ *Óváros tér 5* ☎ *88/329–695* ▤ *AE, MC, V.*

★ $ ✕ **Szürkebarát Vendéglő.** The plain off-white walls of the Gray Monk Tavern may be less than inspiring, but the hearty Hungarian fare at this cellar restaurant in the city center more than compensates. For an unusual (but very Hungarian) appetizer, try the paprika-spiced *velős piritós* (marrow on toast); or for a main course you might try roast duck with polenta and steamed cabbage. There's a live Gypsy band on hand every Saturday after 5. ✉ *Szabadság tér 12* ☎ *88/405–888 or 70/316–6763 (mobile)* ▭ *AE, MC, V.*

★ ¢–$ ✕ **Cafe Piazza.** This quaint eatery has vaulted ceilings inside and a terrace filled with umbrella-shaded tables outside. The menu includes pizzas, pastas, and salads, all with celebrity-inspired or other creative titles, including "James Bond" fried Camembert cheese and " 'A' Pollo 13" chicken breast marinated in mustard sauce. Who knew "Bob Marley's favorite" was cold goose liver in goose fat? There is a vast drinks and coffee menu as well. ✉ *Óváros tér 4* ☎ *88/444–445* ▭ *AE, MC, V.*

¢ ✕▥ **Oliva Panzió.** In the heart of downtown Veszprém, the Oliva pension, restaurant, and garden pub is a bit tricky to find, but it's as charming as they come, with dim lighting, clean, cozy rooms, and a friendly staff. The interior of the establishment is decorated in soft Mediterranean colors to relaxing effect. The outside garden has live jazz several nights a week, and the restaurant serves Mediterranean-inspired cuisine. ✉ *Buhim utca 14–16, H-8200* ☎ *88/561–900* 🖷 *88/403–875* ⊕ *www.oliva.hu* ⇆ *11 rooms* ◇ *Restaurant, minibars, in-room data ports, cable TV, pub, parking (fee)* ▭ *DC, MC, V* ❍ *BP.*

Fodor'sChoice
★

¢ ▥ **Éllő Panzió.** In this 18-room pension just southwest of the town center you'll find ubiquitous golden lamp shades coupled with no lack of red—the carpeting, the velvety chairs, and the curtains. Rooms in the newer annex are more spacious than those in the chaletlike main house. Some rooms have two single beds pushed together; the rest have double mattresses or, as in Hungarian, a *francia ágy* (French bed). Service is uniformly friendly, even down to the six polite cats. ✉ *József Attila utca 25, H-8200* ☎ *88/420–097 or 88/565–445* 🖷 *88/561–445* ⊕ *www.ellopanzio.hu* ⇆ *18 rooms* ◇ *Cable TV, dry cleaning, laundry service, free parking, some pets allowed* ▭ *DC, MC, V* ❍ *Closed Christmas–New Year's* ❍ *BP.*

BALATONFÜRED

❷ *18 km (11 mi) south of Veszprém, 115 km (71 mi) southwest of Budapest.*

Fed by 11 medicinal springs, Balatonfüred first gained popularity as a health resort (the lake's oldest) where people with heart conditions and fatigue would come to take or, more accurately, to drink a cure. The waters, said to have stimulating and beneficial effects on the heart and nerves, are still an integral part of the town's identity and consumed voraciously, but only the internationally renowned cardiac hospital has actual bathing facilities.

Today Balatonfüred, also known simply as Füred, is probably the Balaton's most popular destination, with every amenity to match. Above its busy boat landing, beaches, and promenade lined with great plane and poplar trees, the twisting streets of the Old Town climb hillsides thickly planted with vines. The climate and landscape also make this one of the best wine-growing districts in Hungary. Every year in July the most elaborate of Lake Balaton's debutante cotillions, the Anna Ball, is held here.

The center of town is **Gyógy tér** (Spa Square), where the bubbling waters from five volcanic springs rise beneath a slim, colonnaded pavilion. In the square's centerpiece, the neoclassical **Well House** of the Kossuth Spring, you can sample the water, which has a pleasant, surprisingly refreshing taste despite the sulfurous aroma; for the many locals who come here to stock up, a 30-liters-per-person limit is posted. All the buildings on the square are pillared like Greek temples. At No. 3 is the **Horváth Ház** (Horváth House), a former sanatorium that housed uranium miners in the communist era. The house is also where the Szentgyörgyi-Horváth family arranged the first of what was to become the Anna Ball in 1825 in honor of their daughter Anna.

The Anna Ball now takes place every July in another colonnaded building on the square, also a former sanatorium, the **Árkad Hotel** (1802). The day after the ball the elected queen is paraded around town in a horse-drawn carriage. Under the Árkad Hotel's arcades is the **Balatoni Pantheon** (Balaton Pantheon): aesthetically interesting tablets and reliefs honoring Hungarian and foreign notables who either worked for Lake Balaton or spread the word about it. Among them is Jaroslav Hašek, the Czech author of the *Good Soldier Schweik,* who also wrote tales about Balaton.

On the eastern side of the square is the **Állami Kórház** (State Hospital), where hundreds of patients from all over the world are treated. Here, too, Rabindranath Tagore, the Indian author and Nobel Prize winner, recovered from a heart attack in 1926. The tree that he planted to commemorate his stay stands in a little grove at the western end of the paths leading from the square down to the lakeside. Tagore also wrote a poem for the planting, which is memorialized beneath the tree on his strikingly animated bust: WHEN I AM NO LONGER ON EARTH, MY TREE,/LET THE EVER-RENEWED LEAVES OF THY SPRING/MURMUR TO THE WAYFARER:/THE POET DID LOVE WHILE HE LIVED. In the same grove are trees honoring visits by another Nobel laureate, the Italian poet Salvatore Quasimodo, in 1961, and Indian prime minister Indira Gandhi, in 1972. An adjoining grove honors Soviet cosmonauts and their Hungarian partner-in-space, Bertalan Farkas.

Trees, restaurants, and shops line the **Tagore sétány** (Tagore Promenade), named after the Nobel Prize–winning poet Rabindranath Tagore. It begins near the boat landing and runs for nearly a kilometer (almost ½ mi).

A stroll up **Blaha Lujza utca** from Gyógy tér will take you past several landmarks, such as the **Blaha Lujza Ház** (Lujza Blaha House), a neoclassical villa built in 1867 and, later, the summer home of this famous turn-of-the-20th-century actress, humanist, and singer (today, it's a hotel). The sweet little **Kerek templom** (Round Church), consecrated in 1846, was built in a classical style and has a truly rounded interior.

An Arts Festival North of Balaton

HUNGARY'S VALLEY OF THE arts festival, the largest summer arts event in the country, is hosted annually by six villages spread across the Eger Creek Valley, north of Lake Balaton between Balatonfüred and Badacsony. The 10-day event, beginning the last Friday in July, features works from an estimated 3,500 local and foreign artists. Another 800 dance, theater, and concert performances are held at makeshift stages in meadows, churches, caves, and even along streets. There are also musical walks through the forest and numerous puppet shows for children. Villages hosting the event—Kapolcs, Monostorapáti, Öcs, Pula, Taliándörögd, and Vigántpetend—are literally transformed into outdoor walking art shows, and booths and

vendors abound. What began in 1989 as a three-day event has turned into a major draw for Hungarians and visitors alike, with total attendance today around 150,000 people.

One of the festival's aims is to showcase local craftsmanship in the hosting villages, which have histories steeped in pottery and weaving. Additionally, one city elsewhere in Hungary is invited to present its artists, dance troupes, and musicians. Past years have included groups from Szolnok, Debrecen, and Szeged. For a list of events and programming, contact: **Kapolcs Polgármesteri Hivatal** (Kapolcs Mayor's Office; ☎ 87/437-029 ⊕ www.muveszetekvolgye.hu or www.kapolcs.hu).

NEED A BREAK?

The plush **Kedves Café** (✉ Blaha Lujza utca 7 ☎ 87/343-229), built in 1795, was once the favorite summer haunt of well-known Hungarian writers and artists. Now more touristy than literary, it is still one of Lake Balaton's most popular pastry shops.

Where to Stay & Eat

$$–$$$ ✕ **Tölgyfa Csárda.** Perched high on a hilltop, the Oak Tree Tavern has breathtaking views over the steeples and rooftops of Balatonfüred and the Tihany Peninsula. The dining room and menu are worthy of a first-class Budapest restaurant, and nightly live Gypsy music keeps things festive. ✉ *Meleghegy, up the hill at the end of Csárda utca* ☎ *87/343–036 or 30/929–4515 (mobile)* ▤ *MC, V* ⊗ *Closed late Nov.–Apr.*

★ **$–$$** ✕ **Baricska Csárda.** This rambling country-style restaurant has a reed-thatched roof, wood-beamed rooms, vaulted cellars, vine-draped terraces, and views of both vineyards and the lake. The food is hearty yet ambitious: grilled trout, (cat)fish paprikás with spaetzle to soak up the creamy sauce, stuffed cabbage, and staple desserts such as strudels and palacsintas. In summer, Gypsy wedding shows are held nightly under the grape arbors. ✉ *Baricska dülő, off Rte. 71 (Széchenyi út) behind the Shell station* ☎ *87/580–095* ⌂ *Reservations essential* ▤ *AE, DC, MC, V* ⊗ *Closed Nov.–mid-Mar.*

★ **$** ⌂ **Annabella.** The cool, spacious guest quarters in this large, Miami-style high-rise—whose facade is a soothing marine blue despite its communist-era, tower-block nature—are especially pleasant in the summer heat. The resort overlooks the lake and Tagore Promenade and has access to excellent swimming and water-sports facilities. All rooms have balconies; for the best views, request a room on a high floor with a view of the Tihany Peninsula. ⊠ *Deák Ferenc utca 25, H-8230* ☎ *87/889–400* 🖨 *87/889–412 or 87/889–435* ⊕ *www.danubiushotels. com/annabella* ☞ *383 rooms, 5 suites* ⚒ *Restaurant, café, indoor pool, pool, hair salon, massage, sauna, bicycles, meeting room, bar, nightclub, babysitting, laundry service, travel services, free parking* ⊟ *AE, DC, MC, V* ☉ *Closed late Oct.–mid-Apr.* ⊺⊙⊺ *BP.*

$ 🖼 **Marina.** A central beachfront location is the Marina's main draw. Rooms in the homey 12-story building range from snug to small; suites have balconies but suffer from tiny bathrooms and dark bedrooms. Your safest bet is to get a high-floor "Superior" room with a lake view. Or better yet, stay in the "Lido" wing, which opens directly onto the water and where rooms (suites only) get plenty of sun. In 2006 the hotel adopted an "all-inclusive" policy in high season, meaning that rates include all meals. Visits of less than one week are subject to a daily surcharge of 8–10 euros per room. ⊠ *Széchenyi út 26, H-8230* ☎ *87/889–500* 🖨 *87/889–512* ⊕ *www.danubiushotels.com/marina* ☞ *349 rooms, 34 suites, 34 apartments* ⚒ *Restaurant, indoor pool, hair salon, massage, sauna, beach, boating, bowling, bar, pub, nightclub, laundry service, travel services* ⊟ *AE, DC, MC, V* ☉ *Closed Oct.–late Apr.* ⊺⊙⊺ *AI.*

¢–$
Fodor'sChoice
★
🖼 **Club Imola.** Drive through a metal archway etched with the name "Imola" overhead to find a large square of various buildings surrounded by lush green trees, vines, and plenty of outdoor seating terraces and small gardens. The Imola is a quiet break from the hustle of the nearby Balatonfüred strand, even if the din of traffic out on Petőfi Sándor utca never quite fades. The main hotel features clean, wooden-furnished rooms on the small side but at the lower end of the price range. Inside is a huge, new indoor pool with a brand-new Jacuzzi. For longer stays you can also rent a gorgeous duplex apartment with a small balcony, skylights, and loft bedroom. ⊠ *Petőfi Sándor utca 22, H-8230* ☎ *87/341–722* 🖨 *87/342–602* ⊕ *www. imolanet.hu* ☞ *18 rooms, 8 apartments* ⚒ *Restaurant, cable TV, 2 tennis courts, indoor pool, sauna, bar, laundry service, meeting rooms, free parking* ⊟ *MC, V* ⊺⊙⊺ *BP.*

¢ 🖼 **Astoria Hotel.** No relation to the Budapest hotel by the same name, but rather the name of a hotel that existed in this 1869 family mansion from 1910 until 1950, the imposing, yellow-and-white Astoria Hotel reopened in 2006 after extensive renovation that achieved historical authenticity, at least on the outside. Beyond offering simply furnished, modern rooms with shower-equipped bathrooms at a rate similar to that of the nearby Hotel Park, it offers a

---

GO JUMP IN A LAKE

Lake Balaton is a heck of a lot cleaner than the Danube—it looks clean and it feels clean, and indeed it is absolutely divine to swim in. Intensive clean-up efforts in recent decades, combined with a ban on most motorized craft, have assured one of Hungary's least polluted bodies of water.

---

more elegant exterior in a moderately parklike atmosphere, and is just a tad closer to the lake. ⊠ *Jókai utca 28, H-8230* 🖼 *87/343–643* ⊕ *www.hotels.hu/astoria* ⤴ *15 rooms, 2 suites* ⚘ *Restaurant, minibars, cable TV, bar, free parking* ⊟ *No credit cards* ⵙ *BP.*

¢ 🖼 **Blaha Lujza Ház.** Hungary's fin-de-siècle songbird and actress Lujza Blaha spent her summers at this neoclassical villa, which has been converted into a hotel. The rooms are a bit cramped, and there's not much room to negotiate your way around the bed sometimes. However, the front-desk staff is helpful, and the elegant dining room, which functions as a restaurant on summer evenings, is a pleasant place to begin the day with a buffet or cooked breakfast. ⊠ *Blaha utca 4, H-8230* 🖼 *87/581–210 or 87/581–215* 🖨 *87/581–219* ⊕ *www.hotelblaha.hu* ⤴ *22 rooms* ⚘ *Restaurant, in-room safes, minibars, cable TV, gym, bar, free parking, no-smoking rooms; some rooms with no a/c* ⊟ *AE, DC, MC, V* ⊘ *Closed late Dec.–Mar.* ⵙ *BP.*

¢ 🖼 **Hotel Park.** Hidden on a side street in town—but close to the lakeshore—the Park is noticeably calmer than Füred's bustling main hotels. Rooms are large and bright, with high ceilings and tall windows. Suites have large, breezy balconies but small bathrooms. Outside there's a little swimming pool and a playground. ⊠ *Jókai utca 24, H-8230* 🖼 *87/343–203 or 87/342–005* ⊕ *www. hotelpark.hu* ⤴ *27 rooms, 5 suites* ⚘ *Restaurant, gym, sauna, bar, meeting room, free parking* ⊟ *MC, V* ⵙ *BP.*

Sports & the Outdoors

BEACHES   Balatonfüred has three public beaches, most prominent among them the
Ⓒ   **Eszterházy strand** at the end of Liszt Ferenc utca by the Hotel Tagore. Open 9–7 daily from mid–May to mid–September, it costs 500 HUF to enter (plus 300 HUF if you have small valuables to store). Lakeside hotels typically have their own private beaches, with water-sports facilities and equipment or special access to these nearby. At most beaches you can rent sailboards, paddleboats, and other water toys. **Füred Camping** (⊠ Széchenyi utca 24, next to the Marina hotel 🖼 87/580–241), Hungary's largest campground, rents non-motorized boats as well as water toys. Although motorboats are banned from the lake, if you're desperate to water-ski you can try the campground's electric water-ski machine, which tows enthusiasts around a 1-km (½-mi) circle. A two-tow ticket runs around 1,000 HUF.

BICYCLING   In season you can rent bicycles from temporary, private outfits set up
Ⓒ   in central locations around town and near the beaches.

Rent-a-Ride. The company offers hourly, daily, and weekly bicycle rentals. The office is open during the summer season from 9 AM to 4 PM. Bicycle rentals are 350 HUF per hour, 2,400 HUF per day, 12,000 HUF per week. ⊠ Hotel Tagore, Deák Ferenc utca 🖼 30/630–4767 (mobile).

TIHANY & PENINSULA

★ ❸   *11 km (7 mi) southwest of Balatonfüred, 126 km (78 mi) from Budapest.*

The famed town of Tihany, with its twisting, narrow cobblestone streets and hilltop abbey, is on top of the Tihany Félsziget (Tihany Peninsula), which is joined to the mainland by a narrow neck and juts 5 km (3 mi) into the lake. Only 12 square km (less than 5 square mi), the peninsula is not only a major tourist resort—it is, after all, Hungary's closest approximation of a Mediterranean or Adriatic experience—but perhaps the most historic part of the Balaton area. In 1952 the entire peninsula was declared a national park, and because of its geological rarities, it became Hungary's first nature conservation zone. As a result of volcanic activity in the area, there are more than 110 geyser craters, remains of former hot springs reminiscent of those found in Iceland, Siberia, and Wyoming's Yellowstone Park.

The smooth Belső Tó (Inner Lake), 82 feet higher than Lake Balaton, is one of the peninsula's own two lakes; around it are barren yellowish-white rocks and volcanic cones rising against the sky. Though the hills surrounding the lake are known for their white wines, this area produces a notable Hungarian red, Tihany cabernet.

Fodor'sChoice
★ On a hilltop overlooking the Old Town is the **Bencés Apátság** (Benedictine Abbey), whose foundations were laid by King András I (his body lies in the abbey crypt) in 1055. Parts of the abbey were rebuilt in baroque style between 1719

> **HELLO HELLO HELLO**
>
> It's said that from Visszhang domb (Echo Hill), just a brief stroll from the Benedictine Abbey, as many as 16 syllables can be bounced off the abbey wall. With noise from builders and traffic, these days you may have to settle for a two-second echo.

and 1784. The abbey's charter—containing some 100 Hungarian words in its Latin text, making it the oldest written source of the Hungarian language—is kept in Pannonhalma, but a replica is on display in the 11th-century crypt. The contrast between the simple crypt, where a small black crucifix hangs over the tomb of King András, and the abbey's lavish baroque interior—all gold, gilded silver, and salmon—could scarcely be more marked. The altar, abbot's throne, choir parapet, organ case, and pulpit were all the work of Sebestyén Stuhloff. Local tradition says he immortalized the features of his doomed sweetheart in the face of the angel kneeling on the right-hand side of the altar to the Virgin Mary. A magnificent baroque organ, adorned by stucco cherubs, can be heard during evening concerts in summer.

In a baroque house adjoining and entered through the abbey is the **Bencés Apátsági Múzeum** (Benedictine Abbey Museum). The best exhibits are in the basement lapidarium: relics from Roman colonization, including mosaic floors; a relief of David from the second or third century; and 1,200-year-old carved stones—all labeled in English as well as Hungarian. Three of the upstairs rooms were lived in for five days in 1921 by the last emperor of the dissolved Austro-Hungarian dual monarchy, Karl IV, in a futile foray to regain the throne of Hungary. Banished to Madeira, he died of pneumonia a year later. The rooms are preserved with nostalgic relish for Emperor Franz Joseph's doomed successor. The museum is closed from November through March. ⊠ *Első András tér 1* ☎ *87/448–405 abbey, 87/448–650 museum*

500 HUF for abbey and museum ☉ May–Sept., daily 9–5:30; Oct.–Mar., Mon.–Sat. 10–3, Sun. 11–3; Apr., daily 10–4:30. Nov.–Mar., church and lapidarium only.

The **Szabadtéri Múzeum** (Open-air Museum), Tihany's outdoor museum of ethnography, assembles a group of old structures including an un-plastered dwelling house with basalt walls, a thatched roof, verandas, and white-framed windows dating back to the 18th century. Another building is the former house of the Fishermen's Guild, with all kinds of fishing tools on display, including an ancient boat—used until 1934—parked inside. ⊠ *Pisky István sétány 12* ☎ *87/714–960* *360 HUF* ☉ *Apr. 11–June, Tues.–Sun. 10–6; July–Aug., Tues.–Sun. 10–8; Sept.–Oct. 15, Tues.–Sun. 10–6.*

Where to Stay & Eat

★ **$–$$** ✕ **Ferenc Pince.** This thatched-roof restaurant and wine cellar atop the Tihany Peninsula has splendid views of the Balaton and surrounding vineyards. The menu is heavy not only on Balaton fish but also beef straight from Hungary's prized gray cattle as well as poultry, salads, and other national specialities. The real draw, however, is wine tastings in the cellar just below the restaurant, where you can sample numerous wines produced by Ferenc Pince. Wine tastings cost 1,400 HUF to 2,800 HUF per person, depending on how much you sample, and include cheese, sausage, and various breads. ■ TIP➔ **White varietals, for which Balaton is known, are the best choices.** More than 30 different local wines are sold. Reservations are required for tastings. ⊠ *Cserhegy* ☎ *87/448–575, 20/942–3987 (mobile)* ⊕ *www.ferencpince.hu* ▤ *No credit cards* ☉ *Closed Tues. and Oct.–Apr.*

$–$$ ✕ **Pál Csárda.** Two thatched cottages house this simple restaurant right across the street from a simple but attractive outdoor religious site (featuring the stations of the cross). The somewhat predictable staples include *gulyás leves* (goulash soup) and *halászlé* (fish stew). You can eat in the garden, which is decorated with gourds and grape vines. ⊠ *Visszhang utca 19* ☎ *87/448–605* ▤ *AE, DC, MC, V* ☉ *Closed Nov.–Mar.*

★ **$** ⊞ **Club Tihany.** Picture Club Med transposed to late-1980s Central Europe, and you'll have some idea of what to expect at Club Tihany. This 32-acre, parklike lakeside resort stays busy year-round. Accommodations are standard hotel rooms (higher rate for lake views), or individual bungalows with kitchens. The list of activities is impressive—from fishing to thermal bathing in the spa. In summer, when the hotel is filled to capacity, the scramble for the breakfast buffet can be a little unnerving. Club Tihany is a popular conference center (as of this writing, that of the International Cannabis Research Society). MAP is included in the hotel, optional for bungalows. ⊠ *Rév utca 3, H-8237* ☎ *87/538–564* 🖷 *87/448–083* ⊕ *www.clubtihany.hu* ⬐ *330 rooms, 160 bungalows* ♨ *3 restaurants, café, some kitchens, minibars, cable TV with movies, in-room data ports, miniature golf, tennis court, pool, health club, hair salon, spa, beach, boating, fishing, bicycles, billiards, bowling, Ping-Pong, squash, 2 bars, pub, dance club, children's programs (ages 3–17), Internet, meeting rooms* ▤ *AE, DC, MC, V* ⍓ *MAP.*

★ ¢ 🖼 **Adler Inn.** This cozy inn 500 meters from the Balaton shore has a friendly staff and small, clean rooms, each with an outdoor terrace. Outside the inn is a lovely dining area and outdoor pizzeria. The resident basset hound named Salami can usually be found soaking up the sun outside, and he enjoys attention. Rooms are air-conditioned, but there is an extra charge. ⊠ *Felsőkopazhegyi út 1/a, H-8237* ☎ *87/538–000* 🖨 *87/448–755* ⊕ *www.adler-tihany.hu* 🛏 *13 rooms, 2 apartments* ⚐ *Restaurant, pool, hot tub, sauna, free parking* ⊟ *No credit cards* ☉ *Closed Nov.–mid-Mar.* ⦿ *BP.*

Nightlife & the Arts

Well-known musicians perform on the Benedictine Abbey's magnificent organ during the popular summer **organ-concert series** (☎ 87/538–200 for information and tickets), which runs from July to August 20. Concerts are generally held on weekends at 8:30 PM.

Sports & the Outdoors

HIKING Footpaths crisscross the entire peninsula, allowing you to climb the small
🐾 hills on its west side for splendid views of the area or hike down to Belső Tó (Inner Lake). If in midsummer you climb the area's highest hill, the Csúcshegy (761 feet, approximately a two-hour hike), you'll find the land below carpeted with purple lavender. Introduced from France into Hungary, lavender thrives on the lime-rich soil and strong sunshine of Tihany. The State Lavender and Medicinal Herb Farm here supplies the Hungarian pharmaceutical and cosmetics industries.

SWIMMING You needn't book a room at the Club Tihany to take a dip in the beautiful Balaton here. With a one-mile-plus stretch of simply splendid, free swimming off the coastal road that runs along the Tihany Peninsula's eastern side toward Balatonfüred, you might imagine that you're on the Adriatic. Check it out (along with many others on a hot day), but keep a polite distance from the fishermen (and fisherwomen) who also stake out claims to idyllic spots here and there.

OFF THE
BEATEN
PATH

ÖRVÉNYES – This miniature town about 7 km (4½ mi) west of Tihany has the only working *vízi malom* (water mill) in the Balaton region. Built in the 18th century, it still grinds grain into flour while also serving as a tiny museum. In the miller's room is a collection of folk art, wood carvings, pottery, furniture, and pipes. On a nearby hill stand the ruins of a Romanesque church; only its chancel has survived. On Templom utca, a few steps from the bridge, is the baroque St. Imre templom (St. Imre Church), built in the late 18th century. *Water mill* ⊠ *Szent Imre utca 1, Örvényes* ☎ *87/449–360* 🎫 *200 HUF* ☉ *May–Sept., Tues.–Sun. 9–4.*

BALATONUDVARI – About 1 km (½ mi) west of Örvényes is a pleasant beach resort famous for its cemetery, which was declared a national shrine because of its beautiful, unique heart-shape tombstones carved from white limestone at the turn of the 18th century. The cemetery is essentially on the highway, at the eastern end of town; it is easily visible from the road. Balatonudvari's beach itself is at **Kiliántelep,** 2 km (1 mi) to the west.

8

BADACSONY

★ ❹ *41 km (25 mi) southwest of Tihany, 167 km (104 mi) from Budapest.*

One of the northern shore's most treasured images is of Mt. Badacsony (1,437 feet), simply called the Badacsony, rising from the lake. The mysterious, coffinlike basalt peak of the Balaton Highlands is actually an extinct volcano flanked by smaller cone-shape hills. The masses of lava that coagulated here created bizarre and beautiful rock formations. At the upper edge, salt columns tower 180 to 200 feet like organ pipes in a huge semicircle. In 1965 Hungarian conservationists won a major victory that ended the quarrying of basalt from Mt. Badacsony, which is now a nature preserve. Badacsony is really an administrative name for the entire area, and includes not just the mountain but also five settlements at its foot.

The land below Mt. Badacsony has been painfully and lovingly tilled for centuries. There are vineyards everywhere and splendid wine in every inn and tavern. In descending order of dryness, the best-loved Badacsony white wines are rizlingszilváni, kéknyelű, and szürkebarát. Their proud producers claim that "no vine will produce good wine unless it can see its own reflection in the Balaton." They believe it is not enough for the sun simply to shine on a vine; the undersides of the leaves also need light, which is reflected from the lake's mirrorlike surface. Others claim the wine draws its strength from the fire of old volcanoes.

Many restaurants and inns have their own wine tastings, as do the numerous smaller, private cellars dotting the hill. Look for signs saying *bor* or *Wein* (wine, in Hungarian and German, respectively) to point the way. Most places are open from mid-May to mid-September daily from around noon until 9 or 10.

A good starting point for Badacsony sightseeing is the **Egry József Múzeum** (József Egry Museum), formerly the home and studio of a famous painter of Balaton landscapes. His evocative paintings depict the lake's constantly changing hues, from its angry bright green during storms to its tranquil deep blues. ⊠ *Egry sétány 12* ☎ *87/431–044* 💰 *400 HUF* ☉ *May–Sep., Tues.–Sun. 10–6.*

Szegedy Róza út, the steep main street climbing the mountain, is flanked by vineyards and villas. This is the place to get acquainted with the writer Sándor Kisfaludy and his beloved bride from Badacsony, Róza Szegedy, to whom he dedicated his love poems. At the summit of her street is **Szegedy Róza Ház** (Róza Szegedy House), a baroque wine-press house built in 1790 on a grand scale—with thatched roof, gabled wall, six semicircular arcades, and an arched and pillared balcony running the length of the four raftered upstairs rooms. It was here that the hometown girl met the visiting bard from Budapest. The house now serves as a memorial museum to both of them, furnished much the way it was when Kisfaludy was doing his best work immortalizing his two true loves, the Badacsony and his wife. Szegedy, meanwhile, was heavily involved with wine-making, and her homemade vermouth was famous throughout Hungary. ⊠ *Szegedy Róza út 87*

🕾 *87/701–906* 🍽 *360 HUF*
⊙ *May–mid-Oct., Tues.–Sun. 10–6.*

The steep climb to the **Kisfaludy kilátó** (Kisfaludy Lookout Tower) on Mt. Badacsony's summit is an integral part of the Badacsony experience and a rewarding bit of exercise. Serious summitry begins behind the Kisfaludy-ház (Kisfaludy House), a restaurant just above the Rózsa Szegedy House that was once owned by the family of Hungarian poet Sándor Kisfaludy. The trek to the Kisfaludy Lookout Tower begins at the Rózsakő (Rose Stone), a flat, smooth basalt slab with many carved inscriptions. Local legend has it that if a boy and a girl sit on it with their backs to Lake Balaton, they will marry within a year. From here a trail marked in yellow leads up to the foot of the columns that stretch to the top. Steep flights of stone steps take you through a narrow gap between rocks and basalt walls until you reach a tree-lined plateau. You are now at the 1,391-foot level. Follow the blue triangular markings along a path to the lookout tower. Even with time out for rests and views, the ascent from Rózsakő should take less than an hour.

Villa Marica (✉ Herceg F. utca 24 Badacsonylábdihegy 🕾 87/432–876). In this bright yellow, refurbished century-old villa in a bucolic setting just southwest of town (follow the signs from the Balatonládihegy train station), you can taste two or three wines for around 500 HUF, while sampling a dozen or so will run about 2,500 HUF. Among the specialties are the Badacsononyi aszú dessert wine and the *jégbor* (ice wine), made from frozen grapes. If you overindulge you can always check into one of the seven brightly colored rooms (9,000 HUF with breakfast); those in the back have splendid views of Mt. Badacsony. A bit farther afield—in the same direction but in a tiny village just north of Szigliget—is the highly recommended **Szászi-Pince Ökogazdaság** (Szászi Cellar Bio Farm) (✉ Szent György-hegy Hegymagas 🕾 30/997–1919 or 30/989–8788 (mobile), which offers regular tastings. The staff speak English. Call before going.

Where to Stay & Eat

$–$$$ ✕ **Kisfaludy-ház.** Perched above the Szegedy Róza House is this Badacsony institution, once a wine-press house owned by the poet Sándor Kisfaludy's family. Its wine cellar lies directly over a spring, but the main draw is a vast two-tier terrace that affords a breathtaking view of virtually the entire lake. Naturally, the wines are excellent and are incorporated into some of the cooking, such as creamy cold white-wine soup with dried grapes. ⊠ *Szegedy Róza utca 87* ☎ *87/431–016* ⊟ *AE, DC, MC, V* ☉ *Closed Oct.–Apr.*

★ **$–$$$** ✕ **Szent Orbán Borház.** Part of the illustrious Szent Orbán winery, this restaurant overlooks some of the vineyard's 30 acres. On summer days golden light bathes the 19th-century former farmhouse. There are written menus, but charming servers also recite the dishes (in English and other languages), and they'll steer you toward sampling two unique house wines, Budai zöld and Kéknyelű—both based on legendary varietals from Roman times. Smoked goose-liver pâté is frequently available as an appetizer, as is fresh fish from Lake Balaton, including fogas. ⊠ *Szegedy Róza utca 22* ☎ *87/431–382* ⊟ *AE, DC, MC, V.*

$–$$ ✕ **Halászkert.** The festive Fish Garden has won numerous international awards for its fine Hungarian cuisine. Inside are wooden rafters and tables draped with peachy-pink tablecloths; outside is a large terrace with umbrella-shaded tables. The extensive menu has such fresh-from-the-lake dishes as halászlé, and *párolt* (steamed) harcsa drenched with a paprika-dill sauce. There's live gypsy music several nights a week. ⊠ *Park utca 5* ☎ *87/431–113 or 87/431–054* ⊟ *AE, DC, MC, V* ☉ *Closed Nov.–Apr.*

$ ✕⌂ **Club Hotel Badacsony.** A private beach is just a step away from this hotel right on the shore of Lake Balaton. The Club Hotel is the largest in the area. Rooms are bright and clean, the staff extremely helpful, and the outdoor swimming pool is heated in cool weather. ⊠ *Balatoni út 14, Badacsonytomaj H-8258* ☎ *87/471–040 or 87/471–088* ⊞ *87/471–059* ⊕ *www.badacsonyhotel.hu* ⇗ *70 rooms* ⌂ *Restaurant, café, cable TV, tennis court, hair salon, massage, sauna, beach, bar, playground, meeting rooms; no a/c* ⊟ *AE, DC, MC, V* ☉ *Closed Nov.–Apr.* ⎛ *BP.*

FodorśChoice ★

★ ¢ ✕⌂ **Hotel Neptun.** A five-minute walk from the lakeshore, this alpine-looking onetime mansion offers few frills but is a great place to stay for the budget-minded. The spacious rooms have pine floors with throw rugs, pleasantly peach-colored walls, and two single beds pushed together; the century-old building's thick stone walls keep the rooms reasonably cool even in summer, despite the lack of air-conditioning. Most rooms have showers only, some have tubs; in addition to its eleven private rooms, the hotel has five hostel-type rooms with shared bathrooms. Linden trees shade the tranquil garden of the hotel's excellent Hárskert Vendéglő (Linden Restaurant). ⊠ *Római út 156, Badacsonytomaj H-8261* ☎ *87/431–293* ⊞ *87/471–597* ⊕ *www.borbaratok.hu* ⇗ *11 private rooms* ⌂ *Restaurant, cable TV, bar, playground, free parking; no a/c* ⊟ *AE, DC, MC, V* ⎛ *EP.*

GO JUMP IN A LAKE

A veritable national institution that sometimes draws upward of 8,000 participants young and old, healthy and disabled, Hungarian and non-Hungarian alike, the *Balatoni átúszás* (Cross-Balaton Swim) is by far Hungary's most popular swimming event open to the general public. Held on a Saturday in midsummer (usually late July), the 5.2-km (3.3-mi) swim begins on the northern shore, in the village of Révfülöp, and winds up across the lake at Balatonboglár. The registration fee is 3,000 HUF. For details, visit ⊕ www.balaton-atuszas.com.

Sports & the Outdoors

The upper paths and roads along the slopes of Mt. Badacsony are excellent for scenic walking. Well-marked trails lead to the summit. For beach activities, you can go to one of Badacsony's several beaches or head 6 km (4 mi) northeast, to those at Balatonrendes and Ábrahámhegy, combined communities forming quiet resorts.

The largest stalactite cave in western Hungary, the **Csodabogyós-barlang,** was discovered not long ago in the forested hills outside the village of Balatonederics, between Badacsony and Keszthely, and you can now see it for yourself assuming enough people have called beforehand to merit a group tour. "Base tours" take up to 2 hours and cost 5,000 HUF per adult (children 10–18, 3,500 HUF); "extreme tours" take closer to 4 hours and run 8,000 HUF per adult (no children allowed). Call 20/454–7034 for information and to reserve a spot; given sufficient demand, tours take place daily. It's a 40-minute hike uphill to the cave entrance.

SZIGLIGET

★ ❺ *11 km (7 mi) west of Badacsony, 178 km (110 mi) from Budapest.*

The village of Szigliget is a tranquil, picturesque town with fine thatch-roof wine-press houses and a small beach. Towering over the town is the ruin of the 13th-century **Óvár** (Old Castle), a fortress so well protected that it was never taken by the Turks; it was demolished in the early 18th century by Habsburgs fearful of rebellions. A steep path starting from Kisfaludy utca brings you to the top of the hill, where you can explore the ruins, under ongoing archaeological restoration (a sign maps out the restoration plan), and take in the breathtaking views.

Down in the village, the Romanesque remains of the **Avas templom** (Avas Church; ✉ Iharos út, at the intersection with the road to Badacsony), from the Arpad dynasty, still contain a 12th-century basalt tower with a stone spire. The **Eszterházy summer mansion** (✉ Fő tér), just off the main square, was built in the 18th century and rebuilt in neoclassical style in the 19th. Surrounded by a 25-acre park but with a relatively bland interior, it has functioned as Hungary's foremost writers' retreat in recent decades and is closed to the public.

For an unassuming but all the more surprising dining venue in a charming village where you'd expect to find only traditional Hungarian (i.e., heavy on the belly) fare, do stop in at the **Rigoletto Café Pizzeria** (✉ Kossuth utca 62 ☎ 30/560–5001 (mobile). The opera-loving amiable owner, Mária Glavac-Füzy, who spends much of her year in Vienna as a lawyer, here excels in her passion for making not only excellent pizzas—more than 20 types at 1,200 HUF each, from the traditional to the innovative such as Amore (topped by grapes, rosemary, pine nuts, ricotta, and vanilla ice cream)—to authentic Mediterranean salads, and tiramisus that melt in your mouth. Fine local wines are also available. Open from May through August, this welcoming little eatery has a small, bright inner room and several tables out front.

8

KESZTHELY

6 *18 km (11 mi) west of Szigliget, 196 km (122 mi) from Budapest.*

With a beautifully preserved pedestrian avenue (Kossuth Lajos utca) in the historic center of town, the spectacular baroque Festetics Kastély, and a relative absence of honky-tonk, Keszthely is far more classically attractive and sophisticated than other large Balaton towns. Continuing the cultural and arts tradition begun by Count György Festetics two centuries ago, Keszthely hosts numerous cultural events, including an annual summer arts festival. Just south of town is the vast swamp called Kis-Balaton (Little Balaton), formerly part of Lake Balaton and now a nature preserve filled with birds. Water flowing into Lake Balaton from its little sibling frequently churns up sediment, making the water around Keszthely's beaches disconcertingly cloudy. Keszthely is a good place to spend the afternoon, either walking around town or wading along the Balaton shore, but think twice before spending the night, as accommodation is typically so-so and overpriced.

It's a 15-minute, potentially confusing walk from the train station to the center, by the way: Follow Mártírok utja from the station as it curves left until you get to Kossuth Lajos utca; take a right there and go straight, straight, straight. On Fő tér, the main square, you'll see a massive building on your right, one end of which is an impressive little church (originally built in 1396), the other (much larger) end a secondary school. In the mid-16th century the church was expanded into a fortress that the Turks just couldn't capture, try as they did. From here it's a few more minutes down the other side of Kossuth Lajos utca to the Festetics Palace.

The **Pethő Ház** (Pethő House), a striking town house of medieval origin, was rebuilt in baroque style with a handsome arcaded gallery above its courtyard. Hidden deep inside its courtyard is the restored 18th-century **synagogue,** in front of which stands a small memorial honoring the 829 Jewish people from the neighborhood, turned into a ghetto in 1944, who were killed during the Holocaust. ⊠ *Kossuth Lajos utca 22.*

★ Keszthely's magnificent **Festetics Kastély** (Festetics Palace) is one of the finest baroque complexes in Hungary. Begun around 1745, it was the seat of the enlightened and philanthropic Festetics dynasty, which had acquired Keszthely six years earlier. The palace's distinctive churchlike tower and more than 100 rooms were added between 1883 and 1887; the interior is lush. The **Helikon Könyvtár** (Helikon Library) in the south wing contains some 52,000 volumes, with precious codices and documents of Festetics family history. Chamber and orchestral concerts are held in the Mirror Gallery ballroom or, in summer, in the courtyard. The palace opens onto a splendid park lined with rare plants and fine sculptures, which plays host to an annual two-week open-air Shakespeare festival that begins around late July. Just to add to the palace's attractions, as of 2006 its vaulted-brick cellar became home to the **Balatoni Borok Háza** (House of Hungarian Wines), where from 10 to 6 daily you can sample from 50 different wines not only from the Balaton region but from all over Hungary. In the palace you'll pay a supplementary fee of 900 HUF to take photos (non-flash), 1,700 HUF to bring in your video camera. ⊠ *Kastély utca 1* ☎ *83/312–191 or 88/312–192* 💺 *Palace 1,700 HUF, wine cellar 2,500 HUF* ☉ *June–Aug., daily 9–6; Sept.–May, Tues.–Sun. 10–5.*

Supposedly the largest of its kind in Central Europe, Keszthely's **Babamúzeum** (Doll Museum) exhibits some 450 porcelain figurines dressed in 240 types of colorful folk dress. The building has a pastoral look, created not only by the figurines—which convey the multifarious beauty of village garb—but also by the ceiling's huge, handcrafted wooden beams. On the two upper floors are wooden models of typical homes, churches, and ornate wooden gates representative of all regions in and near present-day Hungary that Magyars have inhabited since conquering the Carpathian basin in 896. The museum's pièce de résistance is the life work of an elderly peasant woman from northern Hungary: a 9-yard-long **model** of Budapest's Parliament building, patched together over 14 years from almost 4 million snail shells (which are 28 million years old, no less) originating from the Pannon Sea, which once covered much of Hungary. Despite the address, by the way, the entrance is not off Kossuth utca but right around the block (via a short alleyway called Bakács utca). ⊠ *Kossuth utca 11* ☎ *83/318–855* 💺 *300 HUF, model of Parliament 300 HUF* ☉ *Daily 10–5.*

<table>
<tr><td>

▌ NEED A
BREAK?

</td><td>

With wicker chairs around round glass-topped tables, and outside terraces on each of its two floors, **Café Pelso** (⊠ Fő tér ☎ 83/315–415 ☰ AE, DC, MC, V) is a fine place for a coffee or glass of wine and perhaps a slice of buttery Eszterházy torta or a Dobos szelet.

</td></tr>
</table>

8

Before you even reach Fő tér, though, or on your way back to the train station, you can have a more substantial repast at John's Pub (⊠ Kossuth Lajos utca 46 ☎ 83/510–857 ☰ AE, DC, MC, V), a laid-back spot where you can choose from a wide range of poultry dishes, grilled meats, pizzas, and salads, the main courses averaging around 1,000 HUF.

HÉVÍZ

❼ *6 km (4 mi) northwest of Keszthely, 202 km (126 mi) from Budapest.*

Hévíz is one of Hungary's biggest and most famous spa resorts, with the largest natural curative thermal lake in Europe. Lake Hévíz covers nearly 60,000 square yards, with warm water that never grows cooler than 33°C to 35°C (91.4°F–95°F) in summer and 30°C to 32°C (86°F–89.6°F) in winter, thus allowing year-round bathing, particularly where the lake is covered by a roof and looks like a racetrack grandstand. Richly laced with sulfur, alkali, calcium salts, and other curative components, the Hévíz water is recommended for spinal, rheumatic, gynecological, and articular disorders and is drunk to help digestive problems and receding gums. Fed by a spring producing 86 million liters (22.7 million gallons) of water a day, the lake cycles through a complete water change every 28 hours. Squeamish bathers should be forewarned that along with its photogenic lily pads, the lake naturally contains assorted sludgy mud and plant material. It's all supposed to be good for you, though—even the mud, which is full of iodine and is claimed to stimulate estrogen production in the body. The vast spa park has hospitals, sanatoriums, expensive hotels, and a casino.

The **Hévízi Fürdő** (Hévíz Baths)—that is, the public bath facilities—are in the **Szent András Kórház** (St. Andrew Hospital), a large, turreted medicinal bathing complex on the lakeshore with a large staff on hand to treat rheumatological complaints. ⚠ **Bathing for more than three hours at a time is not recommended.** ⊠ *Dr. Schulhof Vilmos sétány 1* ☎ *83/501–700* ⊕ *www.spaheviz.hu* ⊠ *Main pool 1,200 HUF, tub 1,400 HUF; sheets to dress up in 300 HUF; coin-operated lockers 100 HUF* ⊗ *May–Sept., daily 7–7 (admission until 6, bathing until 6:30); Oct.–Apr., daily 9–4:30.*

The beautifully furnished **Talpasház** (House on Soles) takes its name from an interesting architectural detail: its upright beams are encased in thick foundation boards. Exquisite antique peasant furniture, textiles, and pottery fill the house along with the work of contemporary local folk artists. Some of their work is for sale on the premises, and you can also create your own works on a pottery wheel. Contact the caretaker, Csaba Rezes, who lives next door at No. 15, if the door happens to be closed. ⊠ *Dózsa György utca 17* ☎ *85/377–066 caretaker* ⊠ *200 HUF* ⊗ *Late May–Sept., Tues.–Sun. hours vary (call the caretaker to let you in).*

OFF THE BEATEN PATH

CSILLAGVÁR (Star Castle) – It's worth stopping in Balatonszentgyörgy, 16 km (10 mi) south of Keszthely on the lake's southern shore, to see this castle, hidden away at the end of a dirt road past a gaping quarry. The house was built in the 1820s as a hunting lodge for László, the Festetics family's most eccentric member. Though it's not star-shaped inside, wedge-shaped projections on the ground floor give the outside this effect. Today the castle houses a museum of 16th- and 17th-century life in the border fortresses of the Balaton. ⊠ *Irtási dűlő* ☎ *83/318–855 or 30/227–2272 (mobile)* ⊠ *400 HUF* ⊗ *Mar.–Oct., daily 9–5; Dec.–Feb., daily 9–1. Closed Oct.–Nov.*

Where to Stay & Eat

$–$$ ✕ **Muskátli Restaurant.** Just a couple of minutes' walk from the center of town, the Geranium Restaurant offers traditional meat, poultry, fish, and wild game dishes in a positively pleasant space. The inside, while cramped, is tastefully decorated with antiques, not to mention a big, green, glazed-tile stove; and the airy, covered terrace out front is ringed by red geraniums. ⊠ *Széchenyi út 28* ☎ *83/341–475* ⊟ *AE, DC, MC, V.*

$–$$ 🏨 **Danubius Thermal Hotel Hévíz.** This large, luxurious spa-hotel, a 20-minute uphill walk from the city center and the lake (through a pretty park, if you wish), has its own thermal baths and physiotherapy unit (plus a full dental service). The maroon-and-beige, smallish rooms are modern, air-conditioned, and freshly renovated, and each has a balcony; request one with a view of the adjacent park and Lake Hévíz beyond. Numerous cure packages are available. ⊠ *Kossuth Lajos utca 13–15, H-8380* ☎ *83/889–400 or 83/889–401* 🖷 *83/889–409 or 83/889–402*

⊕ *www.danubiushotels.com/heviz* ⌨ *203 rooms, 7 suites* ⌂ *Restaurant, minibars, cable TV, in-room data ports, indoor pool, outdoor pool, hair salon, massage, sauna, spa, bar, pub, meeting rooms, dry cleaning, laundry service, free parking* ▤ *AE, DC, MC, V* ⦿ *BP.*

$ ▥ **Hotel Palota Hévíz** (Hotel Palace Hévíz). The Art Deco exterior and atrium of this hotel might convey a hint of 1930s glamour, but all those gleaming white surfaces are new, as it is a relatively recent construction. The hotel has thermal baths, various treatments, and its own dental center. Rooms are spacious and include kitchenettes. ⊠ *Rákóczi utca 1–3, H-8380* ☎ *83/542–140* 📠 *83/542–148* ⊕ *www.h-palota.hu* ⌨ *160 rooms* ⌂ *Restaurant, café, indoor pool, hair salon, massage, sauna, bar, some pets allowed* ▤ *AE, DC, MC, V* ⦿ *BP.*

$ ▥ **Kalma Hotel.** This small hotel, which opened in 2004 right in the center of town, is as close as any such accommodation gets to the public baths by the lake (a two-minute walk down the road). The lobby's impressive skylight enhances the airy, convivial atmosphere. The modern, simply furnished rooms are all kitchenette-equipped suites. ⊠ *Rákóczi utca 12–14, H-8380* ☎ *83/545–910* 📠 *83/545–911* ⊕ *www.hotelkalma. hu* ⌨ *43 rooms* ⌂ *Restaurant, cable TV, in-room data ports, massage, sauna, parking (fee)* ▤ *AE, DC, MC, V* ⦿ *BP.*

¢ ▥ **Rogner Hévíz Hotel Lotus Therme.** No expense has been spared at this spa and wellness hotel promoting relaxation and invigoration. In addition to enjoying thermal baths, a fitness center, and various purification and detoxification therapies, you can join in golf and tennis excursions or avail yourself of the in-house dieticians—all very relaxing and invigorating. ⊠ *Lótuszvirág utca 80, H-8380* ☎ *83/500–500* 📠 *83/500–591* ⊕ *www.lotustherme.com* ⌨ *230 rooms* ⌂ *Restaurant, café, cable TV with movies, driving range, miniature golf, putting green, 4 tennis courts, indoor pool, health club, hair salon, massage, sauna, bar, shops, Internet, no-smoking rooms* ▤ *AE, DC, MC, V* ⦿ *BP.*

SIÓFOK

❽ *110 km (68 mi) east of Hévíz, 105 km (65 mi) southwest of Budapest.*

Siófok is the largest city on Balaton's southern shore and a major tourist and holiday center for Hungarians. It is also, arguably, the least beautiful. In 1863 a railway station was built for the city, paving the way for its "golden age" at the turn of the 20th century. In the closing stages of World War II the city sustained heavy damage; to boost tourism during the 1960s, the Pannonia Hotel Company built four of what many consider to be the ugliest hotels in the area. If these were Siófok's *only* ugly buildings, however, there would still be hope for a ray of aesthetic redemption. With the exception of the twin-tower train station and the adjacent business district stretching a few blocks to the *Víztorony* (water tower), dating from 1912, the city is overrun by drab modern structures. Its shoreline is now a long honky-tonk strip crammed with concrete-bunker hotels, discos, go-go bars, and tacky restaurants. So while Siófok is not for those seeking a peaceful lakeside getaway, it is exactly what hordes of action-seeking young people want—an all-in-one playground.

One worthwhile attraction is the **Kálmán Imre Múzeum** (Imre Kálmán Museum), housed in the birthplace of composer Kálmán (1882–1953), known internationally as the Prince of Operetta. Inside this small house-cum-museum are his first piano, original scores, his smoking jacket, and lots of old pictures. ■ TIP→ **An upstairs room exhibiting paintings closes two hours early, so hit that first.** ⊠ *Kálmán Imre sétány 5* ☎ *84/311–287* 🖾 *250 HUF* ⊙ *Apr.–Oct., Tues.–Sun. 9–5; Nov.–Mar., Tues.–Sun. 9–4.*

NEED A BREAK? Opened in 2005 on the main road downtown, close to the train station, **Marcipán Cukrászda** (⊠ Fő utca 17 ☎ 84/310–433) is one of Siófok's best (and few!) pastry shops. Stand or sit at one of several round wooden tables downstairs and sample a tiramisu and/or a chocolately Sacher torta; or head upstairs to the lounge (where the prices are higher).

Where to Stay & Eat

★ $–$$$ ✕ **Calvados Restaurant.** The more elegant of two restaurants across from the Hotel Azúr, the Calvados, which opened in 2006, offers everything from Balaton catfish soup and pike perch to lobster, frogs' legs, and wild game, not to mention traditional Hungarian dishes (some of them rich with Hungary's reputedly low-cholesterol mangalica pork), pizzas, and salads. ⊠ *Erkel Ferenc utca 11* ☎ *30/389–0441 (mobile)* ▤ *No credit cards.*

★ $–$$ ✕ **Csárdás Étterem.** The oldest and one of the best restaurants in Siófok, the Csárdás Étterem consistently wins awards for its hearty, never-bland Hungarian cuisine. House specialties include fish soup, *cigánypecsenye* (grilled pork), and turkey breast with stewed peach. On a hot day the air-conditioning tastes good, too. ⊠ *Fő utca 105* ☎ *84/310–642* ▤ *AE, DC, MC, V* ⊙ *Closed Jan.–mid-Mar.*

★ $$ ✕🛏 **Hotel Azúr.** Buzzing with activity behind its stylish red-brick and glass exterior, much of it conference induced, Siófok's newest and biggest hotel opened in 2004. The standard rooms, though small, each have a balcony, and a cheery tone punctuated with colorful-checkered silky bedspreads. A spa with a full range of services and treatments is complemented by a private beach. ⊠ *Erkel Ferenc utca 2/C, H-8600* ☎ *84/ 501–400* 🖨 *84/501–435 or 84/501–415* ⊕ *www.hotelazur.hu* 🛏 *204 rooms, 18 suites* ⚴ *Restaurant, cable TV, minibars, in-room safes, Wi-Fi, bar, café, spa, sauna, massage, gym, tennis courts, conference center, business center, babysitting, free parking* ▤ *AE, DC, MC, V* ⧦ *BP.*

★ $–$$ 🛏 **Best Western Janus Atrium Hotel.** Almost every room in this bright luxury hotel has been decorated to a different theme, culture, or place—from Thai, Indian, and Japanese to Gustav Klimt (Klimt being especially plush). The two-level suites have rather dark, windowless bedrooms (atop hard-to-climb steps). The hotel's adjoining café, which serves not only drinks but light foods including salads, is delightful; sit in the courtyard out back amid hanging plants and the sound of trickling water. All in all, a fine place to stay, though it is several blocks from the lake. ⊠ *Fő utca 93–95, H-8600* ☎ *84/312–546* 🖨 *84/312–432* ⊕ *www.janushotel. hu* 🛏 *26 rooms, 7 suites* ⚴ *Café, wireless Internet, in-room safes, minibars, cable TV, indoor pool, gym, sauna, bar, meeting rooms, free parking, most rooms no-smoking* ▤ *AE, DC, MC, V* ⧦ *BP.*

¢ ▦ **Hotel Fortuna.** Not far down the road from the Hotel Azúr but much farther down in price, this three-story, faded yellow rectangular block might not have its own beach, but it is only about 100 yards from the lake, while also being removed from the traffic of the city's main street. The rooms are modern and, like the building's facade, awash in a soothing yellow; all have balconies. ⊠ *Erkel Ferenc utca 51, H-8600* ▦▦ *84/ 311–087 or 84/313–476* ⊕ *www.hotelfortuna-siofok.hu* ↵ *41 rooms, 5 suites* ⟨⟩ *Restaurant, bar, playground, meeting rooms; no a/c* ▭ *AE, DC, MC, V* ⦿ *BP.*

Nightlife & the Arts

Siófok is an important destination in the summer for Hungarian youth, who come to party here. Several outdoor raves and musical festivals are usually held between May and August. These outdoor events are advertised by posters plastered across Budapest.

The town remains loyal to Siófok-born operetta composer Imre Kálmán, and hosts popular operetta concerts regularly in summer at the **Kulturális Központ** (Cultural Center; ⊠ Fő tér 2 ▦ 84/311–855).

LAKE BALATON ESSENTIALS

AIR TRAVEL

Hungary's newest international airport is in Sármellék, south of Keszthely near the western tip of Lake Balaton. Although this means that you can now fly there by Ryanair from London, for example, if you wish to spend more of your time in Budapest than on Lake Balaton, this option may well be inconvenient and more costly.

BUS TRAVEL

Frequent bus service links Budapest with Lake Balaton's major resorts. Arrive at the bus station early. You can buy a reserved-seat ticket at the station up to 20 minutes prior to departure, but you can only do so in person; otherwise, buy your ticket directly from the driver. Contact tourist offices or Volánbusz for schedule and fare information. Buses leave from Budapest's Népliget Bus Station.

🎦 **Volánbusz** ⊠ District X, Népliget Bus Station, Üllői út 131, Budapest ▦ 1/382–4900 ⊕ www.volanbusz.hu.

CAR TRAVEL

Driving is the most convenient way to explore the area, but keep in mind that traffic can be heavy during summer weekends. Expressway E71/ M7 (due for extensive repairs as of this writing) is the main artery between Budapest and Lake Balaton, which runs through southwestern Hungary. From Budapest the E71 traverses the lake's southern shore to Siófok and towns farther west. Route 71 joins E71 at Balaton's eastern shore and travels up along the northern shore to Balatonfüred and lakeside towns southwest. The drive from Budapest to Siófok takes about 1½ hours, except on weekends, when traffic can be severe. From Budapest to Balatonfüred is about the same.

FERRY TRAVEL

The slowest but most scenic way to travel among Lake Balaton's major resorts is by ferry, for about 400 HUF per person plus at least 1,000 HUF per car. Schedules for **Balatoni Hajózási Zrt** (Balaton Shipping Co.) are available from most of the tourist offices in the region.

🚢 **Balatoni Hajózási Zrt** (Balaton Shipping Co.) ☎ 84/310−050 in Siófok, 87/342−230 in Balatonfüred, 87/431−240 in Badacsony ⊕ www.balatonihajozas.hu.

TOURS

You can arrange tours directly with the hotels in the Balaton area and with the help of Tourinform offices; these can include boat trips to vineyards, folk-music evenings, and overnight trips to local inns.

FROM BUDAPEST Cityrama takes groups twice a week from April to October from Budapest to Balatonfüred for a walk along the promenade and then over to Tihany for a tour of the abbey. After lunch, you take a ferry across the Balaton and then head back to Budapest, with a wine-tasting stop on the way.

IBUSZ Travel has several day-long tours to Hévíz, Balatonfüred, and Siófok from Budapest; inquire at the office in Budapest.

🚢 **Cityrama** ☎ 1/302−4382 in Budapest ⊕ www.cityrama.hu. **IBUSZ Travel** ✉ District V, Ferenciek tere 10, Around Ferenciek tere, Budapest ☎ 1/485−2700 ⊕ www.ibusz. hu.

BOAT TOURS **Balatoni Hajózási Zrt** (Balaton Shipping Co.) arranges sailing excursions on Lake Balaton. From Balatonfüred, the *Csongor* sets out several times daily in July and August for an hour-long jaunt around the Tihany Peninsula. Most other summer tours depart from Siófok, including the "Tihany Tour" on Saturday at 10 AM, which stops for guided sightseeing in Balatonfüred and Tihany; the "Sunset Tour" is a daily 1½-hour cruise at 7:30 PM, during which you can sip a glass of champagne while watching the sun set. The "Badacsony Tour" departs from Keszthely and goes to Badacsony at 10:30 AM each Thursday.

🚢 **Balatoni Hajózási Zrt.** ☎ 84/310−050 in Siófok ⊕ www.balatonihajozas.hu.

TRAIN TRAVEL

Daily express trains run from Budapest's Déli (South) Station to Veszprém, Balatonfüred, and Siófok. Whether by the more comfy Inter-City (IC) trains or a standard train, you'll be in Veszprém in around 1 hour 50 minutes (1,200 HUF one-way regular train, 1,600 HUF IC). The roughly two-hour trip to Siófok costs 1,200 HUF, and you get to Balatonfüred in around the same time for 1,400 HUF. ■ TIP→ The easiest way to get between Veszprém and Lake Balaton's northern shore is by bus, with hourly routes to and from Balatonfüred; but it's also possible to go by train to either shore, but that will involve a transfer somewhere along the way.

Trains from Budapest serve the resorts on both shores, but there is no train service to Tihany, only a bus from Balatonfüred or a ferry from the southern shore. While most towns are on a rail line, it's inconvenient to decipher the train schedules; trains don't run frequently, so planning connections can be tricky. Since many towns are just a few miles apart, getting stuck on a local train can feel like an endless stop-start cycle. Also bear in mind that, apart from some trains between Budapest and Veszprém, you cannot reserve seats on the Balaton trains—it's first come, first seated. In summer, arrive at the station in Budapest at least a half-hour early and (once you've bought your ticket, of course) hasten to the track once it is displayed if you want a seat.

🚩 The Hungarian State Railway (MÁV) national info line (a local charge from anywhere in the country)–06–40/494–949–may be your best bet, indeed local stations' numbers are increasingly being rerouted to this national line. **Balatonfüred train station** ⊠ Castricum tér, Balatonfüred ☎ 87/343–652. **Siófok train station** ⊠ Millenium tér, Siófok ☎ 84/310–061. **Veszprém train station** ⊠ Jutasi út 34, Veszprém, 2 km [1 mi] outside of town ☎ 15/175–236.

VISITOR INFORMATION

The Balaton Communication and Information Hotline is an excellent source of travel information for the region (in Hungarian only), with a comprehensive Web site (with some English information).

🚩 Tourist Information **Balaton Communication & Information Hotline** ☎ 88/406–963 ⊕ www.balaton.hu. **Balatontourist** ⊠ Tagore sétány 1, Balatonfüred ☎ 87/342–822 or 87/343–471. **Balaton Volán Utazási Iroda** ⊠ Bus station (Jutasi út), Veszprém ☎ 88/420–063. **IBUSZ** ⊠ Fő utca 174, Siófok ☎ 84/315–213. **Tourinform** ⊠ Park utca 6, Badacsony ☎🖷 87/531–013 ⊠ Petőfi utca 68, Balatonfüred ☎ 87/580–480 ⊠ Kossuth utca 28, Keszthely ☎🖷 83/314–144 ⊠ Víztorony, Siófok ☎ 84/315–355 ⊠ Kossuth utca 20, Tihany ☎🖷 87/448–804 ⊠ Vár utca 4, Veszprém ☎🖷 87/404–548. **Zalatour** ⊠ Rákóczi utca 8, Hévíz ☎ 83/341–048.

8

Sopron

WORD OF MOUTH

"We visited Sopron, Kőszeg, Fertőd, Pannonhalma, and Szombathely last fall after seeing Vienna and the Wachau. If you are limited by time and travel, look no farther than Sopron. It is a charming old city . . . with a great, oval-shaped historic center full of very old buildings."

—hardwater

"Sopron is a beautiful town. We were there one afternoon and night. I thought that was enough."

—LLC

"Sopron is about a half hour's drive from Vienna. . . . [At the border] make sure to bypass the truck lane, as many [trucks] have to go through detailed inspections."

—Kittrdg

By Paul
Olchváry

SOPRON, WHICH LIES ON THE AUSTRIAN FRONTIER 222 km (139 mi) west of Budapest, between Lake Ferto (Neusiedlersee in German) and the Sopron Hills, is one of Hungary's most picturesque cities. Nowhere else in the country are there so many monuments in such a small area; literally every other building in the Sopron city center seems to be a historic marker or landmark of some sort. Under an hour away from Vienna by car or train, this small city is a bargain-shopping center for many Austrians who often come for the day—and, indeed, an ideal stopover on a trip between the Austrian and Hungarian capitals. The joke in Sopron is that every day at noon "We play the Austrian national hymn so that the Austrians have to stand still for two minutes while we Hungarians shop." German-speakers also come to Sopron for another reason: dental care. Calling itself the world's dental capital, Sopron claims to have one dentist for every 80 inhabitants. Most signs and menus are in both Hungarian and German, and most people here speak German as a second language. Don't be discouraged, however, if you don't speak German. Employees at Sopron's Tourinform office speak English, and information for museums and other places of interest is almost always in English as well.

There is much more to Sopron, however, than conspicuous consumption by foreigners. Behind the narrow storefronts along Várkerület (City Ring) and within the city walls (one set built by Romans, the other by medieval Magyars) lies a horseshoe-shaped inner city that is a wondrous mix of Gothic, baroque, and Renaissance, mostly set in and around Fő tér, the main square of perfectly proportioned Italianate architecture. Sopron's inspired restoration won a 1975 Europe Prize Gold Medal for Protection of Monuments, and the work continues slowly and carefully.

Sopron is often called Hungary's most faithful town, as its residents voted to remain part of Hungary in 1921 after the Trianon Peace Treaty following World War I shrunk Hungary's size by some two-thirds. Today's city of 60,000 was a small Celtic settlement more than 2,300 years ago. During Roman times, as Scarabantia, it stood on the main European north–south trade route, the Amber Road; it also happened to be near the junction with the east–west route used by Byzantine merchants. In AD 896 the Magyars conquered the Carpathian basin and later named the city Suprun, after a medieval Hungarian warrior. After the Habsburgs took over the territory during the Turkish wars of the 16th and 17th centuries, they renamed the city Ödenburg (Castle on

9

PAUL'S TOP 5

Eszterházy Palace. This magnificent yellow baroque and rococo palace hosted Joseph Haydn as court conductor for 30 years.

Pannonhalma Apátság. This vast Benedictine abbey may be some 1,000 years old, but it still gleams like a gift from heaven.

Tűztorony. The 200-foot-high Fire Tower has foundations dating to the 9th–13th centuries.

Hotel Wollner. This charming 18th-century hotel has been restored to its original splendor.

Soproni Borház. This 300-year-old wine cellar offers tastings of 300 different Hungarian wines.

the Ruins) and made it the capital of the rich and fertile Austrian Burgenland. Ferdinand III, later Holy Roman Emperor, was crowned king of Hungary here in 1625, and at a special session of the Hungarian parliament in 1681 Prince Paul Esterházy was elected palatine (ruling deputy) of Hungary. And always, under any name or regime, Sopron was a relatively fine and prosperous place in which to live.

About the Hotels & Restaurants

Despite throngs of tourists from neighboring Austria and Germany, the selection of quality hotels in Sopron is modest, and many hotels lie well outside the city center—in particular, on the roads leading to the alpine-like hills to the west of town. The best places to stay are either in the Old Town or along the Várkerület, and from either of these areas the city can easily be navigated by foot. Hotel rates may be quoted in either forints or euros.

Dining tends to be casual, and many restaurants have outdoor seating terraces during warmer months, usually from May through September. In addition to several cozy cafés and small eateries offering Hungarian food, Sopron has numerous pizzerias. Food is less pricey than in Budapest but a bit more expensive than in eastern or southern Hungary.

WHAT IT COSTS In Euros & Forints				
$$$$	$$$	$$	$	¢
HOTELS IN EUROS				
over 225	175–225	125–175	75–125	under 75
HOTELS IN FORINTS				
over 56,000	44,000–56,000	31,000–44,000	18,500–31,000	under 18,500
RESTAURANTS IN FORINTS				
over 3,500	2,500–3,500	1,500–2,500	800–1,500	under 800

Hotel prices are for two people in a standard double room with a private bath and breakfast during peak season (June through August). Restaurant prices are per person for a main course at dinner and include 15% tax but not service.

EXPLORING SOPRON

For those who plan to visit as many museums as they can, one collective ticket covering most of Sopron's museums—11 of them, as of this writing—may be purchased at the Storno Ház for 2,000 HUF

Numbers in the text correspond to numbers in the margin and on the Sopron map.

A GOOD WALK

Sopron is best navigated on foot, as nearly every building in the city center has some historic importance attached to it. Starting from the train station, walk straight out the front door, which will lead you directly to Mátyás Király utca. Continue for about ten minutes until you reach Széchenyi tér, the city's largest square. (The tourist information office is located here.) From here, Mátyás Kiraly utca now turns into **Várk-**

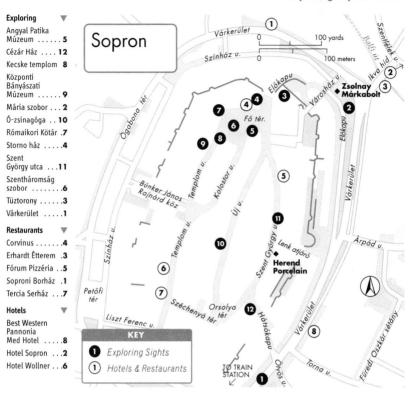

9

erület ❶, Sopron's main boulevard, which is lined with shops, cafés, and dental offices. Continue along this street for about 10 minutes more until you reach the tall **Mária szobor ❷**, which juts into the sky and marks the beginning of Sopron's Old Town.

Keep to the left, past the statue and down the cobblestone Előkapu utca, which leads to Sopron's Old Town. Pass under a concrete archway, where a huge bronze key to the city will be on the right. Above the key is the towering **Tűztorony ❸**. Pass through a narrow, arched wooden passageway under the Tűztorony, and you enter Fő tér, the main square of the Old Town.

The first building to your right is the grandest building in all of Sopron, the **Storno ház ❹**. Across the square, at No. 2, sits the **Angyal Patika Múzeum ❺**. In the center of Fő tér is the **Szentháromság szobor ❻**. Continue walking on the right side of the square, and you will come across the **Rómaikori Kőtár ❼**. Just after the museum, Fő tér turns into Templom utca, and at this junction is the Gothic **Kecske templom ❽**, which according to legend was constructed with treasure unearthed by a goat. Inside the church visit the Középkori Káptalan, a former burial chapel. The ceiling fresco inside the room depicts Franciscan saints and dates back to 1779. A few feet farther along Templom utca, at No. 2, is the **Központi**

Bányászati Múzeum ❾, which displays several centuries of Hungarian mining artifacts in a blue baroque building

From here you can continue down Templom utca, admiring the rows of quaint, colored houses, or you can backtrack to the far-right corner of Fő tér, past the Angyal Patika Múzeum, and take a right down Új utca. At No. 22, is the **Ó-zsi-nagóga** ❿. Continue down Új utca, whose name means "new street" in

> ## WHICH WINES?
>
> Sopron's flagship wine is a red, the indigenous peppery kékfrankos (aka Blaufränkisch). Beyond that, the peppery white zöld veltelini (grüner veltininer), a rarity otherwise in Hungary, is also well worth a try; as are other reds such as zweigelt, cabernet sauvignon, merlot, and pinot noir.

Hungarian but which is actually one of the Sopron's oldest streets. Prior to 1440 it was called Zsidó utca (Jew Street) and was mainly a Jewish neighborhood. Új utca ends at the small Orsolya tér.

As you approach the square, go left across it and take another left onto **Szent György utca** (St. George Street) ⓫. A few feet up the street, at the first corner is the **Cézár Ház** ⓬. If you continue along Szent György utca you'll see several other interesting buildings, including Sopron's richest rococo structure at No. 16 and the Eggenberg Ház two doors down. Across the street is Szent György templom, where a chapel has stood since 1398. Szent György utca leads back to Fő tér.

TIMING   Depending on how many museums you want to visit, the entire walk can easily be done in one afternoon. Although there are many sights in this area, be sure to notice the front doors on nearly every building in the Old Town. Grandiose and unique, each set of doors stands out against the colored backdrop of green, red, and blue-painted buildings.

What to See

❺ **Angyal Patika Múzeum** (Angel Pharmacy Museum). A working apothecary between 1642 and 1647, this museum is filled with old Viennese porcelain vessels and papers pertaining to Ignaz Philipp Semmelweis (1815–65), the Hungarian physician whose pioneering work in antiseptics, while he was in Vienna, made childbirth safer. The building itself dates from the 16th century. A letter by King Lajos II in 1525 forbade the building's demolition—before it became a pharmacy, the building was used mainly for storage—citing the architectural integrity of Fő tér. This letter was Hungary's first ever historic building protection document. If the museum is closed during its posted hours, request entry at the Soproni Múzeum office in the Storno Ház (⇨ see the listing, *below*). ✉ Fő tér 2 ☎ 99/311–327 💰 300 HUF ☉ Apr.–Sept., Tues.–Sun. 10–6; Oct.–Mar., Tues.–Sun. 2–6.

⓬ **Cézár Ház** (Cézár House). The Hungarian parliament met in the upstairs rooms here in 1681; the same space now houses a privately endowed museum, created by the widow of József Soproni-Horváth (1891–1961), a remarkable artist who prefixed his hometown's name to his own so he wouldn't be just another "Joe Croat" (*Horváth* means "Croat," in

Hungarian). Famous for the wonders he worked with watercolors, Soproni-Horváth used the fragile medium to bring large surfaces to life in a density usually associated with oil paintings while depicting realistic scenes, such as a girl grieving over her drowned sister's body. A wine cellar offers the opportunity to sit with a glass of wine. ⊠ *Hátsókapú utca 2* ☎ *99/312–326* 🖃 *300 HUF* ☉ *Thurs., Fri., and Sun. 10–1, Sat. 10–1 and 3–6.*

❽ **Kecske templom** (Goat Church). Legend has it that the early Gothic (1280–1300) church takes its name from a medieval billy goat that scratched up a treasure, enabling the Franciscans to build a church on the site (the Benedictines took over in 1802). More likely, however, the name comes from the figures of goats carved into its crests: the coat of arms of the Gutsch family, who financed the church. The Goat Church has a soaring, pointed, 14th-century steeple, three naves, and its original Gothic choir (betraying French influence). After several rebuildings, there are also a Hungarian Gothic-baroque red-marble pulpit, a rococo main altar, baroque altars, and a painting of St. Stephen by one of the Stornos. The church stands before the Holy Trinity Column in Fő tér. ⊠ *Templom utca 1* 🖃 *Free (donations accepted)* ☉ *Daily 10–noon and 2–5.*

❾ **Központi Bányászati Múzeum** (Central Museum of Mining). Hungarian mining dates back to the 10th century AD; indeed, gold and silver mining played a vital role in the country's trade up until the discovery of the so-called New World, when gold was more often imported. The museum features murals showing the first mine blast in Slovakia in 1627 and the discovery of Hungary's first coal mine near Sopron. Also on hand are the ornamental pieces created by silversmiths that decorated noblemen's tables in jewel-studded splendor, as well as paintings and statues. Tour a nobleman's baroque town house and view various antiquities and works of art, including samples of hundreds of minerals found in the Carpathian basin. ⊠ *Templom utca 2* ☎ *99/312–667* ⊕ *www.kbm.hu* 🖃 *400 HUF* ☉ *Apr.–Oct., Tues.–Sun. 10–6; Nov.–Mar., Tues.–Sun. 10–4.*

❷ **Mária szobor** (St. Mary's Column). With its finely sculpted Biblical reliefs, the column is a superb specimen of baroque design. It was erected in 1745 to mark the former site of the medieval Church of Our Lady, which was destroyed by Sopron citizens in 1632 because they feared the Turks would use its steeple as a strategic firing tower. ⊠ *At the Előkapu (Front Gate).*

NEED A BREAK? Red-velvety chairs, an ornate chandelier, a semi-spiraling wooden staircase, and scrumptious pastry are the hallmarks of the cozy little **Dömötöri cukrászda** (⊠ Széchenyi tér, at the corner of Erszébet utca ☎ 99/506–623) on Sopron's second most famous—and largest—square. In summer there are plenty of tables with umbrellas on an outside terrace. Be sure to notice footwear on the waitresses: open-toed and open-heeled white boots laced halfway up the calf, a popular shoe under communism.

Toothy Tourism

IN ADDITION TO BEING the museum hub of Hungary, Sopron calls itself the world's dental capital, with an estimated one dentist to every 80 residents. Along Sopron city streets, especially the main boulevard, Várkerület, are many dental practices specializing in implants and prostheses. Thousands of Austrians and Germans cross into Sopron on a regular basis for a day at the dentist—at prices 40 to 60 percent cheaper than in their native countries—usually to be combined with shopping or a trip to one of Hungary's thermal spas.

An estimated 1,000 dentists can be found in Sopron and in the nearby border towns of Szombathely and Mosonmagyaróvár. But for the average Hungarian such a dental trip is out of the question, since most Sopron dentists charge, at the very least, Budapest-style prices for

dentistry, which are out of reach of the average Hungarian.

Austrian and German dentists have reported major drops in business. The Austrian Dental Association has even campaigned to ban Hungarian dentists from advertising across the border, while dentists in Austria and Germany publicly rail against Hungarian dentists for poor workmanship, but this hasn't slowed down dental tourism in Sopron. More and more dentists are migrating to the city to set up an office, according to tourism officials. This is good news for Sopron, since the average dental tourist spends several days in Sopron while having his or her teeth fixed, spending money in local shops, attractions, restaurants, and hotels, most of which have a dentist on staff, or at least one they recommend.

⓾ **Ó-zsinagóga** (Old Synagogue). The medieval synagogue, complete with a stone *mikva,* a ritual bath for women, is now a religious museum with old Torahs on display and an exhibit about the World War II deportation of the Jews. Built around 1300, it endured several incarnations over the centuries, including a stint as a hospital (in the 1400s) and a residential building (in the 1700s). Restored in 1973, the existing facade dates from 1734. A plaque honors the 1,640 Jews of Sopron who were murdered by the Nazis—the quiet street that is home to this and another old synagogue a few doors away, at No. 11, became the city's Jewish ghetto in May 1944. Only 274 of Sopron's Jews survived, and today there are scarcely enough to muster a *minyan* (quorum of 10), let alone a congregation. ⊠ *Új utca 22* 🕾 *99/311–327* 🎫 *400 HUF* ☉ *Apr.–Oct., Tues.–Sun. 10–6.*

❼ **Rómaikori Kőtár** (Roman Archaeology Museum). A fine Renaissance courtyard leads to the churchlike vaulted medieval cellar—a perfect setting for the gigantic statues of Jupiter, Juno, and Minerva unearthed beneath the main square during the digging of foundations for the city hall in the late 19th century. On the second floor a separate museum (with identical hours and admission prices) re-creates the living environment of 17th- and 18th-century Sopron apartments. ⊠ *Fő tér 6* 🕾 *99/311–327* 🎫 *500 HUF for each museum* ☉ *Apr.–Sept., Tues.–Sun. 10–6; Oct.–Mar., Tues.–Sun. 10–2.*

4 **Storno Ház** (Storno House). Right on
Fodor'sChoice the exquisite main square, the tur-
★ reted house is the city's finest Re-
naissance-era building. Inside its
two-story loggia is the restaurant
Corvinus (*see* ⇨ Where to Stay &
Eat), which is downstairs; upstairs,
a museum houses a remarkable
family collection of furniture, porcelain, sculptures, and paintings. The
Stornos were a rags-to-riches dynasty of chimney sweeps who, over
several generations bought or just
relieved grateful owners of un-
wanted treasures and evolved into
a family of painters and sculptors
themselves. The dynasty died out in
Hungary in the late 1990s, but a few
remaining distant relatives agreed
with the Hungarian state that nothing should be removed from the
Storno House. On an exterior wall
hangs a plaque commemorating
visits by King Matthias Corvinus
(winter 1482–83) and Liszt Ferenc

> ### IN LIEU OF THE ALPS
>
> After Hungary lost its high moun-
> tains to neighboring states with
> the 1920 Treaty of Trianon, the
> Lövér Hills just to the southeast of
> downtown Sopron—a 40-minute
> walk, though accessible by bus—
> took on all the more significance.
> Commonly referred to in Hungar-
> ian in the plural as the Lövérek,
> the forested hills here are the clos-
> est thing in Hungary to the Alps.
> Even if they aren't nearly as high,
> there are more than a few pines,
> and in places you get a view of
> Austria's Alps over the nearby bor-
> der. Hungarians come here to
> breathe fresh air and, during the
> communist era, perhaps even to
> imagine that they were on the
> other side of the border.

(1840 and 1881). The museum can be visited by guided tour only, given
every half hour (the last tour begins ½ hr before closing). ⊠ *Fő tér 8*
☎ *99/311–327* 🎫 *800 HUF* 🕐 *Apr.–Sept., Tues.–Sun. 10–6; Oct.–Mar.,
Tues.–Sun. 2–6, with tours every ½ hr.*

11 **Szent György utca** (St. George Street). Numerous dragons of religion and
architecture coexist in a somewhat harmonious fashion. The **Erdődy Vár**
(Erdődy Palace), at No. 16, is Sopron's richest rococo building. Two doors
down, at No. 12, stands the **Eggenberg Ház** (Eggenberg House), where
the widow of Prince Johann Eggenberg held Protestant services during
the harshest days of the Counter-Reformation and beyond. But the street
takes its name from **Szent György templom** (St. George's Church), a 14th-
century Catholic church so sensitively "baroqued" some 300 years later
that its interior is still as soft as whipped cream. The church is generally
open daily from 9 to 5; the other buildings are not open to the public.

6 **Szentháromság szobor** (Holy Trinity Column). The centerpiece of Fő tér
is a sparkling, spiraling three-tiered monument aswirl with gilded an-
gels. It represents the earliest (1701) and loveliest baroque monument
to a plague in all of Hungary—in this case, the country's great plague,
which lasted from 1695 to 1701. Kneeling figures carved in the pedestal
represent the married couple who ordered the work from the sculptor.

3 **Tűztorony** (Fire Tower). The symbol of Sopron's endurance—and entrance-
Fodor'sChoice way to the Old Town—is 200 feet high, with foundations dating to the
★ days of the Árpád dynasty (9th–13th centuries) and perhaps back to the
Romans. The tower is remarkable for its uniquely harmonious blend of

architectural styles: it has a Romanesque base rising to a circular balcony of Renaissance loggias topped by an octagonal clock tower that is itself capped by a brass baroque onion dome and belfry. The upper portions were rebuilt after most of the earlier Fire Tower was, ironically, destroyed by the Great Fire of 1676, started by students roasting chestnuts in a high wind. Throughout the centuries the tower bell tolled the alarm for fire or the death of a prominent citizen, and from the loggias musicians trumpeted the approach of an enemy or serenaded the citizenry. Both warning concerts were accompanied by flags (red for fire, blue for enemy) pointing in the direction of danger. Today you can take in good views of the town and surrounding countryside from the top of the tower. ⊠ *Fő tér* ☎ *99/311–327* 💲 *500 HUF* ☉ *May–Aug., Tues.–Sun. 10–8; Apr. and Sept.–Oct., Tues.–Sun. 10–6.*

❶ **Várkerület.** Strolling along the circular boulevard that embraces Sopron's inner core allows you to take in the vibrant harmony of beautifully preserved baroque and rococo architecture and the fashionable shops and cafés of Sopron's thriving downtown business district.

OFF THE
BEATEN
PATH

ESZTERHÁZY PALACE – The magnificent yellow baroque and rococo palace, built between 1720 and 1760 as a residence for the Hungarian noble family, is prized as one of the country's most exquisite palaces. Though badly damaged in World War II, it has been painstakingly restored, making it clear why in its day the palace was referred to as the Hungarian Versailles. Its 126 rooms include a lavish Hall of Mirrors and a three-story-high concert hall, where classical concerts are held throughout the summer (roughly 10 a month, at irregular intervals). Joseph Haydn, court conductor to the Eszterházy family here for 30 years, is the subject of a small museum inside. Slippers—mandatory, to preserve the palace floors—are provided at the entrance. The palace lies 27 km (17 mi) southeast of Sopron, in Fertőd. ⊠ *Haydn utca 2, just off Rte. 85, Fertőd* ☎ *99/537–640* 💲 *1,000 HUF* ☉ *Mid-Mar.–late Oct., Tues.–Sun. 10–6; late Oct.–mid-Mar., Tues.–Sun. 10–4.*

WHERE TO STAY & EAT

★ $–$$$ ✕ **Erhardt Étterem.** Sopron's newest fine-dining rage opened in 2005 on a quiet side street a block from Várkerület, refreshingly removed from the more touristy atmosphere that prevails on the Old Town's main square a few minutes' walk away. Unless a group of young Hungarian (or Austrian) yuppies has reserved one of the cellars for a wine-tasting event (this happens at least once a week), you have your choice in this capacious venue of two brick-vaulted cellars with separate entrances, plus several other rooms, each with a theme (e.g., sailing) and related artwork on the walls; not to mention a pleasant backyard garden. The menu, complemented by an extensive wine list, ranges from traditional Hungarian pork and poultry dishes to French-style cuisine, and fish dishes like catfish paprikás. ⊠ *Balfi utca 10* ☎ *99/506–711* 🚇 *MC, V.*

★ $–$$ ✕ **Corvinus.** The location, in the 700-year-old Storno House off Sopron's delightful cobblestone main square—the city's historic heart—couldn't be better. The Corvinus itself combines a café, pub, pizzeria, and restaurant all in one. Among the specialties are a meaty soup with a baked-on pastry cap, and roast duck with braised red cabbage. Service is formal yet friendly, whether you dine inside under vaulted ceilings or at an outdoor table. ⊠ *Fő tér 7–8* ☎ *99/505–035* ⊟ *AE, DC, MC, V.*

$–$$ ✕ **Tercia Serház.** Located in Sopron's main cultural and conference center on large, lively Liszt Ferenc tér (a short walk south of the Old Town and on the way to the train station), this is one of the largest and most popular restaurants in town. You can enjoy its broad array of cuisine—from breaded veal and gulyás to pork, beef, and poultry dishes as well as pastas—either out front along with so many other people, or in the cellar rooms downstairs. ⊠ *Liszt Ferenc tér 1* ☎ *99/517–550* ⊟ *MC, V.*

¢–$$ ✕ **Fórum Pizzéria.** Only yards from Fő tér, this is the best bet for pizza in the Old Town and possibly in all of Sopron. At relative bargain prices, here you can choose between some 40 pies (between 700 HUF and 1,200 HUF) and a variety of standard dishes including grilled meats and fish. ⊠ *Szent György utca 3* ☎ *99/340–231* ⊟ *AE, DC, MC, V.*

¢–$$ ✕ **Soproni Borház.** This 300-year-old wine cellar just off the city's main
Fodor'sChoice shopping boulevard offers tastings of 300 different Hungarian wines,
★ including some made in Sopron. As you go down the stairs, the heady smell of wood charcoal (presumably for grilling meats) and mustiness exuding from the brickwork evokes a rainy day by a fireplace at a stone lodge in the woods. Your wine is ordered with a plate of accompanying light fare (all under 1,000 HUF), which might include goose liver, salami, pork, sausage, and several types of vegetables. You can also order grilled meats for a bit more (priced by weight). Servers are extremely friendly, and will give you an earful along with each glassful of wine you try. Try the Hungarian *almapaprika* (apple pepper), which is a round yellow pepper soaked in vinegar and spices and marinated for several days. Careful—it can be quite hot. ⊠ *Várkerület utca 15* ☎ *99/510–022* ⊟ *MC, V.*

$ ✕▣ **Hotel Wollner.** Tucked inside the city center, this quiet and charm-
Fodor'sChoice ing 18th-century peach-colored hotel has been restored to its original
★ splendor, as the proud staff will attest. Aside from the exquisite baroque interior, the best thing about the Wollner is a courtyard within the hotel, where there is plenty of outdoor seating amid flowers and greenery. On the wall of the courtyard is a Roman-era cenotaph brought to the hotel by a former owner in 1756. This is a no-smoking hotel, by the way, and that goes even for the restaurant. ⊠ *Templom utca 20, H-9400* ☎ *99/524–400* 🖷 *99/524–401* ⊕ *www.wollner.hu* ↩ *18 rooms* ⌂ *Restaurant, minibars, cable TV, in-room data ports, gym, massage, sauna, bar, wine bar, meeting room, parking (fee); no a/c* ⊟ *AE, DC, MC, V* ❢◗ *BP.*

$ ▣ **Best Western Pannonia Med Hotel.** There has been a hotel here since the 17th century, when the Golden Hind first welcomed stagecoaches traveling between Budapest and Vienna. It was destroyed in a fire but rebuilt in neoclassical style in 1893. With soaring ceilings, dripping chandeliers, and a breakfast room with gilt-edge mirrors and little golden chairs, the hotel is now quite elegant. Standard rooms are comfortable and smart, but they pale in comparison to the handsome suites, which have huge wooden beds and are furnished with antiques. Some services

9

are noteworthy: it's not every hotel that has its own cosmetic-surgery consultant. In keeping with the Sopron spirit, there's also an on-site dentist offering free screenings. ⊠ *Várkerület 75, H-9400* ☎ *99/312–180* 🖷 *99/340–766* ⊕ *www.pannoniahotel.com* 🛏 *48 rooms, 14 suites* ↳ *Restaurant, in-room data ports, pool, gym, hair salon, sauna, spa, bar, meeting rooms, free parking* ▭ *AE, DC, MC, V* ⍾ *BP.*

★ $ ⊡ **Hotel Sopron.** There's no getting around the Hotel Sopron's outdated 1980s-era appearance, so the management wisely emphasizes the panoramic city views and services and amenities. As of this writing, this is the only hotel near downtown with an outdoor pool, and the view of town that's yours while swimming or lounging poolside is marvelous. Many, but not all, of the brown and beige rooms also have great views of Sopron's Old Town. As for services, the hotel can organize everything from wine-tasting tours to scenic train trips, as well as the ubiquitous dental services. And right next door is the hotel's very own wine cellar. ⊠ *Fövényverem utca 7, H-9400* ☎ *99/512–261* 🖷 *99/311–090* ⊕ *www. hotelsopron.hu* 🛏 *106 rooms, 2 suites* ↳ *Restaurant, minibars, cable TV, 2 tennis courts, pool, gym, sauna, Jacuzzi, bar, playground, meeting room; no a/c in some rooms* ▭ *AE, MC, V* ⍾ *BP.*

NIGHTLIFE & THE ARTS

From mid- to late March, Sopron's cultural life warms up during the annual **Tavaszi Fesztivál** (Spring Festival), which coincides with Budapest's famous Spring Festival. On hand are classical concerts, folk-dance performances, and other events. The peak season for cultural events is from mid-June through mid-July, when the **Sopron Ünnepi Hetek** (Sopron Festival Weeks) brings music, dance, and theater performances and art exhibits to churches and venues around town. With its 50th anniversary in 2007, the Weeks will be even bigger and better. Get details from the firm that handles many of Sopron's cultural events, Pro Kultúra Sopron Kht. (☎ 99/517–500 or 99/517–519) or Tourinform, whose main office is in the same building as Pro Kultúra (*see* ⇨ Visitor Information, *in* Sopron Essentials).

SHOPPING

Várkerület is Sopron's main shopping street, where you'll find loads of shops both along the street and in courtyards, where vendors and booths hawk spices, clothing, shoes, and Hungarian wines.

Herend Porcelain Manufactory. Next door to the Herend Village Pottery is a small shop devoted to the famous Herend porcelain, whose history began with a purchase by England's Queen Victoria in 1851, when Windsor Castle ordered a dinner set from the company. ⊠ *Szent György utca 11* ☎ *99/508–712.*

Herend Village Pottery. This shop sells casual dinnerware and ornamentals with highly colorful patterns bearing a more relaxed style and lower prices than the more prized, traditional Herend porcelain found next door. ⊠ *Várkerület 9* ☎ *99/329–681.*

Natura Vinoteka Borszaküzlet. Yards from Várkerület, the main shopping street that partly circles the outside of the Old Town, this is a good place to look for fine Sopron wines, whether the local flagship variety, the peppery red kékfrankos, or the spicy white zöld veltelini. ⊠ *Árpád utca 1* ☎ *06–30/896–6488 or 06–30/411–2973.*

Zsolnay Márkabolt. If you can't make it to the less expensive factory outlet in Pécs, you can purchase exquisite Zsolnay porcelain here. A tiny room lined with glass cabinets displays the delicate wares. ⊠ *Előkapu utca 11* ☎ *99/505–252.*

A STOP IN GYŐR

The largest city in western Hungary, Győr is often called the "Town of Rivers," situated at the confluence of the Rába, Rábca, and Mosoni-Duna rivers. Some 128 km (80 mi) west of Budapest and 94 km (59 mi) east of Sopron, Győr is in the middle of Hungary's *Kisalföld* (Little Plain) and dates back some 2,000 years. With a population of 130,000, it's in the middle of the direct route between Budapest and Vienna and is an automatic train stop along the way to Sopron.

The city has seen occupations by Romans, Tatars, Teutons, and Huns. And even though a former city fortress was built by Italian engineers, it was not strong enough to hold back the Turks, who took Győr in 1594. The fortress was later destroyed by Napoléon Bonaparte.

Downtown Győr, where the three rivers meet, is packed with baroque buildings and museums. As such, it is a downright pleasant place to spend an afternoon or perhaps a night if you can spare the time or want a quick stopover on the way to Vienna. The outskirts of town are mainly industrial, however, much of this owing to the city's geographical location at the rivers' confluence. After the fall of communism, the city was among those in Hungary that became a virtual magnet for various international manufacturers, including Audi; and while this helped the cause of prosperity, it only reinforced Győr's unjustified reputation as a city whose industrial sights obscure its cultural pleasures. (Read: you need only get to the heart of town, and it's as if the industry isn't even there.) Highlights include a 12th-century cathedral and several art museums with renowned collections. If your timing is right, you could also catch a performance by the Győr Ballet, the country's most renowned ballet company.

■ TIP→ If you arrive by train, head straight down either Aradi vértanúk utja or (one to the right) Baross Gábor út several blocks into the historic district. The latter will take you past both Győr's imposing Town Hall and, a block later, the Tourinform office.

What to See

The ancient heart of Győr is at the confluence of the three rivers, called *Káptalan Domb* (Chapter Hill). Here you can see the **Püspöki vár** (Bishop's Palace), the residence of Győr bishops whose oldest section—built on the walls of a Roman fort—dates back to the 13th century. Though little of it is open to the public, it does contain an exhibit dedicated to the life of Bishop Vilmos Apor, shot dead here by Russian soldiers on April 2, 1945, while trying to defend women and girls who sought refuge in the palace. (The exhibit is open and brief tours are held at 10, 12, and 2 Tuesday through Saturday. Check with Tourinform for details.) Káptalan Domb is a good place to wander around, through a maze of fences and wonderfully curved gates surrounding baroque-style homes.

Fodor'sChoice
★
Next to the Püspöki vár is the **Püspöki katedra** (Bishop's Cathedral), which has Romanesque, Gothic, and baroque features. Inside, special ornaments and frescoes of the black altar were painted by A. F. Maulbertsch, who decorated many Hungarian churches in the 18th century. The bishop's throne was a gift from Empress Maria Theresa. The frame of a painting depicting the Blessed Virgin and infant Jesus is considered a rococo masterpiece. Just inside the entrance is **Szent László Chapel** (St. Laszlo Chapel), devoted to the canonized monarch who ruled Győr from 1077 to 1095. Beautifully molded, a 15th-century bust of the saint is an excellent example of medieval Hungarian goldsmithing. ⊠ *Apor Vilmos Püspök tere* ☏ *No phone* 🎫 *Free* ☉ *Daily 9:15–12 and 2–6.*

Directly behind the cathedral is the former bishop's residence that is now the **Borsos Miklós Múzeum.** A prominent 20th-century sculptor, Borsos was a self-taught artist who designed several important Hungarian statues. In the building's courtyard are several bronze and stone figures. ⊠ *Apor Vilmos Püspök tere 2* ☏ *96/316–329* ⊕ *www.gyor-muzeum. hu* 🎫 *300 HUF* ☉ *Tues.–Sun. 10–6.*

Walk down Káptalan Domb to reach **Dunakapu tér** (Danube Gate Square), a waterfront area where grain ships once docked and where open-air markets are still held on Wednesdays and Saturdays. This is also the home of a popular, down-home-style restaurant, the Matróz Dunaparti Kisvendéglő (*see* ⇨ Where to Eat). At the square you will also see an iron weathercock, the symbol of Győr, created by the Turkish army after it took the fortress in 1594.

From Dunakapu tér, Jedlik Ányos utca runs along the western side of the square, ending at **Széchenyi tér** (Szechenyi Square), Győr's main square. Monuments adorning this square—which include an impressive, twin-turreted 17th-century church—are the setting for the annual recreation of a "Baroque Marriage," a traditional ceremony where baroque music is played and participants dress up in ornate wedding outfits and perform for viewers in the square. The marriage is held every August during the Győr Summer Festival.

A former 19th-century spice house, the Iron Stump House now houses the **Patkó Imre Gyűjtemény** (Imre Patko Collection), named in honor of an art historian who collected African and Oceanic applied arts. The museum also has an impressive display of Hungarian and European fine art from the 20th century. A log spiked with nails stands in the corner of the house; it was marked by travelers passing through who noted their journeys on it. Tickets can be purchased around the corner at Széchenyi tér 5, at the Xántus János Múzeum, whose exhibits include local history and Hungarian postage stamps. ⊠ *Széchenyi tér 4 (museum en-*

trance on Stelczer Lajos utca, just around the corner from Széchenyi tér)
☎ 96/310–588 ☜ 400 HUF ☉ May–Sept., Tues.–Sun. 10–6.

Northeast of Széchenyi tér, the **Váczy Péter Gyűjtemény** (Peter Vaczy Collection) is on a small roundabout in a former retirement home. The collection of 17th- and 18th-century paintings, sculptures, and furniture comes from Hungary and all over Europe. Among the most important works in the collection are a 15th-century painting of the Madonna and Child, a biblical scene by Sebastian Bourdon, some 16th-century leather-and-velvet armchairs, a Giacomo Piazetta table, and a richly carved Italian dish holder. ✉ *Nefeljcs köz 3* ☎ *96/318–141* ⊕ *www.gyor-muzeum.hu* ☜ *400 HUF* ☉ *Tues.–Sun. 10–6.*

★ Just off Széchenyi tér in a palace once owned by the Esterházy family, the **Városi Művészeti Múzeum** (City Art Museum) was bestowed in 2005 with a 12-room new permanent collection spanning some 50 years of post–World War I Hungarian art. The Radnai Collection includes everything from József Rippl-Rónai's resplendent *Still Life with Mask* to József Egry's light-pervaded Lake Balaton landscapes, to many other outstanding examples of 20th-century Hungarian painting, sculpture, and graphic art. ✉ *Király utca 17* ☎ *96/322–695* ☜ *500 HUF* ☉ *Tues.–Sun. 10–5.*

Where to Eat

★ **$$–$$$** ✕ **Fonte.** A bit expensive by local standards, this restaurant is in the Hotel Fonte, in the downtown historic district, and has a great reputation among locals as a special-occasion spot. The menu includes a wide range of Hungarian classics plus international dishes, and there is a long wine list to boot. An outdoor terrace offers seating in the summer months, but the soothing beige interior—whose bulb-shaped lamps hang discreetly from low, arched ceilings—is certainly more elegant. ✉ *Schweidel utca 17* ☎ *96/ 513–810* ⊕ *www.hotelfonte.hu* ☰ *AE, DC, MC, V.*

★ **¢–$** ✕ **Matróz Dunaparti Kisvendéglő.** Yards from the foot of the Kossuth Bridge (though with no view of the river, which is obscured by a road out front), the Danube Bank Sailor's Eatery offers down-home cooking at down-home prices. The menu features a sizeable range of fish dishes (several for under 1,000 HUF) plus poultry, pork, and beef standards. The small, thoroughly unpretentious interior—with brick-vaulted ceilings and small wood tables draped with red-and-white-checked tablecloths, and with bunches of garlic and dried pepper and, yes, fishnets, hanging from the ceiling—is surely worth eating in and perhaps even writing home about. ✉ *Dunakapú tér* ☎ *96/336–208* ☰ *No credit cards.*

Nightlife & the Arts

Győri Balett (Győr Ballet). Hungary's most famous and acclaimed ballet company performs regularly at Győr's funky-looking, sharply angled Nemzeti Színház (National Theater). ✉ *Czuczor Gergely utca 7* ☎ *96/ 520–610* ⊕ *www.gyoriszinhaz.hu.*

Győr Nemzetközi Fesztivál (Győr International Festival). The festival takes place in June and July with a series of events, including ballet, theater, folk dancing, folk music, classical music, and a massive handicraft fair. For information, contact the local Tourinform office (*see* ⇨ Visitor Information *in* Sopron Essentials).

OFF THE
BEATEN
PATH

PANNONHALMA APÁTSÁG (Pannonhalma Abbey) – Perched divinely above the countryside on a hilltop roughly 20 km (12 mi) southeast of Győr and 135 km (84 mi) west of Budapest—the vast, 1,000-year-old Benedictine abbey still gleams like a gift from heaven. During the Middle Ages it was an important ecclesiastical center and also wielded considerable political influence. It housed Hungary's first school and is said to be the first place the Holy Scriptures were read on Hungarian soil. It's still a working monastery and school; 60 monks and 320 students live here. A late-Gothic cloister and a 180-foot neoclassical tower are the two stylistic exceptions to the predominantly baroque architecture. A library of more than 300,000 volumes houses some priceless medieval documents, including one of the first known examples of written Hungarian: the 11th-century deed to the abbey of Tihany. Visits are permitted only with a guide, which is included in the admission price. Tours begin every hour on the hour; the last one of the day begins at the closing hour listed below. There are regularly scheduled English and other foreign-language tours at 11 and 1 from late March to mid-November. Occasional organ recitals are held in the basilica in summer. Though it's easiest to drive here, there are three buses Monday–Saturday (at 8, 10, and 12) with a fourth (at 2:10) on Sunday that get you from Győr to the abbey. ⊠ *Off Rte. 82, south of Győr, Pannonhalma* ☎ *96/570–191* 🖷 *96/570–192* ⊕ *www.bences.hu* 🖃 *500 HUF (800 HUF for a foreign-language guide)* ⊗ *Late Mar.–Apr. and Oct.–mid-Nov., Tues.–Sun. 9–4; May, daily 9–4; June–Sept., daily 9–5; mid-Nov.–late Mar., Tues.–Sun. 10–3. Monastery closed Sun. mornings except for those wishing to attend mass; library and yard remain open to tours.*

SOPRON ESSENTIALS

BUS TRAVEL

Buses run between Budapest's Népliget station and Sopron around six times a day and Győr about every half-hour. Prices are calculated by mileage and the type of bus, with newer, more comfortable buses costing more. Although bus and train travel times and costs are roughly equivalent, trains tend to be much more comfortable.

🚌 **Volánbusz** ⊠ District IX, near Üllői út 131, Budapest ☎ 1/219–8063, 1/382–0888 Volánbusz info line ⊕ www.volanbusz.hu.

CAR TRAVEL

By car from Budapest, Győr is approximately 128 km (80 mi) west, along the M1 (E75) motorway, and Sopron is another 94 km (59 mi) along a smaller road, Rt. 85 and, in the last stretch, Rt. 84. Hungary has five toll motorways, referred to as M0, M1, M7, M5, and M3. To drive on these roads, you must first stop at a gasoline station and buy a *matrica* (toll pass), affixing it to the lower left inside of your car's windshield. A matrica valid for four days costs about HUF 1,500. The roads from Győr to Sopron do not require the pass.

TRAIN TRAVEL

The easiest way to get to Sopron is by train, as the entire three-hour trip, with a connection in Győr, offers a lovely view of the western Hungarian countryside and time to enjoy it. Trains running between Sopron and Budapest depart from Budapest's Keleti Pályaudvar (Eastern Train Station) about every 30 minutes throughout the day, the last train to Budapest returning approximately 8 PM from Sopron, about 9 PM from Győr. For train timetables and prices, check out ⊕ www.elivira.hu. Tickets can be bought at any of Budapest's three train stations or at many travel agencies in town.

VISITOR INFORMATION
Tourinform offices have loads of information and brochures on Sopron, Győr, and the surrounding areas. They can also help arrange excursions outside the cities, including trips to Eszterházy Palace and Pannonhalma Abbey. The Tourinform office in Sopron is inside the Liszt Ferenc Kultura Központ, on Széchenyi tér.

🗗 **Tourinform** ⊠ Liszt Ferenc utca 1, Sopron ☎ 99/517–560 ⊕ www.tourinform. sopron.hu ⊠ Árpád utca 32, Győr ☎ 96/311–771.

9

Pécs

WITH VILLÁNY

WORD OF MOUTH

"I spent a lovely two weeks in Hungary last year. I attended a five-day conference in Szeged. Szeged was nice, but five days were WAY too many. Then I traveled to Pécs. This was the highlight of the trip to me. Lovely little city, with a world heritage site, nice pedestrian streets, nice restaurants. We spent three nights there, but really less than two days. Also made a day trip one day to the small wine towns nearby."

—Nuut

By Paul
Olchváry

WESTERN HUNGARY, OFTEN REFERRED TO AS Transdanubia (*Dunántúl* in Hungarian), is the area south and west of the Danube, stretching to the Slovak and Austrian borders in the west and north and to Slovenia and Croatia in the south. It presents a highly picturesque landscape, including several ranges of hills and small mountains. Most of its surface is covered with farmland, vineyards, and orchards—all nurtured and made verdant by a climate that is noticeably more humid than in the rest of the country. Indeed, Hungarians often talk of the southern reaches of *Dunántúl*—the home of a disarmingly atmospheric city, Pécs, and a key wine center, Villány—as their country's little corner of the Mediterranean, despite its being just three hours south of Budapest and, yes, despite the unequivocal absence of any nearby sea.

Pécs (pronounced *paytch*), the southern capital of Transdanubia, dates back to the Roman period, when the city was known as Sopianae and the southern Transdanubia region known as Pannonia. For centuries it was a frontier province and an important stop along the trade route; today it is far richer in Roman ruins than the rest of Hungary. The city played an important role during the Middle Ages as well; in 1009 St. Stephen set up a diocese in Pécs to help cement Christianity among the Magyar tribes. It was a thriving city up until the Turkish Conquest in 1543, and the Turks' 143-year rule left a distinct imprint on the city as well. While the Habsburgs later destroyed or converted many of the Ottoman buildings, Pécs is home to many of Hungary's most important remaining Turkish-era sites. The latter half of the 19th century was important in Pécs, for it saw the rise of local hero Vilmos Zsolnay, whose Secession-style ceramics company would go on to define the city and become one of Hungary's national treasures.

Today Pécs is a vibrant and dynamic university town, rich with historic sites, some of which are on UNESCO's World Heritage list. Already one of Hungary's prettiest cities, Pécs is slowly but surely undergoing an extreme makeover in the run-up to 2010, when it will be "European Capital of Culture" for one year—having beaten out a handful of other Hungarian cities (not to mention other European ones) for this exalted European Union title. Massive construction projects are planned that will, among other things, pedestrianize ever more of downtown and dramatically spruce up a whole host of the city's public spaces (they might start with the bus station and the square in front of the train

10

PAUL'S TOP 5

Pécs Bazilika. This four-spired monument has an utterly breathtaking interior frescoed in shimmering golds, silvers, and blues.

Csontváry Múzeum. The largest museum anywhere dedicated to the work of Mihály Tivadar Csontváry Kosztka.

Bock Pince, Panzió, Étterem. Bock is one of Villány's most celebrated vineyards.

Hotel Millennium Szálló. Renowned Hungarian architect Sándor Dévényi designed this suburban castle.

Jákovali Hászan Múzeum. This is the only Ottoman-era religious building in Hungary with its architecture intact.

station, which are nothing to write home about). As of this writing, controversy was rife over whether Pécs's noble construction plans are on (or behind) schedule, but regardless, as long as funding continues to be available, between 2007 and 2010 the visitor can almost certainly expect to encounter an increasingly attractive Pécs. Even now, though, Pécs packs in a lot: There are early Christian tombs, a magnificent basilica, two mosques dating back to the Turkish occupation, and a handsome synagogue. One can hardly walk a few blocks in Pécs and not see some fanciful Zsolnay tiles adorning a building or roof. On top of that, this small city is home to a half-dozen museums. Three of them— the Zsolnay, Vasarely, and Csontváry—justify a two- or three-day stay in this sparkling, eclectic city in the Mecsek Hills. Once in Pécs, a detour to the nearby town of Villány, in one of Hungary's most fertile wine-producing regions, is a pleasant overnight excursion—that is, if you like the idea of sitting under the stars and tasting some of Hungary's prize vintages.

About the Hotels & Restaurants

There's a good cross-section of hotels available in Pécs and Villány to meet any budget, everything from full-service hotels to modest panzios catering to visiting students. Most hotels quote prices in euros, while some of the smaller panzios use forints for their prices. Although there's no real high season in Pécs—the city is popular year-round— summer does bring many small festivals. The city is also a favorite for Hungarian weddings from April through October, when hotels can get booked solid.

Dining in Pécs can be a much more laid-back affair than in Budapest, and you can expect prices to be significantly lower for a good meal. Although there are a few white-glove restaurants in the city, by and large you'll find dining more informal. The dress code everywhere seems to be smart and casual. Pécs is in the heart of southern Transdanubia, known for its honey, chestnut, and peach production, so don't miss a chance to try one of the many rich desserts made from these local products.

WHAT IT COSTS In Euros & Forints				
$$$$	$$$	$$	$	¢
HOTELS IN EUROS				
over 225	175–225	125–175	75–125	under 75
HOTELS IN FORINTS				
over 56,000	44,000–56,000	31,000–44,000	18,500–31,000	under 18,500
RESTAURANTS IN FORINTS				
over 3,500	2,500–3,500	1,500–2,500	800–1,500	under 800

Hotel prices are for two people in a standard double room with a private bath and breakfast during peak season (June through August). Restaurant prices are per person for a main course at dinner and include 15% tax but not service.

EXPLORING PÉCS

Pécs is best explored on foot, as some of the downtown area is blocked off to cars. The city is small enough to tour in a day but rich enough with attractions that you could spend a leisurely weekend exploring the area. Take time to meander through the side streets for glimpses of the Zsolnay tiles that adorn random buildings throughout the city.

Numbers in the margin correspond to numbers on the Pécs map.

A GOOD WALK

Begin at the base of Széchényi tér, where you can admire the distinctive eosin tile of the **Zsolnay Fountain** ❶. Walk up the hill past the Nádor Szálló, once the most famous hotel in Pécs but now shuttered, though under renovation at this writing. Across from the hotel is the **Belvárosi plébánia templom** ❷, a former 15th-century mosque that still retains its distinctive form. Go uphill from the main square along short, windy Szepesy Ignác utca and turn left on Káptalan utca, where you will find most of the city's important museums. On the right is the **Zsolnay Múzeum** ❸; to the left is the **Vasarely Múzeum** ❹. Walk to the end of the street and turn left; down the hill toward Janus Pannonius utca, where you'll find the **Csontváry Múzeum** ❺. From there, go right (left if you're exiting the museum) to Dóm tér and the **Pécs Bazilika** ❻. A ticket to the basilica will get you into the tiny Peter and Paul Catacombs (to the right side of the basilica), where you can see Christian frescoes from the fourth century. To the left of the basilica is the diocese residence, and on the left balcony there's a metal statue of a somewhat wobbly-looking Franz Liszt, the great composer. Liszt became a devout Catholic in his later days, after a rabble-rousing youth, and paid frequent visits to the bishop of Pécs; however, the statue reminds us that it's far from certain that Liszt's Catholicism went hand in hand with a sober and austere life. Given that the statue is known locally as *a hányás* (the barf), it's likely that he didn't suddenly become a teetotaller.

Exit Dóm tér—you might want to stop to rest first in the pleasant park out in front of the basilica—and walk back toward Janus Pannonius utca and enter Szent István tér. You will be walking among the early Christian cemetery chapels and tombs from the fourth century that are in a long process of excavation. Here is where you'll find the World Heritage Site of the **Ókeresztény mauzóleum** ❼. Bear to the right to leave the burial grounds by walking down the hill on St. István tér until you get to Ferencesek utca. Stay on the right side until you reach the intersection with Korház tér, and then continue to walk down Rákóczi út. You can get a good look of Pécs's Roman walls from here. If you continue down Rákóczi út, you will see on your right the **Jákovali Hászan Múzeum** ❽ on the site of a Turkish mosque. Walk around to the back, and you can still see at the original minaret. Backtrack to Ferencesek utca and walk back to Széchényi tér.

■ TIP➜ Baranya County's Museum Directorate has an umbrella Web site, www.jpm.hu, where info can be had on most of Pécs's museums. The venues covered include the Csontváry and Vasarely museums plus a couple of others.

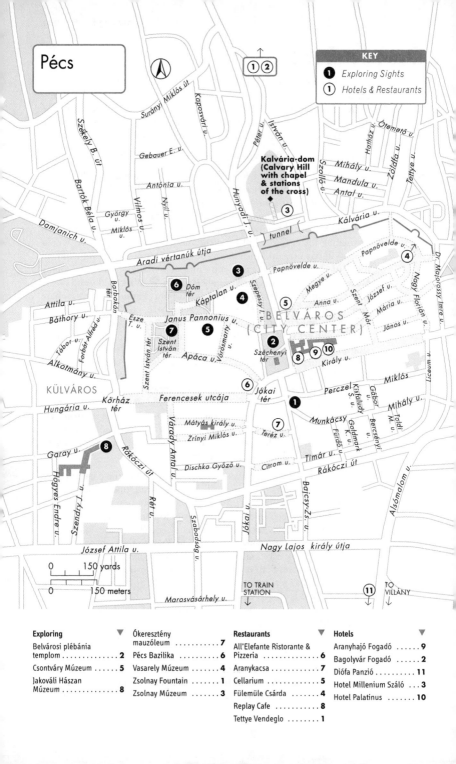

Pécs

KEY
- **1** Exploring Sights
- **①** Hotels & Restaurants

Kalvária-dom (Calvary Hill with chapel & stations of the cross)

BELVÁROS (CITY CENTER)

KÜLVÁROS

tunnel

Dóm tér

Káptalan u.

Janus Pannonius u.

Szent István tér

Apáca u.

Széchenyi tér

Jókai tér

Ferencesek utcája

0 ——— 150 yards
0 ——— 150 meters

TO TRAIN STATION

TO VILLÁNY

TIMING   Pécs can get hot in the summer months, but the city will be less crowded because of the depleted student population. However, autumn is the most pleasant time to visit Pécs and neighboring Villány, when both towns have wine festivals.

What to See

❷ Belvárosi plébánia templom (Inner City Parish Church). Széchenyi tér is crowned by a delightful 16th-century former Turkish mosque. Dating from the years of Turkish occupation (1543–1686), the mosque is now a Catholic church, which you might infer from the cross that surmounts the gilded crescent atop the dome. Despite the fierce religious war raging on its walls—Christian statuary and frescoes beneath Turkish arcades and *mihrabs* (prayer niches)—this church, also known as the Gazi Khassim Pasha Jammi, remains the largest and finest relic of Turkish architecture in Hungary. This is a venue for occasional organ recitals in summer. ⊠ *Széchenyi tér* ☎ *72/321–976* 🎟 *Free* ☉ *Mid-Apr.–mid-Oct., Mon.–Sat. 10–4, Sun. 11:30–4; mid-Oct.–mid-Apr., Mon.–Sat. 11–noon, Sun. 11:30–2.*

❺ Csontváry Múzeum (Csontváry Museum). Mihály Tivadar Csontváry
Fodor'sChoice Kosztka (1853–1919) was a pharmacist who worked, as he put it, to
★   "catch up with, let alone surpass, the great masters." An early expressionist and forerunner of surrealism, Csontváry's work even influenced Picasso. His paintings can be seen today almost exclusively here and in a room of the Hungarian National Gallery in Budapest.

The paintings in the five rooms of this museum are arranged in chronological order, to show Csontváry's progression from soulful portraits to seemingly conventional landscapes executed with decidedly unconventional colors to his 1904 *Temple of Zeus in Athens*—about which Csontváry said, "This is the first painting in which the canvas can no longer be seen." After a 1905 tryout in Budapest, Csontváry was ready for a 1907 exhibition in Paris, which turned out to be a huge critical success. Not long after finishing his last great epic painting, *Mary at the Well in Nazareth* (1908), his ego got the best of him and he went a tad mad, too. The magnificent painting of his that Hungarians probably cherish most, and which has been interpreted as a symbolic self-portrait—*The Solitary Cedar*—is also here. Though his canvases grew ever larger, Csontváry finished nothing that he started after 1909 except a patriotic drawing of Emperor Franz Joseph, completed at the start of World War I in 1914. Indeed, the final room is filled only with sketches. After he died in Budapest in 1919, his canvases were about to be reused as furniture covers when a collector from Pécs named Gedeon Gerlóczy rescued them for 10,000 HUF. The museum, one of the three major galleries in Pécs, sits just around the corner from its peers. ⊠ *Janus Pannonius utca 11* ☎ *72/310–544* 🎟 *600 HUF* ☉ *Tues.–Sun. 10–6.*

★ **❽ Jákovali Hászan Múzeum.** Just beyond the ancient city wall to the west, this 16th-century Turkish mosque is the only Ottoman-era religious building in Hungary with its original minaret and architecture intact. (Another mosque of the same period became the Belvárosi plébánia templom, a Catholic church.) The museum itself has a few artifacts from the

10

Turkish period, plus a few Iznik ceramics. The mosque is still active, used today by Muslim students living in Pécs. ⊠ *Rákoczi út* ☎ *No phone* 💷 *240 HUF* ☉ *Tues.–Sun. 10–6.*

❼ Ókeresztény mauzóleum (Early Christian Mausoleum). In front of Pécs Basilica is a serene little park, and just beyond is the fourth-century tomb, Hungary's largest and most important early Christian mausoleum and a World Heritage Site. Some of the subterranean crypts and chapels date to its earliest days; the murals on the walls (Adam and Eve, Daniel in the Lion's Den, the Resurrection) are in remarkably good condition. ⊠ *Szent István tér* ☎ *No phone* 💷 *350 HUF* ☉ *Tues.–Sun. 10–6.*

❻ Pécs Bazilika (Pécs Basilica). One of Europe's most magnificent cathe-
Fodor'sChoice drals was promoted from mere cathedral to basilica rank after Pope John
★ Paul II's visit in 1991. At the beginning of the 19th century, Mihály Pol-
lack directed the transformation of the exterior, changing it from baroque to neoclassical; its interior remained Gothic. Near the end of the 19th century, Bishop Nándor Dulánszky decided to restore the cathedral to its original, Árpád-period style—the result is a four-spired monument that has an utterly breathtaking interior frescoed in shimmering golds, silvers, and blues. Entry to the basilica includes the Peter and Paul Catacombs next door. ⊠ *Szent István tér* 💷 *700 HUF; 1,000 HUF for Eng-
lish-language tour* ☉ *Apr.–Oct., weekdays 9–5, Sat. 9–2, Sun. 1–5;
Nov.–Mar., Mon.–Sat. 10–4, Sat. 10–1, Sun. 1–4.*

❹ Vasarely Múzeum (Vasarely Museum). The pioneer of Op Art (who left Hungary as a child and spent the rest of his life in Paris) was born Győző Vásárhelyi in 1908 in this house, which has been turned into something wild, as much a funhouse as a museum. The first hall is a corridor of visual tricks devised by his disciples, at the end of which hangs a hyp-
notic canvas of shifting cubes by Jean-Pierre Yvaral. Upstairs, the illu-
sions grow profound: a zebra gallops by while chess pieces and blood cells seem to come at you. ⊠ *Káptalan utca 3* ☎ *72/324–822* 💷 *600 HUF* ☉ *Tues.–Sun. 10–6.*

❶ Zsolnay Fountain. At the foot of Széchenyi tér, the grand sloping monumental thoroughfare that is the pride of the city, stands the dainty, pe-
tite Art Nouveau majolica temple. The fountain is guarded by shiny ox-head gargoyles made of green eosin porcelain that gush pure drinking water piped into Pécs via Roman aqueducts. It was built in 1912 by the famous Zsolnay family, who pioneered and developed their unique porcelain art here in Pécs.

▌ **NEED A BREAK?** A short walk down pedestrians-only Király utca, opening from Széchenyi tér, is the **Caflisch Cukrászda** (⊠ Király utca 32 ☎ 72/310–391), an elegant but cozy café established in 1869—in a building dating to 1789—with tiny round, mar-
ble-top tables and small chandeliers. It's open until 10 PM.

★ **❸ Zsolnay Múzeum** (Zsolnay Museum). Occupying the upper floor of the oldest surviving building in Pécs, the building housing the museum dates from 1324; it has been built and rebuilt over the years in Romanesque, Renaissance, and baroque styles during its checkered history.

A stroll through the rooms is a merry show-and-tell waltz through a revolution in pottery that started in 1851, when Miklós Zsolnay, a local merchant, bought the site of an old kiln and set up a stoneware factory for his son Ignác to run. Ignác's brother, Vilmos, a shopkeeper with an artistic bent, bought the factory from him in 1863, imported experts from Germany, and, with the help of a Pécs pharmacist for chemical-glaze experiments and his daughters for hand-painting, created the distinctive namesake porcelain.

While the museum's permanent space is temporarily closed until around 2008, a choice sample of its permanent collection is on display in a neighboring building. The complete collection includes Vilmos's early efforts at Delft-blue handmade vases, cups, and saucers; his two-layer ceramics; examples of the gold-brocade rims that became a Zsolnay trademark; and table settings for royal families. Be sure to look up and notice the unusual Zsolnay chandeliers lighting your way. The Zsolnay store in the center of Pécs, at Jókai tér 2, sells a wide selection of contemporary ceramics. ⊠ *Káptalan utca 4 (back to its original address, Káptalan utca 2, by around 2008)* ☎ *72/514–040* 🖳 *500 HUF* ☉ *Tues.–Sun. 10–6.*

Zsolnay porcelán gyár (Zsolnay Porcelain Factory). If you haven't had enough Zsolnay after visiting the Zsolnay Museum, join the groups of tourists (usually German or Hungarian) braving heavily trafficked Zsolnay Vilmos utca to visit the company's factory, where gleaming monumental towers and statuary of seemingly pollution-proof porcelain hold their own among giant smokestacks. On a hill behind the factory stands the ultimate monument to the dynasty's founder, who died in 1900: the **Zsolnay Mausoleum** (☎ 06–30/929–7803), with the bones of Vilmos and his wife in a blue ceramic well and, over the doorway, a relief of Vilmos, with disciples resembling his wife, daughters, and son kneeling before him. The mausoleum is open by appointment only; there's a number listed on its front door for a guided tour (it's the cell phone for the enterprising tour guide, who will ask for a donation of around 600 HUF).

The factory can be visited by guided tour only—groups must number between 10 to 30—but you can tag along on an already scheduled group tour even if you're just an individual or a smaller group. Contact either the factory or Tourinform (*see* ⇨ Visitor Information *in* Pécs Essentials) to determine whether a tour is scheduled during your visit to Pécs. Reservations with the factory must be made by e-mail or fax; as of this writing the person to address was Mrs. Józsefné Sólya. ⊠ *Zsolnay Vilmos utca 37* ☎ *72/ 507–652 factory tour information*

"SZIA!"

It may sound like it, but this most common of all friendly greetings in Hungarian neither means nor derives from "See you!" Used between people who are already on friendly terms–or who are approximately the same age and wish to be on informal terms–or by a person speaking to someone younger or to someone they have a cozy work relationship with, *szia* (pronounced "see-ya") means both "Hi!" and "Bye" depending, of course, on the circumstances.

10

🖷 72/313–645 ⊕ *www.zsolnay.hu* 🖃 *Factory: individual, English-language tours 5,000 HUF per person, English-language group tours (min. 10 people) 1,000 HUF per person.*

AN EXCURSION TO VILLÁNY

30 km (19 mi) south of Pécs.

The sleepy town of Villány, south of Pécs and nestled in the low, verdant Villányi Hills, is the center of one of Hungary's most famous wine regions. Roman ruins uncovered in the surrounding area attest to a long history of wine production in this region. Today the Villány-Siklós wine region covers more than 2,000 hectares. Villány's exceptional red wines are heralded both here and abroad; its merlots, cabernets, and ports give their French, Italian, and Portuguese peers a run for the money. Many wine cellars offer regular wine tastings, and an overnight trip to Villány is a worthwhile way to sample a few of the best vintages. The town is clustered with friendly *pincék* (cellars) and *panziók* (pensions), and most owners will be happy to tell you about winemaking in the region as you taste. The Villány vineyards are best known for rich red wines such as kékoportó, kékfrankos, cabernet franc, and merlot. You can get a list of Villány wine cellars from the Pécs Tourinform office (*see* ⇨ Visitor Information *in* Pécs Essentials).

If you wish to learn about the wine before imbibing, stop in at the **Bor Múzeum** (Wine Museum) for a look at the history of the region's viticulture, which dates back some 2,000 years. This impressively deep cellar is a great place to cool off on a hot day, and the English-language text is excellent. ⊠ *Bem utca 8* 🖀 *72/492–130* 🖃 *Free* 🕓 *Tues.–Sun. 9–5.*

Getting to Villány—a plain-looking town that's surprisingly hushed much of the year, though summer weekends and, yes, autumn grape-harvest time can get busy—is easiest by car. From Pécs, getting there by bus is complicated and time-consuming, as it almost invariably means a transfer in Siklós. By train it's not so bad, even though finding your way into town from the station can be a headache. Unless you stay the night, you'll have time only for a quick lunch and wine-tasting before retracing your steps to the station. Carry a bottle of water and wear a wide-brimmed hat on a hot, sunny day. If you do arrive from Pécs by rail, go left on the main road that passes by the station (i.e., in the direction of the train)—most other people should be going this way, too—and keep walking 15–20 minutes as the road curves right and finally enters the surprisingly small, wine-cellar-dominated town center. If you think you're lost, say "Centrum?" (*sent*-room) to someone, and (assuming they know) they'll point the way.

WHERE TO STAY & EAT

$–$$$ ✕ **Aranykacsa.** Not surprisingly, the Golden Duck has long been a favorite with duck-loving locals and visitors alike. And yet this elegant restaurant, which has one relatively intimate, pub-like room with dark

Villány Wine Cellars

CLOSE UP

MOST WINE CELLARS ARE OPEN for tastings all day on Saturday, although some close at midday, so it's best to make your way to Villány during the week or Saturday morning. The town has a well-marked wine route, and it's easy to make your way to most establishments on foot.

Bock Pince (⊠ Batthyány utca 15, Villány 🕾 72/492–919) offers a wide range of Villány wines in its celebrated cellar. The wine bar is a sophisticated step up from some of the other tasting rooms in town.

Some of the finest cabernet sauvignon being made in Hungary comes from **Gere Attila Pince** (⊠ Erkel F. utca 2/a, Villány 🕾 72/492–839), in a dull little suburban neighborhood right next to the vineyards. Once here, don't

miss a chance to taste the local *kékoportó*, a versatile dry table wine.

Günzer Tamás Pince Borozó (⊠ Baross Gábor utca 79, Villány 🕾 72/493–163) is turning out some exciting wines, including a crisp Mont Blanc cuvée blended from chardonnay and irsai oliver grapes and a first-rate cabernet franc. The wine cellar offers tastings in a cozy country room.

Three doors down from the Günzer Tamás Pince Borozó, you'll recognize the friendly **Szende Pince** (⊠ Baross Gábor utca 87, Villány 🕾 72/492–396) in the center of the wine route by its charming wooden tables and flower boxes spilling over with geraniums. Inside, taste away while seated on sheepskin-draped rustic wooden benches.

---

hues and another, more formal, light-hued room decorated with fine Zsolnay porcelain, offers not just several mouth-watering duck dishes—such as roast duck with dried prunes and almonds in red-wine sauce—but also scrumptious wild game and an assortment of more traditional Hungarian fare. ⊠ *Teréz utca 4* 🕾 *72/518–860* 🖃 *AE, MC, V.*

$$ ✕ **Cellarium.** Possibly the only restaurant in Hungary with its own newspaper (published rarely but generally on hand, and always about itself plus some ads), the Cellarium is a huge, and hugely popular if slightly touristy, cellar establishment yards from Széchenyi tér (off the main road leading north from the square). The extensive menu of traditional fare from grilled meats, fish, and wild game includes such specialties as "cock's ball stew garnished with dill and cottage-cheese (i.e., curd-cheese) dumplings (i.e., spaetzle)." The impressive wine list includes notables from nearby Villány. ⊠ *Hunyadi út 2* 🕾 *72/314–453* 🖃 *AE, DC, MC, V.*

$–$$ ✕ **All'Elefante Ristorante & Pizzeria.** This bustling Italian pizzeria opens onto a main square in downtown Pécs. The menu includes some 20 kinds of pizza, many pastas, and a wide range of salads, as well as more traditional meat, poultry, and fish dishes. ⊠ *Jókai tér 6* 🕾 *72/216–055 or 72/532–189* 🖃 *MC, V.*

★ $–$$ ✕ **Fülemüle Csárda.** A *csárda* is a rustic inn, usually found on a highway or crossroads in the Hungarian countryside. As you make your way from Pécs south to Villány, you'll pass this brown-and-white restaurant on your left next to a stream on a hilly terrain covered with vineyards. It's

10

a good place to get old-fashioned, Hungarian peasant food, like *bográcsgulyás* (stew cooked in kettle on an open fire). ✉ *Villány kültelek* ☎ *72/492–939* ▭ *AE, MC, V.*

$–$$ ✕ **Replay Cafe.** Hip students as well as visiting art historians can be found at this popular downtown bar and restaurant not far from Széchenyi tér whose wall frescoes give you your fill of socialist realism. They come for the first-rate pizzas, American-style bacon cheeseburgers, ham and eggs, and draft beer. Tables are filled late into the evening on weekends with a lively crowd. ✉ *Király utca 4* ☎ *72/210–531* ▭ *AE, MC, V.*

$–$$ ✕ **Tettye Vendéglő.** For a country-style lunch or dinner a hefty (25-minute) hike uphill or 10-minute bus ride (take No. 33 from Széchenyi tér to its 2nd-last stop, Tettye tér) on a hillside above Pécs's historic center, try this rustic *vendéglő* (restaurant serving home cooking). Aside from the pleasant views, you'll find mostly traditional Hungarian and other fare of special appeal to local Swabians—smoked meats, Wiener schnitzel, and goose liver, for example—with poultry dishes also available. ✉ *Tettye tér 4* ☎ *72/532–788* ▭ *AE, MC, V.*

★ ¢ ✕▦ **Bock Pince, Panzió, Étterem** (Bok Wine Cellar, Pension, and Restaurant). Bock is one of Villány's most celebrated vineyards, and indeed, you will find Bock *kékoportó* and royal cuvée in many of Hungary's best restaurants. The pension arranges wine tastings and dinners in an elegant attached restaurant, and you can buy a case quite reasonably when you leave. Rooms are tastefully decorated and well equipped. Since October 2005 the pension has also operated a four-room annex in a building a five-minute walk down the road; while closer to Villány's main street, these rooms are of course farther from the main pension and its restaurant. ✉ *Batthyány utca 15, Villány H-7773* ☎ *72/492–919* ⎙ *72/592–010* ⊕ *www.bock.hu* ⤶ *12 rooms, 3 suites ⌂ Restaurant, cable TV, sauna, meeting room, wine bar* ▭ *AE, MC, V* ❙⃝❙ *BP.*

¢–$ ▦ **Hotel Palatinus.** While Art Nouveau is found throughout Hungary, for some pure Art Deco, check out this hotel in downtown Pécs. The grand public areas—lobby, sweeping staircases, restaurant, and ballroom—are all stunning; the detail of the peacock mosaic in the breakfast room particularly so. Rooms are somewhat disappointing after the public areas but are reasonably well equipped; most are superiors, and while these are around 20 euros more than the (cramped) standards, they are certainly more spacious. The hotel's popular all-you-can-eat Sunday brunch (1,000 HUF) features a rich array of traditional Hungarian appetizers and main courses, not to mention live folk music. Since the ballroom can get noisy during weddings, ask if a wedding is scheduled during your planned visit and request a room on an upper floor. ✉ *Király utca 5, H-7621* ☎ *72/889–400* ⎙ *72/889–438* ⊕ *www.danubiusgroup. com/palatinus* ⤶ *88 rooms, 6 suites ⌂ 2 restaurants, minibars, massage, sauna, parking (fee)* ▭ *AE, DC, MC, V* ❙⃝❙ *BP.*

¢ ▦ **Aranyhajó Fogadó.** The Golden Ship Inn is a hotel housed in a pretty yellow medieval building in the heart of pedestrian Király utca and right next door to the Palatinus hotel. The small but modern rooms are traditionally furnished and well equipped; those at the higher end of the price scale have views of Király utca below, the others look out onto the courtyard. The location can't be beat for sightseeing near Széchenyi tér. The restaurant has a popular terrace that spills out onto the street and is shaded under a big awning in summer. ✉ *Király utca 3, H-7621* ☎ *72/310–263* 🖷 *72/212–733* 🌐 *www.aranyhajo.hu* 📞 *19 rooms* 🍴 *Restaurant, minibars, cable TV; no a/c* 🖃 *AE, MC, V* ⏹ *BP.*

★ ¢ 🏨 **Bagolyvár Fogadó.** Nestled in the Mecsek Hills well above Pécs, the Owl Castle Inn is an exquisite little hotel that feels more like a folk museum (even if its buildings are all fairly new). With pinewood floors, the rooms are furnished in rustic styles characteristic of the region or subethnic group of Hungary or neighboring Transylvania whose name is displayed on its door. Add to this a fine restaurant—in a pseudo-cellar with vaulted ceilings, decorated with stuffed animals galore—that specializes in wild game, fish, and fresh salads; a wine press; a nice little garden; and, yes, a vineyard. The main drawbacks: the out-of-the-way location; the odor of cigarette smoke in some rooms; and a huge, paved parking area that detracts from the otherwise green atmosphere you're in. Most easily reached by car (5 minutes from downtown), the inn can also be reached by taking bus No. 33 to the last stop (past the Tettye vendéglő and walking uphill 10 minutes from there. ✉ *Felsőhavi dűlő 6/1, H-7627* ☎ *72/513–213* 🖷 *72/513–212* 🌐 *www.bagolyvarpecs.hu* 📞 *19 rooms* 🍴 *Restaurant, minibars, cable TV; no a/c in some rooms* 🖃 *No credit cards* ⏹ *BP.*

¢ 🏨 **Diófa Panzió.** Opened in 2005 by Tamás and Zsolt Gere, two cousins of the proprietor of another (nice and similarly priced but, well, not quite so nice) nearby pension, the shower-equipped rooms at the Walnut Tree Pension are mostly modern, but two feature rustic, antique-looking furniture and all have bright, cheery colors. No minibars, but there's a well-stocked fridge in the exceptionally wide, airy hallway that all the rooms are on. ✉ *Diófás utca 1, Villány H-7773* ☎ *72/592–009* 🖷 *72/592–109* 🌐 *www.geretamas.hu* 📞 *9 rooms* 🍴 *Restaurant, wine bar* 🖃 *AE, MC, V* ⏹ *BP.*

★ ¢ 🏨 **Hotel Millennium Szálló.** Renowned Hungarian architect Sándor Dévényi designed this chintzy suburban castle on Kálvária hill, amidst a nature reserve and just outside the Old City wall. The rooms are pleasantly low-key, and four of them look out onto the four spires of the Pécs Basilica. It's a quick five-minute walk to downtown from here. ✉ *Kálvária utca 58, H-7625* ☎ *72/512–222* 🖷 *72/512–223* 🌐 *www.hotelmillennium.hu* 📞 *25 rooms* 🍴 *Restaurant, minibars, pool, laundry service, Internet, free parking, some pets allowed, no-smoking rooms* 🖃 *AE, DC, MC, V* ⏹ *BP.*

WALK LIKE A LOCAL

To enjoy a short but sweet walk that most locals know and love, head up Hunyadi utca from Széchenyi tér to the traffic light a couple of blocks away, cross the intersection, and then climb the steps to your right (off Hunyadi utca). Before long you'll see another (short) series of steps, this time on your left—these lead up to the top of Kalvária-domb (Calvary Hill), where you'll find a little white chapel from 1814 and 12 stations of the cross that Jesuits erected here even earlier, on the site of a previous 13th-century chapel. Though the chapel is generally closed, if you turn around you will be rewarded with an impressive view of Pécs.

10

NIGHTLIFE & THE ARTS

September brings harvest-related festivities such as classical concerts, folk-music and dance performances, and a parade or two to venues in and around Pécs. Inquire at the local Tourinform office (*see* ⇨ Visitor Information *in* Pécs Essentials) for specifics. Tourinform publishes a monthly arts and events calendar in English, and can help with further schedule and ticket information.

★ **Áfium.** Hands down, this is Pécs's most atmospheric, nay, bohemian cellar pub-cum-restaurant. With antique paintings and photos all over its walls, and intimate lighting under its vaulted ceilings, this scrumptious little secret right along downtown's main drag is an ideal spot for an evening (or daytime) beer, glass of Villány wine, or bite to eat—and English is reportedly spoken here by many. ⊠ *Irgalmasok utcája 2* ☎ *72/511–434.*

> **LOCKS OF LOVE**
>
> So what's the deal with all those locks along Janus Pannonius utca? Well, those two huge clumps of locks locked to locks locked to building walls—one clump midway up the street and another toward the end symbolize the locals' faith in the binding nature of their loves. Look closer and you'll see the names of the lovers at issue inscribed into the locks.

Fregatt Arizona Pub. This pub—whose display includes a carved eagle, Indian, and rifle, all under a low, vaulted ceiling—has plenty of Guinness on tap. ⊠ *Király utca 21* ☎ *72/511–068 or 72/511–069.*

Murphy's Pub. Accented by dark wood and polished brass, this Irish pub keeps an ample supply of Guinness on tap. ⊠ *Király utca 2* ☎ *72/325–439.*

Pécsi Nemzeti Színház (Pécs National Theater). This theater is the main venue for regular performances by the Pécs Symphony Orchestra and the theater's own opera and modern ballet companies. It is closed from late May until September. ⊠ *Színház tér 1* ☎ *72/211–965.*

SHOPPING

Kirakodóvásár (Flea Market). Pécs's large flea market provides great browsing and bargain-hunting among its eclectic mix of goods—from used clothing and handcrafted folk art to antiques and fresh vegetables. It's held every day (from 5 AM until 2 PM), but weekends draw many more sellers, and the first Sunday of every month is best for quantity and variety, especially in terms of antiques. To get there, take bus No. 50 from the train station to Vásár té. ⊠ *Vásár tér, at Megyeri út* ☎ *72/516–161.*

Király utca, a vibrant, pedestrian-only street lined with beautifully preserved romantic and baroque facades, is Pécs's main shopping zone, full of colorful boutiques and outdoor cafés. For a slightly less bustling but likewise key shopping street, head across Széchenyi tér from Király utca to **Jókai tér** and, just beyond, **Ferencesek utca.**

Zsolnay Márkabolt. The best place in the whole country to buy exqui-site Zsolnay porcelain is in Pécs. At the Zsolnay factory's own outlet, the company offers guaranteed authenticity and the best prices on the full spectrum of pieces—from tea sets profusely painted with colorful, gold-winged butterflies to white-and-night-blue dinner services. ⊠ *Jókai tér 2* ☎ *72/310–220.*

PÉCS ESSENTIALS

BUS TRAVEL

There's regular bus service from Budapest to Pécs several times a day from Népliget station. Infrequent buses to Villány depart from Pécs; un-like the trains, they'll get you right to the village center, but because you must transfer in Siklós, figure on much longer (around 1½ hours) get-ting there.

CAR TRAVEL

Traveling around Transdanubia is most easily done by car. Pécs and Bu-dapest are directly connected by Route 6, which continues on to the Croa-tian border. Villány is a short excursion by car, about 19 mi southeast of Pécs, and is a beautiful drive through the wine country.

INTERNET

Mátrix Internet Kávézó. The service (as of this writing) is glum-faced, and if you don't take a seat, you'll miss the Hungarian-language sign on the inside door of the toilet stall informing you of the 50 HUF toi-let fee (which you will be charged for). That said, this sometimes smoky venue deep in a courtyard off Pécs's main shopping street is otherwise a perfectly fine place to log on—as of this writing it's practically the only place downtown to do so. The cost is reasonable, at 5 HUF / minute. ⊠ *Király utca 15* ☎ *72/214–487.*

🚉 **Pécs train station** ⊠ Indóhász tér ☎ 72/312–443.

TAXI SERVICE

Your best bet in Pécs is the well-established **Volán Taxi** (☎ 72/333–333). A trip between the train station and Széchenyi tér (where taxis park) costs around 800 HUF.

TRAIN TRAVEL

There are good rail connections from Budapest to Pécs and Villány. The trip—by InterCity (IC) trains, which run several times daily—takes 3 hours to Pécs. One such daily route from Budapest goes on to Villány. From Pécs to Villány—a route also served by local trains (some of them at highly inconvenient times if you want to head back the same day)—takes around 50 minutes. It's a good 20-minute walk from the Villány station to the village center (for directions, *see* the description of Villány).

VISITOR INFORMATION

🚉 **Tourinform** ⊠ Széchenyi tér 9 ☎ 72/213–315.

IBUSZ ⊠ Király utca 11 ☎ 72/212–157 can help book private rooms in Pécs.

10

The Great Plain

WORD OF MOUTH

"I like Debrecen for its Protestant character and appearance. You can enjoy this bastion of [Calvinism] right out in the east of Catholic Europe, just short of Orthodox Europe. . . . Szeged is a good choice for a day trip. The city was destroyed by floods about 120 years ago, and was rebuilt in a lavish, nineteenth-century baroque style."

—ben_haines_london

"Debrecen couldn't be more different from Budapest. It really is a 'town' in every essence of the word. Small, pretty, one main huge square with a clock tower, etc. . . . Just to warn you, though . . . other than a couple of hotel and restaurant staff, you're on your own as far as English goes."

—isabela

www.fodors.com/forums

By Paul
Olchváry

HUNGARY'S GREAT PLAIN—THE NAGYALFÖLD—stretches south from Budapest to the borders of Croatia and Serbia and as far east as Ukraine and Romania. It covers an area of 51,800 square km (20,000 square mi) and is what most people think of as the typical Hungarian landscape—even if much of the rest of Hungary is in fact quite hilly, and the two-thirds of its territory that it lost to neighboring countries in the 1920 Treaty of Trianon was mostly mountainous. Almost completely flat, the Great Plain, in its vast open spaces between its small cities and numerous villages, is the home of shepherds and their flocks and, not least, splendid horses and the *csikósok,* their riders. The plain has a wild, almost alien air; its sprawling villages consist mostly of one-story houses, though there are many large farms. Divided into two almost equal parts by Hungary's second-largest river, the Tisza, the Plain also contains several of Hungary's most historic cities. Because much of the region was never occupied by the Turks, it contains a wealth of medieval remnants.

As you near the region, you will soon find yourself driving in a hypnotically straight line from Budapest through the dream landscape of the Hortobágy, a grassy *puszta* (prairie), Hungary's answer to the U.S. Wild West. Here the land flattens out like a palacsinta fresh out of the pan, opening into vast stretches of dusty grassland interrupted only by stands of trees and distant thatch-roof *tanyák* (ranch homes). The only detectable movement here comes from the herds of *racka* (a breed of sheep) or cattle drifting lazily across the horizon, guided by shepherds and their trusty *puli* (herd dogs). Covering almost

> ### PAUL'S TOP 5
>
> **Hortobágy Nemzeti Park.** A great expanse of dusty grassland interrupted only by primeval breeds of sheep drifting across the horizon.
>
> **Pongrácz Major.** Hungary's ultimate dude ranch experience replete with stables and cowboys.
>
> **Cifrapalota.** Built in 1902 this is a perfect example of Kecskemét's unique architecture.
>
> **Szeged.** Its series of redolent old squares, are bustling with people on summer days.
>
> **Debrecen's Calvinist heritage.** This small city's Great Church and Reformed College add up to a centuries-old Protestant stronghold.

200,000 acres, the Hortobágy became the first of Hungary's four national parks, in 1973. Its flora and fauna—including primeval breeds of longhorn cattle and racka sheep, prairie dogs, and *nóniusz* (horses)—are all under strict protection.

Numbers in the margin correspond to numbers on the Great Plain map

About the Hotels & Restaurants

Hotels in the Great Plain region—those outside of the towns, at least—tend to be a tad more rustic than in other parts of Hungary and often have "Wild West" interiors; you're likely to see pictures of horses and the puszta scattered across the walls. Some hotels are also less frequently renovated than their counterparts in more monied regions such as the Balaton and the Danube Bend; but the accommodations we recommend in this chapter are either refreshing exceptions to this rule or comfy despite this. Most hotels, which usually quote rates in forints, are open year-round and can also help arrange horseback riding and hiking trips in the area.

Restaurants in the region serve typical Hungarian food: fried vegetables, meats, and basic salads. Menus will often be translated into both English and German. Dress is casual. Restaurants also tend to open and close earlier along the Great Plain than in Budapest; most every place will be closed by 11 PM. Prices are typically cheaper in this region than anywhere else in Hungary, but that does not mean the quality of the food is lower; indeed, it is often prepared with much care and skill. Make sure to try traditional Hungarian goulash and *halaszlé* (fish soup), a Szeged specialty made with carp (a cherished fish in much of Europe) that is famous across Hungary.

WHAT IT COSTS In Euros & Forints				
$$$$	**$$$**	**$$**	**$**	**¢**
HOTELS IN EUROS				
over 225	175–225	125–175	75–125	under 75
HOTELS IN FORINTS				
over 56,000	44,000–56,000	31,000–44,000	18,500–31,000	under 18,500
RESTAURANTS IN FORINTS				
over 3,500	2,500–3,500	1,500–2,500	800–1,500	under 800

Hotel prices are for two people in a standard double room with a private bath and breakfast during peak season (June through August). Restaurant prices are per person for a main course at dinner and include 15% tax but not service.

DEBRECEN

❶ *226 km (140 mi) east of Budapest.*

With a population of just over 200,000, Debrecen is Hungary's second-largest city. Though it has considerably less clout than Budapest, Debrecen was Hungary's capital twice. In 1849 it was here that Lajos Kossuth declared Hungarian independence from the Habsburgs; in 1944 the Red Army liberated Debrecen from the Nazis and made the city the provisional capital until Budapest was taken.

Debrecen has been inhabited since the Stone Age. It was already a sizable village by the end of the 12th century, and by the 14th an important market town. It takes its name from a Slavonic term for "good earth," and, indeed, much of the country's wheat, produce, meat, and poultry has been produced in this area for centuries.

Today Debrecen is a vibrant, friendly city, with a sizable population of young people attending its esteemed universities. There's only one tram line (appropriately numbered 1), but it runs fast and frequently in a nearly straight line from the railroad station along downtown's main thoroughfare—the broad, and partly pedestrian, Piac utca—and out to the Nagy-

The Great Plain

erdő (Great Forest), a giant city park. Also worth checking out but easy to miss is Batthyány utca, a lively little shopping street just one block to the east of (and parallel to) Piac utca. All in all, Debrecen is a good place to spend a day before heading out to the puszta—or, as in the case of many travelers, on the way to or from a journey farther east to Transylvania. For almost 500 years Debrecen has been the stronghold of Hungarian Protestantism—its inhabitants have called it "the Calvinist Rome." In 1536 Calvinism began to replace Roman Catholicism in Debrecen, and two years later the **Református Kollégium** (Reformed College) was founded on what is now Kálvin tér (Calvin Square). Early in the 19th century the college's medieval building was replaced by a pillared structure that provides a vivid lesson in Hungarian religious and political history: the facade's busts honor prominent students and educators as well as religious reformers John Calvin and Huldrych Zwingli. Inside, the main staircase is lined with frescoes of student life and significant moments in the college's history (all painted during the 1930s in honor of the school's 400th anniversary). At the top of the stairs is the **Oratory**, which has twice been the setting for provisional parliaments. In 1849 Lajos Kossuth first proclaimed Hungarian sovereignty here, and the new National Assembly's Chamber of Deputies met here during the last stages of the doomed revolution. Kossuth's pulpit and pew are marked, and two rare surviving flags of his revolution hang on the front wall. Some relics from 1944 line the back wall. Also worth seeing are the college's **library,** which rotates exhibitions of illuminated manuscripts and rare Bibles, and two **museums.** The first museum, the Student History Museum, commemorates Hungarian intellectuals who studied at the college, while the Religious History Museum showcases jewelry, embroidered clothes, and painted furniture. ⊠ *Kálvin tér 16* ☎ *52/414–744, Ext. 1923* ☝ *300 HUF* ☉ *Tues.–Sat. 10–4, Sun. 10–1.*

Fodor's Choice
★

Because the Oratory in the Reformed College was too small for a large crowd, Lajos Kossuth reread his declaration of independence by popular demand to a cheering public in 1849 in the twin-turreted, orange-yellow **Nagytemplom** (Great Church). The most famous building in Debrecen, the Great Church opened its doors in 1821 after more than a decade of construction on the design of Mihály Pécsi; it was built on the site of a 14th-century church that had burned down in 1802. As befits the austerity of Calvinism, the church is not exactly teeming with decoration—but with all the baroque architecture throughout Hungary, you may welcome the contrast. The church's massive organ was made in Vienna in 1838, and the sanctuary is the site of frequent concerts. ⊠ *Kálvin tér 4* ☎ *52/412–694* ☝ *Church 200 HUF* ☉ *Jan.–Mar., Mon.–Sat. 10–noon, Sun. 11–1; Apr.–Oct., weekdays 9–4, Sat. 9–1, Sun. after 10 AM worship–4; Nov.–Dec., Mon.–Sat. 10–noon, Sun. after 10 AM worship–1.*

The **Déri Múzeum** (Déri Museum) was founded in 1930 to house the art and antiquities of a wealthy Hungarian silk manufacturer living in Vienna. Its two floors are devoted to local history, archaeology, and weapons as well as to Egyptian, Greek, Roman, Etruscan, and Far Eastern art. On the top floor are Hungarian and foreign fine art from the 15th to the 20th century, including the striking (and huge) *Ecce Homo* by Mihály Munkácsy and, on loan since 2000, two similar scenes from the life of Christ by the same famous 19th-century artist. In front of the museum are allegorical bronze statues by Ferenc Medgyessy, grand prize winner at the 1937 Paris World Exhibition. ⚠ **The museum has a separate room for temporary exhibits; while that carries a separate ticket price as of this writing, a forceful ticket lady might insist that this be paid along with the ticket for the permanent collection.** ⊠ *Déri tér 1* ☎ *52/417–561* ☝ *300 HUF Munkácsy room, permanent collection 400 HUF, temporary exhibit 300 HUF* ☉ *Apr.–Oct., Tues.–Sun. 10–6; Nov.–Mar., Tues.–Sun. 10–4.*

A smaller but still somewhat dazzling variation on Budapest's new Palace of the Arts, the **Köcsey Központ** (Kólcsey Center) opened right behind the Déri Múzeum in spring 2006 as Debrecen's grand new cultural-cum-convention center—a venue for everything from concerts and theatrical performances to exhibitions and, yes, conventions. Right next door is Debrecen's newest (if possibly blandest) large hotel. ⊠ *Hunyadi János utca 1–3* ☎ *52/518–497 or 52/518–4000* ⊕ *www.kolcseykozpont.hu.*

Debrecen's main artery, **Piac utca** (Market Street), is a wide and long boulevard that runs from the Great Forest to the railroad station. Its history goes back to the Middle Ages, when handfuls of outdoor vegetable and meat markets lined the road here. However, its architectural face began to take shape only in the first decades of the 19th century, under the impact of classicism. The majority of the existing buildings date from the beginning of 20th century, and you'll see several examples of the influence of Secessionism and eclecticism.

At the corner of Széchenyi utca, the **Kistemplom** (Small Church)—Debrecen's oldest surviving church, which was built in 1720—looks like a rococo chess-piece castle on the outside; and the three-aisle baroque interior, with a pleasant wood aroma, is well worth a look. This Calvinist venue is known to locals as the *csonka templom* (truncated church), because its onion dome blew down in a gale in 1907. ⊠ *Révész tér 2* ☎ *52/342–872* ◷ *Tues.–Sat. 10–6, Sun. 8:30–11 AM.*

Across the street from the Kistemplom is the **Megyeház** (County Hall), built between 1911 and 1912 in Transylvanian Art Nouveau style, a darker and heavier version than what was popular in Paris, Munich, and Vienna. The ceramic ornaments on the pink facade are Zsolnay majolica. Inside, brass chandeliers illuminate the stairs and halls, spotlighting the symmetry and delicate restraint of the interior. In the Council Hall upstairs, stained-glass windows by Károly Kernstock depict seven leaders of the tribes that conquered Hungary in AD 896. ⊠ *Piac utca 54* ☎ *52/ 507–550* ◷ *Mon.–Thurs. 8–4, Fri. 8–1.*

★ The **Tímárház** (Tanner House), in a restored 19th-century building, is the center for preserving and maintaining the ancient folk arts and craft traditions of Hajdú-Bihar county. In its delightful, small complex you can wander into the artisans' workshops and watch them creating exquisite pieces—from impossibly fine, intricately handmade lacework to colorful hand-loomed wool rugs. The artisans—among the best in the country—encourage visitors of all ages to try their hand at the crafts. The complex's showroom displays magnificent leather whips, heavy wool shepherd robes, and other examples of the county's traditional folk art; the embroidered textiles are some of the best you'll see anywhere. Although the displayed pieces are not for sale, the staff can help you contact the artists to custom-order something. A tiny gift shop, however, does sell a small selection of representative goods at great prices. ⊠ *Nagy Gál István utca 6* ☎ *52/321–260* ◷ *200 HUF* ◷ *June–Oct., Tues.–Fri. 10–6, Sat. 10–2; Nov.–May., Tues.–Fri. 10–5, Sat. 10–2.*

The 19th-century **Vörös templom** (Red Church) is as remarkable a Calvinist church as you'll find anywhere in Europe. On the outside it seems to be an undistinguished redbrick house of worship, built with the usual unadorned interior, but the church celebrated its 50th anniversary at the zenith of the applied-arts movement in Hungary. Its worshipers commissioned artist Jenő Haranghy to paint the walls with biblical allegories using no human bodies or faces (just an occasional limb) but rather plenty of grapes, trees, and symbols. Giant frescoes covering the walls, ceilings, niches, and crannies represent, among other subjects, a stag in fresh water, the Martin Luther anthem "A Mighty Fortress Is Our God," and the 23rd Psalm (with a dozen sheep representing the 12 Tribes of Israel and the 12 Apostles). The Red Church is open only during religious services (10 AM on Sunday and religious holidays), but you might try for a private church visit from the deaconage on Kossuth Lajos utca. The church is a 10-minute walk from the Megyeház along Kossuth Lajos utca. ⊠ *Méliusz tér* ☎ *52/325–736.*

Debrecen's one tram line runs out to the **Nagyerdő** (Great Forest), a huge city park with a zoo, a sports stadium, swimming pools, an artificial rowing lake, a thermal-spa-cum-luxury-hotel (the Termál Hotel Debrecen), an amusement park, restaurants, and an open-air theater. Also here is the photogenic Kossuth Lajos University, its handsome neo-baroque facade fronted by a large pool and fountain around which six bronze nudes pose in the sun; it would be a shame to visit Debrecen and not see this. The university is one of the few in Central Europe with a real campus, and every summer, from mid-July to mid-August, it hosts a world-renowned Hungarian-language program.

Where to Stay & Eat

★ $–$$ ✕ **Lucullus Étterem.** While dining in the red-velvety, high-backed chairs in the elegant wooden booths of this small cellar restaurant you may feel just a bit like that Roman general and epicure Lucullus himself. This spot may not have much local flavor, but it has won awards for its good food, including "flamed dishes" prepared at your table, a small but choice selection of lamb, goose, fish, wild game, and more; and one particularly lavish house speciality, turkey breast stuffed with goose liver, prepared in a walnut-almond batter and served with a garnish of stewed fruit. ⊠ *Piac utca 41* ☎ *52/418–513* ▤ *AE, DC, MC, V.*

★ $–$$ ✕ **Serpince a Flaskához.** Once you've managed to find this very popular pub only yards from Piac utca—there's only a menu by the door, no sign—you will find yourself in a ravishingly rustic cellar with vaulted ceilings that's tastefully decorated in a completely unpretentious manner befitting the Great Plains. For a light meal, try a *palócleves,* a thick, piquantly sourish meat-and-potatoes soup with tarragon and caraway. For something heavier, perhaps the *birka* lamb paprikás is the way to go. ⊠ *Miklós utca 4* ☎ *52/414–582* ▤ *AE, DC, MC, V.*

★ $ 🏨 **Cívis Grand Hotel Aranybika.** Art Nouveau classic on the outside, inside the Hotel Golden Bull is a bit of a patchwork quilt. Designed by Hungary's first Olympic champion, Alfréd Hajós, it is the oldest hotel in Hungary (the original was built in the 17th century). Parts of the lobby, like the neo-baroque doorway to the cocktail bar, are gorgeous, as is the airy and elegant restaurant. Brown and beige leftover renovations from the 1970s spoil the effect a bit, but the hotel's location in the center of Debrecen is excellent. The guest rooms in the old Grand section of the hotel are being spruced up, while those in the newer "tourist" wing are a bit on the institutional side. The hotel also contains the Béla Bartók Concert Hall. ■ TIP➡ Most rooms are no-smoking, but the 4th floor is a big exception. Also, most rooms have no minibars. ⊠ *Piac utca 11–15, H-4025* ☎ *52/508–600* 🖷 *52/421–834* ⊕ *www.civishotels.hu* ➪ *205 rooms, 4 suites* ♿ *Restaurant, café, indoor pool, gym, sauna, spa, casino, business services, meeting rooms; no a/c in some rooms* ↻◎ *BP* ▤ *AE, DC, MC, V.*

A Legendary Little Tree

11

CLOSE UP

A SOMEWHAT WEEDY-LOOKING but flowering, willow-like little tree stands unceremoniously by a low, wrought-iron fence behind the left rear corner of Debrecen's Nagytemplom. You'd be forgiven for passing this leafy weakling by, but know that you'd be passing by one of this famously Protestant city's most treasured historic relics. According to local tradition, sometime back in the 18th-century a Calvinist minister named Bálint got into quite a scrap at this very site over religion with a Catholic priest called Ambrosius. All riled up, the latter broke a branch off a nearby tree, stuck it into the ground, and said, scornfully, "Something will come of your religion only when this grows into a tree!" That branch did grow into a tree. Unlike mostly Catholic Hungary, Calvinism flowered in Debrecen, which—along with Transylvania immediately to the east—became a stronghold of Hungary's version of this religion. According to locals, this legendary little tree is also a hardy one; during Hungary's October 1956 revolution a Russian tank ran right over it, but it survived. This may account for its battered appearance.

$ ⬚ **Termál Hotel Debrecen.** Other hotels may be attached to spas, but this hotel is actually located within a medical spa. You can detect the (not unpleasant) smell of alkaline chloride as soon as you check in at the front desk. Amenities span the seasons: in summer you can swim in a large outdoor pool; in winter you can warm yourself by the library fire. The decorators have gone a bit wild with pinkish beige and paisley in the guest quarters, but with a balcony in each room overlooking the Great Forest, that's a minor quibble. ⊠ *Nagyerdei park 1, H-4032* ☎ *52/514–111 (ask for recepció)* 🖶 *52/311–730* ⊕ *www.aquaticum.hu* ➷ *56 rooms, 40 suites* ⚖ *Restaurant, snack bar, indoor pool, sauna, spa, bar, meeting rooms* ⦿ *BP* ⊟ *AE, DC, MC, V.*

★ ¢ ⬚ **Korona Panzió.** This cheery little inn is just down the street from the Great Church. The immaculate rooms are a great value and have contemporary furnishings and terraces. Breakfast costs an extra 1,000 HUF. ⊠ *Péterfia utca 54, H-4026* ☎ *52/535–260* 🖶 *52/535–261* ⊕ *www.hotels.hu/koronapanzio1* ➷ *16 rooms* ⚖ *Cable TV, in-room VCRs; no a/c, no smoking* ⦿ *EP* ⊟ *No credit cards.*

The Arts

Debrecen Tavaszi Fesztivál (Debrecen Spring Festival). The biggest annual event runs from around mid-March, packing in some three weeks of concerts, dance, and theater performances, as well as special art exhibits. Events are held at Bartók Hall and other venues about town. The biannual **Bartók Béla Nemzetközi Kórusverseny** (Béla Bartók International Choral Festival), scheduled next for July 2008, is a competition for choirs from around the world, and provides choral-music aficionados with numerous full-scale concerts in the **Kölcsey Központ** (Kólcsey Center). Jazz fans can hear local ensembles as well as groups from around Hungary and abroad during the **Debreceni Jazz Napok** (Debrecen Jazz Days) around mid-September. One of the city's favorite occasions is the **Debreceni Virágkarnevál** (Flower Carnival) on St. Stephen's Day (August 20), Hungary's national holiday, when a festive parade of flower-encrusted floats and carriages makes its way down Debrecen's main street along the tram line all the way to the Nagyerdő Stadium.

Csokonai Theater. One of Debrecen's main cultural venues, this imposing, bright-yellow classical-Romantic edifice (1861–65) is devoted to theater, opera, and dance productions (though none in English). ⊠ *Kossuth utca 10* ☎ *52/417–811* ⊕ *www.csokonaiszinhaz.hu.*

Főnix Rendezvényszervező kht. (Phoenix Events Planning Co.). Call this agency, located in the Köcsey Központ cultural and conference center, for information on Debrecen's many festivals. ⊠ *Hunyadi János utca 1–3* ☎ *52/518–400.*

Sports & the Outdoors

A visit to the Great Plain is hardly complete without at least some contact with horses. There are several horseback-riding outfits outside Debrecen on the puszta. Contact the Debrecen office of Tourinform (*see* ⇨ Great Plains A to Z) to arrange excursions.

★ ♻ **Mediterrán Élményfürdő** (Mediterranean Bath Experience). Hungary's first indoor thermal water park opened its doors for business in Debrecen in July 2003, to the delight of children everywhere and the tune of $8.7 million in construction. The air temperature inside is a steamy 98.6 degrees Fahrenheit and, despite the fact that Debrecen lies in a flat and arid region, the interior attempts to look and feel like the Mediterranean. Beneath the large glass dome are whirlpool baths, spiraling water slides, an underground water cave, and a rock-climbing wall. Tropical plants and palm trees are everywhere, and interior walls are painted with Egyptian-style murals. ⊠ *Nagyerdei Park 1* ☎ *52/514–174* ⊕ *www. aquaticum.hu* 🎫 *1,799 HUF for min. 2 hours, 9 HUF/min. beyond that* ⊙ *Daily 10–10.*

♻ **Nagyerdei Lido.** Debrecen's Nagyerdő (Great Forest) bubbles with thermal baths and pools. The general swimming area (the *strand*) here has a large swimming pool, a wave pool, and two thermal pools; and the main thermal bath complex (separate entry) has six pools. ⊠ *Nagyerdei Park 1* ☎ *52/514–100* 🎫 *Strand 800 HUF, thermal baths 650 HUF until 1 PM, 970 HUF until 8 PM* ⊙ *Daily 7 AM–8 PM.*

HORTOBÁGY

❷ *39 km (24 mi) west of Debrecen, 187 km (116 mi) east of Budapest.*

The main gateway and visitor center for Hortobágy National Park is the village of Hortobágy, the most famous settlement on the puszta. Traveling from Debrecen, you'll reach this town just before you cross the Hortobágy River. ∎ **TIP→ There's no train service, but there are around 7 buses daily from Debrecen; it's a comfortable, approximately 45-minute ride.**

Thermal Tourism

11

THE DEBRECEN GOVERNMENT, capitalizing on Hungary's rich thermal traditions, hopes to make Hungary synonymous with water tourism. With an estimated 1,300 underground thermal springs—a third of which are employed at various spas across the country—Hungary is in a unique position to do so. Only Japan, Iceland, France, and Italy can boast similar thermal water capacity.

The Romans were the first to capitalize on Hungary's thermal waters in the first century, when they built baths on the banks of the Danube River. The tradition was continued under Turkish rule during the 16th and 17th centuries. As development of thermal baths continued in Hungary, the United Nations took notice, and in the 1970s the "Thermal Project" institute was established in Budapest, charged with promoting development of the baths and planning programs to utilize the practice in other countries. Today there are more than 100 spas and bathhouses across Hungary, and in 2006, the Hungarian Government earmarked 7 billion HUF for the restoration of several baths, including Budapest's Gellért, the Széchenyi, and the Lukács by late 2008.

Before heading out to the prairie itself, you can take in Hortobágy's own sights: a prairie museum, its famous stone bridge, and the historic Hortobágyi Csárda inn.

Fodor'sChoice
★

At 196,800 acres, **Hortobágy National Park** encompasses the largest continuous grassland in Europe. A major part of the area is formed by natural habitats, meadows, and small and large marshes. Natural wetlands occupy one-third of the park, while artificial wetlands, called fishponds, were created on 14,400 acres in the last century on the worst-quality grazing lands and former marshes. These fishponds are vital to the 342 types of birds registered in Hortobágy National Park, of which 152 specifically nest there.

The park has three different types of terrain: forest, marshland, and grassland, and three trails are open to the public, one in each different type of terrain. **Halastó Nature Trail** (✉ Rte. 33, between Km 64 and 65) passes through fishponds 5 km (3 mi) west of Hortobágy that were created in 1915. The ponds are now the habitat for pygmy cormorants, glossy ibis, and spoonbills. The marshes of **Egyek-Pusztakócs** (✉ Rte. 33, at Km 55) can be traversed on a dirt bike path, a former salt road, that begins at the parting of the Egyek. Among the birds you'll likely spot are ducks, grebes, and terns. Bikes can be borrowed at the Western Rest-House, which is the starting point of the trail. A day-long bike rental runs around 2,000 HUF. **Szálkahalom Nature Trail** (✉ Rte. 33, at Km 79) goes through the grassland grazing areas, and you are likely to spot herds of nónius horses, Hungarian grey cattle, water buffalos, and racka sheep. The Hortobágy Tourinform office, which shares a building with the national park's new visitor center, is both an information resource and place to purchase tickets; (Tourinform ⊠ Petőfi tér 13 ☎ 52/589–321 ⊕ www.hnp.hu)

Crossing the Hortobágy River is one of the puszta's famous symbols: the curving, white-stone **Kilenc-lyukú híd** (Nine-Hole Bridge). It was built in the early 19th century and is the longest stone bridge in Hungary. ⊠ *Rte. 33 at Petőfi tér.*

Built in 1699, the **Hortobágyi Csárda** (Hortobágy Inn) has been a regional institution for most of the last three centuries. Its construction is typical of the Great Plain: a long, white stone structure with arching windows, brown-wood details, and a stork nest—and occasionally storks—on its chimney. The restaurant is quite popular. ⊠ *Petőfi tér 2* ☎ *52/369–201* ⊙ *Closed Oct.–mid-Feb.*

For a glimpse into traditional Hortobágy pastoral life, visit the **Pásztormúzeum** (Shepherd Museum), across the street from the Hortobágy Inn. Exhibits focus on traditional costumes and tools, such as the shepherds' heavy embroidered cloaks and carved sticks. The area beside the museum is a tourism center for the area, bustling with visitors and gift stands. ⊠ *Petőfi tér 1* ☎ *No phone* 🖾 *500 HUF* ⊙ *May–Sept., daily 9–6; Oct. and Apr., daily 10–4; mid-Mar. and Nov., daily 10–2; Dec.–mid-Mar., by appointment only.*

Where to Eat

★ **$–$$$** ✗ **Hortobágyi Csárda.** Old flasks and saddles, antlers, and dried corn-and-paprika wreaths hang from the walls and rafters of this traditional Hungarian roadside inn. With a menu oriented toward local specialties with organic, Hortobágy meat, this is the place to order the regional specialty, savory *Hortobágyi húsospalacsinta* (Hortobágy pancakes), which are filled with beef and braised with a tomato-and-sour-cream sauce. Follow the pancakes with *bográcsgulyás* (spicy goulash soup puszta-style, with meat and dumplings). Veal paprikás and solid beef and lamb *pörkölt* (thick stews with paprika and sour cream) are also recommended, as are the sweet curd-cheese and apricot-jam dessert pancakes. ⊠ *Petőfi tér 2* ☎ *52/369–201* ⊟ *AE, DC, MC, V* ⊙ *Closed Oct.–mid-Feb.*

KECSKEMÉT

❸ *191 km (118 mi) southwest of Debrecen, 85 km (53 mi) east of Budapest.*

With a name roughly translating as "Goat County," this sprawling city of 120,000 smack in the middle of Hungary never fails to surprise unsuspecting first-time visitors with its elegant landmark buildings, interesting museums, and friendly, welcoming people. As far back as the 14th century, Kecskemét was a market town, and under Turkish rule in 1439 it was a *khas* (exclusive) city, which meant it received favorable treatment and was spared much of the devastation rendered on other Hungarian cities at the time. Thus, Kecskemét was able to flourish as other cities were destroyed and deserted. That said, as a votive pillar in front of the Katona József Theater attests, an 18th-century plague claimed the lives of two-thirds of the city's population.

11

A 10-minute walk from the train station will get you to the splendid and verdant main square, Szabadság tér (Liberty Square). This soon becomes Kossuth tér, which is marred only by two faceless but incredibly well-kept cement-block buildings, one of which houses the city's McDonald's (a true sign this is not just a dusty prairie town anymore); the other with lovely flowers all over its balconies. Home of the elite Kodály Institute, where famous composer and pedagogue Zoltán Kodály's methods are taught, the city also maintains a fairly active cultural life.

> ## BIG, OLD, OR GREAT?
>
> It's easy to confuse the older **Church of St. Nicholas** on the main square with the more prominent, bright yellow, and much younger **Nagy Templom** (Big Church or Great Church). To make matters more confusing, locals often call the likewise Roman Catholic Nagy Templom the *öreg templom* (Old Church), neither because it is in fact that old nor because they think it is—but because they associate bigness with oldness.

Although raising goats was an economically viable livelihood early on for many in this region of formerly none too fertile soil, Kecskemét and environs ironically came to distinguish itself eventually not so much for goats as for fruit. Although climatic conditions and the soil today are not nearly as ideal as they once were for producing apricots, Kecskemét still milks its reputation as the fruit center of the Great Plain for all it's worth—in particular when it comes to producing *barack pálinka,* a smooth yet tangy apricot brandy that can warm the heart and blur the mind in just one shot. Ask for home-brewed *házi pálinka,* which is much better (and often stronger) than the commercial brews.

A short drive from town takes you into the expansive sandy grasslands of Kiskunság National Park, the smaller of the two protected areas (the other is Hortobágy National Park) of the Great Plain. You can watch a traditional horse show, do some riding, or immerse yourself in the experience by spending a night or two at one of the inns out on the prairie.

★ The **Magyar Fotográfia Múzeum** (Hungarian Photography Museum) is one of only a few museums in Hungary dedicated solely to photography. With a growing collection of more than 500,000 photos, documents, and pieces of equipment, it is the country's most important photography center. The temporary exhibits in its single but spacious room, which change every two months or so, focus on both fine works by such pioneers of Hungarian photography as André Kertész and Brassaï—all of whom moved out of Hungary and gained their fame abroad—as well as contemporary Hungarian (and sometimes non-Hungarian) international photographers; recent exhibits have included the works of the Hungarian master Dénes Rónai (1875–1964) and historical photographs by the nation's aristocrats. ⊠ *Katona József tér 12* ☎ *76/483–221 or 76/ 508–258* ⊕ *www.photomuzeum.hu* 💷 *400 HUF* ☼ *Wed.–Sun. 10–5.*

The handsome Moorish-style former synagogue anchoring one end of Liberty Square is beautifully restored but has been stripped of its original purpose. Today it is the headquarters of the **House of Science and**

Technology, with offices and a convention center, but on its top floor it also houses a small collection of Michelangelo sculpture reproductions from Budapest's Museum of Fine Arts. ☒ *Rákóczi út 2* ☎ *76/487–611* 🖪 *Free* ☉ *Weekdays 10–4.*

Fodor's Choice Kecskemét's most famous building is the **Cifrapalota** (Ornamental Palace),
★ a unique and remarkable Hungarian-style Art Nouveau building built in 1902. A three-story cream-colored structure studded with folksy lilac, blue, red, and yellow Zsolnay majolica flowers and hearts, it stands on Liberty Square's corner like a cheerful cream pastry. Once a residential building, it now houses the **Kecskeméti képtár** (Kecskemét Gallery), with an excellent display of artwork by Hungarian fine artists as well as occasional international exhibits and some space devoted to local history and traditions. The ceiling of the main room on the second floor is something to behold, not least its peacocks: imagine what it was like for the family that lived here. ☒ *Rákóczi út 1* ☎ *76/480–776* 🖪 *300 HUF Tues.–Sat., free on Sun.* ☉ *Tues.–Sun. 10–5.*

▌ **NEED A BREAK?**

You can treat yourself to fresh pastries or ice cream at a café that shares our name, the **Fodor Cukrászda** (Fodor Confectionery; ☒ Szabadság tér 2 ☎ 76/497–545). It's right on the main square and is open from March through late December. We like more about this café than the name and its red-velvety chairs amid typically Kecskemétian apricot walls; try the Tejszínes mákos, a poppy seed–laced, cream-rich sponge cake, or the butter-and-walnut-rich Eszterházy cake.

Built between 1892 and 1896 by Ödön Lechner in the Hungarian Art
★ Nouveau style that he created, the **Városház** (Town Hall) is one of its finest examples. Window frames are arched here, pointed there, and the roof, peppered with tiny copper- and gold-color tiles, looks as if it has been rained on by pennies from heaven. In typical Lechner style, the outlines of the central facade make a curving line to a pointed top, under which 37 little computer-driven bells in a screened-in balcony of sorts add the finishing visual and aural touch: every hour from 9 AM to 4 PM (hours may vary on Fridays and weekends), they flood the main square with the ringing melody of the "Rákóczi March," a patriotic 18th-century tune later orchestrated by Berlioz and adapted by Liszt in one of his *Hungarian Rhapsodies*. Note also the goat occupying center stage in the city's coat of arms on the building's facade. The building's **Dísz Terem** (Ceremonial Hall), on the second floor, is a spectacular palace of glimmering gold-painted vaulted ceilings, exquisitely carved wooden pews, colorful frescoes by Bertalan Székely (who also painted the frescoes for Budapest's Matthias Church), and a gorgeously ornate chandelier that floats above the room like an ethereal bouquet of lights and shining brass. The hall is open only to tour groups that have made prior arrangements; call in advance or, since the person at the other end of the line might not speak English, ask Tourinform for help or ask your hotel to help book a visit if you're staying in town. ☒ *Kossuth tér 1* ☎ *76/513–513, Ext. 2263* 🖪 *Ceremonial hall 300 HUF* ☉ *Mon.–Thurs. 8–4, Fri. 8–1. Ceremonial Hall by appointment only.*

The oldest building on Kossuth tér is the **Szent Miklós templom** (Church of St. Nicholas), known also as the Barátság templom (Friendship Church) because of St. Nick's role as the saint of friendship. The church, the oldest in the city, was built in Gothic style in either the 13th or 15th century (a subject of debate). What is not debated is that it was rebuilt in baroque style during the 18th century. Once you pass through the elaborate wrought-iron gate and through an attractive little courtyard out front, note the interior's apricot hues, which are typical of many an edifice in downtown Kecskemét. ⊠ *Kossuth tér 5.*

The unusual, one-of-a-kind **Szórakoténusz Játékmúzeum és Műhely** (Szórakoténusz Toy Museum & Workshop) chronicles the history of Hungarian toys with almost 18,000 archaeological pieces such as stone figures and clay toys from medieval guilds. The museum also hosts changing international exhibits. In the workshop, artisans create traditional toys and invite you to try to make toys yourself. Next door to the toy museum (in the same building) is the small **Magyar Naív Művészek Múzeum** (Hungarian Naive Art Museum), where you can see a collection of this simple style of painting and sculpting created by Hungarian artists. You can get here via a 5-minute walk to a less than inspiring neighborhood of concrete apartment blocks on the outskirts of downtown. ⊠ *Gáspár András utca 11* ☎ *76/481–469 Toy Museum, 76/324–767 Naive Art Museum* 🖾 *400 HUF Toy Museum, 150 HUF Naive Art Museum* ☉ *Toy Museum Tues.–Sun. 10–12:30 and 1–5; Naive Art Museum Tues.–Sun. 10–5. Toy Workshop alternate Sat. 10–noon and 2:30–5, alternate Sun. 10–noon.*

> ## WORD OF MOUTH
>
> "We drove to Szeged, which is a lovely town but essentially built in the style of a western European capital. Kecskemét is a completely different story. The town is extremely appealing, with beautiful architecture that seems to have a Hungarian touch—it would be a good base for visiting the puszta."   —Michael

OFF THE BEATEN PATH

PIAC (Market) – Kecskemét is Hungary's fruit capital, and it's worth experiencing the region's riches first-hand by visiting the bustling market, where—depending on the season—you can indulge in freshly plucked apples, cherries, and the famous Kecskemét apricots. Provided there is no sudden spring freeze, apricot season is around June through August. It's about 2 km from the city center. ⊠ *Along Budai utca, near corner of Nagykörösi út* ☉ *Tues.–Sat. 6–noon, Sun. 6 AM–11 AM.*

Where to Stay & Eat

$–$$$$ ✕ **Túróczy Étterem.** Probably the closest thing to a Viennese coffeehouse on the Great Plain is this Art Nouveau room with a restaurant-sized menu. From the terrace out front, facing parklike Liberty Square, you can hear birdsong; inside it's pop songs that seem intended primarily to entertain the waitstaff. The menu runs the gamut from traditional fare—such as veal paprikas and catfish "grilled on garlic" and served with *túrós csusza* (pasta with curd-cheese, topped off with bacon bits)—to, yes, Buffalo chicken wings. ⊠ *Szabadság tér 2* ☎ *76/509–175 or 76/509–174* ⊟ *MC, V.*

★ $ ✕ **Kisbugaci Étterem.** This cozy, csárda-style eatery tucked away on a side street a 10-minute walk from the main square is warm and bright. The inner area has wood paneling and upholstered booths; the outer section has simple wooden tables covered with locally embroidered tablecloths and matching curtains. Food is heavy, ample, and tasty, whether it's "outlaw" paprikas with barley-shaped, egg-based pasta; tripe stew with crushed potatoes; turkey breast; or goose liver. Request a plate of dried paprikas—usually crumbled into soup—if you really want to spice things up. ⊠ *Munkácsy utca 10* ☎ *76/322–722 or 76/486–782* ⊟ *MC, V* ⊘ *No dinner Sun.*

¢–$ ⊡ **Aranyhomok Wellness Hotel.** The staff of the Golden Sand is cheerful and friendly, and Kecskemét is right on your doorstep at this hotel on a small square close to the city center. Although it doesn't require an overheated imagination to envisage this concrete-bunker-style hotel as a resting place for communist-era bureaucrats, these days the balconies overlooking the main square are all adorned with flowers, ironically rendering what may be the prettiest such facade in Hungary. Most rooms have pared-down blond-wood furnishings, generic gray wall-to-wall carpeting, and small bathrooms. ■ **TIP**➡ Six rooms on each floor have air-conditioning (at no extra charge); the other rooms can get stuffy in the summer. All doubles have balconies; those overlooking the main square cost around 50% (7,000 HUF) more. The "wellness center" has a 12-meter pool, Jacuzzi, steam bath, sauna, and massage services. ⊠ *Kossuth tér 3, H-6000* ☎ *76/503–730* ⊠ *76/530–731* ⊕ *www.hotelaranyhomok.hu* ⊷ *111 rooms, 4 suites* ⟡ *Restaurant, minibars, gym, casino, laundry service, meeting rooms, travel services, indoor pool, some pets allowed* ⊟ *AE, DC, MC, V* ⟊ *BP.*

★ ¢ ⊡ **Fábián Panzió.** It's hard to miss this positively pink villa just a couple of blocks from the main square. Once inside, the pink (though muted) continues, mixing with white, turquoise, and lavender. The friendly owners keep their pension immaculate: floors in the tiny entranceway are polished until they look wet, and even the paths through the blooming back garden are spotless. Rooms are in the main house and in a comely one-story motel-like building in the garden. The largest and quietest rooms are in the back. Air-conditioning is available, but costs extra (1,000 HUF a night: reasonable given utility rates in Hungary), and the same goes for the bicycles. The hotel can book you a visit to Town Hall, and it keeps on hand a notebook full of local restaurant menus. ⊠ *Kápolna utca 14, H-6000* ☎ *76/477–677* ⊠ *76/477–175* ⊕ *www.hotels.hu/fabian* ⊷ *10 rooms* ⟡ *Minibars, cable TV, bicycles, laundry service* ⟊ *BP* ⊟ *No credit cards.*

¢ ⊡ **Pongrácz Major** (Pongrácz Manor). For total puszta immersion, spend

FodorsChoice

★ a night or two at this Great Plain ranch, about 25 km (16 mi) outside of Kecskemét. The manor, which sits adjacent to a complex of whitewashed buildings with reed roofs, has small, simple, comfortable rooms. The stables house some 70 horses; in addition to riding yourself, you can watch resident champion csikósok perform daredevil stunts and stage

11

mock 1848-revolution battles in full hussar dress. Anglers can try their luck in the nearby lake; the restaurant's kitchen will cook your catch (one fish per day); and gypsy (roma) musicians will entertain you as you eat. The ranch is popular, so reserve ahead. ⊠ *Kunpuszta 76, H-6041 Kerekegyháza* ☎ *76/710–093* 🖻 *76/371–240* ⊕ *www.pongraczmajor. hu* 🛏 *31 rooms (26 with bath), 4 suites* ♨ *Restaurant, 2 tennis courts, pool, sauna, fishing, bowling, horseback riding, squash, tennis, meeting room* 🚫 *No credit cards* ⊙ *Closed Jan.–Mar.*

The Arts

Kecskemét's annual **Tavaszi Fesztivál** (Spring Festival) is held from midMarch to early April, and includes concerts, dance performances, theater productions, and art exhibits by local and special guest artists from around the country and abroad. Every two years in July the city hosts a giant children's festival, **Európa Jövője Gyermektalálkozó** (Future of Europe Children's Convention), during which children's groups from some 25 countries put on colorful folk-dance and singing performances outside on the main square; the next one will take place in 2008.

Katona József Theater. With an imposing votive pillar out front from 1742 commemorating the 1738–39 plague that wiped out a third of the city, this theater—whose beautiful, late-baroque style calls to mind Budapest's Vígszínház (Comedy Theater)—is known for its excellent dramatic productions (in Hungarian) and also hosts classical concerts, operas, and dance performances during the Spring Festival and other celebrations. ⊠ *Katona József tér 5* ☎ *76/501–170 or 76/501–177* ⊕ *www.katonaj.hu.*

Kodály Zoltán Zenepedagógiai Intézet (Zoltán Kodály Music Pedagogy Institute). In a former Franciscan monastery, the school often holds student and faculty recitals, particularly during its international music seminar in mid- to late July, which is held in every odd-numbered year. ⊠ *Kéttemplom köz 1* ☎ *76/481–518.*

BUGAC

❹ *46 km (29 mi) south of Kecskemét, 120 km (74 mi) southeast of Budapest.*

The Bugac puszta, declared by UNESCO as a bioreserve for its unique flora and fauna, is the central and most-visited section of the 127,200-acre **Kiskunsági Nemzeti Park** (Kiskunság National Park)—the smaller sister of Hortobágy National Park (farther northeast); together they compose the entire Great Plain. Bugac puszta's expansive, sandy, impossibly flat grassland scenery has provided Hungarian poets and artists with inexhaustible material over the centuries. Although the dry, open stretches may seem numbingly uniform to the casual eye, the Bugac's fragile ecosystem is the most varied of the entire park; its primeval juniper trees, extremely rare in the region, are the area's most protected and treasured flora. Today Bugac continues to inspire visitors with its strong equestrian traditions and the fun but touristy horse shows and tours offered within its boundaries. The park's half-hour traditional horse show takes place twice daily, around 11 and 2. You can also wander around the area and peek into the Kiskunság National Park Museum, which has exhibits about pastoral life on the prairie. ■ TIP→ Note that areas of the park farther away from Bugac can be accessed for free; the park center in Kecskemét has maps (with English text) that describe the various short trails (whose signs also include English text). ☒ *Kiskunság National Park Management Center, House of Nature, Liszt Ferenc utca 19, Kecskemét* ☎ *76/501–596* ☒ *Park entrance: off Rte. 54 Bugac* ⊕ *www.knp.hu* ☒ *Including horse show: 1,100 HUF (entry on foot) or 2,500 HUF (entry on horse-drawn carriage); without horse show 700 HUF (entry on foot); 200 HUF, House of Nature (in Kecskemét)* ⊙ *May–Oct., weekdays 8–4, weekends 8–1.*

Where to Eat

$–$$$ ✕ **Bugaci Csárda.** Bugac's most famous and popular restaurant is a tourbus magnet, but is still considered a mandatory part of a puszta visit. It's at the end of a dirt road just past the park's main entrance, in a traditional whitewashed, thatch-roof house decorated inside with cheerful red-and-white folk embroideries. Here you can feast on all the Hungarian staples. ☒ *Rte. 54, at the park entrance, Bugac* ☎ *76/372–522* ☲ *No credit cards* ⊙ *Closed Nov.–Mar.*

Sports & the Outdoors

The region specializes in equestrian sports, and several companies offer horseback-riding lessons, trail rides, and horse-carriage rides.

☽ **Bugac Tours.** Through its office at the Karikás Csárda (Karikás Inn) inside Kiskunság National Park, Bugac Tours organizes horseback-riding trips, horse-show excursions, barbecue dinners, and visits to local ranch homes and farmhouses. ☒ *Karikás Csárda, Bugac* ☎ *76/575–112* ☲ *76/575–114.*

☽ **Bugaci Ménes.** Also located inside Kiskunság National Park, Bugaci Ménes breeds sport horses, sheep, and grey cattle, but is most famous for horse shows it puts on for tourists. ☒ *Off Rte. 54, Bugac* ☎☎ *76/575–028.*

☽ **Juhász és Társa.** The company regularly presents traditional horsemanship shows, including the "Puszta Five," an internationally known equestrian team. Visitors can attend courses under the instruction of László Juhász, a world champion in equestrian stunts and driving. ☒ *Móritz utca 5, Bugac* ☎ *76/372–583.*

SZEGED

➎ *87 km (54 mi) south of Kecskemét, 171 km (106 mi) southeast of Budapest.*

The city of 165,000 at the junction of the Tisza and Maros rivers is the largest and by far the liveliest in southern Hungary. Although Szeged owes its origin to the Tisza River, the river has also been its ruin. In 1879 a disastrous flood known by the residents simply as "the water," destroyed the old Szeged in just one night. It's ironic then, to say the least, that Szeged is called "The Sunshine Town," after its average 2,100 hours of sunshine a year. With international assistance the city was rebuilt, and out of gratitude Szeged's ring boulevards bear the names of the cities that helped (Vienna, Moscow, London, Paris, Berlin, Brussels, and Rome).

Historical excavations show the probability that Szeged was once the seat of Atilla, the king of the Huns, in the 5th century. The city later became a Turkish stronghold after it was conquered in 1543. Under Turkish rule Szeged continued to develop, and became a center for trade in southern Hungary, especially given its favorable location along the Tisza River. In 1686, with help from Austrian forces, Szeged was liberated from the Turks. But Hungarians were not happy with Austrian rule either, and in 1704 they tried to take back the city. However, they had poor weaponry, and their rebellion was easily put down. Under Austrian rule Szeged served as a military outpost.

Szeged's darkest hour, known as the Great Flood, came in 1879, when melting snow caused the Tisza and Maros rivers to burst with extra water and smash open a dyke near the outskirts of town. The entire city was nearly washed away, and when it was over 150 people had died and only 265 houses remained standing—5,458 were destroyed. Since 1931 Szeged has held its Open-Air Festival in memory of those lost in the Great Flood.

Aside from the flood, however, Szeged is famous for two other things: paprika and salami. Szeged's paprikas are useful not only in goulash kettles but also in test tubes. Local biochemist Albert Szentgyörgyi won the Nobel Prize in 1937 for his discoveries about vitamin C, extracted from his hometown spice. In late summer and early autumn, you can see rack after rack of red peppers drying in the open air all over town. World-famous Pick salami also comes from Szeged.

Szeged may hold relatively few individual architectural delights unique to Hungary, but its large town center—rich with turn-of-the-20th-century buildings and a series of attractive old squares—makes for a lively atmosphere rivalling that of both Eger and Pécs (even if it does lack the hills, nearby wine country, and Turkish monuments that give those towns their special draw). In summer its main squares are bustling with people who seem to have forgotten that they're not in some Adriatic or Mediterranean towns of like size; and during the school year students from the city's schools and universities continue to liven up the streets, cafés, and bars.

■ **TIP➜** You can save yourself the 25-minute trudge into downtown from Szeged's recently restored, beautiful train station by buying a *vonaljegy* (vohn-awl-jedy) (ticket) for 140 HUF at the public transport kiosk right outside the station and hopping aboard Tram No. 1, which passes by frequently. Go 5 stops to Széchény tér.

Numbers in the margins correspond to numbers on the Szeged map.

❻ The heart of the city center is made up of the large **Széchenyi tér,** shaded with plane trees, and the adjacent **Klauzál tér,** which is not green but much more bustling with people and likewise surrounded by imposing buildings.

KEY

① *Exploring Sights*

① *Hotels & Restaurants*

Szeged

The most notable of Szeged's structures is the bright yellow, neo-baroque **⑦ Városház** (Town Hall; ✉ Széchenyi tér 10), built at the turn of the 19th century and, after suffering major damage during the flood of 1879, reconstructed by well-known, eclectic Art Nouveau architect Ödön Lechner. Its spectacular clock tower with a terrace and a roof of colored tiles is visible from afar. Across Széchenyi tér from the Town Hall stands the **⑧** pale-green **Hotel Tisza** (✉ Wesselényi utca 4). Although the guest rooms and lobby look tired and worn, the hotel's lovely—and still quite active—concert hall was the site of many piano recitals by legendary composer Béla Bartók. Its restaurant was a favorite haunt of famous poet Mihály Babits.

⑨ Anna Spa. After a good long time without, Szeged in 2004 again became the proud owner of its very own thermal baths right in the heart **Fodor's Choice** of downtown. A 5-minute walk from Széchenyi tér, the now immaculately restored Anna Spa was the site of the Turkish-style Városi Gőzfürdő (City Steam Bath) built back in 1896, which operated for decades. Today this palatial-looking building includes a natural thermal pool (complete with built-in chess tables), a sauna, and more on your right as you enter; and a "wellness" center on your left, which includes saunas, a steam room, and several thermal pools that massage you as you wade. The full 1,300 HUF admission allows you entry to

11

both sides of the complex. ⊠ *Tisza Lajos körút 24* ☎ *62/422–820 or 62/487–711* ⊕ *www.szegedifurdok.hu* ☑ *1,300 HUF (900 HUF 9 PM–midnight)* ⊘ *Weekdays 6 AM–8 PM, weekends 8 AM–8 PM; Mon., Wed., Fri., and Sat. 9 PM–midnight.*

⑩

Fodor's Choice

★

The ground floor of the two-story **Pick Szalámi és Szegedi Paprika Múzeum** (Pick Salami and Szeged Paprika Museum) is devoted entirely to the history of the Pick company and its salami production. Knives and tools used in the process are on display—which could turn your stomach—as are videos showing the production of salami and audio recordings of former workers at the Pick factory. Upstairs is loads of information on paprika, including information about the picking and planting of the peppers and their numerous health benefits. In return for the museum fee, visitors are treated to samples of salami and free postage anywhere in the world for a postcard from the company. ⊠ *Felső Tiszapart 10* ☎ *20/980–80005* ⊕ *www.pickmuzeum.hu* ☑ *400 HUF* ⊘ *Tues.–Sat. 3–6.*

NEED A BREAK?

Grab a hot strudel stuffed with apple, poppy seed, or even peppery cabbage at the counter of **Hatos Rétes** (⊠ Klauzal tér 6 ☎ 62/420–121). This bakery-cum-café is a popular spot, not only for a quick snack but also *óriás palacsinta* (giant stuffed crepes) that come either savory (ham, cheese) or sweet (plum, raspberry, chestnut). This is also among the few places in Hungary that serves decaffeinated coffee. Also well worth a try for its larger and more delectable selection of pastries and fresh-squeezed orange juice is the **Cappella Cukrászda** (⊠ Kárász utca 6 ☎ 62/559–966), a larger, more crowded café a few yards away where the square meets Kárász utca.

⑪ Beneath the archways surrounding **Dóm tér** (Cathedral Square), which was built in 1920, is a row of 90 statues of Hungary's most famous scientists, politicians, and other noteworthy personalities.

★ **⑫** Szeged's most striking building is the **Fogadalmi templom** (Votive Church), an imposing neo-Romanesque, twin-steepled brick edifice that was built between 1912 and 1929 in fulfillment of a municipal promise made after the 1879 flood. One of Hungary's largest churches, more commonly called the Dóm (Cathedral), it seats 6,000 and has a splendid organ with 9,040 pipes, one of the biggest in Europe; the church's bell is the second-largest in the country. The church forms the backdrop to the annual Szeged Open-Air Festival, held in the vast Dóm tér. A performance of a different sort takes place here daily at 12:15 PM, when the mechanical figures on the church's clock put on their five-minute show to music. During excavations for the Votive Church, Szeged's oldest building, the Dömötör, was discovered; it's estimated to have been built between the 11th and 13th centuries. ⊠ *Dóm tér* ☎ *62/420–157 church* ☎ *62/420–953* ☑ *Church 400 HUF, crypt 150 HUF* ⊘ *Church weekends 9–6, Sun. 12:30–6. Crypt—with advance arrangement only.*

⑬ Szeged's neoclassical **Régi Zsinagóga** (Old Synagogue) was built in 1839. On its outside wall a marker written in Hungarian and Hebrew shows the height of the floodwaters in 1879, an estimated 3.8 meters high. It took four months for water to recede and the town to dry up completely.

It is open only rarely for special events. ⊠ *Hajnóczi utca 12* ⊙ *Apr.–Sept., Sun.–Fri. 9–noon and 1–6 (often closes earlier on Fri.).*

★ ⑭ The **Új Zsinagóga** (New Synagogue), finished in 1905, is Szeged's purest and finest representation of the Art Nouveau style. Its wood and stone carvings, wrought iron, stained-glass windows, and spectacular dome are all the work of local craftspeople. A memorial in the entrance hall honors Szeged's victims of the Holocaust. The New Synagogue is not far from the smaller Old Synagogue. ⊠ *Gutenberg utca 20, at Jósika utca* ☎ *62/423–849* 🖾 *200 HUF* ⊙ *Apr.–Oct., Sun.–Mon. 9–noon and 1–5; Nov.–Mar., Sun.–Mon. 9–2.*

⑮ The eclectic **Móra Ferenc Múzeum** (Ferenc Mora Museum), named after one of Szeged's early-20th-century writers and museum curators, sits at the foot of the Tisza Bridge, which connects the two sides of the city. The museum displays artifacts found during various excavations dating back to when Hungary was first settled. In addition to natural-science displays, you'll also see works by contemporary Hungarian sculptors. ⊠ *Roosevelt tér 1–3* ☎ *62/549–040* 🖾 *400 HUF* ⊙ *Oct.–June, Tues.–Sun. 10–5; July–Sept., Tues.–Sun. 10–6.*

OFF THE BEATEN PATH

NEMZETI TÖRTÉNETI EMLÉKPARK – The ultimate in monuments to Hungarian history and pride is the enormous National Historic Memorial Park in Ópusztaszer, 29 km (18 mi) north of Szeged. It was built on the site of the first parliamentary congregation of the nomadic Magyar tribes, held in AD 895, in which they agreed to be ruled by mighty Árpád. Paths meander through an open-air museum of traditional village and countryside architecture—including two farmsteads, a fisherman's house, a forester's house, a school, a windmill, and more. The main draw, however, is the **Feszty Körkép** (Feszty Cyclorama), an astounding 5,249-foot, 360-degree panoramic oil painting depicting the arrival of the Magyar tribes to the Carpathian basin in the 9th century AD— effectively, the birth of Hungary. It was painted between 1892 and 1894 by Árpád Feszti and exhibited in Budapest to celebrate the Magyar Millennium. Sixty percent of it was destroyed during World War II, and it wasn't until 1991 that a group of art restorers brought it here and started a painstaking project to resurrect it in time for Hungary's millecentennial celebrations in 1996. Today, housed in its own giant rotunda, the painting is viewable as part of a multimedia experience: groups of up to 100 at a time are let in every half-hour for a 25-minute viewing of the painting, accompanied by a recorded explanation and, at the end, a special sound show in which different recordings are played near different parts of the painting—galloping horses, trumpeting horns, screaming virgins, rushing water—appropriate to the scene depicted. The attraction is so popular that on summer weekends it's a good idea to call ahead and reserve a spot (timed tickets are given for specific shows). The explanation is in Hungarian, but English-language versions on CD, available at the entrance, can be listened to on headphones before or after the viewing. The cyclorama is the only park attraction open in winter. ⊠ *Szoborkert 68, Ópusztaszer* ☎ *62/275–133 or 62/275–055* ⊕ *www.opusztaszer.hu* 🖾 *1,900 HUF* ⊙ *Apr.–Oct., daily 9–6; Nov.–Mar., daily 9–4.*

Where to Stay & Eat

$–$$ ╳ **John Bull Pub.** No, it's neither typically nor stereotypically Hungar-
Fodor'sChoice ian, but it's extremely popular with locals—with good reason. It's *good.*
★ Winner of Hungary's "Pub of the Year" award in 1998, Szeged's John
Bull opened in 1996 on a bustling side street between Széchenyi tér and
the cathedral, and serves up a whole host of delicious dishes from fish
to steak to Wiener schnitzel to the
elaborate Pittsburgh veal ribs with
pan-fried potato wedges (served
with goose-liver pâté, ham, and
red-wine mushroom ragout, among
other things). If you're up for
dessert, be sure to try the túrós
palacsinta, oven-baked palacsintas
filled with sweet-curd cheese and a
thick, heavenly-sweet vanilla cream.
✉ *Oroszlán utca 6* ☎ *62/484–217*
🚫 *AE, DC, MC, V.*

★ **$–$$** ╳ **Matuzsálem Kávézó és Étterem.**
Originally the site of Szeged's first
printing press, this 1810 neoclassical building seems fated to be the
home of various restaurants for the
foreseeable future. The Botond, a
longtime favorite here, came under
new ownership and a new name in
2005. Its successor, the Matusela
Cafe & Restaurant, may be a tad
touristy but it does serves up a wide

FREE THIRST/AILMENT QUENCHER
At any time of day, cross Széchenyi tér, going past the Town Hall (on your left), and take a left onto Vörösmarty utca. Walk a minute or so on the right side of the street to the corner of Tisza Lajos körút, where you can't miss Szeged's famous Anna *forrás* (spring). The water streaming out of four metal pipes here is reportedly curative—which is why some old ladies are given to splashing it all over their faces—but it tastes great, too. The water issuing from three of the four taps is thermal but still perfectly drinkable.

array of decent poultry, beef, and pork dishes, with more than a few
traditional favorites such as veal paprikás and Tatar beefsteak thrown
into the mix. For 100 HUF extra your soup can be served in a hollowed-
out loaf of bread. The terrace out front, which faces leafy Széchenyi tér,
is a pleasant spot to dine. ■ TIP➔ Be sure to turn right (to the restaurant's
one interior room) as you walk inside; a left will land you in a casino.
✉ *Széchenyi tér 13* ☎ *62/420–435* 🚫 *AE, DC, MC, V.*

¢ 🏨 **Dóm Hotel.** Ideally located a block from the cathedral on the way to
Szeged's bustling squares, this small hotel has mostly bright (and a couple of darkish) rooms with silky, apricot bedspreads, standard modern furnishings, and yellow and blood-orange walls. Note that one room faces
the gray side of a building, and another gets little light on account of a
big tree near the window. All rooms but one are no-smoking (and according to a friendly clerk, even that one's smoking days may be numbered).
✉ *Bajza utca 6, H-6725* ☎ *62/423–750* 🌐 *www.domhotel.hu* ⬅ *15
rooms, 2 suites* ⬧ *Restaurant, minibars, cable TV, sauna, meeting room,
in-room data ports, laundry service, free parking* 🚫*AE, DC, MC, V* ⓘ❘*BP.*

¢ 🏨 **Marika Panzió.** This friendly inn sits on a historic street in the Alsóváros
(Lower Town), a five-minute drive from the city center. Cozy rooms have
light-wood paneling and larger-hotel amenities, including color TVs, mini-

bars, and air-conditioning. The back garden has a small swimming pool. ☒ *Nyíl utca 45, H-6725* 🏠 *62/443–861* ⊕ *www.kronikaspark.hu* 🛏 *9 rooms* ☖ *Minibars, cable TV, pool, laundry service, free parking* ▭ *AE, DC, MC, V* ⊙️ *BP.*

The Arts

Szeged's own symphony orchestra, theater company, and famous contemporary dance troupe form the solid foundation for a rich cultural life. Chamber-music concerts are often held in the conservatory and in the historic recital hall of the Hotel Tisza. The city's concert season runs from September to May.

Szeged Nemzeti Színház (Szeged National Theater). The city's main theater stages Hungarian dramas, as well as classical concerts, operas, and ballets. Just to the left of the theater is a statue of Hungary's most famous gypsy musician, Pista Dankó. ☒ *Deák Ferenc utca 12* 🕾 *62/479–279.*

❻ **Szegedi Szabadtéri Játékok** (Szeged Open-Air Festival). Szeged's most important annual event, drawing crowds from around the country, is the annual festival, a tradition established in 1931 in remembrance of the great flood. The festival lasts from mid-July through mid-September. The gala series of dramas, operas, operettas, classical concerts, and folk-dance performances by

> **TIME IN TUNE**
>
> At No. 5 Dóm tér, right across from the main entrance of the Fogadalmi templom (Votive Church), is a building whose facade displays one of Hungary's most beautiful musical clocks. Compliments of local clockmaker Ferenc Csúri and woodcarver József Kulai, the clock—whose doors open on the hour, every hour, to reveal a music-accompanied procession of university council bigwigs and graduating students in their smartest, most colorful outfits—was first put into action in 1936.

Hungarian and international artists is held outdoors on the vast cobblestone Cathedral Square. The line-up always includes outstanding performances of Hungary's great national drama, Imre Madách's *Tragedy of Man*. Classical music groups from the seven cities that assisted in Szeged's rebuilding are also on hand for performances. Tickets are always hot commodities, so plan far ahead. ☒ *Festival Ticket Office, Deák Ferenc utca 28–30* 🕾 *62/554–710* ⊕ *nemzetiszinhaz.szeged.hu.*

Shopping

You'll have no trouble finding packages of authentic Szegedi paprika in all sizes and degrees of spiciness in most of the city's shops. Szeged's other famous product is its excellent salami, which has been made by the local Pick salami factory since 1869.

Pick Factory Outlet. You'll find an extensive salami selection at the company store, which has two outlets in town. ☒ *Mars tér Vásárcsarnok (Food Market on Mars Square)* 🕾 *62/425–256* ☒ *Maros utca 21, next to the factory* 🕾 *62/421–879.*

THE GREAT PLAIN ESSENTIALS

11

BUS TRAVEL

Volánbusz operates service from Budapest's Stadion terminal to towns throughout the Great Plain. Local buses connect most towns within the region. Hajduvolán has three direct routes daily between Debrecen and Szeged—which, though at least four hours (and around 3,000 HUF a ticket), may be more convenient than getting between the two cities by train, as the rail alternative involves more transfers.

Stadion Bus Station ⊠ District XIV, Hungária körút 48–52, Eastern Pest, Budapest ☎ 1/251-0125 or (Volánbusz info line) 1/382-0888 ⊕ www.volanbusz.hu Ⓜ M2: Stadion

CAR TRAVEL

From Budapest, Route 4 goes straight to Debrecen, but it's faster to take the M3 expressway and switch to Route 33 midway there; the M5 goes to Kecskemét and Szeged.

The flat expanses of this region make for easy, if eventually numbing, driving. Secondary Route 47 runs along the eastern edge of the country, connecting Debrecen and Szeged. It's easy to drive between Debrecen and Kecskemét via Route 4 through Szolnok before you drop south in Cegléd. The puszta regions of Bugac and Hortobágy are accessible from Kecskemét and Debrecen by well-marked roads.

INTERNET

Cafe DataNet. If you're hankering to log on in Debrecen, you can do so for 7 HUF per minute from 8 AM to 10 PM or 5 HUF per minute from 10 PM to midnight at this spot just a couple of blocks from the main drag, Piac utca. ⊠ *Kossuth utca 8, Debrecen* ☎ *52/536–724.*

Matrix. Open 24 hours in the bustling center of Szeged near Klauzál tér, the Matrix is a fine place to log on. While kids in the back of the store play computer games, up front there are plenty of machines for the reasonable price of 5 HUF per minute. ⊠ *Kárász utca 5, Szeged* ☎ *62/423–830.*

Cityrama ⊠ District V, Báthory utca 22, St. Stephen's Basilica, Budapest ☎ 1/302-4382 in Budapest ⊕ www.cityrama.hu. **IBUSZ Travel** ⊠ District V, Ferenciek tere 10, Around Ferenciek tere, Budapest ☎ 1/485-2700 in Budapest ⊕ www.ibusz.hu.

TOURS

Cityrama runs a daylong tour several times a week to the Great Plain from Budapest. It begins with a sightseeing walk through Kecskemét, then heads out to the prairie town of Lajosmizse for drinking, dining, Gypsy music, carriage rides, and a traditional csikós horse show. The cost is €72 per person.

IBUSZ Travel also operates a full-day tour out to the Great Plain, to Lajosmizse, first taking in Kecskemét's sights. The tour is likewise €72 per person.

From around the first week of July through the end of August, the national shipping company MAHART PassNave offers one-hour boat rides along the Tisza River in Szeged at 5 PM for 800 HUF on Wednesdays, Fridays, and Sundays. Call 62/425–834 or 06–30/338–7024 (mobile) for more info.

TRAIN TRAVEL

Service to the Great Plain from Budapest is quite good; daily service is available from the capital's Nyugati (West) and Keleti (East) stations. Intercity (IC) trains, the fastest choice, run between Budapest and Debrecen, Kecskemét, and Szeged; they require seat reservations, which will almost certainly be sold to you automatically if you ask for an IC ticket.

■ TIP➔ **Check to be sure you are given two ticket-like slips of paper—one is actually the ticket, the other is the reservation.**

The train ride to Debrecen from Budapest is around three hours, and the Debrecen train station is about a 10-minute walk from the city center. The train from Budapest to Kecskemét is about one hour, while the trip to Szeged from Budapest by rail is 2½ hours.

Connections within the region are via the rail junctions in Szolnok and Cegléd, in the geometric center of the Great Plain. The Szeged train station is a 30-minute walk from the town center, but you can also take a tram; the Kecskemét station is 15 minutes from the center; and the Debrecen station is practically in the center, a few blocks from the main square. The train ride from Szolnok to Debrecen takes about 90 minutes. The trains for Kecskemét are on the Szeged line; the trip between the towns takes roughly an hour. From Kecskemét you can also take a narrow-gauge train service to Kiskunmajsa, another village on the puszta, aboard a "nostalgia" train with old engines and carriages.

🚂 Train Stations As in all parts of Hungary these days, rather than calling local stations directly it's easier simply to dial the state railway company MÁV's national info line (local charges nationwide), at 06/40-49-49-49. **Debrecen train station** ⊠ Petőfi tér 12, Debrecen ☎ 52/346-777. **Kecskemét train station** ⊠ Kodály Zoltán tér 7, Kecskemét ☎ 76/322-460. **Kecskemét narrow-gauge train station** ⊠ Halasi út 19, Kecskemét ☎ 76/504-308. **Szeged train station** ⊠ Tisza pályaudvar, Indóház tér, Szeged ☎ 62/420-136.

VISITOR INFORMATION

🚩 **Tourinform** ⊠ Piac utca 20, Debrecen ☎ 52/412-250 🖨 52/535-323 ⊠ Petőfi tér 13 (in the national park visitors center) Hortobágy ☎🖨 52/589-321 ⊠ Kossuth tér 1, Kecskemét ☎ 76/481-065 ⊠ Dugonics tér 2, Szeged ☎ 62/488-699.

Northern Hungary

By Paul
Olchváry

Northern Hungary stretches from the Danube Bend, north of Budapest, along the northeastern frontier with Slovakia as far east as Sátoraljaújhely. It is a clearly defined area, marked by several mountain ranges of humble height but considerable scenic beauty. Rising well above the stereotype that Hungary is all about its Great Plain, the highest peaks reach 3,000 feet and are thickly wooded almost to their summits. Grottoes and caves abound, as well as thermal baths. In the state game reserves it's not uncommon to spot herds of dainty little roe deer, the much larger red deer (a European counterpart of the American elk), wild boars, and eagles.

Historically, the valleys of northern Hungary have always been of considerable strategic importance, as they provided the only access to

PAUL'S TOP 5
Eger Vár. Eger's famous fortress saw catacombs added in the 16th century that allowed its few defenders appearing at its various ends to trick attacking Turks.
Hotel Senator Ház. A charming inn with guest rooms a pleasant modern contrast to the historical-bric-a-brac-filled lobby.
Rákóczi-pince. Tokaj's most famous wine cellar is also Europe's largest.
Aggtelek National Park. Its biggest cave, Baradla, 24 km (15 mi) long, contains the continent's largest stalactite system.
Ős Kaján. A friendly French-turned-Hungarian couple has created a homey atmosphere here.

the Carpathian Mountains. The city of Eger, renowned throughout Hungarian history as one of the guardians of these strategic routes, retains its splendor, with many ruins picturesquely dotting the surrounding hilltops. What's more, this is one of Hungary's great wine-growing districts, with Eger contributing the "Magyar nectar" and Tokaj producing the "wine of kings."

Numbers in the margin correspond to numbers on the Northern Hungary map.

WHAT IT COSTS In Euros & Forints				
$$$$	**$$$**	**$$**	**$**	**¢**
HOTELS IN EUROS				
over 225	175–225	125–175	75–125	under 75
HOTELS IN FORINTS				
over 56,000	44,000–56,000	31,000–44,000	18,500–31,000	under 18,500
RESTAURANTS IN FORINTS				
over 3,500	2,500–3,500	1,500–2,500	800–1,500	under 800

Hotel prices are for two people in a standard double room with a private bath and breakfast during peak season (June through August). Restaurant prices are per person for a main course at dinner and include 15% tax but not service.

HOLLÓKŐ

★ ❶ *100 km (62 mi) northeast of Budapest.*

UNESCO lists this tiny village in the hills close to the Slovakian border as one of its World Heritage Sites because of its unique medieval structure and the age-old Palóc (ethnographic group indigenous to northern Hungary) cultural and handcrafting traditions still practiced today by its 400 inhabitants. The most famous of these traditions is its Easter celebration, when villagers dress in colorful embroidered costumes. During this time, thousands of visitors descend upon the village.

Pocket-size though it may be, Hollókő is authentically enchanting: old whitewashed houses, some of them built in the 17th century, cluster together on narrow cobblestone pathways; directly above them loom the hilltop ruins (restored in the mid-1990s) of a 13th-century castle. If you enter the village by car, which is the easiest way to get there unless you go on a bus tour from Budapest, you will probably be directed up to a parking area on the hillside a short walk from the village's historical center below; the village center is closed to most outside traffic. The parking fee, good for the entire day, is around 500 HUF. For information on Hollókő's Easter festivities and other events, contact the village's cultural foundation (*see* ⇨ Visitor Information *in* Northern Hungary Essentials).

Where to Stay & Eat

$–$$ ✕ **Muskátli Vendéglő.** Named for the bright red and pink flowers lining its windowsills, the Geranium Restaurant is a cozy little eatery on Hollókő's main street. Specialties include *palócgulyás*, a rich local goulash thick with chunks of pork, potatoes, carrots, and wax beans that makes for a good, quick meal. You can also get *nógrádi palócpecsenye* (pork cutlets bathed in mustard-garlic sauce). ☒ *Kossuth út 61* ☎ *32/379–262* ▭ *MC, V* ⊗ *Closed Mon. in Mar.–Dec. and Mon.–Wed. in Jan.–Feb.*

¢–$ ▦ **Kastély Szirák.** One of Hungary's best country-house hotels was built in 1748, on the foundations of a 13th-century knights' hostel, for Count József Teleki, an art patron who created a vast library and covered the main hall with frescoes depicting Ovid's *Metamorphoses*. A newer wing houses ground-floor rooms that, though lower-priced than those in the main building, were restored by 2006 with period furnishings. You can also go horseback riding, even if you're not a guest. The hotel lies about 35 km (22 mi) from Hollókő along Route 21 and then some lovely side roads; or, put another way, 90 km (56 mi) northeast of Budapest. A world away from the luxury of the hotel is the unassuming village center just down the road, where you may see local *Romas* (Gypsies) riding horse-drawn wagons. ☒ *Petőfi út 26, H-3044 Szirák* ▦▦ *32/485—300 or 32/485–285* ⊕ *www. kastelyszirak.hu* ⤳ *21 rooms, 4 suites* ⌂ *Restaurant, cable TV, tennis court, sauna, horseback riding, meeting rooms; no a/c* ▭ *AE, DC, MC, V* ⏁ *BP.*

EGER

80 km (50 mi) east of Budapest.

Surrounded by vineyards and with more than 175 of Hungary's historic monuments—a figure surpassed only by Budapest and Sopron—the picture-book baroque city of Eger is ripe for exploration. The city of 60,000, which lies in a fertile valley between the Mátra Mountains and their eastern neighbor, the Bükk Range, has borne witness to much history, heartbreak, and glory. It was settled quite early in the Hungarian conquest of the land, and it was one of five bishoprics created by King Stephen I when he Christianized the country almost a millennium ago.

In 1552 the city was attacked by the Turks, but the commander, István Dobó, and fewer than 2,000 men and women held out for 38 days against 80,000 Turkish soldiers and drove them away. One of Hungary's great legends tells of the women of Eger pouring hot pitch onto the heads of the Turks as they attempted to scale the castle walls (the event is depicted in a famous painting now in the National Gallery in Budapest). Despite such heroism, however, Eger fell to the Turks in 1596 and became one of the most important northern outposts of Muslim power until its reconquest in 1687.

Today, restored baroque and rococo buildings line Eger's cobblestone streets, making for excellent strolling and sightseeing. Dobó István utca, which

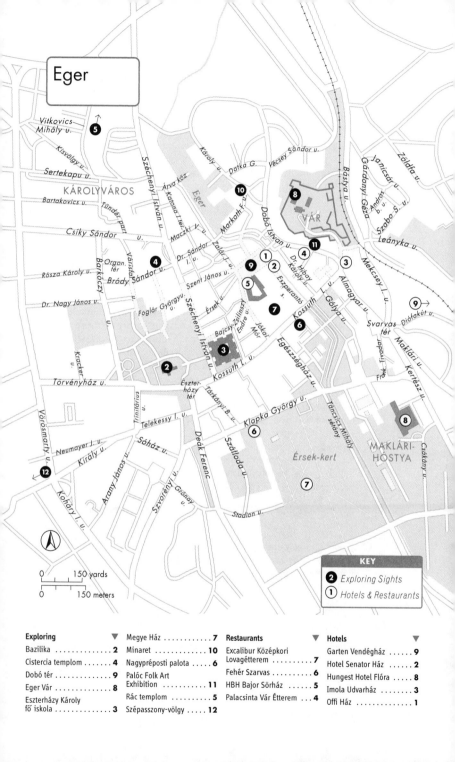

Eger

runs right under the castle walls, is not to be missed. The spacious, lovely city park and the adjacent outdoor swimming complex make cooling off (or warming up, in a thermal pool) aesthetically as well as physically soothing. Wherever you wander, make a point of peeking into open courtyards, where you may happen upon otherwise hidden architectural gems.

Numbers in the margin correspond to numbers on the Eger map.

★ **❷** The grand, neoclassical **Bazilika,** the second-largest cathedral in Hungary, was built in the center of town early in the 19th century. It is approached by a stunning stairway flanked by statues of Sts. Stephen, László, Peter, and Paul—the work of Italian sculptor Marco Casagrande, who also carved 22 biblical reliefs inside and outside the building. Ironically, perhaps, a few yards to the left of the main steps leading up to the Bazilika—on what appears to be its property—is a popular wine bar built into the high brick wall that flanks each side of the steps. From May 15 through October 15, organ recitals are held Monday through Saturday at 11:30 AM and Sunday at 12:45 PM. It's best to visit when no masses are taking place—from 9 until 6. ⊠ *Eszterházy tér* ☎ *36/515–725* 💲 *Free* ☉ *Daily 8–8.*

☾ ❸ The baroque building opposite the basilica, which covers the entire block, is a former lyceum, now the **Eszterházy Károly főiskola** (Károly Eszterházy Teachers College). The handsome library on the second floor has a fine trompe-l'oeil ceiling fresco that provides an intoxicating illusion of depth. The fifth floor houses an observatory, now an astronomical museum: here you'll find a horizontal sundial with a tiny gold cannon, which, when filled with gunpowder, used to let out a burst at exactly high noon. Also here, the noonday sun, shining through a tiny aperture, makes a palm-size silvery spot on the meridian line on the marble floor. Climb higher to the grand finale, a "Specula Periscope," or Camera Obscura, on the tenth floor: in a darkened room, a man manipulates three rods of a periscope—in operation since 1776—to project panoramic views of Eger onto a round table. Children squeal with delight as real people and cars hurry and scurry across the table like hyperactive Legos. Tickets can be purchased at the porter's office as you enter. ⊠ *Eszterházy tér 1* ☎ *36/520–400* 💲 *Library 500 HUF, astronomical museum and camera obscura 600 HUF* ☉ *Apr.–Sept., Tues.–Sun. 9:30–3:30; Oct.–Mar., weekends 9:30–1:30.*

❹ Eger's rococo **Cistercia templom** (Cistercian Church) was built during the first half of the 18th century. A splendid statue of St. Francis Borgia kneeling beneath Christ on the cross dominates the main altar, which dates to 1770. The church can be visited only during mass; other times it can be viewed only through the locked gate. ⊠ *Széchenyi utca 15* ☎ *36/511–240* 💲 *Free* ☉ *Mass weekdays at 7:15 and 8 AM, Sun. at 8 and 10 AM and 7 PM.*

❺ The light, lovely, dove-gray 18th-century **Rác templom** (Serbian Orthodox Church) contains more than 100 icon paintings on wood that look as though they were fashioned from gold and marble. The church sits on a hilltop north of the city center. ⊠ *Vitkovits utca 30* ☎ *36/320–129* 💲 *300 HUF* ☉ *Tues.–Sun. 10–4, but often opens earlier and closes later.*

6 The **Nagypréposti palota** (Provost's House) is a small rococo palace still considered one of Hungary's finest mansions, despite abuse by the Red Army (soldiers ruined several frescoes by heating the building with oil). The building now serves as the European headquarters of the International Committee of Historic Towns (ICOMOS). Alas, it is not open to the public. ✉ *Kossuth Lajos utca 4.*

12

During a brief stay in Eger (1758–61), German artist Henrik Fazola graced many buildings with his work, but none so exquisitely as the wrought-iron twin gates that, facing each other just inside the entryway of the **Megye Ház** (County Council Hall), frame the inner entrances to the building's two wings. Sent to Paris in 1889 for the international exposition, the richly ornamented, mirror-image gates—which have not only numerous flowers and leaves but clusters of grapes and a stork with a snake in its beak—won a gold medal 130 years after their creation. On the wall to the right of the building's street entrance, a sign indicates the level of floodwaters during the flooding of the Eger stream on August 31, 1878. Similar signs can be seen throughout this area of the city. ✉ *Kossuth Lajos utca 9* ☉ *Weekdays 9–5, often later.*

7

> **WORD OF MOUTH**
>
> "Eger, aside from being a wonderful baroque city has the best ruby dry reds I've had. Called Bikaver (Bull's Blood), so far it's beaten any of the Chianti's I've tried as well as samples I've had from other regions. Of course, that's a taste thing, but what a great place for tasting. −clifton

8 **Eger Vár** (Eger Castle) was built after the devastating Tatar invasion of 1241–42. When Béla IV returned from exile in Italy, he ordered the erection of mighty fortresses like those he had seen in the West. Within the castle walls an imposing Romanesque cathedral was built and then, during the 15th century, rebuilt in Gothic style; today only its foundations remain. Inside the foundation area, a statue of Szent István (St. Stephen), erected in 1900, looks out benignly over the city. Nearby are catacombs that were built in the second half of the 16th century by Italian engineers. By racing back and forth through this labyrinth of underground tunnels and appearing at various ends of the castle, the hundreds of defenders tricked the attacking Turks into thinking there were thousands of them. The Gothic-style **Püspök Ház** (Bishop's House) contains the castle history museum and, in the basement, a numismatics museum where coins can be minted and certified (in English). Also here are an art gallery displaying Italian and Dutch Renaissance works; a prison exhibit, near the main entrance; and a wax museum, depicting characters from the Hungarian historical novel *Eclipse of the Crescent Moon,* about Hungary's final expulsion of the Turks. ⚠ **Videotaping and picture-taking are not allowed inside the museums, but are OK (at no charge) on the castle grounds.** ✉ *Dózsa György tér* ☎ *36/312–744* ⊕ *www.egrivar.hu* 🎫 *Castle with castle history museum, art gallery, and prison exhibit 1,000 HUF; numismatics museum 300 HUF; wax museum 350 HUF; castle grounds only 400 HUF* ☉ *Castle grounds Apr.–Oct., daily 6 AM–8 PM; Nov.–Mar., daily 6–5. Museums Apr.–Sept., Tues.–Sun. 9–5; Oct.–Mar., Tues.–Sun.*

Fodor'sChoice ★

9–3. Prison exhibit and catacombs Apr.–Sept., Tues.–Sun. 9–5 (catacombs remain open on Mon.). Wax museum daily 9–6.

⑨ Downtown, picturesque **Dobó tér** is marked by two intensely animated statues produced in the early 20th century by a father and son: *Dobó the Defender* is by Alajos Stróbl, and the sculpture of a Magyar battling two Turks is by Stróbl's son, Zsigmond Kisfaludi-Stróbl.

Dobó tér's famous statues flank the pale-pink **Minorita templom** (Minorite Church; ☎ 36/516–613), which with its twin spires and finely carved pulpit, pews, and organ loft is considered one of the finest baroque churches in Central Europe. It's open daily from 10 to 6.

> ## WHICH WINES?
>
> Though Eger has long been most famous for a dry, fiery red that mixes at least three of nine grapes, Bikavér (Bull's Blood), this is also a great region for the likewise red, peppery kékfrankos (aka Blaufränkisch), not to mention three whites in particular: the sweet királyleánka (muscat-like bouquet with full body and light acidity), muscat ottonel, and, yes, chardonnay.

Ⓒ The **Kisvonat**, a miniature train that actually runs on wheels, leaves from Dobó tér every hour on the hour for an approximately 40-minute tour of Eger's historical sights. ⊠ *Dobó tér* ☎ *34/487–381 or 20/388–6241* 🎫 *500 HUF* ☉ *Apr.–Oct. and late Dec.–early Jan., daily 9–5 or later.*

⑩ A bridge over the Eger stream—it's too small to be classified as a river—leads to an early-17th-century Turkish **minaret,** from the top of which Muslims were called to prayer. After the Turks were driven out of Hungary in the late 1600s, an effort was made to topple the minaret using no fewer than 400 oxen. The venture failed, and it became Europe's northernmost surviving Turkish structure. ⊠ *Knézich K. utca* ☎ *36/410–233 or 70/202–4353* 🎫 *200 HUF* ☉ *Apr.–Oct., daily 10–6.*

⑪ In a tranquil courtyard right under the castle wall, the **Palóc Folk Art Exhibition** is a charming, three-room museum displaying traditional carvings, embroidery, folk costumes, furniture, pillows, and pottery of the Palóc region. ⚠ **You must pay a fee to use your camera and a larger one to use your video camera.** ⊠ *Dobó Istvan utca 12* ☎ *36/312–744* 🎫 *200 HUF; photography fee 1,000 HUF per camera; video fee 2,000 HUF per camera* ☉ *Apr. 15–Sept., Tues.–Sun. 9–5.*

Eger wine is renowned beyond Hungary. The best-known variety is *Egri Bikavér* (Bull's Blood of Eger), a full-bodied red wine. Other outstanding vintages are the Medoc Noir, a dark red dessert wine; Leányka, a delightful dry white; and the sweeter white Muskotály. The place to sample them is the **⑫ Szépasszony-völgy,** a vineyard area on the southwestern edge of Eger's city limits. More than 200 small wine cellars (some of them literally holes-in-the-wall) stand open and inviting in warm weather, and a few are open in winter, too. You may be given a tour of the cellar, and wines will be tapped from the barrel into your glass by the vintners themselves at the tiniest cost (but it's prudent to inquire politely how much it will cost before imbibing).

12

OFF THE
BEATEN
PATH
SZILVÁSVÁRAD – About 25 km (16 mi) from Eger up into the Bükk Mountains bring you to this village, one of Hungary's most important equestrian centers. For more than 500 years the white Lipizzaner horses have been bred here, and every year on a weekend in early September they prance and pose in the Lipicai Lovasfesztivál, an international carriage-driving competition held in the equestrian stadium. At other times you can see them grazing in the village fields.

The proud history of the Lipizzaner horses is covered at the **Lipicai Múzeum** (Lipizzaner Museum; ⊠ Park utca 8 ☎ 36/564–400). Admission is 400 HUF, and the museum is open from April through October, daily except Wednesday from 9 to noon and 1 to 4. Szilvásvárad is also a popular base for hiking and bicycling through the surrounding gentle green hills of Bükk National Park.

Where to Stay & Eat

\$\$–\$\$\$ ✗**Excalibur Középkori Lovagétterem.** Eger's medieval dining rage is well worth a try—if not necessarily for the slightly gimmicky atmosphere complete with waiters in knightly costumes, why then for the hearty fare and an excuse to visit the lovely city park. With candlelit rustic wooden tables, benches, chairs, and plates, the spacious dining room and outdoor (albeit nonmedieval) seating area are, on the whole, a pleasant setting in which to delight in dishes with colorful names both in Hungarian and English—from "Sir Galahad's Festive Feast" (charcoal-grilled pig leg with garlic) to "crispy roast duck," "crispy roast pig legs," and so forth. Dinner only from Monday to Thursday. ⚠ There's an unabashedly modern restaurant in the same building that you might easily enter by mistake (entrance to the left; Excalibur's is to the right), whose loud pop music might undermine the medieval magic a tad. ⊠ *Érsekkert 1, in city park* ☎ *36/427–754* ▤ *AE, MC, V.*

★ **\$\$–\$\$\$** ✗ **Fehér Szarvas.** The name of this homey rustic cellar, a longtime Eger dining landmark, means "white stag," and game is the uncontested specialty. Favorites include venison fillet served in a pan sizzling with goose liver and herb butter; wild boar with juniper berries in red wine sauce; rabbit (presumably not wild) spiced with thyme; and knuckle of lamb (no, not wild either) with mushroom-bacon sweetbreads. The many antlers, skulls, skins, and mounted birds hanging from rafters and walls—not to mention the two little stuffed goats by the entrance—make the inn look like Archduke Franz Ferdinand's trophy room. ⊠ *Klapka György utca 8* ☎ *36/411–129* ▤ *AE, MC, V.*

\$–\$\$ ✗ **HBH Bajor Sörház.** For substantial Hungarian (and, it seems, Bavarian) fare, it's impossible to beat the popular HBH Bavarian Beer Tavern, which has a great location on Dobó tér. The cuisine ranges from traditional Hungarian fare such as veal paprikash to Bavarian-style knuckle of ham. Any of these will go down smoothly with a glass of Bull's Blood—or perhaps a Munich Hofbräuhaus, the beer that gives the restaurant its initials. ⊠*Bajcsy Zsilinszky utca 19, at Dobó tér* ☎ *36/515–516* ▤ *AE, MC, V.*

\$ ✗ **Palacsinta Vár Étterem.** The Palacsinta Castle Restaurant is *the* place to have your fill, and how, of Hungary's famous rolled-up pancake, the *palacsinta*. In this hip little cellar establishment (pleasantly cool on a hot summer day), adorned with funky wall art from Dalí prints to a display of cigarette packs to a stamp collection (and an aquarium full of live fish), you can choose from any of more than two dozen varieties, from the "Boss's Favorite"—a potato-flour palacsinta filled with (pork) knuckle ragout, beans, cabbage, and sour cream—to vegetarian (indeed, egg-free) sorts including the "Spring Pancake" (ewe cheese with dill and chives), to traditional, sweet, jam-filled palacsintas. Servings are lavish, prices quite reasonable. ■ TIP→ **If you order a meat- or vegetable-filled palacsinta, you might ask them to take it easy on the salt.** ⊠ *Dobó utca 9* ☎ *36/413–980* ⊟ *AE, DC, MC, V.*

$ 🏨 **Hungest Hotel Flóra.** Fully refurbished in 1999, Eger's largest hotel is right next to the city's spacious Strandfürdő (open-air baths) and roughly across the street from the city's beautiful indoor swimming complex, a few blocks from the main square. Though it's a bit removed from the charm of Eger's historic city center and its more intimate, smaller accommodations, the hotel is a good choice if you prefer a big, bright, modern, full-service lodging. Besides, it has a pleasant, somewhat alpine-like exterior that ameliorates its otherwise chain-hotel nature. Ask for a room facing the parklike open-air baths. Though the hotel also has its own spa facilities, guests have free access to the public baths as well. ⊠ *Fürdő utca 5, H-3300* ☎ *36/320–211 or 36/513–300* 🖶 *36/320–815* ⊕ *www. hunguesthotels.hu* 🛏 *124 double rooms, 48 singles, 4 suites* △ *Restaurant, minibars, cable TV, exercise equipment, thermal bath, sauna, meeting rooms; no a/c in some rooms* ⊟ *AE, DC, MC, V* ⦿ *BP.*

★ **$** 🏨 **Imola Udvarház.** Apartments at the most upmarket small hotel in Eger are pricey for this town, but the location, facilities, and pleasant, spacious self-catering quarters justify the tariff. Imola Udvarház practically sits on the steps up to the castle, and the oak- and wicker-furnished apartments are spotless yet homey; the smaller ones have balconies, and some apartments have nice views of the main square. The hotel restaurant offers a hundred different wines. Breakfast is extra. ⊠ *Dózsa György tér 4, H-3300* 🖶 *36/516–180* ⊕ *www.imolanet.hu* 🛏 *6 apartments* △ *Restaurant, café, kitchens, minibars, cable TV, in-room data ports, bar, meeting room, parking (fee)* ⊟ *AE, DC, MC, V* ⦿ *EP.*

★ ¢ 🏨 **Garten Vendégház.** This informal, family-run pension is named after its splendorous garden full of lilacs, geraniums, and acacias. It's on top of a rural hill, a 15-minute walk from Eger's main square. Rooms are furnished in pine and have a refreshing, piney fragrance in consequence; some have kitchenettes. The suite, with an eat-in kitchen, is great for families. The genuinely friendly owners, Olga and Sanyi, can arrange tennis at the neighboring courts. If the main house is full, guests can be lodged in a separate, newer, slightly less atmospheric but likewise pine-scented building in a garden a few blocks away, a bit closer to the town center. Breakfast is 800 HUF extra. ⊠ *Legányi utca 6, H-3300* ☎ *36/ 420–371* ⊕ *www.gartenvendeghaz.hu* 🛏 *10 rooms, 1 suite* △ *Some kitchens, cable TV; no a/c, no room phones* ⊟ *No credit cards* ⦿ *EP.*

¢ 🏨 **Hotel Senator Ház.** This little inn, a lovely 18th-century town house, sits on Eger's main square. Whimsical paintings by Budapest artist András Győrffy hang in all the guest rooms, which are decidedly more modern than the small, historical-bric-a-brac-filled lobby might have you believe and are tastefully decorated in pale tans and whites. Rooms 14 and 15 have the nicest views of the main square; reserve well ahead. ⊠ *Dobó tér 11, H-3300* ☎ *36/320–466* 🖶 *36/411–711* ⊕ *www.*

Fodor's Choice
★

hotels.hu/senatorhaz ⏎ *11 rooms* ⛶ *Restaurant, minibars, cable TV, free parking* ☰ *MC, V* ⦿| *BP.*

★ ¢ ▦ **Offi Ház.** Picturesque Dobó tér has not one but two picturesque inns. With a yellow-brick exterior and suites tastefully furnished with reproduction furniture, the Offi has a silver-service restaurant, decorated with a series of sugar sculptures, including a full-size grandfather clock that actually keeps the correct time. Downstairs you can eat a pub lunch in a somewhat smoky, more basic dining room. The difficult-to-find hotel entrance is through its downstairs restaurant, the Arany Oroszlán (Golden Lion). ⊠ *Dobó tér 5, H-3300* ☎☎ *36/518–210 or 36/518–211* ⊕ *www.offihaz.hu* ⏎ *3 rooms, 2 suites* ⛶ *2 restaurants, cable TV, minibars* ☰ *AE, DC, MC, V* ⦿| *BP.*

Festivals & Nightlife

Festivals

From June to mid-September live bands sometimes play folk music for free out on Kis Dobó tér, part of Eger's main square.

Agria Nyári Játékok (Agria Summer Festival). The festival, which runs from July to early September, includes folk-dance and theater performances as well as concerts of everything from Renaissance music to jazz to laser karaoke. Performances are held in various locations.

Szüreti Napok Egerben (Eger Harvest Festival). In early September, the three- to four-day festival celebrates the grape harvest with a traditional harvest parade through the town center, ample wine tastings in the main squares, appearances by the crowned Wine Queen, and an outdoor Harvest Ball on Dobó tér.

Ünnepi Hetek a Barokk Egerben (Festival Weeks in Baroque Eger). For two weeks every summer, beginning around late July, a cultural festival of classical concerts, dance programs, and more takes place in Eger's venues and streets and squares.

Nightlife

Hippolit Club & Restaurant. Eger's most popular upscale dance club is said to be a favorite, particularly among twenty- and thirty-something revelers. The dance floor is open on Friday and Saturday from midnight to 4 AM, while the adjoining restaurant, which serves a wide range of traditional fare, is open 7 days a week until midnight. It is conveniently located a couple of blocks from Dobó tér and right next door to Eger's outdoor food market. Just upstairs is a popular restaurant. ⊠ *Katona tér 2* ☎ *36/412–452.*

Old Jack's Pub. The popular English-style pub—with a choice little selection of food on hand, too, from Norwegian pike-perch and asparagus with Parmesan cheese—is in a bright red, house-like building just outside the center of town. ⊠ *Rákóczi út 28* ☎ *36/425–050.*

Sports & the Outdoors

Bicycling

The forested hills of Bükk National Park around the village of Szilvásvárad, north of Eger, comprise some of the country's most popular mountain-biking terrain.

Mountain Bike Kölcsönző. Rentals, maps, route advice, and tour guides are available at Csaba Tarnai's bike shop. Mountain bikes are available for rental at the Szilvásvárad shop at 900 HUF per hour, 1,200 HUF for 2 hours, and 200 HUF more for each additional hour up to 5 hours; or 2,000 HUF for 6–24 hours. Tarnai's shop in Eger rents hybrids, too. ⊠ *Szalajka-völgy út, Szilvásvárad, at entrance to Bükk National Park in the Szalajka Valley* ☎ *30/335-2695* ⊠ *Ege*zségház utca 11, Eger.

Hiking

Bükk National Park, just north of Eger, has plenty of well-marked, well-used trails. The most popular excursions begin in the village of Szilvásvárad. The Tourinform in Eger (*see* ⇨ Visitor Information *in* Northern Hungary Essentials) can provide a hiking map and suggest routes according to level of difficulty and duration.

Horseback Riding

A famous breeding center of the prized white Lipizzaner horses, the village of Szilvásvárad is the heart of the region's horse culture, but you needn't stray far from the heart of Eger to ride horses.

Állami Ménesgazdaság. At the State Stud Farm you can not only have a look at the approximately 250 Lipizzaner studs, but if you shell out 2,000 HUF or more, you can go on carriage rides, learn how to drive a carriage yourself, and watch special Lipizzaner shows. ⊠ *Egri utca 16, Szilvásvárad* ☎ *36/564-400.*

Mátyus Udvarház. This convenient stable can accommodate your every equestrian need. Taking the reins into your own hands in the yard for 30 minutes costs around 2,000 HUF; if an instructor guides the horse it's more like 2,300 HUF; and a ride a bit farther out (holding your own reins) with a guide is about 4,000 HUF per hour. Kids can ride a pony for approximately 200 HUF per short round. A one-hour carriage ride for up to five people costs some 6,000 HUF. ⊠ *Off Noszvaji út (about 2 km [1.5 mi] outside of downtown Eger in a conspicuously marked location on the right-hand side of the road to the town of Noszvaj)* ☎ *36/517-937 or 06-20/957-0806.*

Swimming

Termál fürdő. Eger's thermal baths are in a vast, shaded, lovely park in the center of town. You can pick where to plunge from among six outdoor pools of varying sizes, temperatures,

---

TURKISH DELIGHTS

After their 1596 seige of Eger, the Turks stayed 91 years, and although their departure was no doubt welcomed by many Hungarians, they did leave behind two public baths. One, an attractive cupola-crowned edifice—on aptly named Fürdő utca (Bath Street), right beside the city's lovely, outdoor Termál fürdő thermal bath and swimming sports complex—presently serves patients with prescriptions, but is due for thorough restoration. It should be fully accessible to the public at large from late 2008. The other, the Valide Sultana Bath, which was a steam bath, is an archaeological site—on Dózsa György tér across from the Imola Udvarház hotel—but it, too, is set for complete restoration by 2008 or not long thereafter.

and curative powers. All-day admission costs 950 HUF; it costs 600 HUF extra for two hours in the *élmény fürdő* (adventure baths), a combination open-air and closed facility that includes a Jacuzzi, underwater massage, and even a waterfall. That's not to mention the Wellness House, whose Jacuzzi, sauna, solarium, and massages (extra charge) can be yours for 950 HUF. The baths are open May–September on weekdays 6 AM–8 AM and 8:30 AM–7:30 PM, and weekends 8 AM–6 PM; the Wellness House, daily 10–6. For a 1,000 HUF deposit you get a locker key (with your locker number on it). ⊠ *Petőfi Sándor tér 2* ☎ *36/411–699 or 36/314–142.*

> **WORD OF MOUTH**
>
> "I've been to a lot of caves; it is really something I like to do. But I've never seen caves like this. First of all, the entire cave was still very much 'alive.' Calcified water was dripping everywhere, and I mean everywhere. . . . This was a spooky cave."   –alyssamma

Shopping

Bornivó. This is the place to stop for a decent variety of local and national wines, including a choice selection of reds, whites, and rosés from more than 12 of Eger's best wineries and some terrific wines from the Tokaj and Villány regions. It's one storefront down from the Dobós Cukrászda café. ⊠ *Széchényi utca 8* ☎ *36/517–221.*

Egri Galéria. In this bright, spacious gallery you'll find works by contemporary artists—paintings, ceramics, blown glass, and more—from all over Hungary. ⊠ *Érsek utca 8.*

AGGTELEK NATIONAL PARK

⓭ *75 km (47 mi) north of Eger, 155 km (97 mi) northeast of Budapest via the motorway and secondary roads, 200 km (125 mi) from Budapest via the motorway and major roads.*

One of the most extensive cave systems in Europe lies at Aggtelek, right on the Slovak border. Containing the largest stalactite system in Europe, the largest of the caves, Baradla, is 24 km (15 mi) long, extending well into Slovakia; its stalactite and stalagmite formations are of extraordinary size—some more than 49 feet high. In one of the chambers of the cave is a 600-seat concert hall, where classical concerts are held every summer. When the lights are left off for a brief period—and they will be during a tour—you experience the purest darkness there is; try holding your hand up to your face. No matter how hard you strain, you won't see it.

There are three entrances to Baradla Cave: in the town of Aggtelek, at Vörös-tó (Red Lake), and in the village of Jósvafő. Guided tours vary in length and difficulty, from the short, one-hour walks beginning at either Aggtelek or Jósvafő to the five- to eight-hour, 7-km (4½-mi) exploration from Aggtelek that ends at Jósvafő. One-hour tours are conducted several times daily.

The two-hour tour, which leaves from Jósvafő, is considered the best. The group meets at the Jósvafő ticket office, then takes a public bus (fare covered by tour admission) to the Vörös-tó entrance, from which you make your way back to Jósvafő underground.

Although all tours are conducted in Hungarian, written English translations are available at the ticket offices. Requests for the long (five- to eight-hour) tour must be sent in writing to the National Park headquarters at least two weeks ahead of time, so the unmaintained sections can be rigged with proper lighting; a minimum of five adults must sign up for the long tour for it to be conducted. The caves are open year-round—they maintain a constant temperature, regardless of the weather. Keep in mind that it's chilly and damp underground—bring a sweater or light jacket and wear shoes with good traction. Tickets available at one of three ticket offices: in Aggtelek, Jóvafő, or at the Vörös-tó entrance, midway between the Aggtelek and Jósvafő (about 5 km [3 mi] from each) in a conspicuously marked location along a forested road (no street address or phone for this ticket office as of this writing). Those traveling by bus should note that the bus will stop at the Vörös-tó entrance if signaled to do so. It's not usually necessary to make tour reservations in advance, but you should call to confirm exact tour times, particularly if you are coming all the way from Budapest. ⊠ *Baradla oldal 1, Aggtelek* 🖀 *48/503–003* ⊕ *www.anp.hu* ✉ *Tengerszem oldal 3, Jósvafő* 🖀 *48/506–009* ✍ *Short tours 1,000 HUF–1,500 HUF, long tours 4,000 HUF–6,000 HUF per person (5 to 10 persons minimum)* ☉ *Mid-Apr.–Sept., daily 10–6; Oct.–mid-Apr., daily 10–4; the last tour leaves 1 hr before closing.*

TOKAJ

 117 km (73 mi) east of Eger, 187 km (123 mi) northeast of Budapest.

This enchanting village is the center of Hungary's most famous wine region. It's home to the legendary Aszú wine, a dessert wine made from grapes allowed to shrivel on the vine. Aszú is produced to varying degrees of sweetness, based on how many bushels of sweet grape paste are added to the wine essence, the already highly sweet juice first pressed from them; the scale goes from two *puttonyos* (bushels) to nectar-rich six puttonyos.

The region's famed wines, dubbed (allegedly by Louis XV) the "wine of kings and king of wines," are typically golden yellow with slightly brownish tints and an almost oily texture. They've been admired outside of Hungary since Polish merchants first became hooked in the Middle Ages. In 1562, after a few sips of wine from the nearby village of Tállya, Pope Pius IV is said to have declared, "*Summum pontificem talia vina decent*" ("These wines are fit for a pope"). Other countries—France, Germany, and Russia included—have tried without much success to produce the wine from Tokaj grapes. (The secret apparently lies in the combination of volcanic soil and climate.) Still, this hasn't kept them from occasionally marketing their own "Tokaj" brands, something that riles Hungarians no end. The branding of Tokaj wines was a major issue for Hungary as the country negotiated its entry into the EU in 2004.

The surrounding countryside is beautiful, especially in October, when the grapes hang from the vines in thick clusters. Before or after descending into the wine cellars for some epic tasting, be sure to pause while the bells toll at the lovely baroque Roman Catholic church (1770) on the main square and wend your way along some of the narrow side streets winding up into the vineyard-covered hills: views of the red-tile roofs and sloping vineyards are like sweet Aszú for the eyes. If you can still focus after a round of wine tasting, be sure to look up at the top of lamp-posts and chimneys, where giant white storks preside over the village from their big bushy nests. They usually return here to their nests in late April or May after wintering in warmer climes.

The third floor of the **Tokaj Múzeum** (Tokaj Museum), housed in a late-18th-century building, displays objects connected with the history of wine production in the region—including, among other things, an impressive collection of Tokaj wine and brandy bottles from the 18th and 19th centuries and an exhibit of "fake Tokaj" bottles from various countries. There's also a film room where you can watch a video (in English or Hungarian) about Tokaj wine. If you could use a break from Tokaj's ubiquitous wine theme, however, you'll also find exhibits of ecclesiastical art and the history of the country. The museum's tranquil, flowery garden is a soothing place to take a breather, and the second floor hosts a summer concert series. ⌂ *Bethlen Gábor utca 7* ☎ *47/352–636* 🖙 *400 HUF* ☉ *Tues.–Sun. 11–4.*

NEED A BREAK?

Halász Cukrászda (⌂ Rákóczi Ferenc út 16), also known as the Café Halász (Fisherman's Café), is a small but pleasant place to stop for coffee and a pastry before or after heading into the city center; for it is situated toward the head of the main street. The decent selection of pastries includes, notably, a scrumptious Eszterházy cake. Order at the counter.

Fodor's Choice
★

Tokaj's most famous wine cellar, the more than 500-year-old **Rákóczi-pince** (Rákóczi Cellar), is also Europe's largest, comprising some 1½ km (1 mi) of branching tunnels extending into the hills (today, about 1,312 feet are still in use). It was here that King János Szapolyai was elected by the Hungarian Diet in 1526—proof positive that Tokaj really is the "wine of kings." You can sample Tokaj's famed wines and purchase bottles of your favorites for the road (most major credit cards are accepted). Standard cellar tours, which include tasting of six different wines and some *pogácsa* (salty biscuits) are usually given every hour on the hour (in English at no extra cost—but best to confirm tours 24 hours in advance), and English-language pamphlets are also available. Off-season tours are by reservation only (you need to

WHICH WINES?

White, to be sure, but you're far from the world of chardonnay. In addition to the region's superlative dessert wines (Aszú) made from desiccated, botrytized grapes, you might well find yourself tasting one of its hallmark table wines made from the grapes that together constitute Aszú: the fiery, floral furmint or the aromatic, spicy, acidic hárslevelű.

make the arrangement at least a week in advance), at varying costs, depending on the size of the group. ⊠ *Kossuth tér 15* 🕾 *47/352–408* 🖃 *2,200 HUF* ⊙ *Mid-Mar.–early Oct., daily 10–6, sometimes later; early Oct.–mid-Mar., by reservation only.*

The Várhelyi family offers wine tastings in the cool, damp cellar of their 16th-century house, called **Hímesudvar.** After the initial tasting, you can purchase bottles of your favorite wines and continue imbibing in their pleasant garden. A standard sampling includes six different wines. If you don't see anyone on arriving, don't hesitate to ring the bell. ⊠ *Bem út 2* 🕾 *47/352–416* 🖃 *2,000 HUF and up* ⊙ *Daily 10–9.*

Where to Stay & Eat

The local Tourinform office (*see* ⇨ Visitor Information *in* Northern Hungary Essentials) can book you a room in a private home as well as in other hotels and pensions in the area. Private rooms in the few quiet streets right behind the village center, for example, range between 6,000 HUF and 9,000 HUF—generally less than those in the town's main hotels (whose prices are quite reasonable, to be fair).

$$–$$$
Fodor'sChoice
★
✕ **Ős Kaján.** Getting to one of Hungary's best little restaurants without a car is a pain in the neck—but if you have a car and you're in the Tokaj area, don't pass up the opportunity. A friendly French-turned-Hungarian (but also English-speaking) couple, Pascal Leeman and wife Anne Roy, have created a homey atmosphere indeed in several rooms of a former *parasztház* (peasant house) that you can wander through until you find one whose particular style of furniture, art, and bric-a-brac makes you feel right at home. The cuisine is Hungarian, but uniquely so: an on-site garden provides a splendorous mix of herbs and fruits to lend the cuisine a special touch, and here, at least, you can be pretty confident that the raw ingredients are not mass-produced across the EU. The small menu, which varies by season, features everything from fish and game to poultry, lamb, and duck. ■ TIP➔ **Every Saturday night for about six summer weeks the restaurant hosts outdoor concerts (1,500 HUF) by some of Hungary's best jazz, blues, and folk musicians.** By car from Tokaj, the drive takes 20–25 minutes. ⊠ *Kossuth utca 14–16, Tolcsva* 🕾 *47/384–195* ✎ *Reservations essential* ▤ *AE, MC, V* ⊙ *Closed Mon. and Feb. 20–Dec. 20.*

$$
Fodor'sChoice
★
✕🏨 **Count Degenfeld Castle Hotel.** With perhaps the exception of fake-marble plastic trash cans in the bathrooms, not a forint was spared in turning this once-neglected countryside mansion into one of Hungary's most elegant luxury hotels and best bargains. Countess Maria Degenfeld's personal, meticulous touch shows in every nook and cranny. Immaculate rooms have period Italian, cherry-wood furnishings, Chagall prints adorn walls, beds are covered with hypoallergenic duvets, and silky red curtains carefully hide radiators. Rooms in the front have terraces that overlook the first-floor patio restaurant and the gardens. The first-floor salon has not only Venetian chandeliers but also one of two original paintings depicting Emperor Francis Joseph with Sissi (Elizabeth), Queen of Hungary, as newlyweds. The Gróf Degenfeld ($–$$$), on the small square in the palace, is Tokaj's most elegant restaurant. The lavish interior tastefully evokes a Tokaj of centuries past—though some-

CLOSE UP

A Noble Line and a Noble Wine

12

THERE ARE ALMOST TOO MANY Degenfeld counts and countesses to count, but one thing is certain: Hungary—and Tokaj in particular—wouldn't be quite the same without this legendary family. Originally from Switzerland, the Degenfelds fled in AD 850 when Leonárd Degenfeld murdered the Bishop of Lausanne. Over the next several hundred years the family's various branches established themselves in a territory ranging from present-day Germany to Transylvania. In present-day Hungary, one Degenfeld base was Szirák, where in the 19th century the family purchased an imposing country house from the Teleki family. (This is today a hotel, the Kastély Szirák.) The other base was Tokaj.

In 2000 Count Sándor Degenfeld came to Tokaj to mark the opening of the onetime family palace (the Degenfeld Palota) as Tokaj's finest restaurant. He remarked that, although his great-great-grandparents had come from German-speaking lands, the Degenfelds became true Hungarian patriots and had done much to establish Tokaj's international reputation. Indeed, back in 1857 Count Imre Degenfeld helped establish a prominent school for vintners in the family mansion in Tarczal. This branch of the family fled back to Germany from Hungary at the end of World War II. Under communism, the building housed a state-run agricultural cooperative and fell into disrepair. However, with a huge investment from the family—and under the watchful eye of Countess Maria Degenfeld, who lives near Munich—it reopened in 2003 as the lavish Count Degenfeld Castle Hotel. The house's vineyard has since been re-establishing itself as a producer of some of the Tokaj region's finest wines.

---

times with pop music in the background. A multicourse meal might include an appetizer of rose hip–flavored wild boar carpaccio with apple slices and beetroot salad, and a main course of pike-perch fried with goat cheese on a potato patty with grape-and-celery sauce. Reservations are necessary for the restaurant. ⊠ *Terézia kert 9, Tarczal 3915* 🖃 *47/580–400 for hotel, 47/552–202 for restaurant* 🖃 *47/580–401* ⊕ *www.hotelgrofdegenfeld.hu* ⭢ *20 rooms, 1 suite* ⌂ *Restaurant, minibars, cable TV, 2 tennis courts, pool, gym, hot tub, sauna, wine bar, meeting room, some pets allowed* ⊟ *AE, MC, V* ⧧ *BP.*

¢ ✕⌦ **Millennium Hotel.** One of many hotels and restaurants around Hungary named after the 1,000th anniversary of Hungarian statehood opened in the millennium year 2000. You can't miss its round, bastionlike tower as you enter Tokaj on the main street from the train station. Rooms are bright and spacious, offering two simple beds and bathrooms with showers only. Some rooms afford a view of the Tisza River, although (unlike the older, more worn-looking Hotel Tokaj down the road) none have terraces. The suite, with a plush velvety sofa and armchairs to sink into as well as a lovely bathtub, is in the bastion. Its decent little restaurant ($–$$) specializes in poultry and game dishes. ⊠ *Bajcsy-Zs. út 34, H-3910* 🖃 *47/352–247* 🖃🖃 *47/552–091* ⊕ *www.tokajmillennium.hu* ⭢ *14 double* *rooms, 4 suites ⌂ Restaurant, café, cable TV, minibars, Jacuzzi, massage, sauna, meeting room, free parking; no a/c ⊟ AE, DC, MC, V ⦿ EP.*

★ ¢ ☒ **Toldi Fogadó.** This historic building with a pleasantly rustic interior is right in the town center. A new, more modern-looking wing opened in 2003, adding 14 rooms plus a swimming pool with an opening roof. The rooms are clean and spacious, with pictures of Tokaj above the beds. Unlike the 6 rooms in the older wing, which have full baths, the new rooms have showers only—but the new wing is no-smoking. ⊠ *Hajdú köz 2, H-3910* ☎☎ *47/353–403* ☏ *47/353–402* ⊕ *www.toldifogado. hu* ➲ *20 rooms ⌂ Restaurant, minibars, cable TV, pool, Jacuzzi, sauna* ⊟ *AE, DC, MC, V* ⦿ *BP.*

NORTHERN HUNGARY ESSENTIALS

BUS TRAVEL

Most buses to northern Hungary depart from Budapest's Stadion station, a fairly modern, presentable-looking transport hub. Getting to Eger by bus is even easier than it is by train: beginning around 6:25 AM and then leaving every 30 to 45 minutes until evening, buses depart from the Stadion station and take about two hours to reach Eger. The Eger–Budapest runs follow a similar schedule, but the last bus of the day leaves before 7 PM on weekdays and Saturday, around 8 PM on Sunday. As for Tokaj, going by bus is a bit of a hassle (relatively time-consuming and sometimes requiring more than one transfer); if you're not driving, go by train (one transfer, in Miskolc).

Getting to Aggtelek by bus from Budapest takes nearly five hours, but service begins around 6 AM or shortly after from Budapest's Stadion station; as long as you get a seat, it's a comfortable ride. That said, you will have just five hours to spend there, at most, as the last bus back to Budapest leaves shortly after 4 PM (an earlier bus leaves around 3 PM), though it somehow manages to reach Budapest in one hour less time than it takes to get to Aggtelek. If you're visiting Eger, though, Aggtelek is a much easier day-trip: a bus leaves around 8:45 AM and gets to Aggtelek 2½ hours later; though the return to Eger is a bit complicated, with a transfer either in Miskolc or Ózd; the last buses leave in the late afternoon or early evening, depending on the season.

🚌 **Stadion Bus Station** ⊠ District XIV, Hungária körút 48–52, Eastern Pest, Budapest ☎ 1/251-0125 or (Volánbusz info line) 1/382-0888 ⊕ www.volanbusz.hu Ⓜ M2: Stadion.

CAR TRAVEL

The M3 expressway is the main link between Budapest and northern Hungary, cutting toward the northeast and Ukraine. Construction has been underway for years; it is, at this writing, already more than halfway to the border, somewhere beyond the Tisza River. There's an exit near Füzesabony, from where you can drive north about 20 km (13 mi) to Eger. Smaller roads through the Bükk Mountains north of Eger are winding but in good shape and wonderfully scenic—this is the best way to see the region. You can go on toward Tokaj either by taking the M30 expressway, which soon hooks up with the smaller, older Route 3 north toward Miskolc, from where Route 37 branches eastward toward Tokaj and Sárospatak. Shorter on the map but perhaps a bit longer in fact: continue on the M3 past the Tisza River, then take secondary roads northeast toward Tokaj.

The most convenient way to reach Aggtelek is by car. From Budapest, take the M3 motorway east, and then turn up toward Miskolc on the M30, which soon becomes Route 26. Route 26 will take you past Miskloc to Sajószentpéter, from where you continue north on Route 27 and turn west after about a half hour for the final leg of the journey. From Eger, rather than head initially east, toward Miskolc, you can take a shortcut by secondary roads due north toward Route 26, then other secondary roads the rest of the way.

TOURS

IBUSZ Travel offers its all-day "Eger Wine Region" tour leaving from Budapest on Tuesdays and Thursdays from May through October for €80. The excursion involves a thorough look at downtown Eger including the fortress, a hearty lunch, and wine-tasting in Szépasszonyok völgye on the city outskirts.

IBUSZ Travel ☎ 1/485-2700 in Budapest ⊕ www.ibusz.hu.

TRAIN TRAVEL

Trains between Eger and Budapest (about 2 hours travel time) run several times daily from Keleti Station, with a transfer in Füzesabony. Direct trains run frequently all day between Budapest and Miskolc, the travel time on the fastest of these, the Intercity (IC) routes, being likewise around 2 hours.

Several daily trains connect Miskolc with Sárospatak and with Tokaj. Szilvásvárad and Eger are easily accessible from each other by frequent trains.

The Eger train station lies about 1 km (½ mi) from the center of town (a 20-minute walk). Miskolc's station is about 15 minutes by bus or tram from the center of town, and Tokaj's is about the same distance from the village center.

Last but not least, if you want to combine a trip to northern Hungary with one to the Great Plain, you can also get between Tokaj and Debrecen by train several times a day in roughly 1½ hours, with a transfer in Nyíregyháza.

As in all parts of Hungary these days, rather than calling local stations directly it's easier simply to dial the state railway company MÁV's national info line (local charges nationwide), at 06/40-49-49-49; indeed, in most cases, if you do call directly, you'll immediately be connected to the national info line, anyway. **Eger train station** ⊠ Állomás tér 1, Eger ☎ 36/314-264. **Miskolc train station** ⊠ Tiszai pályaudvar, Miskolc ☎ 46/412-665.

VISITOR INFORMATION

Hollókőért közalapítvány ⊠ Kossuth utca 68, Hollókő H-3176 ☎☎ 32/579-010. **Tourinform** ⊠ Bajcsy Zsilinszky út 9, Eger ☎ 36/517-715 ☎ Baradla oldal 13, Aggtelek ☎ 48/503-000 ☎ Serház utca 1, Tokaj ☎ 47/352-259.

UNDERSTANDING BUDAPEST

BUDAPEST AT A
GLANCE

BOOKS & MOVIES

HUNGARIAN
VOCABULARY

BUDAPEST AT A GLANCE

Fast Facts

Type of government: Democracy, with chief mayor, four deputy mayors, and a 67-member city council administering a metropolitan government, each of the city's 23 districts electing its own mayors and representatives for district affairs
Population: 1.8 million
Population Density: 3,387 people per square km (8,758 people per square mi)

Median age: Female 43.7, male 39.0
Crime rate: Down 1.4% from 2001–02; 105,000 reported offenses
Language: Hungarian (official)
Ethnic groups: Hungarian 92%; other 6%; German 1%; gypsy 1%
Religion: Catholic 56%; unaffiliated 23%; Protestant 19%; Jewish 1%; other 1%

Geography & Environment

Latitude: 47.5° N (same as Seattle, Washington; Ulan Bator, Mongolia; Quebec City, Canada)
Longitude: 19° E (same as Stockholm, Sweden)
Elevation: 102 meters (337 feet); highest point: János Hill 527 meters (1,729 feet)
Land area: 525 square km (203 square mi) city; 2,250 square km (869 square mi) metro
Terrain: City split by the Danube River, with Buda on a series of hills on the

right bank and Pest on the flatland on the left bank
Environmental issues: Budapest and the rest of Hungary are cutting carbon-dioxide emissions in accordance with the Kyoto Treaty, air quality has been under close watch since 1994; wastewater treatment is slowly ending outlet of untreated sewage into the Danube River

Economy

Per capita income: Average take-home pay 1.0 million HUF ($4,842)
Unemployment: 2.4%
Work force: 743,673; government 20%; manufacturing and processing 14%; trade and repairs 13%; real estate and business related services 11%; transport, warehousing, post, and telecommunications 10%; education

8%; health care and social services 8%; other 6%; financial activities 4%; construction 4%; accommodation and catering 3%
Major industries: Banking, electronics, farm machinery, food processing, pharmaceutical products, publishing, extiles, tourism, transportation

BOOKS & MOVIES

Although Hungarians have played a central role in the intellectual life of the past century, their literary and cinematic masters are less well known abroad than their luminaries in other arts, such as Béla Bartók in music and André Kertész in photography.

When Imre Kertész won the 2003 Nobel Prize in Literature, for *Fateless* and other novels, he was the first Hungarian to achieve this distinction but certainly not the first regarded by his compatriots as worthy. Novelist and poet Dezső Kosztolányi was prominent in Europe after World War I and admired by Thomas Mann. Some years earlier, the great novelist Gyula Krudy created the most memorable character in modern Hungarian literature, the hopelessly romantic gentleman Szindbád. In his novel *Azarel*, Károly Pap, who perished in the Holocaust, wrote with piercing candor about growing up Jewish. In the 1960s and '70s, István Örkény penned his popular novellas and *One Minute Stories*. Later in the Communist era, novelist and dissident György Konrád reflected on intellectual life under totalitarianism in *The Loser*. In her 1987 novel *The Door*, Magda Szabó explores the relationship between a writer and her housekeeper.

The 1990s saw the extraordinary literary revival of Sándor Márai, whose many books—most of which he published by 1945—include the fictional memoir *Confessions of a Bourgeois* and the novella *Embers*. Márai fled Hungary after World War II; he died in California in 1989. Among Hungary's greatest contemporary novelists are Péter Nádas, whose magnum opus is the Proustian *Book of Memories*; Péter Eszterházy, whose inventive prose has inspired a generation of younger Hungarian writers while also earning him enormous popularity; and László Krasznahorkai,

whose labyrinthine novels have likewise been critically acclaimed.

Writers of Hungarian descent abroad have certainly helped interpret Hungary for the outside world. The English novelist Tibor Fischer's *Under the Frog* is set in Hungary under Communism. In *Budapest 1900,* the American historian John Lukacs provides an elegant, illustrated look at Hungary's capital in a golden age. Austrian-Hungarian journalist Paul Lendvai's *The Hungarians* is a novel-like encapsulation of 1,000 years of nationhood.

Though it is difficult to express its beauty in English, Hungary's poetry is really at the heart of its literature. Some 20th-century greats, whose work has appeared in fine translations, are Endre Ady, Attila József, Miklós Radnóti, János Pilinszky, Sándor Weöres, and Ágnes Nemes-Nagy.

Turning to film: István Szabó (*Mephisto*; Oscar, 1981) and Miklós Jancsó are best known abroad among Hungarian directors. Péter Bacsó's *The Witness* is a disarming satire of Communism made in the late 1960s but kept from the general public for years. The 1970s yielded Károly Makk's *Love* and Zoltán Huszárik's *Sindbad*, both masterpieces. Péter Gothár, who rose to fame in the 1980s, produced a moving treatment of the aftermath of the 1956 revolution in *Time Stands Still*. Márta Mészáros's films masterfully explore women's lives. Ildikó Enyedi gained international recognition beginning in the late 1980s with her cosmic-ironic fairy tales, including *My Twentieth Century*. One of several recent films that have garnered international prizes is György Pálfi's *Hukkle*, on the explosive undercurrent of village life.

Hungary may look small on a map, but it is a universe of great literary and cinematic art that is still expanding.

HUNGARIAN VOCABULARY

Tricky double consonants (with English equivalents as they appear in the pronunciation guide below):

gy = a one-syllable "dy" sound (a quick *dya*—indicated in the pronunciation guide below as *dy*)
ly = y (as in "yard")
ny = a one-syllable "ny" (a quick *nya*—indicated below as *ny*)
ty = a one-syllable "ty" (a quick *tya*—indicated below as *ty*)

Tricky vowels:

ö = the "i" in a short, snapped out "*Sir!*" (pronounced with slightly rounded lips)
ő = the "i" in a long "s*iiiir*" (pronounced with very rounded lips)
ü = no clear English equivalent; like the "ü" in the German expression "*über alles*" (pronounced with slightly rounded lips)
ű ř a longer form of the "ü" (pronounced with very rounded lips)

English	Hungarian	Pronunciation
Basics		
Yes/no	Igen/nem	**ee**-gen/nem
Please [when asking for something]	Kérem (szépen)	**kay**-rem (**say**-pen)
Please [to get the attention of someone; e.g., a waiter]	Legyen szives	**le**-dyen **see**-vesh
Thank you (kindly)	Köszöszöm (szépen)	**kuh**-suh-nuhm (**say**-pen)
Excuse me	Elnézést	**el**-nay-zaysht
Sorry [for doing something]	Bocsánat	**boh**-chah-nut
Hello [not too formal]	Szervusz	**ser**-voose
Hi [informal, chummy; commonly used]	Szia	**see**-ya
Good evening	Jó estét	**yo**-esh-tate
Goodbye [formal]	Viszontlátásra	**vees**-ohnt-lot-osh-ruh
Goodbye [informal]	Viszlát	vees-**lot**
Do you speak English?	Beszél angolul?	**bess**-ale un-goal-ool
I don't understand.	Nem értem.	**nem** air-tem
I would like . . .	Szeretnék . . .	**ser**-et-nake
How much does it cost?	Mennyibe kerül?	**men**-yee-beh kair-uhl
Help!	Segitség!	**sheh**-geet-shaig

Meeting People

My name is . . .	[stress on name] . . . a nevem.	uh ne-vem
What is your name? [literally]	Mi a neve?	**me** uh ne-ve
Where are you from?	Honnan van?	**hone**-un-vun
What is your occupation?	Mi a foglalkozása?	**me** uh foge-lull-koze-ahsh-uh
Let's have a coffee.	Kávézunk egyet.	**kah**-vaze-oonk e-*dy*et

Numbers

One	egy	e*dy*
Two	kettő	**ket**-tuh
Three	három	**hah**-rome
Four	négy	nay*dy*
Five	öt	uht
Six	hat	hut
Seven	hét	hate
Eight	nyolc	*ny*olts
Nine	kilenc	**kee**-lents
Ten	tíz	teez
One hundred	száz	sahz
One thousand	ezer	**ez**-zer

Days of the Week

Sunday	vasárnap	**vuh**-shahr-nup
Monday	hétfő	**hate**-fuh
Tuesday	kedd	ked
Wednesday	szerda	**ser**-duh
Thursday	csütörtök	**chit**-ir-tik
Friday	péntek	**pain**-tek
Saturday	szombat	**soam**-but

Food

A restaurant	az étterem	uhz **eht**-teh-rem
The menu	az étlap	uhz **ate**-lup
The check, please.	a számlát kérem.	uh **sahm**-lot **kay**-rem
Breakfast	reggeli	**reg**-ell-ee

Budapest
Essentials

There are planners, and there are those who fly by the seat of their pants. We happily place ourselves among the planners. Our writers and editors try to anticipate all the issues you may face before and during any journey, and then they do their research. This section is the product of their efforts. Use it to get excited about your trip to Budapest, to inform your travel planning, or to guide you on the road should the seat of your pants start to feel threadbare.

GETTING STARTED

We're really proud of our Web site: Fodors.com is a great place to begin any journey. Scan Travel Wire for suggested itineraries, travel deals, restaurant and hotel openings, and other up-to-the-minute info. Check out Booking to research prices and book plane tickets, hotel rooms, rental cars, and vacation packages. Head to Talk for on-the-ground pointers from travelers who frequent our message boards. You can also link to loads of other travel-related resources.

▌ RESOURCES

ONLINE TRAVEL TOOLS

Several Web sites will be helpful to travelers going to Budapest. All the sites listed below have an English-language translation option, though you may have to click on an American or British flag to activate it. The Hungarian news agency's (MTI) English-language Web site has daily news plus a backlog of earlier articles. Web sites of the *Budapest Sun, Budapest Business Journal,* and *Budapest Times* have news articles and features, plus bits of current tourist information like the restaurant guide in *Budapest Sun.* The Mayor of Budapest's Web site has current city-related news features plus notes about upcoming cultural events and festivals and general visitor information, and the Tourinform site has a broad range of information on Hungary. The Travellers Youth Hostels Web site has tips and information for the globe-roaming budget set. *Budapest In Your Pocket*'s Web site has some useful visitor information and articles for tourists;

a more extensive print version is available at newsstands. The Hungary Page has, well, just about everything.

All About Budapest **Budapest Tourism Office** ⊕ www.budapestinfo.hu/en. **Budapest Business Journal** ⊕ www.bbj.hu. **Budapest In Your Pocket** ⊕ www.inyourpocket.com. **Budapest Sun** ⊕ www.budapestsun.com. **Budapest Times** ⊕ www.budapesttimes.hu. **The Hungary Page** ⊕ www.thehungarypage.com. **Office of the Mayor of Budapest** ⊕ www.budapest.hu. **MTI** ⊕ www.english.mti.hu. **Tourinform** ⊕ www.hungary.com or www.itthon.hu. **Travellers Youth Hostels** ⊕ www.backpackers.hu.

Budapest's Main Sights Online **Budapest Thermal Baths** ⊕ www.spasbudapest.com. **Esztergom Basilica** ⊕ www.bazilika-esztergom.hu. **Eger Castle** ⊕ www.egrivar.hu. **Herend Porcelain Museum** ⊕ www.porcelanium.com. **Holocaust Memorial Center** ⊕ www.hdke.hu. **Hortobágy National Park** ⊕ www.hnp.hu. **Hungarian Museums umbrella site** ⊕ www.museums.hu. **Hungarian National Gallery** ⊕ www.mng.hu. **Museum of Fine Arts** ⊕ www.szepmuveszeti.hu. **Palace of the Arts** ⊕ www.mupa.hu.

Currency Conversion **Google** ⊕ www.google.com does currency conversion. Just type in the amount you want to convert and an explanation of how you want it converted (e.g., "14 Swiss francs in dollars"), and voilà. **Oanda.com** ⊕ www.oanda.com also allows you to print out a handy table with the current day's conversion rates. **XE.com** ⊕ www.xe.com is a good currency conversion Web site.

Safety **Transportation Security Administration** (TSA) ⊕ www.tsa.gov

Time Zones **Timeanddate.com** ⊕ www.timeanddate.com/worldclock can help you figure out the correct time anywhere in the world.

Weather **Accuweather.com** ⊕ www.accuweather.com is an independent weather-forecasting service with especially good coverage of hurricanes. **Weather.com** ⊕ www.weather.com is the Web site for the Weather Channel.

WORD OF MOUTH

After your trip, be sure to rate the places you visited and share your experiences and travel tips with us and other Fodorites in Travel Ratings and Talk on ⊕ www.fodors.com.

Other Resources CIA World Factbook
⊕ www.odci.gov/cia/publications/factbook/
index.html has profiles of every country in the
world. It's a good source if you need some
quick facts and figures.

VISITOR INFORMATION
Within Hungary, Tourinform has continued to expand and smarten up its act. It
has numerous offices in Budapest and outposts throughout the country. Its toll-free
tourist-information telephone hotline operates 24 hours a day. For off-hours help
in person, you can visit the Non-Stop
Hotel Service travel agency, the only such
office open 24 hours a day.

DISCOUNTS & DEALS
In Budapest the popular Budapest Card,
developed by the Tourism Office of Budapest in the late 1990s, entitles holders to
unlimited travel on public transportation;
free admission to many museums and
sights; and discounts on various services
from participating businesses. The cost at
this writing was 5,200 HUF for two days,
6,500 HUF for three days; one card is
valid for an adult plus one child under 14.
It is available at many tourist offices, hotels, travel agencies, and metro ticket counters. A similar pass called the Hungary
Card gives discounts to museums, sights,
and services across the entire country.
Tourinform ☏ 1/438-8080 (24-hr hotline),
80/630-800 (24-hr toll-free recorded information within Hungary), 36-30/303-0600 (24-hr
hotline from abroad) ⊕ www.hungary.com or
www.itthon.hu. **Tourism Office of Budapest**
☏ 1/322-4098 ☏ 1/302-8580 ☏ 1/488-0475
⊕ www.budapestinfo.hu.
In the U.S.: Hungarian National Tourist Of-
fice of New York ☏ 212/695-1211 ☐ 212/207-
4103 ⊕ www.gotohungary.com.

▮ THINGS TO CONSIDER

GOVERNMENT ADVISORIES
As different countries have different world
views, look at travel advisories from a range
of governments to get more of a sense of
what's going on out there. And be sure to

> **WORD OF MOUTH**
>
> Many areas are best seen on foot, so take
> a pair of sturdy walking shoes and be pre-
> pared to use them. High heels will present
> considerable problems, not only on cob-
> blestone streets but also on buses and
> trams that offer a less than steady ride.

parse the language carefully. For example,
a warning to "avoid all travel" carries more
weight than one urging you to "avoid
nonessential travel," and both are much
stronger than a plea to "exercise caution."
A U.S. government travel warning is more
permanent (though not necessarily more serious) than a so-called public announce-
ment, which carries an expiration date.

▮ TIP→ Consider registering online with the
State Department (https://travelregistration.
state.gov/ibrs/), so the government will know
to look for you should a crisis occur in the
country you're visiting. The U.S. Department
of State's Web site has more than just travel
warnings and advisories. The consular information sheets issued for every country have
general safety tips, entry requirements (though
be sure to verify these with the country's embassy), and other useful details.
General Information & Warnings Australian
Department of Foreign Affairs & Trade
⊕ www.smartraveller.gov.au. **Consular Af-**
fairs Bureau of Canada ⊕ www.voyage.gc.
ca. **U.K. Foreign & Commonwealth Office**
⊕ www.fco.gov.uk/travel. **U.S. Department of**
State ⊕ www.travel.state.gov.

GEAR
Although fashion was all but nonexistent
under 40 years of communist rule, these
days residents of Budapest, especially
young people, are dressed in the latest
Western trends. Don't worry about packing lots of formal clothing: a sports jacket
for men and a dress or pants for women
are appropriate for an evening out. Everywhere else you'll feel comfortable in casual pants or jeans.

Hungary enjoys all the extremes of an inland climate, so plan accordingly. In the

higher elevations winter can last until April, and even in summer the evenings will be on the cool side. And don't forget that umbrella, for showers, while certainly not a daily occurrence, are not at all unheard-of.

SHIPPING LUGGAGE AHEAD

Imagine globetrotting with only a carry-on in tow. Shipping your luggage in advance via an air-freight service is a great way to cut down on backaches, hassles, and stress—especially if your packing list includes strollers, car seats, etc. There are some things to be aware of, though. First, research carry-on restrictions; if you absolutely need something that's impractical to ship and isn't allowed in carry-ons, this strategy isn't for you. Second, plan to send your bags several days in advance to U.S. destinations and as much as two weeks in advance to some international destinations. Third, plan to spend some money: it will cost least $100 to send a small piece of luggage, a golf bag, or a pair of skis to a domestic destination, much more to places overseas. Some people use Federal Express to ship their bags, but this can cost even more than air-freight services. All these services insure your bag (for most, the limit is $1,000, but you should verify that amount); you can, however, purchase additional insurance for about $1 per $100 of value.

Luggage Concierge ☎ 800/288-9818 ⊕ www.luggageconcierge.com. **Luggage Express** ☎ 866/744-7224 ⊕ www. usxpluggageexpress.com. **Luggage Free** ☎ 800/361-6871 ⊕ www.luggagefree.com. **Sports Express** ☎ 800/357-4174 ⊕ www. sportsexpress.com specializes in shipping golf clubs and other sports equipment. **Virtual Bellhop** ☎ 877/235-5467 ⊕ www. virtualbellhop.com.

PASSPORTS & VISAS

Only a valid passport—one still valid for at least six months at the time of entry, that is—is required of U.S., British, Canadian, Australian, and New Zealand citizens entering Hungary.

PASSPORTS

We're always surprised at how few Americans have passports—only 25% at this writing. This number is expected to grow in coming years, when it becomes impossible to re-enter the United States from trips to neighboring Canada or Mexico without one. Remember this: a passport verifies both your identity and your nationality—a great reason to have one.

U.S. passports are valid for 10 years. You must apply in person if you're getting a passport for the first time; if your previous passport was lost, stolen, or damaged; or if your previous passport has expired and was issued more than 15 years ago or when you were under 16. All children under 18 must appear in person to apply for or renew a passport. Both parents must accompany any child under 14 (or send a notarized statement with their permission) and provide proof of their relationship to the child.

There are 13 regional passport offices, as well as 7,000 passport acceptance facilities in post offices, public libraries, and other governmental offices. If you're renewing a passport, you can do so by mail. Forms are available at passport acceptance facilities and online.

The cost to apply for a new passport is $97 for adults, $82 for children under 16; renewals are $67. Allow six weeks for processing, both for first-time passports and renewals. For an expediting fee of $60 you can reduce this time to about two weeks. If your trip is less than two weeks away, you can get a passport even more rapidly by going to a passport office with the necessary documentation. Private expediters can get things done in as little as 48 hours, but charge hefty fees for their services.

■ TIP➔ Before your trip, make two copies of your passport's data page (one for someone at home and another for you to carry separately). Or scan the page and e-mail it to someone at home and/or yourself.

U.S. Passport Information **U.S. Department of State** ☎ 877/487-2778 ⊕ http://travel. state.gov/passport.

TRIP INSURANCE

What kind of coverage do you honestly need? Do you even need trip insurance at all? Take a deep breath and read on.

We believe that comprehensive trip insurance is especially valuable if you're booking a very expensive or complicated trip (particularly to an isolated region) or if you're booking far in advance. Who knows what could happen six months down the road? But whether or not you get insurance has more to do with how comfortable you are assuming all that risk yourself.

Comprehensive travel policies typically cover trip cancellation and interruption, letting you cancel or cut your trip short because of a personal emergency, illness, or, in some cases, acts of terrorism in your destination. Such policies also cover evacuation and medical care. Some also cover you for trip delays because of bad weather or mechanical problems, as well as for lost or delayed baggage. Another type of coverage to look for is financial default—that is, when your trip is disrupted because a tour operator, airline, or cruise line goes out of business. Generally you must buy this when you book your trip or shortly thereafter, and it's only available to you if your operator isn't on a list of excluded companies.

■ TIP→ Expect comprehensive travel-insurance policies to cost about 4% to 7% of the total price of your trip (it's more like 12% if you're over age 70). A medical-only policy may or may not be cheaper than a comprehensive policy. Always read the policy's fine print to make sure you are covered for the risks of most concern to you. Compare several policies to make sure you're getting the best price and range of coverage available.

If you're going abroad, consider buying medical-only coverage at the very least. Neither Medicare nor some private insurers covers medical expenses anywhere outside of the United States except Mexico and Canada (including time aboard a cruise ship, even if it leaves from a U.S. port). Medical-only policies typically reimburse you for medical care (excluding treatment related to pre-existing conditions) and hospitalization abroad, and provide for evacuation. You still have to pay the bills and await reimbursement from the insurer, though.

Trip Insurance Resources

INSURANCE COMPARISON SITES		
Insure My Trip.com		www.insuremytrip.com
Square Mouth.com		www.quotetravelinsurance.com
COMPREHENSIVE TRAVEL INSURERS		
Access America	866/807-3982	www.accessamerica.com
CSA Travel Protection	800/873-9855	www.csatravelprotection.com
HTH Worldwide	610/254-8700 or 888/243-2358	www.hthworldwide.com
Travelex Insurance	888/457-4602	www.travelex-insurance.com
Travel Guard International	715/345-0505 or 800/826-4919	www.travelguard.com
Travel Insured International	800/243-3174	www.travelinsured.com
MEDICAL-ONLY INSURERS		
International Medical Group	800/628-4664	www.imglobal.com
International SOS	215/942-8000 or 713/521-7611	www.internationalsos.com
Wallach & Company	800/237-6615 or 504/687-3166	www.wallach.com

BOOKING YOUR TRIP

Unless your cousin is a travel agent, you're probably among the millions of people who make most of their travel arrangements online. But have you ever wondered just what the differences are between an online travel agent (a Web site through which you make reservations instead of going directly to the airline, hotel, or car-rental company), a discounter (a firm that does a high volume of business with a hotel chain or airline and accordingly gets good prices), a wholesaler (one that makes cheap reservations in bulk and then re-sells them to people like you), and an aggregator (one that compares all the offerings so you don't have to)? Is it truly better to book directly on an airline or hotel Web site? And when does a real live travel agent come in handy?

ONLINE

You really have to shop around. A travel wholesaler such as Hotels.com or Hotel-Club.net can be a source of good rates, as can discounters such as Hotwire or Priceline, particularly if you can bid for your hotel room or airfare. Indeed, such sites sometimes have deals that are unavailable elsewhere. They do, however, tend to work only with hotel chains (which makes them just plain useless for getting hotel reservations outside of major cities) or big airlines (so that often leaves out upstarts like jetBlue and some foreign carriers like Air India). Also, with discounters and wholesalers you must generally prepay, and everything is nonrefundable. And before you fork over the dough, be sure to check the terms and conditions, so you know what a given company will do for you if there's a problem and what you'll have to deal with on your own.

■ TIP➜ To be absolutely sure everything was processed correctly, confirm reservations made through online travel agents, discounters, and wholesalers directly with your hotel before leaving home.

Booking engines like Expedia, Travelocity, and Orbitz are actually travel agents, albeit high-volume, online ones. And airline travel packagers like American Airlines Vacations and Virgin Vacations—well, they're travel agents, too. But they may still not work with all the world's hotels.

An aggregator site will search many sites and pull the best prices for airfares, hotels, and rental cars from them. Most aggregators compare the major travel-booking sites such as Expedia, Travelocity, and Orbitz; some also look at airline Web sites, though rarely the sites of smaller budget airlines. Some aggregators also compare other travel products, including complex packages—a good thing, as you can sometimes get the best overall deal by booking an air-and-hotel package.

WITH A TRAVEL AGENT

If you use an agent—brick-and-mortar or virtual—you'll pay a fee for the service. And know that the service you get from some online agents isn't comprehensive. For example, Expedia and Travelocity don't search for prices on budget airlines like jetBlue, Southwest, or small foreign carriers. That said, some agents (online or not) *do* have access to fares that are difficult to find otherwise, and the savings can more than make up for any surcharge.

A knowledgeable brick-and-mortar travel agent can be a godsend if you're booking a cruise, a package trip that's not available to you directly, an air pass, or a complicated itinerary including several overseas flights. What's more, travel agents that specialize in a destination may have exclusive access to certain deals and insider information on things such as charter flights. Agents who specialize in types of travelers (senior citizens, gays and lesbians, naturists) or types of trips (cruises, luxury travel, safaris) can also be invaluable.

A top-notch agent planning your trip to Russia will make sure you get the correct visa application and complete it on time; the one booking your cruise may get you a cabin upgrade or arrange to have bottle of champagne chilling in your cabin when you embark. And complain about the surcharges all you like, but when things don't work out the way you'd hoped, it's nice to have an agent to put things right.

■ TIP→ Remember that Expedia, Travelocity, and Orbitz are travel agents, not just booking engines. To resolve any problems with a reservation made through these companies, contact them first.

Local agencies in Budapest can help you book excursions, hotel rooms, and train and airline tickets for travel beyond the city. **Agent Resources American Society of Travel Agents** ☎ 703/739-2782 ⊕ www.travelsense. org.

Budapest Travel Agents American Express ⊠ District V, Deák Ferenc utca 10, Around Deák Ferenc tér ☎ 1/235-4330 ⊟ 1/235-4339. **Getz International** ⊠ District V, Falk Miksa utca 5, Parliament ☎ 1/312-0645 or 1/312-0649 ⊟ 1/312-1014. **IBUSZ Travel** central branch ⊠ District V, Ferenciek tere 10, Around Ferenciek tere ☎ 1/485-2700 or 06-40/428-794 ⊕ www.ibusz.hu. **Vista Travel Center** main office ⊠ District VI, Andrássy út 1, Around Andrássy út ☎ 1/452-3636 ⊟ 1/429-9925 ⊠ District II, Mammut shopping mall, Lövőház utca 2-6, Around Moszkva tér ☎ 1/315-1105 ⊕ www.vista.hu.

■ AIRLINE TICKETS

Most domestic airline tickets are electronic; international tickets may be either electronic or paper. With an e-ticket the only thing you receive is an e-mailed receipt citing your itinerary and reservation and ticket numbers. The greatest advantage of an e-ticket is that if you lose your receipt you can simply print out another copy or ask the airline to do it for you at check-in. You usually pay a surcharge (up to $50) to get a paper ticket, if you can get one at all. The sole advantage of a paper ticket is that it may be easier to endorse over to another airline if your flight is canceled and the airline you booked with can't accommodate you on another flight.

■ TIP→ Discount air passes that let you travel economically in a given country or region must often be purchased before you leave home. In some cases you can only get them through a travel agent.

The least expensive airfares to Budapest must usually be purchased well in advance; flights on major airlines are usually cheaper if booked for round-trip travel. The flock of new budget airlines serving Hungary offers fantastic fares from major European hubs like London, Paris, and Amsterdam, most priced on a one-way basis (⇨ European Airlines, *below*). With a little geographical creativity and some flexibility, you can save yourself quite a bit of money. Most budget airlines offer cheaper tickets if you book online; tickets purchased over the phone usually involve a surcharge. When shopping around for fares, be sure to calculate in taxes if they're not included; they can often add over $100 to your final fare. Airlines generally allow you to change your return date for a fee; most low-fare tickets, however, cannot be changed and are nonrefundable. Sometimes you can find better rates and have more schedule options if you fly in and out of Vienna, just a two- to three-hour bus or train journey from Budapest.

EuropebyAir's Flight Pass system offers $99 one-way fares for country-hopping between many European cities, including direct flights connecting Budapest with Brussels and Venice. Taxes are not included and restrictions apply. Check their Web site for specifics.
Air Pass Info FlightPass ☎ 888/321-4737 EuropebyAir ⊕ www.europebyair.com.

■ RENTAL CARS

When you reserve a car, ask about cancellation penalties, taxes, drop-off charges (if you're planning to pick up the car in one city and leave it in another), and surcharges (for being under or over a certain age, for additional drivers, or for driving across state or country borders or beyond

10 WAYS TO SAVE

1. Nonrefundable is best. If saving money is more important than flexibility, then nonrefundable tickets work. Just remember that you'll pay dearly (as much as $100) if you change your plans.

2. Comparison shop. Web sites and travel agents can have different arrangements with airlines and offer different prices for exactly the same flights.

3. Beware those prices. Many airline Web sites—and most ads—show prices *without* taxes and surcharges. Don't buy until you know the full price.

4. Stay loyal. Stick with one or two frequent-flier programs. You'll rack up free trips faster and you'll accumulate more quickly the perks that make trips easier. On some airlines these include a special reservations number, early boarding, access to upgrades, and roomier economy-class seating.

5. Watch those ticketing fees. Surcharges are usually added when you buy your ticket anywhere but on an airline Web site.

6. Check early and often. Start looking for cheap fares up to a year in advance, and keep looking until you see something you can live with.

7. Don't work alone. Some Web sites have tracking features that will e-mail you immediately when good deals are posted.

8. Jump on the good deals. Waiting even a few minutes might mean paying more.

9. Be flexible. Look for departures on Tuesday, Wednesday, and Thursday (typically the cheapest days to travel), and check prices for departures at different times and to and from alternative airports.

10. Weigh your options. What you get can be as important as what you save. A cheaper flight might have a long layover, or it might land at a secondary airport, where your ground transportation costs might be higher.

a specific distance from your point of rental). All these things can add substantially to your costs. Request car seats and extras such as GPS when you book.

Rates are sometimes—but not always—better if you book in advance or reserve through a rental agency's Web site. There are other reasons to book ahead, though: for popular destinations, during busy times of the year, or to ensure that you get certain types of cars (vans, SUVs, exotic sports cars).

■ TIP➔ Make sure that a confirmed reservation guarantees you a car. Agencies sometimes overbook, particularly for busy weekends and holiday periods.

You should not rent a car if you do not plan to leave Budapest itself, because of traffic and parking concerns. However, a car can be convenient for traveling around the country—not so much for visiting smaller cities, which can easily be reached by train or bus and are all quite walkable, but for zipping around the countryside between these cities, and taking in smaller towns and villages, at your leisure.

Rental rates are high in Hungary. Daily rates for automatics begin around $50 to $60 plus 50¢ per kilometer (½ mi), quoted in euros or forints. Personal, theft, and accident insurance (this is coverage beyond the ordinary CDW for theft and is not required but recommended) runs an additional $25 to $30 per day. Rates for manual-transmission cars are lower. Rates tend to be significantly lower if you arrange your rental *from home* through the American offices. Locally based companies usually offer lower rates.

Your driver's license may not be recognized outside your home country. You may not be able to rent a car without an International Driving Permit (IDP), which can be used only in conjunction with a valid driver's license and which translates your license into 10 languages. Check the AAA Web site for more info as well as for IDPs ($10) themselves.

CAR-RENTAL INSURANCE

Everyone who rents a car wonders whether the insurance that the rental companies offer is worth the expense. No one—including us—has a simple answer. It all depends on how much regular insurance you have, how comfortable you are with risk, and whether or not money is an issue.

If you own a car, your personal auto insurance may cover a rental to some degree, though not all policies protect you abroad; always read your policy's fine print. If you don't have auto insurance, then seriously consider buying the collision- or loss-damage waiver (CDW or LDW) from the car-rental company, which eliminates your liability for damage to the car. Some credit cards offer CDW coverage, but it's usually supplemental to your own insurance and rarely covers SUVs, minivans, luxury models, and the like. If your coverage is secondary, you may still be liable for loss-of-use costs from the car-rental company. But no credit-card insurance is valid unless you use that card for *all* transactions, from reserving to paying the final bill. All companies exclude car rental in some countries, so be sure to find out about the destination to which you are traveling.

■ TIP→ Diners Club offers primary CDW coverage on all rentals reserved and paid for with the card. This means that Diners Club's company—not your own car insurance—pays in case of an accident. It doesn't mean your car-insurance company won't raise your rates once it discovers you had an accident.

Some countries require you to purchase CDW coverage or require car-rental companies to include it in quoted rates. Ask your rental company about issues like these in your destination. In most cases it's cheaper to add a supplemental CDW plan to your comprehensive travel-insurance policy (⇨ Trip Insurance *under* Things to Consider *in* Getting Started, *above*) than to purchase it from a rental company. That said, you don't want to pay for a supplement if you're required to buy insurance from the rental company.

10 WAYS TO SAVE

1. Beware of cheap rates. Those great rates aren't so great when you add in taxes, surcharges, and insurance. Such extras can double or triple the initial quote.

2. Rent weekly. Weekly rates are usually better than daily ones. Even if you only want to rent for five or six days, ask for the weekly rate; it may very well be cheaper than the daily rate for that period of time.

3. Don't forget the locals. Price local car-rental companies as well as the majors. Fox Autorent, for example, has "unlimited-mileage weekend + 1 day" specials, and rates include free delivery and pickup of the car anywhere in Budapest.

4. Airport rentals can cost more. Airports often add surcharges, which you can sometimes avoid by renting from an agency whose office is just off airport property.

5. Wholesalers can help. Investigate wholesalers, which don't own fleets but rent in bulk from firms that do, and which frequently offer better rates.

6. Look for rate guarantees. With your rate locked in, you won't pay more, even if the price goes up in the local currency.

7. Fill up farther away. Avoid hefty refueling fees by filling the tank at a station well away from where you plan to turn in the car.

8. Pump it yourself. Don't buy the tank of gas that's in the car when you rent it unless you plan to do a lot of driving.

9. Get all your discounts. Find out whether a credit card you carry or organization to which you belong has a discount program. And confirm that such discounts really are a deal. You can often do better with special weekend or weekly rates.

10. Check out packages. Adding a car rental onto your air/hotel vacation package may be cheaper than renting a car separately.

Car Rental Resources

AUTOMOBILE ASSOCIATIONS		
U.S.: American Automobile Association (AAA)	315/797-5000 most contact with the organization is through state and regional members	www.aaa.com
National Automobile Club	650/294-7000 membership open to CA residents only	www.thenac.com
LOCAL AGENCIES		
CentRent	06-20/541-1035 or 06-20/541-1034 (both mobile)	www.centrent.hu
Fox Autorent	1/382-9000 1/411-0395	www.fox-autorent.com
Recent Car	1/453-0003	www.recentcar.hu
LOCAL OFFICES OF MAJOR AGENCIES		
Avis	1/318-4240 1/296-6421	www.avis.hu
Budget	1/214-0420 1/296-8197	www.budget.hu
Europcar	1/328-6464 1/421-8370; also known in Hungary as EUrent	www.europcar.hu
Hertz	1/296-0999 1/266-4361 1/296-7171; Ferihegy Repülőtér, Terminal 2B also known in Hungary as Mercur Rent-a-Car	www.hertz.com
National Car Rental	1/477-1080 1/296-6610; also known in Hungary as National Alamo Hungary	www.nationalcar.hu
MAJOR AGENCIES		
Alamo	800/522-9696	www.alamo.com
Avis	800/331-1084	www.avis.com
Budget	800/472-3325	www.budget.com
Hertz	800/654-3001	www.hertz.com
National Car Rental	800/227-7368	www.nationalcar.com
WHOLESALERS		
Auto Europe	888/223-5555	www.autoeurope.com
Europe by Car	212/581-3040 in New York or 800/223-1516	www.europebycar.com
Eurovacations	877/471-3876	www.eurovacations.com
Kemwel	877/820-0668	www.kemwel.com

You must be 21 to rent a car in Hungary; some agencies rent superior-model cars only to drivers over 25, and some charge extra for all models driven by those who are under 25. Most countries, including Hungary, require that you have held your driver's license for at least a year before you can rent a car. Keep in mind that Hungarian law states that children under 16 may not travel in the front passenger seat, and that car seats are compulsory for infants and toddlers and must be placed in the back seat of the car.

Cars rented from the Budapest airport carry an 11% to 12% surcharge; be sure to ask whether it is included in your initial price quote. If you are renting in winter, ask about additional "winter upkeep" charges. Additional insurance is sometimes required if you drive the car into certain countries, such as Romania, Bulgaria, and Serbia. Car seats can be rented with the car for about €9 per day. Some firms have a surcharge for drivers under 25; Hertz charges an extra €10 per day (to a maximum of €50 per rental, plus V.A.T.) on all models.

■ TIP→ You can decline the insurance from the rental company and purchase it through a third-party provider such as Travel Guard (www.travelguard.com)–$9 per day for $35,000 of coverage. That's sometimes just under half the price of the CDW offered by some car-rental companies.

■ VACATION PACKAGES

Packages *are not* guided excursions. Packages combine airfare, accommodations, and perhaps a rental car or other extras (theater tickets, guided excursions, boat trips, reserved entry to popular museums, transit passes), but they let you do your own thing. During busy periods packages may be your only option, as flights and rooms may be sold out otherwise. Packages will definitely save you time. They can also save you money, particularly in peak seasons, but—and this is a really big "but"—you should price each part of the package separately to be sure. And be aware that prices advertised on Web sites

and in newspapers rarely include service charges or taxes, which can up your costs by hundreds of dollars.

■ TIP→ Some packages and cruises are sold only through travel agents. Don't always assume that you can get the best deal by booking everything yourself.

■ GUIDED TOURS

Guided tours are a good option when you don't want to do it all yourself. You travel along with a group (sometimes large, sometimes small), stay in prebooked hotels, eat with your fellow travelers (the cost of meals sometimes included in the price of your tour, sometimes not), and follow a schedule. But not all guided tours are an if-it's-Tuesday-this-must-be-Belgium experience. A knowledgeable guide can take you places that you might never discover on your own, and you may be pushed to see more than you would have otherwise. Tours aren't for everyone, but they can be just the thing for trips to places where making travel arrangements is difficult or time-consuming (particularly when you don't speak the language). And remember that you'll be expected to tip your guide (in cash) at the end of the tour.

Recommended Companies Exclusive City Tours ☎ 06-20/982-3157 ⊕ www.citytour96. com. **IBUSZ** ⊠ District V, Ferenciek tere 10, Around Ferenciek tere ☎ 1/485-2700 or 06-40/428-794 ⊕ www.ibusz.hu.

TRANSPORTATION

■ BY AIR

In May 2006 Delta Airlines became the second carrier—alongside Malév Hungarian Airlines—to offer nonstop service between the U.S. and Budapest, with flights from New York. These flights fill up very quickly during the summer, so book well in advance. Malév flies nonstop to Budapest from New York–JFK and well as from Toronto.

Travel time to Budapest can vary greatly depending on whether or not you can get a nonstop flight. A nonstop flight from NYC to Budapest is approximately 9 hours. Most trips from the U.S. require a change at Frankfurt, London, Paris, Prague, Zurich, Amsterdam, or Vienna and can take up to 15 hours. Direct flights from London to Budapest take between 2 and 3 hours.

Ferihegy Airport is small, modern, and easy to navigate. The main and newer facility, Terminal 2, has long hosted larger commercial airlines; the older part, Terminal 1, was renovated by 2005 and is the main gateway for budget airlines. Check-in counters for flights to North America open three hours before departure, but under normal circumstances arriving two hours ahead is plenty of time. For shorter-haul flights, arrive between one and two hours before departure.

Airlines & Airports Airline and Airport Links.com ⊕ www.airlineandairportlinks.com has links to many of the world's airlines and airports.
Airline Security Issues Transportation Security Administration ⊕ www.tsa.gov has answers for almost every question that might come up.
Air Travel Resources in Budapest

AIRPORTS

Ferihegy Repülőtér (BUD), by far Hungary's largest commercial airport, is 24 km (15 mi) southeast of downtown Budapest. All non-Hungarian airlines operate from Terminal 2B, Malév from Terminal 2A. The older part of the airport, Terminal 1, reopened in 2005 after thorough renovation and is the main terminal for low-cost airlines flying to European destinations. There are also commercial airports with regular, albeit relatively limited, service at Sármellék, near the western end of Lake Balaton (e.g., Ryanair flights from London Stanstead several times weekly as of May 2006, and other regular flights from Germany, Austria, and Denmark); and in Debrecen (e.g., daily service from Budapest in addition to charter flights).

Airport Information Balaton Airport 📞 83/355-500 (airport), 1/302-0908 (head office, Budapest) ⊕ www.flybalaton.com. **Debrecen Airport** 📞 52/520-8102 ⊕ www.airportdebrecen.hu. **Ferihegy Repülőtér** 📞 1/235-3888, 1/296-9696, or 1/296-7000 flight information ⊕ www.bud.hu.

GROUND TRANSPORTATION

Many hotels offer their guests car or minibus transportation to and from Ferihegy, but all of them—except the Hilton on Castle Hill—charge for the service. You should arrange for a pickup in advance. If you're taking a taxi, allow anywhere from 25 minutes during non-peak hours to an hour during rush hours (7 AM–9 AM from the airport, 4 PM–6 PM from the city).

Sadly, at this writing numerous taxis at the airport were grossly overcharging. If you must take a taxi, your best option is to call Főtaxi or Buda Taxi from a pay phone and order one. Főtaxi has a toll-free number, so you don't need to use a coin or phone card. Both companies are trustworthy and offer fixed rates from and to the airport; destinations in Pest cost around 4,000 HUF, in Buda at least 4,500 HUF. Always get a receipt.

Most travelers—locals and tourists alike— use the Airport Minibus, which provides convenient door-to-door service between

NAVIGATING BUDAPEST

As in Paris, neighborhoods in Budapest are known and referred to locally not by name but by their district number, the equivalent of the Paris arrondissement. The standard format for street addresses is: first the district number—on maps Roman numerals designate each of Budapest's 22 districts, while on envelopes the middle two numerals of the four-digit zip code indicate the district (e.g., a specific neighborhood in District VII might have a 1072 zip code)—followed by the word "Budapest" (sometimes followed by the Roman numeral, just to be certain); and then the street name and street number. For the sake of clarity, in this book the word "District" precedes the Roman numeral. For easier reference, we've also delineated and named neighborhoods (⇨ What's Where at the front of this book). Although the lower-numbered districts are generally downtown and the farther you go into the outskirts in all directions the higher the district number, it's not quite as simple as that: the first several numbers—Districts I (including Castle Hill), II, and III—are in Buda and border the Danube, while District IV somehow ended up in northern Pest (along the Danube) well away from downtown, and Districts V through IX are all wholly or at least partly in downtown Pest (parts of V and IX border the river). Whereas District X is in eastern Pest, far from the Danube, some areas of downtown Buda by the river fall within District XI.

Districts V, VI, VII, and some of IX are in downtown Pest; District I includes Castle Hill, Buda's main tourist district.

You will find few reminders among street names of the era of communist rule, when streets and squares were named after Soviet heroes and concepts. If you look carefully at street signs, you may still find some with the old names crossed out with a triumphant red line. Today many of Budapest's streets and squares are named after famous Hungarian composers, poets, and painters, reflecting the nation's strong regard for music and the arts.

Keep in mind that Hungary numbers building levels starting from zero (i.e., the ground floor is 0, next floor up is 1, etc.).

The following translations will help you in your navigating:

út (sometimes *útja*) means road or avenue

utca (u.) means street

tér (sometimes *tere*) means square

körút (krt.) means ring road

körtér and *körönd* mean circle

kerület (ker.) means district

emelet (em.) means floor

földszint (fsz.) means ground floor

the airport and any address in the city. To get to the airport, call to arrange a pickup at least 12 hours before your flight leaves. To get to the city, make arrangements at the Airport Minibus airport desk and wait nearby until the driver calls out your address; the wait is usually about 10 minutes. Service to or from either terminal costs 2,300 HUF per person; the discounted round-trip fare is 3,900 HUF. Credit cards (AE, MC, V) are accepted. ■ TIP→ If you plan to buy a Budapest Card (*see below*) during your stay, you can purchase it at the minibus desk and immediately receive the card's 15% discount on your fare. Since it normally shuttles several people at once, remember to allow time for a few other pickups or drop-offs.

Airport Minibus ☎ 1/296-8555. **Buda Taxi** ☎ 1/233-3333 ⊕ www.budataxi.hu. **Főtaxi** ☎ 1/222-2222 or 06-80/222-222 toll-free ⊕ www.fotaxi.hu.

FLIGHTS

A wide variety of American and European airlines offer connecting service from North America, including Aer Lingus (through Dublin or Shannon), Air France (through Paris), Austrian Airlines (through Vienna), British Airways (through London Heathrow and Gatwick), Czech Airlines (through Prague), KLM in partnership with Northwest (through Amsterdam), LOT (through Warsaw), and Lufthansa (through Frankfurt, Berlin, or Munich).

If you are already in Europe or if you are traveling from the U.K., there are many more options for flying to Budapest on low-cost carriers that have begun operating out of several of London's airports. However, it is difficult for travelers from North America to make quick connec-

tions between Heathrow (where most flights from the U.S. land) and Gatwick, Stansted, or Luton (where many of these cheap flights originate). Most of these airlines book tickets only on their Web sites—and bear in mind that a separate ticket within Europe (on an airline other than the one that got you to the U.K.) means that you must abide by more restrictive baggage restrictions (often one checked bag weighing a maximum of 20 kilograms (44 pounds).

Airline Contacts American Airlines ☎ 1/266-6222 in Budapest, 800/433-7300 ⊕ www.aa.com. **British Airways** ☎ 1/777-4747 in Budapest, 800/247-9297 in the U.S. ⊕ www.britishairways.com. **Czech Airlines** (CSA) ☎ 1/318-3175 in Budapest, 800/223-2365 in the U.S. ⊕ www.czechairlines.com. **Delta Airlines** ☎ 800/221-1212 for U.S. reservations, 800/241-4141 for international reservations ⊕ www.delta.com. **Malév Hungarian Airlines** ☎ 06-40/212-121 (from anywhere in Hungary), 1/235-3888 in Budapest, 800/223-6884 in the U.S. outside NYC, 212/566-9944 in the U.S. in NYC ⊕ www.malev.hu. **USAirways** ☎ 800/428-4322 for U.S. reservations, 800/622-1015 for international reservations ⊕ www.usairways.com.

European Airlines Easyjet ☎ 0871/750-0100 in U.K., calls charged at 10p per minute ⊕ www.easyjet.com connects Budapest with London (Luton), Berlin, and Dortmund. **Sky Europe** ☎ 1/777-7000 in Budapest, 0207/365-0365 in U.K. ⊕ www.skyeurope.com flies between Budapest and Amsterdam, Dubrovnik, London (Stansted), Milan, Paris, Rome, Split, Venice, Warsaw, and Zurich. **Wizz Air** ☎ 1/470-9499 in Budapest ⊕ www.wizzair.com flies between Budapest and Athens, Barcelona (Girona), Brussels (Charleroi), London (Luton), Paris (Beauvais), Prague, Rome (Ciampino), and Stockholm (Skavsta).

■ BY BOAT

From late July through early September, two swift hydrofoils leave Vienna daily at 8 AM and 1 PM (once-a-day trips are scheduled mid-April–late July and Septem-

---

WORD OF MOUTH

Ask the local tourist board about hotel and local-transportation packages that include tickets to major museum exhibits or other special events.

ber–October). After a 5½-hour journey downriver with a stop in Bratislava, the Slovak capital, and views of Hungary's largest church, the cathedral in Eszter-gom, the boats head into Budapest via its main artery, the Danube. The upriver journey takes about an hour longer. Combined hydrofoil-train and hydrofoil-bus trips are also available for those who prefer that one leg of their trip be by land.

Schedules are available at the MAHART PassNave office and on its Web site, as well as at most hotels, travel agencies, and tourist information offices. Tickets (€75 one-way, €99 round-trip) are reserved through the MAHART PassNave Web site or by phone. They can be purchased by credit card via phone or the Web site, or they can be purchased in person at the check-in counter by cash or credit card (MC, V).

MAHART PassNave ☎ 1/484–4005 or 1/484–4025 ⊕ www.mahartpassnave.hu.

∥ BY BUS

TO AND FROM HUNGARY

Getting to Hungary by bus from other European cities is fairly easy, and typically accomplished from Western Europe with Eurolines, Europe's main coach line. Routes run between London and Budapest, for example, several times a week, and take approximately 24 hours. Service within Hungary is generally timely, especially on routes originating in Budapest and most other cities; but be prepared for modest delays at intermediate points. All routes, both domestic and international, are no-smoking.

Most buses in Hungary are run by the state-owned Volánbusz company, which is in partnership with Eurolines, Europe's main coach line. Long-distance buses link Budapest's Népliget bus station with most cities in Hungary as well as major cities in Europe. ∥ TIP→ **Some routes tend to be crowded, so if you travel by bus, buy your tickets as far in advance as possible, either at the station or at a Volánbusz travel agency.** The

Budapest–Vienna route is especially popular. That said, on many domestic routes originating in cities outside of Budapest you can buy a ticket only from the bus driver as you board, so on these routes you don't want to be the last in line.

Buses to the eastern part of Hungary depart from the Stadion station in eastern Pest; those to western Hungary generally leave from the Népliget station, also in eastern Pest. For the Danube Bend, buses leave from the bus terminal at Árpád Bridge, near the northern end of Margaret Island, also in Pest. Quality-wise, buses in all areas are a bit of a mixed bag: most are modern and quite comfortable, and even air-conditioned; though some buses appear to be holdovers from the communist era and can get quite hot on warm summer days if the a/c isn't working (though they usually have curtains you can pull closed to block the sun). Domestic routes have no toilets, but many do make pit stops of 5 minutes or more every hour or two (but do confirm before wandering off!).

Long-distance coaches are generally comfortable, but in warm weather it's worth asking about air-conditioning, as some don't have it. Smoking on board is prohibited on both domestic and international routes.

There are no classes on buses in Hungary. Although on some older buses you won't be able to move your seat back much, in general you can expect a moderate degree of legroom and mostly clean seats upholstered in fabric you don't stick to it on hot summer days (with some exceptions).

With the exception of one-month passes of interest primarily to locals, there are no multiday passes or multitrip bus passes available for travel between cities within Hungary. That said, children under 6 travel for free.

Schedule and fare information is available online in English on the Volánbusz Web site. Should a telephone inquiry in English not work, which is a distinct possibility, you might ask for help at your hotel.

Of course, you can also go in person to the bus station or, more conveniently, to the Volánbusz travel office in downtown Pest, which handles most, but not all, bus routes.

Bus Information The general information line for Volánbusz, for both domestic and international routes, is 1/382-0888.

Bus Stations & Ticket Offices **Árpád Bridge bus station** ☎ 1/329-1450. **Népliget bus station** ☎ 1/219-8030 for information, 1/219-8020 international ticket office. **Stadion bus station** ☎ 1/251-0125. **Volánbusz Travel Agency** ☎ 1/318-2122 or 1/267-6243 ⊕ www.volanbusz.hu.

BUDAPEST BY BUS & TRAM

Trams (*villamos*) and buses (*autóbusz*) are abundant and convenient, covering the entire city from around 5 AM to 11 PM or a bit later, after which time there are special all-night runs on key thoroughfares (some every 15 minutes, others only once an hour). Though trams and buses are comfortable, you might well have to remain standing and grab a handhold for lack of a seat; both can get crowded, particularly after around 7 AM and then throughout the day until early evening (some downtown routes, in particular those along the ring boulevards, can get crowded even in the evening, when younger people in particular are out and about). Trolley-bus stops are marked with red, rectangular signs that list the route stops; regular bus stops are marked with similar light blue signs. (The trolley buses and regular buses themselves are red and blue, respectively.) Tram stops are marked by light blue or yellow signs. When getting on a bus or tram, if the doors don't open automatically right away, press the green or red button next to the door to open it.

A one-fare ticket (185 HUF) is valid for only one ride in one direction on any form of public transportation, including the metro; a "transfer ticket" (320 HUF) allows you to make one transfer. ("Ticket," by the way, is *jegy*, pronounced "ye*dy*" in one quick syllable. Try English if that doesn't work.) You can also purchase a day ticket (*napijegy*, pronounced "nup-ee-yedy" for 1,150 HUF, a three-day "tourist ticket" (*három-napos bérlet*, pronounced "hahr-ome nup-oshe bare-let") for 2,500 HUF, or a one-week ticket (*egy-hetes bérlet*, [seven-day pass]) for 3,400 HUF, all of which allow unlimited travel on all services within the city limits. Bulk ticket books in 10- and 20-piece (*tízes tömb* [teez-esh temb] or *huszas tömb* [hoos-ush temb] at 1,665 HUF and 3,145 HUF, respectively) units are also available; don't tear the tickets from their binding after validating them or else you'll run into trouble with the undercover checkers. Most lines run from 5 AM and stop operating at 11 PM, but there is all-night service on certain key routes. Consult the separate night-bus map posted in most metro stations for all-night service.

Schedules, though not available in printed form (unless you print out from the Web site of the Budapest Transport Company, commonly known by its Hungarian acronym BKV ["bay-kah-vay"]), are posted at stops, and buses and trams generally stick to them, although rush-hour traffic and occasional breakdowns do sometimes throw a wrench into the otherwise smoothly functioning mechanism of public transport in the capital.

In Budapest tickets are widely available in metro stations and at many newsstands and (sometimes malfunctioning) sidewalk automats. The accepted method of payment is cash. Your best bet is simply to buy a pass, which you can do at a metro station. If you do opt to buy individual tickets instead (do so if you'll take only a handful of rides during the day and saving a couple of dollars is an issue), each ticket must be validated on board by inserting it, downward-facing, into the little device provided for that purpose, then pulling the knob; with newer devices, just insert the ticket. (When you do so, some locals on board who are riding without validating their tickets—there are always a few of them—may become alarmed, thinking that you've seen a ticket checker, or that you *are* the ticket checker. But that's life.) ■ **TIP**→ Hold on to whatever ticket you have throughout the length of the ride; spot checks by undercover checkers—who slip on red armbands just before getting down to their highly unpopular task—are numerous and often target tourists.

Paying on board is possible only on a few bus and tram lines in Budapest, and even on those it may be unreliable, as drivers occasionally run out of tickets; at this writing the cost was 210 HUF a ticket, compared to 185 HUF tickets purchased in advance. In many smaller Hungarian cities on-board ticket purchasing is a good alternative, though likewise a bit more expensive than buying a ticket beforehand. **Bus Information** Short of consulting the schedules at individual stops, the easiest way to get info is to ask a local; or log onto BKV's Web site, which has user-friendly English-language content. There are no bus stations for service within the city. BKV has a customer service-phone number (used rarely by locals for transport info), but you may not get someone who speaks much English. **BKV** ☎ 1/461-6688, Ext. 4 ⊕ www.bkv.hu.

Eventually, by the way, Budapest's public transport system may well adopt magnetic tickets and passes. At this writing, however, the capital's human ticket-checkers had little to fear in terms of job security: the cost and complications of effecting such a major overhaul mean it is unlikely in the immediate future.

∎ BY CAR

Although driving in Budapest is a bad idea, and visiting most individual smaller cities is easy by train or bus, driving is the most convenient way to get from Eger to Tokaj, for example, or to travel between Debrecen and Szeged without having to return to Budapest (though there are a couple of buses each day that will also save you the trouble). Of course, assuming you

can afford the time and the high fuel cost, and are not rattled by the prospect of encountering Hungarian drivers who pass whenever the opportunity does or does not present itself, a car will allow you to explore the countryside at your leisure. It's a small country, so even driving from one end to the other is manageable.

The main routes into Budapest are the M1 from Vienna (via Győr), the M3 from around Polgár (southeast of Miskolc), the M5 from south of Kecskemét, and the M7 from the Balaton region; the M3 and M5 are being upgraded and extended to Hungary's borders with Ukraine and Serbia, respectively, and yet another motorway is under construction north from the M3 to Miskolc, eventually destined for Slovakia. Like any Western city, Budapest is plagued by traffic jams during the day, but motorists should have no problem later in the evening. Motorists unaccustomed to sharing city streets with trams should pay extra attention. You should be prepared to be flagged down numerous times by police conducting routine checks for drunk driving and stolen cars. Be sure all your papers are in order and readily accessible; unfortunately, the police have been known to give foreigners a hard time.

GASOLINE

Gas stations are plentiful in Hungary, and many on the main highways stay open all night, even on holidays. Major chains, such as MOL, Shell, and OMV, have Western-style, full-facility stations with restrooms, brightly lit convenience stores, and 24-hour service. Lines are rarely long, and supplies are stable. Unleaded gasoline (*bleifrei* in German or *ólommentes* in Hungarian) is available at all stations (leaded fuel is no longer sold in Hungary) and is usually the 95-octane-level choice. At this writing, fuel was around 300 HUF per liter ($5.33 per gallon). Credit cards are widely accepted, and you should automatically get a receipt. If you don't, ask for a *blokk* (pronounced "blowk").

PARKING

Gone are the "anything goes" days of parking in Budapest, when cars parked for free practically anywhere in the city, straddling curbs or angled in the middle of sidewalks. Now most streets in Budapest's main districts have restricted, fee-based parking; there are either parking meters that accept coins and give you a ticket to display on your dashboard (usually for a maximum of two hours) or attendants who approach your car as you park and charge you according to how many hours you intend to stay. Hourly rates range between 120 HUF and 400 HUF. In most cases, parking in these areas overnight (generally after 6 PM and before 8 AM weekdays and after noon on Saturday) and all day Sunday is free. The minimum parking time is 15 minutes; the maximum in one place, two to three hours.

For longer parking in one spot, your best bet downtown is a parking garage. There are garages in central Pest's District V at Szervita tér, Aranykéz utca 4–6, and underground at Szabadság tér. Lots and garages are easy to find by following the standard blue "P" signs marking their entrances. There is also P+R (Park and Ride) parking near some metro stations, such as Árpád híd in northern Pest, but these are on the outskirts of downtown (not a good option if your hotel is downtown). Finally, note that illegally parked cars are liable to have a wheel clamped, meaning that the car stays there until you pay; if this happens, an information sheet including English text should be on your windshield explaining what to do.

Away from Budapest, smaller towns usually have free parking on the street and some hourly fee lots near main tourist zones. Throughout the country, no-parking zones are marked with the international no parking sign: a red circle with a diagonal line through it.

ROAD CONDITIONS

There are four classes of roads: expressways (designated by the letter "M" and a single digit), main highways (a single digit), secondary roads (a two-digit number), and minor roads (a three-digit number). Expressways, highways, and secondary roads are generally in good condition. The condition of minor roads varies considerably; keep in mind that tractors and horse-drawn carts may slow you down in rural areas. In planning your driving route with a map, opt for the larger roadways whenever possible; you'll generally end up saving time even if there is a shorter but smaller road. It's not so much the condition of the smaller roads but the kind of traffic on them and number of towns they pass through (where the speed limit is 50 kph [30 mph]) that will slow you down. If you're in no hurry, however, explore the smaller roads.

At this writing, Hungary was continuing a massive upgrading and reconstruction of many of its expressways, gearing up for its role as the main bridge for trade between the Balkan countries and the former Soviet Union and Western Europe. To help fund the project, tolls are collected on several routes. Toll roads include the M1, which runs west from Budapest toward Vienna; the M3, which runs northeast, providing access via connecting routes to both Miskolc and Debrecen, but with the main route, once construction is complete, directed toward Ukraine (at this writing it's already more than halfway there, southeast of Miskolc); the M5, from Budapest to south of Kecskemét at this writing, and eventually on to Szeged and from there to Serbia; and the M7, which goes southwest toward Lake Balaton, where it turns narrow once again but eventually becomes a full-fledged motorway once more as you near Croatia, welcoming all those vacation-minded Hungarians driving so eagerly to the Adriatic Sea.

ROADSIDE EMERGENCIES

In case of a breakdown, your best friend is the telephone. Try contacting your rental agency or the national breakdown service. If your rental car is stolen, try the agency (assuming you have the papers) and, of course, the police.

Emergency Services Hungarian Automobile Club's breakdown service ☎ 188.

RULES OF THE ROAD

Hungarians drive on the right and observe the usual European rules of the road (but they revel in passing). Although at this writing there was no detailed English-language text readily available on traffic rules, if you keep a few things in mind you'll be fine. Unless otherwise noted, the speed limit in developed areas is 50 kph (30 mph), on main roads 90 to 110 kph (55 to 65 mph), and on highways 130 kph (78 mph). Stay alert: speed-limit signs are few and far between. Developed areas are marked by a white rectangular sign with the town name written in black; slow down to 50 kph (or less if so marked) as soon as you pass one. You can speed up again once you pass a similar sign with the town name crossed out in red. Seat belts are compulsory (front-seat belts in lower-speed zones, both front and back in higher-speed zones), as is the use of headlights outside of cities or towns. Children under 16 may not travel in the front passenger seat; infants and toddlers must sit in a car seat in the back seat of the car. Holding a mobile phone while driving is illegal; headsets are OK. Drinking alcohol is prohibited—there is a zero-tolerance policy, and penalties are severe.

Tolls must be paid ahead of time, which gives you a sticker (*matrica*) displayed on the upper left corner of your windshield. These come in 4-day, 10-day, monthly, and yearly increments; toll stations verify them electronically as you drive through. Stickers can be bought at all gas stations, but NOT at tollbooths themselves. Be sure to ask for and keep the receipt (*blokk*, pronounced "blowk"). In summer spot-checks are frequent. If you're not in a hurry, you can also always take the free route that was replaced by the toll road.

WORD OF MOUTH

Speed traps are numerous, so it's best to observe the speed limit; fines start from the equivalent of $50, but they easily climb higher. In an effort to forestall bribe-taking, the time-honored practice of on-the-spot payment for violations was abolished in 2000, so police must now give accused speeders an invoice payable at post offices. (Remember this if you feel innocent and an officer suggests an on-the-spot "discount.") Spot checks are frequent as well, and police occasionally try to take advantage of foreigners, so always have your papers on hand.

▌ BY SUBWAY

Service on Budapest's subway system—locally called the *metro*—is inexpensive (for Western visitors, anyway), fast, and frequent (even the escalators are fast!); stations are easily located on maps and streets by the big letter "M" (for metro). *Bejárat* means entrance; *kijárat* means exit. Tickets valid on all forms of mass transportation within the boundaries of Budapest can be bought at hotels, metro stations, newsstands, and kiosks—but metro stations are least likely to run out and therefore your best bet. Metro fares are the same as bus and tram fares (⇨ Getting Around Budapest by Bus & Tram, *above*). Special metro-only tickets are also available in several varieties, but it's generally not worth the confusion and the minimal cost difference. **Tickets must be validated** in the time-clock machines in station entrances and should be kept until the end of the journey, as there are frequent checks by undercover inspectors; the fine for traveling without a ticket is 2,500 HUF plus the fare.

Line 1 (marked FÖLDALATTI), which starts downtown at Vörösmarty tér and follows Andrássy út out past Gundel restaurant and City Park, is an antique tourist attraction in itself, built in the 1890s for the Magyar Millennium; its yellow trains with tank treads still work. Lines 2 and 3 were built 90 years later. Line 2 (red) runs from the eastern suburbs, past the Keleti (East) Railway Station, through the city center, and under the Danube to the Déli (South) station. One of the stations, Moszkva tér, is also the terminus for the Várbusz (Castle Bus). Line 3 (blue) runs from the southeastern suburbs to Deák tér, through the city center, and northward to the Nyugati (West) station and the northern suburbs. All three lines meet at the Deák tér station and run every few minutes from 4:30 AM to shortly after 11 PM.

Subway cars are comfortable, though they are often so crowded during the day that you won't find a seat. Smoking is strictly prohibited anywhere within the area of the metro (generally, beyond the ticket-validating machines located above the escalators); and this rule is enforced.

TICKET/PASS	PRICE
Single Fare	185 HUF
Day Ticket	1,150 HUF
3-Day Tourist Pass	2,500 HUF
One week	3,400 HUF

Subway Information BKV Customer Affairs Office ✉ District VII, Akácfa utca 18, Around Blaha Lujza tér ☎ 1/461-6688, Ext. 4 ⊕ www.bkv.hu.

▌ BY TAXI

There are plenty of honest taxi drivers in Budapest but a few too many dishonest ones. If you follow these guidelines you should be able to avoid being one of the many frustrated travelers taken for a ride. Whenever possible, do as locals do and order a taxi by telephone—even if you're on the street. Főtaxi now has a toll-free number, which can be called from any pay phone without using any coins. All the companies we list have English-speaking operators. City Taxi and Főtaxi are especially good with English and handling for-

eigners. You will be asked for the address, your name, and a contact phone number; if you're at a pay phone, give them the number written on the phone if it's visible. The taxi usually appears in 5 to 10 minutes, and the driver will ask you to confirm your name. Most locals open the front door and hop in the passenger seat next to the driver. If you're at a restaurant, you can ask your waiter to call you a cab, but be sure to specify which company or companies you want. Don't be shy: this is common practice in Budapest.

Hailing a taxi on the street is tricky, as the available ones will tend to be the sharks trolling for tourists. If a gleaming, unmarked white Mercedes offers to take you, don't get in! The reliable ones are easy to spot (but most of them on the streets are occupied by telephone customers): their company logo and phone number will be displayed clearly all over the car—again, it's safest to wait for one of the companies listed below. You're more likely than not to find one at a *taxi állomás* (taxi stand) (pronounced, "tuck-see ah-lome-osh").

All legitimate taxis must have a working meter; make sure it is running when you start out. The charge is by distance and time, not by passenger; while taxis are not allowed to charge separate fees for luggage, any help the driver gives you with luggage means that the tip you include with the fee can be on the high end (or higher) of the usual 10%–15%.

If you hail a taxi on the street, the base fare at this writing was no more than 300 HUF during the day and 420 HUF at night. Added to this are 220 HUF per kilometer by day or 336 HUF at night, plus 60 HUF per minute when not in motion by day, 84 HUF at night. Larger companies, including those we recommend, often charge lower rates, especially when called in advance. When you order a taxi by phone, the per-kilometer rate falls by 10% or more per kilometer.

Be especially wary at the airport and train stations, where many visitors run into trouble. *Never* go along with someone who approaches you on the platform (⇨ Ground Transportation in Airports, *above*). Outside the train station will be a line of taxis; look there for one of the reliable ones. If you don't find one, call from a pay phone.

Another tip: if you're on a tight budget, avoid taking official hotel taxis, as they tend to be very expensive. Visitors stranded on Castle Hill should avoid the Hilton taxicabs, shiny as they may be, for this reason. **Taxi Companies BudaTaxi** ☎ 1/233-3333. **City Taxi** ☎ 1/211-1111. **Fő taxi** ☎ 1/222-2222, 06-80/222-222 toll-free. **Radio Taxi** ☎ 1/377-7777. **6x6 Taxi** ☎ 1/266-6666.

▌ BY TRAIN

International trains—and there is a steady stream of them, from all directions—are routed to two stations in Budapest. Keleti Pályaudvar (East Station) receives most international rail traffic coming in from the west, including Vienna. Nyugati Pályaudvar (West Station) handles a combination of international and domestic trains. Déli handles trains to the Lake Balaton region and to Pécs. Within Hungary, there is frequent and convenient rail service to many smaller cities and towns on the many routes that radiate in all directions from Budapest.

Snacks and drinks are often not available on trains, so pack a lunch for the road; train picnics are a way of life. For more information about rail travel, contact or visit MAV Passenger Service.

Many domestic trains have only second-class (*másod osztály,* pronounced "mah-should oh-sty") cars. First class (*első osztály,* pronounced "ell-she oh-sty"), which costs around 50% more, will give you somewhat larger seats, fewer fellow passengers crowding in and slicing their odorous salami beside you, and velvety upholstery that you won't stick to on a hot summer day, unlike the vinyl-like seat fabric found in most second-class cars. On generally newer Intercity (IC) trains even

---

SMOKIN' SEATS

All trains have no-smoking sections or cars, and rarely do smokers feel empowered to light up where they shouldn't—they'll eventually be told not to. When buying tickets for domestic travel on relatively fast Intercity (IC) trains, you will automatically be sold a seat in a no-smoking section unless you request otherwise. Just to be sure, confirm this if you prefer clear air around you. If you are a smoker and you are in a smoking car but notice that no one else in your compartment is smoking (it's possible that there were no more no-smoking seats left), it is considered polite to step into the corridor before lighting up.

---

second class is considerably more comfortable than the same class on older trains that ply slower routes.

For travel only within Hungary, Eurail offers a Eurail National Pass, which costs $83 for any 5 days of travel within a 15-day period, or $98 for 10 days within a one-month period. There is also MÁV's own 7- and 10-day *turista bérlet* (tourist pass) good for either seven or 10 days (13,180 HUF and 18,960 HUF, respectively) of second-class travel, available directly from the MÁV office. Such a pass may be economical if, during a short stay, you take separate trips from Budapest to Eger, Pécs, and Lake Balaton, for example.

The European East Pass, available outside of Europe, may be used on the national rail networks of Hungary, Austria, the Czech Republic, Poland, and Slovakia. The pass covers anywhere from five to 10 days of unlimited first- or second-class travel within a one-month period; a five-day first-class pass costs $226, second-class costs $160.

Hungary is also covered by the Eurail-pass, which provides unlimited first-class rail travel, in all of the participating countries of Europe, for the duration of the pass. Purchase rail passes in the U.S. and Canada from either ACP Rail, Euro Railways, or Rail Europe. Service charges can vary dramatically, so be sure to shop around.

Domestic fares are based on distance traveled, minus a series of complicated discounts for which foreigners are mostly ineligible. Information staff at the Budapest train stations and MAV Passenger Service office should, in theory, be able to help you with ticket information as well as sell you tickets. If you have trouble communicating, you can ask for help at any tourist information office or travel agency listed below. MÁV's English-language Web site, called "ELVIRA," has current domestic schedule and fare information in English, as does its 24-hour telephone hotline, and is a good place to start.

Travel by train from Budapest to other large cities or to Lake Balaton is cheap and efficient. ■ TIP→ Avoid *személyvonat* (local trains), which are extremely slow; instead, take Intercity (IC) trains or *gyorsvonat* (express trains). On timetables, *vágány* (tracks) are abbreviated with a "v"; *indul* means departing, and *érkezik* means arriving. Trains get crowded during weekend travel in summer, especially to Lake Balaton; you're more likely to have elbow room if you pay a little extra for first-class tickets—assuming first class is an option on your train.

All major credit cards can be used to pay for tickets at Budapest train stations, but at domestic ticket windows you won't make friends with the locals in line behind you at rush hour if you opt to pay for a ticket amounting to 1,000 HUF (roughly $5) with plastic rather than cash. Practically all locals pay with cash, and at many

stations in smaller cities and in the countryside this is your only option.

Intercity (IC) trains—which ensure relatively comfy, clean, and fast service on domestic routes to the largest towns outside of Budapest—require a *helyjegy* (seat reservation, roughly pronounced "heyyedy" as two distinct syllables). But you should automatically receive one at the time of purchase, for around 500 HUF extra beyond the normal cost of the ticket for the distance you're going. ■ TIP→ Before leaving the ticket window, though, check to see that you get two ticket-like slips of paper: one is your ticket, the other your seat reservation.

MAV Passenger Service ☒ District VI, Andrássy út 35, Budapest ☎ 06–40/49–49–49 central information line (local charge from anywhere in Hungary) ⊕ www.elvira.hu.

Rail Passes ACP Rail International ☎ 866/938-7245 ⊕ www.eurail-acprail.com. **Euro Railways** ☎ 866/768-8927 ⊕ www.eurorailways.com. **Rail Europe** ☎ 877/257-2887 in the U.S., 800/361-7245 in Canada ⊕ www.raileurope.com.

Train Stations Keleti Pályaudvar (East Railway Station) ☒ District VIII, Baross tér. **Nyugati Pályaudvar** (West Railway Station) ☒ District V, Nyugati tér. **Déli Pályaudvar** (South Railway Station) ☒ District XII, Alkotás utca.

DISCOUNTS

Only Hungarian citizens are entitled to student discounts on domestic train fares; however, all senior citizens (men over 60, women over 55) are eligible for a 20% discount.

ON THE GROUND

■ COMMUNICATIONS

INTERNET

Cybercafes ⊕ www.cybercafes.com lists over 4,000 Internet cafés worldwide.

PHONES

The good news is that you can now make a direct-dial telephone call from virtually any point on earth. The bad news? You can't always do so cheaply. Calling from a hotel is almost always the most expensive option; hotels usually add huge surcharges to all calls, particularly international ones. In some countries you can phone from call centers or even the post office. Calling cards usually keep costs to a minimum, but only if you purchase them locally. And then there are mobile phones (⇨ *below*), which are sometimes more prevalent—particularly in the developing world—than land lines; as expensive as mobile phone calls can be, they are still usually a much cheaper option than calling from your hotel.

CALLING WITHIN HUNGARY

Dial "198" for directory assistance for all of Hungary. There is usually someone on hand who can speak English. You can also consult *The Phone Book*, an English-language telephone directory full of important Budapest numbers as well as cultural and tourist information; it's provided in guest rooms of most major hotels and at many restaurants and English-language bookstores. The slim but information-packed city guide *Budapest in Your Pocket* lists important phone numbers; it appears six times a year and can be bought at newsstands and hotels.

On their way to extinction but still around, coin-operated pay phones accept 10-HUF, 20-HUF, 50-HUF, and 100-HUF coins; the minimum initial amount is 20 HUF. Given that these phones often swallow up change without allowing a call in ex-change, however, it's best when possible to use gray card-operated telephones, which outnumber coin-operated phones in Budapest and the Balaton region (⇨ Calling Cards, *below*). Every three minutes will cost you at least 20 HUF.

Budapest's area code for land-line phone numbers is 1, but from within the city you need only dial the seven numbers that follow. From outside the city you must first dial 06 and wait for the buzzing tone, then dial 1 followed by the seven numbers. Should you need to dial a mobile-phone number—beginning with 06 followed by either 20, 30, or 70, depending on the service provider, and seven more numbers—bear in mind that you'll be charged at least three times more for such a call.

CALLING OUTSIDE HUNGARY

Cellular-phone numbers are treated like long-distance domestic calls: dial 06 before the number (when giving their cellular phone numbers, most people include the 06 anyway).

Direct calls to foreign countries can be made from Budapest and all major provincial towns by dialing 00 and waiting for the international dialing tone; on pay phones the initial charge is 60 HUF.

The country code for Hungary is 36. When dialing from outside the country, drop the initial 06 prefix for area codes outside of Budapest. The country code for the United States is 1.

Access Codes AT&T ☎ 06/800-01111. **World Phone** ☎ 06/800-01411. **Sprint** ☎ 06/800-01877.

CALLING CARDS

Traditional calling cards—available at post offices and most newsstands and kiosks—come in units of 800 HUF and work by being inserted into the telephone's card slot. The units are then withdrawn, at a rate of approximately 20 HUF every three minutes.

324 < **On The Ground**

LOCAL DO'S & TABOOS

CUSTOMS OF THE COUNTRY

There is a very large population of elderly people in Budapest, and chivalry towards them is customary, even among young people. When riding public transportation it is polite to give your seat to an elderly person, man or woman. This should be done discreetly, by simply getting up and moving aside; the man may not wish to be perceived as weak, the woman prefer not to be thought of as elderly.

As in some other parts of Europe, personal space may be less generous than you're used to, which is to say that you should not be disconcerted by locals standing embarrassingly close to you while talking.

Discussing such matters as one's religion is generally taboo—many Hungarians are so firmly secular, anyway, that broaching religion would strike them as strange. Unlike an American, a Hungarian will rarely ask a stranger, "So, what do you do? Where are you from?" Conversations about world affairs, art, politics, economics, and the weather are much more common. If you do initiate a conversation on a more personal note, though it may seem odd to the local, it may well be refreshing to find a stranger actually interested in them.

Given that public transport cannot always be counted on to get you places right on time, few Hungarians will even notice if you're a half-hour late for a lunch or dinner invitation, for example. Although locals are not famous for punctuality, this does not mean that they do not generally keep to schedules. They do. If you think you'll be delayed by more than 30 minutes or so, a phone call is in order. In Budapest it's best to arrange to meet where it is possible to sit down rather than on a streetcorner, lest one party should be kept standing for too long.

GREETINGS

Hungarians are traditionally polite and well-mannered people—certainly when dealing with non-Hungarians. It is customary to greet people upon entering and exiting a store or restaurant rather than just walking in and out without a word. A general greeting of jo napot kivánok/jo estét (good day/good evening) when you enter and viszontlátásra when you leave will suffice. You'll likely hear the same in response from the storekeeper, or else szija, an informal, combination "hi/bye" that is used especially by young people.

Except in business situations, both women and men double-kiss, once on each cheek, in greeting. Men generally shake hands.

LANGUAGE

One of the best ways to avoid being an obvious tourist is to learn a little of the local language. You need not strive for fluency; even just mastering a few basic phrases is bound to make chatting with the locals more rewarding.

Older people generally speak some German, and many younger people speak at least rudimentary English, which has been the most popular language to learn since around 1990, once Russian was no longer compulsory in schools. It's a safe bet that anyone in the tourist trade—especially in hotels but also in many restaurants—will speak at least one of the two, if not both, languages. In outlying areas of the country noticeably fewer people speak English than in Budapest.

When giving names, Hungarians put the family name before the given name, thus János Szabó (John Taylor) becomes Szabó János.

See Hungarian Vocabulary.

Another option—one that, significantly, also allows you to make low-cost international calls (e.g., around 10¢ or less per minute to the U.S.)—is to purchase a prepaid calling card from any general shop, newsstand, or post office; it can be used for local as well as international phone calls and works with a toll-free access number, so you don't need coins to use it at a pay phone. But most companies that offer such cards impose a modest surcharge if you do use them from a pay phone. At this writing the so-called "Bla-Bla" card offered the best rates; other good options include the Neo card and Touristfon. Since more and more such cards have appeared in recent years, the best thing to do is shop around by comparing the fine print on the brochures for such cards that are available about town (generally there is English text).

MOBILE PHONES

If you have a multiband phone (some countries use different frequencies than those used in the United States) and your service provider uses the world-standard GSM network (as do T-Mobile, Cingular, and Verizon), you can probably use your phone abroad. Roaming fees can be steep, however: 99¢ a minute is considered reasonable. And overseas you normally pay the toll charges for incoming calls. It's almost always cheaper to send a text message than to make a call, since text messages have a very low set fee (often less than 5¢).

If you just want to make local calls, consider buying a new SIM card (note that your provider may have to unlock your phone for you to use a different SIM card) and a prepaid service plan in the destination. You'll then have a local number and can make local calls at local rates. If your trip is extensive, you could also simply buy a new cell phone in your destination, as the initial cost will be offset over time.

▌ TIP→ If you travel internationally frequently, save one of your old mobile phones or buy a cheap one on the Internet; ask your cell-phone

company to unlock it for you, and take it with you as a travel phone, buying a new SIM card with pay-as-you-go service in each destination. **Cellular Abroad** ☎ 800/287-5072 ⊕ www.cellularabroad.com rents and sells GMS phones and sells SIM cards that work in many countries. **Mobal** ☎ 888/888-9162 ⊕ www.mobalrental.com rents mobiles and sells GSM phones (starting at $49) that will operate in 140 countries. Per-call rates vary throughout the world. **Planet Fone** ☎ 888/988-4777 ⊕ www.planetfone.com rents cell phones, but the per-minute rates are expensive.

▌ CUSTOMS & DUTIES

You're always allowed to bring goods of a certain value back home without having to pay any duty or import tax. But there's a limit on the amount of tobacco and liquor you can bring back duty-free, and some countries have separate limits for perfumes; for exact figures, check with your customs department. The values of so-called "duty-free" goods are included in these amounts. When you shop abroad, save all your receipts, as customs inspectors may ask to see them as well as the items you purchased. If the total value of your goods is more than the duty-free limit, you'll have to pay a tax (most often a flat percentage) on the value of everything beyond that limit.

You may import duty-free into Hungary 250 cigarettes or 50 cigars or the equivalent in tobacco, 1 liter of spirits, and 1 liter of wine. In addition to the above, you are permitted to import into Hungary goods valued up to 27,000 HUF (personal items and appliances such as cameras, and laptops are not figured into this sum).

Objects considered to be of museum value—certain works of art or antiques marked *védett*—cannot be taken out of the country. Take care when you leave Hungary that you have the right documentation for exporting goods. Keep receipts for any major purchases. Upon leaving, you are entitled to a refund of up to 18% of value-added tax (V.A.T., or ÁFA by its

Hungarian acronym) on new goods (i.e., not works of art, antiques, or objects of museum value) that appear on one invoice with a value of 45,000 HUF or more (V.A.T. inclusive). For details, ⇨ Taxes.

Information in Hungary Hungarian Customs & Finance Guard ☎ 1/456-9500 ⊕ www.vam.hu. **Tourinform** ☎ 1/438-8080 (24-hr hotline) or 06-80/630-800 (24-hr toll-free recorded information) ⊕ www.hungary.com or www.itthon.hu.

U.S. Information U.S. Customs and Border Protection ⊕ www.cbp.gov.

▌DAY TOURS & GUIDES

You won't find the streets and squares of downtown Budapest overflowing with freelance tour guides vying for your business. IBUSZ and EUrama are two well-established agencies that can provide individual guides for specially arranged tours. Exclusive City Tours, which offers a three-hour automobile tour of Budapest for up to three persons at a somewhat exclusive price of around €170, specializes in more personalized tours both in Budapest and elsewhere in Hungary.

Recommended Tours/Guides EUrama ✉ Hotel InterContinental, District V, Apáczai Csere János utca 12-14, Around Váci utca ☎ 1/327-6690 ⊕ www.eurama.hu. **Exclusive City Tours** ☎ 06-20/982-3157 ⊕ www.citytour96.com. **IBUSZ** ✉ District V, Ferenciek tere 10, Around Ferenciek tere ☎ 1/485-2700 or 06-40/428-794 ⊕ www.ibusz.hu.

BOAT TOURS

The Legenda company offers hour-long *Danube Legend* sightseeing cruises that depart nightly at 8:15 from mid-March through April and in October and three times nightly (at 8:15, 9, and 10) from May through September. The cost is 4,200 HUF. From November through December—except December 24–26 but including December 27–30—and New Year's Day, there are cruises only at 6:30 PM. Guests receive headphones with recorded explanations of the sights (available in 30 languages), as well as a free drink. Boats depart from Pier 6–7 at Vigadó tér. It's wise to double-check the schedule to avoid missing the boat.

Legenda also has six two-hour *Duna-Bella* cruises a day, most of which include a one-hour walk on Margaret Island. Recorded commentary is provided through earphones. The tour, which costs 3,600 HUF, is offered July and August eight times a day; May through June and in September six times a day; and mid-March through April and October through mid-December once a day. Boats depart from Pier 6–7 at Vigadó tér.

From early April to early September at noon every day Legenda's boats leave from the dock at Vigadó tér on 1½-hour cruises between the railroad bridges north and south of the Árpád and Petőfi bridges, respectively. The trip operates only on Friday, Saturday, Sunday, and holidays in April, then daily until early September. From late April to mid-June there is an additional tour leaving every day at 7:30 PM. Tickets are around 1,800 HUF.

Another company, MAHART Passnave, operates one-hour *Duna Corso* cruises that commence from Vigadó tér pier and take in the sights between Margaret Bridge to the north to the National Theater to the south, with commentary in four languages. The tours, which cost 2,400 HUF, run every day from May to October 1 and depart hourly from 10 AM to 7 PM, with additional tours at 8:30 and 9:30. In low season (late March through late April and late September through late October) the last tour is at 5 PM.

Danube Legend and *Duna-Bella* ☎ 1/317-2203 reservations and information. **MAHART PassNave** ☎ 1/484-4013 (main info line) or 1/318-1223 (boat landing at Vigadó tér) ⊕ www.mahartpassnave.hu.

BUS TOURS

Program Centrum conducts two- and three-hour bus tours of the city that operate all year (no two-hour tour from November through March) and cost 5,000 HUF and 6,500 HUF, respectively. Holders of the Budapest Card get big discounts. Starting from Erzsébet tér, the tours take in parts of both Buda and Pest. The company can also provide private English-speaking guides on request. EUrama also offers a three-hour city bus tour (6,500 HUF per person). IBUSZ runs a variety of city-highlight tours, some including interior tours of Parliament or the Great Synagogue, some with extras such as post-tour wine tasting. All three agencies also offer full- and half-day bus excursion tours outside of Budapest. Budatours runs two-hour city tours on its open-top buses daily May through September for 4,300 HUF. All bus tours have commentary in English, but ask whether it's recorded or live if it's important to you.

Budatours ☎ 1/374-7070 or 1/353-0558 ⊕ www.budatours.hu. **EUrama** ☎ 1/327-6690 ⊕ www.eurama.hu. **IBUSZ** ☎ 1/485-2700 or 06-40/428-794 ⊕ www.ibusz.hu. **Program Centrum** ☎ 1/317-7767 or 1/318-4446 ⊕ www.programcentrum.hu.

BICYCLE & SEGWAY TOURS

For something different, you can try Yellow Zebra's 3½-hour English-language bicycle tour taking in the major sights of Buda and Pest (via designated bike lanes and less-trafficked streets). The cost is 5,500 HUF. For something even more different, there's Budapest's only Segway tours operation, run by the same company out of its shop behind the Opera House: for 12,000 HUF you get 30–45 minutes of training plus a roughly 2-hour tour of downtown; tours usually 10 AM and 6:30 PM, but call beforehand to confirm.

Yellow Zebra Bike Tours ☎ 1/269-3843 or 1/266-8777 ⊕ www.yellowzebrabikes.com.

WALKING TOURS

Absolute Walking Tours, run by the same company that operates Yellow Zebra Bike Tours, has broken the mold for guided walking tours in Central Europe. The company offers not only historical and general-interest tours but also creatively executed theme tours, such as the "Ham-

mer & Sickle Tour" and a "Budapest Dark Side" night tour. The 3½-hour Budapest walk costs 4,000 HUF (free for kids under 15). No reservations are necessary; just show up at one of the two designated starting points, rain or shine. From June through August, tours start at 9:30 AM and 1:30 PM in front of the yellow church on Deák tér, and at 10 AM and 2 PM from the steps of the Műcsarnok on Heroes' Square. From September through May tours go just once a day: 10:30 AM from Deák tér and 11 AM from Heroes' Square (in January call ahead, as tours don't run every day; there are no tours on December 25 and 26). Private theme tours can be specially arranged.

Chosen Tours offers several options, including a two-hour walking tour of Budapest's onetime Jewish neighborhood (6,500 HUF) and a three-hour combination bus and walking tour (9,000 HUF) called "Budapest Through Jewish Eyes," highlighting the sights and cultural life of the city's Jewish history. Tours run daily except Saturday and include free pickup and drop-off at central locations. Arrangements can also be made for off-season tours, as well as custom-designed tours.

Absolute Walking Tours ☎ 1/269-3843 ☎ 1/266-8777 ⊕ www.absolutetours.com. **Chosen Tours** ☎☎ 1/355-2202.

WINE TOURS

IBUSZ Travel offers its all-day "Eger Wine Region" tour leaving from Budapest on Tuesdays and Thursdays from May through October for €93. The excursion involves a thorough look at downtown Eger including the fortress, a hearty lunch, and wine-tasting in Szépasszonyok völgye on the city outskirts. Exclusive City Tours, meanwhile, offers more personalized service (at a higher price), with one-day tours of Eger or Tokaj for approximately 80,000 HUF for up to three people.

Exclusive City Tours ☎ 06-20/982-3157 ⊕ www.citytour96.com. **IBUSZ** ✉ District V, Ferenciek tere 10, Around Ferenciek tere ☎ 1/485-2700 or 06-40/428-794 ⊕ www.ibusz.hu.

▌ELECTRICITY

The electrical current in Hungary is 220 volts, 50 cycles alternating current (AC); wall outlets generally take plugs with two round prongs. Consider making a small investment in a universal adapter, which has several types of plugs in one lightweight, compact unit. Most laptops and mobile phone chargers are dual voltage (i.e., they operate equally well on 110 and 220 volts), so require only an adapter. These days the same is true of small appliances such as hair dryers. Always check labels and manufacturer instructions to be sure. Don't use 110-volt outlets marked FOR SHAVERS ONLY for high-wattage appliances such as hair-dryers.

Bring an adapter for your laptop plug. Adapters are inexpensive, and some models have several plugs suitable for different systems throughout the world. Some hotels lend adapters to guests for use during their stay.

At the airport, be prepared to turn on your laptop to prove to security personnel that the device is real. Security X-ray machines can be damaging to a laptop, and keep computer disks away from metal detectors.

Steve Kropla's Help for World Traveler's ⊕ www.kropla.com has information on electrical and telephone plugs around the world. **Walkabout Travel Gear** ⊕ www. walkabouttravelgear.com has a good coverage of electricity under "adapters."

▌EMERGENCIES

If you need a doctor, ask your hotel or embassy for a recommendation, or contact FirstMed Centers, a private, American-standard clinic located in central Buda and staffed by English-speaking doctors offering 24-hour emergency service. The clinic accepts major credit cards and has direct billing agreements with numerous international insurance companies. In an emergency you can call for a general ambulance or call American Clinics International and they will arrange for one for you.

Profident Dental Services is a private, English-speaking dental practice consisting of Western-trained dentists and hygienists, with service available until 10 PM except Sundays. S.O.S. Dent, another private English-speaking dental clinic, offers 24-hour care.

Most pharmacies (*gyógyszertár*) close between 6 PM and 8 PM, but several stay open at night and on weekends, offering 24-hour service, with a small surcharge for items that aren't officially stamped as urgent by a physician. You must ring the buzzer next to the night window and someone will respond over the intercom. Staff are unlikely to speak English, so try to get at least a rough translation of what you need before you go. A small extra fee (100 HUF–200 HUF) is added to the bill. Late-night pharmacies are usually found across from the train stations.

Hungarian hospitals don't have dedicated general emergency rooms that one can just walk into. If you call an ambulance, the paramedics assess you and, based on your condition and location, take you to the relevant department of the hospital, where you are immediately treated. Hungarian doctors are well trained, and most speak English or German. Generally speaking, state hospitals, although more or less hygenic and staffed by reliable, well-meaning professionals, are certainly not in tip-top condition compared to most hospitals in the North America and Western Europe. So we recommend that you go elsewhere if possible. The private Telki Hospital just outside of Budapest or one arranged by the American Clinic are the best options.

Doctors & Dentists FirstMed Centers ⊠ Hattyúház, District I, Hattyú utca 14, 5th floor, Around Moszkva tér ☎ 1/224–9090 ⊕ www. firstmedcenters.com. **Profident Dental Services** ⊠ District VII, Karoly Köröt 1, Around Deák Ferenc tér ☎ 1/342–2546. **S.O.S. Dent** ⊠ District VI, Király utca 14, Around Király utca ☎ 1/267–9602.

U.S. Embassy U.S. Embassy ⊠ District V, Szabadság tér 12, Parliament ☎ 1/475–4400 ⊕ www.usembassy.hu.

General Emergency Contacts Ambulance
☎ 104. **Police** ☎ 107 or 112.
Hospitals & Clinics Telki Hospital ✉ Telki
kórház fasor 1, Telki ☎ 1/459-6555 or 26/372-
300.
Pharmacies with 24-hour service District II
✉ Frankel Leó út 22, Around Batthyány tér
☎ 1/212-4311. **District VI** ✉ Teréz körút 41,
Around Nyugati Train Station ☎ 1/311-4439.
District XII ✉ Alkotás utca 1/b, Around Déli
Train Station ☎ 1/355-4691.

█ HEALTH

You may gain weight, but there are few
other serious health hazards for the traveler in Hungary. Tap water may taste bad
but is generally drinkable; when it runs
rusty out of the tap in an old building or
the aroma of chlorine is overpowering, it
might help to have some bottled water
handy.

█ HOURS OF OPERATION

Banks are generally open Monday–Thursday until 3 or 4; most close by 2 on Friday. Businesses tend to be open later, until
4:30–5 weekdays, though many close by
early to mid-afternoon on Friday, the same
goes for government offices. Post offices
are a different story, however: in Budapest
you can mail your postcards on weekdays
from 8 to as late as 7 or even 9 at a few
post offices, though most are open only
until 5 or 6. A few are open until 2 or even
later on Saturdays; all are closed on Sundays.

HOLIDAYS

January 1; March 15 (anniversary of 1848
Revolution); Easter Sunday and Easter
Monday (in March, April, or May); May
1 (Labor Day); Pentecost Monday (also
known as Whitsun Monday; Whitsunday
is the seventh Sunday after Easter); August
20 (St. Stephen's and Constitution Day);
October 23 (1956 Revolution Day); December 24–26.

█ MAIL

Airmail letters and postcards generally
take seven days to travel between Hungary
and the United States, sometimes more
than twice as long, however, during the
Christmas season. At this writing, postage
for an airmail letter to the U.S. costs 220
HUF; an airmail letter to the U.K. and
elsewhere in Western Europe costs 190
HUF; airmail postcards to the U.S. cost 160
HUF and to the U.K. and the rest of Western Europe, 130 HUF.

Most post offices in the capital are open
on weekdays from 8 AM until 6 PM, some
as late as 8 PM; practically all are closed
on weekends. In the countryside, where
post offices are likewise closed on weekends for the most part, post offices tend
to close earlier; in many villages they shut
their doors by around 3:30 PM.

Budapest's main post office is downtown
near both Deák tér and Váci utca. The post
offices near Budapest's Nyugati (West)
and Keleti (East) train stations stay open
on weekdays until 8 PM and 9 PM, respectively; on Saturdays the former is open
until 6 PM, the latter until 2 PM; and both
are closed on Sunday. █ TIP➔ The American Express office in Budapest has poste
restante services—or "client mail," as they call
it—for cardholders, but they will not accept
packages.
Main Branches American Express ✉ District
V, Deák Ferenc utca 10, Budapest ☎ 1/235-
4330. **Downtown Budapest post office**
✉ District V, Magyar Posta 4 sz., Városház
utca 18, Budapest. **Keleti post office** ✉ District VIII, Baross tér 11/C, Budapest. **Nyugati
post office** ✉ District VI, Teréz körút 51,
Budapest.

SHIPPING PACKAGES

DHL, FedEx, and UPS all operate in Budapest, but you'll have to contact them directly, as stores that offer shipping have
yet to make their mark on Hungary's capital. Overnight service is possible to the
U.K. but not always to the U.S., which
might take two days. Express service to

Australia and New Zealand can take three to four days. All services are expensive (starting at around $50 for an overnight document to the U.K.).

Express Services DHL ☎ 06-40/454-545 ⊕ www.dhl.hu. **FedEx Hungary** ☎ 0629/ 551-900 or 0640/980-980 ⊕ www.fedex. com/hu. **UPS** ☎ 06-40/98-98-98 or 1/877- 0000 ⊕ www.ups.com.

∎ MONEY

A week in Budapest might run you any-where from around $1,800 or less—if you find an airfare of less than $1,000, stay in a moderately priced hotel (€70 or so) or a private room (as little as €30 a night), and don't dine too lavishly—to well up-wards of $3,000 if spending is not so much of an issue.

Though most restaurants and hotels accept credit cards, as do many chain supermar-kets these days, cash is still king when it comes to small purchases. The easiest way to handle money in Budapest is to with-draw forints directly from your home bank account at one of the city's many ATMs. Many banks will cash American Express and Visa traveler's checks, but stores and restaurants are unlikely to ac-cept them as payment. American Express has a full-service office in Budapest. There are also several Citibank branches, offer-ing full services to account holders. For in-formation on taxes, *see* Taxes.

When possible, unless you are in a large food store (which should have plenty of cash on hand to make change with), avoid making small purchases with bills of 5,000 HUF or more. Doing so might result in a little huff from the cashier or a kind re-quest for something smaller. Tipping should always be done in forints, since re-ceiving money in dollars only represents a complication for most locals; they'll have to take it to a bank to exchange it.

A cup of coffee (i.e., a single shot of espresso) will run you anywhere between 100 HUF and 350 HUF, depending on whether you're at a train-station snack bar or an elegant café; a somewhat more American-style (i.e., more water but weaker) *hosszu kávé* (long coffee) might run a bit more. A glass *pohár* of beer will be 200 HUF–300 HUF; a mug *korsó*, 300 HUF–500 HUF. A sandwich at a snack bar or café costs 200 HUF–400 HUF, a one-mile taxi ride will be around 600 HUF (base fare + distance); a visit to a thermal bath will cost you at least 2,000 HUF al-together. Although the permanent collec-tions of most Budapest museums can be seen for free these days, those that still charge, and those museums with tempo-rary exhibits worth a look, might ask you for 500 HUF to 1,000 HUF or more.

Prices throughout this guide are given for adults. Substantially reduced fees are al-most always available for children, stu-dents, and senior citizens.

∎ TIP→ Banks never have every foreign cur-rency on hand, and it may take as long as a week to order. If you're planning to exchange funds before leaving home, don't wait until the last minute.

ATMS & BANKS

Your own bank will probably charge a fee for using ATMs abroad; the foreign bank you use may also charge a fee. Neverthe-less, you'll usually get a better rate of ex-change at an ATM than you will at a currency-exchange office or even when changing money in a bank. And extract-ing funds as you need them is a safer op-tion than carrying around a large amount of cash.

∎ TIP→ PIN numbers with more than four digits are not recognized at ATMs in many countries. If yours has five or more, remem-ber to change it before you leave.

ATMs are common in Budapest and more often than not are part of the Cirrus and Plus networks. You can withdraw forints only (automatically converted at the bank's official exchange rate) directly from your account. Instructions are available in En-glish. Some levy a 1% or $3 service charge; ask your bank about its surcharges before you travel. Outside of urban areas, machines are scarce and you should plan to carry enough cash to meet your needs. **American Express** ✉ District V, Deák Ferenc utca 10, Around Deák Ferenc tér ☎ 1/235–4330 🖶 1/267-2028 ✉ District I, Dísz tér 8, Castle Hill. **Citibank** ✉ District V, Vörösmarty tér 4, Around Váci utca ☎ 1/288-2352 ✉ District V, Báthori utca 12, Parliament ☎ 1/301-2700.

CREDIT CARDS

Throughout this guide, the following abbreviations are used: **AE**, American Express; **DC**, Diners Club; **MC**, MasterCard; and **V**, Visa.

It's a good idea to inform your credit-card company before you travel, especially if you're going abroad and don't travel internationally very often. Otherwise, the credit-card company might put a hold on your card owing to unusual activity—not a good thing halfway through your trip. Record all your credit-card numbers—as well as the phone numbers to call if your cards are lost or stolen—in a safe place, so you're prepared should something go wrong. Both MasterCard and Visa have general numbers you can call (collect if you're abroad) if your card is lost, but you're better off calling the number of your issuing bank, since MasterCard and Visa usually just transfer you to your bank; your bank's number is usually printed on your card.

If you plan to use your credit card for cash advances, you'll need to apply for a PIN at least two weeks before your trip. Although it's usually cheaper (and safer) to use a credit card abroad for large purchases (so you can cancel payments or be reimbursed if there's a problem), note that some credit-card companies *and* the banks that issue them add substantial percentages to all foreign transactions, whether they're in a foreign currency or not. Check on these fees before leaving home, so there won't be any surprises when you get the bill.

■ TIP➔ Before you charge something, ask the merchant whether or not he or she plans to do a dynamic currency conversion (DCC). In such a transaction the credit-card *processor*

(shop, restaurant, or hotel, not Visa or MasterCard) converts the currency and charges you in dollars. In most cases you'll pay the merchant a 3% fee for this service in addition to any credit-card company and issuing-bank foreign-transaction surcharges.

Dynamic currency conversion programs are becoming increasingly widespread. Merchants who participate in them are supposed to ask whether you want to be charged in dollars or the local currency, but they don't always do so. And even if they do offer you a choice, they may well avoid mentioning the additional surcharges. The good news is that you *do* have a choice. And if this practice really gets your goat, you can avoid it entirely thanks to American Express; with its cards DCC simply isn't an option.

All major credit cards are accepted in Hungary, but don't rely on them in smaller towns or less expensive accommodations and restaurants. The most commonly accepted cards are MasterCard and Visa.

Reporting Lost Cards American Express ☎ 800/992-3404 in the U.S. or 336/393-1111 collect from abroad ⊕ www.americanexpress.com. **Diners Club** ☎ 1/488-888 in Budapest or 800/234-6377 in the U.S. or 303/799-1504 collect from abroad ⊕ www.dinersclub.com. **MasterCard** ☎ 0680-012-517 in Budapest, 800/622-7747 in the U.S. or 636/722-7111 collect from abroad ⊕ www.mastercard.com. **Visa** ☎ 0680-011-272 in Budapest, 800/847-2911 in the U.S. or 410/581-9994 collect from abroad ⊕ www.visa.com.

CURRENCY & EXCHANGE

Hungary joined the European Union (EU) in 2004, but it still uses the forint (HUF or Ft.)—and this will be the case until sometime after 2010 (read: no earlier, but perhaps not until 2014), when, if the government's domestically unpopular efforts at budget belt-tightening meet stipulations, it will eventually be allowed to adopt the euro. There are bills of 200, 500, 1,000, 2,000, 5,000, 10,000, and 20,000 forints and coins of 1, 2, 5, 10, 20, 50, and 100 forints.

At this writing, the exchange rate was approximately 213 HUF to the U.S. dollar, 188 HUF to the Canadian dollar, 396 HUF to the pound sterling, and 271 HUF to the euro. There is still a black market in hard currency, but changing money on the street is risky and illegal, and the bank rate almost always comes close. Stick with banks and official exchange offices. Banks may charge a commission, but their rates tend to be much better than those at exchange offices. If you're lured into an exchange office by an attractive advertised rate, be sure to read and ask about special conditions and service charges before putting any money down. There are also many cash-exchange machines in Budapest, into which you feed paper currency for forints, but this can feel too risky for those with a healthy distrust of machines. Most bank automats and cash-exchange machines are clustered around their respective bank branches throughout downtown Budapest.

It can help to have some local currency before you leave. If your local bank doesn't offer this service, you can order some foreign currency before you leave from International Currency Express or Travelex.

■ TIP➔ Even if a currency-exchange booth has a sign promising no commission, rest assured that there's some kind of huge, hidden fee. (Oh . . . that's right. The sign didn't say no *fee*.) And as for rates, you're almost always better off getting foreign currency at an ATM or exchanging money at a bank.

TRAVELER'S CHECKS & CARDS

Some consider traveler's checks the currency of the cave man, and it's true that fewer establishments accept them these days. Nevertheless, they're a cheap and secure way to carry extra money, particularly on trips to urban areas. Both Citibank (under the Visa brand) and American Express issue traveler's checks in the United States, but Amex is better known and more widely accepted; you can also avoid hefty surcharges by cashing Amex checks at Amex offices. Whatever you do, keep track of all the serial numbers in case the checks are lost or stolen.

Banks in Hungary will exchange traveler's checks, but stores and businesses hardly ever accept them.

American Express now offers a stored-value card called a Travelers Cheque Card, which you can use wherever American Express credit cards are accepted, including ATMs. The card can carry a minimum of $300 and a maximum of $2,700, and it's a very safe way to carry your funds. Although you can get replacement funds in 24 hours if your card is lost or stolen, it doesn't really strike us as a very good deal. In addition to a high initial cost ($14.95 to set up the card, plus $5 each time you "reload"), you still have to pay a 2% fee for each purchase in a foreign currency (similar to that of any credit card). Further, each time you use the card in an ATM you pay a transaction fee of $2.50 on top of the 2% transaction fee for the conversion—add it all up and it can be considerably more than you would pay when simply using your own ATM card. Regular traveler's checks are just as secure and cost less.

American Express ☎ 888/412–6945 in the U.S., 801/945–9450 collect outside of the U.S. to add value or speak to customer service ⊕ www.americanexpress.com.

▌ RESTROOMS

While the restrooms at Budapest's Ferihegy Airport may sparkle and smell of soap, don't expect the same of those at Hungarian train and bus stations—which, by the way, usually have attendants on hand who collect a fee of at least 50 HUF. Especially outside Budapest, public restrooms are often run-down and sometimes rank. Pay the attendant on the way in; you will receive toilet tissue in exchange. Since public restrooms are generally few and far between, you will sometimes find yourself entering cafés, bars, or restaurants primarily to use their toilets; when doing so, unless it happens to be a bustling fast-food place, you should probably order a little something.

Find a Loo The Bathroom Diaries ⊕ www. thebathroomdiaries.com is flush with unsanitized info on restrooms the world over—each one located, reviewed, and rated.

▌ SAFETY

Crime rates are still relatively low in Budapest and the rest of Hungary, but travelers should beware of pickpockets in crowded areas, especially on public transportation, at railway stations, in western fast-food chains like McDonald's and Burger King, and in big hotels. In general, always keep your valuables with you—in open bars and restaurants, purses hung on or placed next to chairs are easy targets.

The Hungarian word for "help" is *segítség,* pronounced sheh-geet-shayg. The word for "police" is *rendőr,* pronounced rend-er.

Male tourists are the target of Budapest's most prevalent local scam, which is generally staged in the Váci utca area: a pair of women (but sometimes more, sometimes only one) approach the tourist in a casual, friendly way, sometimes acting as locals, sometimes pretending to be just visiting Budapest. They eventually suggest having a drink to continue the conversation, and take the man to a colluding bar or café, where all is well until the bill arrives with outrageously high prices and his female companions have conveniently left their wallets at home. When the victim protests, the waiter claims the group ordered some special, expensive version of whatever drinks were had and soon several of the waiter's large, intimidating colleagues join the conversation. If your ego clouds your judgment enough so that you do end up sitting down somewhere with such new "friends," don't allow anyone to order anything without choosing it from a menu with prices, even if your companions offer to treat you— and don't assume the extra zeroes are just typos!

Note that Hungarian police will *NEVER* ask you for money, neither as a fine nor to "inspect" or count your currency; if they do, refuse and seek help—they may be con artists impersonating officers.

If you do become a victim of a crime while in Hungary, you can contact White Ring (Fehér Gyűrű), a crime-prevention and victim-protection organization dedicated to helping foreigners with everything from free legal advice and counseling to help filing reports and replacing stolen documents. During peak tourist seasons, the main office of Tourinform has a police officer on hand to help visitors with crime and safety issues.

■ **TIP→** Distribute your cash, credit cards, IDs, and other valuables between a deep front pocket, an inside jacket or vest pocket, and a hidden money pouch. Don't reach for the money pouch once you're in public.

Tourinform ⊠ District V, Sütő utca 2, Around Deák Ferenc tér ☎ 1/317–9800, 1/438–8080, or 80/630–800 24-hr toll-free hotline within Hungary. **White Ring** ⊠ District V, Szt. István körút 1, Around Nyugati Train Station ☎ 1/ 472–1161 or 1/312–2287. **U.S. Embassy in Budapest** ⊕ www.usembassy.hu.

▌ TAXES

As a tourist in Hungary you will generally encounter two kinds of tax. Value-Added Tax (VAT) of 5% to 25% (at this writing) is included in the price of most consumer goods and services. An additional tourist tax is added to hotel bills in some parts of the country—it's 3% in Budapest.

V.A.T. in Hungary is also called ÁFA and ranges from 5% to 25% depending on the type of goods or service. At this writing, most general consumer goods are taxed at 15%, and most other services and products, including hotel fees, car-rental costs, and gasoline, are taxed at a whopping 25%. Upon leaving the country you are entitled to a refund of up to 18% of value-added tax on new goods (i.e., not works of art, antiques, or objects of museum value) that appear on each invoice you have whose value is 45,000 HUF or more (V.A.T. inclusive). The goods in question must leave the country within 90 days of their purchase, and the refund must be requested within 183 days of the purchase. **Be sure to request a V. A.T. refund form,** V.A.T. refund envelope, and detailed invoice from the store where you made your purchase; ask them for instructions, too, on how to proceed. Keep your credit-card receipt, too, or the receipt from where you exchanged your money into forints if you paid in cash (ATM receipt, if applicable). Present these documents, along with the relevant goods purchased, to a customs officer before you leave Hungary (at the airport or train station). The documents will be stamped to prove the goods are leaving the country. You can then get a cash refund (in forints) at the V.A.T. refund agency in the airport, or apply by mail later for a credit-card refund. A service charge is subtracted from all refunds. If the goods in question are packed in your luggage, be sure to tell the check-in agent before you check your bags that you want to get a VAT refund on goods in your luggage. They will arrange access.

For more information, pick up a tax-refund brochure from any tourist office or hotel. For further Hungarian customs information, inquire at the Hungarian Customs and Finance Guard office (1/456-9500). If you have trouble communicating, call Tourinform's 24-hr hotline at 1/438–8080 for help.

Global Refund is a Europe-wide service with 225,000 affiliated stores and more than 700 refund counters at major airports and border crossings. Its refund form, called a Tax Free Check, is the most common across the European continent. The service issues refunds in the form of cash, check, or credit-card adjustment.

V.A.T. Refunds Global Refund ☎ 800/566-9828 ⊕ www.globalrefund.com.

▌TIME

Hungary is within the Central European Time (CET) zone, which for most of the year is one hour ahead of Greenwich Mean Time and six hours ahead of Eastern Standard Time in the United States. The nation springs its clocks forward by an hour to adjust to Daylight Savings Time in the wee hours on the last Sunday in March, and falls back, so to speak, on the last Sunday of October.

▌TIPPING

Tipping is ubiquitous in those areas of life where a service is rendered or the opportunity otherwise presents itself, and it is appreciated even if the receiving party (whose regular salary is probably pitiful) doesn't always show it. Most often it is done by making it clear when paying that you don't need the change (just nod and say *köszönöm* (thank you), pronounced "kuh-suh-num"). If your bills are too big for that, then somehow specify the amount of change you expect. Beyond the usual categories of persons tipped (*see below*), discreet tips that round out the total to the next convenient figure are often given to newspaper sellers and sometimes even store clerks: if an English-language newspaper comes to 580 HUF, pay 600 HUF and say *köszönöm* or just leave, and that's that. The same goes for snack bars where you are served at a counter; give 120 (or even 150) HUF for a 100 HUF cup of espresso, 220 or 250 HUF if the total comes to 200 HUF, and so on.

Taxi drivers and hairdressers expect 10% to 15% tips; porters should get 200 HUF to 400 HUF. Coatroom attendants receive 50 HUF to 100 HUF, as do gas-pump attendants if they wash your windows or check your tires; dressing-room attendants at thermal baths receive 50 HUF to 100 HUF for opening and closing your locker. Gratuities are not included automatically on bills at most restaurants; when the waiter arrives with the bill, you should immediately add a 10% to 15% tip to the amount, as it is not customary to leave the tip on the table.

INDEX

PHOTO CREDITS

Cover Photo (Opera house, Budapest): *Jim Doberman/The Image Bank/Getty Images.* 7, *Kevin Foy/Alamy.*
8, *Ingolf Pompe/Alamy.* 12, *Sergio Pitamitz/age fotostock.* 14, *Angelo Cavalli/age fotostock.* 15, *McPHOTO/
Alamy.* 16, *Brian A. Gauvin/viestiphoto.com.* 17 (left), *Eddie Gerald/Alamy.* 17 (right), *Ingolf Pompe/Alamy.*

NOTES

NOTES

NOTES

NOTES

NOTES

NOTES

NOTES

NOTES

NOTES

NOTES

ABOUT OUR WRITERS

Susan MacCallum-Whitcomb first visited Budapest in the late 1980s, when she was still a grad student—and it was still a communist capital. Clearly both have changed a lot in the intervening years. Now a full-time travel writer, Susan zips around the globe writing for Fodor's as well as for top-selling Canadian newspapers and magazines (*The National Post, Globe and Mail, Wedding Bells, Homemakers, Money-Sense* . . . you get the picture).

Betsy Maury, a former senior editor with the U.S. publisher Bantam Doubleday Dell, moved to Budapest in 1999 and has made the Magyar capital her home ever since. Her enthusiasm for the national cuisine—as well as a love of Hungarian wines—keeps her busy exploring the cosmopolitan city in search of interesting restaurants. She travels widely throughout Central Europe, working as a freelance writer. This year Betsy shared her insights on where to eat and where to shop in her favorite city.

Paul Olchváry is a writer and translator of many Hungarian books into English and a contributor to the first editions of *Fodor's Budapest* and *Fodor's Croatia & Slovenia.* Formerly a senior copy writer at Princeton University Press, he lived in Hungary throughout the 1990s, initially in Pécs and later, beginning in 1992, in Budapest. A native of western New York who lives in both his log cabin north of Budapest and in various reaches of the northeastern United States, he is currently completing a book-length fable recounting the life stories of several wine grapes (including at least one Tokaj). While in Hungary, in addition to translating, he taught English at a university, reported on politics under a fellowship with the U.S. embassy, and was founding editor of a news service called *Hungary Around the Clock.* Paul wrote Exploring Budapest, The Danube Bend, The Great Plain, Northern Hungary, Pécs, Sopron, Books & Movies, and Language.